ESSAYS IN

THE SCIENCE OF CULTURE

In Honor of Leslie A. White

BOARD OF ADVISORS

Robert Anderson
Richard K. Beardsley
Stephen C. Cappannari
James B. Griffin
Betty J. Meggers
William W. Newcomb, Jr.
Elman R. Service
Albert C. Spaulding

Leslie A. White

* * * * *

ESSAYS IN
THE SCIENCE OF CULTURE

In Honor of

LESLIE A. WHITE

IN CELEBRATION OF HIS SIXTIETH BIRTHDAY
AND HIS THIRTIETH YEAR OF TEACHING
AT THE UNIVERSITY OF MICHIGAN

EDITED BY

GERTRUDE E. DOLE
Columbia University

AND

ROBERT L. CARNEIRO
American Museum of Natural History

*

New York

THOMAS Y. CROWELL COMPANY
Established 1834

＊ ＊ ＊ ＊

CONTENTS

Contents

* * * * *

PREFACE

The essays in this volume are presented as a tribute to Leslie A. White in celebration of his sixtieth birthday and his thirtieth year of teaching at the University of Michigan. These essays are meant to honor Dr. White not only by being dedicated to him but also by contributing to the science of anthropology.

During the thirty years that Dr. White has taught anthropology at Michigan he has had a profound influence on his students. While they do not think of themselves as constituting a "Whitean school," many of them nevertheless heartily subscribe to the body of coherent and illuminating principles he has developed. Dr. White's work, however, has not so greatly influenced others in the profession until relatively recently. Thus, as late as 1953 one anthropologist wrote, "Though White's views [have] become considerably publicized by vigorous presentation, no professional following has fallen in behind him." [1] To the extent that this statement was true when it was written, it reflected the fact that the ideas which Dr. White has so forcefully propounded were at variance with the prevailing currents of anthropological theory. Also it must be recognized that until a decade or so ago, few of Dr. White's students had become professional anthropologists, and those who had were publishing relatively little.

An increasing number of anthropologists are now coming to recognize the value of Dr. White's work and to accept his views. A comment recently made by another anthropologist, not himself a student or colleague of Dr. White, is indicative of this trend: "A major defender of evolutionary theory in anthropology when most voices were raised in opposition, White has had the rare pleasure of seeing his once unpopular views taken up by many younger anthropologists." [2]

---

[1] Felix Keesing, *Culture Change,* p. 40. Stanford, Stanford University Press, 1953.
[2] Morton H. Fried. Explanatory footnote to the reprinting of White's article, "The Expansion of the Scope of Science," in *Readings in Anthropology,* vol. 1, pp. 15–16n. New York, Thomas Y. Crowell Company, 1959.

The idea of assembling a group of essays to honor Dr. White was conceived in 1955 and was first discussed during a visit with Robert and Alma Anderson in August of that year. At that time it occurred to us that the best way to honor Dr. White would be by demonstrating his influence, and that this might best be done through essays written by his students. Accordingly, beginning in May, 1956, exploratory letters were written to a number of his former students. Some of the persons to whom we wrote at that time pointed out that Dr. White had had considerable influence on his colleagues as well and suggested that they too be invited to contribute essays. This suggestion was taken, and the project was expanded to include those who had been professionally associated with him at the University of Michigan. The response to our invitation to submit essays was enthusiastic, and a large number of scholars indicated a desire to participate in the enterprise. However, many were unable to do so because of lack of time.

It was originally proposed that the organizing theme of the volume be ethnological theory. But since adherence to such a theme might exclude contributions by archeologists who had studied under Dr. White, it was suggested to us that we broaden the theme to culture theory. In soliciting articles, therefore, we requested that each essay be written as a contribution to culture theory. However, authors were not held to this request, and a few of the papers in the volume do not conform to the suggestion.

In order to assist authors in the final preparation of their essays, a Board of Advisors was formed. The persons who agreed to act as Advisors were Robert Anderson, Richard K. Beardsley, Stephen C. Cappannari, James B. Griffin, Betty J. Meggers, William W. Newcomb, Jr., Elman R. Service, and Albert C. Spaulding. These Advisors read the original drafts of papers submitted and made editorial suggestions for revision. We would like to express our appreciation to them for the valuable assistance they rendered to the project.

We are indebted to Mary White for helping us to compile Dr. White's bibliography. She generously gave of her energy to this task not long before her tragic death. We are grateful also to Volney H. Jones for making available to us additional bibliographic information. We owe a particular debt of gratitude to Elman R. Service, who has helped us not only as a member of the Board of Advisors but also in innumerable instances when information, advice, and support were needed.

We should like to thank the Wenner-Gren Foundation for Anthropological Research, Inc., for a grant to help defray some of the expense of publication.

GERTRUDE E. DOLE
ROBERT L. CARNEIRO

* * * *

Harry Elmer Barnes

FOREWORD

MY PERSONAL FRIENDSHIP FOR LESLIE WHITE

It has given me much pleasure to accept the invitation of~this *The editors of*
Festschrift to write the Foreword as a deserved testimonial to an
able scholar, a devoted and earnest teacher, and a courageous man. It is
both a personal satisfaction and a professional privilege. I have known
Leslie Alvin White intimately for more than a third of a century, and one
of my chief professional interests has been the history and methodology
of the social sciences, the field to which Professor White has made such
notable and consistent contributions.

My first contact with Leslie White came in 1923 when I was a visiting
professor of history at the summer school of the University of California
in Los Angeles. Leslie had just finished his undergraduate work at Columbia University the previous month and, with his lifelong roving intellectual curiosity, had decided to see what of interest he could pick up on the
opposite coast of the Continent. I am not aware just what prompted him
to come up and introduce himself after one of the early meetings of my
class in intellectual history, but it was probably the discernment of some
underlying mental affinity, for we have both been relatively adventurous
and independent dissenters with respect to conventional attitudes on
public affairs and the accepted academic dogmas. Perhaps he came up
because he desired sympathy and encouragement at the moment. His
other course that summer, one in philosophy, was conducted by Professor
Frank Thilly, a man of a quite different intellectual temperament from
that of either Leslie or myself. He was one of the most distinguished professors in the faculty of Cornell University, a true gentleman and scholar

of the old school. But his dogmatic metaphysical approach, embracing a combination of Kant, Hegel, and the German idealists, was anathema to Leslie, who had the temerity to challenge the professor and try to argue matters out with him during classtime. Finally, a truce was arranged through which there was a tacit agreement that Thilly would pass Leslie if he would just keep quiet during the lectures. Indeed, they agreed not to speak to each other until the end of the session.

A person of such intellectual traits was, naturally, one to attract my interest and loyalty, and Leslie has had both to an ever increasing degree in the more than three decades which have followed. After we both returned East that autumn, we met again at The New School for Social Research where I was lecturing, in addition to teaching at Smith and Amherst. Leslie was taking special work at The New School along with regular graduate studies at Columbia. I had urged him to enroll in some courses there taught by William Isaac Thomas, formerly of the University of Chicago, a man whom I had long admired and with whom I enjoyed valued friendly relations.

My contact with Leslie was actively maintained while he was a graduate student at the University of Chicago and a professor at the University of Buffalo, and has continued during the years since 1930 when he has so long ably served on the staff of the University of Michigan.

We were kept together not only by mutual respect and affection but also by such things as incidental aspects of Leslie's anthropological interests. When I lived near Auburn, New York, in the 1930's, Leslie might stay at our house overnight while by day he wandered along the paths presumably taken by Lewis Henry Morgan in his studies of Indian remains on the shores of Cayuga Lake, particularly around Aurora, now the seat of Wells College. Morgan brought us together again far later and in an area remote from central New York. When I was a visiting professor at Washington State College in Pullman, Leslie was my guest in October, 1954. He had been retracing, so far as it could be done by automobile, the course taken by Morgan in his expedition to the headwaters of the Missouri River. By the time he reached Pullman, he had covered nearly twice the direct mileage from Ann Arbor to Pullman. His numerous and prolonged researches in the Morgan materials in Rochester, New York, also encouraged visits to us not only in Auburn but also in Cooperstown, where we lived for some fifteen years after leaving the Auburn region in 1939. Nor was the visiting all one-sided. Over the years I frequently lectured in the Chicago area and when possible arranged to stop off in Ann Arbor for a day or so. A good visit was even more certain when

I lectured in Michigan, as I did rather frequently during the 1930's. After 1930, when Leslie married the beautiful and charming Mary Pattison, we always enjoyed their joint companionship, whether in Auburn, Cooperstown, or Ann Arbor. Their last visit was paid to us at Malibu, California, when they were on their way from New Mexico to Leslie's visiting professorship at the University of California at Berkeley in January, 1957.

So much for a brief review of our personal relationships, which were always close, loyal, and devoted. Our ideological affinity and harmony was no less pronounced. We shared a healthy skepticism toward prevailing popular policies, and in no major crisis in domestic or world affairs since 1923 have Leslie and I ever found ourselves on opposite sides of the fence. Although I was usually far more widely identified with dissent in the public mind, Leslie always stuck by me even when it must have caused him some embarrassment and concern. One such occasion was in May, 1940, when he introduced me and I gave a strongly anti-interventionist address to a great throng in Rackham Auditorium at the University of Michigan, much to the delight of most of the students and the dismay of many of the faculty, some of whom, like the militant geologist William H. Hobbs, stalked out of the room.

An even greater test of his loyalty and courage came on the evening of this same day. On Leslie's recommendation, I had been invited to be the annual Social Science Lecturer. The invitation had been extended in March, and the faculty committee had suggested that I talk about the European war and its relation to American policy. If the phony war of September, 1939, to April, 1940, had continued through the lecture date, my lecture very likely would not have stirred violent reactions on the part of members of the social science faculty. But in the interval Hitler had launched his drive westward and was already threatening to break through the Maginot Line. Strong emotions had begun to surge up in the bosoms of even supposedly calm and detached scholars. My lecture, while actually highly factual, moderate, and restrained, stirred a more acrimonious reaction than anything of the kind in the previous history of the University of Michigan. Leslie could easily have backed away and protected himself by alleging astonishment and shock at my realism and candor. But he stood his ground and adhered strongly to the principle of freedom of speech even in the face of martial ardor on the part of the faculty. The echoes of that lecture lingered on at Ann Arbor. In the autumn of 1944 when my wife was doing some important work for the Ford Motor Company at Willow Run, she found a room with the family of a professor at the University of Michigan. As soon as the professor discovered the actual identity of her husband, he compelled her to move out at once. Leslie and Mary graciously took her into their own home.

A related reason for affinity and sympathy between us has been the fact that, in regard to both scholarly matters and public affairs, we have been alike in defending what have often been minority positions. This led us to devote much of our scholarly and literary efforts to controversial writing. Fortunately, our views usually coincided, and even when they did not they rarely clashed directly. For the most part, we encouraged each other in our major controversial enterprises. I urged Leslie on in his then-minority efforts in behalf of culturology and cultural evolution, and he approved my activities in behalf of "revisionism" relative to the causes of the two World Wars, even though he did not feel too sure that the establishment of truth about this matter would be likely to affect very deeply the cultural pressure for more and bigger wars. I recall one sagacious if humorous remark he made in this connection about 1946. I had revealed to him my intention to devote most of my remaining years to the correction of the mythology relative to the responsibility for the outbreak of World War II and our entry into it, and had stressed the great difficulties and handicaps facing any such program. Leslie agreed, and then observed: "Go ahead; maybe you can do it; Jack did!"—having reference to the legendary achievements of Jack the Giant-killer.

While I have not been a professional anthropologist, my interest in the subject was aroused in my undergraduate years. As a graduate student at Columbia, Harvard, and elsewhere, I did about as much course work in that field as is usual on the part of those who take their doctorate in anthropology. The subject has always greatly interested me, especially in its historical and theoretical aspects, and if I had not been so much absorbed in history in my early academic life I might have become an anthropologist instead of an historian. At any rate, my contact with anthropology gave Leslie and myself mutual academic and intellectual interests and enabled me to comprehend what he was doing in the field and to have a proper appreciation of his achievements, especially since his major concern was with the theoretical phases and evolutionary applications of anthropology. I read the manuscript of the first article he ever wrote in the field of anthropology, one titled "Personality and Culture," and recommended that he send it to *The Open Court*, where it was published in 1925. Since I had personally met and listened to most of the leaders of the original Boas School during my years at Columbia, I was also acquainted with Leslie's chief opponents in his later theoretical and methodological battles, an acquaintance which gave an added personal import and interest to the spirited professional debate that has been going on for some thirty years.

EDUCATIONAL EXPERIENCE

To turn from personal matters to professional items, it is logical and sensible first to consider Dr. White's educational interests and career. These throw much light on his later activities and writings as a scholar and teacher. The following information has been obtained in writing directly from Dr. White; hence, it may be regarded as authentic and final.[1]

Even before he entered high school in Zachary, Louisiana, he had decided to become a teacher and had formed a rather clear idea of what he believed would constitute his academic career: he would become a physicist or an astronomer. These desires and decisions he developed from reading a small book his father had used in college, *Natural Philosophy*, then the usual designation for physics. The book was an introduction to this field. About the same time, his father took him outdoors one night on the family farm near Lane, Kansas, to show and explain to him Halley's Comet, which was flaming across the sky in 1910. Dr. White's earliest intellectual heroes were Galileo, Newton, Kepler, and Halley. By the time he graduated from high school in 1916, it had become a foregone conclusion with him that he would enter Louisiana State University and major in physics, although once or twice he momentarily entertained the idea that he would like to be a physician. Sickness after graduation from high school, followed by service in the Navy during World War I, postponed his entry into the university until September, 1919.

In the interval, his experiences in the war brought about a profound change in his intellectual interests and turned him toward psychology

---

[1] Dr. White sent me this information in the summer of 1959, but he had no knowledge that this *Festschrift* was being prepared or that I requested this information for use therein. I told him, quite honestly, that I was gathering information for a possible future expansion of my *Historical Sociology*. I am happy to be able to state that I informed Mrs. White in May, 1958, of the plan for a *Festschrift* and of my promise to write the Foreword. Her gratification over this information was very evident, especially about the *Festschrift*.

While dealing with these matters, I would like to express my gratitude to two of Dr. White's associates in the Michigan Department, Professors Elman R. Service and Marshall D. Sahlins, and to two of his former students and the editors of the *Festschrift*, Dr. Gertrude E. Dole of Columbia University and Dr. Robert L. Carneiro of the American Museum of Natural History, for their indispensable assistance in furnishing me with detailed information about Dr. White and the Anthropology Department.

and the social sciences. As he expressed it: "The War changed my life purpose and outlook profoundly. I discovered, somehow, during the War that all I had been taught, formally and informally, about my society, my country, and related subjects, was a gross distortion of reality. I therefore determined, when I entered college, to find out why *peoples* behave as they do. My love for physics was not extinguished; it was merely pushed into the background. I majored in history and political science during my freshman and sophomore years at Louisiana State University, thinking they would answer my new and big questions for me. They did not, and I turned to psychology, sociology and philosophy during my junior and senior years at Columbia University, to which I had transferred." Dr. White studied at Louisiana State from 1919 to 1921, and at Columbia from 1921 to 1923, receiving his bachelor's degree there in 1923. He took no courses in anthropology as an undergraduate at Columbia, nor did he take any there as a graduate student, where he received his master's degree in 1924. He continued to concentrate in psychology, sociology, and philosophy, and wrote his master's thesis in psychology under the direction of Professor Robert S. Woodworth.

But even before he finished his senior year, he struck out boldly and diversely in his effort to understand the behavior of "peoples," mainly at The New School for Social Research in New York City, where he took courses from 1922 to 1924. Here, he really began his study of anthropology under Alexander Goldenweiser, the most lucid lecturer among Boas' disciples, and the veteran sociologist William I. Thomas, who had been a student of primitive society for a generation and whose *Source Book for Social Origins,* published in 1909, had long been a classic in both sociology and anthropology. Dr. White also took courses in economics under Thorstein Veblen, in behavioristic psychology under John B. Watson, and in psychiatry under Frankwood E. Williams, among others. He even took two courses in clinical psychology at Manhattan State Hospital for the Insane at Ward's Island, and for a time toyed with the idea of entering the field of psychiatry by way of clinical psychology. But he abandoned this notion and in 1924 decided to go to the University of Chicago and study sociology so that he might learn more about peoples. He soon found, however, that he was not learning much about peoples in his sociology courses, so he shifted his major interest to anthropology.

Dr. White wrote his doctoral dissertation, "Medicine Societies of the Southwest," under the direction of Professor Fay-Cooper Cole, and received his Ph.D. degree in 1927. His dissertation produced a bitter academic controversy between Professor Cole and the sociologist Professor Ellsworth Faris. This provided the chief reason for division of the previously unified department into two distinct departments—sociology and anthropology. Dr. White thus describes his interests and motivations between the time he left The New School and his achievement of the doctorate at Chicago: "I still remained interested in what I then called 'peoples' (rather than 'culture'). Therefore, I went to the University of Chicago to study sociology. I quit sociology because I found that it seemed to me all theory and little fact. I jumped out of the sociological frying pan into the fire of anthropology only to find that the anthropologists had plenty of facts but no ideas." But, as we have noted, he stuck with anthropology until he received his doctorate. When he began to teach the subject he enriched it with plenty of ideas, most of which for years enraged the dominant groups among American anthropologists.

It is instructive to note that Dr. White's concern with anthropology came late in his life as a university student. Neither Morgan, Tylor, nor Boas was an intellectual star in his youthful mental galaxy. When he did start to study the subject, and right down through the period of finishing his work for the doctorate, he read, studied, believed, and extolled the doctrines of the Boas School, to the demolition of which he has devoted most of his later academic and professional life. His early interest in the exact sciences certainly had something to do with his later rigorous adoption of the scientific frame of reference in his writings and his broad and precise knowledge of the interrelation of the sciences. His work in psychology and philosophy helped to produce his unusual ability to analyze problems of anthropological theory with keenness and precision. The importance of his psychological training was evident in the first article on anthropology that he ever published, the critical treatment of "Personality and Culture." Further, although as a graduate student he found sociology too theoretical, there can be no doubt that his sociological studies in earlier years were an enormous aid to him when his own work in anthropology became deeply involved in theory, especially theories of social evolution. Since W. I. Thomas was an unusually keen and astute student of methodology, it is quite possible that the courses taken with Thomas at The New School influenced Dr. White more than the sociology classes he attended at the University of Chicago. He has implied to me several times that this was the case. His youthful interest in medicine may have had something to do with his early anthropological concern with primitive Indian medicine societies.

TEACHING EXPERIENCE AND ACADEMIC CAREER

In 1927, Dr. White was appointed to his first teaching position, that of instructor in sociology and anthropology at the University of Buffalo, where his work fell mainly in the field of anthropology. He was promoted to assistant professor the next year. In 1930, he came to the University of Michigan as assistant professor of anthropology and has remained in this institution and department ever since. He was appointed to replace Julian Steward. He was promoted to associate professor in 1932. Despite the fact that the next decade was one of the more active periods of his life in research, teaching, and writing, his promotion to a full professorship was delayed until 1943. Colleagues attribute this mainly to criticism of his relentlessly scientific attitude by Catholic churchmen and other conservative religious groups in the state. The fact that he was professionally earnest almost to the point of quasi-belligerence in his early days at Michigan and was not an aggressive "mixer" in faculty society may also have had something to do with the delay in promotion. He became acting chairman of the Anthropology Department in 1936 and was made chairman in 1944; he voluntarily retired as chairman in 1957. His position has always been in the College of Literature, Science and the Arts and was never subordinated to the Museum of Anthropology. Although he was listed as assistant curator and later associate curator of the Museum, this had no relation to the Museum budget.

Under Dr. White's direction and guidance, the Department of Anthropology at the University of Michigan has grown from a one-man affair in 1930 to one of the outstanding departments in the United States or the world with a total staff of seventeen in 1959, some of them, to be sure, provided by budgetary arrangements with other departments. It is today the largest teaching staff maintained by any anthropology department in the United States. The first addition to the staff was Dr. Mischa Titiev, who joined in the spring of 1936. The next full-time additions were Dr. Richard Beardsley in 1947 and Dr. Frederick Thieme in 1948. Drs. Griffin, Greenman, and Spaulding, Professor Jones, and Mrs. Aga-Oglu joined the Museum staff at different times, and began to teach part-time in the Anthropology Department as the student body grew. By 1949, all of the above members of the Museum staff were teaching in the department and had their respective titles in it.

The present large staff is well distributed among the various branches of the general field of anthropology: ethnology, physical anthropology, archaeology, and linguistics. The department not only embraces all the main fields of anthropological interest and the most important specialties and geographic areas within each, but also represents diversified training in leading departments throughout the United States. It is not an ingrown department, as might have been expected of one built up mainly by one man. Of the total staff, only two men, Drs. Elman R. Service and Marshall D. Sahlins, were undergraduate students of Dr. White in ethnology at Michigan, and both of these men did graduate work and received their doctoral degrees at Columbia University. Most of the leading departments of anthropology in the country are now represented on the staff at Michigan: Harvard by five, Columbia by four, Chicago by four, and California by one.

Student interest and participation in the Anthropology Department have developed in proportion to the increase in the size of the staff and the diversity of course offerings. But the growing student interest, the resulting demand for courses, and the need for a larger staff were for years due chiefly to the unusual attraction that Dr. White's courses have offered to an ever larger number of students since 1930. When he came to Michigan, even the undergraduate courses in anthropology were small, and there was only a handful of graduate students. His two famous undergraduate courses, "The Evolution of Culture" and "The Mind of Primitive Man," were already drawing about 250 students each some twenty years ago. They are still among the most heavily attended of the non-required courses given at the University of Michigan. In reporting on Dr. White's services as a teacher to an important university committee in 1957, a committee of the Anthropology Department called special attention to "the importance of these courses not merely for anthropology concentrates but also for the general educational functions of the Literary College." There are about thirty undergraduate "concentrates" or majors in the department today and approximately fifty full-time graduate students.

Until 1951, only the master's degree was given strictly under the auspices of the Department of Anthropology. The doctor's degree was conferred on Emerson Greenman in 1927 and on James Griffin in 1936, but these men occupied positions in the Museum of Anthropology, had previous degrees from other institutions, and received their doctoral degrees by special arrangement. Two doctor's degrees, through arrangements with other departments, were later awarded to William Haag and Frederick Matson, but the first doctorate conferred independently by the Anthropology Department was awarded to Robert Anderson in 1951. The increased interest and enrollment in the graduate work is reflected by the fact that a total of twenty-five doctorates have been awarded since 1951. The chapters in this *Festschrift,* contributed by his colleagues and former students, reveal and underline the diversity of anthropological interests and achievements which have been stimulated and supported by the department under Dr. White's inspiration and guidance.

Despite his interest and activities in teaching, research, and writing, Dr. White has been very conscientious in discharging his administrative duties, both as regards matters within the department and the relations of the Anthropology Department with other departments and with the university as a whole. He has taken these responsibilities very seriously, never slighting them to make article or book deadlines. Yet he never went to the extreme of being dictatorial in administrative affairs or of seeking to dominate departmental activities and policies unduly. He has not hesitated to delegate administrative functions and has been notable for his loyal support of the decisions of those staff members to whom such functions have been delegated. The university authorities and alumni have learned to appreciate Dr. White's contributions to the substance, integrity, and expansion of intellectual interests and achievements at Michigan. Whereas his promotion to a full professor was delayed for some eleven years (1932–1943), he was one of five members of the university staff to whom the Distinguished Faculty Achievement Award, one of the outstanding university honors within the power of the institution, was granted. He received this award in 1957, and was one of the first five to be so honored.

The extent to which the Anthropology Department has appreciated Dr. White's scholarly leadership, his cooperative attitude with colleagues, and his administrative talents is well illustrated by the following excerpt from the letter that the departmental committee wrote to the Distinguished Faculty Achievement Awards Committee setting forth Dr. White's qualifications:

As an administrator Professor White has served his University well. Under Professor White's chairmanship the Department has been built up with discrimination and foresight, and under his guidance it operates as an effective, balanced unit. Professor White's conspicuous achievements as a scholar, his capacity to kindle enthusiasm and loyalty among a large group of students, and his harmonious administration of a fast growing department constitute an all-around performance of high distinction in the service of the University. Yet, though his unyielding assertion of scientific truth as he sees it has established his indubitable eminence around the world in his profession, he remains an unassuming and softspoken person among his colleagues and students. The harmony among the staff under him is high.

Although Dr. White has rendered a large service to the university through his administrative talents and the conscientious discharge of his duties connected with building and guiding an ever growing department, the main basis of his achievements and of the subsequent growth of the department has been his success as a classroom teacher. While his lectures are utterly devoid of the histrionic and the sensational in either approach or delivery, he is one of the more popular teachers at the University of Michigan and in the field of anthropology anywhere. This has been due in large part to his own intense personal interest in his subject and the deadly earnest but lively manner in which he presents his material. These attitudes seem to permeate most of his students, and his classes even attract many who anticipate or have been warned that their convictions are likely to be hostile to Dr. White's materials and attitudes. He usually gains their respect and confidence, and many who came to scoff have remained to praise, if never to pray. His concentration on the announced subject matter of the course is notable, and he rarely strays off into extraneous or irrelevant matters for effect or evasion. His presentation is clear, forceful, incisive, unequivocal, and uncompromising, but never arrogantly dogmatic. Even when criticizing those who hold opposing views, he always quotes their opinions or statements at length and with accuracy before offering his own criticisms or refutations. He never resorts to the frequent and easy method of setting up fanciful straw men and toppling them over with sophistry. Yet he is invariably forthright and uncompromising in the positions he takes on scientific issues. His firm but unprovocative stand against the attempts of the Catholic Church to muzzle his teaching has done much to strengthen the cause of academic freedom at the University of Michigan.

In short, Dr. White's popularity and effectiveness as a teacher have been due almost wholly to sheer intellectual appeal. To his own classroom earnestness and intensity has been added the fact that the problems and ideas with which he deals in his two large undergraduate courses are intrinsically important, thought-provoking, and usually controversial. In other words, they are "live" courses, even if they rarely deal extensively with current events. Dr. White is one of the minority of anthropologists who insist that anthropology does not cease with a study of the culture of the stone ages but is relevant to the understanding of even the latest implications of exploiting energy in an atomic era. Although there is nothing of the rhetorical showman about Dr. White in the classroom, his presentation is anything but dull and heavy or in any way conducive to somnolence on the part of students. His form of expression is lively, admirably chosen, and always cogent, frequently interspersed with sharp wit and cleverly adapted sarcasm. He makes his students feel that they are mutually engaged in a joint intellectual enterprise of much immediate and practical importance even though the actual theme may be an item from a most remote period. He can make the complicated relationship systems of primitive society seem for the moment as relevant as the jurisdictional disputes of contemporary labor unions.

If Dr. White never attempts to make a circus out of his courses, he also sees to it that his students are not encouraged to indulge in levity or laxity. He demands the undivided attention of students in his undergraduate courses, and it is usually offered quite spontaneously. His seriousness and dignity are joined to a somewhat defensive attitude when lecturing to his large undergraduate classes, caused in part, perhaps, by the fact that over the years there have always been some students in these classes who are filled with suppressed hostility to his bold and forthright handling of controversial topics. There is little argument in his undergraduate classes, for Dr. White is not notably receptive to, or tolerant of, views markedly different from his own, especially if these dissident opinions are traditional and uninformed, or mere heckling. In his graduate courses, which are attended mainly by students more familiar with anthropology and more sympathetic with his point of view, he is less on the defensive and more receptive to discussion, although even here he does not encourage vigorous dissent from his basic positions. It is probable that another reason for his being somewhat on the defensive in his teaching is that throughout most of his academic career, he has been battling for theories and interpretations that have been minority opinions in the anthropological profession.

If Dr. White is not given to wasting time in futile argument with uninformed or irate undergraduates in the classroom, he has been extremely liberal in giving his time to serious students who come to his office for information or consultation. The demands on his time in this respect have been far greater than in the case of any of his colleagues in the department. In addition to serving as departmental chairman, he did all the counseling and program-planning for graduate students in the department for many years. He is notably kind and sympathetic to worthy students who seek his guidance, and moreover, he has been extremely liberal and generous in the matter of having students in his home. Indeed, he has frequently invited whole classes of advanced students to his house for dinner.

What I have said in the preceding paragraphs accurately characterizes the nature of Dr. White's methods and achievements as a teacher of anthropology. But it is summarized, livened up, and brilliantly appraised in far better manner than I could do it in a statement sent at my request by one of Dr. White's brilliant and appreciative graduate students, himself now a university teacher of anthropology:

At Michigan, Leslie White came to teach two kinds of courses. The first consisted of immensely popular offerings with titles such as *The Evolution of Culture,* and *The Mind of Primitive Man.* Students from every walk of campus life flocked to these lectures and formed a large, if sometimes tense, audience.

Now any large school has its share of prima donnas, and the University of Michigan is no exception. Some of these gentlemen—notably heavenstorming romantics out of literature, converted Thomists out of philosophy, and the moodier type of analyst out of psychology—bridled at certain arguments in White's brand of anthropology. So they told their students, and the students, very naturally, attempted to carry the war to the floor of White's classroom. These students were in for a painful surprise.

Over the years, White developed the lightning-witted acidity one usually associates with the House of Commons. A student, equipped with a loaded question that he thought would demolish White and all his works, was outmanned, outgunned, and usually outflanked. Some of them probably still carry the scars. It follows from all of this that White's lectures were often lively, to put it mildly, and to those who were sympathetic, thoroughly enjoyable.

In his other kind of courses, the more specialized offerings for students in anthropology and the social sciences, Leslie White almost seemed another person. No one could ask for a more patient, painstaking, and genial instructor. He had all of that humility before the unknown that sets apart the truly perceptive man, a wonderful curiosity in anything and everything, and great personal charm. Off the campus, he was something more and perhaps better than all these things: he and his wife Mary were good friends to all their students.

Dr. White's scholarship and his ability to enlist the excited interest of earnest students have been widely recognized in the academic world. He has served as a visiting professor in a number of the leading departments of anthropology in the United States—Chicago, Yale, Columbia, Harvard, and California—and even for one year in Yenching University in Peiping, China. These invitations have been the more remarkable in that Dr. White's fundamental positions in anthropological theory were in more or less direct opposition to those held by the men who dominated the departments in which he was asked to teach.

Harry Elmer Barnes

OUTSTANDING CONTRIBUTIONS TO
ANTHROPOLOGY AND SOCIAL SCIENCE:
CULTURE, CULTUROLOGY, CULTURAL EVOLUTION

Before considering in some detail the main contributions of Dr. White to the social sciences in general and to anthropology in particular, it may be well to list those achievements and contentions for which he is best known and for which he is likely to be longest remembered. These are (1) first and foremost, the revival and rehabilitation of the doctrine of cultural evolution in a discriminating manner, validated and buttressed by a wider range of information than was available to the older, classical evolutionists, and clarified by a more closely reasoned analysis than any of the earlier evolutionists were able to bring to bear on the subject; (2) the further development and precise definition of the concept of culture as the core of anthropological interest and investigation; and (3) the forceful presentation of the contention that culture, in both its descriptive phases and its evolutionary development, must be entrusted to a new and independent science, namely, culturology, which, if not the whole of anthropology, is surely its largest and most important sector.

In the light of the fact that Dr. White will probably go down in the history of anthropology as the outstanding protagonist and practitioner of cultural evolution in the middle third of the present century, if not in the whole century, it is interesting and important to consider just how he arrived at this uncompromising but productive position and attitude. While he became well acquainted with the general theory of evolution and its application in various fields of science and philosophy during his undergraduate years, the doctrine seems to have played no part whatever in his earlier anthropological contacts and attitudes. Indeed, as a beginning student of the subject, chiefly under Alexander Goldenweiser and William I. Thomas, his original orientation in the field was strongly Boasian and anti-evolutionary. This approach was continued in his graduate work at the University of Chicago under Fay-Cooper Cole and Edward Sapir, both of whom had taken their doctorates under Boas. Most of the literature that he read in the field of anthropology prior to taking his doctorate in 1927 was that produced by the Boas School. In the light of his long and vigorous debates with Robert H. Lowie, it is interesting to learn that Dr. White states that of all this type of material,

Lowie's vigorously anti-evolutionary, anti-Morgan volume, *Primitive Society,* exerted the greatest influence upon him at this time. He has informed me that during this period he read virtually none of the works of the classical anthropologists and the older evolutionists, such as Morgan, Tylor, Frazer, Letourneau, Lippert, and the like, because his teachers informed him that such books had become "obsolete," and at the time he had no reason to question this estimate.

It is rather generally supposed by most students of ethnological theory who comment on Dr. White's position that he suddenly and accidentally happened upon a copy of Morgan's *Ancient Society* and from this was struck by a blinding flash of light that converted him instantly from a partisan of the Boas School to a crusader against its major tenets, much as St. Paul was converted on his way to Damascus. As a matter of fact, his conversion to evolutionism was a slow process and the product of several converging factors.

First of all was his early experience in formal instruction in anthropology at the University of Buffalo. Since he found that it was difficult for him to expound and defend the anti-evolutionary position even though he still adhered to it, he soon felt compelled to abandon his belief in anti-evolutionism. As he put it in a letter to me: "When I went to the University of Buffalo to teach I found that I could not defend, with facts and logic, the anti-evolutionist position I had acquired from Goldenweiser *et al.* After a time, I found that I could no longer believe in it." He repeats this essentially on page ix of the Preface to *The Evolution of Culture.* I am able to understand this explanation very well, for it duplicates precisely my own experience when I came to try to teach traditional classical economics in college courses. It all went well so long as I was instructing uninformed and innocent sophomores in the liberal arts college. But when I had to deal with a class of seniors from the engineering college, who had been around and gathered some contact with reality, I was compelled rather abruptly to reconsider my former approach to economic facts and theory.

The second important influence was that of a young colleague, the brilliant and learned philosopher Marvin Farber, who had joined the staff of the University of Buffalo the year before Dr. White came there. Farber had taken some anthropology as a student at Harvard and in extensive foreign study thereafter and was especially interested in the subject of evolution in general. He did much to undermine Dr. White's already fading confidence in the extreme anti-evolutionary arguments advanced by Lowie in *Primitive Society.*

Another impulse was a by-product of some interest in field work. When Dr. White went to Buffalo he found that a reservation for the Seneca Indians was nearby, and he took his students to study their life, ways, and traditions. This led him to read Morgan for the first time—at the outset not *Ancient Society* but the *League of the Iroquois*. This book encouraged him to read Morgan more thoroughly and completely and, as he puts it, "I found that far from being the kind of person that Lowie pictured him to be, he was really a remarkable scholar, savant and personality." The study of Morgan naturally suggested reading several of the other great evolutionists, but no others attracted his admiration and devotion as much as Morgan, with the possible exception of Sir Edward Burnett Tylor. In the case of Tylor the influence was greater with respect to the concept of culture than with regard to evolutionary doctrine.

The final step in Dr. White's conversion to enthusiastic evolutionism was a tour through Russia and Georgia in 1929, during which he first made his acquaintance in any thorough manner with the literature of Marx and Engels, particularly those portions dealing with the nature and development of civilization. In his treatment of the origins of the family, Engels had made especially wide use of the views of Morgan on social evolution and thus tended to impress Dr. White still further with the validity and importance of the evolutionary approach. The writings of Marx and Engels also helped to reveal the reasons that Morgan's theory of the role of property in cultural development was so vigorously attacked by Catholic scholars and by capitalist historians and economists.

Hence, by the time Dr. White came to teach at the University of Michigan in 1930, he had shuffled off his earlier Boasian anti-evolutionary orientation and had espoused the evolutionary approach. Much of his theoretical writing since that time has been devoted to a spirited and constructive debate with leading members of the Boas School, but for the last decade he has shifted his theoretical discussions more to a definition of the field of culture, and to the delimitation of the science of culture—culturology.

If Morgan became the main personal inspiration to Dr. White's evolutionary approach, a comparable influence must be assigned to Tylor with respect to his emphasis on the vital significance of culture in anthropological perspectives and operations. Dr. White frequently cites Tylor's classic and pioneer definition of culture in his great work *Primitive Culture:* "Culture . . . is that complex whole which includes knowledge, beliefs, art, morals, law, customs, and any other capabilities and habits acquired by man as a member of society." If Dr. White had developed his interest in culture earlier, doubtless Professor Alfred L. Kroeber would have been his first mentor in this field, for Kroeber's famous article on "The Superorganic" appeared in 1917 and was a commonplace in anthropological jargon and discussion among the members of the Boas School long before Dr. White entered Columbia or The New School. As it was, Kroeber's influence came later than that of Tylor, and was supplemented by that of Émile Durkheim and Wilhelm Ostwald. These men also helped him to discern the need for, and propriety of, a special science to study the nature and development of culture, which he has christened culturology, although he later found that the term had already been used in precisely the same connotation by the famous chemist Ostwald as early as 1915. It is somewhat curious that Dr. White appears to have known little about the work of men like Julius Lippert, Maksim Kovalevsky, Franz Carl Müller-Lyer, Alfred Vierkandt, and Alfred Weber, whose views were as fertile and cogent as those of Tylor, Durkheim, Kroeber, and Ostwald. At any rate, they do not appear to have stimulated Dr. White, and their stimulus was not needed.

In short, Dr. White's notable efforts to describe the nature and processes of cultural evolution and to delimit, develop, and defend the related theory represent bringing to fruition, on the basis of a richer and fuller body of knowledge and more complete theoretical comprehension, the pioneer work of Morgan and Tylor. In one of his most recent publications, "The Concept of Evolution in Cultural Anthropology" (1959a), Dr. White has discussed this matter in thorough and learned fashion. It will be impossible to present here in any adequate detail Dr. White's conceptions of culture, culturology, cultural evolution, and related subjects, or his contributions to these fields. An introductory treatment of these matters constitutes a substantial book of over four hundred pages— his *The Science of Culture*—and even this volume treats rather sparsely the nature and import of cultural evolution or the laws and processes of culturology. But we can outline the essentials of his approach, doctrines, and convictions, and indicate their significance for the present status and future development of anthropology and the social sciences.

First, we may turn to the nature of culture, which is basic in Dr. White's ideology and working equipment. Culture is uniquely human; no other animal possesses culture, for culture depends upon the ability to use symbols, an ability strictly limited to mankind. Dr. White called attention to the basic importance of symbolic behavior in an article published as early as 1940. That this article attracted a great deal of favorable attention is demonstrated by the fact that it has been reprinted in some six collections of articles aside from Dr. White's own collection, *The Science of Culture*. He describes the importance of the symbol and symbolic behavior thus:

> The thesis that we shall advance and defend here is that there is a *fundamental* difference between the mind of man and the mind of non-man. This difference is one of kind, not of degree. . . . Man uses symbols; no other creature does. An organism has the ability to symbol or it does not; there are no intermediate stages.
>
> A symbol may be defined as a thing the value or meaning of which is bestowed upon it by those who use it. . . . All symbols must have a physical form; otherwise they could not enter our experience. . . .
>
> All culture (civilization) depends upon the symbol. It was the exercise of the symbolic faculty that brought culture into existence and it is the use of symbols that makes the perpetuation of culture possible. Without the symbol there would be no culture, and man would be merely an animal, not a human being. Articulate speech is the most important and characteristic form of symbolic behavior (1949b:25, 33).

Culture comprises all products of the human use of symbols—symboling—when viewed and operating in their extrasomatic context, that is, when separated from direct and immediate relationship to the human organism: "Things and events dependent upon symboling comprise ideas, beliefs, attitudes, sentiments, acts, patterns of behavior, customs, codes, institutions, works and forms of art, languages, tools, implements, machines, utensils, ornaments, fetiches, charms, and so on. . . . Culture is the name of things and events dependent upon symboling considered in an extrasomatic context" (1959c:246–247). If these are considered in their somatic context, that is, their immediate relation to human beings, then they manifest "human behavior," quite a different level and category within the meanings and responsibilities of social science.

Dr. White's conception of the uniqueness of culture—the one product that man does not share with the animal world—naturally leads to his contention that the study of culture requires an equally unique science or discipline to describe, analyze, and evaluate it, the science he has appropriately christened "culturology." Earlier writers, from Lippert and Tylor onward, and even others before them, had clearly implied this, but Dr. White appears to have been the first *anthropologist* specifically to use the term "culturology." If he was not literally the first to suggest and employ the term, he was certainly the earliest to define, defend, and develop it. He is as much entitled to rank as the "father" of culturology as Auguste Comte was to be regarded as the father of sociology. Several of Comte's predecessors had anticipated most of his ideas, including at least roughly even his hierarchy of the sciences and his notion of the nature and lofty status of sociology. Of course, neither Dr. White nor any of his disciples would claim that he invented the culturological perspective; he *named* it for anthropology. Nor has he been its sole practitioner; many culturological studies were carried out before 1947, whether they were specifically called culturological or not.

Dr. White believes that Ostwald, a world-famous chemist, was the first to use the term culturology precisely in the manner that Dr. White defines it and with the identical implications. This was embodied in two essays published in 1915. But no anthropologist had ever picked up the term, developed it, and applied it fruitfully until Dr. White began to do so in his classes a decade and a half ago and set forth his convictions on the matter in his article on "The Expansion of the Scope of Science" in 1947. It was not until nearly two years later that he came across Ostwald's essays, a discovery which appears to have aroused considerable excitement and given him added gratification and confidence. As he once wrote me: "I am sure that no other *one* treatise on cultural evolution ever gave me the excitement of discovery that Ostwald's 1915 discourse on culturology did." Since culture, not social life, is the one unique and the most distinctive product of mankind, culturology should therefore be regarded as the supreme science and should supplant sociology at the apex of the sciences. Dr. White's 1947 essay is reminiscent in a broad way of Comte's famous discussion of the hierarchy of the sciences a century and a quarter earlier.

While one may readily concede the validity of Dr. White's argument for the place and need of the science of culturology, it must be admitted that it is today mainly a promising aspiration—a fruitful and challenging program, much like sociology was in the days of Comte. Culture is said by Dr. White, probably quite correctly, to have its own unique processes, laws, trends, and the like, which are of the greatest importance in explaining the human past, informing us how mankind has arrived at the present world impasse, and suggesting what the prospects may be for the immediate and remote future. But neither Dr. White nor any of his followers among culturologists or anthropologists have as yet told us much about what these processes, laws, and trends really are or illustrated and demonstrated them in detail from the experience of the past or present conditions. Nor has even Dr. White, in the first volume of his brilliant and learned *The Evolution of Culture,* gone very far in this direction beyond emphasizing the relation of the volume of available energy and its successful utilization to the grades or types of culture, the rapidity of the changes in cultures, and the trends in their development. This fruitful conception of the relation of energy to cultures and their evolution he had set forth back in 1943.

One must admit that most of the "laws" of culturology which have thus far been committed to print are those embodied in the books of the classical evolutionists of the last century. A "new" or revitalized science should furnish us with new laws, or at least should investigate, evaluate, revamp, and extend the processes, laws, and trends related to culture that were set forth in works of an older, less informed, and more uncritical generation nearly a century ago. In short, culturology has a most logical claim to existence, a well demarcated and most promising field and body of responsibilities, but thus far it remains chiefly a challenge to the culturologists of our day and the future. The paucity of its achievements to date is probably in large part due to the negative attitude toward most of the assumptions and problems of culturology taken by the Boas School in the United States and its counterparts in Europe. Whatever its other merits and achievements, anthropology in the first third of the twentieth century was pretty much of a culturological desert. There is little doubt, however, that this relative vacuum will soon be filled, and quite impressively—in considerable part by Dr. White and his students. In fact, this *Festschrift* is mainly composed of culturological studies which explicate the processes, laws, and trends of cultural evolution. A systematic treatment of the subject by two of Dr. White's students, Drs. Sahlins and Service, *Evolution and Culture*, is likely to be published before this *Festschrift* appears.

Dr. White was impressed with the importance of evolutionary doctrine and processes in general even before he began to study anthropology and became ever more conscious of its significance; hence, it is not surprising that he came to regard the evolution of culture as the outstanding problem in dealing with its manifestations. As he expresses it in the Preface to his *The Evolution of Culture:* "It would be curious, indeed—more, it would be incomprehensible—if this theory [evolution], which has been so fundamental in the biological sciences, so fruitful and illuminating in the physical sciences, where it is coming to be used more and more in astronomy and physics, and in many of the social sciences, should not find a place in cultural anthropology" (1959b:viii–ix).

His own contribution to making culturology something more than a promising forecast of a fundamental approach to human understanding lies chiefly in the cultivation of the evolution of culture. He goes to some length in emphasizing the fact that cultural evolution, as he understands and expounds it, is a faithful continuation, without any theoretical break, of the evolutionary theories and principles of the classical evolutionists, such as Morgan, Tylor, and their associates. His work is *evolutionism,* not *neoevolutionism.* The main difference lies in the greater body of information available to the evolutionist today and in the more astute theoretical analysis that can now be applied to the problems of cultural evolution. Dr. White puts this succinctly as follows: "Neoevolutionism is a misleading term: it has been used to imply that the theory of evolution today is somehow different from the theory of eighty years ago. We reject any such notion. The *theory* of evolution as set forth in this work does not differ one whit in principle from that expressed in Tylor's *Anthropology* in 1881, although of course the development, expression, and demonstration of the theory may—and does—differ at some points" (1959b:ix). He would retain the "stages theory" of cultural evolution that was a fundamental tenet of classical evolutionism: " 'Evolutionary stages' is a realistic and scientifically valid concept; progress in cultural change is something that can be defined in objective terms and measured by an objective standard or standards, and . . . therefore, cultures can be evaluated and graded in terms of 'higher,' 'more advanced,' etc. . . . Stages are merely the succession of significant forms in the developmental process" (1947a:165, 179).

The main novelties in Dr. White's approach to cultural evolution and his proposed cultivation of this field lie in the temporal scope of his perspective, and in the emphasis he places upon the importance of the role of energy in cultural evolution. Most of the older evolutionists tended to limit their work mainly to a consideration of cultural development during the preliterary period, although some did come down as far as the origins of civil society in the ancient Near East, and Morgan, Tylor, and Spencer made some references to classical times and even to the modern age. Indeed, Tylor made at least passing reference to the practical value of considering the whole period of human existence. He closed his famous *Anthropology* with this sentence: "The knowledge of man's course of life, from the remote past to the present, will not only help us to forecast the future, but may guide us in our duty of leaving the world better than we found it." Dr. White proposes not only to carry his detailed study of cultural evolution down to the present day but also to apply its principles to the prediction of the main cultural trends of the next century.

In a very real sense, Dr. White's emphasis on the importance of the harnessing and exploitation of energy in cultural evolution is not a fundamental departure from the doctrines of the classical evolutionists, especially Morgan, who laid primary stress upon technology as the chief factor in cultural development and social progress. The increase in the amount of available energy that is harnessed and used is directly related to technological advances and is the most important service of technology.

Dr. White contends that "The best single index by which all cultures can be measured is the amount of energy harnessed per capita per year. This is the common denominator of all cultures" (1947a:187). The extent to which energy is harnessed and successfully exploited determines the rapidity and complexity of cultural evolution. In the effective utilization of energy not only the technological equipment but also the social organization to exploit technology must be considered: "Culture has grown as the amount of energy harnessed per capita per year has been increased. But *amount* of energy is not the only significant factor in cultural development, although it is the most important and fundamental one. The *means* by which energy is harnessed is also significant. This factor is expressed in the efficiency of tools and machines, and in the social organization of their use. With the amount of energy remaining constant, the amount of need-serving goods and services produced will vary with the efficiency of expenditure of the energy" (1949a:377).

In treating the general framework and historical panorama of cultural evolution, interpreted in terms of improvements in the provision and exploitation of energy, Dr. White finds that there have been two outstanding periods of advance: (1) the agricultural revolution, based on the domestication of animals and the beginnings of agriculture, which took place near the end of the preliterary age and helped to usher in civil society; and (2) the great fuel revolution which was a phase of the industrial revolution that began to get under way noticeably in the eighteenth century, although it had its roots in previous centuries: "The first significant advance in culture was achieved when animals were brought under domestication, or plants under cultivation, or both. Plants and animals are of course forms and magnitudes of energy; and the arts of agriculture and animal husbandry are means of laying hold of this energy and of putting it to man's use, just as hydroelectric plants are means of harnessing the energy of rivers. . . . With the harnessing of fuels, especially of coal and oil, in steam and internal combustion engines, civilization took the next great step forward. And now a new source of energy has been tapped: the nucleus of the atom" (1949a:376–377).

While the conquest of energy has been the most important item bringing man from the Eolithic Period to the atomic age, its ultimate effect upon the human race will depend upon the extent to which the existing culture permits it to be used for constructive purposes. Cultural evolution has made civilization and brought it down to its present stage, but it can also extinguish both mankind and his culture if allowed to turn against them. As Dr. White expresses this near the end of his eloquent paper on "Man, Culture, and Human Beings," delivered on December 27, 1958, as Vice-President of the Anthropology Section of the American Association for the Advancement of Science: "Culture has given man power and control. But the price for this is bondage for the human race. We are carried along inexorably in culture's grip, and must face what'er's to come. And now, in this day, when culture holds out the prospect that we are no longer Earth-bound, but may journey to moons and planets, it also holds over us a threat most dire. Long ago, man might have perished but for culture's aid. Today, he may be extinguished *because* of culture, vanishing from the earth in the incandescence of thermonuclear explosion. . . . The time of decision is probably near at hand."

Dr. White goes to some pains to differentiate between the historical and the evolutionary culturological approach to a study of the past. The former describes events that are unique as to time and space, while the latter generalizes relative to classes of phenomena: "The historic process and the evolutionist process are alike in that both involve temporal sequences. They differ, however, in that the historic process deals with events determined by specific time and space coördinates, in short with *unique* events, whereas the evolutionist is concerned with classes of events independent of specific time and place. . . . The one particularizes, the other generalizes" (1945:230).

It was inevitable that Dr. White's vigorous exposition of the fundamental nature of the concept of culture, of the need for an independent science of culturology, and of the validity and overwhelming importance of the evolutionary approach to the study of culture would bring him into sharp and extensive controversy with many other anthropologists. He was almost a solitary figure in the early days of this lively discussion and debate. The older evolutionists were mainly dead or in retirement, and the succeeding generation of anthropologists were nearly all supporters of the anti-evolutionary tenets of the Boas School in the United States and its European counterparts. But Dr. White was not to be intimidated, and he took on the mightiest in the anthropological clan of the period.

It is not an exaggeration to say that, aside from the writer of this Foreword in his revisionist work on World War II, no social scientist of merit and integrity has ever engaged in a more one-sided contest, numerically considered, than Dr. White did. Nor has anyone in the anthropological field emerged in more creditable fashion and with more apparent respect and good will on the part of his opponents, however far they may have remained from being converted to the evolutionary position or to Dr. White's view of the nature of culture and culturology. This has been due in large part to the intense earnestness of Dr. White's attitude, his serious approach to the problems, his concentration upon facts and theory, and his avoidance of facetiousness and personal invective. He attacked attitudes and convictions rather than personalities, and he attacked with rugged honesty and complete fairness. Those who wish to follow his debates and controversies will find them listed conveniently on pages xi–xiv of the "Author's Note" to *The Science of Culture,* in footnote 9 on page ix of the Preface of his *The Evolution of Culture,* and in his 1959 article on "The Concept of Culture" in the *American Anthropologist.*

In his theoretical writings on anthropology, Dr. White has exhibited other notable traits and made many significant contributions, but in the space available it has seemed best to stress those which are of outstanding importance and to which Dr. White has made the most unique and enduring contribution. Such are his clear conception of culture, the nature, need, and contributions of culturology, and the validity of an unabashed evolutionary approach to cultural change and development. We can here do no more than to proceed to list some of the other characteristic traits or phases of his writings.

One of the more fundamental of these is the basic frame of reference of all of his writings and teaching, namely, a clear analysis of the method and philosophy of science and his forceful declaration of rigorous adherence to the scientific method in his own writings, a dedication which he has fulfilled with remarkable consistency and courage. One of his best statements of this attitude is contained in his article "Science Is *Sciencing,*" which originally appeared in 1938 and was reproduced with some additions as the first chapter of *The Science of Culture.* He has examined and rejected all theological and metaphysical explanations of phenomena. He has been especially, but not unjustifiably, harsh on the doctrine of free will. Dr. White has written in suggestive and illuminating fashion on the interrelation, filiation, and hierarchy of the sciences and in defense of the autonomy and independence of the science of culture—culturology—which he would place at the apex of the hierarchy. This has brought upon him some criticism from colleagues and others in the profession who are partisans of the interdisciplinary approach in the social sciences.

Next to his adherence to the scientific point of view, the most important item in Dr. White's assumptions and methodology is his espousal of a consistent and valiant historical materialism. This is not derived from Marx or any other brand of traditional ideology but from the common-sense assumption that the basic item of all culture is "the business of living," or the problem of survival. All other aspects of culture, however noble and commendatory, are additions, embellishments, and accretions. His emphasis on the importance of technology and on the outstanding product of technology—energy—follows naturally and logically from this initial subscription to historical materialism.

Also notable in Dr. White's historical materialism is the emphasis which he lays upon property and property relations as being perhaps the outstanding trait and characteristic of civil society (since the preliterary age): "All civil societies are organized on the basis of property relations. . . . Property is the foundation of civil society; its forms and processes are the morphology and physiology of the body politic. It is the common denominator into which all social classes above the tribal level of social development can be translated. The status of every individual, every class, is a function of property relations. Everything has the form or function of property; one is himself an item of property or is a property owner. In civil society property is the measure of all men" (1959b:329–330). This emphasis on property, following the precepts of Morgan, is about the only position for which Dr. White is criticized by some of his disciples. That civil society is organized exclusively, or even primarily, on the basis of property relations is a dubious statement. Few of the early primitive states were based on extensive private property or free trade, nor were even the Mediterranean states prior to the Greece of Aristotle's time. The immense importance of property relations cannot be denied, but to make them the core of social relationships is going a little too far.

Another of Dr. White's main tenets in which he departs from the view of most social scientists is his contention that mankind cannot control the course of cultural evolution—that culture, as he expresses it, "has reduced mankind to submission and bondage." He has adopted an adamant and uncompromising doctrine of cultural determinism in which economic factors are of predominant importance. This position, of course, makes short shrift of the "great man" theory of history and the notion of the primary role of genius in determining the course of historical development. According to his assumptions, the eminence and influence of a personality will depend upon the degree to which he is adjusted and adapted to the cultural environment: "A man of extraordinary native ability may live and die unknown unless the proper cultural materials and circumstances are at hand to realize his potentialities. Conversely, a certain combination of cultural events might make a man of rather ordinary talents appear to be a genius" (1946:87).

Dr. White's antagonism to the "personality" interpretation of culture is in harmony with his basic doctrine of cultural determinism. Although he was the first anthropologist to write an article entitled "Personality and Culture" (1925), he has consistently opposed the personality and culture movement within anthropology and its attempts to explain cultures and cultural patterns as a product of personality, an interpretation for which writers like Edward Sapir, Ruth Benedict, and Clyde Kluckhohn are best known. His rejection of the tenets of this popular recent trend in anthropology is the more remarkable in the light of the extensive attention he gave to psychology in his predoctoral academic work.

While thus far main stress has been laid on Dr. White's theoretical work, his writings and anthropological activities have by no means been confined to this area of intellectual endeavor. He has published four monographs based on extensive field work among the Pueblos of the Southwest over the last quarter of a century. The fifth, just now being completed, that on the Pueblo of Sia, is the most extensive and impressive. He also conducted a field school among the Pueblos for a brief period in the 1930's. Some critical commentators on Dr. White's writings have complained that he has rarely brought any reference to his field work into his theoretical materials. They have held that it is the more remarkable that he should have failed to do so, since he has commented rather harshly on the tendency of anti-evolutionary anthropologists to describe the classical evolutionary school unfairly as armchair scholars mostly devoid of field experience.

This criticism hardly holds water. It is rather difficult to understand how descriptive material on the Keres Indians of the Pueblos in New Mexico could be extensively introduced into any comprehensive theoretical treatment of the symbol, cultural evolution, or culturology. One would hardly criticize Darwin for describing Galapagos turtles or some rare bird he saw in the Argentine and then failing to return to them in detail in a general treatment of biological evolution. Dr. White's monographs on the Keres Indians are in the standard tradition of the reporting of field work—to describe that particular culture so that other field workers will not need to go there and do likewise. They are not supposed to be of any notable theoretical import. It might, however, have been wise for Dr. White to protect himself from devious or uninformed critics by at least some minimum but relevant reference to his field work in his theoretical monographs.

PUBLICATIONS AND PUBLICATION PROGRAM

With the possible exception of the time put on his monumental work on *The Evolution of Culture,* a vast four-volume enterprise of which the first appeared in 1959, it is probable that Dr. White has given more time to his biographical and quasi-biographical studies than to any other topic. Here we have in mind his intensive investigation of the life and work of Lewis Henry Morgan, the outstanding evolutionist among the classical anthropologists. He has not only exhausted the literary sources relative to Morgan but has also tried literally to retrace Morgan's footsteps in the areas where he traveled and did his field work. He has already published *Extracts from the European Travel Journal of Lewis H. Morgan* (1937); *Pioneers in American Anthropology: The Bandelier-Morgan Letters, 1873–1883,* a two-volume work (1940); an excellent chapter on Morgan's contributions to historical sociology in the volume which I edited, *An Introduction to the History of Sociology* (1947); and numerous articles dealing with Morgan's life and theories and the source material on these. The University of Michigan Press has just brought out his *Morgan's Indian Journals, 1859–1862,* the significance of which one commentator has equated with those of Lewis and Clark.

All of Dr. White's researches and publications on Morgan have been pointed up toward the definitive biography of this distinguished anthropologist and publicist, and at least emotionally this enterprise rates in the mind of Dr. White on a par with his *The Evolution of Culture.* There is little doubt that the study of Morgan, if completed according to expectations, will constitute the most impressive biography ever written of an anthropologist and will provide quite a different picture of Morgan from that presented in the criticisms of the anti-evolutionary writers of the first half of this century. It will also demonstrate that Morgan was a remarkably active, able, and interesting personality, entirely aside from his evolutionary writings.

While I have in several places called attention to one or another of

Dr. White's publications, it is desirable to bring them together here briefly, although this list must be limited to books and monographs. A full bibliography of his writings, including the numerous articles and reviews, has been prepared by the editors, and is to be found on pages 486–497 of this volume.

First to be noted are his monographs on the Keres Indian Pueblos of New Mexico: *The Acoma Indians* (1932), *The Pueblo of San Felipe* (1932), *The Pueblo of Santo Domingo, New Mexico* (1935), *The Pueblo of Santa Ana, New Mexico* (1942). The monograph on the Pueblo of Sia is being completed for publication in 1960, and will be a fitting achievement to commemorate his sixtieth birthday. The first volume of his *magnum opus, The Evolution of Culture,* carrying the treatment to the breakup of ancient pagan society, was published early in 1959. Mention has already been made of the three books he has edited on the life and activities of Morgan: the extracts from Morgan's European travel journal (1937), the Bandelier-Morgan letters (1940), and Morgan's Indian journals (1959).

The original plan was to publish *The Evolution of Culture* in two large volumes. In this form, I personally examined the massive and impressive manuscript of some 2,500 pages of carefully edited and well-written material. While readers for publishers thought well of the work, the increased postwar publishing costs made it impractical for any publisher to consider bringing out a work of this size without a large subsidy, no matter how highly the content of the book might be esteemed. Since no such subsidy was forthcoming, a tentative solution was worked out whereby the material dealing strictly with the evolution of culture would be edited carefully, deleted somewhat, and published in two volumes, with the dividing point to come at the end of the Roman Empire in the West. Then the long section on the fuel revolution, which would make a sizable volume in itself, would be published as a separate volume, to be followed by a final one that would draw the leading conclusions from the preceding three and apply them to a forecast of the main trends in cultural evolution during the next hundred years. If carried through as planned, this four-volume enterprise will constitute the most substantial and extensive project produced by any anthropologist of the present century with the exception of the late Sir James G. Frazer, and its scientific validity, of course, far exceeds that of Frazer's volumes. To this will doubtless be added the monumental biography of Morgan.

Although his monographs, articles, and reviews add up to an impressive total of pages, even friendly commentators have hitherto tended to regard Dr. White's literary output as more distinguished for its quality than for its quantity, but now with the essential completion of the four-volume project described above even the quantitative display is impressive. Certainly, few scholars have taken more pains with their writing than Dr. White. Until very recently, he wrote out everything in long-hand with a fountain pen, although he is a rapid and expert typist. It took me more than two decades to convince him that he should at least type his material. I was never able to persuade him that he could and should dictate much of his material, in first draft at least, to Mrs. White, who was a professionally trained secretary. He made a few halfhearted experiments at this and then gave up the effort. Both his longhand and typed drafts are always carefully edited and revised before being systematically retyped, and even these neat second copies are often revised and retyped once more. The result has been that all his publications are thoroughly polished. His style is lucid and keen, with a gratifying minimum of unnecessary verbiage. The reader is never left in any doubt as to his meaning. His prose is vivid, often characterized by striking turns of phrase. It sometimes attains real eloquence and sheer beauty of expression, as perhaps most notably in his December, 1958, paper on "Man, Culture and Human Beings," delivered as the vice-presidential address before the American Association for the Advancement of Science. This is the more remarkable in that the paper was prepared at a time of crushing domestic tragedy.

With the exception of his monographs on the Pueblos and *The Evolution of Culture*, the majority of Dr. White's writings have been, in differing degrees of intensity, material of a controversial nature. In the process he has developed what even his unconverted enemies have conceded to be a masterly controversial style. It is regarded by many as especially effective by virtue of its restraint and what is commonly conceded to be good taste. I have already called attention to the respect he has gained, even among his enemies, by his fairness in quoting fully and honestly the material he is about to attack. At any rate, few are likely to question the statement that Dr. White is the most prolific, talented, and effective controversial writer among all living American anthropologists.

ACADEMIC AND PROFESSIONAL HONORS

Casual reference has been made from time to time to the professional honors that have been conferred on Dr. White. Some of the outstanding ones may be listed here. In the strictly academic field, the foremost was the Distinguished Faculty Achievement Award given to him by the University of Michigan in 1957. This award had greater honorific significance in that 1957 was the first time that it was given. Attention has been called to the invitations to serve as a visiting professor at Columbia University, Harvard University, Yale University, the University of Chicago, the University of California, and Yenching University in Peiping, China. He was elected Chairman of Section H (Anthropology) and Vice-President of the American Association for the Advancement of Science in 1957, delivering the retiring address in December, 1958. Another testimonial to his status and achievements was the award of the Viking Fund Medal and $1,000 for outstanding contributions to the field of general anthropology for 1959. The winners of the Viking award in general anthropology are chosen each year by a committee of anthropologists representing the American Anthropological Association. Granted by the Wenner-Gren Foundation, the only American organization of its kind devoted to the promotion of research and publication in the field of anthropology, the award gives three medals each year: one for general anthropology, one for physical anthropology, and one for archaeology. One eminent anthropologist has observed to me that the delay in granting Dr. White the award deprived it of much honorific significance, since it should have been given to him a decade or more ago, if at all.

By far the most impressive public recognition of the significance of Dr. White's work came in 1947. The United States Rubber Company was for the time being sponsor of the broadcasts of the New York Philharmonic Society Concerts in Carnegie Hall on Sunday afternoon. The program was divided in two parts, and the interval between them was utilized to provide some distinguished scientist the opportunity to present the bearing of his subject on public life and well-being. Chosen to represent the social sciences, Dr. White delivered a brilliant, concise discourse on cultural evolution, with special reference to the significance of the harnessing and exploitation of energy. It was entitled "Energy and the Development of Civilization," and was published in *The Scientists Speak,* edited by Warren Weaver (1947), pp. 302–305; in two Technocratic magazines; and in digest form in *Time* Magazine.

BRIEF CRITICAL APPRAISAL
OF DR. WHITE'S WORKS AND IDEAS

In the light of the fact that I have written in rather enthusiastic and somewhat laudatory fashion about the career and achievements of Dr. White, skeptics may suspect that I can see no wrong in his work and regard it as having been carried out under divine guidance. Since Dr. White has engaged in more important and dignified controversial writing than any other living American anthropologist, those who doubt the validity of his attitudes and interpretations surely have ample data at hand written by those who question them. I do not pretend that my opinions about the merits and accuracy of Dr. White's assumptions and performance are infallible.

On the basis of as much information as any other living social scientist possesses on the general tenets and trends in social science in contemporary times and of rather more relevant information about anthropology than most social scientists who are not professional anthropologists have at their command, I can say that I go along with all of his major premises and the fertile exploitation he has made of them: the importance of the concept of culture, the basic significance of symboling, the need for, and the rational nature of, culturology, the validity of the doctrine of cultural evolution, and the general conception of cultural determinism if the latter is restrained by fact and logic.

My own experience with, and reactions to, the theory of cultural evolution went through a rather different development from those of Dr. White. In my junior and senior years in college I read virtually all the books of the classical evolutionists—at least those which had been written in English or translated into that language: Morgan, Tylor, Brinton, Spencer, Frazer, Letourneau, Westermarck, Sumner, Howard, and the like. When I started graduate work at Columbia University in 1915 I enrolled in the courses of Alexander Goldenweiser, the most erudite and eloquent of the disciples of Franz Boas, and my enthusiasm for the evolutionists was rather sadly deflated. At that time I also became personally acquainted with Robert H. Lowie and later read with avidity his *Primitive Society*. This finished the evolutionists for me at the time, and in a number of places I quoted Lowie's assaults on Morgan and evolutionism with much gusto.

At that moment Dr. White and I were at one in our repudiation of evolutionism. Thereafter, my attention became more and more diverted to social, intellectual, and diplomatic history, and I paid less attention to anthropological disputes beyond reading reprints which Dr. White and a few other anthropologist friends sent me from time to time. My firm conviction that Dr. White is both honest and intelligent led me to suspect that perhaps there was more to evolutionism than Lowie's famous funeral oration, echoed in his controversies with Dr. White, would imply. Careful reading of the controversial articles by Dr. White and much personal conversation with him further persuaded me. All this has not led me to believe that his views are the word of God, and he would be dubious about them if they were. But I am convinced of their general soundness, cogency, and permanent value.

It has already been pointed out that as of today, culturology still remains mainly a rich province of social science that has been little more than surveyed as to boundaries with a valid claim staked out. Its vindication and full development remain chiefly a task for the future, but there is already evidence of reasonably rapid and impressive success in carrying out this enterprise, as witnessed among other things by the work of Dr. White and his colleagues, for example, notably in this *Festschrift* and the book on *Evolution and Culture* by Professors Sahlins and Service.[2]

I would depart from the tenets and philosophy of Dr. White only in respect to the extremes to which at times he appeared to me to carry cultural determinism by overlooking in his "high, wide, and handsome" generalizing exercises the importance of personal and fortuitous factors in the determination or conditioning of historical events. Even in an extreme version, of course, this attitude is a valuable corrective of the dominant dogmas in conventional historical writing as to the primary importance of personal acts and influences in historical experience. If one were compelled to choose between extremes in these two opposing interpretations, I would have no hesitation in lining up behind even an inflexible cultural determinism, but I do not believe that this is necessary.

By and large, culture is the determining factor in the evolutionary process and the development of civilization. But within this larger framework there remains an ample field for the operation of personal factors and accidental occurrences. I tended to share Dr. White's monolithic views of cultural, or at least social, determinism until, more or less by accident, I was diverted into the field of diplomatic history about the

[2] See also the symposium *Evolution and Anthropology: A Centennial Appraisal.* Washington, D.C., The Anthropological Society of Washington, 1959.

time I first met Dr. White. In fact, the first systematic lecture I ever gave in this field was in the course that he attended in the summer of 1923, and no member of the class was more approvingly excited than he. It dealt with the revisionist correction of the causes of World War I. To be sure, my studies in diplomatic history for a third of a century have not dislodged my adherence to belief in the broad validity of cultural determinism. The fact that I have been the most prolific expositor of the doctrine of cultural lag as the outstanding cause of institutional maladjustments and social problems amply attests to this.

It would be impossible to discuss this vital matter adequately in the space available, but the issues involved can be at least briefly illustrated by reference to the causes of war in 1914. The settlement of group disputes by warfare had been a basic item in the cultural heritage of mankind since late primitive society. Cultural determinism was also very evident in the basic institutions of the early twentieth century: nationalism, racialism, militarism, economic rivalry, imperialism, and the like, which encouraged international disputes and their settlement by recourse to arms. It was also powerfully present in the diplomatic traditions and usages, even in the new influences on diplomacy, such as the power of the new popular press which did so much to inflame Europe from 1900 to 1914, and in the technology of war at the time. But the cultural background of 1914 and the cultural heritage of the chief agents of the advent of hostilities in August, 1914, had remained essentially constant for some decades before 1914 without producing any general war. No realistic explanation of the outbreak of war in 1914 can overlook the items of personality and accident in the five weeks between the assassination of the Austrian Archduke on June 30, 1914, and the launching of hostilities at the beginning of August. It required about six hundred pages of my *Genesis of the World War* just to summarize these adequately, and I do not intend to repeat it here. Not only were there such major personal items involved as Sir Edward Grey's devotion to the English policy of the balance of power on the Continent of Europe, Izvolski's passionate espousal of the desire to get the Straits leading out of the Black Sea, and Poincaré's determination to recover Alsace-Lorraine; such seemingly minor matters as Sazonov's being able to sneak into an interview with the Tsar behind the back of the Minister of Agriculture were of great importance also. Most authorities believe that this led the Tsar to revive his order for the general mobilization of the Russian military forces, an act which brought on the war when it was just beginning to appear that diplomacy might produce a peaceful settlement.

To be sure Dr. White, with his extensive knowledge of psychology and psychiatry and a more comprehensive command of historical data than is the case with many anthropologists, has recognized all this, notably in his articles that are reprinted with amplification in chapters VI and VIII of his *The Science of Culture*. Indeed, on pages 227 to 230 of this book he makes out an impressive case for the importance of personal and fortuitous items in human experience. My main criticism lies in the fact that when Dr. White launches into his grandiose and eloquent theorizing about cultural determinism, he seems to forget most of this, and culture becomes to him a sort of bulldozer or juggernaut which buries from perceptible discernment the personal and the fortuitous. It is just unfortunate that, in this instance, he does not let his right hand know what his left hand has done. I have argued this at length with him, and he always accuses me of mixing culture and history. My answer is that unless one *does* mix cultural determinism with all valid and relevant historical data, there can be no adequate understanding of any important segment of historical experience. Generalizations are surely very important, but they possess little practical significance unless they contribute directly to a better understanding of specific historical situations. In any of these it requires a great deal of careful thought to determine the relative influence of the cultural heritage and the personal and fortuitous elements involved. Even this can never get far beyond superior guesswork. At every time and place, the cultural background and human behavior are intertwined and interlaced in creating policy and action. To seek to separate them other than by formal definition is as futile as it is misleading.

When cultural determinism is pushed to a needless extreme it ceases to be a scientific interpretation. Culturology then becomes a sort of grandiose mysticism or a fatalistic, neopredestinarian theology, something that Dr. White vigorously and justly repudiates under those specific names. Undeviating and unremitting cultural determinism is something akin to the transcendental grace of God. But there is no need of pushing cultural determinism to an unreasonable extreme that rules out or pushes aside the personal and fortuitous. In creating the larger patterns and stages of human development and destiny, culture reigns supreme, and that assurance should satisfy any reasonable culturologist, whose real task is to understand and expound the processes of cultural change. My only complete dissent from Dr. White lies in our divergent conceptions of the possible role of the social sciences in social reform. In the *Scientific Monthly*, March, 1948, he wrote: "No amount of development of the social sciences would increase or perfect man's control over civilization by an iota." I am as irrevocably committed to the precise opposite of this as Dr. White is to the reality of culture and the validity of cultural evolution.

RECOGNITION AND HONORS FOR AN HONEST AND CONSISTENT DISSENTER

In this Foreword I have called attention to many interesting matters connected with the personal and academic career of Dr. White, but the one item which seems to me to be by all odds the most remarkable is the fact that, so far as I know, Dr. White is the only notable dissenter in the academic world who has also been accorded as many academic honors and as much academic recognition as he would have been likely to receive if he had been the usual weak and meek conformist. Indeed, I know of few other academic personages who have shown a comparable amount of courage and professional skepticism and have been able to hold their posts, to say nothing of being showered with honors. The dissent of the more notable figures in academic martyrdom in the United States, such as E. Benjamin Andrews, Edward A. Ross, Scott Nearing, Arthur W. Calhoun, Ralph E. Turner, *et al.*, was limited and trivial compared to that of Dr. White. He not only challenged the overwhelmingly dominant dogmas and trends in his own professional field but also resisted unflinchingly what has usually been the most powerful force in intimidating academicians and limiting academic freedom, namely, ecclesiastical obscurantism. He has warmly espoused the economic determinism that caused Charles Beard so much trouble, and has invariably taken an intelligent and skeptical attitude toward the dominant public idiocies of our day. Never in his classroom teaching, in his administrative responsibilities, in his relations within the university, or in his expressions of opinion on public affairs has he suppressed his honest opinions and yielded to expediency or ambition.

I find myself completely at a loss to explain this unique phenomenon in American academic history, surely without parallel in the present century and even less likely to have occurred in any other century, back to Abelard and Socrates. The recognition of Dr. White's integrity, earnestness, devotion to truth, repudiation of personal ambition and expediency, and total absence of personal vindictiveness may throw some light on the situation but, all combined, they offer no adequate explanation. I can only focus attention on this extraordinary fact and leave it to others to ponder. Whatever the total explanation, the demonstration of the devotion of the University of Michigan to academic freedom must not be overlooked or left without adequate praise. Yet this does not explain the numerous invitations to lecture in the seats of the mighty who were vigorously opposed to his views. It might be suggested that his scholarship and integrity were recognized, but Charles Beard was also recognized for these qualities on four continents for decades. Yet could any sane and informed person imagine Beard's being invited to lecture on the causes of World War II and American intervention during the 1940's at Columbia, Yale, Harvard, Chicago, or California? The analogy is not strained. Whatever the reasons for this virtually unparalleled situation, my delight over it is exceeded only by my mystification and lack of comprehension.

BIBLIOGRAPHY

WHITE, LESLIE A.

1943 "Energy and the Evolution of Culture." *American Anthropologist,* 45:335–356.

1945 "History, Evolutionism and Functionalism: Three Types of Interpretation of Culture." *Southwestern Journal of Anthropology,* 1:221–248.

1946 "Kroeber's 'Configurations of Culture Growth.'" *American Anthropologist,* 48:78–93.

1947a "Evolutionary Stages, Progress, and the Evaluation of Cultures." *Southwestern Journal of Anthropology,* 3:165–192.

1947b "The Expansion of the Scope of Science." *Journal of the Washington Academy of Sciences,* 37:181–210.

1949a "Ethnological Theory." In *Philosophy for the Future: The Quest of Modern Materialism,* ed. by R. W. Sellars, V. J. McGill, and M. Farber, pp. 357–384. New York, The Macmillan Company.

1949b *The Science of Culture.* New York, Farrar, Straus and Company.

1959a "The Concept of Evolution in Cultural Anthropology." In *Evolution and Anthropology: A Centennial Appraisal,* pp. 106–125. Washington, D.C., The Anthropological Society of Washington.

1959b *The Evolution of Culture.* New York, McGraw-Hill Book Company, Inc.

1959c "The Concept of Culture." *American Anthropologist,* 61:227–251.

ESSAYS IN

THE SCIENCE OF CULTURE

In Honor of Leslie A. White

✳ ✳ ✳ ✳

David F. Aberle

UNIVERSITY OF MICHIGAN

THE INFLUENCE OF

LINGUISTICS ON EARLY CULTURE

AND PERSONALITY THEORY

I. INTRODUCTION

In this essay I shall try to describe the impact of linguistics on early writing in the field of culture and personality: to discuss why language was used as a model for theories of culture, what assumptions about culture were made by extension from this model, and what difficulties arose from these assumptions.[1] Although I shall largely restrict my attention to Ruth Benedict and Edward Sapir, many of the comments I make have a far wider applicability, not only to other theorists in the field of culture and personality, but to many current approaches to cultural theory in general.

The topic is appropriate for an essay in honor of Leslie A. White, both

---

[1] I am much indebted for helpful and clarifying discussions and criticisms in the course of preparing this paper to E. Kathleen Gough Aberle, Robert Carneiro, Gertrude Dole, Herbert H. Paper, Marshall Sahlins, Elman Service, and Albert C. Spaulding. The ideas here expressed had their inception some years ago, and are influenced by Bernard Barber, Albert K. Cohen, Marion J. Levy, Jr., Talcott Parsons, and Francis X. Sutton, although they themselves might be surprised by the result. In certain respects this essay also follows lines suggested by Pitirim A. Sorokin's analysis of types of cultural integration (Sorokin 1937:3–53). I am indebted to the Horace H. Rackham School of Graduate Studies of the University of Michigan for released time in Spring of 1958 under a Ford Foundation Grant Program, during which period this paper was written.

· 1

because of his interest in the history of anthropological theory and because the first known paper entitled "Personality and Culture" was written by White (White 1925).[2] It was a plea for the use of cultural (including in that term what some would call social and situational) variables, to replace the physiological and neurological variables which were then prominent in many texts in academic psychology. It contained no word of the impact of personality on culture. By the time the reader has finished the present essay, he may feel that it has returned to White's position.

I shall be primarily concerned with Benedict and Sapir, although Franz Boas will also receive some attention. The period under analysis stretches from 1911 and the first volume of the *Handbook of American Indian Languages* (Boas 1911) to 1938 and the last of Sapir's publications in the field of culture and personality.

II. BACKGROUND

It seems fairly evident that Boas and many of his followers rejected most of the theoretical currents in cultural and social science of the times. (The reasons for the rejection fall outside the scope of this paper.) There have been many comments on the Boasians' hostility to, or neglect of cultural evolution. Such works as Lowie's *History of Ethnological Theory* (1937) and Benedict's lectures on anthropological theory as I heard them in 1940–41, indicate that French sociology as represented by Durkheim, and Lévy-Bruhl was also rejected or was accepted only in the form of piecemeal propositions. Functionalism in the manner of Radcliffe-Brown or of Malinowski was similarly unacceptable. Thurnwald's theoretical work seems to have made no impact, and there is no evidence that German sociology as represented by Weber received any significant attention during the years under discussion. The rejection or neglect of these various theoretical positions occurred in some instances prior to the development of culture and personality as a field; in other cases rejection accompanied the development of the field of culture and personality. Such orientations meant that during the period under discussion, most

---

[2] My attention was first called to this paper by Kluckhohn and Murray, who remark, "In 1925, Dr. Leslie A. White published an article called Personality and Culture in *The Open Court*. Dr. White was then a student of the linguist-anthropologist, Professor Edward Sapir. . . ." (Kluckhohn and Murray 1948:xii). In fact, however, the paper appeared in March, whereas Sapir came to Chicago in Fall of 1925, after a summer at Columbia (Benedict 1939:466–67) and its preparation was not influenced by Sapir.

of the currents of theory which made it possible to think of culture as an organization, as a system, either synchronically or diachronically, made no headway among the Boasians. In spite of individual exceptions to this generalization, it seems to me to be true on the whole.

In what terms, then, was culture to be analyzed? Boas and his followers considered that it was to be seen as a result of two factors, an historical factor and a psychic one. As for history, no culture can be understood solely by reference to its current situation. As a result of the accidents of history, it has had contacts with a variety of other cultures. These other cultures provide the pool of potential cultural material on which a culture can draw. Since there is no general basis for predicting what cultures will have contact with what others, the historical factor has an accidental and fortuitous character. With respect to the psychic factor (hereafter called psyche), there are qualities of men's minds—whether general tendencies to imitate or specific attitudes held by a particular group—which determine whether or not any available cultural item will be borrowed. Although contacts are unpredictable, the laws of psychology may account for acceptance and rejection. Hence the laws of culture are psychological laws. Thus culture is an emergent only in the sense that it is an historical precipitate, something more than a situational product. This position is represented by such writings as Boas' 1930 essay on social science methodology (Boas 1940:267–268), Sapir's focus in 1916 on historical and psychological explanations of culture in the introduction to *Time Perspective* (Mandelbaum 1949:391–392), and Benedict's remarks on history and psychology in *Patterns of Culture* (Benedict 1934:231–232). For all three writers the question was, how much is to be explained by history and how much by psyche. Under these circumstances, of course, problems of history and historical reconstruction were seen as particularly important. Although the sequence of culture contacts might be planless, history and the study of diffusion would tell us what the sequence was. And psychological problems were important, since a grasp of psychological principles would explain the selection of traits from the pool made available by contacts. This was the opening wedge for students of culture and personality.

As it happens, these and other orientations toward cultural phenomena proved particularly stimulating for the development of descriptive linguistics. The history-psyche dichotomy was absorbed without difficulty. The section on linguistic drift in Sapir's *Language* (1921) makes it quite clear that for Sapir drift is to be understood both in terms of long-range directional trends (history) and in terms of such factors as speakers' needs for pattern congruence, resulting in extension of one linguistic form at the expense of another, needs for pattern maintenance, and so on (psyche). Hence the analysis of language could go on within the context of Boasian assumptions about culture.

Parenthetically, this seems to me to account for the seeming paradox that Sapir, working successfully with language, "the most massive and inclusive art we know, a mountainous and anonymous work of unconscious generations" (Sapir 1921:235), could nevertheless deny the concept of the superorganic (Sapir 1917). He maintained that cultural phenomena stand in the same relationship to psychology as geological phenomena do to physics: it is not that the laws of physics do not apply to geological formations, or the laws of psychology to cultures, but that they do not account "conceptually," but only "concretely" for the particular phenomena encountered (a mountain range, a culture): that is, they explain, say, the fact of folding in a mountain range, but not the existence or particular form of that range. Nowhere is there evidence that he placed any reliance on cultural or social laws—only in particular congeries of materials and the underlying psychological laws. Sapir could work in this way with language; difficulties, we shall see, arose when culture was thus viewed.

Yet Boasian negativism and particularism proved very fruitful in the development of descriptive linguistics. Boas rejected oversimple theories of the development of language and categorizations of language, and waged war against ethnocentric models for the analysis of language. By insisting that the phonology and morphology of every language must be analyzed uniquely in their own terms, he provided the critical key for the linguistic study of "exotic" languages. The value of this strategy was amply manifest as early as 1911, with the publication of Part I of the *Handbook*.

We have already seen that Boas and his followers rejected a variety of possible approaches to culture—of analogies for thinking about culture: the analogy of biological evolution, the analogy of the biota, the analogy of the functioning organism. Given a striking early success in one field of cultural analysis, linguistics, it would appear natural that the analogy adopted would be that of language. I am not arguing that the approach to language developed in independence of thinking about culture and was then applied to culture. Rather I am saying that certain general assumptions made about culture, including language, proved particularly fruitful for work in linguistics, and that success and more detailed theoretical development in linguistics made the extension of assumptions derived from linguistics to total culture exceedingly tempting. Indeed, until very recently most of the parallels drawn between language and total culture have begun with language and been extended to culture: it is far commoner to find sentences which say, "As in language, so in culture," than to find those which say, "As in culture, so in language." [3]

III. THE LINGUISTIC ANALOGY

It is now necessary to select for discussion certain salient characteristics of language as viewed by Boas and Sapir (and indeed by many other linguists) and to show that parallels were drawn, explicitly and implicitly, between language, in these respects, and total culture. In this way the significance of the linguistic model for cultural theory can be demonstrated. It should be said that this is *not* an effort to present the most recent and sophisticated views on these subjects, but rather to represent the point of view both of Sapir, a linguist, and of Benedict, a nonlinguist, during Sapir's life and the first half of Benedict's professional career. The truth of the propositions about language is not critical, although many of them would be considered valid by linguists today. I shall list seven features of language and seven corresponding cultural analogies, commenting critically on some of the analogies. Part *a* of each of the following numbered paragraphs will deal with language, part *b* with cultural parallels, and part *c* with criticism.

1a. Language is characterized by the fact that it selects a small number of actualizations from a large number of possibilities. The range of phonetic possibilities is enormous, but only a small number of phonemes is actually used by any language. The range of grammatical principles is also vast, but the principles used in any given language are few.

1b. By the same token, culture is selective. No given culture utilizes more than a tiny fraction of the total range of known human behavior.

It is in cultural life as it is in speech; selection is the prime necessity. In culture . . . we must imagine a great arc on which are ranged the possible interests provided either by the human age-cycle or by the environment or by man's various activities. A culture that capitalized even a considerable proportion of these would be as unintelligible as a language that used . . . [all

---

[3] To avoid confusion, I should say at this point that although I must speak of "language and culture," I do not regard language as noncultural or culture as nonlinguistic. I am speaking of language as it is analyzed by linguists, and of culture as including linguistic behavior—but linguistic behavior viewed as a communicative device rather than as a set of phonological and morphological principles.

the known sounds]. Its identity as a culture depends upon the selection of some segments of this arc. Every human society everywhere has made such selection in its cultural institutions. Each from the point of view of another ignores fundamentals and exploits irrelevancies. One culture hardly recognizes monetary values; another has made them fundamental in every field of behavior. In one society technology is unbelievably slighted even in those aspects of life which seem necessary to ensure survival; in another, equally simple, technological achievements are complex and fitted with admirable nicety to the situation (Benedict 1934:23–24).

1c. Benedict's use of the linguistic analogy is explicit in this passage. She argues that selection is necessary in culture, as in language, for coherent interaction to occur. It is perfectly true that there must be limitation in cultural "form" and "vocabulary" for any group in direct communication. But as total cultures become more complex and heterogeneous, as groups become more differentiated, the over-all set of patterns for a complex culture can be exceedingly elaborate, to the degree that it is hard to see any limits for that *total* culture set by selectivity alone. In the contemporary United States, or in eighteenth-century India, how much of the total cultural complex is determined by a selectivity based on a need for coherent interaction (cf. Aberle 1950)?

This, however, is not the basic problem posed by the analogy. Linguistic selectivity is based on the fact that random sound-production would make communication impossible. The question of *which* sounds are selected is fundamentally unanswerable for any particular language, except in terms of a prior state plus change over time. We do not, and need not try to account for the origins of a particular selection, but need only acknowledge its existence. To adopt such a position for total cultures is almost too easy a path. Benedict seems to tell us that cultures select so as not to be unintelligible or chaotic, that we know the range of materials from which they select, as we know the range of sounds from which languages select, and that we know what they have selected— and that the inquiry can stop there.

This point of view ignores the fact that selection in cultures is not simply a reduction in random behavior, that on the contrary it has other important adaptive functions in addition to making face-to-face relationships intelligible. Benedict denies this: some cultures, she says, do not trouble to work on their technology; others do. This view is not sufficient. In linguistics, given the prior state of a language, the linguist can sometimes account for a later stage on the basis of the accommodations of elements to their internal environment. But with cultures, elements accommodate not only to one another but to the external environment. If a group is located in an environment where agriculture is possible, and is then driven into one where agriculture is impossible, then the "selection" of hunting and gathering as a primary basis for subsistence is not surprising, nor is it based on the need for reduction of random behavior. If a nonagricultural group is living in an environment where agriculture is possible, and is exposed to agriculture, then in most instances it must either "select" agriculture or face expulsion from the area through intercultural competition. Selection in culture, then, rests on factors which go well beyond the issue of reduction of random behavior. It is not adequate to document the fact of selection and the nature of the selection, and to treat it as arbitrary but interesting.

2a. Language is patterned. Indeed a treatment of the traits of a language is meaningless without a consideration of their arrangement (cf. Sapir in Mandelbaum 1949:33–60). Similarly, elements cannot be adequately analyzed except in the context of the pattern of which they form a part.

2b. Culture is patterned; traits can be understood only by reference to their arrangement, and cannot be understood apart from their context. Sapir makes the link between language and culture explicit—as well as telling us that language is the most helpful model for understanding cultural patterning. In an essay written in 1929 Sapir says that both language and culture are patterned, but culture patterns are harder to grasp; so language will show the way (Mandelbaum 1949:164–165).

3a. Some of the most important linguistic patterns are unconscious ones: the speaker does not recognize them except under very special circumstances (cf. Boas 1911: esp. 69–70).

3b. Some of the most important cultural patterns are unconscious —or the "real" basis for their formation is unconscious. In this area Sapir does not so much assert the utility of linguistics for an understanding of total culture, as handle both language and other behavior under the same rubric, in "The Unconscious Patterning of Behavior in Society" (1927—Mandelbaum 1949:544–559).

Boas' views on this matter are of particular interest because they show so early a concern with the utility of linguistics for an understanding of culture. He wrote, "Linguistic phenomena never rise into the consciousness of primitive man, while all other ethnological phenomena are more or less clearly subjects of conscious thought" (Boas 1911:63). Linguistic categories are one such area of unconscious thought. Other cultural categories, which bring together rules of etiquette, objects viewed with disgust, attitudes toward modesty, and the like, may, like linguistic categories, originate in similarly unconscious fashion.

It seems necessary to dwell upon the analogy of ethnology and language in this respect, because, if we adopt this point of view, language seems to be one of the most instructive fields of inquiry in an investigation of the formation of the fundamental ethnic ideas. The great advantage that linguistics offer in this respect is the fact that, on the whole, the categories which are formed always remain unconscious, and that for this reason the processes which lead to their formation can be followed without the misleading and disturbing factors of secondary explanations [what today would be called rationalizations], which are so common in ethnology, so much so that they generally obscure the real history of the development of ideas entirely (Boas 1911:70–71; see also 72–73).

The unconscious patterns found in language, then, will help us to understand the patterning of culture, where, for one reason or another, the patterns or their underlying rationale (as opposed to actor's explanation) are more difficult to grasp.

4a. Every language is a unique configuration. There are no general categories for the analysis of all languages. (I do not wish to make this position ridiculous. Phonology, grammar, and syntax are, of course, properties of all languages, as Boas, Sapir, and all other linguists would insist. But no specific phonology, grammar, or syntax is found in all languages; no categories such as the dative, sex gender, mood, tense are general phenomena.) The fundamental process of analysis must be to find the system of categories in the language in question and to describe it. By the same token, the unique configurations thus discovered cannot be compared point for point, but only as wholes (except when we are considering related languages).

This position is well represented in Boas' introduction to the *Handbook* (1911:81) and in Sapir's *Language* (1921:125). In this connection, I do not wish to imply that linguists do not in fact compare languages or parts of languages typologically. Indeed Sapir made such comparisons (1921:127–156). Nevertheless, there was a prevalent attitude among this group of theorists that different languages were fundamentally noncomparable.

4b. Every culture is a unique configuration. There are no general categories for analysis, in the same sense that there are none for languages. The process must be to discover and describe the unique cultural configuration. Comparison must utilize cultural wholes.

I can find no passage in Benedict or Sapir which makes explicit use of a parallel between language and culture in this respect, but can only show that Benedict's attitude toward culture is similar to that expressed by Sapir and Boas toward language in the citations provided above. For Benedict, Zuni, Kwakiutl, and Dobu cultures "are not merely heterogeneous assortments of acts and beliefs." "They differ from one another not only because one trait is present here and absent there, and because another trait is found in two regions in two different forms. They differ still more because they are oriented as wholes in different directions. They are travelling along different roads in pursuit of different ends, and these ends and these means in one society cannot be judged in terms of those of another society, because essentially they are incommensurable" (Benedict 1934:223). Furthermore, I cannot document my assertion that for Benedict general categories for comparing parts of cultures with one another were of trivial importance, save by stating that she conveyed this impression both in her course on anthropological theory and in her various area courses. I think, however, that many of my readers will recognize both the idea of the inutility of part-comparisons and the parallel idea of cultural incommensurability as being a part of the spirit of the times. I believe that the prestige of the linguistic analogy made such ideas far more comfortable for cultural theorists than would otherwise have been the case.

4c. The difficulty with the assumption of "incommensurability" is that, if it is taken literally, scientific work becomes impossible. If two objects or events are truly incommensurable, then no further statements can be made about them in the same universe of discourse. The less imposing claim that two objects or events (in this instance two cultures) can only be compared "as wholes" can be an almost equally serious stumbling block, although it need not be. It may mean that only attributes of each total system can be compared usefully, and that attributes of parts of the system which do not apply to the whole cannot be so usefully compared. If that is what is meant, the scientist's task is to develop a systematic list of attributes for the comparison of the wholes. But what seems to have happened in the case of cultures treated by Benedict and Sapir is the "comparison" of nonsystematic descriptions of certain cultures. All that emerges is some governing principle—dominant pattern, ethos, or what have you, like the Apollonian label, which is "compared with"— that is, described in the same work as—another such principle, say Dionysian. In the case of language, the insistence on incommensurability or on comparison of wholes, then, resulted in the emergence of descriptive linguistics, but in the case of culture it had the effect of retarding the development of general frameworks for the comparison and contrast of cultural systems.

5a. Languages change through "drift." Drift has three characteristics which are important for present considerations. First, although inspection of historical tendencies tells us the direction of drift (say, toward positional emphasis in English), there is no a priori basis for predicting the direction of drift. Second, changes are consistent, not random, so that the result of change is not chaos but either the "same" pattern with different content, or a shift to a different pattern. Third, change frequently gives rise to greater consistency: out of several available patterns one is chosen for dominant emphasis.

The linguistic drift has direction (Sapir 1921:165). What is the primary cause of the unsettling of a phonetic pattern and what is the cumulative force that selects these or those particular variations of the individual on which to float the pattern readjustments we hardly know (Sapir 1921:195–196). It is obvious that a language cannot go beyond a certain point in this randomness. Many languages go incredibly far in this respect, it is true, but linguistic history shows conclusively that sooner or later the less frequently occurring associations are ironed out at the expense of the more vital ones. In other words, all languages have an inherent tendency to economy of expression (Sapir 1921: 38–39). Thus analogy not only regularizes irregularities that have come in the wake of phonetic processes but introduces disturbances, generally in favor of greater simplicity or regularity, in a long established system of forms. These analogical adjustments are practically always symptoms of the general morphological drift of the language (Sapir 1921:203).

5b. Cultures also change through drift. The reasons why they drift the way they do are either unimportant or incomprehensible, but the result is often greater consistency.

In discussing the development of styles of writing, Sapir said in 1921, "It is not otherwise with language, with religion, with the forms of social organization. Wherever the human mind has worked collectively and unconsciously, it has striven for and often attained unique form. The important point is that the evolution of form has a drift in one direction, that it seeks poise, and that it rests, relatively speaking, when it has found this poise" (Mandelbaum 1949:382). "The drift of culture, another way of saying history, is a complex series of changes in society's selected inventory—additions, losses, changes of emphasis and relation" (Sapir 1921:233). Sapir continues by saying ". . . we shall do well to hold the drifts of language and of culture to be non-comparable and unrelated processes" (Sapir 1921:234). But here he is not rejecting the analogy of drift as such, but the idea that the drift of a particular language is related in any causal or functional way to the drift of the culture associated with the speakers of that language: he is saying not that we cannot speak of cultural drift on the analogy of linguistic drift, but that the two processes do not go on *pari passu*.

Benedict makes the analogy explicit in her "Configurations of Culture in North America" (1932).

It is, however, the reality of such configurations that is in question. I do not see that the development of these configurations in different societies is more mystic or difficult to understand than, for example, the development of an art style. Many cultures have never achieved this thoroughgoing harmony. There are peoples who seem to shift back and forth between different types of behavior. . . . But the fact that certain people have not . . . [achieved consistency], no more makes it unnecessary to study culture from this angle than the fact that some languages shift back and forth between different fundamental grammatical devices in forming the plural or in designating tense, makes it unnecessary to study grammatical forms (1932:26–27).

Both Sapir and Benedict, then, made explicit analogies between linguistic drift and cultural process. Benedict did not, of course, argue that *all* cultures showed a drift toward consistency, but in discussing this drift, she compared it with linguistic drift. I cannot point out further explicit comparisons between linguistic and cultural drift made by Benedict and Sapir, but it is worthwhile quoting one key passage in which Benedict makes use of the concept of cultural drift.

The cultural situation in the Southwest is in many ways hard to explain. With no natural barriers to isolate it from surrounding peoples, it presents probably the most abrupt cultural break that we know in America. All our efforts to trace out the influences from other areas are impressive for the fragmentariness of the detail; we find bits of the weft or woof of the culture, we do not find any very significant clues to its pattern. From the point of view of the present paper this clue is to be found in a fundamental psychological set which has undoubtedly been established for centuries in the culture of this region, and which has bent to its own uses any details it imitated from surrounding peoples and has created an intricate cultural pattern to express its own preferences. It is not only that the understanding of this psychological set is necessary for a descriptive statement of this culture; without it the cultural dynamics of this region are unintelligible. For the typical choices of the Apollonian have been creative in the formation of this culture, they have excluded what was displeasing, revamped what they took, and brought into being endless demonstrations of the Apollonian delight in formality, in the intricacies and elaborations of organization (Benedict 1930:581).

David F. Aberle

Discussion of several features of this quotation must be deferred. The noteworthy point for present purposes is that Benedict treats cultural drift as an autonomous process. She considers it important to discover the nature of the fundamental configuration and to describe the direction of the drift (toward a more and more harmonious Apollonian pattern), but she does not ask why the drift takes a particular direction. This corresponds exactly to the linguist's attitude toward linguistic drift.

5c. The criticism of the concept of cultural drift as used by Benedict and Sapir is identical with the criticism of the concept of selectivity (*1c* above), since the two concepts are closely allied. For example, there is no mention of the environmental, technological, and economic factors which might account for a portion of the selective nature of the drift. Benedict seems to feel no need to mention them—just as it would be unnecessary in linguistics to inquire why one pluralizing device was winning out over others, provided one could demonstrate that one such device was in the ascendancy. Benedict seems to see all the cultural apparatus of the Plains, of the Circumpueblo area, and of the Colorado River, as available to the Puebloans—who either refused to take it on or transformed it, because they had an Apollonian bent. She does not point out the significance of ecology: that the Puebloans occupied reusable agricultural land, which they had to defend, had a culture primarily based on agriculture, irrigated their lands, did not have dense herds of buffalo immediately available in their area, etc., whereas the Plains Indians did have such herds, could use the horse efficiently to hunt them, occupied nonagricultural or marginally agricultural lands, and found predation easy and defense of a sharply delimited area unnecessary. The facts of ecological succession or ecological adaptation in the Pueblo area are not treated as important. It should be noted, however, that when she wrote, Southwestern archeologists tended to make more of a mystery of the origins of Southwestern culture than would be the case today.

6a. No language is inherently "superior" or "inferior" to another as an adaptive or an expressive vehicle: in terms of morphology all languages are potentially capable of carrying the same informational "load," although a given language may not have the lexicon for certain messages, if these messages are not required. Even though it may be possible to speak of grammatical complexity or simplicity, there is no association between complexity and communicative capacity. One language is no more "primitive" than another—either in the sense of being simpler, or in the sense of representing an earlier, less developed stage of communication.

6b. As adaptive systems, cultures cannot be described as "superior" or "inferior" nor called "simple" or "complex" or "primitive" or "civilized" except by putting the words in quotes.

6c. There is a sense in which cultural relativism is a valid position: science does not provide answers to questions of ultimate values. There is no scientific sense in which we can say that nineteenth-century American culture is "better" than Plains Indian culture. But again the question of adaptation arises when we consider total cultures, in a way that it does not when we consider linguistic phonology and morphology. American English may not be a superior communicative device compared with Omaha. But plough agriculture and its accompaniments are superior *as an adaptation in the American prairies* to buffalo hunting and gathering: American culture successfully competed with and annihilated Plains culture when the two attempted to utilize the same environmental niche.

Cultures can be ranked with respect to energy utilization, and there are associations between energy utilization and other features of culture (White 1949:363–393). But even when languages are ranked with respect to complexity (for example, Greenberg 1954:192–220), no special corollaries have been discovered. Cultures can be ranked with respect to the number of role systems, the elaboration of the division of labor, the size of the group integrated within one cultural system, and so on (cf. Naroll 1956). There are no parallels in linguistic systems.

In sum, the morphology of any given language is equivalent to any other as a communicative device. But although any culture may be an adequate—that is, a feasible—adaptation for a particular environment, it is frequently possible to say quite straightforwardly whether a hunting and gathering, or an agricultural economy will be competitively superior in a particular setting. As in the case of selection and drift, the analogy between language and culture breaks down insofar as adaptation and ecological, technological and economic considerations do not have linguistic analogues. (In fact, however, there are analogues for communication systems, though not for natural languages. Cf. Greenberg 1957:56–65.)

7a. The grammar and phonology of a language analyzed by a linguist consist of the shared speech-patterns of a speech community. They are derived by analyzing the patterns of speech of a series of individual speakers and factoring out the shared patterns from the various idiolects. We do not derive the dative from speaker A and the accusative from speaker B. The idiolect is, loosely speaking, isomorphic with the language. This proposition I regard as so fundamental to linguistic research as to require no documentation.

7b. A culture consists of the shared behavior of the members of a group.[4] It also is derived by examining the behaviors (including descriptions of behavior, conversation, etc.) of the members of a group and factoring out the shared patterns from the various idiosyncratic behaviors. The outlook of the individual—his cultural idiolect—is isomorphic with the culture. Although, as I think I can later show, this outlook pervades the work of Sapir and Benedict (See Section IV), I cannot demonstrate that the linguistic analogy was used in this connection. I believe that no such analogy was used precisely because the assumption here was entirely implicit: no other view of culture was imagined.

7c. This, of course, although an implicit analogy, is the most critical misapplication of the linguistic model. There are *three* terms in fact to a consideration of linguistic materials: idiolect, language (or dialect), and system of communications. People do not *share* a system of communication, they *participate* in it, precisely because they occupy *different* positions in the communications chain. The organization of a communications system is different in kind from the organization of an idiolect or a dialect; it has no isomorphism with either.

There are three corresponding terms for the analysis of a culture: cultural idiolect, shared culture, and cultural system. And cultural system, again, is a matter in which individuals participate. It is not a matter of sharing. This distinction is easily obscured in the most primitive cultures, since to some degree every member *knows* about the cultural behavior involved in other roles, but the distinction is still there. Even the cultural *system* of a simple Shoshonean group involves relationships of asymmetry and reciprocity. It involves the interaction of, not the sum of, the cultural behavior of males and of females, of children and adults and aged.

If the insistence on *shared* behavior is maintained in the analysis of complex cultural systems, confusion arises rapidly. It leads to an insistence that it is nonsense to speak of American culture, since so many groups have such different beliefs, ideologies, and habits. Alternatively, it leads to a definition of an American culture which consists only of those things which all, or almost all, Americans share: belief in the ballot box,

---

[4] By the "shared" speech patterns of a speech community, I refer to patterns of phonology or morphology found in similar or nearly identical form in the speech of each member of the community. By "shared" behavior I refer to linguistic or non-linguistic activities manifest in similar or near-identical form by each member of the group. It may be objected that no one *really* meant that the patterns were shared by *all* members of the group, that obviously there are at a minimum age and sex differences; to this the reply must be made that the problem was not dealt with in sufficiently explicit a fashion. It may also be claimed that by "sharing" some theorists refer to common understandings, not common behavior. Again, there has not been sufficient care to make this explicit, if that is the intention.

knowledge of American English, use of cash, etc. But it is precisely the interlocking of *different* cultural items *not* uniformly diffused through the population which permits American culture to function as a system: for example, the relationship between mathematics, engineering, and mechanical skills that makes a factory possible. Indeed, it is a requisite for the functioning of a highly differentiated cultural system that the members who participate in the system *cannot* share all the items that make up the culture complex.

It is here that linguistics, which could proceed using only history and psyche for the analysis of linguistic phenomena, was utterly misleading as an analogy for the understanding of culture. The inability of the Boasians to come to terms with cultural *systems,* masked by the success of linguistics, led to difficulties which have plagued the development of culture and personality theory ever since—and indeed the development of cultural theory.

IV. EARLY CULTURE AND PERSONALITY THEORY

It now becomes necessary to shift to a chronological treatment of essays by Sapir and Benedict in the area which has become known as "culture and personality." As a preliminary, there are a few points that I should like to clarify.

First, I am *not* attempting to make a critique of descriptive or comparative linguistics, of Sapir as a linguist, of the Whorfian hypothesis, or anything of the sort. I do not assert that the linguistic model was the sole source of the approach to culture of Boas, Benedict, and Sapir. Nor am I saying that *all* analogies between language and total culture are false and misleading. Indeed it is true that language and culture are patterned, are selective, involve unconscious elements (elements of which speakers or members of the culture are unaware), and so on. I have tried to make clear the particular points at which I consider the analogies to be misleading, incorrect, or incomplete. Nor do I claim that there is no value in the work of Benedict or Sapir, or that an understanding of an individual's organization of the cultural materials available to him is valueless (cf. Aberle 1951). I would claim, however, that the unwillingness or inability to come to grips with culture as a system in any sense except a set of congruences analyzed from the point of view of the actor in the system was a serious source of confusion in culture and personality theory.

I would not argue that Benedict and Sapir were incapable of analyzing cultural systems as such. Sapir's 1915 essay on Northwest Coast social organization (Mandelbaum 1949:468–487) and Benedict's "Marital Property Rights in Bilateral Society" (1936) alone would refute such a suggestion. I would claim, however, that this was not the approach that either one found most congenial, and that the central tendency of their work is correctly described in this essay. This tendency is manifest in their concern for ritual, mythology, folklore, ideology, and style, and in their relative lack of interest in economics, political systems, and the organization of kinship relationships. In this section I shall no longer be concerned with establishing the use of a linguistic model, but instead with some of the problems raised by cultural theory, and by culture and personality theory, developed in the context of the assumptions mentioned in Section III.

By 1916, in his *Time Perspective,* Sapir had already divided the universe of explanation of cultural phenomena into historical and psychological factors or explanations. This dichotomy persisted throughout his professional career, although the weight which he was disposed to give to psychological versus historical factors varied from time to time. It should be said that sometimes Sapir uses the word "psychological" to refer to explanations based on the immediate operation of men's minds. Such explanations of cultural phenomena he always eschewed. Culture was always to be explained in part historically, but increasingly, psychological factors operating through time rather than immediately, were invoked.

In *Time Perspective* Sapir shows his concern with meaning rather than with function and system: "If any general point should have come out more clearly than another in the course of our discussion, it is the danger of tearing a culture element loose from its psychological and geographical (i.e., distributional) setting" (Mandelbaum 1949:462). A reply to an article of Dewey's published in 1916 displays his historical bias and his rejection of culture as a system: "Each of the aspects of social life, say philosophy, or music or religion, is more definitely determined in form and content by the past history of that aspect . . . than by its co-existence with the other aspects of that life" (Sapir 1916:2). There is, however, a foreshadowing of the position he was to take in "Culture, Genuine and Spurious": "A constant but always very imperfectly consummated tendency is present towards the moulding of these more or less distinct strands into a fabric; countless modifications and adaptations result, but the strands nevertheless remain distinct" (*loc. cit.*).

By 1917, it was to meaning that Sapir turned for understanding unsolved anthropological problems: an understanding of symbol-formation in the unconscious, he felt, would prove "indispensable for an approach to the deeper problems of religion and art," presumably because psychoanalysis affords some possibility of understanding the phenomena of the mind as an organized whole—unlike academic psychology (Mandelbaum 1949:523–524).

A review of Lowie's *Primitive Society* in 1920 contains a rejection of evolutionism and of "psychological" explanations. The psychology to which he objects, however, is the tendency to explain institutions as arising out of universals of the human mind. Indeed Sapir puts evolutionism in the class of psychological explanations, presumably basing this criticism on certain elements in Morgan's and Bastian's thinking, although they are not mentioned. Evolutionism is psychological for Sapir because he sees it as a tendency to view cultural phenomena as arising from "germs of thought" operating under similar conditions. His answer to these approaches is Lowie's particularistic, diffusion-based historicism: ". . . what if a widespread social feature . . . can be shown . . . to be not the immediate and universal psychological response that we would have it, but an originally unique, local phenomenon that has gradually spread by cultural borrowing over [a] continuous area?" (Sapir 1920:378). Nevertheless, it was to psychology in history that Sapir turned for his explanations, and indeed had already turned, in "Culture, Genuine and Spurious," which was begun by 1919 and published in full in 1924.

This essay is crucial for the understanding of the development of culture and personality theory. Sapir begins by distinguishing three views of culture. One is the layman's—the view which uses culture as a synonym for education and refinement of taste. Another is the traditional ethnological view: "any socially inherited element in the life of man, material and spiritual" is cultural (Mandelbaum 1949:309). Sapir wishes to add to these his own view, which is culture as a world outlook. His view "aims to embrace in a single term those general attitudes, views of life, and specific manifestations of civilization that give a particular people its distinctive place in the world. Emphasis is put . . . on how what is done and believed functions in the whole life of that people, on what significance it has for them." "Culture thus becomes nearly synonymous with the 'spirit' or 'genius' of a people," but these terms, Sapir says, are psychological, whereas "culture includes . . . a series of concrete manifestations" of this spirit (Mandelbaum 1949:309–311).

In a sentence Sapir now states the core conception of Benedict's *Patterns of Culture*. "A mode of thinking, a distinctive type of reaction, gets itself established, in the course of a complex historical development, as typical, as normal; it serves then as a model for the working over of new elements of civilization" (Mandelbaum 1949:311). Here we have a gifted linguist's understanding of cultural development, after the model of language: a pattern—like affixing—gets somehow established; the pattern is an orientation toward the world, not a system of relationships among culture traits or among social roles; new items are accommodated to that pattern. There is no need to explain the source of the pattern.

As examples he uses French and Russian culture. In the case of the French he focuses on such characteristics as "clarity, lucid systematization, balance, care in choice of means, and good taste" and finds reflections of French "genius" in the nature of aesthetic movements, the quality of musical style, attitudes toward religion, and "the strong tendency to bureaucracy in French administration" (Mandelbaum 1949:312–313). One can be impressed with the intuitive flash which allies bureaucracy and musical style, but the treatment of these two elements of culture on the same level and in the same terms makes sense only in the light of Sapir's avowed view of culture as "general attitudes." Sapir's statement may dazzle, but it begs more questions than it raises as to the nature and sources of the characteristics of French bureaucracy, and I cannot in fact imagine what next steps should be taken, in the light of Sapir's statement, to understand the phenomenon. This tendency to bring together many institutional areas under one configurational rubric, without a proper understanding of the systematic character of any of the areas involved, was to be a source of confusion in culture and personality theory for several decades: the inability to separate a cultural system from an individual outlook—or in my earlier terms, to separate the analogue of a communications system from the analogue of a language.

Sapir's interest in configuration, expressed in "Culture, Genuine and Spurious," developed as a preoccupation with a drive toward formal elegance in culture—a "form libido" as he once called it (Mandelbaum 1949:527; the essay appeared in 1921). Meantime his interest in the source of configurations made him increasingly concerned with psychology, and specifically with psychoanalysis. The concern with a drive toward form arises again in an essay on "Anthropology and Sociology" (1927), where it is introduced to explain parallel developments that do not rest on diffusion. "We can only glance at a few of these formal convergences . . . which we believe to be of common interest to anthropology, to sociology, and to a social psychology of form which has hardly been more than adumbrated" (Mandelbaum 1949:339). He compares the internal solidarity and external hostility of Naga clans, Northwest coast villages, and modern nations. "In each case a social group-pattern —or formal 'image,' in psychological terms (clan, nation)—so dominates feeling that services which would naturally flow in the grooves of quite other intercrossing or more inclusive group patterns . . . must suffer appreciable damage" (Mandelbaum 1949:339). Here Sapir makes the attitudes of individuals, shared to be sure, account for social forms. But clearly this analysis will not long prove satisfactory: he will eventually be driven to account for the kinds of feelings by finding out more about the kind of persons involved. There is a further and more elaborate treatment of form libido with reference to the neat arrangements of clans, band camps, and the like, in various primitive societies, and the analogy from Sapir's views of linguistic process is evident (Mandelbaum 1949:344). More important for culture and personality theory is Sapir's concern with "the possible transfer of a psychological attitude or mode of procedure which is proper to one type of social unit to another type of unit in which the attitude or procedure is not so clearly relevant" (Mandelbaum 1949:342). This point of view has its parallel in Sapir's comments on "analogical adjustments in language," quoted earlier.

An example of pattern transfer is to be found in the Roman Catholic Church bureaucracy, which is probably a

carry-over of the complex structure of Roman civil administration. That the Jews and the evangelical Protestant sects have a far looser type of church organization does not prove that they are, as individuals, more immediately swayed by the demands of religion. All that one has a right to conclude is that in their case religion has socialized itself on a less tightly knit pattern, a pattern that was more nearly congruent with other habits of their social life (Mandelbaum 1949:343).

Apparently the Protestants just lost their bureaucratic habits. Whatever this example and the earlier one prove about the social process, they seem to me to indicate that for Sapir the presence, absence, and form of institutions are to be explained in terms of their congruence with a particular world view of the members of the society in which they appear (or do not appear). Sapir sums up by saying that he sees a "germ of a social philosophy of values and transfers that joins hands in a very suggestive way with such psychoanalytic concepts as the 'image' and the transfer of emotion" (Mandelbaum 1949:343). By 1927, then, Sapir was building analogies not just between language and culture, but between personality processes and culture.

The full tide of Sapir's use of personality psychology, however, comes in the essays published between 1932 and 1938. The analysis of his writings during this period can focus only on some features of his thinking which are particularly relevant for present purposes and cannot do justice to the entirety of his thought. (Thus I must pass by his pungent and still useful criticisms of psychoanalytic approaches to primitive data.) These essays are increasingly concerned with grasping the organization of the individual's private world. Sapir points out, for example, that two individuals of ostensibly similar social position may live in quite different perceived worlds. He becomes increasingly concerned with what he regards as the failure of standard ethnographies—not merely their failure to deal with the world outlook of various cultures, but their unwillingness to treat of individual variation in outlook.

In 1932 Sapir says, "The more closely we study this interaction [of systems of ideas which characterize the total culture and systems established in individuals], the more difficult it becomes to distinguish society as a cultural and psychological unit from the individual who is thought of as a member of the society to whose culture he is required to adjust" (Mandelbaum 1949:518–519). "Personality organizations . . . at last analysis are psychologically comparable with the greatest cultures or idea systems . . ." (Mandelbaum 1949:521). The isomorphism between personality system and cultural system has now become an explicit element in his theoretical approach. By 1934, in his essay entitled "Personality," he writes:

The socialization of personality traits may be expected to lead cumulatively to the development of specific psychological biases in the cultures of the world. Thus Eskimo culture, contrasted with most North American Indian cultures, is extraverted; Hindu culture on the whole corresponds to the world of the thinking introvert; the culture of the United States is definitely extraverted in character. . . . Social scientists have been hostile to such psychological characterizations of culture but in the long run they are inevitable and necessary (Mandelbaum 1949:563).

By 1932, then, the direction of drift is determined by the cumulative bias of socialization.

By 1934 the revolt against cultural process as such has become explicit. In "The Emergence of a Concept of Personality in a Study of Cultures" we find:

. . . if we are justified in speaking of the growth of culture at all, it must be in the spirit, not of a composite history made up of the private histories of particular patterns, but in the spirit of the development of a personality. The complete, impersonalized 'culture' of the anthropologist can really be little more than an assembly or mass of loosely overlapping idea and action systems

which . . . can be made to assume the appearance of a closed system of behavior (Mandelbaum 1949:594). The anthropologist should not fear the "concept of personality, which must not . . . be thought of . . . as a mysterious
entity resisting the historically given culture but rather as a distinctive configuration of experience which tends always to form a psychologically significant
unit and which, as it accretes more and more symbols to itself, creates finally
that cultural microcosm of which official 'culture' is little more than a metaphorically and mechanically expanded copy" (Mandelbaum 1949:595).

Acceptance of this view, says Sapir, will force the consideration of new
problems, and especially of problems of socialization practices. He suggests the study of a child's acquisition of culture patterns from birth until ten years of age, to see how, and out of what materials, the child
forms a significant world. "I venture to predict that the concept of culture
which will then emerge, fragmentary and confused as it will undoubtedly
be, will turn out to have a tougher, more vital, importance for social thinking than the tidy tables of contents attached to this or that group which
we have been in the habit of calling 'cultures'" (Mandelbaum 1949:597).
Culture, finally, becomes unreal for Sapir: it is only a convenient and
fallacious way of talking about the sum of individual behavior. Its causes
are to be sought in socialization patterns.

This view becomes even clearer in "Why Cultural Anthropology Needs
the Psychiatrist" (1938):

To the extent that we can . . . speak of causative sequences in social phenomena, what we are really doing is to pyramid, as skillfully and as rapidly
as possible, the sorts of cause and effect relations that we are familiar with in
individual experience, imputing these to a social reality which has been constructed out of our need for a maximally economical expression of typically
human events. It will be the future task of the psychiatrist to read cause and
effect in human history. He cannot do it now because his theory of personality
is too weak and because he tends to accept with too little criticism the impersonal mode of social and cultural analysis which anthropology has made
fashionable (Mandelbaum 1949:576–577).

We have gone, then, from the analogy of language and culture, to the
germ of *Patterns of Culture* found in "Culture, Genuine and Spurious,"
to the idea of cumulative drift dominated by a pattern somehow selected
and established; from there to the equating of psychological forces
(image, transfer) with social forces, and finally to a search in personality development for the source of the forces—the basis of the drift.
Culture and personality have been made isomorphic at last, in the same
degree that idiolect and dialect are for the linguist. And throughout these
last essays runs a fatigue and disgust with the *membra disjecta* of tradi-

tional ethnography divorced from cultural theory. From rejection of cultural systems, we have come at last to the individual as the source of, or the homologue of the cultural pattern.

Treatment of Benedict's work will be somewhat briefer—not that she is a less significant figure, but because some of the major points to be discussed have already been dealt with in Section III. Furthermore, in Sapir's case I have dealt with writings published from 1916 to 1938, whereas in Benedict's, I attempt to cover only the years 1922–34, and especially 1928–34. A rounded treatment of Benedict's thought should follow through to her last works, but the interest in this paper is not the intellectual life of particular theorists; it is the development of a trend in theory.

Benedict's two earliest publications, "The Vision in Plains Culture" (1922) and "The Concept of the Guardian Spirit in North America" (1923) are concerned with showing the "non-organic" quality of various religious trait complexes: the lack of necessary connection among the traits. After the fact we can see that she is also showing how each particular exemplification of the vision or the guardian spirit is related to some general feature of the culture in question. Indeed, the paper on the vision quest has the germ of the approach of *Patterns of Culture:* "The ritualistic system of the Blackfoot, then, offers a perfect example of the enormous formative power of a once-established pattern, and its tendency toward indefinite self-complication" (Benedict 1922:17–18).

The positive stress on configurations, rather than the emphasis on the lack of organic quality of a trait complex, becomes a dominant note in "Psychological Types in the Cultures of the Southwest" (Benedict 1930).[5] (The key passage of this paper has already been discussed in Section III.) Benedict saw the Apollonian ethos as a "psychological set" at this

[5] This paper was delivered in September of 1928 but published in 1930. There are a number of parallels between it and Sapir's 1928 paper on religion (Mandelbaum 1949: 346–356). These and other parallels led me to be concerned with the question of when Sapir and Benedict began to use each other's work. I am much indebted to Margaret Mead for information on this score. She informs me that Benedict wrote her paper on the vision quest before she met Sapir, and probably before she had read "Culture, Genuine and Spurious." From 1922 on they did work closely together and influenced each other. There is a good deal of correspondence between 1922 and 1926, and Sapir visited New York fairly often during part of this period, since his first wife was then ill and in New York. [Margaret Mead's *An Anthropologist at Work, Writings of Ruth Benedict,* appeared in 1959, too late for me to use in revising this paper, which had gone to the editors in final form in October of 1958. Sapir's comments on some of Benedict's work, Benedict's on Sapir's, and Mead's elucidation of the background of *Patterns of Culture* would have made it possible to deal with certain major differences between Sapir's and Benedict's theoretical positions. Here, however, my primary interest is in their similarities.]

time (cf. Benedict 1930:572, 581). She says of the various Southwestern groups she has described,

these cultures, though . . . made up of disparate elements fortuitously assembled from all directions by diffusion, are none the less over and over again in different tribes integrated according to very different and individual patterns. The order that is achieved is not merely the reflection of the fact that each trait has a pragmatic function that it performs. . . . The order is due rather to the circumstances that in these societies a principle has been set up according to which the assembled cultural material is made over into consistent patterns in accordance with certain inner necessities that have developed within the group (Benedict 1932:2).

History and psyche again! Diffusion provides the content; configuration determines the organization. As a trait is borrowed, quite frequently it "is reworked to express the different emotional patterning characteristic of the culture that has adopted it" [6] (Benedict 1932:7).

So the inner necessity is not a matter of systematic organization, but of psyche, of emotional necessity—of *Weltanschauung*. She goes on to make the assumption of individual-culture isomorphism: "Cultural configurations stand to the understanding of group behavior in the relation that personality types stand to the understanding of individual behavior" (Benedict 1932:23). In psychology, it is now recognized that behavioral items only make sense in the context of personality configuration:

If this is true in individual psychology where individual differentiation must be limited always by the cultural forms and by the short span of a human lifetime, it is even more imperative in social psychology where the limitations of time and of conformity are transcended. The degree of integration that may be attained is of course incomparably greater than can ever be found in individual psychology. Cultures from this point of view are individual psychology thrown large upon the screen, given gigantic proportions and a long time span (Benedict 1932:24).

The configurations of particular cultures cannot be explained by reference to general human nature:

Another and greater force has been at work that has used the recurring situations of mating, death, provisioning, and the rest almost as raw material and elaborated them to express its own intent. This force . . . we can call within that society its dominant drive [7] (Benedict 1932:26).

---

[6] The concept of "reworking" of foreign materials also has its parallel in linguistic theory. Since this point is not critical in the present essay, I have omitted a full length treatment of it from Section III and mention it here only in passing.

[7] There is another minor parallel between language and culture, suggested here and elsewhere in Benedict's work. The vocal apparatus determines the range of available sounds from which particular phonemic systems select, and the human condition provides the range of experiences from which culture patterns are drawn and selectively elaborated.

David F. Aberle

She concludes:

These dominant drives are as characteristic for individual areas as are house forms or the regulations of inheritance. We are too handicapped yet by lack of relevant descriptions of culture to know whether these drive-distributions are often coextensive with distributions of material culture, or whether in some regions there are many such to one culture area defined from more objective traits (Benedict 1932:27).

Although Benedict here suggests the possibility of some ecological fit of her configurations, she does not develop the idea. Indeed, as I have shown, the "Psychological Types" paper expresses some astonishment at the differences of psychological orientation between the Pueblos and the Plains, without ever adverting to the gross technological, economic and environmental differences between them for an explanation. Nevertheless, she does not fall back on socialization patterns to account for the configurational drives. She takes essentially the position I have ascribed to the linguist: she observes the pattern and its power to rework materials over time, but does not attempt to account for differences of patterns between cultures.

From a theoretical point of view, *Patterns of Culture* is simply an elaboration of "Psychological Types" and "Configurations of Culture." Again we find the history-psyche dichotomy.

The difficulty with naive interpretations of culture in terms of individual behavior is not that these interpretations are those of psychology, but that they ignore history and the historical process of acceptance or rejection of traits. Any configurational interpretation of cultures also is an exposition in terms of individual psychology, but it depends upon history as well as upon psychology. It holds that Dionysian behaviour is stressed in the institutions of certain cultures because it is a permanent possibility in individual psychology, but that it is stressed in certain cultures and not in others because of historical events that have in one place fostered its development and in others have ruled it out. At different points in the interpretation of cultural forms, both history and psychology are necessary; one cannot make the one do the service of the other (Benedict 1934: 232–233).

For Benedict, as for Boas and Sapir, the distinctive thing about a culture is not that it is a system organized in a different way from an individual personality, but that it has a history—that it is an accretion—that it is not and cannot be created *de novo* in each generation. The protest is against *immediate* psychological explanation, not against psychological explanation. Only, psychology is not enough; a series of unknown accidents have determined the selective principles operating in any given culture, the accidents of history.

But for Benedict, the nonlinguist, the ontogenetic considerations which began to concern Sapir at the end of his life remained insignificant. Sapir, who did not ask the source of positional emphases in English, did ask for the source of Eskimo extraversion—in the cumulative biases of socialization. Benedict, the nonlinguist, maintained the linguist's position to a considerable degree—to locate the pattern and demonstrate its effect, but not to ask for its source. Mead has justly observed that even in Benedict's last book, *The Chrysanthemum and the Sword,* child-rearing was a relatively unimportant element in the presentation (Mead 1949:461).

V. THE "CULTURE" OF CULTURE
AND PERSONALITY

To use a model of culture based on the analogue of language is not necessarily wrong, but it is frequently incomplete and misleading. In linguistics it is not wrong to analyze a language as a phonological or morphological system, to profess ignorance as to the origins of grammatical devices or drift tendencies, nor is it wrong to write grammars. By the same token, it is not wrong to examine the ideas, attitudes and values of members of a society, nor to show the harmonies among these orientations and the ways in which they seem to govern behavior in several spheres of life. It would be wrong, however, to write a monograph entitled "The Communications Network among the Bathonga" which referred only to phonology, morphology, and lexicon and which did not discuss who communicates with whom, when, and about what. A description of a language may be essential to understand the content of communication, but it does not provide information about the network of communication. This network is participated in, not shared by the members of the group. In the same way, the most important systematic characteristics of culture, such as the relationships between technology and environment, between the product of this interaction and economic structures, between these structures and political units, and so on, do not emerge from a description of a set of value-orientations. They cannot. These are two different types of systems. When they are confused (for the cultural system I have mentioned cannot be ignored by even the hardiest psychologizer), the confusion seems to drive theorists to various sorts of efforts at solution—none of them satisfactory.

The first solution is that of obfuscation: of attempting to obliterate the difference between individual and culture, sometimes by maintaining that they are isomorphic, sometimes by maintaining that they are an identity, sometimes by claiming that cultures are just like individuals except that they have longer histories. Benedict's position lies somewhere in this range. This solution destroys the field of culture and personality by providing it with nothing to relate to anything else. To the degree that culture and personality are identical, there is no interaction between them.

The second solution arises out of the feeling that there is something to explain, and not merely to document. It involves an effort to explain the sources of the configurations (again, remember, value-attitudes) which are seen as straining for expression and dominating new cultural materials in a given culture. In the long run, it is not intellectually very satisfying simply to maintain that the configurations result from the vagaries of history. The temptation is then to turn to socialization patterns, to the early patterning of personality, as a source of the cultural configuration. To this solution Sapir turned toward the end of his life, although he cannot be said to have adopted it wholeheartedly or without qualification. This solution is reductionist. It assumes that the cultural order can be explained by the orientations of its component individuals, which creates a special kind of problem, since the issue of why the individuals continue to share the same orientations must arise again. (The same problem can arise from the "isomorphic" view.)

The third solution denies that there is a problem. It is the "chicken and egg" solution. Its proponents point out that no individual is born outside a culture. The individual is born in a culture, is socialized to find it congenial (or perhaps to find it uncongenial), and therefore strives to maintain it (or change it). The circle is complete, and therefore, it is said, the question of where to break into it for descriptive purposes is arbitrary. Oddly enough, however, those who maintain this view either "break" the circle at the point where the child's socialization starts, or stress the importance of socialization for perpetuation or change.

Now, in fact, it is becoming increasingly apparent that we cannot find cases where changes in socialization, occurring prior to other major changes in a cultural system, have resulted in such changes. On the other hand, myriad other sources of cultural change press for attention. And finally, it seems highly reasonable to regard socialization changes as responses to other changes. Therefore the point at which we should break into the "circle" is the description of the on-going adult system of relationships in its ecological context. This will "explain" socialization. Socialization itself explains the how, not the why of stability and never explains major features of change. It may account for the nature of adjustment to or resistance to change. The third solution, which attempts to do away with the problem, eventually betrays its psychologistic bias.

It might appear from what has been said that this essay is an effort to destroy the entire area of culture and personality studies as a legitimate field of scientific enquiry. The intention, however, is rather to give to the field a properly delimited sphere of endeavor, within which there is ample room for adequate research. The viable core of culture and personality studies is the analysis of the impact of the cultural system (*not* of a *Weltanschauung* alone) as a technological, economic, or political organization on the individual through the mediation of socialization patterns and as that organization affects him in his adult life. This analysis must be carried out in terms appropriate to personality theory—whether in terms of drives, defenses, cognitive orientations, motives, or of personality theory not yet available. Essentially, although my language differs from his, I am proposing a field of endeavor very like that outlined by White in 1925.

As White then said, and as Mead and others have often said, the variations in cultural systems promise us a greater opportunity to measure the impact of various factors on the development and functioning of personality than any laboratory setting imaginable in the present cultural order. The adaptation of personality systems, as realities in their own right, to cultural systems, as realities in their own right, is a subject of no small interest and importance for personality theory. It also has its special interest for anthropology. This adaptation does not account for the content, organization, or process of change of a culture, but it does tell us something of the "physiology" of a culture—of how culturally relevant incentives and inhibitions are produced in persons. There is also some reason to believe that an understanding of the dynamics of modal personality types (themselves the products of cultural systems) may assist us in the study of expressional devices in different cultural systems— matters of ritual idiom, gesture, some features of art style, recreation, and the like. Some research in this area looks promising, but too little objective work is yet available for a definite judgment. Unfortunately, the earlier work in culture and personality tended to reduce all aspects of culture except those obviously related to the biological survival of the individual organism to expressional elements, and hence to lapse into one or another of the confusions discussed above.

In sum, culture and personality theory developed in the vacuum created by the rejection of perspectives which saw culture as a system, either synchronically or diachronically. This theoretical approach rested in part on an analogy between total culture and language. Benedict and Sapir were among the earliest proponents of this view of culture, but the explicit and implicit assumptions they employed remain with us and trouble us today. Indeed the temptation to fall back on the linguistic model in other forms than those I have mentioned arises again and again, whenever culture seems too perplexing. A viable study of culture and personality, capable of dealing with cause and effect in definite terms, will be built on an appropriate model of culture, which represents it as an organized, symbolically mediated mode of adjustment of human groups to their environment. But needless to say, the personality investigations which proceed within this context must similarly be built on a frank recognition of personality systems, and on an appropriate and sophisticated personality theory and methodology of study. For if culture is not a macrocosm of personality, neither is personality a microcosm of culture.

BIBLIOGRAPHY

ABERLE, DAVID F.
  1950 "Shared Values in Complex Societies." *American Sociological Review*, 15:495–502.
  1951 "The Psychosocial Analysis of a Hopi Life-History." *Comparative Psychology Monographs*, 21 (1).
BENEDICT, RUTH F.
  1922 "The Vision in Plains Culture." *American Anthropologist*, 24:1–23.
  1923 "The Concept of the Guardian Spirit in North America." *Memoirs of the American Anthropological Association*, 29.
  1930 "Psychological Types in the Cultures of the Southwest." *Proceedings of the Twenty-Third International Congress of Americanists* (New York, 1928), pp. 572–581.
  1932 "Configurations of Culture in North America." *American Anthropologist*, 34:1–27.
  1934 *Patterns of Culture.* Boston, Houghton Mifflin Company.
  1936 "Marital Property Rights in Bilateral Society." *American Anthropologist*, 38:368–373.
  1939 "Edward Sapir." *American Anthropologist*, 41:465–477.
BOAS, FRANZ
  1911 "Handbook of American Indian Languages. Part I." *Bureau of American Ethnology Bulletin*, 40.

1940 *Race, Language and Culture.* New York, The Macmillan Company.

GREENBERG, JOSEPH H.

1954 "A Quantitative Approach to the Morphological Typology of Language." In *Methods and Perspectives in Anthropology: Papers in Honor of Wilson D. Wallis,* ed. by Robert F. Spencer, pp. 192–220. Minneapolis, University of Minnesota Press.

1957 *Essays in Linguistics.* Chicago, The University of Chicago Press.

KLUCKHOHN, CLYDE and HENRY A. MURRAY, eds.

1948 *Personality in Nature, Society, and Culture.* New York, Alfred A. Knopf, Inc.

LOWIE, ROBERT H.

1937 *The History of Ethnological Theory.* New York, Farrar and Rinehart, Inc.

MANDELBAUM, DAVID G.

1949 *Selected Writings of Edward Sapir in Language, Culture and Personality.* Berkeley, University of California Press.

MEAD, MARGARET

1949 "Ruth Fulton Benedict 1887–1948." *American Anthropologist,* 51:457–468.

1959 *An Anthropologist at Work, Writings of Ruth Benedict.* Boston, Houghton Mifflin Company.

NAROLL, RAOUL

1956 "A Preliminary Index of Social Development." *American Anthropologist,* 58:687–715.

SAPIR, EDWARD

1916 "Culture in the Melting Pot." *The Nation Supplement,* Section II. Thursday, Dec. 21, 1916, pp. 1–2.

1917 "Do We Need a 'Superorganic'?" *American Anthropologist,* 19:441–447.

1920 "Primitive Society." [Review of Robert H. Lowie, *Primitive Society.*] *The Freeman,* 1:377–379.

1921 *Language.* New York, Harcourt, Brace and Company.

SOROKIN, PITIRIM A.

1937 *Fluctuation of Forms of Art.* (*Social and Cultural Dynamics,* vol. 1) New York, The American Book Company.

WHITE, LESLIE A.

1925 "Personality and Culture." *The Open Court,* 39(3):145–149.

1949 *The Science of Culture.* New York, Farrar, Straus and Company.

✳ ✳ ✳ ✳

Richard N. Adams

MICHIGAN STATE UNIVERSITY

AN INQUIRY INTO

THE NATURE OF THE FAMILY

Science can study only what is.

LESLIE WHITE,

IN AN UNDERGRADUATE LECTURE, 1943

Literature on the human family appearing during the past decade has taken a decided swing away from the earlier simple classificatory goals of identifying lineality, locality, descent groups, and formal kin structures. The new direction, as has been noted by many persons active in the movement, has been towards examining the phenomenon within wider dimensions. No longer, for example, is it possible to speak simply and securely of matrilocality or of patrilocality without extensive and adequate analysis of the precise configurations standing behind the activities of the members of the particular society concerned (Fortes 1949; Goodenough 1956). In a very real sense many of the formerly analytic terms have become heuristic and descriptive.

With respect to the form of the nuclear family, however, there has been little evidence of increased interest in fundamentals. Concern here is as ancient as any in the field of social organization, but treatments of it continue to be predominantly expressions of profound convictions, buttressed by more or less convincing logical arguments stemming from a variety of theoretical premises. A recent example of this may be found in Weston LaBarre's *The Human Animal* (1954), an absorbing and provocative though unconvincing argument for the absolute necessity and inevitability of a continuing nuclear family. A more rigorous argument with the same conclusion but based on different kinds of evidence is contained in G. P. Murdock's *Social Structure* (1949). Murdock claims, on the basis of an examination of 250 societies, that there are no cases where the nuclear family is not the fundamental unit or cell upon which all further familial and kin elaborations are based. Both before and after Murdock's study, exceptions to this picture were cited, specifically the Nayar of Malabar (Linton 1936; Gough 1952; Cappannari 1953), but in principle Murdock's judgment has met with general approval. Even an examination of the *kibbutz* led Spiro (1954) to conclude that whereas the *kibbutz* may have eliminated the nuclear family, it did so only through converting the entire community into a single large *gemeinschaft*.

The purpose of the present essay is to question whether some arguments in support of this general view are satisfactory and to do so through a review of selected cases in which the nuclear family is manifestly only one type of basic form. This is in accord with, but varies in focus from, the interest expressed by Marion Levy (1955) when he asked whether the nuclear family was "institutionalized" in all societies. Levy pointed out that even though the statuses of father, mother, spouse, sister, and brother may be present, they may not function as a nuclear family unit. He gave as an example the case of the traditional Chinese family. In the present paper the position is taken that social organization is flexible enough to permit different forms of the family to exist simultaneously. These different forms may not even take care of the same general functional needs of the total society, and in many cases certain of the standard nuclear family statuses (that is, mother-wife, father-husband, unmarried children) may not function at all. So far as present evidence indicates, there is no question but that these statuses are present in the society; rather it is a question of how they are filled and how they function. The flexibility of social organization permitting the appearance of different family forms rests on the fact that there are more elemental forms of the family than the nuclear, and that different forms may function in relation to different aspects or characteristics of the total social structure.

The cases to be discussed are taken from contemporary Central and South America. We are intentionally treating only this material (and omitting the Nayar and similar cases) because it better illuminates the propositions we wish to explore. Studies in Latin America have increasingly indicated that while most contemporary family systems of that region reckon descent bilaterally, there are many instances where family forms other than the nuclear are operative. The nuclear family is generally replaced in these circumstances by a group based on what we will call the maternal dyad, a residential unit composed of a mother and one or more children. As is the case in many nuclear family residences, these dyad households may also have a variety of other members present, both kin and non-kin.

Our interest will focus on two dyad forms: the maternal dyad, just described; and an adult dyad, composed of a man and woman, which we shall clumsily call the sexual or conjugal dyad. This dyad may be based simply on the sexual act, or may be further sanctioned by marriage. There is a third dyad, the paternal (composed of father and one or more children) which we will not treat here. It is with no intent of minimizing the importance of this dyad in the world at large that it is minimized here, but simply because it does not appear in significant numbers apart from the nuclear family in our data.[1] The identification of the maternal dyad, as distinct from the nuclear family, is made on the basis of the fact that there is no husband-father regularly resident. The cases used here are based on a distinction made between households with a woman head and those with a man head. This identification in terms of the sex of household heads stems from the nature of census data from which much of the information is derived. While having both theoretical and practical disadvantages, it serves sufficiently well for present purposes. The presence of woman-headed households (in these bilateral societies) is being used here as an index to the prevalence of the maternal dyad family form, and man-headed households as an index to the prevalence of the nuclear family form. While some woman-headed households are doubtless due to widowhood, the percentage of widows seldom exceeds 5 per cent of the women in the society, and, of course, many widows are not heads of households. While some man-headed households may be paternal dyads and not nuclear families, the number is not significant in all cases where specific information is available.

SOME CASES FROM LATIN AMERICA

In his recent monograph on the community of Villa Recôncavo, Bahia, Brazil, Harry W. Hutchinson (1957) defines an entire social class segment of his community in terms of the fact that it is composed of woman-

---

[1] It would perhaps be well to note at this point that not only the paternal dyad, but many other forms both of family elements and artificial or pseudo-kin relationships are pertinent to the discussion as it progresses. In the interests of brevity, I am raising these principles for discussion, and am intentionally not pursuing here all the lines of exploration they suggest.

headed households. Ninety (31 per cent) of the 290 households in the community were reported to be of this type in the 1950 census. Although Hutchinson says (1957:151) that, "The composition of these households almost defies classification," he promptly notes that 55 of them (19 per cent of the total number of families, and 61 per cent of the 90) are "composed of mothers and children, with the addition in some cases of relatives and an *agregado* as well as boarders." The other households in this class, Hutchinson describes as "left overs" from other families or marital unions. Although Hutchinson evidently feels that these families offer the scientist nothing but confusion, the fact that they were sufficiently distinct to move him to the extreme of categorizing them as an entirely separate "social class," and the fact that they do manifest a considerable consistency with respect to the presence of the dyad family indicate that they do not defy classification.

The Services, in their report on Tobatí, Paraguay (1954), indicate that what they call "incomplete" families form a prominent part of the community. Of a total of 292 families, only 133 (45.5 per cent) are complete nuclear families (with or without additional members); of the remainder, 113 (38.8 per cent of the total) are woman-headed households. This detailed report gives a somewhat higher woman-headed household rate than Emma Reh's earlier study (1947) of the Paraguayan community of Piribebuy where she estimated that 60 per cent of the families were complete and 33 per cent were headed by women. Since there are almost as many woman-headed households as man-headed households in Tobatí, there is little doubt that the maternal dyad is the basis of a highly significant portion of the household units.

Although national statistics for Brazil and Paraguay were not available to the writer, there is evidence from other areas that the presence of maternal dyad families is not a matter of limited or local significance. In Central America, 1950 census data are available for four countries concerning the relative number of families recorded as having women as heads of households:

Country	Number of Families	Per cent of Families with Woman Heads
Guatemala	561,944	16.8
El Salvador	366,199	25.5
Nicaragua	175,462	26.0
Costa Rica	143,167	17.2

Within this general picture for Central America, there is great variation both with respect to area and to ethnic types. Ethnically, there is a marked difference between Guatemalan departments (a department is equivalent to a U.S. state) where the population is heavily Mayan Indian, and departments occupied predominantly by Spanish Americans, called Ladinos. In the predominantly Indian departments (so classified because 70 per cent or more of their population was registered as Indian in the 1950 census) the total percentage of families with women as heads runs between 10 per cent and 20 per cent. Only two of the seven departments of this type had percentages greater than 15 per cent. Outside these departments, the percentage ran as high as 35 per cent. While the woman-headed household rate of the Ladino population is generally higher than that of the Indians, there is also a pronounced difference from one region to another within the Ladino area. In El Salvador a block of six departments (out of a total of thirteen) has percentages between 25 per cent and 30 per cent, while three Pacific coastal departments of Nicaragua run over 30 per cent. Although lack of data from Honduras (Honduras census data on heads of household were not tabulated by sex) makes a large blank in the Central American picture, the material from the aforementioned four countries makes it perfectly evident that woman-headed families are a widespread and common form in Ladino society. There is evidence from one area, El Salvador, that there is also a significant difference between urban and rural populations in this respect. (Urban is defined in the Salvadorean census as pertaining to a municipal or district capital town; the population outside of these towns is rural.) While only 20.3 per cent of the Salvadorean rural families have women heads, 34.7 per cent of the urban families are of this type.[2]

The presence, then, of woman heads of households in Central America is not a confused and random situation but is definitely associated with the Ladino population, is concentrated in certain regions, and is probably more commonly associated with town dwellers than with rural populations (Adams 1957).

Another region from which there has been an increasing number of reports of dyad families is the Caribbean and the Guianas. Of the studies that have appeared in recent years one in particular has addressed itself to this issue and should concern us here. Raymond T. Smith (1956)

---

[2] While this urban-rural comparison superficially compares with the material cited by Franklin Frazier for Negro families of the United States, caution should be observed since the Salvador data do not make the same distinctions between "owners" and "tenants" and, more important, between "rural farm" and "rural non-farm," as Frazier makes. See Frazier (1939:570–1).

studied three Negro towns in British Guiana in which the percentage of woman heads of households was as follows:

Town	Number of Households	Per cent of Households with Woman Heads
August Town	275	37.1
Perseverance	103	16.5
Better Hope	71	29.2

Many accounts of West Indian societies have indicated the presence of these families (as in the work of Herskovits, Campbell, Simey, and Henriquez) but for present purposes we will restrict ourselves to the work of Smith.

These cases from Paraguay, Brazil, Central America, and British Guiana give ample evidence that in contemporary populations with bilateral descent systems woman-headed households are quite common. We infer, especially from those cases which have been described in some detail, that this is an index to an almost equally high incidence of families that have the maternal dyad as their basic unit.

THE UNIVERSAL FUNCTIONS APPROACH

The problem now is to arrive at a theoretical framework that will make these data intelligible. As literature on the family is extensive, we will restrict ourselves to a limited number of theories concerning the status of the nuclear family. The writers of particular interest to us here are Murdock, Parsons, and R. T. Smith.

Murdock's Multiple-Function Approach

Murdock's major reasons for seeing the nuclear family as a universal and inevitable phenomenon are that it was present in all the societies in his original sample for *Social Structure* (1949), and that logically it seemed to him that the family fulfilled a number of functions better than any other conceivable agency. The four functions he regards as primary (although he would doubtless allow others for any specific society) are "fundamental to human social life—the sexual, the economic, the reproductive, and the educational." Murdock is quite explicit in saying that "Agencies or relationships outside of the family may, to be sure, share in the fulfillment of any of these functions, but they never supplant the family" (1949:10). The immediate issue that arises from Murdock's propositions is whether in fact other agencies have not frequently taken over the functions that he regards as being uniquely served by the nuclear family. In reading Murdock, one gathers that he is referring not only to the presence of a nuclear family in all societies, but also to its pervasiveness among household groups in all societies. The implication is that its absence is considered by him to be an abnormal situation. When he says that "no society . . . has succeeded in finding an adequate substitute for the nuclear family, to which it might transfer these functions," one cannot help concluding that almost everyone in all societies must therefore rely on the nuclear family to fulfill these functions.

The cases cited earlier make it clear that large segments of some contemporary societies do not have functioning nuclear families, and that the nonnuclear family segments cannot fruitfully be cast aside as "abnormal" or "disorganized," but are regular, viable, family units in a regular, functioning society. With respect to the four functions listed by Murdock, we simply find that other social agents do in fact take over the functions for extended periods; precisely who may do it varies from one society to another. The educational function may be taken care of by the mother, other relatives, chums, schools, and so on. The rationale that a male child must have a resident father in order to learn to be a man does not hold in fact. The economic function may be handled by the mother and the children as they grow older; to this can be added grandparents, brothers, and other relatives who help either regularly or periodically. And, of course, the sexual function is handled well by other married men, boarders, visitors, friends, and so forth. The reproductive function does not need the father's presence; a midwife is more useful. While there is no denying the social necessity of the functions that Murdock has delineated, there is evidence that some families can achieve them without the presence of someone identified as a "father-husband."

Parsons' Dual-Function Approach

In a recent collection of papers Talcott Parsons (1955) has expressed the opinion that the multiple-functions approach is not adequate to explain the basic necessity of the nuclear family. In its place, he offers another functional explanation. There are, he feels, two functions, and two functions only, that are necessary everywhere and account for the universal presence of the nuclear family. One of these concerns, which Murdock calls the "educational," is namely the necessity of providing socialization of the child. The other (not on Murdock's list, but again he probably would not deny its potential importance) consists of the constant development and balancing of the adult personality which is achieved because of the constant interaction between spouses. Parsons singles out this second function as being of particular importance in explaining the restrengthening of the American (U.S.A.) nuclear family today.

Since Parsons proposes these two functions as being essential everywhere, any documented instance in which they are not operative should be sufficient to cast doubt on his thesis. Such an instance is provided by R. T. Smith's detailed study of the British Guiana Negro family. While Smith would hold that the nuclear family does have universality in the sense that all the statuses therein are recognized, he makes it clear in his study that some households remain with women as heads for extended periods, often for the greater part of the adult life of the woman concerned. He adds, furthermore, that even when men are attached to the household, it is precisely during this period that the "men spend a considerable amount of time working away from home and they do not take any significant part in the daily life of the household . . . There are no tasks allotted to a man in his role as husband-father beyond seeing that the house is kept in good repair, and providing food and clothing for his spouse and the children" (1956:112–113). The function of socio-psychological integration assigned by Parsons to the husband-wife relationship would have considerable difficulty operating if the husband were absent most of the time. The specific functions that Smith assigns to the husband-father are economic. Parsons' argument for the universality of the nuclear family is basically no stronger than that of Murdock since the functions delineated by both can be taken care of by other agents in the society, or by other members of the family.

The fundamental weakness in Murdock's and Parsons' points of view is that they take functions that may be "imperatives," "universal functions," or "basic prerequisites" for a society, and try to correlate them with functions that are fulfilled by the nuclear family. Since it is mistakenly believed that the nuclear family form is found everywhere, that is, a universal, it must therefore be correlated with some universal requirement of human society. It is correct that there are social prerequisites, and that the nuclear family has numerous functions; but to correlate the two is a deduction that is not empirically supported.

A STRUCTURAL APPROACH

Another approach to the problem of the significance of the woman-headed household and maternal-dyad families is taken up in Smith's study (n.d.). Following the lead of his mentor, Meyer Fortes, Smith regards the family as something to be studied empirically and within a temporal as well as spatial framework (Fortes 1949) and not a hard-shelled cell that forms the building unit of all kin-based social structure. Unlike Murdock and Parsons, Smith has approached the family from the point of view of the ethnographer and not the ethnologist or comparative sociologist, and studied a society where the dyad family and woman-headed households are normal. Much of Smith's work is of interest, but we will concentrate here on some major propositions referring to the woman-headed households.

Smith reports that the woman-headed household in British Guiana Negro society almost always goes through a stage during which there is a man attached to it.[3] A family starts in a nuclear form, and later develops into the maternal dyad form when the man leaves. Smith goes on to propose that there is a basic "matri-focal" quality in the familial relations so that it is relatively easy for a family to be reduced to the maternal dyad type; the husband-wife relationship and the father-child relationship are much less important than is the mother-child relationship. The weak character of the husband-father role is related to a situation in the general social structure in British Guiana. General social status is conferred through ascribed membership in an ethnic-class group. The specific occupation of the husband, in the lower class, confers no prestige, and hence the children have nothing to gain from their fathers in this matter. This is made more obvious by comparing the lower class Negroes

---

[3] This temporal difference was also noted in a survey of El Salvador in terms of residence pattern: "even though the patterned residence at the time of marriage or beginning to live together may be neo-local, the subsequent departure of the man of the family leaves it a domestic establishment based on the fact that the woman lives there. It is, if you like, matrilocality by-default." And further: "The solidarity of the Salvadorean nuclear family was reported in some places (Texistepeque and Chinameca) to be increased after the birth of children. This does not, however, seem to hold in all cases in view of the numerous cases in which the woman has retained her children and the man has gone elsewhere" (Adams 1957:460–461).

with members of the higher class. In the latter, the occupation of the father is of importance for the general social status of the entire family, and the father is considered an indispensable part of the family. Smith correlates the presence of the woman-headed household with a social status system in which the father can achieve no superior status.

Smith's work provides an important structural analysis of the significance of the woman-headed household and shows that the maternal dyad can and does exist effectively in spite of the theoretical positions of Murdock and Parsons. Parsons, who had access to Smith's study prior to the preparation of his own paper, failed to see the full implications of the Guiana material (Parsons 1955:13f.). The fact that the Guiana family may include a man long enough to get a household institutionalized in the local society and to undertake the procreation of children, does not mean that the man is present to fulfill either of the functions that Parsons tries to hold as being "root functions" that "must be found wherever there is a family or kinship system at all. . . ."

THE ELEMENTAL FAMILY UNITS: DYADS AND NUCLEUS

In rejecting the propositions advanced by Parsons and Murdock in favor of a structural approach, their position concerning the elemental importance of the nuclear family is also cast into doubt. If "functions" do not explain the absence of the nuclear family in some situations, they can hardly be called upon to support the claim of universality for that form. No matter how fruitful this position has been in reference to other problems in social structure, we must seek an alternative view here.

The nuclear family comprises three sets of relationship that are identifiable as dyads. There is the relationship based on coitus between a man and a woman, and which may be identified as the sexual dyad until or unless it is recognized as a marital union, in which case it becomes a conjugal dyad. There is, second, the maternal dyad, composed of mother and child, that presumably begins at the time of conception but is not of great social significance as a dyad until parturition. And third, there is the paternal dyad, between father and child, that is identified specifically because of the relationship established by the sexual or conjugal dyad. Both the sexual and conjugal dyad, on the one hand, and the maternal on the other, have clear cut correlates in biological activity. The paternal does not. So no matter what importance it may hold in a given society, at the present level of analysis it must be looked upon as a dyadic relationship of a different order; it exists not by virtue of a biological correlate, but by virtue of other dyads. Once given these dyads (all three, the sexual-conjugal, maternal, and paternal) there are important economic functions that may be assigned them. Infant dependency through nursing is, after all, an economic relationship as well as a biological one. But the economic cooperation and interdependency that may be assigned beyond this level is clearly a socially defined activity with no immediate biological correlates.

If we reject the idea that the nuclear family is the fundamental "atom" in the social "molecule," or the irreducible unit of human kin organization, and take initially the two dyads with biological correlates as two distinct components which must each be present at certain times, but not necessarily always or simultaneously, we will be approaching a view of the elements of social organization which is less biased by contemporary social system philosophy. If we allow that the nuclear family is not the minimum model for the building of subsequent structures, then we can see that it is basically, as Lowie partially suggested (1948:215), an unstable combination of two simpler elements, each of which is also unstable and temporal. This allows us to look at more complex forms without the bias of assuming the nuclear family always to be present, and to seek excuses for its absence. There is a significance to be attached to the nuclear as well as the dyad forms, but it is distinctive. The conjugal or sexual dyad is particularly significant because it is the reproductive unit of the society; the maternal dyad is the temporal link between successive generations of adult dyads. While theoretically the two kinds of dyads can operate independently at all times, the society would be a sadly disjointed affair were they to do so. Their combination into a nuclear family provides generational relationships for all concerned. Since such combinations can be a short-lived activity for the individuals involved, and actually may occupy only a limited time, most people are theoretically available most of the time to focus on the dyadic relationships.

The reason that human societies have supported the nuclear family in such abundance can be found at the level of social analysis. Like all animals, human beings live not only in families, but in larger aggregates which, following general usage, can generically be called *communities*. A community cannot maintain stability and continuity solely with such unstable and temporal forms as dyads for elemental units. Seen from this point of view, the nuclear family becomes one combination that, if on nothing more than a random basis, must inevitably occur from time to time. It is the simplest way of joining the two dyads. Since the mother is the only adult in the maternal dyad, and the wife is the only female in the sexual dyad, they can be jointed most readily by identifying the wife with the mother. Once this identification is made, the nuclear unit is created and can fulfill many potential functions. But while its occurrence is inevitable, its continuation is by no means inevitable because each of the dyads alone can also fulfill some functions, and there are, in addition, presumably other societal agents that can also fulfill them. The nuclear family therefore becomes only *one of the ways* the community maintains itself. For some functions and under some circumstances, individuals may be effective agents; for others the elemental dyads are more efficient; for yet others the nuclear family may serve, and still others find other kinds of groups more useful. There are, in short, *alternative* ways in which the basic kin units can be used and combined for continued maintenance of the community.

The social universals of human society are not, then, as has been held by many students, the nuclear family and the community, but rather the community and the two dyads. The nuclear family is, in a sense, a structural by-product of the nature of the dyads, but one which is almost inevitable, even if for the briefest period. However, beyond these, the dyads may be subject to a variety of combinations to further the continuity of the community. The case described by Spiro (1954) as existing in the *kibbutz*, and the details of the woman-headed households of the British Guiana Negroes described by Smith should not be interpreted as being exceptions to a principle of nuclear family universality, but as positive illustrations of how dyads may and do operate outside of the nuclear family.

Before turning to the final points of the paper, we should deal briefly with other possible dyadic forms. Two candidates for basic forms are the paternal and sibling dyads. The appearance of a paternal dyad, as was mentioned earlier, is a result of the joining of the maternal and sexual dyads in the easiest way they can be joined. It is a logical derivative, a potential focus of social emphasis and available for further combinations itself. The sibling dyad is logically somewhat similar, being a derivative of the joining of two maternal dyads through the presence of a common mother. Again, once created it serves as a potential focus of emphasis and can combine with other dyads. While logically other dyads can be derived through further combinations, it is not within the scope of this essay to take the next step, and begin a logical and exhaustive construction of the possible combinations and derivative combinations of dyads, triads, quadics, and so on. It seems reasonable, however, to assume that such an analysis would lead us far in the creation of models of social structure, and offer insight into the actual forms that kin groups take in human society.[4]

It should not be thought that the concept of the dyad in social structure has gone unnoticed in social anthropology. Its significance, however, has usually been in descriptive terms rather than as an analytical tool. A. R. Radcliffe-Brown, certainly a pioneer in structural studies, pointed out on a number of occasions that the basic elements of social structure were dyadic:

> I regard as a part of the social structure all social relations of person to person. For example, the kinship structure of any society consists of a number of such dyadic relations, as between a father and son, or a mother's brother and his sister's son. In an Australian tribe the whole social structure is based on a network of such relations of person to person, established through genealogical connections (1952a:191; see also 1952b:52–53).

But Radcliffe-Brown's view was somewhat different from that proposed here, as he also held that, "The unit of structure from which a kinship system is built up is the group which I call an 'elementary family,' consisting of a man and his wife and their child or children, whether they are living together or not" (1952b:51). The nuclear family, as a constellation of statuses, served as the central block although, unlike Murdock and Parsons, Radcliffe-Brown did not hold that this unit must everywhere exist.

While Radcliffe-Brown saw in the "elementary family" three kinds of social relationships, "that between parent and child, that between children of the same parents (siblings), and that between husband and wife as parents of the same child or children" (1952b:51), he did not expressly project these as potential analytical units that could themselves be examined apart from the nuclear family context and considered as distinctive building blocks. On the other hand, Radcliffe-Brown did, in his principles of "the unity of the sibling group" and "the unity of the lineage," recognize the theoretical significance of a society's placing emphasis upon a given set of relationships that, in terms of the present discussion, we would see as a "sibling dyad" and either the maternal or paternal dyad. He did not carry it farther at the time of the essay in question to include the husband-wife dyad as also being a potential

---

[4] Analysis based on triadic and quadic relations has already been started in communications research.

center of emphasis, nor did he distinguish between other maternal and paternal relations.

THE WOMAN-HEADED HOUSEHOLD
AND THE TOTAL SOCIETY

The thesis presented by Smith concerning the reasons for the appearance of the woman-headed household provides an analysis that on the surface fits well into the present argument. Over a single life cycle of Guiana Negroes the sexual or conjugal dyad tends to come into play strongly only at limited periods—for procreation and for support of the woman with infant. As a woman becomes free of dependent infants, the conjugal relation can and often does disappear or change its character. This dyad is weak because the members are part of an ethnically distinct, lower class community in which there is no status differentiation possible between males, and hence, little that one man can offer a family or son over what another can offer. According to this analysis we would expect to find similar developments in other similar situations. However, the data from Latin America do not support the extension of the analysis. Three examples will indicate the nature of the variations.

The first involves a comparison of the Guatemalan Indians and neighboring Ladinos. The former have predominantly nuclear families while the latter have a significantly high proportion of woman-headed households. The populations involved hold comparable positions within the total social structure, but the Indians in particular are similar to the Guiana Negroes in being a lower class ethnic group within which the status of the father does not necessarily give status to the son. There is some variation in this matter, and a situation comparable to that of the Guiana Negroes is to be found less among the more traditional Indians than among the more acculturated ones. Among both Indians and Ladinos some segments of the population work on plantations, some live in independent villages, and some are part-time subsistence farmers and part time laborers. Both have the same general concept of land tenure, and both live within the same general national context. But, it will be remembered, in the predominantly Indian departments the percentage of households with women as heads is considerably lower than that of the Ladino departments.

Although Indians and Ladinos live under similar conditions, the Ladino family is much closer to the model Smith sets up for the British Guiana Negroes than is the Mayan Indian family. The difference lies in what Smith has referred to in the Guiana situation as the "marginal nature of the husband-father role" that gives rise to a "matrifocal system of domestic relations and household groupings." Shifting the theoretical focus from the structure of the family to the values associated with it is in one sense a shorthand method of indicating that somewhere the structure, in spite of overtly similar conditions, is different. Thus, presumably the Indians have within the structure of their total community certain features which stress the father-husband role, but they are not necessarily the same features whose absence causes the weak role in the Guiana Negro situation.

Smith reports another case in a later paper (n.d.) in which he says that the East Indian residents of British Guiana (like the Guatemalan Mayan Indians) have retained a strong father-husband role in spite of the similarity to the Negroes in their general circumstances. "Quite apart from their historical derivation the ideal patterns of [East] Indian culture and family life have themselves become an object of value in distinguishing Indians from their nearest neighbors in the ethnic status system, the Negroes." If Smith is interpreting his Guiana data and I my Guatemalan material correctly, the reasons behind women-headed households among the Guiana Negroes are relative to the structure of the particular society. Values associated with one phase or aspect of the social structural system may in fact conflict with or contradict values stemming from or associated with other aspects. Thus in many Guatemalan Indian situations, where the population works on coffee plantations, the nuclear family is not sustained through variable social status derived from the father, but is important economically. During the five or six months of harvest, the wife also brings in a significant income through picking coffee. This means that a man with a wife has access to a larger income than one without a wife.

Societies, in which families exist, offer many faces, and the form a specific family takes must integrate with as much of the total system as possible. Total systems are complex and seldom completely self-integrated, so some aspects will be more significant for the family form of some parts of the population, while other aspects prove to be more important for others. There is thus room for variation in the form a family may take simply because different families may be answering to different structural features.

The last case involves the Guiana Negroes and the Ladinos themselves, both societies in which two distinctive forms of the family appear within similar total structural situation. Smith reported, and the censuses for Central America show, that within these populations there are variations in the degree to which the woman-headed household occurs. If Smith's argument with respect to the relation between the dyadic Negro household and the total system is valid, we must then account for the presence of some continuous nuclear families. The answer here is probably the same as that just discussed. Within the total structure, there is room for variation, and we must assume that in spite of the structural features appearing to be the same, we are not identifying those features which the different family forms are answering to.

The evidence from the present cases does not provide us with a clear enough picture to delineate with precision why some families go one way and some go another. It is here that we must rest our case simply by preferring to place our confidence in the structural approach to solve the issue as over and against the "universal functions" preferred by other writers. We need to seek out facts pertaining to a number of situations:

1. We need to delineate the types of structural aspects which can differentially affect family forms within a single class or ethnic societal group, or both.

2. Given this, we need then to establish the principles which will hold for such relationships within any society.

SUMMARY AND CONCLUSIONS

The preceding discussion has been exploratory, working on the hypothesis-building level. The following summary remarks are made in the light of the same approach.

1. The concept of "functions" as being activities necessary to the maintenance of the species, society, or individual personality is one which is not satisfactory to explain the various forms that the family may have in a given society. The economic, sexual, reproductive, and educational functions as outlined by Murdock, or the socialization and adult-personality-maintaining functions of Parsons may be taken care of by the nuclear family under some circumstances and not under others. We cannot agree with Parsons that there are "root functions" everywhere associated with the nuclear family. If there are such things, they would probably be better identified in terms of the community and the dyads. The search for universal functions has unfortunately become an activity

not unlike the continuing search for human instincts: it is not that there are none, but that it is misleading unless it is correlated with structure.

2. A theoretical analysis of the human family must not start with the assumption that the nuclear family is a basic cell or atom, but rather that there are two distinct dyadic relations that go into the formation of the nuclear family as well as into other family forms. While the concept of the nuclear family is doubtless useful for many kinds of social analysis, the fact that it fails in analyzing some family forms means we must look further. A full understanding of family form requires an analysis beginning with dyads. With this kind of approach, it may well prove that the nuclear family has not had the extensive ramifications which have been attributed to it heretofore. By adding other dyads, we are in a position to reanalyze kin and family structure as well as to pursue more analytically the nature of intrafamilial and other interpersonal relationships. It has been recognized that the nuclear family, as found among apes and men, is essentially a very primitive form. It is not surprising to find that man's culture elaborates on the dyadic possibilities of the family, and produces forms intricate and fantastic.

3. Smith's work among the British Guiana Negroes gives us a most important insight into the structural correlates of the woman-headed household in that society. It leads us to the next step, which is to seek the structural correlates which will explain why woman-headed households sometimes appear and sometimes do not within apparently a single structural system. One step in this explanation is to have recourse to the theoretical position that the other aspects of the total social structure may be working adversely to those which are producing a nuclear or a dyadic emphasis. The emphasis thus placed, however, must have structural correlates, even if they are merely reflective of some structural aspect that is about to disappear. In this case we need more research into the exact nature of form and structure relationships, both in a synchronic and a diachronic context.

4. The final general position to be derived from the preceding discussion is that it is neither necessary nor valid to attempt to find a single normal structural form for the family within a society. That there *may* be only one is possible; but the assumption that there *can* be only one is unfruitful. The conviction that there is only one right way is older than social science, but it continues to make itself felt today. Many sociologists and anthropologists have regarded the woman-headed household as an abnormal, incomplete, or disorganized form of the family. This has contributed to the argument that the nuclear family is an in-

dispensable, basic, stable, family type, and that its absence must therefore represent a breakdown. If we accept the notion, however, that the basic relational elements of the family are dyadic, and that the nuclear family is a more complex arrangement but one which is probably even less significant temporally than its dyad components, then we are in a position to see women-headed households as alternative or secondary norms rather than forms of disorganization. The assertion that the nuclear family successfully fulfills certain functions is perfectly valid. But the reverse assertion that other social forms can never suitably fulfill these functions is both empirically and theoretically invalid.

The denial of this reverse assertion is also important for our approach to other cultural forms. The search for a fundamental cell or building block of kin organization leads not only to a misplaced emphasis on the nuclear family, but towards a biased approach in the study of the entire family system. As Goodenough (1956) has pointed out with respect to residence, there are ethnographic ways of seeing things, and there are ethnological ways of seeing the same things. Just as the desire to discover cross-cultural regularities has led to forcing an ethnological straight jacket on a society's residence rules, so it has led to misleading assumptions concerning the identification of the nuclear family as the minimum structural form of family organization. If we look into other aspects of culture, it seems likely that we should assume that all cultural forms are alternatives (in the Lintonian sense) until a given form can be demonstrated to be universal by the ethnographers. To assume that a form, because it is a variant, is abnormal, is to evade the task before us. The first job of science is, after all, to study what *is*, not what might, or could, or should be.[5]

BIBLIOGRAPHY

ADAMS, RICHARD N.
1957 "Culture Surveys of Panama—Nicaragua—Guatemala—El Salvador—Honduras." *Panamerican Sanitary Bureau, Scientific Publications*, 33.
CAPPANNARI, STEPHEN C.
1953 "Marriage in Malabar." *Southwestern Journal of Anthropology*, 9:263–267.

---

[5] I am indebted to William Davenport, Iwao Ishino, Raymond T. Smith, Nancie Solien de González, John Useem and the editors of this volume for critical readings of earlier drafts of this paper.

FORTES, MEYER

1949 "Time and Social Structure: An Ashanti Case Study." In *Social Structure; Studies Presented to A. R. Radcliffe-Brown*, ed. by Meyer Fortes, pp. 54–84. Oxford, Clarendon Press.

FRAZIER, E. FRANKLIN

1939 *The Negro Family in the United States*. Chicago, The University of Chicago Press.

GOODENOUGH, WARD H.

1956 "Residence Rules." *Southwestern Journal of Anthropology*, 12: 22–37.

GOUGH, E. KATHLEEN

1952 "Changing Kinship Usages in the Setting of Political and Economic Change among the Nayar of Malabar." *Journal of the Royal Anthropological Institute*, 82:71–88.

HUTCHINSON, HARRY WILLIAM

1957 *Village and Plantation Life in Northeastern Brazil*. The American Ethnological Society. Seattle, University of Washington Press.

LaBARRE, WESTON

1954 *The Human Animal*. Chicago, The University of Chicago Press.

LÉVI-STRAUSS, CLAUDE

1956 "The Family." In *Man, Culture, and Society*, ed. by H. L. Shapiro, pp. 261–285. New York, Oxford University Press.

LEVY, MARION J., JR.

1955 "Some Questions about Parsons' Treatment of the Incest Problem." *The British Journal of Sociology*, 6:277–285.

LINTON, RALPH

1936 *The Study of Man*. New York, D. Appleton-Century Company, Inc.

LOWIE, ROBERT H.

1948 *Social Organization*. New York, Rinehart & Company.

MURDOCK, GEORGE P.

1949 *Social Structure*. New York, The Macmillan Company.

PARSONS, TALCOTT

1955 "The American Family: Its Relations to Personality and to the Social Structure." In *Family, Socialization and Interaction Process*, by Talcott Parsons and Robert F. Bales, pp. 3–33. Glencoe, The Free Press.

RADCLIFFE-BROWN, A. R.

1952a "On Social Structure." In *Structure and Function in Primitive Society*, pp. 188–204. Glencoe, The Free Press.

1952b "The Study of Kinship Systems." In *Structure and Function in Primitive Society,* pp. 49–89. Glencoe, The Free Press.

REH, EMMA

1946 *Paraguayan Rural Life.* Washington, D.C., Institute of Inter-American Affairs.

SERVICE, ELMAN R., and HELEN S. SERVICE

1954 *Tobatí: Paraguayan Town.* Chicago, The University of Chicago Press.

SMITH, RAYMOND T.

1956 *The Negro Family in British Guiana: Family Structure and Social Status in the Villages.* London, Routledge and Kegan Paul.

n.d. "Family Structure and Plantation Systems in the New World." Paper presented at the Seminar on Plantation Systems of the New World, San Juan, Puerto Rico, 1957.

SPIRO, MELFORD E.

1954 "Is the Family Universal?" *American Anthropologist,* 56:839–846.

Robert Anderson

UNIVERSITY OF UTAH

REDUCTION OF VARIANTS

AS A MEASURE OF

CULTURAL INTEGRATION

Kroeber and Kluckhohn remark in their survey of the history and status of the culture concept that ". . . there seems to be general agreement that every culture possesses a considerable degree of integration both of its content and its forms, more or less parallel to the tendency toward solidarity possessed by societies. . . ." (1952:159). Definitions of cultural integration are numerous. The general notion in most of them is exemplified by Linton's "mutual adjustment between culture elements" (1936:348) and Kroeber's "accommodation of discrete parts, largely inflowing parts, into a more or less workable fit" (1948:287).

It is difficult, however, to find useful suggestions about specific mechanisms of integration and clearly isolated processes leading to an integrated state. Beyond asserting that they exist, how does one recognize adjustment or accommodation? Precisely what takes place? And how does one measure this progressive phenomenon? The refractory nature of the problem can be gauged from Linton's pioneer discussion of integration in *The Study of Man* (1936).

"By the *process of integration,*" Linton wrote, "we mean the progressive development of more and more perfect adjustments between the various elements which compose the culture. By *degree of integration* we mean simply the extent to which such adjustments have been perfected at any given point in the cultural continuum" (1936:348).

The situation by which Linton attempted to illustrate integrational dynamics was a complex one which he was familiar with at first hand—the changes in Tanala society which followed introduction of rice irrigation. After describing Tanala society as it existed under dry rice cultivation, and then under wet rice cultivation, Linton asserted that the evident transformation "can be traced back step by step and at every step we find irrigated rice at the bottom of the change. It created a condition which necessitated either a modification of pre-existing patterns or the adoption of patterns already developed in the neighboring tribes who had had a longer time to meet these problems" (Linton 1936:353).

It is clear, however, that Linton's Tanala case convincingly demonstrates the primacy of technology in bringing about culture change, rather than elucidating the factors of integration itself. In his discussion there are no specific criteria for isolating the phenomenon of cultural integration and no measure for any particular stage of it beyond observational "tendencies," "accommodations," and "consistencies" (1936:352, 355, 358).

To be sure, the concept of technology as the independent variable is a valid and useful and even indispensable one in a general theory of culture (White 1949:365 *et seq.*). However, the concept is misused if by means of it one intends, as Linton appears to in the Tanala case, to explain the "progressive development of more and more perfect adjustments" or to measure "the extent to which such adjustments have been perfected at any given point."

In analyzing the phenomenon of integration, it would seem that a beginning might be made in a more limited segment of culture than its entire socioeconomic system, as Linton tried to do. Furthermore, isolation of even one characteristic accompanying integration within a segment of culture would be a step toward understanding the general phenomenon. It is assumed here that both culture as a whole and any particular culture are systems, and that a process or mechanism applicable to one segment ought to be applicable and operative generally. The only other assumption that needs to be made now rests upon the generally accepted view, implicit in the statements quoted in the first paragraph of this essay, that integration, viewed as process, is progressive. The assumption is that, other things being equal, older complexes and elements will be better integrated into their surrounding system than newer ones.

I have set myself the problem, then, of devising an explanatory principle of integration. I shall do this by isolating a contrasting trait of well-integrated and less well-integrated ritual complexes—the exhibition of lesser and greater numbers of variant behaviors—and by demonstrating a mechanism by which the two states are produced.

Parenthetically, I hold that certain requirements should be met by a cultural mechanism which is proposed as an explanatory principle. It should be explicitly cultural, which is to say, superorganic and not socio-psychological, in its reference; the process it postulates should be concrete and identifiable, and it should be phrased in an abstract manner which will permit wide application and testing. Finally, it should be amenable to measurement. It is needless to state that the principle suggested is offered as an hypothesis. It is, however, patently capable of verification or disproof in the field.[1]

I term it the principle of reduction of variants, defining variants simply as alternative and interchangeable elements. The principle may be phrased formally in this fashion: Reduction or increase in the number of variants operative in given situations is a function of the degree of integration of the complex of which they are parts. As integration of a complex proceeds, the number of variants in given situations is reduced. Other things being equal, the degree of integration is indicated positively by the extent to which element bundles reduce their component variants in each case toward unity, and negatively, by the extent to which the variants increase toward infinity. (Rarely, if ever, might one expect to find elements invariant in every respect; and beyond a point, multiplication of variants would result in disintegration of the pattern."

The principle and its related notion of contrasting integrational states can best be clarified by sketching the ethnographic situation in which they occurred to me. This was the Sun Dance of two western tribes.

Among the northern Cheyenne, informants with whom observations of the Sun Dance were checked, occasionally were asked, "Why did So-and-so perform this particular act at this particular time?" The answer generally took the form, "You have got to do it this particular way." If pressed on the matter, the informant might relate the act of myth episode as rationale ("This was the way Sweet Medicine did it."), or assert that there would be supernatural displeasure and intervention for breach of procedure ("A big wind would come up, or somebody might get sick.").

Among the Northern Ute, on the other hand, when an informant was

---

[1] Morris E. Opler has discussed critically a number of contemporary concepts "aimed at better describing the content of culture and accounting for its integration" (Opler 1948:107). As I see it, these in the main either are oriented around patterns and configurations, which remain in the area of the historical—the unique and concrete—or they employ the notion of drives which are purposive or psychological in connotation.

asked why a particular act was performed and, in this case, why there were a number of variants, the reply was, "They can do what they want to do about that."

These expressions reflected what was in effect a limited number of variants among the Cheyenne, and a relatively large number among the Ute. The Cheyenne, it might be said, had reduced the appropriate alternatives.

The notion of reduction itself is not new. Kroeber (1948:370–374) applied it to the development of the alphabet under the term "invention by reduction-segregation." Linton adumbrated it without label or theoretical exploration in his paper, "The Comanche Sun Dance," published the year before *The Study of Man.* He did not, so far as I can ascertain, pursue it in the latter work. There may be other uses of the notion of which I am not aware.[2] It is convenient, however, to devise an initial test of the principle as I have phrased it by extending Linton's observation on the same body of material, the Sun Dance of the Plains Indians.

Linton's informants among the Comanche described to him details of dances they had witnessed and heard about which suggested considerable variation and choice in such elements as details of painting of dancers, construction of the Sun Dance lodge, and limited breaking of fast. Linton concluded: "I believe that the rather wide variation in certain details of the Sun Dance, such as form of the lodge, can best be explained by the assumption that the Comanche had not had the Sun Dance long enough to establish a complete and integrated pattern for the ceremony. If so, many of the details of particular Sun Dances might be determined largely by the officiating medicine man's knowledge of the Sun Dance ritual of neighboring tribes, especially the Kiowa and Cheyenne" (1935:427).

The conclusion is germinal but not so useful as it might be, inasmuch as it is neither formalized nor pushed beyond this single ethnographic situation. Furthermore, it actually begs the question as to how an integrated pattern would have established itself out of the diversely derived elements if the Comanche had had the Sun Dance longer than they did.

With reference to the general principle as I have stated it, the Comanche situation may be oriented in this fashion: Other things being equal, integration (the progressive adjustment between elements) may

---

[2] It should be noted that discussions of integration generally are allied with the notion of function. The two, however, are analytically separable, and I have avoided here involvement with the problem of function. Papers in which alternatives are examined in relation to function include Firth's essay of 1954 and the well-known "Manifest and Latent Functions" by Merton (reprinted 1957).

be expected to have proceeded farther in an old complex than in a more recently adopted one. A corollary of integration is reduction in the number of variants at specific points in the complex. The Comanche dance, however, exhibited a number of variants or alternatives at specific points (painting, form of lodge, and so on). This contrasts with the situation in other tribes among which the Sun Dance is known to be old and hence presumably well integrated. Therefore, the Comanche Sun Dance was in a relative sense recently adopted, and not old within the culture.

That tribes known to have old and presumably well-integrated Sun Dances do indeed show suggestive contrasts with the Comanche can be demonstrated. In its general form, the dance is too well known to require description here. Indeed, the literature pertaining to it is extensive enough to have served as a vehicle for analysis of approaches to ethnographic materials through several phases of American ethnology (Bennett 1944).

In his classical study published in 1921, Spier deduced, on the basis of the distribution of its elements, that the Arapaho and Cheyenne were the originators and disseminators of the dance. This conclusion was confirmed and elaborated by Driver and Kroeber (1932). In comparison with Plains tribes as a whole, then, the Arapaho and Cheyenne had relatively old dances. If integration is progressive and other factors are considered equal, these dances should have been maturely integrated at the time of their description by Dorsey (1903, 1905). And if our principle is valid, the complexes should exhibit a firm pattern, with few variants in those aspects of the ceremony selected because of their comparability with the material in Linton's brief account of the Comanche. These situations are the selection and cutting of the center pole (the core feature); the form of the lodge; and ritual painting.

Among the Arapaho, who should choose the pole was made explicit: "The duty of the selection of the pole falls by custom not only to the most famous warriors of the tribe, but to those few who have served as scouts and have been successful in raids against the Pawnee" (Dorsey 1903:77–78). Among the Cheyenne, "The formal and ceremonial location of the center-pole by custom falls to the lot of a Cheyenne who has had the distinction, when acting as a spy, of striking an enemy inside his tipi" (Dorsey 1905: note, p.82). (When Dorsey observed the Cheyenne dance, only two old men with these qualifications were alive, and presumably because they were unable to serve, "a priest and chief" acted as surrogate in one performance. The fact that there had been an explicit qualification obviously remained fresh in memory, however.)

It is apparent from Dorsey's accounts that in both tribes there was precise protocol for cutting the pole. Among the Arapaho, the principal cutters were two women, one the wife of the director of the dance who "personates" (Dorsey's term) the Arapaho tribe, and the other the female director of the dance (Dorsey 1903:24–25, 80). Among the Cheyenne, "chiefs only may participate in bringing the pole to the camp circle," and the first to strike the pole was "*necessarily* [italics supplied] one who had run an enemy through with a knife or an axe," after which the chiefs cut the tree (Dorsey 1905:111).

Now compare Linton (1935:421) on the Comanche: "There seems to have been no ceremony attending . . . selection [of the center pole]. It was cut, in various instances, by a virtuous Comanche woman, . . . a virtuous captive woman, and a captive man who had a number of war deeds to his credit." (As we shall argue below, "there seems to have been no ceremony" and similar phrases, actually may be taken to mean that there was a large but unknown number of unformalized variants.)

For the two tribes with older Sun Dances, there was apparently one appropriate form of lodge in each case: Among the Arapaho, sixteen poles arranged in a circle around the center pole, each joined to it by a rafter and to each other by cross bars, the whole lodge inclosed by cottonwood boughs standing upright on the ground and leaning on the cross bars (Dorsey 1903:96). Among the Cheyenne, tipi covers were spread over a similar lodge frame (Dorsey 1905:120). The Comanche lodge, however, varied from dance to dance: "In one case the entire lodge was covered with cottonwood brush. In another only the walls were filled in with brush, the roof being left open" (Linton 1935:422).

With respect to the painting of Arapaho and Cheyenne dancers, there are well-defined variations in successive dances, but a basic pattern prescribes continuing elements. Among the Arapaho, for instance, "With all paints is worn a black dot on the nose, for the buffalo calf, and tear symbols under the eyes" (Dorsey 1903:172). That there are specific Cheyenne patterns and that their number is limited and stable is indicated by this significant sentence: "A variation in this [the "White-black" or "Cyclone"] paint may be worn by those who have missed none of the paints during the dance; they have the privilege of having their right arm painted entirely black with an extra large sun symbol on the breast, and an extra large moon symbol on the back" (Dorsey 1905:173).

That the Cheyenne had rigidly prescribed procedures with respect to a limited number of appropriate paints is indicated further by Grinnell in an illuminating passage. Most of the participants at the closing segment of the dance he observed wore the traditional Hail paint, but some displayed an innovation associated with the Ghost Dance. Grinnell (1923, II:281) reports: "The dance was now soon to end, and Little Hawk [the leader] called out, 'Those who are wearing the old Cheyenne paint are not to wash it off; others may do as they please.'" Here my thesis may be extended to explain behavior with respect to older and newer elements within the same complex: With traditional, well-integrated elements, there was no variation in procedure (no washing off of the Hail paint). With newer and less well-integrated elements one did as one pleased, which is to say that variant behavior was present and expectable.

The case for the presence of multiple variants in younger and presumably less well-integrated Sun Dances is strengthened further by such information as is available on the Sun Dance of another tribe, the Northern Ute, who adopted it from the Wind River Shoshone as late as 1890 (Stewart 1942:349; Jones 1955:241).

In recent years there has been little formality with respect to pole selection and cutting. "The center-pole, a cottonwood, is chosen, prayed over, and cut down by a work group headed by the dance leader" (Jones 1955:245). In 1912, Lowie was able to learn nothing specific as to who cut the tree, although shooting at the pole by a warrior, and a sham battle, preceded the cutting (Lowie 1919:407). These elements later were confirmed by Stewart (1942:349). The lodge form, however, has been variable. Today the Ute erect a lodge with twelve poles around its circumference and run stringers to each of them. In 1912, Lowie (1919:407) recorded this: "My interpreter said that no rafters had been used that season, though they were employed in the construction of previous lodges. . . ." There was, in other words, variation in lodge form two decades after adoption of the dance by the Ute. With respect to painting, Stewart reports (1942:349), "Dancers may paint with any color according to their desires." Jones (1955:247) notes, "Some paint their faces and bodies, and others do not, depending on the instructions they have received in their dreams."

Thus the Ute dance, so far as our information goes, is most like that of the Comanche in exhibiting alternatives or variants.[3] Although we have

---

[3] Marvin K. Opler in a stimulating paper has argued the contrary for the Southern Ute. That tribe, he says, closely integrated dance elements into its own culture. "In a real sense, the Ute never borrowed the sun dance of the Plains at all. Rather, they seized upon its existence, hastening to reinterpret it in the light of their own religious experience. Readapted to fit their own needs, the ritual swung out of its Plains orbit

no reliable information on the date of adoption of the Sun Dance by the Comanche, we know it to be later than that of the Arapaho and Cheyenne. That the Ute dance is more recent than the other three is well documented.

The Sun Dance evidence, then, tends to meet expectations and to support the principle. If the assumption that integration is a progressive phenomenon is correct, older Sun Dances will be more maturely integrated than younger dances, other things being equal. The old Arapaho and Cheyenne dances stand in contrast with the younger ones of the Comanche and Ute. The former exhibit a relatively small number of alternatives or variants at specific points, the latter a relatively large number. Considered as process, this means that integration (Kroeber's "accommodation of discrete parts . . . into a more or less workable fit") proceeds, at least in one of its aspects, through the progressive reduction of variants.

If the principle of reduction is established firmly through means such as this, we may measure the degree of integration (Linton's "extent to which such adjustments have been perfected at any given point in the cultural continuum") of one complex as compared with another by the relative number of variants exhibited at given points. This is, perhaps, a step toward the desideratum voiced recently by Beals in a critique of acculturation studies—"accurate conceptualization of processes" and their "empirical identification" (Beals 1953:637). For the propositions expressed here are indeed capable of verification or disproof.

Having formulated a principle relevant to cultural integration and having given it an initial test, I want now to orient it with respect to a particular kind of interpretation of human behavior and to suggest a broader implication. This principle is a tool which will help us to understand the nature of variant behaviors, which too often tend to be dismissed as random, unpredictable, and indeterminate.

It is an axiom of the culturological approach to the interpretation of human behavior that although the individual is relevant to the culture process, to the ongoing movement of the natural things we label cultural, he is irrelevant to an explanation of that process. He is, as White says, "a

---

and was reinvented to meet the needs of a Basin culture" (Opler 1941:571). My view and Opler's are in part complementary in that Opler's emphasis is upon changing function, an aspect which, as noted above, I have chosen to hold in abeyance in order to focus attention upon integration through reduction. Furthermore, I have discussed relationships within the Sun Dance, while Opler is concerned with the relation of the complex as a whole to the rest of Ute culture. Admittedly, however, there is a conflict of interpretations here with respect to the degree of integration among the Ute of the Plains-derived elements themselves.

catalytic agent that makes the interactive culture process possible," and "a medium of expression of the culture process" (1949:181). The same may be said of groups considered as collections of individuals; the collectivity as well as the individual is irrelevant to an explanation of culture process; indeed, the size, nature, and behavior of the collectivity is a function of culture in no less or greater degree than that of the individual. Culture may be regarded as "a thing *sui generis*," explainable in terms of itself.

We have already referred to the striking expressions of Cheyenne and Ute informants when speaking of behaviors within their respective Sun Dances—"You have got to do it in this particular way," and "They can do what they want about that." We take them as indices of the separate integrational states of the dances at the time they were observed. Furthermore, these statements may be thought of as functions of the culture process in particular times and places, as signs arising out of those separate states, impersonal indicators of fuller and lesser integration.

It is more useful to consider the expressions as cultural data in this sense than as assertions of personal will upon which behavior follows. Even if one removes the ontological implications and regards the expressions as summations of values in order to construct a value-centered theory for the explanation of cultural facts such as Sun Dance behaviors, no advantage is gained, and something is lost.

One might, for instance, assert that the expressions show that the Cheyenne value formality, that they have a fondness for tidying up loose ends of religious and social behaviors, and it is therefore consistent that they weave their ceremonies in firm patterns. It might be averred, on the other hand, that the Ute hold freedom and license as more desirable than restraint, so it is to be expected that they encourage innovation and diversity. At worst, the insertion of values leads to an inverted sequence of cause and effect. Values are derivative and conjunct, not causal. At best, their addition is superfluous and distracting. There still remains the task of accounting for the disparate values.

Now it might be assumed that the Ute, whose actions are ostensibly random and unpredictable, and who rationalizes his "choice" by informing us, "I can do what I want to about that," is demonstrating cultural motivation and determinacy to a lesser degree than the Cheyenne who feels he must perform a specific ritual motion. Such an assumption would be unproductive and misleading.

It is more useful to view the situation in this way: Surrounding every behavioral situation is a penumbra of potentially appropriate alternatives which are elements of the specific cultural whole, whether tribal or regional. All of the alternatives are parts of systems. Each individual may be regarded as the point of intersection of several systems—inorganic, organic, and superorganic, and within the latter, of familial, economic, ritual, and other subsystems (White 1949:364). And finally, either within a single subsystem or crosscutting several of them, we may distinguish the specific clusters of elements that we label Sun Dance, or Peyote ritual, or Shoshone shamanism.

In a strongly integrated cluster, the reduced alternatives or variants act repetitively and with sufficient force to make themselves and their pattern readily apparent to the observer. This is the situation in the Cheyenne dance.

On the other hand, in a loosely integrated complex or cluster, elements pertaining more largely to other complexes and systems, that is, variants not eliminated in the integration process, may impinge and motivate. Thus, one may find in the Comanche dance variant elements derived from the Kiowa and Cheyenne. They belong to the Plains regional system, but neither variant has become firmly operative in the Comanche dance to the exclusion of the other. Both have force as motivators of behavior. Similarly, one may observe today in the Northern Ute dance variants derived from the Basin shamanistic complex—numerous dream motivations for individual paints, and a variety of bodily manipulations for healing. Both regional clusters or complexes, Basin shamanism and Plains Sun Dance, each with a freight of numerous variants, crosscut Ute ritualism, intersect in the individual Ute dancer, and variously motivate his actions. All of the variants have cultural reality, and may have an impact upon a human receptor.

By loose analogy, the Cheyenne and Arapaho performer of the Sun Dance is like a well-informed and skilled chess player who works within the stable rules of a developed and integrated game; the Ute and Comanche, by the same token, is a novice whose attention is diverted by distractions not immediately integral to the game—that is, by parts of other systems.

A day taken up by the Sun Dance among the Ute has the same number of minutes as a day taken up with its performance among the Cheyenne. The minutes are full of content in both instances. The performers are doing something so long as they are in the dance, whether it is engaging in fantasy, or joking with bystanders, on the one hand, or meticulously enacting a pipe protocol or applying a required paint on the other.

But there is no need to regard the fantasy or the joking as without relevance. They may appear to be aberrant and random, and viewed solely from the center of a given ceremonial pattern, they may be so. But the fantasy may be comprehensible in the context of shaminism, another and intersecting cultural pattern, and thus it is no less culturally determined and determinable than the behavior toward the pipe. Conceivably, the fantasy may have no shamanistic or other cultural meaning, and perforce can be viewed at a given time in a psychological, which is to say, organic and noncultural, context. But once the fantasy acquires symbolic, arbitrary, cultural meaning, it assumes the properties of any cultural fact and exercises cultural force. From that point, it may be viewed as an element, unitary or variant, within one or another system or pattern. Similarly, an act of joking may be comprehended as an element in a familial, or kinship, or associational system, activated as the system intersects other systems in the human receptor, the dancer. It does not escape the net of cultural determinism by reason of its apparent absence of integration in a ceremony.

Now the ethnographer, prepared by observation of performances roughly similar to the one he anticipates viewing, or armed with information from published materials, seeks to sort out acts which appear relevant to a known pattern. The others he dimisses. Or, if he encounters a new ceremony, he seeks to discern the pattern with reasonable economy of time and labor, discarding what he assumes to be irrelevancies. This is justifiable, insofar as his task is to introduce order into his materials. But in so doing, he may be neglecting the materials which illuminate process.

Firth has written recently, "Here is our great problem as anthropologists—to translate the acts of individuals into the regularities of social process. How do we do it?" (Firth 1954:10). One way to translate the acts of individuals into *cultural* process is to demonstrate that diffuse individual acts may be regarded as responses to variants. As one seeks to understand behavior in a ceremony as an aspect of process, the infrequent variant may be as important as the established unitary element. Acts of individuals seemingly irrelevant to a specific pattern also have their motivations. The motivations are variants marginal to the complex itself, or they are positioned within other systems, cultural and noncultural. These may become linked with the pattern, first as permissible variants in a cluster, and finally as elements with exclusive force. We may regard the expression, "You have got to do it this particular way," and its accompanying behavior, as end products of the reduction of variants, summed up in the principle I have postulated. They are acts of individuals, but they are translatable into the regularities of cultural process. What is the source of variant behaviors? They may come from outside of a given cultural system or from within. The ancient and honorable processes of diffusion and invention suffice to account for most occurrences of innovation. Linton's suggestion, for instance, that the medicine-man-leader of one Comanche dance was familiar with the Cheyenne forms, and that a second Comanche at another time was acquainted with Kiowa procedures, can be comprehended as separate instances of diffusion. Neither diffusion nor invention, however, nor sheer time within which individuals act, account by themselves for subsequent integration. Once variants exist in a system, reduction may be assumed to be operative as a mechanism leading to integration, and their progressive diminution may be used as a measure of the degree of integration.

BIBLIOGRAPHY

BEALS, RALPH
  1953 "Acculturation." In *Anthropology Today*, prepared under the chairmanship of A. L. Kroeber, pp. 621–641. Chicago, The University of Chicago Press.
BENNETT, JOHN W.
  1944 "The Development of Ethnological Theory as Illustrated by Studies of the Plains Sun Dance." *American Anthropologist*, 46:162–181.
DORSEY, GEORGE A.
  1903 "The Arapaho Sun Dance; the Ceremony of the Offerings Lodge." *Field Columbian Museum, Anthropological Series*, 4.
  1905 "The Cheyenne. II. The Sun Dance." *Field Columbian Museum, Anthropological Series*, 9(2):57–186.
DRIVER, HAROLD E. and A. L. KROEBER
  1932 "Quantitative Expression of Cultural Relationships." *University of California Publications in American Archaeology and Ethnology*, 31:211–256.
FIRTH, RAYMOND
  1954 "Social Organization and Social Change." *Journal of the Royal Anthropological Institute*, 84:1–20.
GRINNELL, GEORGE BIRD
  1923 *The Cheyenne Indians, Their History and Ways of Life*. 2 vols. New Haven, Yale University Press.

JONES, J. A.
  1955 "The Sun Dance of the Northern Ute." *Bureau of American Ethnology Bulletin,* 157 (*Anthropological Papers,* 47):203–263.
KROEBER, A. L.
  1948 *Anthropology.* Revised edition. New York, Harcourt, Brace and Company.
KROEBER, A. L., and CLYDE KLUCKHOHN
  1952 "Culture. A Critical Review of Concepts and Definitions." *Papers of the Peabody Museum of American Archaeology and Ethnology, Harvard University,* 47(1).
LINTON, RALPH
  1935 "The Comanche Sun Dance." *American Anthropologist,* 37:420–428.
  1936 *The Study of Man.* New York, D. Appleton-Century Company, Inc.
LOWIE, ROBERT H.
  1919 "Sun Dance of the Shoshoni, Ute, and Hidatsa." *Anthropological Papers of the American Museum of Natural History,* 16(5):387–431.
MERTON, ROBERT K.
  1957 *Social Theory and Social Structure.* Revised edition. Glencoe, The Free Press.
OPLER, MARVIN K.
  1941 "The Integration of the Sun Dance in Ute Religion." *American Anthropologist,* 43:550–572.
OPLER, MORRIS E.
  1948 "Some Recently Developed Concepts Relating to Culture." *Southwestern Journal of Anthropology,* 4:107–122.
SPIER, LESLIE
  1921 "The Sun Dance of the Plains Indians: Its Development and Diffusion." *Anthropological Papers of the American Museum of Natural History,* 16(7):451–527.
STEWART, OMER C.
  1942 "Culture Element Distributions: XVIII. Ute-Southern Paiute." *Anthropological Records,* 6(4):231–356.
WHITE, LESLIE A.
  1949 *The Science of Culture.* New York, Farrar, Straus and Company.

✳ ✳ ✳ ✳

Richard K. Beardsley

UNIVERSITY OF MICHIGAN

SHINTO RELIGION AND

JAPANESE CULTURAL EVOLUTION [1]

Shinto's beliefs and practices are very much alive today in Japan, together with those of Buddhism, which claims among its followers the very persons who practice Shinto. All but a fraction of religiously inclined Japanese participate in both Buddhist and Shinto ritual. Present day manifestations of Shinto, however, far from making up a unified, systematic creed, exhibit striking diversities and ambiguities. Some forms are quite recent in origin whereas others date from remote, even prehistoric times. Many are difficult to trace to their roots because of the fragmentary nature of evidence, especially those from prehistoric times. Yet one is tempted to search the past, if only to be able to determine whether the present day melange of ritual and belief can be disentangled and seen as parts of one religious system or whether the label "Shinto" is simply a convenient catchall title for a potpourri of unrelated supernaturalistic elements.

Much speculation on Shinto has assumed that the religion began as a pure, self-consistent cult but suffered degeneration in later centuries. This is an *a priori* hypothesis with little supporting evidence. Rather more empirical than this are ethnological hypotheses which account for some modern diversities by tracing them to hypothetical migrations or waves of cultural diffusion to Japan in early times. However stimulating and posi-

[1] I owe to Eiichirō Ishida, Masao Oka, and numerous other Japanese colleagues much of my perception of Japanese religion, however limited. I am obliged for certain specific data to Dr. G. Raymond Nunn, Far Eastern Library, University of Michigan.

tive these hypotheses are, they concern themselves almost entirely with the earliest manifestations of Shinto and leave our question as regards present day Shinto largely unanswered, though suggesting that it may be made up simply of bits and pieces of primitive belief. What is offered in this paper is an evolutionary view that considers Shinto to be a continuing religious system and that deals with recent as well as ancient variants of Shinto worship in the context of Japanese culture as a whole.

In asserting this evolutionary view of Shinto, we do not reject or contradict the ethnological argument that diverse beliefs and rituals have been borrowed from outside areas. We do contend, however, that they were incorporated into a religious system that harmonized with Japanese culture at the time. Nor do we argue for the evolution of Shinto itself, independent of all other cultural phenomena. By demonstrating that main features of Shinto are responses to evolutionary developments in Japanese culture as a whole, we produce an evolutionary hypothesis for comprehending Shinto. The attempt made here is by no means a final summary of research. Rather, it is a speculative work paper suggesting a program for future research. It outlines stages of development in both general culture and religion, recognizable from summary inspection of evidence, which make the apparent ambiguities of Shinto more comprehensible. It is hoped that these suggestions will stimulate further research along the same line.

Before examining individual phases of Shinto, we present a sketch of the general nature of this religious system, together with some assurance that it has not been at any time radically transformed by alien religious creeds. Such assurance may be all the more necessary in view of the peculiarities of Shinto as compared with the world's major religions, for Shinto has no explicit creed; the most common forms lack a scripture or unifying dogma; they present no code for moral guidance; they have no epistemological explanation for major human problems such as death. Consequently, they have seemed peculiarly formless and inchoate to students approaching them as they would the major doctrinal religions. It may be unnecessary to specify that, notwithstanding the absence of the foregoing features, Shinto's beliefs and practices are nonetheless unequivocally religious inasmuch as they presuppose the existence of supernatural beings or forces. It can be said, in addition, that the various forms of Shinto have a family resemblance, a characteristic style or overtone that colors their somewhat variant views of the universe. This style might likely have been broken by close contact with Buddhism, a powerful religion with great absorptive capacity which has been popular in Japan for more than twelve centuries. It is true that at various times Buddhist temples have absorbed Shinto shrines and vice versa; also, that numerous features of belief or ritual have been interchanged between the two cults in Japan. Notwithstanding such syncretism, however, the great majority of religious Japanese are able to practice Shinto and Buddhism simultaneously as two distinct cults without confusion. The two religions, instead of competing, have come to complement one another, articulating together to provide a full religious life for the everyday Japanese worshiper.

The distinctive style linking together all the main variants of Shinto is illustrated in the following brief outline of Buddhism and Shinto, which states only the most general, contrastive features of each one without reference to their respective sect or local variations.

Buddhist philosophy starts with the premise that all existence is pain. Carnal appetites and passions produce and perpetuate this pain. Buddhist doctrine shows how to transcend bodily desires and achieve release from the pain of existence. Buddhism's most sacred supernal beings, the Buddha and Bodhisattvas, were originally human beings; by meditation, self-discipline, or inspiration, they actually transcended material existence, though they retain tremendous power to aid mankind, as do certain pre-Buddhist divinities who were converted to the faith. Citing these illustrious examples, Buddhism offers the Japanese worshiper his real reward in afterlife, compared to which his life on earth is only a delusory, transitory phenomenon. The worshiper honors his ancestors, for they have already escaped from existence, and he should gladly anticipate the time when he will join them. Reincarnation plays little role in Japanese Buddhism; ceremonies serve primarily to communicate with and honor one's particular ancestors. Death anniversaries for each ancestor are celebrated theoretically up to the forty-ninth year after his demise; at four annual ceremonies (New Year, Spring and Fall Equinox, Midsummer), also, each household honors all its forebears collectively, using bells, incense, and lighted candles or a small fire, a prayerbook and a rosary. Offerings are of rice, water, fresh fruits, and vegetables; offensive and forbidden alike as offerings or as food for the worshiper are meat, fish, and sake or other liquors.

Standard Shinto ritual contrasts at every point with what has just been described. Whereas family ties link each person to his Buddhist temple, community residence links him to his Shinto shrine. The shrine, in a sense, belongs to everyone in a village or district. Whereas one uses Buddhism to insure welfare after death, he uses Shinto to secure welfare here and now in this world. The flavor of Shinto is one of joy in living. Worshipers approach the shrine more or less literally as revelers, and set out feasts with drinks and delicacies—including the very fish and sake that are not tolerated under Buddhism. The young men, especially, drink enough sake to achieve a state of jolly inebriation—and mystic communion—at important ceremonies. Ceremonies serve both to give thanks for the present health and well-being of all living things within the community and to appeal for future protection against disease and calamity. Ritual takes place at some sacred spot, usually the precincts of a shrine, which is the locus of a *kami*— a key concept in Shinto, but an ambiguous one, to be discussed below. The *kami*, be it a manifestation of impersonal power like mana, a personalized spirit, a high god with human personality, or a deified hero, is beneficent and protective. It is present in the shrine during ceremonies, being embodied in certain objects (*shintai*, "body of the kami") of bronze or more perishable treasures kept in the shrine's innermost recess. The *kami* safeguards the well-being of all persons and things in the district pertaining to its shrine, not merely of active worshipers and their families. Thus, while Buddhism in Japan is a personal or family religion to provide for a blissful afterlife, Shinto mostly functions as a community religion to protect a particular neighborhood in the present world. Even in special cases in which Shinto worship is not performed by and for the community, it preserves most other characteristics named here.

With the foregoing general features in mind, we may now examine the major phases of Shinto in their postulated evolutionary sequence, summarizing each against the background of Japanese culture in the relevant time period. Three main phases are recognized: (1) a cult of local powers and local spirits, associated with early phases of prehistoric Yayoi culture; (2) a cult of personalized spirits and gods, associated with the emergence of aristocracy in protohistoric and early historic centuries; (3) a phase marked by two developments, (a) appearance of evangelistic sects, corresponding to the rise of an entrepreneurial class and dissolution of the feudal regime, and (b) invention of a nationalist supercult, corresponding to the emergence of a modern nation-state in the nineteenth century.

1. LOCAL POWERS AND LOCAL SPIRITS

The beginnings of Shinto are found among the beginnings of Japanese culture itself. The period of Yayoi culture (ca. 300 B.C.–A.D. 350), though by no means first in the Japanese archaeological sequence, is nonetheless the period in which the basis of Japanese culture was formed and, with it, the beginnings of the native religion. Yayoi culture provides the first evidence for the veneration of local powers and local spirits in the style which eventually was to evolve into modern Shinto.

The Yayoi culture, bearer of rice agriculture to Japan, was preceded by several thousand years of preagricultural habitation grouped into two main divisions: Pre-Ceramic and Jomon cultures. We have little evidence, indeed, on which to describe or even to speculate concretely about the religion of these peoples. For all we know, it may have been not unlike Yayoi religion in general categorical terms; for example, religion of the primitive Ainu in Hokkaido, who may descend at least in part from one facet of late Jomon culture, is also based on belief in local spirits and powers. Yet, in its details, Ainu cult is quite apart from Shinto, and the extinction of Pre-Ceramic and Jomon cultures without perceptible residue in Japanese culture makes any contributions from them to Japanese religion unlikely. Hence, we look to Yayoi culture for the basis of Japanese Shinto.

Yayoi culture began to replace Jomon culture about 300 B.C., bringing numerous elements of settled village life along with agriculture. Excavations show wooden, grass-thatched houses grouped into hamlets which were small at first but larger in size and number as agriculture became more efficient and widespread. Iron, though in use early, rarely has been preserved, whereas numerous bronze implements survive from the later phases of Yayoi culture.

The Yayoi bronzes give some clues to the religion of the time. They consist mainly of mirrors (often imported), bells, spears, and halberds with broad, paper-thin blades. Significantly, all these forms are so impractical that they seem clearly designed for ceremony rather than everyday use. Moreover, they seem rarely, if ever, to have been personal property. Evidence suggests, in fact, that no dominant group or class existed to own such treasures; rather that the villages operated collectively as communities of near-equals in socioeconomic position. The bronzes supposedly were kept as communal property, perhaps as symbols in the community shrine. This speculation is based on several bits of evidence. One, coming from outside of Japan, is a near-contemporary Chinese report (from the dynastic chronicle, the Wei-chih) on nearby south Korean villages. The report mentions that certain objects, which were the collective symbols of an autonomous group of hamlets, were guarded specifically in the communal shrine where they validated the ceremonial and judicial functions exercised, with weak authority, by the village elders. Society in these hamlets seems decidedly to have been unstratified. Secondly, in Japan itself, though no Yayoi structure has been identified yet as a shrine, most bronzes themselves are found under curious conditions; they are secreted in hideaways distant from any community as if to be protected from harm, and are not infrequently battered as if by conquerors anxious to destroy or invalidate their "power." As we shall see from the following period, conquerors' symbols are apt to have been substituted in worship for those of the vanquished as a symbol of subordination or incorporation. Thirdly, we have the commonplace phenomenon today of modern shrines in which are kept *shintai* (embodiment of the *kami*) which often enough are of bronze or other precious materials. A certain proportion of the objects themselves and their shrines may literally survive from Yayoi times, though many, of course, are much more recent.

These bits of evidence just cited suggest the existence in Yayoi times of the type of cult represented today by *ujigami*, or tutelary spirit shrines which are ubiquitous in Japan. The *kami* of such a shrine protects the *uji* or body of worshipers, who comprise all residents of a particular area. This *kami* is a localized force or power—or, alternatively but less commonly, a personalized spirit. At most seasons, the *kami* is secluded on a peak, in a woods, or at some other landmark, but on ceremonial occasions it resides or vests its power in the sacred objects (*shintai*) at the heart of the shrine. The *kami*, consequently, has a dual location, one in the shrine conveniently close to the villages of worshipers, the other in a spot which may have no manmade marker. Should a branch shrine be built (not too far away) and sanctified by transferring part of the *shintai*, the *kami* visits it as well. Certain *kami* are more powerful or even ubiquitous, so that widely scattered shrines go by their names; but others are quite narrowly localized.

We are inclined to suppose that *ujigami* ritual loomed important in Yayoi hamlets just as it does in today's farm villages. Today's villages must act together in irrigation and other economic activities; they reassert their sense of communality by joint shrine worship, the same hamlets being represented for each activity. But Yayoi supernaturalism is unlikely to have consisted exclusively in worship at *ujigami* shrines. Other common elements of present-day Shinto, as well, may date from this phase of Japanese cultural development, and will be listed forthwith, not because we possess concrete archaeological evidence on the question but because these features are as ubiquitous throughout Japan as *ujigami* worship, and because typologically or stylistically they harmonize with *ujigami* ritual in concept and practice. They all have a clear, definite relation to the passage of seasons, as do *ujigami* rituals; they are performed by the community for its general welfare; they presuppose supernatural forces or spirits that have no real anthropomorphic features or personality and that are, by nature, benign and protective. The ceremonies are basically prophylactic or purificatory. Five festivals celebrating the several seasons comprise a set collectively termed the *sekku;* Seven Grasses for winter, Cherry Blossom for early spring, Iris for late spring, Bamboo for midsummer, and Chestnut for fall. Each, in earlier times, promoted fertility and insured that nature would successfully complete the seasonal transition, though these ritual implications have been weakened or lost in recent times. Their flower-names are probably Chinese inspired; the ceremonies themselves, however, have no evident connection with Chinese ceremonies. A second class of rituals, now much changed or in disuse, was important in village life up to the last century for the safeguarding or purification of women and children; of these the Doll Festival (Girls' Day) and Boys' Day survive in altered form as nationally popular festivals. A third set, still much practiced in the countryside, honors specific nonanthropomorphic spirits that have specialized protective powers: *Yakujin* guards against disease, *Ushi-no-kami* safeguards domestic beasts, *Jijin* protects the riceland through the growing season, retiring to the mountains as *Yama-no-kami* after each harvest. All these foregoing ceremonies are presumed to derive from the primal phase of Shinto identified in the period of Yayoi culture.[2]

2. DEIFIED HEROES AND HIGH GODS

A second phase of Shinto development, the founding of shrines to heroes, great family heads, and high gods, occurred as an aristocracy emerged in Japanese society, and is considered here to be functionally a response to the rise of aristocrats. Shortly after A.D. 300, in several richer parts of the Japanese country-side, great earthmound tombs began to blossom among the Yayoi rice fields. These ostentatious sepulchers, which ushered in the

---

[2] Buddhism now almost monopolizes ancestor worship in Japan; in other regions it makes little or nothing of ancestor reverence, but the ancestor cult in Japan is a focus for Buddhism. One is tempted to suggest, on the strength of its stylistic parallels with the *ujigami* cult, that the ancestor cult was absorbed by Buddhism out of early Shinto. The ancestors resemble *ujigami* in their essential benevolence and their periodic visits to the community (or the home itself) each year to bless their living descendants; like the *ujigami*, they are entertained with food and praise. Masao Oka groups ancestors or souls with four other primal categories of supernatural beings in his reconstruction of early Japanese supernaturalism (in Ishida *et al.* 1958:60–63). Our suggestion, however, concerns the basic concept, not the modes of worship. As to the actual ritual of Bon, the main midsummer ancestral ceremony, it seems derived from non-Buddhist Indian ritual, specifically from Ganges valley worship of the goddess Kali which has quite detailed parallels.

Tomb Period, give abundant evidence of the rise of an elite class nourished from the labor of commoners who continued living much as before in their villages. A few early tombs and other bits of evidence indicate that social stratification had already begun in the late Yayoi period, perhaps had even progressed rather far. This evidence is not yet well explored. But, in the archaeological period of Tomb culture and the early historic period, at any rate, society clearly included a class of aristocrats.

Some aristocrats, almost certainly, were immigrant soldiers of fortune who introduced customs from the continent. Others rose out of local village society. By elaborating in-marriage within their class, they gave rise to the so-called "clans" (*uji*) among the aristocracy of early historic times. (see Beardsley, Hall, and Ward 1959: 33–34 for further summary of the nature of the *uji*.) Eventually, the Yamato *uji* achieved hegemony beginning with Jimmu, the first "emperor" according to legend. An interesting problem recently raised, incidentally, is whether Jimmu may have been one of the migrants, out of China, rather than being of the local aristocracy; the suggestion comes from a study of Chinese sources, not from Japanese archaeology directly or from the early Japanese semilegendary histories, the Kojiki (A.D. 745) and Nihonshoki (A.D. 810).

The rising aristocrats administered an increasingly complex society, in which occupationally specialized villages have been identified archaeologically in the fourth and fifth centuries A.D. Individual or family land ownership included rights to land won by conquest. Larger domains incorporated clearly defined districts governed by commanders, who were subchieftains or nobles. We suggested earlier that sacred symbols of a victorious community were placed for worship in the shrines of other communities which they had subjugated; from the Tomb period we have evidence that mirrors of a particular type, emblems of a given noble family, were sent to subordinate or subjugated nobility for them to perform proper ceremonies of worship. Tremendous amounts of manpower were expended in building earth tombs and megalithic burial crypts as monuments for distinguished leaders, before the Tomb culture came to its end in the seventh century A.D. Among all of these developments, a feature of principal interest for the study of religion is the emergence of individuals of great social consequence, chieftains and leaders powerful enough to manipulate human affairs for great harm or good.

Shinto religion reflects this development with two features that seem likely to date from this period. One is the founding of shrines to the spirit of heroic ancestors of great family lines. The other is the development of a narrative mythology of high celestial gods and goddesses who, like the

Olympian deities of classical Greece, have a wide range of human temperaments and quirks of personality.

An illustration of the first development is the great shrine of Kibitsu and several small nearby shrines in Okayama Prefecture in western Japan, near the Inland Sea. Kibitsu Shrine is the major shrine of southern Okayama; though rebuilt several times after conflagrations, as happens to any ancient shrine in Japan, it still rests on stone foundations laid in the Nara period (A.D. 710–845), which perhaps cover still more ancient remains. The *kami* of this shrine is Prince Kibitsu-hiko, one of the four conquering generals dispatched by the late fourth century Yamato emperor, Sujin, to enlarge his realm. The shrine is on the hillside which was Kibitsu's stronghold for his major battle, according to local legend:

Kibitsu's main opponent, Ura, was wounded by a dextrously aimed arrow from Kibitsu's bow. He tried to escape by turning into a pheasant; Kibi became a hawk and chased him through the woods. Just as the hawk dove to make his kill, the pheasant leaped into a creek and became a carp. But before the carp could disappear, Kibitsu took shape of a cormorant, dived, and delivered the final blow. Blood gushing from the dying carp colored the stream and gave it the name, Chisuigawa ("Blood-drinking Creek") (Beardsley, Hall, and Ward 1959:35).

Smaller shrines exist today on the bank of Chisui Creek and at other spots connected with this folkloristic "magicians' contest." None is of the size or importance of the shrine to Kibitsu-hiko, which, with two more recent branches, is the *ujigami* shrine over the whole region, called Kibi, conquered by this semi-legendary general and thereafter ruled for a time by his direct descendants and their branches.

The conceptual pattern of the Kibitsu shrine is repeated on a still more august level in Japan's foremost national shrines, imperial family shrines to the high gods and heroes who, alike, are presumptive imperial ancestors. The celebrated imperial sword, the mirror, and the sacred stones, sacred symbols that validate the imperial right to rule, are shrine symbols or *shintai* housed in three localities: Kōtai Jingū in Ujiyamada City, Mie Prefecture, one of the much-visited pair of Ise shrines to the sun-goddess, Amaterasu, houses the bronze mirror; Atsuta Jingū, in Nagoya City, Aichi Prefecture, houses the bronze sword; the necklace of stones is kept in the Imperial Court in Tokyo. Some nine other family shrines in central Japan or in Tokyo are dedicated to other ancestral *kami*, ranging from the high god Susano-o through the first emperor, Jimmu, up to the nineteenth century emperor and empress Meiji. The Meiji Jingū in Tokyo is very recent, of course; one or two other shrines may not antedate the historical period;

but the majority were probably founded protohistorically. Parts of the complex may be still older. Were a prehistorian to examine the three major imperial symbols, the sword, the mirror, and the jewels, he might find them to be literal relics from Yayoi times.

Closely linked to the enshrinement and deification of imperial ancestors is the second main feature of the protohistoric phase of Shinto evolution: a cosmology of high gods who, by definition, are ancestors of the imperial family. Japan's earliest records, the Kojiki and Nihongi, described these gods and their genealogical connection with the imperial family. These records are not so much impartial histories as partisan documents glorifying the Yamato rulers, suppressing facts about any rival rulers and their *kami* and distorting other facts and traditions to achieve a convincing genealogy. However suspect some of their reportage may be, we can be sure they did not invent deities, that Shinto concepts had already come to include celestial beings with the power to transform, to create land and sea, to control storms and the fertility of crops, and otherwise to affect natural phenomena. These *kami* are like humans in personality. Their marriages, deaths, quarrels, and expeditions comprise a cosmology markedly different from the superworld of generalized *kami* postulated for early Yayoi times. Nonetheless, this new Shinto, with *kami* worshiped in the same manner as before and safeguarding the welfare of their worshipers in the same way, clearly has its evolutionary roots in the Shinto of prehistoric times.

3A. EVANGELISTIC SECTS

The next recognized transformation of Shinto, creating a third evolutionary phase of the cult, occurred after a lapse of a millennium, and came about as a response to the crystallization of an entrepreneurial economy. Two distinct new forms arose, one on the heels of the other in the nineteenth century. Each had its own distinctive etiology: evangelistic sects respond to the principle of enterprise and profit displayed by the new commercial class, whereas the supercult known as State Shinto is directly related to the coming into being of the nation-state under a bureaucracy headed by the emperor. Both the social and the political phenomena of this period, however well each may be isolated for analysis, must be considered dependent, in turn, on a single development: emergence of commerce on the principle of enterprise. Hence they are regarded here as two aspects of a single evolutionary phase, not as successive and independent phases. For convenience, however, each will be discussed separately.

We need not follow socioeconomic history through the decline of the early aristocracy and the gradual crystallization of a system of feudalism up to the nineteenth century because, for all the vastness of change, no corresponding revolution in Shinto is recognizable. Buddhism had its great period of development through the medieval centuries in Japan; its sects provided ideological backing for the various contending groups and classes. Shinto, by continuing to serve its former functions, seems to have met demands placed on it without radical transformation. Religious historians have pointed to many specific changes, of course, notable among which were syncretistic adjustments to Buddhism and an upsurge of shamanistic phenomena such as spirit possession. Some combination of these phenomena may be responsible for the medieval cult of *goryōshin*, malevolently inclined spirits of the dead credited with the authorship of all manner of personal and social ills, who were diagnosed by female shamans and repelled or exorcised by Buddhist magic. Though interesting as a variant on the belief in *kami*, distinguished especially by its conception of evil *kami*, the *goryō* cult does not seem to constitute a radical departure from preexisting patterns of Shinto. It certainly is less of a transformation, at any rate, than is either of the nineteenth century phenomena about to be discussed. We consider, first, the social events that prepared a propitious environment for the rise of Sect Shinto.

Medieval feudalism had lacked any firm central government. It was modified in the early 1600's by establishment of a sternly centralized military government under the Tokugawa family serving as marshals (*shoguns*). Relative prosperity in the following two centuries revived internal trade, encouraged city growth, and stimulated the rise of a new class whose strength eventually did much to crack open the military state from the inside. This was the commercial class composed of merchants and artisans or, more broadly, of townsmen committed to the newly emerging money economy. The prospering townsmen, or *chōnin*, struggled free from their humble status notwithstanding the government's discriminatory treatment aimed at restoring the feudal equilibrium. As they grew wealthy, they patronized new forms of art, literature, and theater. The Kabuki drama and wood block prints, typical *chōnin* arts, gave voice to their nonfeudal values. Careful study has shown that the important *chōnin* did not themselves lead the overthrow of the shogunate in 1868 because, having done well under the decadent feudal order, they tended, as individuals, to oppose the destruction of modified feudalism. Yet they were the idealogical forebears of the entrepreneurs and businessmen who set about modernizing Japan in the late nineteenth century. And in their time there sprang up the first of a rash of new religious sects which gave a quite new setting to the old Shinto beliefs. Though gods or all-powerful principles of these sects bore the names of Shinto *kami,* their doctrines were those of personal salvation or enlightenment, and they earnestly sought converts in a manner quite foreign to any earlier forms of Shinto worship.

These sects have been well studied as social psychological phenomena but very little in terms of their common cultural characteristics. Nor have they been related in detail to socioeconomic events of the nineteenth and twentieth centuries. Hence, comment here must be ventured tentatively, in default of historical detail. Each sect sprang up without direct connections to others, over a time span ranging from 1833 to the present day. The Tenri sect, earliest and now the largest, with over two million followers, dates from 1833. Its founder was Miki Nakayama, daughter of a Buddhist priest near Nara. After an unhappy early married life, she experienced a series of visions which brought her enlightenment and provided the basic doctrines of her sect. The first preaching of the Konkō doctrine was separated by a quarter century and a hundred and twenty miles from the Tenri sect. Konkō was founded in 1859 in Okayama by a mystic leader known as Taijin Konkō after he began receiving revelations. Only slightly later and in the same province, the sun-goddess Amaterasu, herself, brought enlightenment to Munetada Kurozumi, son of a Shinto priest, who then went out to gather converts to his Kurozumi sect. Other revealed doctrines gathered followers in the following decades despite periods of disapprobation or persecution by the government. Their number, totalling more than thirty, has risen since the close of World War II with the appearance of new sects such as the so-called Dancing Sect (Odori-kyō) or the reformulation of older sects, an example being the PL Kyōdan (Perfect Liberty Sect) which stemmed from the Hitonomichi-kyō (Man's Way Sect).

Each sect among these "New Religions" has its particular links to Shinto belief and practice; most claim primarily to offer a clearer vision of the *kami.* Yet, as a group, they bring totally unprecedented principles and practices to Shinto. They are based on ecstatic revelation, an innovation in itself. They offer a moral code or, at least, a standard to live by. They proselytize for converts and gather their believers into congregations for regularly scheduled services, sometimes once each week. Some promise salvation, others seek enlightenment on earth. In these divergent characteristics there is more than a slight taste of Christianity or, more narrowly, of Protestantism. Chronology is awkward for any simple explanation based on borrowing of Christian ideas, for the earliest sects far antedate the arrival of the first Protestant Christian missionaries in Japan (John Liggins and C. M. Williams, in 1859); alternatively, one is tempted to look for antecedents back to the so-called Christian Century (1549–1649) when Francis Xavier and his fellow Catholic missionaries built a Christian community of an estimated 500,000 converts. Between 1650 and the early 1800's, however, every open expression of Christianity had been rigidly suppressed in Japan. Without the support of further research, there seems only a faint possibility of influence in the formation of Tenri or other Shinto sect doctrines from Catholic teachings, from Catholic converts who survived covertly near Nagasaki, or from the closely guarded Dutch traders based in Nagasaki through the decades in question. Should such outside inspiration ever be documented, it will not alter the fact that the new concepts took hold in the nineteenth century among persons who were now prepared to accept such assumptions, thanks to the success of entrepreneurial thinking. Such persons were more mobile psychologically than their fathers; they were not mentally committed to a given occupation simply because it was hereditary in their family, but were prepared to switch, individually, to a different line of worship (as to a different line of goods) if it offered greater benefits. The "New Religions" offer not only salvation but also good health, physical comfort, and prosperity of one's earthly affairs. Their style of doctrine and worship seems as admirably attuned to the new *chōnin* as the doctrines of Protestantism were to the bourgeois class in northwestern Europe three centuries earlier. For this reason, they are here regarded as an ideological response to the evolution of individualistic enterprise and commerce in Japan.

3B. THE NATIONALIST SUPERCULT

Among the first steps in establishing a government for the Meiji Emperor in 1868, when the last Tokugawa Shogun was removed, was the creation of a Department of Shinto. Previous rulers, it is true, had similarly taken care of shrines that validated the imperial rule. Imitating the imperial pattern, the shoguns had completed a resplendent shrine to their own *kami* at Nikko, and it behooved the imperial government to restore ancient shrines to their proper eminence. However, the Department of Shinto took on new functions. The new government displayed an unprecedentedly nationalistic, centralizing fervor, feeling itself beset not only by major economic and political crises but also by external threat—conquest or dismemberment by the European nations who were in the act of carving up China. Whereas the Tokugawa regime, though the first to succeed in uniting all Japan, had knit their conquests together as a family demesne, not as a nation, the Meiji regime from its birth was the government of a nation-state. Its officers were not vassals but bureaucrats under a law code. Its citizen-subjects were to pay taxes directly to the central government, were to bear arms for national defense, and were to give their first loyalty directly to the state and its sovereign. In this last item we see a compromise between feudal loyalty to persons and the concept of patriotism. Not quite daring to rely on its citizens' abstract patriotism, the guiding oligarchy fostered a cult of personal loyalty to the sovereign. Thus was State Shinto born.

Bureaucratic reshuffling turned the Department of Shinto (1868) into the Shinto Ministry (1871) and then into the Ministry of Religion (1872) before incorporating its functions into the octopus Home Ministry, the all-powerful ministry of domestic affairs (1877). Within the first two years, in 1870, an imperial rescript clearly stated the government's intention to establish a national cult based on worship of the sun goddess. The Department of Shinto had already organized shrines for the first time into a nationwide hierarchy, placing imperial family shrines in the top rank and following downward with one official shrine for each prefecture, one for each county, and two or three for each of the recently redistricted villages and towns; a state-paid priesthood, similarly ranked, provided a guardian for each shrine; precise ceremonial was prescribed for each shrine. The new hierarchy omitted many of the thousands of small local shrines, of course, and the Department of Shinto undertook to discourage worship at them in order to be able to supervise directly all religious activity. Now, to create a national supercult, the Department simply rededicated each shrine in its official hierarchy to the sun goddess or another divinity on the approved list; further, by prescribing ceremonies for each, the Department aimed to prevent the little communities from simply continuing the traditional rituals appropriate to their local *kami*. Beyond this, a portrait of the emperor was enshrined in every school and public office in the nation and minutely detailed ceremonies were invented for worship of this living *kami*. Stories of the exaggerated sanctity built up for these ceremonies and for the portraits themselves are probably too well known to need repetition here.

To validate this brand new national supercult, a veneer of antiquity was needed. Scholars were encouraged to burrow into ancient records and publish interpretations justifying the actions of the Department of Shinto and its successors. Also, campaigns were launched to softpedal or crush other forms of worship, including the new Shinto sects, Christianity, and Buddhism. The more severe measures provoked waves of outspoken protest and resistance from the cults concerned, forcing the government periodically to relax its pressure; the unorganized mass of people maintained a passive resistance to most attempts to wipe out traditional local cults even though they complied with the new regulations. Thus, the supercult never absorbed all of Shinto ceremonial even in its period of greatest intensity during World War II. When it was abolished, at the close of the war, as one of the first acts of the Supreme Commander of the Allied Forces in the Pacific, virtually all forms of popular worship were still alive though disorganized, and they sprang back into activity. State Shinto at present is moribund, though perhaps not dead. Various nationalist and ultraconservative groups are anxious to revive it and may succeed in doing so, given extreme conditions of international tension, a depression, or other severe crisis, for nationalistic Shinto, being a state-inspired cult, is intimately dependent on the course of political events.

CONCLUSION

Shinto's concepts and practices, as many students have discovered, do not lend themselves to easy and brief definition. The ethical flavor in Sect Shinto is absent from other forms. The localism inherent in most varieties of popular worship makes their export outside of Japan difficult, even ridiculous; yet overseas Japanese were able to practice State Shinto when it was propagandized among them, and certain sects, notably Tenri, are winning converts even among non-Japanese Californians, Southeast Asians, and others. Thus, what characterizes some facets of Shinto proves contradictory to the nature of other facets.

The attempt to define *kami*, a central concept, illustrates the elusiveness of Shinto from the descriptive point of view. What is *kami?* Etymologically, the word is a locative that merely signifies "up, above, superior," and in some contexts it becomes a title for persons of superior rank, carrying this basic meaning. In other contexts it denotes a force, supernatural and impersonal, that invests certain places or objects. In still others it is a spirit, invisible and formless, whose worshipers can entertain and please it as they could not were it purely impersonal. Still other occasions present the *kami* of an ancient hero as the spirit to be worshiped, and yet other *kami* are eternal high gods vested with human personality. Translations of Christian writings use *kami* for God, which is a concept vastly different from that of a local spirit with very limited powers and no ethical connotations. *Kami,* viewed definitionally, is an extremely ambiguous concept.

Evidence has been reviewed here, however, which indicates that current Shinto concepts and practices date from various periods in Japan's past. These phenomena of varied character were functionally attuned to socioeconomic and political assumptions during the several periods of Japan's cultural evolution. The various beliefs fall into place when viewed in this evolutionary context, being derived from one of the three stages recognized at the present writing. *Kami,* our example above, is an impersonal force or a localized spirit in terms of cult forms of the prehistoric phase; it is a disembodied hero or high god in the context of protohistoric cult developments; it is apt to be an ethical deity or moral force for worshipers in the proselyting sects that have arisen since 1800. State Shinto added nothing to the *kami* concept; its contribution—nullified for the present—was a hierarchical organization of selected fragments of the preexisting cult in the service of political nationalism. Further research probably will succeed in multiplying or modifying the three stages now defined. In so doing, they may throw new light on general features of Japanese culture, and so confirm the utility of the evolutionary interpretation of Shinto.

BIBLIOGRAPHY

BEARDSLEY, RICHARD K., JOHN W. HALL and ROBERT E. WARD
  1959 *Village Japan.* Chicago, The University of Chicago Press.
ISHIDA, EIICHIRŌ, MASAO OKA, NAMIO EGAMI and ICHIRŌ YAWATA
  1958 *Nihon Minzoku no Kigen (Origin of the Japanese People).* Tokyo, Heibonsha.

* * * *

John Buettner-Janusch

YALE UNIVERSITY

THE STUDY OF NATURAL

SELECTION AND THE ABO(H)

BLOOD GROUP SYSTEM IN MAN

INTRODUCTION

The history of attempts to solve particular problems in science often reveals to us how science in general develops. We are all too prone to consider science divorced from the influences of social ideologies. Yet it is possible to demonstrate that scientists frequently, indeed usually, project something of their social philosophy into their views of the nature of science and the nature of the problems which science should solve. The metaphysical position of a scientist and the quasi-scientific conceptions of the nature of man, the universe, reality, and other such large categories of experience determine the ways in which individuals engaged in scientific investigation will respond to the problems which confront them and to the solutions which are proposed by other scientists. The gathering of evidence is not the only way in which science examines problems. One of the most important aspects of the development of science is the increase in sophistication and understanding of the nature of what it is that science does. Physical anthropology has been a singularly unsophisticated participant in the biological and social sciences. The difficulty of viewing its major subject—man—with the necessary detachment, the preoccupation with descriptive minutiae of individual men, and the misunderstanding of the implications of genetic and evolutionary theory are partly responsible and partly symptoms of the state of scientific thinking about man at the historical period when physical anthropology was formalized.

The central problem of the science of physical anthropology is to characterize human variation and to relate such a variation to human evolution. A major part of the research effort in physical anthropology since the time of Broca in France (1863; 1875) and S. G. Morton in the United States (1839; 1844) has been directed to describing the superficial similarities and differences among men. The color of skin, hair and eyes, the dimensions of the femur, thorax, skull, and pelvis of thousands of individuals from hundreds of populations are recorded in a myriad of indices and tables. Very little work has been done to ascertain the genetic structure of human populations. The study of the biological parameters of human behavior has been given scant attention. The theoretical study of selection in man has been the concern of geneticists and even they have examined few human traits that are molded by this evolutionary process.

A number of notable studies have been made in an attempt to show the relationship between a variety of traits and the conditions of the environments in which the bearers of these traits lived. The relationship between body size and climate (Newman 1953), the association between complexion and the susceptibility to disease (MacDonald 1911–12), the effect of climate, temperature, and solar radiation on skin color (Woodruff 1912; Love and Davenport 1919), the correlation between shape and size of nose and eye and the air temperature and amount of sunlight and the habitat (Coon, Garn, and Birdsell 1950; Coon 1954) have been cited as examples of the operation of selection. These studies have provided a vast amount of information supporting the view that man is physically as well as culturally adapted to ecological conditions. Dobzhansky has noted (1950), as have others, that human skin color has a definite geographical gradient, and suggestions have been made that the amount of fat, the hair form, and the blood groups follow similar gradients.

In this paper I plan to discuss certain current problems in physical anthropology which are related to an understanding of natural selection as the major factor that produces evolutionary change. These problems surround the study of the way in which natural selection controls population frequencies of the ABO blood groups. In the discussion of these problems I intend not only to describe their present status but also to inquire about considerations, usually thought to be irrelevant to scientific inquiry, that influenced the kind of research and theory-construction which went into their solution.

Organic evolution, according to modern genetic theory, occurs through four processes: mutation, natural selection, genetic drift, and migration. The final process, migration, is the method by which interbreeding between populations occurs. Natural selection is called *creative* because it selects new forms within a population that are to constitute that population in the future. Mutation brings about new traits: selection works upon the fortuitous expression of such new traits to pick out those that will maintain the continuity of the species or population in an ever-changing environment. This procedure applies to man as well as to other organisms.

There has been a tendency upon the part of eugenicists, and others, to discount the effect of natural selection upon civilized human populations. The advance of civilization, increasing man's ability to control natural phenomena, including disease, has been cited as a factor in reducing the effect of selection, for example, Rittenhouse (1913), Shrubsall (1914). Furthermore, a peculiar social philosophy, often called "social Darwinism," attributed implications to Darwinian theory which it did not have. This is not the place to develop a discussion of social Darwinism. However, such phrases as "survival of the fittest," "the struggle for existence," and the "elimination of the unfit" are slogans of the rather heterogeneous group of philosophies which are legitimately lumped under the rubric "social Darwinism." These implications obscured the biological theory of natural selection with respect to man. The "unfit" are not eliminated, the "fittest" do not necessarily survive. One must inquire into what it is that the writer or speaker means when he uses terms like *the fittest*, which are appropriate to theological or moral but not to scientific discourse.

Over thirty years ago S. J. Holmes commented as follows: "The literature on natural selection in man is somewhat peculiar in that most of the writers who have contributed to it have apparently not had the subject of natural selection in mind at all" (1924). Holmes had in mind the fact that most investigators did not study selective death rates or differential susceptibility to morbid conditions with respect to hereditary traits in human populations. E. B. Ford has pointed out that man is a species that shows balanced polymorphism with respect to the ABO

blood groups (1940). More recently, Allison (1954a; 1955) has demonstrated the same situation exists in the case of the sickle cell trait and
the abnormal and sickle cell hemoglobins. Balanced polymorphism is
maintained by natural selection, and it can be taken as *prima facie*
evidence that one should look for a specific selective mechanism. Polymorphism is the condition that exists when two or more discontinuous
forms of a single species share the same habitat and the frequency of the
least common of them is too great to be accounted for by the effect of
natural mutation. If this polymorphism maintains itself from generation
to generation it is in a state of balance, and the process which maintains
this balance is natural selection (Ford 1940; 1957).

Specific genetic traits which exhibit polymorphism in human populations include the ABO blood group phenotype (Ford 1957), the sickle
cell trait and associated abnormal hemoglobins (Allison 1954a; 1954b;
1954c), and the gene for the ability to taste PTC (phenylthiocarbamide)
(Allison and Nevanlinna 1952; Lugg and Whyte 1955; Lugg 1957). There
are two general classes of traits with a distribution among human groups
that suggests the hypothesis that their frequencies are due to natural
selection. One class includes traits whose frequencies show distinct
geographical or ecological gradients; the other class contains traits in
respect to which various human populations are polymorphic. It is the
latter I shall discuss here.

The specific problems discussed below are based on the hypothesis that
the ABO blood group system in man is subject to the forces of natural
selection. Despite the fact that we can argue *a priori* that this system is
subject to selection because it exhibits balanced polymorphism, nevertheless, one must view this statement as an hypothesis. Details of statistical and laboratory investigations of this hypothesis have been published
elsewhere (Buettner-Janusch 1957).

The investigation of the ABO blood groups and natural selection
presents us with a very intriguing episode in the history of anthropology
and medicine. The point of view from which this episode is analyzed
here is stated by the following question. Why has there been resistance
to and lack of interest in the idea that the frequencies of the various
blood groups in different human populations are due to selection? I do
not think that I can provide a precise answer to the question but I believe
that it is difficult to explain the history of this problem on strictly rational
and scientific grounds. Metaphysics and vested interests both played their
role in shaping research in this area.

EARLY WORK ON ABO BLOOD GROUPS AND SELECTION

Maternal-Fetal Incompatibility

Perhaps the earliest published work which can now be claimed part of the study of blood groups and natural selection was made by Dienst in 1905. He suggested that eclampsia (toxic disease of late pregnancy marked by convulsions and coma) is due to the transfusion of incompatible blood from the fetus into the mother's circulation. He made the following statement (1905:356):

Es sollen nun im folgenden noch weitere Stützpunkte aufgezählt werden, die für die zunächst überraschende neue Eklampsiehypothese sprechen, nach der also die Eklampsie nichts anderes wäre als eine Transfusion heterogenen Kindsblutes in den mütterlichen Kreislauf, die durch eine Kommunikation beider Kreislaufsysteme, oder, noch allgemeiner ausgedrückt, durch ein Undichtsein der Placenta ermöglicht worden wäre.[1]

He proceeded to do just that. Earlier he had published data which supported this theory, and he had been severely criticized by medical men for daring to advance such a monstrous hypothesis. Dienst performed a series of ingenious experiments with the placentae of women giving birth. He injected methylene blue dye into the umbilical artery or vein at the placenta while it was still attached. The blue dye showed up in the urine of the mother. This was interpreted—legitimately, it might be added—as demonstrating a connection between maternal and fetal circulations. He was able to show that the blood and serum of mothers suffering from eclampsia usually laked (hemolyzed) or agglutinated the cells of their children. He was able to produce lesions resembling those of eclampsia in experimental animals transfused with incompatible blood.

Within weeks after the publication of his 1905 paper, Dienst was attacked by Liepmann (1905) who used the peculiarly old fashioned argument that to believe a mother's blood should injure her child or

---

[1] In the following, there must be enumerated the theory which underlies the surprising new hypothesis of eclampsia. According to this, eclampsia would be nothing else than the transfusion of heterogeneous blood from the child into the mother's circulation. This is feasible through a communication between both systems of blood circulation, or in other more general words, through an increased permeability of the placenta.

vice versa was postulating the existence of a biological monstrosity. In other words, if this *could* happen, women would not be able to bear children. Nature would not permit it. Liepmann's words are quaint and are worth quoting (1905:484):

> Ad 2) Das mütterliche Blut verhält sich zum kindlichen Blute wie das Blut "zweier verschiedener Spezies." . . . Eine individuelle Verschiedenheit ist also bewiesen, aber nicht die biologische Ungeheuerlichket von Dienst, der direkt ausspricht, dass in bestimmten Fällen mütterliches und kindliches Blut sich verhalten, wie das Blut zweier Spezies.[2]

It is of great interest that Dienst changed his opinion about the pathogenesis of eclampsia. Not, however, in response to the exhortation of Liepmann, but in the light of further experimental and clinical work. Various investigators showed that methylene blue injected subcutaneously into pregnant women would appear in the urine of their infants. The women in these experiments produced intact placentas and did not suffer eclampsia. Dienst took the trouble to examine placentae of some of these women microscopically and was able to state with assurance that the placentae were intact. Further experimental work of his own convinced him of the inadequacy of his theory to cover these exceptions. Particularly convincing, apparently, was his inability to repeat the pathology of eclampsia a sufficient number of times in experimental animals transfused with incompatible blood.

In 1908 Dienst reported several inconsistent results which led him to retire from the discussion. The placenta of an eclamptic woman was subjected to a detailed microscopic analysis and no rupture or "leak" could be found. Furthermore, eclamptic women were occasionally found in his clinical work whose sera did not lake or agglutinate the cells of their children.

The extraordinary thing about Dienst's work is that it aroused small interest and that he abandoned it in a rather casual way. Ehrlich and Morgenroth (1900), for example, had suggested that important clues for determining the pathogenesis of eclampsia lay in the study of blood hemolysins, agglutinins, and precipitins. Other investigations threw out suggestions of a similar sort during the first few years of this century, but after Dienst's work almost nothing more appeared in print bearing on the problem.

Liepmann's attack on Dienst indicates the difficulty many prominent

---

[2] The maternal blood would relate to the fetal blood as the blood of a different species. An individual difference might be proven, but not the biological monstrosity of Dienst, according to whose opinion in certain instances the maternal and fetal blood behave like the blood of two different species.

investigators had with the concept of maternal-fetal incompatibility. The biological monstrosity Dienst is accused of postulating is this very incompatibility. How could there be children if the maternal environment was antagonistic to the fetus? Only traumatic or abnormal conditions could be conceived of as affecting abortion and eclampsia; the normal physiology of the organism could not. This is the way in which biological processes were and are conceived by a large number of investigators. Nature does not make mistakes: natural processes, the normal physiology of the organism, are not responsible for pathogenic states. I shall discuss the general implications of this below.

In 1923 McQuarrie and Ottenberg independently revived Dienst's argument. Ottenberg, for that matter, had worked on the problem from Dienst's point of view from 1911. However, when Dienst published his large set of experimental data Ottenberg felt that he had been forestalled. He therefore did not publish his early findings and confined himself to expanding and confirming Dienst's work. This took a number of years. He and his associates published their first results in 1915. He found fewer lesions after incompatible transfusions than Dienst and he found that they were confined to the kidney. It was not until 1923, after reviewing his earlier work, that Ottenberg realized that the technical problems of adequately transfusing a sufficient quantity of incompatible blood by the direct method into the experimental animals were responsible for the rather meager results.

McQuarrie (1923) reported on a series of toxemic women in whom he showed that incompatibility between maternal and fetal blood groups was enormously more frequent than in a series of normal pregnant women. Allen reviewed the question in 1926 and presented a much larger set of data. His review was based on a large series of clinical cases and apparently contradicted the findings of McQuarrie. His decisive analysis had, in all probability, much to do with the fact that the question was again dropped for a number of years. Unlike the response of Liepmann, Allen's point of view toward the problem was rationalistic. If incompatibility is the factor which resulted in eclampsia and abortion, then why is incompatibility not always accompanied by such serious pathological results?

Here we bring up another important and interesting point. Allen's doubts about the hypothesis of blood incompatibility were not expressed as a consequence of a certain anthropocentric world-view. Rather, he uses a statistical argument, one which is still seriously used against the hypothesis that differential fertility and differential death rates are related to blood group incompatibility. Both positive and negative findings in studies of this sort are not very convincing until a functional relationship has been demonstrated between trait and advantage or disadvantage. Even negative findings should not be taken as conclusive since a more sophisticated understanding of the functional relationship may reverse the conclusions implied by such a negative statistical study. I shall return to this point later in the essay.

The major *scientific* argument against the theory that eclampsia was due to blood incompatibility between mother and fetus was based on the theory of a placental barrier. The placenta was and is interpreted as a defense mechanism for the fetus. Demonstration that iso-hemaglutinins or other materials could pass through it from the mother to the fetus or *vice versa* was not easy. Dienst had proved it could occur in eclamptic mothers. Other investigators repeated the observation on pregnant women who produced normal infants. This suggested to them that fetal and maternal blood could mingle *without* resulting in eclampsia. Unlike either the anthropocentric point of view alluded to above, or the statistical approach which tests associations between a condition and an inherited trait, this approach of Dienst attempted to deduce and describe a *mechanism* leading to the condition perceived. He looked for a system in eclamptic women which permitted the stimulation of the mother's antibody-producing system by fetal antigens to produce antifetal hemolysins or agglutinins. Dienst believed that an abnormal permeability of the placenta was sufficient to explain his observations.

It seems that the concept of a placental barrier played as important a role as some of the less rational ideas touched upon in focusing attention on the problem of serological incompatibility and eclampsia. Progress in understanding the role of serological incompatibility and various diseases of pregnancy and of *neonates* was made along two general lines. On the one hand, investigators were looking for the mechanics for transmitting antigens and antibodies between mothers and fetuses despite the placental barrier. On the other hand, the antigenicity of human blood was studied as a cause of neonatal jaundice and hemolytic disease.

In 1926 Hirszfeld and Zborowski demonstrated that isohemagglutinins traversed the placental barrier from mother to fetus. Polayes *et al.* (1929a; 1929b) independently confirmed this observation. By 1936 Jonsson and others reported on the antigenic properties of human blood. Sporadic reports of neonatal jaundice of hemolytic disease, perhaps due to ABO isoimmunization, were made during the decade 1929 to 1939. Isoimmunization is the production of the immune antibodies by an individual due to stimulus by antigenic proteins he himself elaborates. In the case of a pregnant woman isoimmunization is the process by which the female produces antibodies in response to the antigenic proteins of her fetus. In 1941 Levine and Polayes identified an immune atypical intergroup hemolysin. A group A mother went into a transfusion reaction after she had delivered a group B anemic infant. In this case, the incompatibility apparently reacted upon both of the organisms.

Levine (1943) published a general summary article in which he showed a definite relationship between spontaneous abortion and ABO isoimmunization. Between 1942 and 1949 Aubert *et al.*, Wiener, Kelsall, Halbrecht, Polayes, Boorman *et al.*, and others published data suggesting A and B antigens induce isoimmunization in RH positive women. Generally, the resulting neonatal condition was described as similar to *erythroblastosis fetalis* when not identical with it. Levine (1943) and Halbrecht (1944) demonstrated statistically that most cases of *erythroblastosis fetalis* occurring in infants born to RH positive mothers occur in heterospecific pregnancies—pregnancies in which the ABO type of a mother is incompatible with that of the fetus she is carrying.

The general reader will forgive me for the excursion into biological nomenclature. The details are not important for the purpose of this essay. It is important to point out that research into the problem of eclampsia and *erythroblastosis fetalis* as a condition of blood-group incompatibility eventually produced important additions to understanding of the function and physiology of the blood groups.

It is safe to suggest that the whole medical problem of *erythroblastosis* and the anthropological problem of factors affecting the frequencies of blood group genes would have been much more advanced had Dienst's approach in his suggested solutions been legitimate. One of the difficulties that confronted investigators was the double nature of the problem. A condition affecting the *neonate* and its mother had to be related to incompatible serology, *and* a mechanism by which the incompatible serology led to the morbid condition had to be demonstrated. The statistical arguments of Allen, for example, had to be met. Just what sort of mechanism is it that works in certain cases of incompatibility and not in others?

This question has not yet been answered to the satisfaction of all. However, the problem is under intensive research in a number of laboratories and clinics. It is extremely interesting to note how the approach to the problem has evolved in the past fifty-odd years. At first, the conception of incompatibility was rejected because it contravened good biological thinking. Second, it did not meet statistical test, that is, there were cases of incompatibilities that did not show the morbid conditions. Finally, research had disclosed a mechanism in incompatible pregnancies which will produce the morbid condition. The problem is to understand why there are apparent exceptions. But with a mechanism demonstrated to account for the pathology of neonatal jaundice and eclampsia in the mother, it is possible to design and execute experiments which will extend understanding of the nature of the substances involved. Furthermore, it is possible to investigate defenses which the organism can mobilize when threatened by incompatibility.

It is unfortunate for anthropology that research of this sort is so often considered solely medical or biological or immunological. Techniques may come from one or another of the disciplines involved, but the problem and its implications are of central importance to anthropology, cultural and physical. The investigation of the pathology associated with inherited traits such as the blood groups is the essence of investigating natural selection in human populations.

During the period when Dienst was attempting to determine the relation of maternal-fetal blood group incompatibility to eclampsia, forensic medicine and anthropology developed important applications of human serology. A demonstration by the Hirszfelds (1919) that frequencies of the ABO phenotypes differed among populations of different ethnic origin was an important event for anthropology. The use of blood groups in paternity cases and in identification work and the analysis of blood stains in criminal cases became an important part of medico-legal work. From the point of view of the courts, it was impossible to accept evidence from blood groups unless assurance could be given that they remained permanent throughout life and that there was no variation of any sort in inheritance and identification of specific blood groups.

Anthropologists, too, were interested in genetic traits that distinguished races and that were impervious to environmental effects. In other words, they were interested in traits that were not subjected to the forces of natural selection. The blood groups seemed to meet these requirements. Innumerable papers distinguishing or relating populations in various parts of the world on the basis of blood group frequencies were published. Boyd presented a definitive survey of them in 1939. These early studies were based on an assumption which now seem anti-evolutionary and antiscientific; namely, that traits which distinguish human populations (or races) are nonadaptive. In other words, the way to characterize human evolution and human raciation (or divergence of populations) consequent to it, was to select traits not subject to the evolutionary process. The reason for choosing these traits is obvious: they have nothing to do with human evolution but rather characterize, once and for all, different human populations (e.g. Ashman 1950). One of the classical aims of physical anthropology was to provide a catalogue or a taxonomy of the subpopulations, or races, of man. Such a classification, meeting logical criteria, can be constructed only if some defining characteristic (such as the frequencies of ABO phenotypes) is found.

Insufficient technical development and inadequate understanding of the theory behind a new idea in science or a new discovery in science will often be cited as the apparent reason for the abandonment by scientific workers of a line of investigation that later proves to be fruitful. This is not a reasonable way to account for the lack of interest in the work of Dienst and for the lack of interest in the whole problem area of the physiology and function of the blood groups. An attitude of mind, a vested interest it might be called, rather than an ignorance of technology or a blindness to the implications of theory, was crucial. The development of blood group work in forensic medicine and anthropology and the problems which were attacked produced such an attitude. The functional study of antigens and antibodies was ignored because it did not seem relevant to the major purpose of pursuing human serology in anthropology and in forensic medicine. The various blood groups systems which were discovered were extremely useful in identification work and in racial studies. The genetics of the systems was being clarified; and the techniques for identifying an individual's blood group were simple and repeatable by modestly trained technicians. Therefore, it seemed, a sound technique for genetically classifying *Homo sapiens* was at hand. Many studies were published which used the ABO frequencies to reconstruct the history of population movements and to elucidate the racial history of Europe, e.g., Wiechmann and Paal (1926); Ashman (1950).

It was not until 1953 that a prominent immuno-geneticist pointed out the value of studying the distribution and function of blood groups from the point of view of natural selection. Boyd (1953) wrote effectively about the absurdity of using nonadaptive traits in the study of human evolution and raciation. Since then several investigators, notably Brues (1954), Glass (1954, 1956), Ford (1957), and Ceppellini (1955b), have taken the stand that the most important work in anthropological studies of the blood groups is examination of possible selective factors which could have produced present population frequencies. Haldane (1949)

TABLE 1. EARLY STUDIES OF THE ASSOCIATION BETWEEN

Authors [*]	Date	Country	Condition	Number	Results
CARCINOMA					
Alexander	1921	England	Malignant tumor	50	O less, AB, B greater than population frequencies
Buchanan and Higley	1921	Great Britain	Malignant disease	292	No differences
			Pernicious anemia	457	No differences
			Chronic ulcers	172	No differences
Pfahler and Widmann	1924	Canada	Malignant disease	314	No differences
Johannsen	1925	Denmark	Malignant tumors	263	Very small differences, B and O smaller than population frequency
Johannsen	1925	Denmark	Uterine cancer	107	A greater, B less than in pregnant controls
Weitzner	1925	Germany	Carcinoma	84	O less than, AB greater than population frequency
Hoche and Moritsch	1926	Germany	Carcinoma	176	AB greater than population frequency
Bendien	1926	Netherlands	Carcinoma	110	O less than, AB greater than population frequency
Hirschfeld and Hittmair	1926	Germany	Carcinoma	150	No differences
Schiff	1926	Germany	Malignant tumors	263	No differences; same proportions as normal controls *from same locality*
Oppenheim and Voight	1926	Germany	Malignant tumors	108	No differences
Goldfeder and Fershing	1937	U.S.A.	Malignant tumors	300	No differences
SYPHILIS					
Amsel and Halber	1925	Germany France	Positive Wassermann	1736	O less than population frequency
Straszynski	1925	Germany	Positive Wassermann	618	O less than, AB greater than normals
				325	Larger percent O recovered with treatment

[*] References are cited in bibliography.

Authors	Date	Country	Condition	Number	Results
			SYPHILIS (cont.)		
Wiechmann and Paal	1926	Germany	Positive Wassermann	500	O less than, AB larger than population frequency
Gundel	1927	Germany	Syphilis	2665	No differences. B and AB less often recovered, took longer to achieve negative Wassermann
Diamantopoulos	1928	Greece	Syphilis	405	No differences
Naito	1928	Japan	Syphilis	small	No differences
Leveringhaus	1927	Germany	Positive Wassermann	454	No differences
Perkel and Israelsson	1928	Russia (Odessa)	Syphilis	721	O persons less frequent, achieved negative Wassermanns most quickly. B, AB more frequent among *paralysis progressiva* patients, O least frequent among paralytics
			OTHER		
Hollo and Lenard	1926	Germany	Tuberculosis	200	No differences
Alperin	1926	Germany	Tuberculosis	515	No differences
Chi-Pan	1924	China	Tuberculosis	60	No differences
			Syphilis	111	No differences
			Typhoid	130	No differences
Hermanns and Kronberg	1927	Germany	Hyperthyroidism	403	No differences though O slightly elevated
Kraus and Medvei	1929	Austria	Hyperthyroidism	100	No differences
Hilgers, Wohlfeil, and Knötzke	1928	Germany	Typhus	223	O greater than normals
Mironescu and Stefanoy	1926	Germany Roumania	Typhus	small	No differences, sample too finely subdivided for significant results
Diamantopoulos	1928	Greece	Influenza, typhus, malaria, dengue	535	No differences
Snyder	1929	U.S.A.	Malaria	100	A less than, B greater than normal
			Syphilis	100	No differences
			Migraine	500	No differences
			Polydactyly (only Negroes)	50	A less, B greater than normal

has published a largely speculative account of the effect of disease on evolution. His comments on testing the association of disease in human serological traits are stimulating. He believes that, if correlations exist between certain diseases and these genetically well-known serological traits, we can then understand the effect of disease in molding human evolution.

Diseases and the ABO Blood Groups

We turn now to the history of attempts to demonstrate another kind of selective mechanism which affects the ABO blood group antigens. During the period 1918–1929 many studies of possible associations between A, AB, B, O phenotypes and a variety of morbid conditions were published. Most of these observations were inconclusive. The studies most readily accessible in the literature are summarized in Table 1. Repetition of the observations by other investigators seldom confirmed the original findings. Snyder (1929) concluded that the evidence showed no direct or important associations between the ABO groups and disease. As late as 1943 Wiener expressed the opinion that any associations found were the result of a mixture of different ethnic strains and not the result of a physiological action of the blood groups substances.

Wiener (1943; 1956) argues that if two populations with different frequencies of the ABO genes are mixed and the one with the higher frequency of one gene, say gene B, has an elevated frequency of cancer, and if an association between cancer and blood group B is found, the association is fortuitous. Since most modern European and American populations are of mixed ethnic origin, associations between the ABO blood groups and diseases are due to these ethnic factors. Positive results obtained in the examination of associations between diseases and blood groups is due to ethnic stratification in the population from which the patients were derived. This argument is not convincing, particularly in the light of Ceppellini's (1955a; 1955b) discussion of the problem and his evidence. It is interesting to note, however, that Wiener has continued his outspoken opposition to such investigations (Wiener and Wexler 1956).

The ethnic stratification argument must now cover several different examples of correlations between morbidity and blood group antigens. In other words, too many different ethnic stratifications must be postulated to account for the various associations between blood groups and disease. Furthermore, Clarke *et al.* (1957) published evidence showing the extreme unlikelihood of stratification with respect to duodenal ulcers and the ABO blood groups in Great Britain. Clarke's group pursued the argument in great detail and demonstrated that, as far as Great Britain is concerned, there would have to be one ethnic stratification which would account for the association between blood group O and duodenal ulcers and another stratification which would account for the association between blood group A and gastric carcinoma. The latter stratification would have to run counter to the known ethnic make-up of the British population. Therefore, I suspect that little stress will be placed upon this ethnic argument in the future.

A most interesting series of papers are summarized in Table 2. The thirty years of investigations by Jungeblut and Smith (1916–1947) on the relation between paralytic poliomyelitis and the ABO blood group system should be noted particularly. Their studies show decreased frequency of blood group B among persons suffering from paralytic poliomyelitis. They also show a significant association between nonsecretion of water soluble ABO(H) group-specific substances and paralytic poliomyelitis. One of the puzzling facts in reviewing the history of human blood group serology and disease is the apparent vacuum into which these studies fell, although carried out for over thirty-five years. Almost no attention was given by specialists in forensic medicine or physical anthropology, two disciplines which might be expected to be extremely interested in such findings. In fact, almost all of these papers were published in journals specializing in the study of poliomyelitis. One can only speculate about the reasons for ignoring them. I suspect they were read with the point of view indicated above: nothing affects the blood groups.

It is quite true that medical specialists and anthropologists did turn their attention to the study of associations between the blood groups and a variety of human biological traits. For example, correlation studies between standard anthropometric indices and blood groups produced no significant results (Facaoaru and Ramneantzu 1937; Kossovitch 1928; Klein and Osthoff 1926). Some old and fascinating ideas about the association between blood groups, pigmentation and eye color were tested by Ramneantzu and Facaoaru (1937) and by McConnail (1938) with results that were not statistically significant. Finally, attempts to show a relation between body build and blood groups ended inconclusively (Vuori 1929; Hilgers, Wohlfeil and Knötzke 1928). Reasons may be given for the failure of these studies to produce useful data. First, the majority of morphological "racial" traits and anthropometric indices are

TABLE 2. STUDIES OF ABO BLOOD GROUP

Authors [*]	Date	Country	Condition	Number	Results
Jungeblut and Smith (cited in Jungeblut, Karowe, and Braham 1947)	1916	U.S.A.	Paralytic polio.	208	O greater than, B less than controls
Madsen, Engle, Jensen and Freuchen	1936	Denmark	Polio.	1118	No difference from controls. B markedly more frequent among males, 2:1 ratio after age 20
Grooten and Kossovitch	1930	France	Polio.	78	A greater, B, O less than controls. Controls were other sick children
Foa (cited in Jungeblut, Karowe, and Braham 1947)	1931	Italy	Polio.	22	B less than A greater than controls. Marked difference
Shaw	1932	U.S.A.	Polio.	100	O greater, B less than controls
Jungeblut and Smith	1932	U.S.A.	Polio. (all)	343	B less than controls (slight)
			paralytic	236	B less than controls (marked)
			abortive	107	B less than controls (slight)

[*] References are cited in bibliography.

not the result of simple gene systems, nor are they so clearly genetically determined as are the blood groups. It is likely that a number of gene systems determine eye color, pigmentation of the skin, and head breadth respectively. Second, the characters given morphological identity or those described by an anthropometric index are usually constructed from several anatomical parameters and may be extremely susceptible to environmental influences. Relatively small changes in diet or physical activity may have a major effect upon the way a morphological trait is classified. This applies particularly to studies of body build or physical type in relation to the blood groups.

A much more important kind of study that might be expected to lead to an understanding of the action of selective mechanism on the blood

DISTRIBUTIONS AMONG POLIOMYELITIS PATIENTS

Authors *	Date	Country	Condition	Number	Results
Hatzky	1933	Germany	Polio. (all)	136	B greater than controls
Bloetevogel and Bloetevogel	1934	Germany	Paralytic polio.	366	B, A less than, O greater than controls
Erb, Doyle, and Heal	1938	Canada	Polio. (all)	703	No difference from controls (other sick children)
			paralytic	427	B less than, O greater than controls
			abortive	276	No differences
Kleinschmidt	1939	Germany	Polio. (all)	309	B less than controls
			paralytic	211	B less than controls
			abortive	98	B less than controls (slight)
Fanconi *et al.*	1945	Switzerland	Polio. (all)	507	B less than controls, A greater than
Jungeblut, Karowe, and Braham	1947	U.S.A.	Paralytic polio.	220	B less than controls, A and O greater than controls. **Non-Secretors much greater than controls

* References are cited in bibliography.
** Statistically significant.

groups has been the investigation of genetic linkage between the ABO and other genes. Linkage relationships have most often been sought between pathological, rare, recessive traits and the blood group genes. Most of this work has been inconclusive or negative with respect to the ABO blood groups (see Race and Sanger, 1954, for a detailed discussion of this point). Mohr (1951) showed the first definite example of linkage between two sets of blood group genes when he demonstrated linkage between the Luther and Lewis blood groups. A presentation of the details of this demonstration or a discussion of Luther and Lewis blood group antigens is unnecessary here. It is only necessary to record the fact that this demonstration of linkage relationships among the blood groups and diseases has potentially important implications for an understanding of natural selection.

RECENT WORK ON THE ABO BLOOD GROUPS AND SELECTIVE MECHANISMS

In recent years a series of advances has been made in investigation of associations between disease and the ABO blood groups. Table 3 summarizes the studies of morbid conditions for which statistical associations with the ABO blood group system have been demonstrated. The study

TABLE 3. DISEASE CONDITIONS ASSOCIATED WITH ABO BLOOD GROUP PHENOTYPES

Condition	Blood Group Phenotype	Number of Studies [*]	Countries
Duodenal Ulcer	O	8	England, Scotland, U.S.A., Denmark, Norway, Austria
Gastric Ulcer	O	8	England, Scotland, U.S.A., Denmark, Norway, Austria
Stomach Carcinoma	A	8	England, Scotland, U.S.A., Australia, Austria, Norway, Switzerland
Pernicious Anemia	A	4	England, Scotland, U.S.A., Denmark
Diabetes Mellitus	A	2	England, Scotland
Brain Tumors (Chromophobe adenomas of the pituitary)	O	1	U.S.A.
Rheumatic Fever	Non-Secretors in excess	1	Great Britain
Paralytic Poliomyelitis	B significantly reduced Non-Secretors in excess	11	Italy, England, U.S.A., Denmark, Germany, France

[*] The sources for these data are listed in the references.

of these conditions is not as advanced as the study of maternal-fetal ABO incompatibility. The mechanisms by which one or another ABO phenotype makes the organism more susceptible to the various morbid conditions listed have not been demonstrated. Indeed, only the most general speculative beginning has been made on this aspect of the problem. One thing is certain, however: the associations hold. They have been demonstrated by a variety of investigators for different populations. The probability of sampling error has been reduced to a negligible figure.

It is no longer possible to dismiss the various differences in ABO phenotype frequencies among populations as due simply to "ethnic" factors. A question that no one seems to have asked is how did the differences arise in the first place? Ceppellini (1955) has noted that significant differences in the frequencies in ABO phenotypes exist among neighboring villages in Sicily. This certainly requires some kind of functional explanation and cannot be attributed to "ethnic" factors.

It is not only among studies of the association of the ABO blood groups and disease conditions that great advances have been made in the past years. Table 4 is the summary of a number of studies in which

TABLE 4. SUMMARY OF SOME FERTILITY SURVEYS WITH
RESPECT TO MATERNAL-FETAL INCOMPATIBILITY
AND THE ABO BLOOD GROUPS *

Author	Country	Date	Results
Waterhouse and Hogben	Great Britain	1947	Pooled 12 published sets of family data. Deficiency of A children in A male x O female, and of B children in B male x O female matings reported.
Boorman	Great Britain	1950	2,000 consecutive admissions to maternity hospital had an apparent excess of homospecific pregnancies over expectations.
Bryce *et al.*	Australia	1950	O mothers A children; B mothers children than expected. AB women more fertile than others.
Sjöstedt *et al.*	Sweden	1951	B, AB women in excess in abortion series. 433 matings tested.
Johnstone	Great Britain	1954	No deficit of A *or* B children in 2578 heterospecific matings.
Kirk *et al.*	Australia	1955	O mothers A *and* B children. 16,179 mother-child pairs.
Grubb and Sjöstedt	Sweden	1955	737 matings analyzed. No differences in ABO and RH incompatibility between aborting and normal couples.
Matsunaga	Japan	1955	10–14% deficiency of A and B children in heterospecific matings. No change in ABO frequencies in two generations.
Matsunaga and Itoh	Japan	1958	1429 couples on Hokkaido; 21% mortality of children with phenotypes incompatible with mother.

* Sources will be found in the references.

fertility with respect to the ABO(H) blood group system has been examined. The surveys summarized there are based on the postulate that male-female or mother-fetus incompatibility with respect to the ABO blood group system will result in reduced fertility for such matings and in an increased rate of abortion. Again, a detailed discussion of the data is not relevant to the major argument here. The data are presented to

TABLE 5. SUMMARY OF STUDIES OF AGE AND SEX RATIO AND THE ABO BLOOD GROUPS *

Author	Date	Country	Number	Results
Sanghvi	1951	India (Bombay)	1,330	Sex ratio high among all off-spring of B mothers, among group O offspring of O mothers. Sex ratio low among off-spring of A mothers, among all A offspring.
		U.S.A. (New York)	864	Same as Bombay data.
Allan	1953	Ulster and England	59,371	Low sex ratio in group B with increasing age.
	1954	Scandinavia	12,611	High sex ratio among ill B males; high sex ratio among all B males.
Johnstone	1954	England	2,429	Same as Sanghvi. No deviation among O offspring of O mothers.
Cohen and Glass	1956	U.S.A.	4,538	Similar to those of Sanghvi and Johnstone. Pooled data to get significant results.
Shield *et al.*	1958	Australia	11,508 (Melbourne) 3,967 (Perth)	No significant deviations of sex ratio in either city. Pooled data indicate possible deviation among offspring of A and B mothers.

* Sources will be found in the references.

show that we are able to make an extremely good case for maternal-fetal and male-female incompatibility as a selective mechanism of considerable importance with respect to the ABO(H) blood group system.

Table 5 is a summary of several intriguing studies which have investigated the possibility that a deviation in the sex ratio at birth may be due to an effect of the ABO blood group genes. It can be seen that the results are contradictory, and a recent review of the problem by Edwards (1957) casts considerable doubt on the validity of the statistical assumptions used in gathering the data for all of them. Shield, Kirk, and Jakobowicz (1958) recently published the findings of a survey of a large number of Australian births in which they have been unable to find any influence on the sex ratio at birth by the ABO blood group genes. They point out that, in order to demonstrate statistical significance for such an effect, over 100,000 births would have to be studied.

This brings me back to a point which is related to the major theme of the paper, the way in which natural selection on man is studied in physical anthropology. Not only do the dominant ideologies or vested interests of a scientific profession control the way in which new ideas will affect research or the direction in which it will go, but preoccupation with statistics is a factor of no small importance in this story. No statistical study, no matter how sophisticatedly it may be executed, how carefully the paired sib method is used, or how extensive the controls are, can provide us with the information that is crucial to an understanding of how natural selection operates on the ABO(H) system in man. Such studies are nonetheless necessary and must come before we can even begin to search for mechanisms. However, now that there is strong evidence that differential morbidity is associated with the four phenotypes in the blood group system, it is time to go into the laboratory and test speculations and theories about the function of the ABO blood groups. Now that there is excellent evidence that fertility is impaired with respect to ABO incompatibility, laboratory and clinical studies seem to be next on the agenda. And they are properly on the agenda of physical anthropologists.

In this connection it is worth citing some very recent work done by Gullbring (1957) and by myself. We have been able to show that sperm from males of A, B, or AB blood type can be agglutinated by the commercial anti-A and anti-B sera. Gershowitz *et al.* (1958) have been able to show that the anti-A and anti-B hemagglutinins occur in the cervical secretions of women, and Matsunaga and I (through personal communication) have been able to show that these antibodies occur in some other body fluids, notably saliva. Confirmation of this work is necessary, of course. It is cited here to show that if one takes his cue from statistical studies and goes into the laboratory, some startling and interesting leads for research on this problem of natural selection in man are likely to be found.

CONCLUSION

If the theory of evolution is the principal organizing idea of anthropology, then it is of critical importance that such work as reviewed above be a central concern of physical anthropology. If the description of human variation is a traditional part of physical anthropology, it must be so because the description will develop a better understanding of the nature of the evolutionary process in the genus *Homo*. Description must now be supplemented or replaced by laboratory investigations of mechanism and function.

Anthropologists, committed to study the implications of the theory of evolution as applied to man's organism and man's culture, must lead the way in the examination of the functional nature of those traits characterizing the racial or population differences among men. Notable contributions have been made by anthropologists in providing a rational understanding of man's relationship to the rest of the order Primates. One hundred years after Darwin's great book the *Origin of Species* (1859), physical anthropologists, among others, have produced the fossil evidence which demonstrated that the explanation Darwin sketched out for the evolution of man and other species was sound. It is time to carry on this task and to attempt to understand the social and ideological forces which affect the carrying out of scientific work. It is time for physical anthropologists to produce the studies which will show how the evolutionary process, so elegantly described by modern mathematical population genetics (Fisher 1930; Li 1955; Kempthorne 1957), affects the variation which they have been so effective in describing.

SUMMARY

This account of the history of evolutionary studies of the ABO blood group genes focused upon certain major episodes, and is an interpretation of them. First, it was pointed out that a particular metaphysical conception of nature prevented the full appreciation of the work of Dienst on eclampsia. Second, the conception of evolutionary processes and the concern with racial classification led to a search for traits unaffected by natural selection. The ABO phenotypes were picked because they were believed to meet this criterion. Third, statistical surveys proved to be the clue to many important problems that are now directing research into the selective forces that affect the frequencies of the ABO genes. Finally, important new data from recent experimental, laboratory investigations of evolutionary problems were presented and their significance was discussed.

BIBLIOGRAPHY

ALEXANDER, W.
   1921 "An Inquiry into the Distribution of the Blood Groups in Patients Suffering from 'Malignant Disease'." *British Journal of Experimental Pathology*, 2:66–69.
ALLAN, T. M.
   1953 "Blood Groups and Age Groups." *Lancet*, 2:456.
   1954 "Blood Groups and Age Groups." *Lancet*, 1:292–293.
ALLEN, W. M.
   1926 "Interagglutination of Maternal and Fetal Blood in Late Toxemias of Pregnancy." *Bulletin of the Johns Hopkins Hospital*, 38:217–336.
ALLISON, A. C.
   1954a "Notes on Sickle-cell Polymorphism." *Annals of Human Genetics*, 19:39–51.
   1954b "Protection Afforded by Sickle-cell Trait against Subtertian Malarial Infection." *British Medical Journal*, 1:290–294.
   1954c "The Distribution of the Sickle-cell Trait in East Africa and Elsewhere, and Its Apparent Relationship to the Incidence of Sub-tertian Malaria." *Transactions of the Royal Society for Tropical Medicine and Hygiene*, 48:312–318.
   1955 "Aspects of Polymorphism in Man." *Cold Spring Harbor Symposia on Quantitative Biology*, 20:239–255.
ALLISON, A. C. and H. R. NEVANLINNA
   1952 "Taste Deficiency in Lappish and Finnish Populations." *Annals of Eugenics*, 17:113–114.
ALPERIN, M. M.
   1926 "Über die Beziehungen zwischen Blutgruppen und Tuberkulöse." *Beiträge zur Klinik der Tuberkulöse*, 64:500–509.
AMSEL, R. and W. HALBER
   1925 "Ueber das Ergebnis der Wassermannschen Reaktion innerhalb verschiedener Blutgruppen." *Zeitschrift für Immunitätsforschung, Originale*, 42:90–98.

ASHMAN, R.
1950 "Origins of Blood Groups ABO, and the European Mongoloid Problem." *American Journal of Physical Anthropology*, n.s. 8:427–452.

AUBERT, E. F., J. B. COCHRANE, and M. E. ELLIS
1945 "An Unusual Case of Erythroblastosis Foetalis." *British Medical Journal*, 2:648–649.

BENDIEN, S. G. T.
1926 "Haemagglutingehalte van het Bloedserum bij carcinompatiënten." *Nederlandsche Tijdschrift fur Geneeskunde*, 1:2856–2858.

BLOETEVOGEL, H. and W. BLOETEVOGEL
1934 "Blutgruppe und Daktylogramm als Konstitutionsmerkmale der Poliomyelitiskranken." *Zeitschrift für Kinderheilkunde*, 56:143–169.

BOORMAN, K. E.
1949 "An Analysis of the Blood Types and Clinical Condition of 2000 Consecutive Mothers and Their Infants." *Annals of Eugenics*, 15:120–131.

BOORMAN, K. E., B. E. DODD, and R. H. TRINCK
1950 "Haemolytic Disease of the New Born Due to Anti-A Antibodies." *Lancet*, 1:1088–1091.

BOYD, W. C.
1939 "Blood Groups." *Tabulae Biologicae*, The Hague, 17:113–240.
1953 "The Contributions of Genetics to Anthropology." In *Anthropology Today*, prepared under the chairmanship of A. L. Kroeber, pp. 488–506. Chicago, The University of Chicago Press.

BROCA, P. B.
1863 *Sur les caractères des cranes basques.* Paris, V. Masson.
1875 "Instructions craniologiques et craniométriques." *Société d'Anthropologie de Paris, Mémoir*, 2.

BRUES, A. M.
1954 "Selection and Polymorphism in the ABO Blood Groups." *American Journal of Physical Anthropology*, n.s. 12:559–597.

BRYCE, L. M., R. JAKOBOWICZ, N. MACARTHUR, and L. S. PENROSE
1950 "Blood-group Frequencies in Mother and Infant Samples of the Australian Population." *Annals of Eugenics*, 15:271–275.

BUCHANAN, J. A. and E. T. HIGLEY
1921 "The Relationship of Blood Groups to Disease." *British Journal of Experimental Pathology*, 2:247–255.

BUETTNER-JANUSCH, J.
1957 "The Distribution of ABO Blood Groups in a Sample of Hospital

Patients Receiving Blood Transfusions." *American Journal of Physical Anthropology,* n.s. 15:341–356.

CEPPELLINI, R.
1955a "The Usefulness of Blood Factors in Racial Anthropology." *American Journal of Physical Anthropology,* n.s. 13:389.
1955b "Discussion of Allison's Paper." *Cold Spring Harbor Symposia on Quantitative Biology,* 20:252–255.

CHI-PAN, LI
1924 "A Study of Fifteen Hundred Chinese Blood Groups." *National Medical Journal of China,* 10:252–261.

CLARKE, C. A., R. B. McCONNELL, and P. M. SHEPPARD
1957 "ABO Blood Groups and Duodenal Ulcer." *British Medical Journal,* 1:758–759

COHEN, B. H. and B. GLASS
1956 "The ABO Blood Groups and the Sex Ratio." *Human Biology,* 28:20–42.

COON, C.
1954 "Climate and Race." *Smithsonian Institution Annual Report for 1952–1953:277–298.*

COON, C., S. M. GARN and J. B. BIRDSELL
1950 Races: A Study of the Problems of Race Formation in Man. Springfield, Illinois, Charles C Thomas, Publishers.

DIAMANTOPOULOS, J.
1928 "Die Blutgruppen bei verschiedenen Krankheiten." *Deutsche Medizinische Wochenschrift,* 54:1839–1840.

DIENST, A.
1905 "Das Eklampsiegift." *Zentralblatt für Gynäkologie,* 29:353–364.
1908 "Die Pathogenese der Eklampsie und ihre Beziehungen zur normalen Schwangerschaft, zum Hydrops und zur Schwangerschaftsniere." *Archiv für Gynaekologie,* 86:314–386.

DOBZHANSKY, T.
1950 "The Genetic Nature of the Differences Among Men." In *Evolutionary Thought in America,* ed. by Stow Persons, pp. 86–155. New Haven, Yale University Press.

EDWARDS, J. H.
1957 "A Critical Examination of the Reputed Primary Influence of ABO Phenotype on Fertility and Sex Ratio." *British Journal of Preventive and Social Medicine,* 11:79–89.

EHRLICH, P. and J. MORGENROTH
1900 "Ueber Haemolysine." *Berliner Klinische Wochenschrift,* 37:453–458.

ERB, I. H., H. S. DOYLE, and F. C. HEAL
 1938 "Blood Groups in Poliomyelitis." *Canadian Public Health Journal,*
    29:441–442.
FACAOARU, J. and P. RAMNEANTZU
 1937 "Das Verhältnis zwischen Rassen und Blutgruppen bei der Sieben-
    bürgischen Bevölkerung." *Congrès International d'Anthropologie
    et d'Archéologie Préhistoriques,* Bucharest, 17:337–339.
FANCONI, G., H. ZELLWEGER, and A. BOTSZTEJN
 1945 *Die Poliomyelitis und ihre Grenzgebiete.* Basel, Benno Schwabe.
FISHER, R. A.
 1930 *The Genetical Theory of Natural Selection.* Oxford, The Univer-
    sity Press.
FORD, E. B.
 1940 "Polymorphism and Taxonomy." In *The New Systematics,* ed. by
    Julian Huxley, pp. 493–513. Oxford, The Clarendon Press.
 1957 "Polymorphism in Plants, Animals and Man." *Nature,* 180:1315–
    1319.
GERSHOWITZ, H., S. J. BEHRMAN and J. V. NEEL
 1958 "Hemagglutinins in Uterine Secretions." *Science,* 128:719–720.
GLASS, B.
 1954 "Genetic Changes in Human Populations, Especially Those Due
    to Gene Flow and Genetic Drift." *Advances in Genetics,* 6:95–139.
 1956 "On the Evidence of Random Genetic Drift in Human Popula-
    tions." *American Journal of Physical Anthropology,* n.s. 14:541–
    556.
GOLDFEDER, A. and J. L. FERSHING
 1937 "Iso-agglutinins in Association with Malignant Growths." *Ameri-
    can Journal of Cancer,* 29:307–312.
GROOTEN, O. and N. KOSSOVITCH
 1930 "Sur les groupes sanguines chez les enfants poliomyélitiques."
    *Comptes Rendus Hebdomadaires des Séances et Mémoires de
    la Société de Biologie,* 105:428–429.
GRUBB, R. and S. SJÖSTEDT
 1955 "Blood Groups in Abortion and Sterility." *Annals of Human
    Genetics,* 19:183–195.
GULLBRING, B.
 1957 "Investigation on the Occurrence of Blood Group Antigens in
    Spermatozoa from Man, and Serological Demonstration of the
    Segregation of Characters." *Acta Medica Scandinavica,* 159:169–
    172.

GUNDEL, M.

1927 "Bestehen der Zusammenhänge zwischen Blutgruppe und Lues-disposition sowie zwischen Blutgruppe und Erfolge der Lues-therapie?" *Klinische Wochenschrift,* 6:1703–1705.

HALBRECHT, I.

1944 "Role of Hemo-agglutinins Anti-A and Anti-B in Pathogenesis of Jaundice of the New-born (Icterus Neonatorum Praecox)." *American Journal of the Diseases of Children,* 68:248–249.

1948 "Le role du facteur Rhesus dans la pathogenise de l'icterus neonatorum praecox." *Schweizer Medizinscher Wochenschrift,* 78:592–593.

HALDANE, J. B. S.

1949 "Disease and Evolution." *Symposium sui Fattori Ecologici e Genetici della Speciazione negli Animali, La Ricerca Scientifica,* 19:1–11.

HATZKY, K.

1933 "Untersuchungen über die Blutgruppenverteilung be Poliomye-litikern." *Münchener Medizinische Wochenschrift,* 130:1973–1974.

HERMANNS, L. and J. KRONBERG

1927 "Blutgruppe und Krankheitsdisposition." *Münchener Medizinische Wochenschrift,* 74:967–969.

HILGERS, W. E., T. WOHLFEIL, and F. KNÖTZKE

1928 "Beiträge zur Blutgruppenforschung." *Klinische Wochenschrift,* 7:2101–2104.

HIRSCHFELD, H. and A. HITTMAIR

1926 "Über Blutgruppenbestimmungen bei Krebskranken." *Medizin-ische Klinik,* 22:1494–1496.

HIRSZFELD, L. and H. HIRSZFELD

1919 "Serological Differences between the Blood of Different Races. The Result of Researches on the Macedonian Front." *Lancet,* 2:675–679.

HIRSZFELD, L. and H. ZBOROWSKI

1926 "Gruppenspezifische Beziehungen zwischen Mutter und Frucht und elektive Durchlässigkeit der Placenta." *Klinische Wochenschrift,* 1:1152–1157.

HOCHE, O. and P. MORITSCH

1926 "Zur Frage der Blutgruppenspezifität der malignen Tumoren und deren gruppenspezifische Bekämpfung." *Mitteilungen aus den Grenzgebieten der Medizin und Chirurgie,* 39:409–414.

John Buettner-Janusch

HOLLO, J. and W. LENARD
1926 "Gibt es einen Unterschied in der Häufigkeit der einzelnen Blutgruppen bei Lungentuberkulösen und bei gesunden Menschen?"
Beiträge zur Klinik der Tuberkulöse, 64:513–514.

HOLMES, S. J.
1924 "A Bibliography of Eugenics." *University of California Publications in Zoology,* 25.

JOHANNSEN, E. W.
1925 "Classement de sujets affectés de tumeurs malignes selon les
isoagglutinines de leur sang." *Comptes Rendus Hebdomadaires
des Séances et Mémoires de la Société de Biologie,* 92:112–115.

JOHNSTONE, J. M.
1954a "Heterospecific Pregnancy." *British Journal of Preventive and
Social Medicine,* 8:117–123.
1954b "Sex Ratio and the ABO Blood Group System." *British Journal
of Preventive and Social Medicine,* 8:124–127.

JONSSON, B.
1936 "Zur Frage der heterospezifischen Schwangerschaft." *Acta Pathologica et Microbiologica Scandinavica,* 13:424–433.

JUNGEBLUT, C. W., H. E. KAROWE, and S. B. BRAHAM
1947 "Further Observations on Blood Grouping in Poliomyelitis." *Annals of Internal Medicine,* 26:69–75.

JUNGEBLUT, C. W. and L. W. SMITH
1932 "Blood Grouping in Poliomyelitis; Its Relation to Susceptibility
and Neutralizing Property of Convalescent Serum." *Journal of
Immunology,* 23:35–47.

KELSALL, G. A.
1944 "Erythroblastosis Due to A-B-O Incompatibility." *Medical Journal
of Australia,* 2:236–238.

KEMPTHORNE, O.
1957 *An Introduction to Genetic Statistics.* New York, John Wiley &
Sons, Inc.

KIRK, R. L., M. KIRK and N. S. STENHOUSE
1953 "Differential Fertility between Women of Blood Groups O and
A." *British Journal of Preventive and Social Medicine,* 7:1–8.

KIRK, R. L., J. W. SHIELD, N. S. STENHOUSE, L. M. BRYCE and R. JAKOB-
OWICZ
1955 "A Further Study of A-B-O Blood Groups and Differential
Fertility among Women in Two Australian Maternity Hospi-
tals." *British Journal of Preventive and Social Medicine,* 9:104–
111.

KLEIN, W. and H. OSTHOFF
1926 "Haemagglutinine, Rasse, und anthropologische Merkmale." *Archiv für Rassen und Gesellschaftsbiologie,* 17:371–378.

KLEINSCHMIDT, H.
1939 *Die uebertragbare Kinderlähmung.* Leipzig, S. Hirzel.

KOSSOVITCH, M. N.
1928 "Relations entre les groupes sanguins des Arméniens et les autres caractéristiques anthropométriques de cette race." *Institut International d'Anthropologie* (Amsterdam, 1927), 3:439–444.

KRAUS, H. and C. V. MEDVEI
1929 "Die Blutgruppenverteilung bei Hyperthyroidismus." *Münchener Medizinische Wochenschrift,* 76:493.

LEVERINGHAUS, H.
1927 "Die Bedeutung der menschlichen Isohämagglutination für Rassenbiologie und Klinik." *Archiv für Rassen und Gesellschafts Biologie,* 19:1–19.

LEVINE, P.
1943 "Serological Factors as Possible Causes in Spontaneous Abortions." *Journal of Heredity,* 34:71–80.

LEVINE, P. and S. H. POLAYES
1941 "An Atypical Hemolysin in Pregnancy." *Annals of Internal Medicine,* 14:1903–1908.

LI, C. C.
1955 *Population Genetics.* Chicago, The University of Chicago Press.

LIEPMANN, W.
1905 "Zur Dienst'schen Eklampsietheorie." *Zentralblatt für Gynäkologie,* 29:481–486.

LOVE, A. G. and C. B. DAVENPORT
1919 "A Comparison of White and Colored Troops in Respect to Incidence of Disease." *Proceedings of the National Academy of Science,* 5:58–67.

LUGG, J. W. H.
1957 "Taste-thresholds for Phenylthiocarbamide of Some Population Groups. II. The Thresholds of Two Uncivilized Groups Living in Malaya." *Annals of Human Genetics,* 21:244–253.

LUGG, J. W. and J. M. WHYTE
1955 "Taste Thresholds for Phenylthiocarbamide of Some Population Groups. I. The Thresholds of Some Civilized Ethnic Groups Living in Malaya." *Annals of Human Genetics,* 19:290–311.

MACDONALD, D.
1911–12 "Pigmentations of the Hair and Eyes of Children Suffering

from the Acute Fevers, Its Effects on Susceptibility, Recuperative Power, and Race Selection." *Biometrika,* 8:13–39.

MADSEN, T., E. T. ENGLE, C. JENSEN, and I. FREUCHEN
1936 "Blood Grouping and Poliomyelitis; Report Based on 1118 Cases in 1934 Epidemic in Denmark." *Journal of Immunology,* 30:213–219.

MATSUNAGA, E.
1955 "Intra-uterine Selection by the ABO Incompatibility of Mother and Foetus." *American Journal of Human Genetics,* 7:66–71.

MATSUNAGA, E. and S. ITOH
1958 "Blood Groups and Fertility in a Japanese Population with Special Reference to Intra-uterine Selection Due to Maternal-Foetal Incompatibility." *Annals of Human Genetics,* 22:111–131.

McCONNAIL, M. A.
1938 "Blood Groups and Pigmentation." *Nature,* 161:923.

McQUARRIE, I.
1923 "Isoagglutination in New-born Infants and Their Mothers. A Possible Relationship between Interagglutination and the Toxemia of Pregnancy." *Bulletin of the Johns Hopkins Hospital,* 34:51–59.

MIRONESCU, T. and G. STEFANOY
1926 "Beitrag zum Studium der Beziehungen zwischen Blutgruppen und Infektionen." *Seuchenbekämpfung,* 3:138–139.

MOHR, J.
1951 "Estimation of Linkage between the Lutheran and the Lewis Blood Groups." *Acta Pathologica et Microbiologica Scandinavica* 29:339–344.

MORTON, S. G.
1839 *Crania Americana.* Philadelphia, J. Dobson.
1844 *Crania Egyptica.* Philadelphia, J. Pennington.

NEWMAN, MARSHALL T.
1953 "The Application of Ecological Rules to the Racial Anthropology of the Aboriginal New World." *American Anthropologist,* 55:311–327.

OPPENHEIM, F. and R. VOIGHT
1926 "Blutgruppenstudien an der Leiche." *Krankheits Forschung,* 3:306–334.

OTTENBERG, R.
1923 "The Etiology of Eclampsia." *Journal of the American Medical Association,* 81:295–297.

OTTENBERG, R., H. KALINSKI and J. FRIEDMANN
1915 "Experimental Hemolytic and Agglutinatic Transfusions." *Journal of Medical Research*, 33:141–153.

PERKEL, J. D. and M. M. ISRAELSSON
1928 "Blutgruppenverteilung bei Syphilis des Zentralnervenssystem der inneren Organe und der Haut." *Dermatologische Zeitschrift*, 54:261–267.

PFAHLER, G. E. and B. P. WIDMANN
1924 "The Relation of Blood Groups to Malignant Disease and the Influence of Radiotherapy." *American Journal of Roentgenology and Radium Therapy*, 12:47–50.

POLAYES, S. H., M. LEDERER and A. S. WIENER
1929a "Studies in Isohemagglutination. I. Theoretical Considerations." *Journal of Immunology*, 16:469–482.
1929b "Studies in Isohemagglutination. II. The Landsteiner Blood Groups in Mothers and Infants." *Journal of Immunology*, 17:545–554.

RACE, R. R. and R. SANGER
1954 *Blood Groups in Man*. Oxford, Blackwell Scientific Publications.

RAMNEANTZU, P. and J. FACAOARU
1937 "The Blood Groups and the Pigmentation of Iris in the Population from Transylvania." *Congrès International d'Anthropologie et d'Archéologie Préhistoriques*, Bucharest, 17:333–337.

RITTENHOUSE, E. E.
1913 "The Increasing Mortality from Degenerative Maladies." *Popular Science Monthly*, 82:376–380.

SANGHVI, L. E.
1951 "ABO Blood Groups and Sex Ratio at Birth in Man." *Nature*, 168:1077.

SCHIFF, F.
1926 "Hämagglutiningehalt des Blutserums Karzinomkranke 4." *Medizinische Klinik*, 22:455.

SHAW, E. B., M. D. THELANDER, and K. KILGARIFF
1932 "Blood Grouping in Poliomyelitis." *Journal of Pediatrics*, 1:346–348.

SHIELD, J. W., R. L. KIRK and R. JAKOBOWICZ
1958 "The ABO Blood Groups and Masculinity of Offspring at Birth." *The American Journal of Human Genetics*, 10:154–163.

SHRUBSALL, F. C.
1914 "The Relative Fertility and Morbidity of Defective and Normal

Stocks." *Report of the British Association for the Advancement of Science*, 83:680–681.

SJÖSTEDT, S., R. GRUBB and F. LINNELL
1951 "Blood Group Incompatibility and Sterility." *Acta Pathologica et Microbiologica Scandinavica*, 28:375–387.

SNYDER, L. H.
1929 Blood Grouping in Relation to Clinical and Legal Medicine. Baltimore, The Williams & Wilkins Co.

STRASZYNSKI, A.
1925 "Über das Ergebnis der Wassermannschen Reaktion innerhalb verschiedener Blutgruppen bei behandelter Lues." *Klinische Wochenschrift*, 4:1962–1963.

VUORI, A. K.
1929 "Die Vererbung der Blutgruppen und deren Korrelation an anderen konstitutionellen Eigenschaften." *Acta Societatis Medicorum Fennicae "Duodecim." (Suomalaisen Lääkäriseuran Duodecim'in) Toimitukosia*, 12:1–137.

WATERHOUSE, J. A. and L. HOGBEN
1947 "Incompatibility of Mother and Fetus with Respect to the Isoagglutinogen A and Its Antibody." *British Journal of Preventive and Social Medicine*, 1:1–17.

WEITZNER, G.
1925 "Hämagglutiningehalt des Blutserums Karzinomkranker." *Medizinische Klinik*, 21:1960–1961.

WIECHMANN, E. and H. PAAL
1926 "Ueber die Blutgruppen der Kölner Bevölkerung." *Münchener Medizinische Wochenschrift*, 73:606–608.

WIENER, A. S.
1943 *Blood Groups and Transfusion*. 3rd ed. Springfield, Illinois, Charles C Thomas, Publishers.
1956 "Blood Groups and Disease." *Lancet*, 2:1308.

WIENER, A. S. and I. B. WEXLER
1956 "Blood Group Paradoxes. Guest Editorial." *Journal of the American Medical Association*, 162:1474–1475.

WOODRUFF, C. E.
1912 "Blonds and Brunettes in the Tropics." *New York Medical Journal*, 96:721–729.

* * * *

Albert Carl Cafagna

UNIVERSITY OF MICHIGAN

A FORMAL ANALYSIS OF

DEFINITIONS OF 'CULTURE'

INTRODUCTION

The recent pronounced interest in the problem of defining the concept 'culture' is the most promising sign that cultural anthropology is beginning to emerge from the descriptive phase of its brief scientific career. For while a science is still primarily concerned with the collection and description of its data, terminological subtleties are likely to command little attention. When first observing a sacred ritual or a ceremonial dance, an ethnographer does not ask himself, "Let me see, should I record this? Is this an element of culture according to my definition?" Like the workers in any particular field he is able to recognize his data "on sight." Even prior to the appearance of professional anthropologists, there were those who had this same rough and ready ability to distinguish culture traits from other discriminable phenomena. I shall, hereafter, refer to this ability as the "pre-definitional knowledge of culture.

Concern over the adequacy of terminology arises when the workers in a particular discipline attempt to formulate general principles, to work out hypotheses, and to arrive at prediction in order to test these hypotheses. Given pre-definitional knowledge of culture, ethnographers have reported and described their observations in the field with whatever terms seemed most appropriate for their purposes. As a consequence, what was a "tribe" in one monograph was a "nation" in another, and so on. In order to facilitate communication and to make generalization possible, there arose an effort to adopt standard terms to describe similar phenomena among different peoples. This is the preliminary stage in the development of a scientific terminology. But all that was sought for here was the adoption of standard terms to be used cross-culturally. A certain measure of success has been achieved in this endeavor. But as ethnologists go beyond the mere generalization of facts and attempt to formulate hypotheses to account for these descriptive regularities, their concern with terminology goes beyond that of seeking arbitrary agreement in vocabulary.

Since scientific hypotheses must be logically consistent and verifiable, their constituent terms must be so defined as to be compatible with these properties. Thus, we find a growing concern with definitions.

Thus far I have attempted to make two points. First, that despite their disagreement in how to "say" what they mean by the word 'culture,' all cultural anthropologists "know" what a culture trait is when they see one. Second, that this pre-definitional knowledge, while adequate for descriptive purposes, is not sufficient for explanation and prediction.

It is the thesis of this essay that the task of critically evaluating the many prevalent and conflicting definitions of 'culture' will be facilitated by the application of some of the formal rules for definitions developed by philosophers of science. I shall attempt to apply one set of formal rules to several current definitions of 'culture,' and offer some suggestions for improving those definitions whose defects are terminological in nature. In order to introduce this formal analysis, a brief discussion of some of the general principles of the theory of definitions will be presented.

THE NEED FOR DEFINITIONS [1]

The theory of definitions grew out of the need for improving the communicability of natural language. It is characteristic of all natural languages (the languages studied by linguists) that a relatively small set of linguistic elements are made to function in a great variety of contexts and circumstances. The structure of language is such that its elements, together with its formative (phonological) and transformative (grammatical) rules, enable it to present an infinite number of utterances. For example, a common set of words may function in emotive, persuasive, or

---

[1] For some of the ideas and terms used in the first part of this essay, I am indebted to Max Black, Morris Cohen and Ernest Nagel, and Irving Copi.

descriptive discourse. The requirements which any given set of words must meet in order to perform these various functions effectively will, of course, vary considerably from one type of discourse to another. Most words, or even larger linguistic units, possess a certain degree of vagueness, indefiniteness, and ambiguity. These properties enhance the versatility and generality of words and phrases enabling them to meet the varied demands of ordinary discourse.

Vagueness is one important property of language. A word is vague where there are borderline cases such that it is difficult to decide whether or not the word may be applied to them. An example of a vague word is 'bald.' How many hairs must a man have lost before we would call him bald? In general, vagueness is advantageous since it permits discussion on subjects which are not known precisely. For example, it is sufficiently clear in ordinary discourse to use 'fish' to refer to all animals that live in the water. But this usage would not suffice for the zoologist wanting to distinguish between whales and other marine animals. Vagueness in our language reflects vagueness in our knowledge.

Another significant feature of ordinary language is *indefiniteness*. A word is indefinite if it supplies less information in a context in which it occurs than another word might have supplied. For example, the word 'bilateral' in the statement, "The kinship system among western European peoples is bilateral," is indefinite since it supplies less information than 'Eskimo' would. Again, as with vagueness, we are sometimes forced to use indefinite words by indefiniteness in our knowledge.

Perhaps the most important property of ordinary language is *polysemy*. A word is said to be polysemic or multivocal if it has two or more well-established senses or meanings. This feature of words enormously expedites the learning of a language and facilitates communication since it reduces the size of the working vocabulary. A polysemic word is said to be *ambiguous* if the specific sense intended, in an instance in which the word is used, is not made clear by the context. It is customary to speak of the ambiguity of words. Strictly speaking, however, words are polysemic; it is *word usage* that is ambiguous. To illustrate this point, consider the word 'bank.' This word is commonly understood to have at least two senses, the bank of the river, and the savings bank. While it is polysemic, by itself 'bank' is not ambiguous. But the sentence, "I lost it near the bank," is. While polysemy is one of the most essential properties of language, ambiguity, unless held to a minimum, severely restricts the effectiveness of communication.

Ambiguity is perhaps the most persistent obstacle to effective communication. Hence a discussion of some of its most typical forms and the conceptual techniques for reducing their incidence is warranted. Most "dangerous" ambiguities result from a subtle shift or confusion between the competing meanings of a polysemic word. Three of the most frequently encountered types of these confusions are: *word-referent shifts; connotation-denotation shifts;* and *process-product shifts.*

Perhaps the most important source of ambiguities is *word-referent shifts.* This ambiguity, which is sometimes labeled the *use versus mention fallacy,* has been focused upon by the general semanticists. They have called this fallacy "word magic" and consider it the source of the great bulk of muddled thinking. One commits this fallacy when he confuses the use of a word to refer to or mention some *nonverbal entity* with the use of a word to refer to or mention *itself* (a verbal entity). A flagrant example of muddled thinking which has resulted from this type of confusion is the argument presented by some physical anthropologists for the substitution of the word "ethnic" for the word "race." This argument, in effect, runs as follows: "Race has been the cause of the most pernicious acts in the history of mankind; therefore we ought to substitute ethnic for race."

The confusion here results from the fact that in the first instance the word 'race' is *used* to mention a disposition toward prejudice or discrimination, and in the second instance, the word 'race' is itself *mentioned.* "Word magic" is a very apt description of this argument since it tacitly assumes that by changing a word we are changing deep-rooted attitudes and habits. A clear distinction between the use and mention of a word can be maintained if single quotation marks are placed around any word mentioned, for example, 'Bill' has four letters, rather than Bill has four letters.

Another persistent cause of fallacies is *connotation-denotation shifts.* An example of this type of ambiguity is contained in the statement, "The word mermaid is meaningful; therefore mermaids exist." This statement involves a confusion between two senses of 'meaning.' In one sense, the "meaning" of a word consists of all those *particular objects* to which the word is ordinarily applied. This sense of 'meaning' is usually called *denotation.* In another sense, the "meaning" of a word consists of those *general properties* which a particular object must possess for the word to be properly applied to them. This sense of 'meaning' is usually called *connotation.* Perhaps the distinction between the denotation and the connotation of a word can be clarified by the following example: The denotation of the word 'cultural anthropologist' consists of such particular objects (persons) as A. L. Kroeber, Robert Lowie, and others, while its connotation consists of such general properties (qualifications) as being a student of the science of culture, having done field work among some preliterate people, and so on.

It is customary in philosophical discourse to employ 'meaning' in the sense of connotation since all intelligible words, however vague, indefinite, or ambiguous, have connotation. However, a word need not, and in fact some very common words (for example, 'mermaid') do not, denote. It is important to note, moreover, that there is a fundamental independence between the logical activity of establishing or clarifying the connotation of a word; that is, defining a term, and that of empirically determining its denotation.

The last type of ambiguity we will consider is sometimes referred to as *process-product shifts*. This sort of verbal confusion may arise when a word is commonly understood to mean both a process or activity of some kind and the product or results of that activity. This type of ambiguity is illustrated in the following argument: "Science is a continuously self-correcting activity. Therefore, Harvey's theory of the circulation of blood is not scientific, since it has not been modified in almost three centuries." The weakness in this argument is that it neglects the fact that 'science' is commonly understood to mean a *product*, or body of highly confirmed hypotheses, as well as the *process* by means of which this body of hypotheses was obtained.

THE FUNCTIONS OF DEFINITIONS

I have discussed some of the more important characteristics of the use of words which enable them to meet the varied and complex demands of natural language. It is apparent, however, that the rigorous demands of scientific discourse make it desirable to employ terms whose versatility is held to a minimum.

Definitions may be regarded as conceptual devices for controlling the functions of words. Thus, definitions are commonly employed in the following capacities: (a) in the clarification of vague and indefinite words, (b) in the reduction of ambiguity, and (c) in the explanation of new words in terms of old words. Definitions used in these capacities may be said to function by helping to establish and maintain logical consistency in scientific language. However, there is another and equally important role which definitions may perform in the scientific enterprise. This follows from the fundamental tenet of the philosophy of science that scientific hypotheses be empirically verifiable. According to this basic principle, propositions are scientifically meaningful if and only if they have consequences which are directly or indirectly verifiable by observation. This function is performed by a special class of definitions called "operational definitions," which serve to connect hypotheses with those observations by means of which they may be confirmed.

Before proceeding with the analysis of definitions of 'culture,' it would be well to consider the nature of scientific definitions, the various types of definitions, and finally a formulation of several formal rules for definitions which will be employed in the subsequent discussion.

What are scientific definitions? The first point to be made in addressing this question is that *definitions are about "words," not "things."* Where we ask for a definition of 'culture,' we are asking for an explanation of the use of the *word* 'culture,' not for an empirical characterization of the *phenomenon* culture. This point cannot be overemphasized since the widespread failure to understand it is probably the main reason why anthropologists have made so little progress in arriving at a generally acceptable definition of their central term.

If a definition is an "explanation" of the meaning or the use of a term, what is meant by "explanation"? A definition explains by stating the *necessary and sufficient conditions* for applying (or using) the term in question. By stating the conditions under which a word may be used a definition implicitly establishes the connotation of the word. For example, when George P. Murdock stipulates the rules for using the word 'clan,' the following definition is implied: Let 'CLAN' connote what is connoted by '*any cohesive social group which has a unilinear descent system, a residence pattern consistent with the descent system, and a mechanism for integrating the in-marrying spouses*' (1949:65). Here the necessary condition for designating anything by the word 'clan' is that it be a cohesive social group; the sufficient condition is that it possess the three additional attributes specified above.

All definitions consist of two components: the word to be explained, and the word or set of words used to explain it. These components are usually called the *definiendum* and the *definiens,* respectively. In Murdock's definition stated above the definiendum has been printed in small capital letters and the definiens in italics. Every definition asserts that these two components have equivalent connotations and may be used interchangeably.

While every definition must establish the post-definitional usage and connotation of the definiendum by equating it with the usage and connotation of the definiens, definitions may differ in the nature of the equation they assert (that is, the equation may be a proposition, a stipulation, or an explication) and in whether or not the definiendum is assumed to have a pre-definitional usage. Three types of definitions may be distinguished on this basis.

THREE TYPES OF SCIENTIFIC DEFINITIONS

The first type to be considered may be called *real definitions*. Here a pre-definitional usage of both the definiendum and the definiens is assumed; the definition merely asserts an equation between them. For example, the real definition, 'Sloop' has the same connotation as 'a fore-and-aft-rigged vessel with one mast and a single headsail jib,' is a genuine proposition which may be true or false. Since it asserts that its definiendum and its definiens can be interchanged in all contexts without loss of communication, it is a factual statement which can be tested by asking people how they use the words, observing people's verbal behavior, looking in dictionaries, and so on.

It is important to notice that while the usage of the definiens ought to be "very close" to the usage of the definiendum, it need not be identical. For example, frequently the usage of the definiendum is ambiguous, that is, has unresolved multiple meanings; here, a real definition may reduce the ambiguity of the word by asserting that only one usage, that of the definiens, is equivalent to the usage of the definiendum. A real definition, then, may in some cases analyze the words it defines. Its success, of course, depends upon the definiens having fewer defects than its definiendum.

The second type to be discussed is usually called *nominal definitions*. Nominal definitions attach a connotation to the unknown (definiendum) by means of the known (definiens). In this case, the definiendum is either a new term or an old one used in a new context and is presumed to have no pre-definitional usage. A nominal definition serves the need for economy in technical language since its definiendum is always much shorter than its definiens, for example, let $a^{10} \overset{\text{df}}{=} $ a x a x a x a x a x a x a x a x a x a. A nominal definition is arbitrary; it simply announces an intention to use the definiendum as a synonym for the definiens, hence, there can be no question of its truth or falsity. These definitions, then, are stipulations rather than propositions. A nominal definition is said to be successful if and only if its use enhances the rigor and fruitfulness of the language.

One special class of nominal definitions is the so-called "operational definition." Operational definitions serve to meet the requirements of measurement and verification of scientific hypotheses. A term is said to be operationally defined when it is used to connote properties which are empirically observable and measureable. More accurately, a term is operationally defined if, when contained in a scientific hypothesis, the consequences of that hypothesis are testable by experience. Examples of operational definitions are the definition of 'temperature' as the points along a Fahrenheit scale, and the definition of 'intelligence' as the performance level on an I.Q. test. When Leslie A. White asserts that the degree of evolution of culture can be measured by the amount of energy harnessed per capita per year, he is offering, in effect, an operational definition of 'evolution' (1949:363–397).

The third type to be considered may be called *explicative definitions*. In this case, while the definiendum is assumed to have an established predefinitional usage, the definiens need not. Their essential characteristic is that these definitions always attempt to analyze the terms they define. Consider, for example, the following attempt to explicate the vague term 'bald': Anyone may be called 'bald' to whom the phrase, 'having a hairline that has receded beyond the vertical line perpendicular to the Frankfort Plane where the lines intersect at the tympanic bone,' can be ascribed. This definition, while its definiens clearly transcends established usage, is probably true in that most persons who are ordinarily considered bald also possess the properties specified by its definiens. Furthermore, the adoption of this definition would reduce the vagueness of 'bald' by eliminating many borderline cases. As this illustration suggests, an explication is a hybrid having some of the characteristics of both nominal and real definitions. That is, while they must be compatible with habitual usage, their adoption must serve to sharpen and clarify such usage.

FORMAL CRITERIA FOR DEFINITIONS

The following is a list of rules suggested as a basis for evaluating the formal adequacy of definitions of 'culture.'

1. A definition must establish the connotation of the word it defines.
2. The definiens must be less ambiguous, less indefinite, less vague, and more familiar than the definiendum.

3. The substitution in relevant contexts of the definiens for the definiendum (of real and explicative definitions) must be compatible with ordinary usage and/or enhance the rigor and fruitfulness of such usage.
4. The definiens must connote properties which are at least indirectly confrontable by experience.

ANALYSIS OF DEFINITIONS OF 'CULTURE'

The remainder of this essay is an application of the results of the foregoing discussion to various definitions of 'culture.' The following definitions [2] were selected because individually they are widely held, and collectively they are representative of the diversity of current definitions.

Definitions Stressing Social Heritage

One definition of this type is given by Bronislaw Malinowski, who says: "This social heritage is the key concept of cultural anthropology. It is usually called culture. . . ." (1931:621). Edward Sapir submits a very similar definition when he says 'culture' refers to "any socially inherited element in the life of man, material and spiritual" (1924:402). Ralph Linton agrees by maintaining: "the social heredity is called *culture. . . . culture* means the total social heredity of mankind. . . ." (1936:78).

The above are real definitions since they assert that the connotation of 'culture' is equivalent to the connotation of 'social heritage.' This group of definitions is vulnerable to criticism on several counts. In the first place, the definiens ('social heritage') has not successfully reduced the vagueness of the definiendum ('culture'). For example, the celebration of Christmas would probably be regarded as an element of our social heritage, but contemporary observance of the holiday is far more commercial and less spiritual than that of the previous generation, therefore the question arises, "How similar do the practices have to be before we would regard the one as the heritage of the other?"

Furthermore, these definitions appear to be false since 'social heritage' is not interchangeable with 'culture,' as it is asserted to be. In fact, the

---

[2] Most of the statements which are under analysis in this paper are not explicitly formulated as definitions of the word 'culture.' Rather, they are attempts to state the distinguishing features of cultural phenomena. However, since it is apparent that such statements implicitly define the term, I have regarded them as definitions.

connotation of 'culture' appears to be much more inclusive than that of 'social heritage.' Consider, for example, the formula, $E = mc^2$, known to laymen as Einstein's theory of relativity. At the time of its first publication, this formula was not part of our social heritage, but few anthropologists would deny that it was an element of culture. I feel that the difficulty here arises from a neglect of the ordinary connotation of 'culture' as a *process* as well as a *product*. The connotation of 'social heritage' does not include the processes by means of which new cultural elements are introduced, and old ones modified and transmitted lineally and laterally. Thus, the connotation of 'social heritage,' rather than being equivalent to, appears to be a subset of, the connotation of 'culture.' (See Figure 1.) [3]

The vagueness of 'social heritage' could be reduced by the adoption of an auxiliary explicative or operational definition designed to eliminate borderline cases. For example, one might restrict 'social heritage' to the designation of those things and events whose existence antedates the birth of the eldest member of a particular society and which he regards as having been unchanged throughout his lifetime. It would appear that the process/product difficulty could be overcome by stipulating that 'culture' is to connote in the product sense only, offering evidence that such a modification of ordinary usage would increase the fruitfulness of the concept.

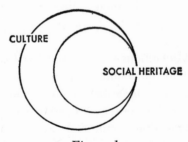

Figure 1

Definitions Stressing Learned Behavior

Definitions which emphasize learned behavior have been employed by many psychologists, sociologists, and anthropologists. Ruth Benedict says: ". . . culture is the sociological term for learned behavior. . . ." (1945:13). Julian Steward suggests: "Culture is generally understood to

---

[3] The use of Venn-like diagrams for this purpose was suggested by Robert Carneiro in a personal communication.

mean learned modes of behavior which are socially transmitted. . . ." (1950:98). According to Allison Davis: ". . . culture . . . may be defined as *all behavior learned by the individual in conformity with a group.* . . ." (1948:59). For Clyde Kluckhohn: "Culture consists in all transmitted social learning" (Kroeber and Kluckhohn 1952:58). Similarly, Charles Hockett maintains: "Culture is those habits which humans have because they have been learned . . . from other humans" (1950: 113).

These are all real definitions which assert that the pre-definitional connotation of 'culture' coincides with that of 'learned behavior.' These definitions do not meet our criterion of interchangeability since the connotation of 'learned behavior' (when restricted to human beings) is much less inclusive than that of 'culture.' These definitions may be said to neglect the "product" sense of 'culture.' For regardless of how they may define 'culture,' few anthropologists fail to include descriptions of tools, weapons, ritualistic paraphernalia, and so on, in their monographs on the grounds that artifacts are not culture traits. The relation between 'learned behavior' and 'culture' may be represented in the following diagram (Figure 2), which illustrates why this group of real definitions is false.

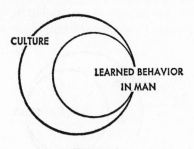

Figure 2

Suggested Modifications

The logical difficulty with these definitions is that there are many contexts in which 'culture' and 'learned behavior' are not interchangeable. I would suggest two alternative ways for improving these definitions. One strategy would be to change the definiens to read 'learned behavior and the products of learned behavior' so that it could be interchanged with 'culture' in far more contexts. Another strategy would be to admit the departure from ordinary usage, regard the definition as an explication, and submit evidence in justification of this departure.

Albert Carl Cafagna

Definitions Stressing Ideas

Some anthropologists have emphasized ideas shared by the members of a society. For Clark Wissler: ". . . culture is a definite association complex of ideas" (1916:197). Similarly, according to James Ford: ". . . culture may be briefly defined as a stream of ideas, that passes from individual to individual by means of symbolic action, verbal instruction, or imitation" (1949:38). Thinking along the same line, Walter Taylor says: "By . . . culture . . . I mean all those mental constructs or ideas which have been learned or created after birth by an individual. . . . Culture . . . consists of ideas" (1948:109).

This group, which I interpret as explicative definitions, fails to meet our third and fourth criteria (that the definiens must be interchangeable with the definiendum and that the definiens must connote properties which are at least indirectly observable). In the first place, the connotation of the definiens, 'ideas' is far less inclusive than the pre-definitional understanding of 'culture.' Some of the same archeologists who define 'culture' in terms of ideas write reports describing unearthed artifacts as "cultural assemblages"; hence there is little reason to believe that this departure from ordinary usage would enhance the fruitfulness of the concept. This is another case where the connotation of the definiens is a subset of the connotation of the definiendum. (See Figure 3.)

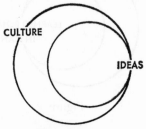

Figure 3

Secondly, and this is more important, these explications of 'culture' in terms of 'ideas' not only violate our fourth rule in that it is impossible to observe ideas, but they introduce the irrelevant issue of the ontological status of culture. No suggestions will be offered for modifying the definitions in this group since their basic defects are not terminological but appear to result from a fundamental misconception of the function of definitions in science.[4]

---

[4] See Goldstein (1957), for a discussion of the inappropriateness of raising ontological issues in anthropology.

Definitions Stressing Shared (or Standardized) Behavior

Explicitly or implicitly, many definitions have placed major emphasis on 'shared behavior.' Geoffrey Gorer says: ". . . culture, in the anthropological sense of the word [is] . . . shared patterns of learned behavior. . . ." (1949:2). Another similar definition is given by Kimball Young, who says: "Culture consists of common and more or less standardized ideas, attitudes, and habits. . . ." (1942:35). Again, we find this notion in Clark Wissler: ". . . culture is . . . the aggregate of standardized beliefs and procedures followed by the tribe" (1929:341).

This group of real definitions is inadequate in several respects. First, they fail to reduce the vagueness of the word 'culture.' How many persons must do a particular thing or have a particular belief before we could call it "shared"? Second, 'shared behavior' (when restricted to human beings) has a much narrower connotation than 'culture,' since it does not embrace artifacts. Third, some phenomena which would clearly be regarded as culture traits are forms of behavior which can be performed only by one person, for example, being a king or queen. The relation between the connotation of 'shared behavior' and that of 'culture' is illustrated in Figure 4.

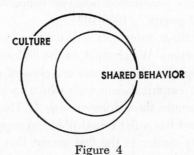

CULTURE

SHARED BEHAVIOR

Figure 4

Suggested Modifications

The vagueness of 'shared behavior' can be reduced by offering auxiliary operational definitions specifying the minimum number or percentage of persons who must exhibit a certain type of behavior before it may be called 'shared.' For example, some purposes would be served by restricting 'shared behavior' to the designation of all acts engaged in by two or more human beings. Other purposes would require that 'shared behavior' be used to designate only those acts which are modal in the entire range of the behavior exhibited by the members of a specific socio-cultural system. The problem of the noninterchangeability of 'shared behavior' and 'culture' in those contexts involving artifacts or unique behavior can be resolved only by arguing that the restriction of the use of 'culture' to those contexts where interchangeability is possible explicates 'culture' by enhancing its clarity and fruitfulness.

DEFINITIONS STRESSING ABSTRACTION FROM BEHAVIOR

Statements that culture is an abstraction from behavior of one sort or another have been made by some anthropologists. Some of the most explicit of such statements are by A. L. Kroeber and Clyde Kluckhohn, who say: "A culture is then an abstraction . . . ." ". . . culture is inevitably an abstraction" (1952:61). ". . . behavior seems . . . to be that within whose mass culture exists and from which it is conceptually extricated or abstracted" (Kroeber and Kluckhohn 1952:156). The psychologist John Dollard says, "Culture is the name given to abstracted intercorrelated customs of a social group" (1939:50). Again, according to David Aberle, *et al.*, "Culture is socially transmitted behavior conceived as an abstraction from concrete social groups" (1950:102).

Before evaluating these statements, a distinction must be made between two senses of 'abstraction.' We abstract, in the first sense, when we isolate or focus attention upon a certain restricted class of empirical data from the larger cluster of empirical data with which they are ordinarily perceived. Take, for example, three different objects. The first is colored blue, is made of wood, and has a flat round platform supported by four legs. The second object is similar to the first except that its color is red and it is made of metal. The third object is similar to both the first and the second but its flat round platform is covered with green leather and is supported by wooden legs. Now if we call all three distinct objects by the common term 'stool' we are abstracting, that is, restricting our attention to the property of having a flat round platform supported by four legs and ignoring those of color and building materials. Thus, we could say the word 'stool' is an abstraction in that its connotation was arrived at through the process of abstracting. Notice, however, that in so doing we have in no way denied the "concrete existence" of the things to which the word 'stool' refers. It is to be noticed further that we have only given an implicit definition of 'stool.' Explicitly, the definition is as follows: 'Stool' connotes what is connoted by 'flat, round platform supported by four legs.'

There is another sense of 'abstraction' which is perhaps better called "hypothesization." As we have seen, when we abstract we merely confine our attention to a restricted class of observable data within a larger class of observable data. In hypothesization, we employ terms to connote certain posited or constructed entities which are in principle unobservable and whose ontological status is mental. (The fallacy of reification is committed if we treat these constructed entities as concrete ones.) Take, for example, the psychoanalytic concepts, "id," "ego," and "superego." These terms signify certain constructed entities which were posited to make some types of behavior intelligible, but they cannot in any sense be said to connote observable properties. In other words, in the first sense, a word is called an 'abstraction' even though it connotes observable properties, because its connotation was arrived at through the process of abstracting. In the second sense, a word is called an 'abstraction' because it connotes "abstract" or hypothesized properties or entities.

As a result of the failure to distinguish between these two senses of 'abstraction,' a fallacious argument has been put forth in some anthropological papers which may be expressed as follows: How can culture determine human behavior if culture is an abstraction? How can an abstraction have causal efficacy? [5]

This argument reveals what has earlier been called the *use versus mention fallacy*. In the statement, "Culture determines human behavior," the word 'culture' is *used* to mention a restricted class of observable phenomena. However, in the statement, "Culture is an abstraction," the word 'culture' is itself *mentioned* (since it is the word which is the abstraction).

In light of the above remarks, the word 'abstraction' in the statement, "Culture is an abstraction from human behavior," may be taken in two different, but often confused, senses, that is, it is ambiguous. If 'abstraction' is understood in what we have called its first sense (that is, the process of determining the connotation of a term by abstracting), then the statement, "Culture is an abstraction," is not a definition of 'culture' at all. That is, it doesn't purport to explain how 'culture' is to be used. It merely makes a rather uninformative assertion about how the connotation of the word was derived (uninformative since the connotations of almost all words are derived by the process of abstraction). On the other hand, if

[5] Three instances of this fallacious argument are given by A. R. Radcliffe-Brown (1940:10–11), A. Irving Hallowell (1945:174–175), and Melford E. Spiro (1951:25).

'abstraction' is used to connote what we have called "hypothesization," then the statement, "Culture is an abstraction from human behavior," is an explication of how the word 'culture' is to be used which has unfortunate metaphysical implications. These explicative definitions assert that 'culture' has the same connotation as certain hypothesized constructs such as 'patterns of behavior,' 'designs for living,' and so on.

Now these definitions, as I have interpreted them, fail to meet our second and fourth criteria. Consider the absurdity of the following statement which results from the substitution of 'patterns abstracted from behavior' for 'culture' in a typical context: "The Clovis fluted points found in New Mexico are among the earliest appearances of patterns abstracted from behavior found in the New World." Hence, these real definitions falsely assert the interchangeability of the definiens (hypothesized 'patterns' or 'designs') and the definiendum ('culture'). Further, these definitions fail to meet our fourth criterion since their definiens do not connote observable data. This group of definitions has an additional defect, previously encountered in those definitions stressing ideas. This deficiency results from the failure to separate the logical question, "How is the word 'culture' used?" from the ontological question, "What is the essence or nature of culture?". I have not offered any suggestions for modifying these definitions since their primary deficiency is not terminological in nature.

Definitions Stressing Superorganic

According to White: "Culture . . . constitutes a supra-biological, or extra-somatic, class of events. . . ." (1949:16). Almost identical statements have been made by Kroeber (1917:192) and Lowie (1936:301). If the above is taken as a definition, it would be classified as a real definition which asserts that 'culture' connotes what is connoted by 'supra-biological,' or 'extra-somatic.' This definition (if it is a definition) would appear to violate our third criterion, since its definiens ('extra-somatic') is not interchangeable with 'culture,' in all contexts as asserted. For example, puberty rites are certainly regarded as culture traits and just as certainly have "somatic" or biological aspects. But the contexts in which the statements under discussion occur make it quite clear that such statements as, "Culture is super-organic," are to be interpreted as hypotheses about how cultural differences may be most fruitfully explained, and not as definitions. In other words, I interpret the above statements as methodological propositions about the *phenomenon* culture which presuppose a definition of the word 'culture.'

A Definition Stressing Name of Class of Things and Events

To my knowledge, statements which explicitly refer to 'culture' as a word whose usage is to be established by fiat have been made only by White [6] who says: "*Culture* . . . is a *word* that we may use to label a class of phenomena—things and events. . . ." (1954:463). According to White, 'culture' is the name of the class of all ". . . things and events dependent upon symbolling. . . ." (1954:464). This must be classified as a *nominal definition* in that the word 'culture' is treated as if it had no pre-definitional meaning. Therefore, there can be no question of its truth or falsity, and this stipulation must be evaluated in terms of its heuristic value, that is, its fruitfulness as a conceptual tool.

In his many essays White has systematically and convincingly laid bare a class of anthropological problems for the explanation of which the human organism may be regarded as a functionally irrelevant factor. The following is synoptic of such problems: How can we account for the observed differences in the customs, institutions, and other aspects of behavior of people in geographically separated areas? Speaking of such problems, White says: ". . . in the whole range and scope of human behavior, differences of custom or tradition can nowhere be correlated in a functional sense with differences of physical structure . . . , therefore, we may regard man as a constant, culture as a variable" (1949:124). Again, White says of the problem of cultural differences, ". . . we can treat them scientifically as if they had an independent existence. In fact . . . [such problems] . . . can be solved most effectively by eliminating the human organism from our consideration entirely" (1949:100). In light of the above, it is reasonable to maintain that the adoption of White's definition of 'culture' should allow at least the logical possibility of referring to cultural phenomena without necessarily referring to the human organism.

Having discerned this one criterion for appraising its heuristic value,

---

[6] In a recent article, Omar K. Moore (1952), has presented a series of alternative nominal definitions of 'culture' in order to illustrate a method of analysis. I feel that the formulistic "model analysis" offered in his paper has little to offer anthropology in its present state of development. While it is true that theoretical physics has been able to develop fruitful empirical interpretations of logico-mathematical calculi, my opinion of the general applicability of such a formalistic method is in agreement with Rudolf Carnap who says: "It is, of course, *logically possible* to apply the same method to any other branch of science as well. But *practically* the situation is such that most of them seem at the present time to be not yet developed to a degree which would suggest this strict form of presentation" (italics mine) (1955:202).

White's definition must now be carefully examined to determine the degree to which it meets the formal requirements for nominal definitions, that is, logical clarity plus fruitfulness. Expressed fully the definition reads: Let 'culture' have the same connotation as 'the class of all things and events dependent upon symbolling.' The phrase 'dependent upon' is indefinite since more information could be supplied by 'necessary condition' or 'sufficient condition.' However, the contexts in which this definition occurs suggests that this phrase may be explicated as follows: Let 'the class of all things and events dependent upon symbolling' have the same connotation as 'the class of all things and events for the occurrence and comprehension of which symbolling is a necessary condition.'

Assuming the validity of the above explication, the next step is to analyze the term 'symbolling.' However, before pursuing the analysis, it must be clearly understood that the logical structure of a nominal definition is such that its definiendum is assumed to have no pre-definitional meaning. Thus, in White's definition, the definiendum 'culture' may be legitimately used to refer to a particular entity *if and only if* the properties which characterize that entity are specifically connoted by the definiens 'the class of all things and events for the occurrence and comprehension of which symbolling is a necessary condition.'

Now the only property connoted by this definiens is that of being a class about whose members nothing is known except that they could neither exist nor have any significance were it not for the unique human ability to use symbols. White describes this ability as the: ". . . creative faculty . . . of freely, actively, and arbitrarily bestowing value upon things. . . ." (1949:29). Furthermore, we are given no criterion for determining by direct observation whether or not any thing or event owes its existence and meaning to this human faculty, that is, is a symbol. In fact, we are told that ". . . a thing which in one context is a symbol is, in another context, not a symbol but a sign. . . . This distinction *must* be made [only] when one bestows value upon . . . [a physical object] . . . or when a previously bestowed value is discovered for the first time. . . ." (1949:26). In other words, the only distinguishing property which is connoted by 'the class of all things and events dependent upon symbolling' is that of being a physical thing or event toward which some human organism is voluntarily responding in some "meaningful" but arbitrary manner. It is therefore logically necessary under White's definition, for 'culture' to be used only when referring to this symbolic relationship between some human organism and some physical thing and event.

Thus, we are directly confronted with the pragmatic paradox that although White has convincingly argued for a broad class of cultural phenomena which can most effectively be explained "by eliminating the human organism from our considerations entirely," the term 'culture,' under his own definition, may not be used to refer to such phenomena.

Suggested Modifications

It has been shown that the adoption of White's definition would impose excessive restrictions upon the use of the word 'culture.' Furthermore, it has been shown that this is a consequence of conceiving of 'culture' as "a word the use of which we have arbitrarily to determine. . . ." (1954: 463) by a stipulative or nominal definition. I suggest the following conceptual modifications for avoiding these consequences. In the first place, while it is certainly true that when it was first introduced into anthropological discourse the usage of the word 'culture' was arbitrarily determined, it is equally certain that, at least since Tylor, the word has had a well-established usage, however vague and ambiguous. Now if 'culture' is admitted to have a pre-definitional usage, then it may be given a real or explicative definition but not a nominal one. Thus the statement: 'Culture' has the same connotation as 'the class of all things and events dependent upon symbolling,' could be taken as a real definition. As we have seen in real definitions, both the definiens and the definiendum have established connotations prior to the assertion of their equation. Hence, we may use 'culture' to refer to all things and events having the properties specified in its pre-definitional connotation,[7] that is, things and events commonly regarded to be culture traits. We may also use 'the class of all things and events dependent upon symbolling' to refer to anything having the properties specified by its connotation, that is, things and events standing in symbolic relationship to the human organism. Now, these words may be so used independently of one another, except when we are evaluating the truth of the definition which asserts that they can be used interchangeably without loss in communication. Once this definition is established through the empirical investigation of word usage, we may reasonably infer from the fact that a particular thing or event is designated by 'culture' that probably that thing or event would be said to have the property of sustaining a symbolic relationship to the human

---

[7] For an illustration of the pre-definitional usage of 'culture,' the reader is referred to the table of contents of George P. Murdock, *et al.* (1950).

organism. It would appear that in addition to conforming to ordinary usage, the interchange of 'the class of all things and events dependent upon symbolling' for 'culture' would reduce the vagueness in the use of the latter term since there are no borderline cases between symbolling and nonsymbolling.

SUMMARY

The recent concern over the problem of defining 'culture' has been interpreted as a sign that cultural anthropology is becoming methodologically self-conscious. Some of the most characteristic features of natural language were discussed in order to illustrate the need for and functions of definitions. This led into a consideration of the nature, types, and formal criteria of definitions. These criteria were used as the basis for evaluating seven alternative formulations of a definition of 'culture.' The results of this analysis revealed that some terminological and conceptual modification is necessary before any of these formulations could be said to meet the formal criteria for definitions.

BIBLIOGRAPHY

ABERLE, DAVID F., ALBERT K. COHEN, ARTHUR K. DAVIS, MARION J. LEVY, JR., and FRANCIS X. SUTTON
   1950 "The Functional Prerequisites of a Society." *Ethics,* 60:100–111.
BENEDICT, RUTH
   1945 *Race, Science and Politics.* Revised edition. New York, The Viking Press.
BLACK, MAX
   1952 *Critical Thinking.* New York, Prentice-Hall, Inc.
CARNAP, RUDOLF
   1955 "Foundations of Logic and Mathematics." *International Encyclopedia of Unified Science,* 1:139–214.
COHEN, MORRIS R. AND ERNEST NAGEL
   1934 *An Introduction to Logic and Scientific Method.* New York, Harcourt, Brace and Company.
COPI, IRVING
   1953 *Introduction to Logic.* New York, The Macmillan Company.

DAVIS, ALLISON
1948 *Social-Class Influences upon Learning.* Cambridge, Harvard University Press.

DOLLARD, JOHN
1939 "Culture, Society, Impulse, and Socialization." *American Journal of Sociology,* 45:50–63.

FORD, JAMES A.
1949 "Cultural Dating of Prehistoric Sites in Virú Valley, Peru." In "Surface Survey of the Virú Valley, Peru," by James A. Ford and Gordon R. Willey, pp. 29–89. *Anthropological Papers of the American Museum of Natural History,* 43(1):1–89.

GOLDSTEIN, LEON J.
1957 "On Defining Culture." *American Anthropologist,* 59:1075–1080.

GORER, GEOFFREY
1949 *The People of Great Russia.* London, Cresset Press.

HALLOWELL, A. IRVING
1945 "Sociopsychological Aspects of Acculturation." In *The Science of Man in the World Crisis,* ed. by Ralph Linton, pp. 171–200. New York, Columbia University Press.

HOCKETT, CHARLES
1950 "Language *and* Culture: A Protest." *American Anthropologist,* 52:113.

KROEBER, A. L.
1917 "The Superorganic." *American Anthropologist,* 19:163–213.

KROEBER, A. L. and CLYDE KLUCKHOHN
1952 "Culture: A Critical Review of Concepts and Definitions." *Papers of the Peabody Museum of American Archaeology and Ethnology, Harvard University,* 47(1).

LINTON, RALPH
1936 *The Study of Man.* New York, D. Appleton-Century Company, Inc.

LOWIE, ROBERT H.
1936 "Cultural Anthropology: A Science." *American Journal of Sociology,* 42:301–320.

MALINOWSKI, BRONISLAW
1931 "Culture." *Encyclopedia of the Social Sciences,* 4:621–646.

MOORE, OMAR K.
1952 "Nominal Definitions of 'Culture.'" *Philosophy of Science,* 19:245–256.

MURDOCK, GEORGE P.
1949 *Social Structure.* New York, The Macmillan Company.
MURDOCK, GEORGE P., *et al.*
1950 *Outline of Cultural Materials.* 3rd edition. New Haven, Human Relations Area Files.
QUINE, WILLARD V. O.
1953 *From a Logical Point of View.* Cambridge, Harvard University Press.
RADCLIFFE-BROWN, A. R.
1940 "On Social Structure." *Journal of the Royal Anthropological Institute,* 70:1–12.
SAPIR, EDWARD
1924 "Culture, Genuine and Spurious." *American Journal of Sociology,* 29:401–429.
SPIRO, MELFORD E.
1951 "Culture and Personality; The Natural History of a False Dichotomy." *Psychiatry,* 14:19–46.
STEWARD, JULIAN H.
1950 Area Research: Theory and Practice. *Social Science Research Council, Bulletin,* 63.
TAYLOR, WALTER W.
1948 A Study of Archaeology. *Memoirs of the American Anthropological Association,* 69.
WHITE, LESLIE A.
1949 *The Science of Culture.* New York, Farrar, Straus and Company.
1954 Review of A. L. Kroeber and Clyde Kluckhohn, "Culture: A Critical Review of Concepts and Definitions." *American Anthropologist,* 56:461–468.
WISSLER, CLARK
1916 "Psychological and Historical Interpretations for Culture." *Science,* 43:193–201.
1929 *An Introduction to Social Anthropology.* New York, Henry Holt and Company.
YOUNG, KIMBALL
1942 *Sociology: A Study of Society and Culture.* New York, American Book Company.

* * * *

Stephen C. Cappannari

WAYNE STATE UNIVERSITY

THE CONCEPT OF PROPERTY

AMONG SHOSHONEANS [1]

Much of the literature pertaining to economic anthropology reveals considerable disagreement concerning the nature of property conceptions among various primitive peoples. Whether the forms
taken by property in diverse cultures may be quantitatively or qualitatively differentiated from those in civil society has been an important
issue. Discussion of this particular question has often generated more
heat than light, especially when it has manifested political controversy
rather than scientific disagreement. (Cf. Herskovits 1952:330.) A phrase
such as "primitive communism," as Herskovits indicates, has become
charged with emotional content, and the discovery of "primitive communism" in low cultures has been used to support the philosophy of devout Communism just as the discovery of "high gods" in low cultures has
been interpreted as being in conformance with the religious view of a
devout Catholic.

In addition to its association with political controversy, the idea of
"primitive communism" is also related to a nonpolitical scientific issue,

[1] The term "Shoshonean" is used here to refer inclusively to all tribes who speak Shoshonean languages and should not be confused with "Shoshoni," the name of one of
these tribes. This paper is, in part, adapted from my Doctoral Dissertation (with the
same title) which was submitted to the University of California (Berkeley) in 1950.
The Kawaiisu ethnographic data referred to were obtained separately in the field
by Maurice L. Zigmond and Stephen C. Cappannari. Dr. Zigmond's field work was
financed by Yale University and mine by the University of California. Subsequent
collaboration with Zigmond was financed by the Wenner-Gren Foundation for
Anthropological Research.

namely, the evolution of culture. In this connection Morgan's early descriptions of "primitive communism" (1881) are strikingly similar to Bunzel's, fifty years later, when she writes of the Zuni:

The economic unit is the household, whose nature and methods of function illustrate admirably certain very fundamental Zuni attitudes. . . . The household owns certain cultivated fields which cannot be alienated. In addition, the various male members individually own certain fields—generally fields recently brought under cultivation—which remain their own after they have severed connection with the household. However, all fields, whether collectively or individually owned, are cultivated by the cooperative labor of the entire male population of the household. The products go into the common storeroom to become the collective property of the women of the household. The women draw on the common stores for daily food and trade the surplus for other commodities. Sheep are owned individually by men but are herded cooperatively by groups of male kindred. When the profits of the shearing are divided a man is expected out of these to provide clothing for himself, his wife and children, including children by previous marriages, and his mother and unmarried sisters, in case they are not otherwise provided for (Bunzel 1932:447).

Evolutionary theorists have drawn from such ethnographic studies of contemporary tribal people as well as from prehistoric data to provide evidence for cultural evolution. Implicit in the varied terminology employed by cultural evolutionists to characterize early stages of cultural development, such as *savagery, societas, kinship society,* and the like, has been the idea of a period of "primitive communism" which precedes (evolutionarily and not necessarily historically) modern society.

If one abandons, on grounds of looseness and ambiguity, such terms as "primitive communism," there remain to the present day many important problems in the characterization of property rights within diverse cultures and in the assessment of their comparative significance. The present paper is concerned especially with a few of the characterizations and interpretations of property rights in the literature examined in the light of data from certain of the Shoshoneans.

It is, then, the thesis of this paper that property rights among some of the Shoshonean speaking groups differ *basically* from property rights among other, more advanced, societies. Among the former, and in contrast to the latter, kinship and personal ties form the basis for access to natural resources and the distribution of goods. This paper is not designed as a study in cultural evolution, but should its thesis be correct, it would be consistent with the evolutionary view that certain contemporary societies exemplify earlier evolutionary stages of cultural development. Furthermore, I shall attempt to demonstrate that distinctions which are pertinent to cultural evolutionary theory or the development of cross-culturally valid economic theory may be obscured by the ethnocentric application of economic terms derived from our own culture to other cultures.

I shall use the term "property" as a thing or service which can satisfy a need, which quantitatively represents human labor and which functions in an economic context. This paper will refer to some of the Shoshonean-speaking groups of North America, most of whom reside in the Great Basin and Plateau, but who inhabit also parts of California and the Southwest. These include the Kawaiisu, Tubatulabal, Ute, Gosiute, Pauite, Shoshoni, and Hopi. Only casual reference will be made to the sedentary agricultural Hopi who differ culturally in a number of important respects from their linguistic affiliates. For sharper contrast with civil society the emphasis here is upon tribes with extremely low cultural status, and there is nothing novel in this characterization of some of these peoples. In a paper discussing cultural connections between Plateau Shoshoneans and California tribes, Lowie writes: "The simpler representatives of this ultra-montane group, stripped of special environmental adaptations, probably came as close as any Indians of recent periods to the primeval North American culture, and this fact, irrespective of the lack of color incident to rudeness, lends to their study a peculiar fascination" (Lowie 1923:156). More recently, Steward's characterization of certain Shoshonean groups similarly emphasizes cultural poverty (Steward 1939a:524).

Among the marginal subsistence tribes who practise no agriculture, the western Kawaiisu of south-central California may be said to "hold" fairly definite territory in the same sense in which they believe their neighboring tribes, such as the Yokuts to the west or the Tubatulabal to the north, hold territory. However, as Steward points out for western Shoshonean groups in general, the boundaries between groups are not usually clearly defined by these Indians themselves. Such "boundaries" may refer to land which is uninhabited and seldom visited by anyone, or it may be land occupied in common by members of two neighboring tribes (Steward 1939b).

The Kawaiisu lack any tradition of migration. Within the territory they occupy are numerous landmarks such as caves, cliffs, springs, rocks, or trees which figure prominently in their mythology. It is the importance of these features to the Kawaiisu which tends to identify them with their territory rather than the exclusion of others.

Scarcity of land *per se* is not here an issue for a Kawaiisu population of perhaps 500 persons. Moreover, the incursion of other groups into Kawaiisu territory was commonly acceptable, as were visits by Kawaiisu, for economic purposes, into territory occupied by others. In their studies of tribal distributions ethnographers have not made it clear that the areas which they assign to groups do not coincide with their areas of economic exploitation. (Cf. Steward 1939b.)

In what sense, then, do rights in land constitute property for the Kawaiisu? It is not so much the land itself that is considered valuable, but the plant and animal life that it yields. "To the hunter, as Sumner aptly remarks, land laws are really game laws" (Seagle 1941:54). For the Kawaiisu, however, it is not easy to establish the presence of such laws. Expeditions for salt, piñons, and obsidian were conducted freely into neighboring territory without any stigma of trespass. Free movement of south central California tribes into occupied territory was not, however, an invariable rule. Kawaiisu skirmishes with the neighboring Yokuts of California (their center was near the present city of Bakersfield), although not common, were by no means unknown. In one such incident, several Kawaiisu men were ambushed and two killed when they entered Yokuts territory to hunt antelope. Continuous hostility between these two groups did not exist for both intertribal trade and marriages did take place. Voegelin (1938) does not mention instances of hostility due to trespass among the neighboring Tubatulabal. The Ute of Utah Lake are reported to own and defend their territory against trespass by other Ute, Paiute, and Gosiute (Steward 1938:227). Similarly, trespass by hunters upon adjacent territory led to fighting among the Surprise Valley Paiute who inhabit the northern border of California and Nevada and southern Oregon (Kelly 1932:70).

Presentation of data from other groups of Shoshonean-speaking hunters would be tedious and would serve only to confirm the picture which is emerging. I agree with Hobhouse that one should not speak of property at all when all the world alike can use something (Hobhouse 1922:7). But here, under special circumstances, members of other tribes may be denied access to occupied territory and in this sense one may speak of holdings in land for these peoples (cf. Hoebel 1949:335). This type of land holding may also be characterized as "inalienable" provided one understands that the question of "alienability" probably never arose here in pre-Caucasian times.

Of more importance for the thesis of this paper is the fact that persons *within* the Shoshonean group have equal access to the resources of nature. Nor do rights in land give rise to political power or control over the services of others, as is the case in some more advanced cultures.

It is evident that habitual utilization of a food area by a people does not itself lead automatically to the notion of excluding others. Steward does, however, suggest that habitual use led to village ownership of pine-nut tracts by the Shoshoni of the Ione and Reese River Valleys in Nevada. He suggests further that the populations were dense, stable, and "able to get all essential foods within a small radius of the village" (Steward 1938: 106). In a case such as this, exclusion of others seems to be largely a matter of convenience. Where pine-nut tracts are abundant, this becomes a system of apportionment which promotes the common good, in that no one has to go far for pine nuts if he restricts himself to the use of tracts located near his own village. The Shoshoni of the Kawich Mountains were directed by one of their chiefs where to gather pine-nuts when they were scarce, but families gathered where they liked in times of abundance (Steward 1938). Under conditions of scarcity, then, a family here may be said to hold a temporary gathering right in that pine-nut tract indicated to them by their chief.

The Shoshoni regulations concerning access to wild food, then, reflect factors of natural scarcity and abundance in terms of promoting the welfare of all members of the group. Hoebel has succinctly summarized Steward's argument as follows:

Steward has given an admirable explanation of the situation in terms of ecological factors. The uncertainty and variability of the pine-nut and wild seed crops are so great that the territories exploited by different groups varied greatly from year to year. When there were good crops in any locality, they ripened so fast and fell to the ground so quickly that the people who ordinarily lived in the area could not possibly gather them all. When a good harvest was promised, they therefore spread the news abroad, so that people whose crops had failed could come to share their bounty with them. "Under such conditions," notes Steward, "ownership of vegetable resources would have been a disadvantage to everyone" (Hoebel 1949:333).

Among these Shoshoni, then, available vegetable resources were utilized in a manner designed to promote equally the survival of all the members of the group.

Kinship and personal ties related to the free gathering of wild foods are not always distributed territorially on the *tribal* level. Steward characterizes the Owens Valley Paiute of northern Nevada as being fairly homogeneous culturally but differentiated by habitat and dialect. He describes these Paiute as being subdivided into political districts ". . . each with communistic hunting and seed rights, political unity, and a number of villages." [2] Trespass by others into the pine-nut territory "owned" by a

---

[2] Steward has employed the term "district" differently in different contexts. "District" connotes political significance as applied to the Owens Valley Paiute but his division of Western Shoshoni Territory into "districts" refers chiefly to natural subsistence areas ". . . having slight solidarity but not all being named" (Steward 1939b:262).

district was resented and led to quarrels or rock throwing although permission to gather nuts was sometimes given to members of other districts (Steward 1933:236, 241).

It should be made explicit here that holdings of pine-nut territory by subdivisions of the Paiute, rather than by larger and tenuous groups of Paiute, does not negate the thesis that access to vegetable resources follows personal and kin ties.

The hunting of animals and allocation of game follow essentially the same lines as presented for gathering. The general picture is one of a hunter sharing his game with a considerable number of relatives, neighbors, and friends, this being greatly emphasized among the Northern Shoshoni. There is considerable variation in the extent of the claim of other persons upon a given hunter's booty. Among the Kawaiisu the head and hide of a deer went to the one of several Kawaiisu hunters whose arrow actually brought down the animal, although its flesh was evenly apportioned. The hunter who seemed reluctant to share his catch with friends and relatives might be subjected to ridicule or ostracism. In some cases he was shamed when those to whom he had been niggardly reciprocated with exaggerated generosity.

The proceeds of communal hunting were distributed in different ways, both with regard to the different game taken and by different tribes. Sometimes the spoils were evenly distributed, while in other instances the organizer of the hunt, or the shaman whose hunting magic lured the game, was rewarded beyond the amount distributed to other participants in the hunt. In the Hopi communal rabbit hunt, a participant was entitled only to the animals he personally dispatched. In some cases, then, the luck or skill of the individual hunter or leader was specially rewarded. On the whole, however, the claims of people, based upon kinship or friendship, upon the spoils of the chase, remains impressive. The network of interpersonal relations was more influential in the distribution of game than was any evaluation of the products of the chase.

The pattern for the distribution of fish is similar to that for game. Where an individual had charge of a trap or weir, he was usually rewarded by a larger share of fish.

In no instance among any of the Shoshonean groups referred to in this paper was land property held for power, in the sense that it gave rise to control over the services of others. (For a discussion of the distinction between use and power see Hobhouse 1922:22; Philbrick 1938:697.)

The existence of personally owned chattels in low cultures has received considerable emphasis in recent ethnographic literature although such personal possessions usually are virtually devoid of economic significance. This emphasis upon private property in personal possessions of primitives does serve to bolster the idea that private property is generally very much alike the world over. By present-day standards, the "personal property" of a Shoshonean was meager indeed. However, Shoshoneans ordinarily "owned" individually some clothing, ornaments, implements, weapons, tools and the like. People commonly lent personal possessions to their children or friends, but in most instances permission to borrow was required. Concerning such chattels elsewhere Lowie states, "Movable property is generally owned by individuals on the principle that one has a right to whatever one has produced." He continues, "This fact is attested by various collectors who found it impossible to buy coveted ethnographica, no matter how commonplace, in the rightful owner's absence" (Lowie 1949:356). A similar explanation for this type of ownership is offered by Hoebel, who terms it "the principle of individual effort" (1949:344; see also Hartland 1924:92). The limitations of this "principle" are evident if we remember that the diamond-cutter does not own a diamond because he has cut it any more than the King's baker owns blackbird pie he has baked for his lord. (For a relevant discussion of metaphysical explanations of culture see White 1949:399–401.) In addition to the "principle of individual effort" Hoebel offers an additional and psychological explanation for certain types of chattels. Rather than referring to the labor expended, he notes the "psychological identity between the artisan and his creation, as though it were an extension of his personality . . . the personal attribute attached to property is an incorporeal element that is almost a property feature in itself" (*ibid.*).

In some cases the artisan may well feel a sense of identity with his creation. But the point is of course that his creation becomes *his* "property" in terms of cultural factors, not psychological ones. The fallacy of this type of explanation has been discussed fully elsewhere (see especially White 1947 and Herskovits 1952:328–9).

There are abundant examples of the coincidence of "manufacture" and "ownership" of objects among Shoshoneans but this does not constitute a necessary connection. Moreover, similar sanctions apply to chattels that have been obtained through inheritance, gift, or trade. The "principle of individual effort" is simplistic and ignores the socio-cultural context within which property acquires meaning. As one sociologist puts it:

The other idea was that a man made a thing his own—providing it was not yet appropriated—by putting his labor into it. But this qualification left the doctrine of property as unrealistic, as remote from the facts of social life, as it was before. . . . It . . . neglected the relation of property to inheritance. It vindicated the property of utopia, not of the present world, or even of the remotest past (MacIver 1946:7, 8).

On the one hand, it is both appropriate and useful to examine cross-culturally property concepts derived from Western industrial society. On the other hand, as has been posited in this paper, the indiscriminate application of terminology derived from industrial societies to simpler peoples may serve to obscure the meaning of property rights among the latter. A striking instance of such misapplication is furnished by anthropological usage of the term "incorporeal property."

Thus, Lowie regards the exclusion of females from the right to eat human flesh, to wear masquerade costumes, or to play sacred flutes, as instances of male incorporeal property (Lowie 1949:361). In similar fashion the right to tell a particular myth, perform a ceremony or to sing a song has been labeled either "incorporeal" property or "intangible" property (Hoebel 1942; Hallowell 1943; Bunzel 1938:348–9). To begin with, the writer believes these terms are misleading even when applied to modern society. But even worse, when used as they have been in the instances just cited, they serve to obliterate useful and important distinctions in the property rights of different cultures.

In the cases cited above, transactions in such "incorporeal" property do not often occur and when they do occur, they lack the commercial significance which characterizes transactions in "incorporeal" property in industrial societies. Not only do the former lack *commercial* significance, they do not even function *economically* at all, in the usual sense of that term. They form part of the "prestige economy" as DuBois has defined that term. In her discussion of the wealth concept she makes the following pertinent distinction:

By subsistence economy is meant the exploitation of the plentiful natural resources available to any industrious individual. . . . By prestige economy on the other hand, is meant a series of social prerogatives and status values. They included a large range of phenomena from wives to formulae for supernatural compulsion. They embraced mourners' privileges and innumerable personal dignities, the disregard of which was cause for compensation regardless of intent (Dubois 1936:50).

Parenthetically, DuBois also makes clear that the "monies" (that is, dentalia, woodpecker scalps, obsidian blades, and so on) of the Tolowa-Tututni served as a medium of exchange primarily in the prestige economy rather than the subsistence economy (*ibid.*). The same applies to the "monies" of the Shoshoneans.

Labeling the right to sing a song or to wear masquerade costumes "incorporeal" property thus obscures the noncommercial and noneconomic nature of such property. These socio-psychological rights in a prestige economy differ qualitatively and quantitatively from "incorporeal" property as the term is generally used by lawyers or economists. Modern "incorporeal" property refers not only to our subsistence economy but plays a major role in it. "As a matter of fact, the total value under our law today of proprietary rights which have no material object is probably enormously greater than the value of such rights in all land and tangible chattels. This modern incorporeal property includes, particularly, promissory notes, bills of exchange, patent rights, and shares of corporate stock" (Philbrick 1938:692). To be sure, it is incorrect to say that such "incorporeal" or "intangible" property really lacks reference to "material objects." Patent rights or stocks are papers but these pieces of paper do stand for hi-fi sets or Chevrolets or portions of steel plants and these are hardly "intangible" or "incorporeal." Misleading as these terms are when applied to modern society, they become grotesque when applied to the cultural level of Shoshoneans.

SUMMARY

The right of access to the resources of nature follows personal and kin ties among Shoshoneans. Shoshoneans have property rights or holdings in land but these differ profoundly from land ownership in modern societies. Among Shoshoneans private ownership of natural resources nowhere excludes people from access to the resources of nature. Nowhere among these Shoshoneans does "ownership" of any sort give rise to coercive power over other persons. If the term "primitive communism" must be abandoned because it has become ambiguous and emotionally laden, a new term should be devised to characterize a way of life, such as that enjoyed by the Shoshoneans and by similar societies. Closer inspection of alleged "incorporeal" property in primitive society reveals such property to be noncommercial, outside the "subsistence economy" and merely part of the "prestige economy." The usage of such terms derived from modern economies and functioning in different contexts, thus obscures fundamental distinctions in different societies. Such distinctions are necessary for the construction of a cross-culturally valid science of economics and for studies in the evolution culture.

BIBLIOGRAPHY

BEAGLEHOLE, ERNEST O.
1937 "Notes on Hopi Economic Life." *Yale University Publications in Anthropology*, 15.

BUNZEL, RUTH L.
1932 "Introduction to Zuñi Ceremonialism." *Forty-seventh Annual Report of the Bureau of American Ethnology* (1929–1930):467–544.
1938 "The Economic Organization of Primitive Peoples." In *General Anthropology*, ed. by Franz Boas, pp. 327–408. Boston, D. C. Heath and Company.

COLTON, HAROLD S.
1934 "A Brief Survey of Hopi Common Law." *Museum Notes, Museum of Northern Arizona*, 7(6):21–24.

DIAMOND, A. S.
1935 *Primitive Law*. London, Longmans, Green and Co.

DUBOIS, CORA
1936 "The Wealth Concept as an Integrative Factor in Tolowa-Tututni Culture." In *Essays in Anthropology Presented to A. L. Kroeber*, pp. 49–65. Berkeley, University of California Press.

FORDE, C. DARYLL
1931 "Hopi Agriculture and Land Ownership." *Journal of the Royal Anthropological Institute*, 61:375–405.

HALLOWELL, A. I.
1943 "The Nature and Function of Property as a Social Institution." *Journal of Legal and Political Sociology*, 1:115–138.

HARTLAND, E. S.
1924 *Primitive Law*. London, Methuen & Co., Ltd.

HERSKOVITS, MELVILLE J.
1952 *Economic Anthropology*. New York, Alfred A. Knopf, Inc.

HOBHOUSE, L. T.
1922 "The Historical Evolution of Property, in Fact and in Idea." In *Property, Its Duties and Rights*, pp. 3–31. New edition. New York, The Macmillan Company.

HOEBEL, E. ADAMSON
1942 "Fundamental Legal Concepts as Applied in the Study of Primitive Law." *Yale Law Journal*, 51:951–963.
1948 "Anthropology of Inheritance." In *The Inheritance of Property and the Power of Testamentary Disposition*, by E. A. Hoebel,

A. A. Friedrich, P. W. Tappan, and J. Nathanson ("The Social Meaning of Legal Concepts," No. 1), pp. 5–53. New York, New York University School of Law.

1949 *Man in the Primitive World.* New York, McGraw-Hill Book Company, Inc.

KELLY, ISABEL T.

1932 "Ethnography of the Surprise Valley Paiute." *University of California Publications in American Archaeology and Ethnology,* 31:67–210.

LEWIŃSKI, JAN ST.

1913 *The Origin of Property and the Formation of the Village Community.* London, Constable & Company Ltd.

LOWIE, ROBERT H.

1923 "The Cultural Connection of California and Plateau Shoshonean Tribes." *University of California Publications in American Archaeology and Ethnology,* 20:145–156.

1949 "Property among the Tropical Forest and Marginal Tribes." *Bureau of American Ethnology Bulletin 143, Handbook of South American Indians,* ed. by Julian H. Steward, 5:351–367

MACIVER, ROBERT M.

1946 "Government and Property." *Journal of Legal and Political Sociology,* 4:5–18.

MORGAN, LEWIS HENRY

1881 "Houses and House-Life of the American Aborigines." *U. S. Geographical and Geological Survey of the Rocky Mountain Region. Contributions to North American Ethnology,* 4.

PARSONS, ELSIE CLEWS, ED.

1936 "Hopi Journal of Alexander M. Stephen." *Columbia University Contributions to Anthropology,* 23, 2 Parts.

PHILBRICK, F. S.

1938 "Changing Conceptions of Property in Law." *University of Pennsylvania Law Review,* 86:691–732.

SEAGLE, WILLIAM

1941 *The Quest for Law.* New York, Alfred A. Knopf, Inc.

STEWARD, JULIAN H.

1933 "Ethnography of the Owens Valley Paiute." *University of California Publications in American Archaeology and Ethnology,* 33:233–350.

1938 "Basin-Plateau Aboriginal Sociopolitical Groups." *Bureau of American Ethnology Bulletin,* 120.

Stephen C. Cappannari

Stephen C. Cappannari

1939a "Changes in Shoshonean Indian Culture." *Scientific Monthly,* 49:524–537.

1939b "Some Observations on Shoshonean Distributions." *American Anthropologist,* 41:261–265.

TITIEV, MISCHA

1944 "Old Oraibi. A Study of the Hopi Indians of Third Mesa." *Papers of the Peabody Museum of American Archaeology and Ethnology, Harvard University,* 22(1).

VOEGELIN, ERMINIE W.

1938 "Tübatulabal Ethnography." *Anthropological Records,* 2(1):1–90.

WHITE, LESLIE A.

1947 "Culturological *vs.* Psychological Interpretations of Human Behavior." *American Sociological Review,* 12:686–698.

1949 *The Science of Culture.* New York, Farrar, Straus and Company.

ZIGMOND, MAURICE L.

1938 "Kawaiisu Territory." *American Anthropologist,* 40:634–638.

* * * *

Robert L. Carneiro

AMERICAN MUSEUM OF NATURAL HISTORY

THE CULTURE PROCESS

In recent years anthropologists have given evidence of becoming increasingly concerned with process as it is manifested in culture. Not only has the term process been employed more frequently in discussions, it has also appeared in the title of a number of theoretical papers (for example, Barnett 1940; Herskovits 1945; Spencer 1958; Steward 1953; White 1948, 1950). Despite this widespread concern with process, however, seldom does an anthropologist tell us exactly what he means or understands by the term when he uses it. What, after all, is process? What is the culture process? How does it differ from history? Are there laws of the culture process? These are questions I should like to consider in this essay.

THE CONCEPT OF PROCESS

Process, as a general phenomenon, may be defined as the interaction through time of the elements of a system as the system changes from one state to another. This interaction proceeds in determinate ways, which is to say that it is an expression of underlying natural laws. In order to make this characterization of process clearer and more distinct let us examine some of its major terms: *elements, system, state of a system,* and *natural laws.*

The *elements* of a system are simply the structural units that make it up. What kinds of units are found in a system depends, first of all, on the nature of the system being examined. If we are dealing with astronomical systems, our units will be such things as planets, asteroids, binary stars, magellanic clouds, spiral nebulae, and the like. If we are studying living systems, our concern will be with organs, glands, muscles, nerves, reflex arcs, and so forth.

Nevertheless, the scientist working within each realm of nature exercises a certain amount of choice regarding the type of units which he will admit to the system he is investigating. He does this arbitrarily—by stipulation—on the basis of his theoretical orientation and his objectives. For example, human psychology and culturology both begin with the same raw data: things and events in the life of the human species.[1] But each science conceptualizes them in a different way. The psychologist sees human behavior in terms of drives, anxieties, repressions, compulsions, projections, and phenomena of a similar sort. The culturologist, on the other hand, focuses his attention on cultural elements as such: the division of labor, cannibalism, hunting magic, plow agriculture, cross-cousin marriage, and the like. To be sure, all cultural elements have psychological concomitants, and the culturologist in no way means to deny or obscure this fact. He simply asserts that cultural elements can be legitimately and fruitfully studied in and of themselves, as a separate, or, more precisely, as a *conceptually separable* class of phenomena.

We may define a *system* as a set of structurally and functionally related elements articulated into a working whole. A system is thus more than its constituent units; it is these *plus* (or better, *times*) their interrelations. Our solar system is not merely the sun, the planets with their respective moons, and the comets and other minor bodies; it consists as well of the ways in which these bodies are related to each other in space and time. By the same token, the 1,447 culture traits listed for the Papago in the California Anthropological Records (Drucker 1941) are not the same thing as the Papago cultural system. Members of the class of phenomena labeled "cultural" are not equivalent to culture as an organization of interacting cultural elements. It is in this sense that "the whole is greater than the sum of its parts."

The entire network of elements and patterns of interrelations of a system at a single point in time constitutes the *state of the system*. A system may be studied and described synchronically, as it exists at one moment in time; or it may be studied diachronically, as it assumes successively different states over time. When one examines a system completely synchronically—as he would, for example, in studying the structure of a

---

[1] "Psychology and culturology deal . . . with biological and extra-somatic aspects respectively of one and the same set of events" (White 1949:145).

crystal, or the categories of relationship shown on a kinship diagram—he sees only pattern or configuration, not process. The essence of process is change of some kind,[2] and for change to occur, time must of course elapse.

Pattern and configuration are not, however, unrelated to process. Indeed we may think of process as a very rapid succession of synchronic states of a system, each one only slightly modified over the preceding one. Viewed in this way a process is much like a motion picture in which one still frame succeeds another, producing the effect of change with continuity. The study of process is, in effect, the study of how the state of a system at one point in time, with its particular patterns and configurations, becomes transformed into a different state at a later point in time. Process, one might say, is pattern undergoing change.

At the root of the order, regularity, and determinateness in the behavior of a system lie *natural laws;* a system may be said to manifest or express these laws. One of the principal objectives in studying ongoing process in a system is to formulate the laws that are operative in it. Scientific understanding of a process is achieved when it can be shown to be the necessary consequence of known laws.

THE CULTURE PROCESS

The culture process can now be defined as the interaction, within a system, of elements belonging to the class of cultural phenomena. This process has been vividly described by Leslie White (1950:76) as

a stream of interacting cultural elements—of instruments, beliefs, customs, etc. In this interactive process, each element impinges upon others and is in turn acted upon by them. The process is a competitive one: instruments, customs, and beliefs may become obsolete and eliminated from the stream. New elements are incorporated from time to time. New combinations and syntheses —inventions and discoveries—of cultural elements are continually being formed. . . .

Considered in its broadest terms the culture process comprises all of the interactions that have occurred among cultural elements throughout the course of human history. If we regard it in this way, the flow of culture is seen as a great and unitary process, embracing all cultural

---

[2] Systems undergo two fundamentally different types of change which may be called *state-restoring* and *state-transforming*. A state-restoring change is one by means of which the system reestablishes a previous condition of balance or equilibrium which has been temporarily disturbed. A state-transforming change is one which brings about a new and different state in the system.

traditions in all periods and all places. We need not of course deal with the process as integral and indivisible. We can arbitrarily, but quite justifiably, delimit a particular segment of the culture process and proceed to investigate it by itself. Thus one can study the culture process in operation over restricted sectors of time and space: in the Nile Valley between 4000 B.C. and 324 A.D., in Western Europe during the Middle Ages, or on the Trobriand Islands in 1915.

In addition to delimiting it spatially and temporally, we can analyze the culture process logically into a number of constituent subprocesses. Just as biologists in their study of the life process as a whole have found it useful to isolate and define a number of more restricted processes, such as digestion, respiration, circulation, and so forth, cultural anthropologists in their study of the total culture process have found it convenient to analyze it into such constituent processes as evolution, invention, diffusion, acculturation, integration, segmentation, and many more. If we were to look at the matter from the point of view of synthesis rather than of analysis, we would say that the culture process as a whole consists of all of these component smaller processes, each of which functions in its own right, and at the same time interacts with and contributes to other processes. As A. L. Kroeber expressed it:

. . . these several processes, which in the abstract seem so neat and distinctive, are found to manifest themselves in association and interwoven. All of them are often at work at once, so that the same phenomenon may be seen as an example of two or three of them. This constant interrelation of processes is characteristic of culture (1948:344).

HISTORY AND THE CULTURE PROCESS

The concept of the culture process as it is entertained in anthropology can perhaps be better understood if we compare it with the concept of past human events held by members of another academic discipline, namely, history. The datum of these two disciplines is the same: "what actually happened," and the unit of "happening" for both is the event. Now each event is of course unique. This is no less true of a drinking bout or a funerary rite observed in the field by an ethnographer than it is of Napoleon's victory at Austerlitz or the destruction of Carthage by the Romans. Each of these events, in its full particularity, happened only once and will never recur.

The uniqueness of historical events is a quality which the professional historian not only recognizes, but apparently finds himself unable to transcend. The historian who studies the death of Caesar deals with it as a singular and distinctive occurrence. To him it is precisely the characteristics setting it off from all other events—the time, the place, the mode of death, the last words of the great man, the thoughts and emotions of those involved—that arouse his interest and command his attention.

The approach of the student of the culture process to this or to any other event is quite different. The uniqueness of historical events is of course not denied, but no longer is it their primary and inescapable feature. In fact, an event now attains significance only as it can be subsumed under a general class of cultural phenomena having other representatives.[3] Caesar's death would thus be placed in the context of political assassinations, or of conflicts for power in autocratic states, or some similar category. Only then would it begin to take on scientific, as opposed to merely historical, interest.

The same point has been made by White using a different example:

> Let us say that we are studying insurrections from the functionalist [in this context, culture process] point of view. We would therefore be interested in insurrection A not because it is unique (which of course it actually is) but precisely because it resembles other insurrections. Time and place are irrelevant; we do not care whether the uprising took place in May or December, in France or in Russia. What we are interested in is insurrections in general; we want to formulate a generalization which will be applicable to all insurrections. We want a universal that will explain the particulars (1945:229).

But merely because anthropologists were the ones who originated and developed the concept of the culture process, it does not follow that all of them have been concerned with this process in their work.[4] Indeed, a good many anthropologists, like most historians, give the impression in their writings that their interest is with cultural facts *in and of themselves*. This concern is, of course, a difficult one to avoid or surpass. The real world, after all, consists of particulars, and it is with these that the scien-

---

[3] In the words of Bertrand Russell, "a fact, in science, is not a mere fact, but *an instance*" (1931:58; italics mine).

[4] For that matter, it must be acknowledged that not all historians have ignored the culture process either. For example, in the writings of James Harvey Robinson, one of the founders of the culturally-oriented "New History," one occasionally finds passages like the following: "every human institution, every generally accepted idea, every important invention is but the summation of long lines of progress, reaching back as far as we have the patience or means to follow them. The jury, the drama, the Gatling gun, the papacy, the letter S, the doctrine of *stare decisis*, each owes its present form to antecedents which can be scientifically traced" (1912:64). As another instance of a historian's awareness of and concern with the culture process the reader is referred to Lynn White's brief but illuminating discussion of the effect of the invention of the spinning wheel on the development and spread of printing (1956:73–74).

tist or the scholar must begin his study. Dealing with details, furthermore, tends to heighten one's awareness of the peculiarity and uniqueness of things. Kroeber studies the history and distribution of the double-headed eagle and, finding it an intricate matter, feels compelled to say: "There is practically nothing in the history of civilization of which we can affirm that it must happen, and which we can therefore predict, except perhaps occasionally on the very threshold of an event. Each case has to be worked out for what did actually happen . . ." (1948:475).

Kroeber, a student of Franz Boas, wrote of his teacher that his "one constant objective" was "process, rigorously determined process" (1935: 541). Nevertheless, if we are to judge by what Boas himself wrote, that which impressed him most about things and events was their particularity and intricacy. After half a century of painstaking and detailed research on myth motifs, needle cases, linguistic texts, and the like, he concluded that "the phenomena of our science are so individualized, so exposed to outer accident that no set of laws could explain them," and again, that "cultural phenomena are of such complexity that it seems . . . doubtful whether valid cultural laws can be found" (1932:612).[5]

To me, Boas' considered judgment seems unduly pessimistic. The rest of the world of nature is, after all, no different in these respects from the world of culture. It, too, is complex, and in it, too, phenomena are individualized. Nevertheless, regularities and laws have been found in the behavior of natural phenomena because they were studied *from the point of view of science*. When things and events are investigated in this way individuality gives way to types and classes, and unique series to formulations of process. This is certainly not a new discovery. The issue was seen clearly and expressed succinctly by Henry Thomas Buckle fully a century ago.

In regard to nature, events apparently the most irregular and capricious have been explained, and have been shown to be in accordance with certain fixed and universal laws. This has been done because men of ability, and, above all, men of patient, untiring thought, have studied natural events *with the view of discovering their regularity:* and if human events were subjected to a similar treatment, we have every right to expect similar results [italics mine] (1857:6).

The tendency to particularize events rather than to generalize from them is, as we have seen, an important difference between the discipline

---

[5] As early as 1904, Boas had already expressed the same opinion: "The grand system of the evolution of culture, that is valid for all humanity, is losing much of its plausibility. In place of a simple line of evolution *there appear a multiplicity of converging and diverging lines which it is difficult to bring under one system. Instead of uniformity the striking feature seems to be diversity*" (1904:522; italics mine).

of history as it is conventionally practiced and the study of the culture process. But there are other differences as well. Perhaps the most important of these is that historians tend to select as their units of attention and description, actions in the lives of *people*. Students of the culture process, on the other hand, fix their attention not on people at all, but on customs, beliefs, tools, rituals, institutions, and so on, which by logical analysis they abstract from the total behavior of people. In a word, their concern is with *culture*.

This difference in the units chosen for description and analysis inevitably influences the way in which the two groups of scholars view the dynamics of the past. The question of determinism in historical events itself often finds anthropologists and historians in opposing camps. As scientists, anthropologists make almost constant use of the principle of determinism in human affairs. Historians, however, while not necessarily denying causation in history outright, frequently tend to minimize its role. Typical of this viewpoint is the remark of the British historian, H. A. L. Fisher, that the "only . . . safe rule for the historian [is] that he should recognize in the development of human destinies the play of the contingent and the unforeseen" (1939:xv).

To be sure, not all historians are so nondeterministic in outlook. Nevertheless, even those historians who accept the play of determinism in history see it operating in a much different manner than do students of the culture process. To conventional historians, the determinants of events are to be sought not in cultural forces but in the personal motivations of individuals: Bismarck's stubbornness, Napoleon's ambition, Richelieu's guile—these are the forces that make events and shape the course of history.

Seeing the motive forces of history on this level can hardly be escaped if, with Carlyle, one conceives of history as "the essence of innumerable biographies." But to the culturologist, whose units of study are, by specification, cultural elements rather than individuals, the causal links between events in the culture process cannot be personal motivations; they are necessarily *other events in the culture process*.

LEVELS OF ANALYSIS OF THE CULTURE PROCESS

We have noted that the culture process can be studied either as a whole or in its several aspects; at varying times and in different parts of the world. Similarly, the operation of the process can be investigated and represented at different levels of generality. One may choose to grapple with rather minute details of the process, or concern himself with the entire process in its broadest sweep. One student may direct his attention to the determinants of kinship terminology, while another may be concerned with the origin and development of civilization. And of course problems at any intermediate level of the culture process may be attacked. In fact the very same event (as "event" is commonly understood) is susceptible of description and explanation at several different levels of analysis. I believe there would be some value in illustrating this point, and I would like to use as an example the Protestant Reformation.

There is, first of all, the occurrence "as it actually happened in history." A description of the Reformation at this level would be phrased in terms of individuals and events in their lives. Since it would thus constitute an individual-biographical level of description, below even the most specific cultural level, we may, in the notational system to be employed here, designate it as L_0. At L_0 the Reformation is seen in terms of persons— Tetzel, Luther, Melanchthon, Zwingli, Calvin, etc.—whose actions generate significant events: the posting of the 95 Theses, the Edict of Worms, the Conference of Marburg, the Diet of Augsburg, and so forth.

If one "recreates" the Reformation in essentially these terms the result is conventional history. But one may choose instead to select or abstract cultural elements and sequences of cultural forms from the historical raw materials. If one focuses on these, a different picture of the Reformation emerges; it now becomes an episode in the culture process. Let us attempt to see what the Protestant Reformation looks like at three successively more general and abstract levels of the culture process, which we may call, respectively, L_1, L_2, and L_3.

At L_1, we see the Reformation as a transformation in the ecclesiastical organization of Northern Europe. At this level of analysis the event appears somewhat as follows: Differences of opinion arise within the Roman Catholic clergy over the propriety of certain doctrines, rites, and practices. The sphere of controversy, furthermore, extends to the basic question of how doctrinal disputes themselves are to be decided. The dissident faction favors personal interpretation of the Scriptures in direct opposition to the traditional and established practice of unique and final interpretation by the Pope. Attempts to modify church tenets and organization from within fail, and the movement ultimately goes outside of the established order and sets up new religious institutions with altered doctrines and practices.

At L_2, the Reformation is perceived not merely as a religious transformation, but as an event in a wider context, involving many other aspects of culture, some of which figure at least as prominently in the event as religious factors themselves. At this level of interpretation we see the institution of the Church being subjected not only to internal strains and stresses over doctrinal matters, but to a complex series of external pressures as well. The growing political power of the German states clashed with the temporal and religious power of the supranational Catholic Church. Secular and ecclesiastical competition arose over the control of church property and the revenues therefrom, the filling of clerical offices, and the like. With the beginning of industrial production and the expansion of commerce, church rules intended to limit economic activity, such as the prohibition on profit making and on the lending of money at interest, and the prescription of a large number of fast days and religious holidays, became unrealistic and unenforceable. The invention of the printing press created a new and effective medium for the dissemination of the radical ideas that were an expression of the growing incongruity between the old socioreligious institutions and the prevailing conditions of life. And so on. The reform which finally took place was, in the words of James Harvey Robinson, "essentially a stage in the disengaging of the modern [secular] state from [the] medieval, international ecclesiastical state. . . ." (1911:5).

This level of explanation not only includes more aspects of the culture process than the previous one, but also treats cultural elements as phenomena of a more general sort. A full description of the Reformation at L_1 would give much attention to particular elements, such as the sale of indulgences and the controversy over clerical celibacy—events more or less unique to the time and place. But at L_2 our concern is with more general phenomena, such as changes in ideas and attitudes brought about by new economic conditions, and the struggle for power between secular and religious institutions—features by no means restricted to sixteenth century Europe.

Nevertheless, while at L_2 many of the elements and forces of the culture process assume the status of recurring phenomena, the particular way in which they combined and interacted in the event known as the Protestant Reformation remains unique. But at L_3, a still higher level of analysis, the event as a whole—the entire Reformation—loses this uniqueness and becomes a member of a general class. At this level the Reformation assumes the characteristics of a well-known phenomenon: readjustment of the socioreligious structure to altered material conditions of existence. The story is a familiar one. The technological and economic aspects of culture change more readily and more rapidly than its social and religious aspects. Inevitably this brings about a disconformity between the two, which, when it reaches a certain magnitude, results in abrupt readjustive changes in social and religious institutions.

In some ways this last explanation is the most satisfactory of all, since it shows a particular occurrence to be an instance of the operation of a known principle or law. However, as has already been stated, one does not have to deal with the culture process at its maximum degree of generality. If our interests and objectives are more restricted, then approach to a cultural event at a lower level of analysis (L_1 or L_2) may be more appropriate and enlightening. And of course our interests and objectives often *are* restricted, and quite legitimately so. The student of the culture process is as entitled to concern himself with the formation of the eight-class system among the Arunta of aboriginal Australia as he is with the origin of the state. There is nothing in the concept of process *per se* that makes it any more characteristic of occurrences in which the phenomena are broad gauged than of occurrences where the phenomena are more narrowly conceived. Process is process, regardless of the level at which we study it.

REPETITION IN HISTORY AND IN THE CULTURE PROCESS

At this point in the argument something needs to be said about the repetition or recurrence of events in history and in the culture process. Let us begin by looking again at the "history of historians." The feeling of most historians seems to be that, contrary to popular notion, "history" does not repeat itself. And to be sure, if we accept the conception of history that sees events in their full particularity and therefore as unique, then history *cannot* repeat itself.

Events can be said to repeat themselves only when they are seen, not as singular occurrences, but as *instances*. This, as we have noted, is precisely the way in which events are conceived in the culture process. Caesar dies just once, but autocratic rulers are murdered again and again. The culture process thus does repeat itself. As a matter of fact, repetition is so common in the process that anthropologists take it as a matter of course. Virtually everywhere they look they see instances of segmentation, territorialization, centralization, secularization, industrialization, detribalization, the overthrow of monarchies, the growth of nationalism, the rise of nativistic movements, and so on.

Recurrences in the culture process go well beyond the repetition of simple or small-scaled events and processes; they are observable in long and complex series of events as well. An example of this may be cited. Julian Steward, in his well-known article, "Cultural Causality and Law" (1949), found that the rise of civilization in various areas of the world was so closely parallel that the phenomenon could be subsumed under the same series of successive stages wherever it had occurred.

Perhaps the most striking and instructive instances of the culture process repeating itself are provided by inventions and discoveries which were made independently and simultaneously two or more times. The meaning of these coincidences has been pointed out by White (1949:169–170) in the following words:

> Nothing demonstrates more clearly the nature of the culture process and its expression in significant episodes of cultural advance . . . than the phenomena of multiple and simultaneous, but independent, inventions and discoveries. . . . A culturological interpretation . . . readily makes them intelligible: when growing and converging lines of cultural development reach a certain point, fusion and synthesis will take place. If culture is advancing on a wide front, these syntheses will find two or more independent and approximately simultaneous expressions. The invention or discovery is explained therefore in terms of a growing and interactive culture process. . . .

LAWS OF HISTORY AND LAWS OF THE CULTURE PROCESS

Few professional historians appear to have made it their primary concern to seek out and set forth the larger trends and patterns of history. Fewer still have ventured to formulate *laws* of history. I know in fact of only two historians who have done so avowedly and explicitly. One of them, Edward P. Cheyney, took the occasion of his presidential address to the American Historical Association to enunciate six "laws of history" (Cheyney 1927:10–22). The other scholar to make such an attempt was the German historian, Kurt Breysig, who formulated no fewer than 35 "laws of history" (*Gesetze der Weltgeschichte*) (Breysig 1927:159–165). By any critical standards both these attempts were unsuccessful. Cheyney's "laws," upon examination, turn out to be either not laws at all in any rigorous sense, or else downright false, or both. Breysig's "laws" are in no instance even framed in the form of scientific laws. They are nothing more than hypothetical stages, most of them highly improbable at that.

Attempts to propound historical laws are, I repeat, not typical of members of the historical profession. The majority of historians have evidently felt as did Eduard Meyer, called in his day "the greatest of living historians" by Harry Elmer Barnes (1925:294), who maintained that "during many years of historical research, I myself have never discovered a law of history, nor have I encountered one found by anyone else" (1924:32).

It should not surprise us that historians have been unsuccessful in formulating generalizations about the course of history which are expressed in the form of scientific laws, and at the same time hold true. This failure appears inevitable in view of the conception of history that prevails among historians.[6] The nature of this conception and its relevance to the problem of "historical laws" was clearly stated by the Rumanian historian, Alexandru Xénopol, when he wrote: ". . . history deals only with phenomena individualized by time, that is to say, those that are produced but once in the course of the ages; . . . such a conception could not give rise to the formation of notions of laws, but only to that of unique and particular series" (1902:292).

If, then, there are no laws of "history," are there laws of the culture process?

We have already noted that cultural anthropologists, as practicing scientists, fully recognize the working of causation in human behavior. And if determinism does operate in this sphere of nature, then culture itself must exhibit a certain lawfulness. Some anthropologists, however, while granting that the course of culture may be strictly determined, have maintained that it comprises so many different cause-and-effect sequences, and forms such a vast and complex fabric that there are few discernible trends, and apparently no laws. And if laws do exist, they are either "obvious" or merely "truisms."[7]

Nonetheless, I believe it can be shown not only that there are laws of

---

[6] "The fact that there are no laws of history is due not to an intellectual weakness on the part of historians, nor to a lack of data, but to the very nature of history itself" (Meyer 1924:35).

[7] Boas, for example, maintained that "the material of anthropology is such that it needs must be a historical science, one of the sciences the interest of which centers in the attempt to understand the individual phenomena rather than in the establishment of general laws which, on account of the complexity of the material, will be necessarily vague and, we might almost say, so self-evident that they are of little help to a real understanding" (1932:612).

culture, but that these laws are more than tautologies or trivialities. I would argue, furthermore, that the reason why their existence is not more commonly recognized is not the complexity of the culture process so much as the lack of concern on the part of many anthropologists with the formulation of such laws. So intent, in fact, have anthropologists been in refuting purported laws of culture that among other social scientists, according to Murdock (1957:251), they have gained the reputation of being "a detestable bunch of bubble-prickers."

Before attempting to give examples of genuine laws of culture it seems appropriate to offer a definition of scientific law in general. A scientific law, as I understand it, is simply a statement of an invariant relation between two or more classes of phenomena under stated conditions. Assuming that this notion of a law is in accord with the consensus of scientific opinion and thus does not have to be defended here, let us present a few propositions about the culture process which appear to qualify as scientific laws.

Probably the proposed cultural law most familiar to anthropologists is that formulated by White (1949:368–369) relating energy and culture: "Other factors remaining equal, culture evolves as the amount of energy harnessed per capita per year is increased, or as the efficiency of the instrumental means of putting the energy to work is increased."

I would suggest that the following proposition is also a law of culture: Once the neolithic level of culture is attained, and warfare becomes intensified and redirected toward conquest and subjugation, the number of autonomous political units in the world decreases, and their size increases.

A third law of culture may be proposed: When a society achieves (a) the technical means for surplus production, and (b) a class of specialists capable of organizing and directing the labor of others, the majority of prisoners taken in war will no longer be killed for cannibalistic or sacrificial purposes, but will be exploited economically as slaves.

THE STATISTICAL FORMULATION
OF CULTURAL LAWS

The results of much of the recent work done in anthropology with the aim of discovering and formulating regularities in culture have been expressed in terms of statistical correlations. It is illuminating to investigate the relation between these correlations (or, more correctly, associations) and cultural laws. Attempts to work out correlations between cultural phenomena are of course nothing new to anthropology, having occupied the attention of students of the culture process from Tylor to Murdock. However, traditional endeavors along these lines almost invariably have had two shortcomings, which in the end come down to essentially the same thing. In the first place, scholars have correlated only single factors with the phenomenon being investigated and explained. And secondly, after obtaining positive correlations, they have tended to rest on their laurels rather than continuing to modify and refine their hypotheses in such a way as to raise the coefficients to the highest possible degree.

That continued refinement of hypotheses by the specification of additional relevant factors will yield correlations approaching +1.00 has been recognized and demonstrated by George P. Murdock in his book, *Social Structure* (1949). The significance of this demonstration for the science of culture is so great and yet so little commented on that I would like to examine the pertinent passages in some detail.

After presenting in tabular form the set of correlations (all of them positive) that he obtained from statistical tests of his 30 Theorems and Propositions, Murdock writes as follows:

Although the above results are perhaps unprecedented in social science, they by no means do justice to the actual possibilities. It must be remembered that multiple factors are operative in every instance, but that in most of our theorems we have isolated only a single factor for analysis. If several factors are taken into consideration at the same time, the magnitude of the coefficients rises appreciably, and usually also their reliability. This can be demonstrated for the social system in our own society (1949:178–179).

Earlier (p. 153), Murdock had found a correlation of +.68 between neolocal residence and the use of lineal kinship terms for the trio of relatives: mother, mother's sister, and father's sister, as well as a correlation of +.56 between the presence of the isolated nuclear family and the use of lineal terminology for the same set of kin.[8] Murdock continues: "If we combine these two factors [neolocal residence and the isolated nuclear family] and add two other characteristic features of our own social structure—strict monogamy and the absence of exogamous unilinear kin groups —we arrive at the results shown in Table 54" (1949:179).

Table 54 shows that the correlation of lineal kinship terminology for mother, mother's sister, and father's sister with the combination of monogamy, isolated nuclear families, neolocal residence, and the absence

---

[8] In kinship terminology of the lineal type, such as our own, mother is called by a distinct term, not applied to any other relative, while mother's sister and father's sister are classed together and called by a term equivalent to 'aunt.'

of exogamous lineages or sibs is an impressive $+.91$. Murdock concludes the discussion by saying: "Similar results are obtainable from an exceedingly large number of similar combinations. . . ." (1949:179).

It is not possible to say *a priori* just how high coefficients of this sort can be raised if still other relevant factors are included in the correlation. Even with the most repeated and painstaking refinements, however, it may never be possible to achieve correlations of $+1.00$. Continued ignorance of some of the relevant variables despite our best efforts and, especially, the existence of a time lag between cause and effect may preclude the formulation of statements of association that hold without any exceptions. Perhaps many of the hypotheses about cultural phenomena in which we will come to have the greatest confidence may never be verified to a degree higher than that represented by a coefficient of the order of, say, $+.95$.

Such propositions, while not laws in the sense of being statements of absolutely invariant relations, might nevertheless be considered statistical laws. This would not necessarily demean their status, for as Hans Reichenbach has pointed out, "statistical laws are not 'less dignified' than causal laws—they are more general forms, among which the causal law represents the special form of statistical correlations holding for 100 percent of the cases" (1951:122).

"Moreover," Reichenbach adds, "causal laws, at least in quantitative form, are never found to hold strictly in observational terms. We do not observe a 100 percent validity; we notice exceptions. Causal laws are introduced by a process of schematization; we assume them to hold for ideal conditions, knowing that the inevitable 'errors of observation' will lead to deviations from the ideal" (1951:122).

The number of highly verified propositions about the culture process is still small. But as cultural phenomena come increasingly to be studied *"with the view of discovering their regularity,"* the body of laws found to hold for the process will inevitably grow. And as it does, the science of culture will gradually come to assume its proper position as a mature and respected scientific discipline.

BIBLIOGRAPHY

BARNES, HARRY ELMER
1925 *The New History and the Social Studies*. New York, The Century Co.

BARNETT, HOMER G.

1940 "Culture Processes." *American Anthropologist,* 42:21–48.

BOAS, FRANZ

1904 "The History of Anthropology." *Science,* 20:513–524.

1932 "The Aims of Anthropological Research." *Science,* 76:603–613.

BREYSIG, KURT

1927 *Der Stufenbau und die Gesetze der Weltgeschichte.* Second edition, enlarged. Stuttgart and Berlin, J. G. Cotta'sche Buchhandlung Nachfolger.

BUCKLE, HENRY THOMAS

1857 *History of Civilization in England,* vol. I. London, John W. Parker and Son.

CHEYNEY, EDWARD P.

1927 *Law in History and Other Essays.* New York, Alfred A. Knopf, Inc.

DRUCKER, PHILIP

1941 "Culture Element Distributions: XVII Yuman-Piman." *Anthropological Records,* 6:91–230.

FISHER, H. A. L.

1939 *A History of Europe.* Revised edition. Boston, Houghton Mifflin Company.

HERSKOVITS, MELVILLE J.

1945 "The Processes of Cultural Change." In *The Science of Man in the World Crisis,* ed. by Ralph Linton, pp. 143–170. New York, Columbia University Press.

KROEBER, A. L.

1935 "History and Science in Anthropology." *American Anthropologist,* 37:539–569.

1948 *Anthropology.* Revised edition. New York, Harcourt, Brace and Company.

MEYER, EDUARD

1924 *Kleine Schriften.* Halle (Saale), Verlag von Max Niemeyer.

MURDOCK, GEORGE PETER

1949 *Social Structure.* New York, The Macmillan Company.

1957 "Anthropology as a Comparative Science." *Behavioral Science,* 2:249–254.

REICHENBACH, HANS

1951 "Probability Methods in Social Science." In *The Policy Sciences,* ed. by Daniel Lerner and Harold D. Lasswell, pp. 121–128. Stanford, Stanford University Press.

ROBINSON, JAMES HARVEY
1911 "The Reformation." *The Encyclopaedia Britannica*, 11th edition,
23:4–22.
1912 *The New History*. New York, The Macmillan Company.

RUSSELL, BERTRAND
1931 *The Scientific Outlook*. New York, W. W. Norton & Company, Inc.

SPENCER, ROBERT F.
1958 "Culture Process and Intellectual Current: Durkheim and Ata-
türk." *American Anthropologist*, 60:640–657.

STEWARD, JULIAN H.
1949 "Cultural Causality and Law: A Trial Formulation of the Development of Early Civilizations." *American Anthropologist*, 51:
1–27.
1953 "Evolution and Process." In *Anthropology Today*, prepared under
the chairmanship of A. L. Kroeber, pp. 313–326. Chicago, The
University of Chicago Press.

WHITE, LESLIE A.
1945 "History, Evolutionism, and Functionalism: Three Types of Interpretation of Culture." *Southwestern Journal of Anthropology*,
1:221–248.
1948 "Ikhnaton: The Great Man *vs.* the Culture Process." *Journal of
the American Oriental Society*, 68:91–114.
1949 *The Science of Culture*. New York, Farrar, Straus and Company.
1950 "The Individual and the Culture Process." *Centennial*, American
Association for the Advancement of Science, pp. 74–81. Washington, D.C.

WHITE, LYNN, JR.
1956 "History: The Changing Past." In *Frontiers of Knowledge in the
Study of Man*, ed. by Lynn White, Jr., pp. 68–78. New York,
Harper & Brothers.

XÉNOPOL, ALEXANDRU D.
1902 "Les Sciences Naturelles & l'Histoire à propos d'un Ouvrage
Récent." *Revue de Synthèse Historique*, 4:276–292.

* * * *

Gertrude E. Dole

COLUMBIA UNIVERSITY

THE CLASSIFICATION OF YANKEE

NOMENCLATURE IN THE LIGHT

OF EVOLUTION IN KINSHIP

INTRODUCTION

A classification is a device to express the interrelation of phenomena. Hence, in classifying his subject matter a scientist
endeavors to emphasize the most significant similarities and differences.
But classifications differ according to the particular relationships which
the classifier wishes to express. It may be that the classes proposed by
one student for his particular purpose obscure relationships which are
considered significant by another. In order to throw light on those
relationships it may be necessary either to group together previously
established classes or to revise the classification by a process of division.
The present paper investigates the utility of this latter process with respect
to certain kinship nomenclatures.

In a comparative study of kinship by Murdock, the nomenclature of
the "Yankees" has been classed with those of the Eskimos and Andaman
Islanders as "lineal" or "Eskimo" (1949:142, 227). This is an apparent
anomaly, since these three peoples represent different levels of cultural
development. The Yankees have one of the most complex cultures known,
while the Andamanese have one of the simplest, a fact that led Murdock

to conclude that there was no necessary association between particular patterns of kinship terminology and levels of culture (1949:200).

Murdock has demonstrated that there is a close relation between kinship nomenclatures and such aspects of social structure as descent, marriage, and residence (1949:141ff.). In this relation the social structure acts as a filter through which factors external to the social system influence the nomenclature. The social structure itself may be modified directly by external factors; but the nomenclature is modified only in response to changes in the social structure (1949:199).

The form which a social structure will take is fundamentally dependent on the type of subsistence technology with which it is associated (Simmons 1937; Murdock 1949:137; White 1949:377–378). In view of this dependence and of the fact that Murdock found a correlation between kinship nomenclatures and some aspects of social structure, we might expect that kinship nomenclatures would show some relation to level of technological development. The possibility arises, therefore, that significant differences may be obscured by classing together the nomenclatures of societies with such different technologies as the Yankee, Eskimo, and Andaman societies have. In order to determine whether or not there are significant differences among these nomenclatures which can be correlated with technological development, let us examine them in some detail, beginning with the Andaman.

ANDAMAN KINSHIP NOMENCLATURE

The Andamanese use particularizing terms for primary relatives. That is, a special term is used for father, mother, brother, sister, son, and daughter, as among Anglo-Americans. But all other relatives are grouped into large classes. Figure 1 shows the pattern to which the Andaman nomenclature belongs.[1] In this pattern a single term is used for individuals of each sex in any single generation outside Ego's nuclear families of orientation and procreation. Thus only two terms are used for the four grandparents and all their siblings; two for all the siblings and cousins of Ego's parents; two for all of Ego's cousins, no matter how distant; two for the offspring of all his siblings and cousins; and two for all persons in the grandchild generation.

---

[1] In Andaman nomenclature as recorded by Man (1883:126, 421ff.), a single term is used for all females of the first and second ascending generations. This is an unusual feature, not shared by other societies with the same type of kinship nomenclature. For the sake of simplicity and clarity, the usual arrangement is represented in Figure 1.

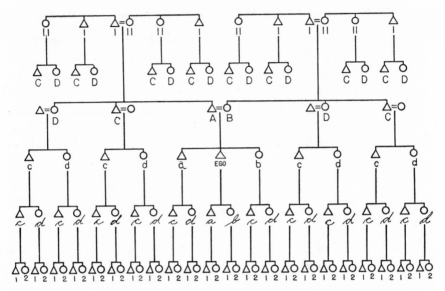

Figure 1. THE PATTERN OF ANDAMAN NOMENCLATURE *

* In this and subsequent diagrams, the terms most frequently used in each generation are represented by a distinctive set of symbols. Thus the terms used primarily in the first ascending generation are represented by A, B, C, D, and so on, while the terms used primarily in Ego's generation are represented by a, b, c, d, and so on. In this way one may see at a glance whether or not terms are used in more than one generation, a characteristic feature of some patterns.

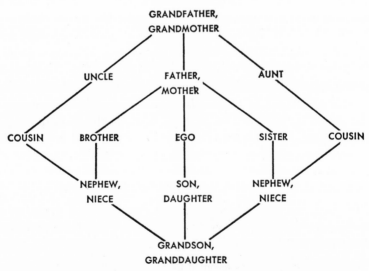

Figure 2. THE CLASSIFICATORY NATURE OF
ANDAMAN NOMENCLATURE

It should be noted that grandparents and grandchildren are lineal relatives to Ego, while the siblings of grandparents and the grandchildren of Ego's siblings and cousins are collateral relatives. In the Andaman nomenclature the lineal and collateral relatives in these generations are classed together by the use of the same terms for grandparents as for their siblings and by the use of the same terms for grandchildren as for their cousins. Classing lineal with collateral relatives is the criterion of classificatory nomenclature as Morgan defined it (1868:451; 1871:277; 1904:82; 1909:416). It has the effect of bringing distant relatives into the sphere of close relationships, as can be seen in Figure 2, an adaptation of a diagram used by Morgan (1871:Plate VIII).

The converging lines indicate that both ascendants and descendants of all collateral relatives are ultimately classed with lineal relatives. Hence Andaman nomenclature is classificatory. In contrast to this, classificatory features are entirely lacking from Yankee nomenclature. In other respects, however, the pattern of Yankee kinship terms resembles the Andaman to some extent.

YANKEE KINSHIP NOMENCLATURE

By 'Yankee nomenclature,' I mean the pattern of kinship terminology currently used among Anglo-Americans. As has been pointed out above, this pattern is not exactly the same as the Andaman. In the Yankee system as in the Andaman, Ego's primary relatives are distinguished from all others by particularizing terms. Also both types of nomenclature have generalizing terms which group together several types of collateral relatives. But here the resemblance ends. In Yankee nomenclature, by contrast with Andaman, no collateral relatives are grouped with lineal. As can be seen from Figure 3, *all* of Ego's lineal relatives are distinguished from their siblings and cousins.

Not only are parents distinguished from aunts and uncles, siblings from cousins, and own children from nieces and nephews; but separate terms are used also to differentiate grandparents from their siblings, own grandchildren from the grandchildren of one's siblings, and so on, to a theoretically infinite degree of ascent and descent. Distinction of lineal from collateral relatives constitutes the principal characteristic of what Morgan called descriptive nomenclature (1871:13).

A further difference between this pattern and the Andaman is that degrees of collaterality are distinguished in all generations in Yankee

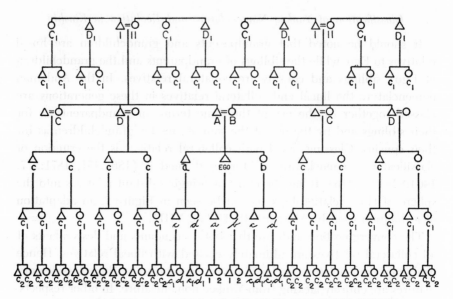

Figure 3. THE PATTERN OF YANKEE NOMENCLATURE

Figure 4. THE DESCRIPTIVE NATURE OF
YANKEE NOMENCLATURE

nomenclature. Members of Ego's own generation may be designated as first, second, third cousins, and so forth, according to the distance of their consanguineal relationship. Moreover, the siblings of lineal relatives are distinguished from their cousins in every instance. Thus while parents' siblings are called "aunts" and "uncles," their cousins are referred to by Ego as "cousins" (properly first cousins once removed).[2] Similarly, the descendants of brother and sister are called "nephews" and "nieces," but the offspring of Ego's cousins are called "cousins" (again first cousins once removed). Hence the descendants of collateral relatives are never brought into the sphere of close relationships. Figure 4, on the opposite page, shows the complete absence of classificatory features in Yankee nomenclature.

The pattern of Yankee terms for collateral relatives in the first ascending and descending generations also differs from the Andaman. It will be recalled that rather than distinguishing aunts and uncles, as well as nieces and nephews, from more distant relatives, Andaman terms group parents' siblings with their cousins, and the same terms are used for the children of Ego's siblings as for the children of his cousins. We can see, therefore, that there are fundamental differences between the Andaman and Yankee nomenclatures, both of which have been referred to as lineal and as Eskimo. Let us consider next the nomenclatures of the Eskimo peoples.

KINSHIP NOMENCLATURES OF THE ESKIMOS

In the nomenclatures used by most Eskimo tribes, parents, children, and siblings are distinguished from all other relatives, as in the Andaman and Yankee patterns. As in these two patterns also, there are generalizing cousin terms. Terms in the grandparent and grandchild generations are classificatory, grouping collateral relatives with lineal.[3] In this feature the nomenclatures of Eskimos resemble the Andaman but differ from the Yankee. The terms for parents' siblings and for the children of Ego's siblings are of quite a different pattern from either Andaman or Yankee.

---

[2] Some of my informants refer to parents' siblings as "second cousins," a usage which may represent an advanced form of the Anglo-American nomenclature pattern. In this paper, however, I use the form which is standard in genealogical research (Brand 1954:369).

[3] In discussing Eskimo nomenclature, Morgan wrote that it was a "classificatory as distinguished from a descriptive system," being "in general agreement with the Ganowánian system in . . . the mergence of the collateral lines in the lineal line, ascending and descending" (1871:277).

Gertrude E. Dole

Instead of two, there are four terms for parents' siblings, and the terms for brother's children differ from those for sister's children.

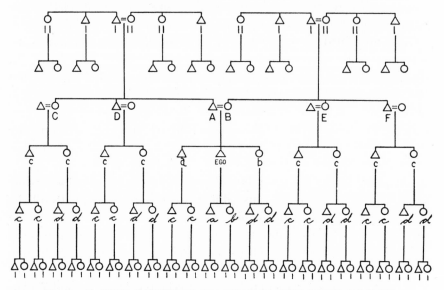

Figure 5. THE PATTERN OF ESKIMO NOMENCLATURES

This pattern was named the Eskimo Type by Spier, who proposed the original classification of Eskimo nomenclatures. He based his classification on the terms for cousins (1925:79). There was, therefore, a precedent for using the name Eskimo for the pattern of cousin terms that is characteristic of Eskimo, Andaman, and Yankee nomenclatures. But Eskimo cousin terms were not classed as lineal either by Spier or by Lowie, who first used this term to describe kinship nomenclatures.

In setting up his own typology shortly after the publication of Spier's, Lowie used the terms for aunts and uncles instead of cousins. On this basis he classed the Eskimo nomenclatures described above as bifurcate collateral because they distinguish patrilateral relatives from matrilateral (bifurcation) and parents from their siblings (collaterality) (Lowie 1929:84, 86). The term lineal was used by Lowie to refer to a very different pattern, namely that which Spier had referred to as the Salish Type (Lowie 1929:86; Spier 1925:75).

The Salish Type is represented by nomenclatures of the Salish, Nootka, and Kwakiutl, which are "characterized by the merging of father's and mother's siblings: that is, there is only one term for 'aunt' and one for 'uncle.' Conversely, there is but one term for nephew and niece. . . .

168 ·

Sibling terms are applied to both parallel and cross cousins" (Spier 1925:74). This pattern is represented in Figure 6.

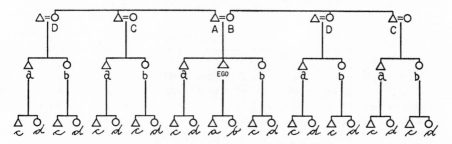

Figure 6. SALISH TYPE OF NOMENCLATURE

In the Salish Type, as in the Andaman and Yankee patterns, parents and offspring, who are lineal relatives, are distinguished from collateral. It is for this reason that Lowie referred to them as lineal. However, in Ego's generation all collateral relatives are classed with siblings, as in the Hawaiian, or generation pattern.

As I mentioned earlier Murdock has recently applied the term lineal, not to the Salish Type (Lowie's lineal pattern), but to Andaman, Eskimo, and Yankee nomenclatures (1949:223). According to Murdock, "the English system is identical in type to the system of the Andamanese Pygmies, the Ona of Tierra del Fuego, and the Eskimos, and is even technically classified as 'Eskimo system'" (1949:100).[4] Of these systems, however, the Andaman and Yankee have lineal aunt and uncle terms, while the Eskimo pattern has bifurcate collateral terms in that generation. Hence Murdock's lineal pattern is not equivalent to any single type in Spier's or Lowie's classifications.[5] Rather it is a composite class comprising nomenclatures from two previously proposed types. (The same is true of Murdock's Hawaiian, or generation, pattern.) The effect of this classifica-

---

[4] Spier did not mention Yankee or Andaman nomenclatures. As we have seen, although the nomenclatures of the Eskimos do have terms which group all cousins together and set them apart from siblings, they had not been classed by Lowie with Andaman and Yankee nomenclatures since they do not have lineal terms in the parental or offspring generations. Rather these generations in Eskimo nomenclatures are bifurcate collateral. This is quite a different pattern from either Yankee or Andaman.

[5] Rivers spoke of a "family system" in which members of the nuclear family are distinguished from all other relatives (1914:77), but this was not clearly described. Kirchhoff's Type A was an ideal type, a modification of Eskimo nomenclatures, and is not comparable in any of the three middle generations to Murdock's lineal pattern. Kirchhoff, however, proposed as another type the pattern of nomenclature used by the Koryak of northeastern Siberia. Curiously enough this pattern coincides with the type Murdock has labeled Eskimo (Kirchhoff 1932:46–50).

tion, therefore, has been to make the traditional classes more inclusive rather than more refined. The interrelation of the three classifications discussed above may perhaps be seen more clearly in the following chart:

CLASSIFICATIONS

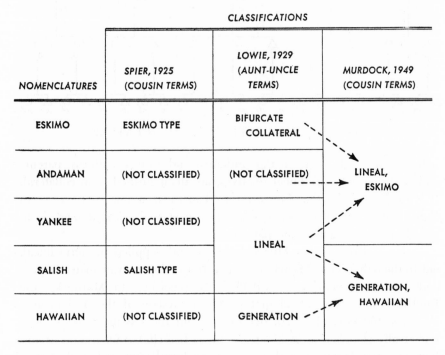

NOMENCLATURES	SPIER, 1925 (COUSIN TERMS)	LOWIE, 1929 (AUNT-UNCLE TERMS)	MURDOCK, 1949 (COUSIN TERMS)
ESKIMO	ESKIMO TYPE	BIFURCATE COLLATERAL	
ANDAMAN	(NOT CLASSIFIED)	(NOT CLASSIFIED)	LINEAL, ESKIMO
YANKEE	(NOT CLASSIFIED)	LINEAL	
SALISH	SALISH TYPE		GENERATION, HAWAIIAN
HAWAIIAN	(NOT CLASSIFIED)	GENERATION	

Figure 7. THE INTERRELATION OF THREE CLASSIFICATIONS

It is possible that when Murdock applied the name lineal to Eskimo nomenclatures, he did so in the belief that the terms of the three middle generations are usually congruent; that is, if the terms of Ego's generation distinguish cousins as a group from siblings, then the terms of the first ascending generation will group together parents' siblings, distinguishing them from parents, and nepotic terms will group together the children of Ego's siblings, distinguishing them from his own children. Lowie had spoken of such "logical coherence" in the pattern of terms in the parental and offspring generations (1929:85), but he had disregarded the pattern of cousin terms. Murdock says of the "Eskimo social organization" that, in addition to having by definition Eskimo cousin terminology and no exogamous unilineal kin groups, "it is characterized by . . . lineal terms for aunts and nieces" (1949:227). Nevertheless, in Murdock's early sample of two Eskimo nomenclatures, this is not the case. The Copper Eskimo niece terms are of the bifurcate collateral pattern. No aunt terms were recorded for this society, and neither aunt nor niece terms were recorded for the other, the Angmagsalik (1949:228). These nomenclatures could be regarded as lineal, therefore, only on the basis of the cousin terms.

However, assuming congruence in the pattern of terms in the various generations of Eskimo nomenclatures is unwarranted. Eskimos do not in any instance have a symmetrical nomenclature of the pattern which Murdock refers to as lineal (1949:142). Rather, in the parental and off-spring generations they usually distinguish paternal from maternal relatives, as well as collateral from lineal (bifurcate collateral); while in Ego's generation distinction is made only between collateral and lineal relatives (lineal, Eskimo). Of the 15 Eskimo nomenclatures for which I have data, all have bifurcate collateral terms in the parental generation except the Aleut and Nunivak, which are bifurcate merging. (See Giddings 1952 for a discussion of variation among Eskimo nomenclatures.)

In setting up his six-class typology based on cousin terms, Murdock refers to his lineal class as Eskimo. He states that this is one of four patterns in his typology that "are well established in the literature and correspond closely to those which Spier calls by the same names" (1949: 223, 226). In Murdock's Eskimo pattern, "FaSiDa and MoBrDa [are] called by the same terms as parallel cousins but terminologically differentiated from sisters; the terms for the two cross cousins are usually, but not always the same" (1949:223). It is apparent that he intended this to be the Eskimo Type of Spier's classification. But Murdock's Eskimo pattern differs from Spier's. Murdock finds that "Eskimo" nomenclature is characterized by lineal aunt and niece terms, while Spier's Eskimo Type had bifurcate collateral aunt and niece terms. The new application of the name Eskimo indicates that a change has occurred in its meaning through the tacit assumption that terms in the parental and offspring generations conform to the pattern of terms in Ego's generation.

In interpreting Lowie's observation of the usual coherence in the patterns of terms in the parental and offspring generations, Murdock classified Eskimo cousin terms as lineal "by extension" (1947:65, 56). Clearly the use of 'lineal' as a label for Eskimo nomenclatures, which Lowie had called bifurcate collateral, extends its meaning beyond that which Lowie proposed for it. Lowie used it to refer to the conceptual separation of lineal *ascendants* and *descendants* from Ego's collateral relatives. As applied to the Eskimo nomenclatures, it refers instead to Ego's generation, implying the separation of cousins as a group from siblings.

CORRELATION OF NOMENCLATURE PATTERNS WITH CULTURAL COMPLEXITY

The Andaman pattern is found also among the Semang and Sakai of the Malay peninsula, and the Chukchee and Koryak of northeastern Siberia. The Eskimo pattern is used by most of the Eskimos, and by the following peoples: Lapp, Maricopa, Ojibwa of Parry Island, Ona, and Yahgan.[6] Nomenclatures of the Yankee type are used by all English-speaking peoples and by most other Indo-Europeans (including the Belgians, Dutch, Flemish, French, Germans, Greeks, Irish, Italians, Portuguese, Spanish, and Welsh). This pattern is found also among such linguistically diverse peoples as the Finnish, Japanese, and the Mayan-speaking Mam of Guatemala. I have suggested elsewhere three structural names for these three nomenclature patterns, Primitive Isolating for Andaman, Secondary Isolating for Eskimo, and Modern Isolating for Yankee (Dole 1957).

In societies with any one of these three patterns, the nuclear family is the only stable residence kin group. This unit is the most important kin group, and it is usually the only significant kin group within a local group. Primitive, Secondary, and Modern Isolating nomenclatures all reflect the unique importance of the nuclear family in the particularizing character of terms for Ego's primary relatives, in contrast to the generalizing terms used for all other relatives. It is precisely because these nomenclatures set off primary relatives that I have suggested the name Isolating for all three patterns.

Another point of similarity is to be found in the marriage customs. In all of these societies, marriage with close cousins, either cross or parallel, is disapproved. Moreover, in all of these societies cousins do not regularly reside with Ego throughout their lives. Correspondingly, all three nomenclatures group cross and parallel cousins together but distinguish them as a group from siblings.

These are significant similarities in the kinship structures and nomenclatures of the simplest and the most complex societies. A typology which groups them in one class emphasizes these similarities. Nevertheless there

---

[6] Although the Yahgan nomenclature has been classed as Hawaiian (Murdock 1949:230, 346), cousins are distinguished as a group from siblings according to Gusinde (1937: 786ff.) and according to Lothrop (1928:161–162), whose data were checked by William Bridges.

are also fundamental differences between some of the nomenclature patterns described above. The Primitive and Secondary Isolating nomenclatures are classificatory, grouping some collateral relatives with lineal; while the Modern Isolating is descriptive, distinguishing all collateral relatives from lineal.

Moreover, all the peoples who have Primitive or Secondary Isolating nomenclatures also have relatively primitive cultures, with very simple social structures. All those which have the Modern Isolating pattern have much more advanced cultures with relatively complex social structures. They are organized into densely populated villages or cities with individual production for profit, money economies, and centralized political control. This distribution immediately suggests a dichotomy of peoples with Primitive and Secondary Isolating nomenclatures on the one hand, and those with Modern Isolating on the other. A division along this line corresponds exactly to the fundamental distinction between classificatory and descriptive nomenclatures.

It would be surprising if such marked differences in culture level were not associated with other differences in kinship nomenclature and kinship structure, that is, the organization of kinship relations. Let us therefore compare the kinship structure of these two major groups of societies and consider its relation to the nomenclature patterns.

In the simple societies with Primitive and Secondary Isolating nomenclatures, the siblings of grandparents and the grandchildren of Ego's siblings are functional equivalents of Ego's grandparents and grandchildren themselves. They may reside with Ego's nuclear family, and Ego shares the responsibility of their support if their own close relatives are unable to provide for them. This is necessary as survival insurance in times of hardship.

By contrast, in the more complex societies with money economy and centralized political control, distant relatives do not share responsibility for subsistence and protection. Ego is not expected to support his grandparents' siblings or the grandchildren of his own siblings. Among Anglo-Americans, for example, relatives who are removed by two or more degrees of consanguinity seldom live near enough to render assistance when there is need, nor indeed are they aware of the need. Responsibility for any but one's primary relatives is incompatible with advanced industrial social organization. Instead, specialized groups of nonrelatives assume progressively more responsibility for those functions which cannot be performed by the nuclear family. The political organization is delegated to protect its citizens from starvation and exposure to the elements in instances of greatest need. It also supplies protection from violence and loss of property. In addition nonpolitical organizations, such as charitable foundations, insurance companies, and industrial pension programs, arise to perform the functions of support and protection which were once performed by large corporate groups of kin. In industrial nations vast numbers of impoverished people would perish if governmental and other non-kin agencies did not provide for them.

Terminological features correspond to this contrast in the degree of dependence on collateral relatives. In the Primitive and Secondary Isolating nomenclatures of the simpler societies, the same terms are used for grandparents and their siblings. Moreover Ego's grandchildren and the grandchildren of Ego's siblings and cousins are all referred to by the same terms. In Modern Isolating nomenclature, on the other hand, grandparents and grandchildren are designated with special terms, emphasizing the social distinctiveness of these lineal relatives.

A feature of the kinship structure which is closely allied to the support and protection of relatives is the inheritance of property. In primitive societies the amount of property inherited by individuals is relatively insignificant. However, in the more complex societies with production for profit and money economies, considerable amounts of individual property may be accumulated. The property accumulated by individuals is transmitted by inheritance to other individuals according to degrees of consanguineal relation. When this occurs, degrees of consanguinity must be reckoned. Early legal records of civilized societies define these degrees with great precision. Correspondingly in Modern Isolating nomenclature parents' siblings are separated from their cousins; the offspring of Ego's siblings are separated from the offspring of his cousins; and first, second, third cousins, and so forth, may be distinguished in precise usage. Primitive and Secondary Isolating nomenclatures, on the other hand, do not distinguish between degrees of consanguinity among collateral relatives.

Another point of contrast between primitive and complex societies is the basis on which social status is established. In the face-to-face contact between relatives which is characteristic of the simple societies with Primitive and Secondary Isolating nomenclatures, age differences are of great importance in establishing social status. In keeping with this significance of seniority, all generation differences are expressed in the nomenclatures. By contrast, Modern Isolating nomenclatures group together several generations of collateral relatives as "cousins." The average American, for example, is uncertain of the "proper" terms of relationship for distant collateral relatives and usually refers to them as "some sort of cousin" (Brand 1954:369). This feature is correlated with the fact that in dense populations with complex social organization and great mobility, there is little face-to-face contact of kin except among the closest relatives. Whereas seniority of kinship relations is of primary importance in primitive societies, in industrial urban societies differences in occupation and property ownership are the principal bases of social status.

From these contrasts we can see that, although all three of the nomenclature patterns compared here emphasize the isolation of the nuclear family, there are differences among them which can be correlated with differences in kinship structure and level of general cultural complexity. Andaman and Eskimo peoples depend on solidarity among lineal and collateral relatives for social security, and the associated kinship nomenclatures class lineal relatives with collateral outside the nuclear family. Because the Andaman and Eskimo nomenclatures have this feature I have referred to them as Isolating, the Andaman as Primitive Isolating and the Eskimo as Secondary Isolating. (The differences in kinship structure between the societies which have Primitive and Secondary Isolating nomenclatures constitute a complex problem which is beyond the scope of the present paper and has been discussed elsewhere [Dole 1957:212ff.].)

Yankee nomenclature is also of an isolating nature. I have referred to it as Modern Isolating to indicate this fact and also that it differs from both the Eskimo and the Andaman patterns in every generation, as can be seen from the accompanying chart, Figure 8. The differences may be summarized as follows: (1) Instead of classing together lineal and collateral relatives in the grandparent and grandchild generations as do the Primitive and Secondary Isolating, Modern Isolating nomenclature differentiates *all* lineal from collateral relatives. This is because property is inherited primarily in a lineal pattern, and because an individual is not responsible for the support and protection of his collateral relatives. (2) In its more precise form, the Modern Isolating pattern expresses differences in degrees of consanguinity among collateral relatives in each generation, which is not true of the Primitive or Secondary Isolating. The function of this feature is to differentiate between relatives according to inheritance rights, especially to subsistence property. (3) Finally, the Modern Isolating pattern groups together collateral relatives of different generations, whereas each generation is terminologically distinct in both the Primitive and Secondary Isolating patterns. In industrial society many people have almost no contact with offspring of their parents' siblings. When this is true, it is not likely that they will be concerned enough with more distant relatives to differentiate them with special nomenclature.

All of these characteristic features of Modern Isolating nomenclature have been brought about in one way or another by specialization of social relations in civilized society.

	MODERN ISOLATING	PRIMITIVE ISOLATING	SECONDARY ISOLATING
GRANDPARENT GENERATION	DESCRIPTIVE	CLASSIFICATORY	CLASSIFICATORY
PARENTAL GENERATION	LINEAL DIFFERENTIATES PARENTS' SIBLINGS FROM THEIR COUSINS	LINEAL GROUPS PARENTS' SIBLINGS WITH THEIR COUSINS	BIFURCATE COLLATERAL GROUPS PARENTS' SIBLINGS WITH THEIR COUSINS
EGO'S GENERATION	EXPRESSES DEGREES OF CONSANGUINITY	GROUPS ALL COUSINS TOGETHER	GROUPS ALL COUSINS TOGETHER
OFFSPRING GENERATION	LINEAL DIFFERENTIATES SIBLINGS' FROM COUSINS' CHILDREN	LINEAL GROUPS SIBLINGS' WITH COUSINS' CHILDREN	BIFURCATE COLLATERAL GROUPS SIBLINGS' WITH COUSINS' CHILDREN
GRANDCHILD GENERATION	DESCRIPTIVE	CLASSIFICATORY	CLASSIFICATORY

Figure 8. COMPARISON OF MODERN ISOLATING WITH OTHER ISOLATING NOMENCLATURES

CONCLUSION

Scientific classification is of course an arbitrary procedure. The criteria one uses to establish classes of phenomena are selected according to one's particular purpose. For this reason classifications differ in the relationships they express. One classification may be preferable for one purpose, while a different one is more useful for another purpose.

Murdock's typology of kinship nomenclatures classes together in an Eskimo pattern nomenclatures which have particularizing terms for primary relatives and generalizing terms for more distant ones. It thereby emphasizes the primary importance of the nuclear family in societies which have this type of nomenclature. But Murdock's Eskimo class comprises nomenclatures of societies which differ among themselves in other features of kinship organization. Furthermore it includes nomenclatures of societies which differ greatly in general cultural complexity. On the basis of his typology one must group together such diverse societies as the industrialized Yankees, the Eskimos, and the Andamanese. Hence such a classification obscures the terminological differences which are correlated with cultural development. This procedure might indeed lead one to conclude that there is no necessary association between nomenclature patterns and culture level.

But one may wish to investigate the relation of nomenclature patterns to the evolution of culture. Evolution has been demonstrated in nearly every aspect of culture. Moreover the concept of evolution has aided so greatly in the understanding of culture that it seems worthwhile to try to utilize it in studying patterns of kinship nomenclature. In order to investigate the relation of nomenclature patterns to cultural development, we need to explore the differences among nomenclatures found in societies at various culture levels. If we approach the classification of kinship terminologies from this point of view, we see that there are significant terminological differences which may be correlated with general cultural development. For this reason I have chosen to divide the class of nomenclatures previously referred to as Eskimo into new classes which reflect culture level.

BIBLIOGRAPHY

BRAND, NORTON F.
  1954 "Genealogy." *The Encyclopedia Americana,* 12:369–370.
DOLE, GERTRUDE E.
  1957 "The Development of Patterns of Kinship Nomenclature." Ph.D. dissertation, Ann Arbor, University Microfilms.
GIDDINGS, J. L., JR.
  1952 "Observations on the 'Eskimo Type' of Kinship and Social Structure." *Anthropological Papers of the University of Alaska,* Vol. 1, No. 1:5–10.

GUSINDE, MARTIN
1937 Die Feuerland-Indianer. Vol. II: Die Yamana. Mödling bei Wien.
KIRCHHOFF, PAUL
1932 "Verwandtschaftsbezeichnungen und Verwandtenheirat." *Zeitschrift für Ethnologie*, 64:41–71.
LOTHROP, SAMUEL KIRKLAND
1928 "The Indians of Tierra del Fuego." *Contributions from the Museum of the American Indian*, No. 10.
LOWIE, ROBERT H.
1929 "*Relationship Terms*." *Encyclopaedia Britannica*, 14th edition, 19:84–89.
MAN, EDWARD HORACE
1883 "On the Aboriginal Inhabitants of the Andaman Islands." *Journal of the [Royal] Anthropological Institute*, 12:69–175, 327–434.
MORGAN, LEWIS H.
1868 "A Conjectural Solution of the Origin of the Classificatory System of Relationship." *Proceedings of the American Academy of Arts and Sciences*, 7:436–477.
1871 "Systems of Consanguinity and Affinity of the Human Family." *Smithsonian Institution Contributions to Knowledge*, 17.
1904 *League of the Ho-dé-no-sau-nee or Iroquois*. New edition, ed. by Herbert M. Lloyd. New York, Dodd, Mead & Co.
1909 *Ancient Society*. Chicago, Charles H. Kerr & Company.
MURDOCK, GEORGE P.
1947 "Bifurcate Merging, A Test of Five Theories." *American Anthropologist*, 49:56–68.
1949 *Social Structure*. New York, The Macmillan Company.
RIVERS, W. H. R.
1914 *Kinship and Social Organisation*. London, Constable & Co.
SIMMONS, LEO W.
1937 "Statistical Correlations in the Science of Society." In *Studies in the Science of Society*, ed. by George P. Murdock, pp. 495–517. New Haven, Yale University Press.
SPIER, LESLIE
1925 "The Distribution of Kinship Systems in North America." *University of Washington Publications in Anthropology*, 1:69–88.
WHITE, LESLIE A.
1949 "Ethnological Theory." In *Philosophy for the Future*, ed. by Roy Wood Sellars, V. J. McGill, and Martin Farber, pp. 357–384. New York, The Macmillan Company

* * * *

Fred Eggan

UNIVERSITY OF CHICAGO

LEWIS H. MORGAN IN

KINSHIP PERSPECTIVE[1]

I

One hundred years ago Lewis H. Morgan discovered that the Algonkian-speaking Ojibwa on the southern shores of Lake Superior had a pattern of grouping relatives similar to that he had earlier recorded among the linguistically unrelated Iroquois Indians of New York state. This discovery stirred his scientific imagination and led him to initiate and carry through a monumental comparative study of kinship systems, which was to have far-reaching and unexpected results. The steps by which he reached his conclusions as to the nature of kinship systems, and their relevance to the history of the American Indians and to the evolution of human society, were first presented in detail in *Systems of Consanguinity and Affinity of the Human Family* (1871), and later developed as a theory of cultural evolution in *Ancient Society* (1877). With these evolutionary conceptions we are not here concerned. They have been reviewed by Bernhard J. Stern (1931), Robert H. Lowie (1936; 1937:54–67), and Leslie A. White (1948), among many others; and White has recently completed a major study of the evolution of culture based

[1] I am indebted to a Ford Foundation Faculty Grant for providing assistance in the preparation of this paper; and to the Center for Advanced Study in the Behavioral Sciences, Stanford, California, for various facilities. I would like to thank my colleagues at the Center, particularly Raymond Firth, Meyer Fortes, and Clifford Geertz, and the editors of this volume for their comments and suggestions, and Mrs. Isabel S. Caro for editorial assistance and advice.

· 179

in part on Morgan's ideas. We believe, however, that Morgan's discoveries in the field of kinship, as presented in *Systems*, have not received the consideration which they deserve.

Anthropologists generally have been uniform in their praise of *Systems*, in contrast to their reactions to *Ancient Society*. Leslie A. White, who considers *Systems* to be "one of the most significant anthropological treatises ever written," notes that it has been called "monumental" by Haddon and Radcliffe-Brown, a "towering monument" by Lowie, and "perhaps the most original and brilliant single achievement in the history of anthropology" by Murdock (White 1957:257, with references). Sol Tax says that *Systems* "rounded out the subject matter of the science of social organization," and "is a contribution that ranks with any in ethnology" (1955:458). And Evans-Pritchard lists *Systems* as one of the "books which we regard as our early theoretical classics" (1951:27).

But despite this high praise few anthropologists or their students read *Systems*. One reason may well be its "monumental" character; indeed Rivers noted that "the very extent of the material he [Morgan] collected has probably done much to obstruct the recognition of the importance of his work" (1914:5). Franz Boas in his pioneer monograph on *The Central Eskimo* (1888) not only did not collect kinship terms but for some reason did not utilize those published by Morgan a decade earlier from the same region. With Boas' later (1896) attack on the comparative method, it was understandable that his students should neglect Morgan, and many of them did, although Kroeber, Lowie, and Spier were notable exceptions. But perhaps the major reason for the neglect of *Systems* is that many students find kinship exceedingly dull. Not until they have collected and interpreted kinship data themselves do they begin to appreciate the magnitude of the task which Morgan accomplished.

II

Morgan was not the first to "discover" kinship systems. According to Tax (1955:445), that honor belongs in modern times to Lafitau, a French Jesuit missionary who described the Iroquois and Huron classifications of consanguineal kindred as early as 1724. Morgan was unaware of Lafitau's researches when he collected the materials later published in *The League of the Ho-dé-no-sau-nee, or Iroquois* (1954), but he presents essentially the same information and adds a brief list of kinship terms in the Seneca language. White has recently published a portion of Morgan's Journal, written in 1859, which presents the circumstances under which he was led to undertake the researches on kinship. In it Morgan notes that "when I first came upon this peculiar system of consanguinity, which was as early as the year 1846 among the Seneca Iroquois, I did not as much as surmise that it extended beyond this Indian family, and much less that it might have important ethnological uses. In other words, I supposed it was a system of their own invention" (White 1957:260).

This was the year that Morgan, as a result of his assistance in the litigation against the Ogden Land Company, was made a member of the Seneca Hawk clan, a circumstance which greatly facilitated his researches on the structure and principles of the league. According to Stern (1931:18) Morgan never actually lived among the Iroquois for any extended period. But he did recognize the social importance of kinship and that the terminology formed a clear and definite system: "These relationships, so novel and original, did not exist in theory, but were actual, and of constant recognition and lay at the foundation of their political as well as their social organization" (Morgan 1954,I:82). He also tried to understand the bilateral, bifurcate-merging kinship system by reference to the matrilineal clan system, though he somewhat confused clan and family: "each tribe [clan] being in the nature of a family, the ties of relationship which bind its individual members together are indispensable" (1954,I:74).

For the next several years Morgan devoted himself to his business interests, and "Indian affairs were laid entirely aside." But in the summer of 1858, while at Marquette on Lake Superior, he met some Ojibwa and obtained their kinship terminology:

To my surprise somewhat, and not a little to my delight, I found their system was substantially the same as that of the Iroquois; thus, by including a second stock language, extending very greatly the area of its distribution. From this time I began to be sensible of the important uses which such a primary institution as this must have in its bearing upon the question of the genetic connection of the American Indian not only, but also upon the still more important question of their Asiatic origin (in White 1957:263).

With this discovery interest in kinship became a principal preoccupation for the next decade. Morgan's basic assumption was that both the Seneca and Ojibwa terminologies "were derived from a common source since it was not supposable that two peoples, speaking dialects of stock-languages as widely separated as the Algonkin and Iroquois, could simultaneously have invented the same system, or derived it by borrowing one from the other" (1871:3).

This assumption, while it simplified Morgan's analysis, also limited his conclusions. By dismissing the alternatives of independent invention and borrowing before testing them against the full data, Morgan lost an important opportunity to contribute to ethnological method. And as Tax (1955:457) has pointed out, he was beginning to use a circular argument, namely, "that kinship terms can be used to reconstruct history because they remain constant, we know they remain constant because they are widespread among people who once were one and who have otherwise changed, and we know they were once one because the kinship systems are the same."

Morgan notes in his Journal the discovery of the same kinship system among the Dakota, and his resolve to pursue the inquiry into kinship in systematic fashion. His first task was to prepare a schedule containing almost every known relationship, which he tested on the Seneca and then sent to missionaries and Indian agents on the various reservations, and to a selected number in other countries. The results were disappointing but enough answers were received to encourage Morgan to visit reservations in Kansas and Nebraska and to collect the necessary data himself. Here he collected twelve schedules, all of which were similar; and from French traders he was able to learn of the existence of the same system among most of the Plains tribes.

On his return from the field he received a letter from an American missionary among the Tamil in India which presented their system of relationship. To Morgan's astonishment it was practically identical with that of the Seneca and he believed "that we had now been able to put our hands upon decisive evidence of the Asiatic origin of the American Indian race" (White 1957:267). He was thus led to extend his inquiry to Asia, Australia, Africa, and to the islands of the Pacific, which he did with the aid of the Department of State and the Smithsonian Institution, while continuing his own field work in both Canada and the United States.

Tax (1955:456–63) has sketched the steps by which Morgan set out to solve the historical problems that he had posed. The American Indian systems he had collected or received from correspondents largely conformed to a single broad type he called "classificatory," since in these systems certain lineal and collateral relatives were classed together, in contrast to Semitic and Celtic nomenclatures which were "descriptive" in character. This broad uniformity of kinship helped convince Morgan that kinship systems were exceedingly stable. When many of the Asian systems were found to be similar to those of the American Indian, Morgan felt he had demonstrated the origin of the American Indian in Asia and their dispersal from a common source.

But with the schedules from the Pacific there were some surprises. The Hawaiian terminological system was "classificatory" to a much higher degree than were the American Indian systems. The Hawaiians normally made no terminological distinctions between relatives of the same generation, those of the first ascending generation being "parents," those of ego's generation being "siblings," and those of the first descending generation being "children," with sex being indicated where necessary by the addition of the terms for male or female. The American Indian systems Morgan was familiar with generally equated the father and the father's brother, and the mother and the mother's sister, but had separate terms for the mother's brother and the father's sister, and for their offspring.

Morgan set out to account for these differences. He had early identified the Iroquois—and most American Indian systems—with a society organized on the basis of clans, in contrast to the European systems which he believed were related to the development of property as an institution. He now set out to find a social system which would fit the Hawaiian pattern of terminology: he found an answer in some notes appended by the Hon. Lorin Andrews, one of the judges of the Hawaiian supreme court: "The relationship of *pinalua* is rather amphibious (*sic*). It arose from the fact that two or more brothers with their wives, or two or more sisters with their husbands, were inclined to possess each other in common. . . ." To which the Rev. Artemus Bishop added: "This confusion of relationships is the result of the ancient custom among relatives of the living together of husbands and wives in common" (Morgan 1871:457). With this apparently authoritative information Morgan concluded that "the Hawaiian custom affords a probable solution of the Hawaiian system of relationship" (1871:457), since the kinship terms were the logical results of such a pattern of marriage.

Morgan assumed that kinship systems arose in connection with social systems, but changed so slowly that they might survive changes in social conditions and thus reflect earlier conditions of society. He had rejected the possibility that the same kinship system could arise independently in separate areas. Since the Malayan (Hawaiian) system could be explained on the basis of a "communal family" and the Ganowanian (American Indian) could develop from the Malayan by the addition of clans, the basis was laid for the development of a series of evolutionary stages, starting from an assumed promiscuity and ending with monogamy. It is this sequence, with its elaborations, which Morgan thought was the crowning achievement of his kinship studies, and which bore the brunt of criticism during the next decades. As White points out (1948:142–43), the theory of family evolution seemed plausible in the light of the evidence available to Morgan, but "the consensus is that Morgan's theory is untenable." And Tax (1955:463) notes that "the assumptions Morgan made, such as that of dependence of kinship terms on social structure and the lag of terminology in social change, are historically more important than the exact sequence of evolution that he set up."

Morgan went on to write *Ancient Society* (1877), based on *Systems* but with a broader conception of cultural evolution as a product of successive inventions permitting increasing control over the sources of subsistence. The debates that ensued involved attacks upon the validity of Morgan's terminologies as evidence: McLennan claimed that "the classificatory system is a system of mutual salutations merely" (1886:273), since he found no evidence in Morgan's work as to any rights or duties related to the terms in the classificatory system; and this criticism was "convincing enough to delay the study of kinship for thirty years" (Tax 1955:464), until Rivers and others revived it by producing the missing evidence.

But if the raw materials on kinship in *Systems* are still of "inestimable value" we might return to these data and see what Morgan missed by pursuing the problems of the ultimate origins of the American Indian and the evolution of human society, rather than the more immediate implications of the data he had assembled. For Morgan the terminological systems were a means to other ends—he was not apparently interested in the concrete, behavioral aspects of kinship as a social system and therefore failed to make certain of the discoveries that lay within his grasp.

III

When Morgan began his comparative investigations of American Indian kinship systems, he quite naturally took the Seneca as his model. But in the interim since the publication of the *League of the Iroquois* in 1851, his conceptions of kinship had advanced considerably. When he re-recorded the Seneca system in December, 1858, he did so with a greatly augmented schedule which approximated a genealogical chart and covered both consanguineal and affinal terms, ranging as far as the fourth collateral line on both sides of ego. This huge schedule, with its more than 200 entries, was unwieldy and difficult to use, but Morgan wanted to cover every possibility. Not until Rivers' invention of the "genealogical method" (1900:74–82) as a result of his researches on the Torres Straits expedition was a better technique developed for recording kinship and other sociological data.

During the years 1859–62, Morgan personally recorded some 56 terminological systems, mainly on Indian reservations in the United States and Canada, and from visitors to Washington, D.C. and New York, as well. During this period of intensive field research, perhaps the first to be devoted to the solution of specific anthropological problems, Morgan made a number of important discoveries about kinship, as well as about other aspects of social organization such as clans. In the first place, he noted the universality of the use of terms of relationship: "I have put the question direct to native Indians of more than fifty different nations, in most cases at their villages and encampments, and the affirmation of this usage has been the same in every instance" (1871:132). Correlated with this usage he found a general reluctance to use or mention personal names, a custom which he believed to contribute to the maintenance of the kinship system.

Yet with all his field experience in collecting terminologies, Morgan's conception of the kinship system was deficient. Despite his long contact with the Iroquois and his adoption by the Hawk clan of the Seneca tribe, Morgan missed an essential aspect of the kinship system—the day-to-day behavior patterns between relatives. He realized that kinship relations were real, and basic to the political and social organization, but he never probed deep enough to lay this foundation bare. If he had gone below the clan level to the world of actual kinship behavior, he would have discovered that particular relatives had rights and obligations beyond inheritance and succession. Had he translated the speeches at his adoption, detailing the rights and duties of relatives, he could have understood better the relations between terminology and behavior, between household and lineage, and between lineage and clan. The history of social organization might then have taken a different course, as Rivers has pointed out (1914:17). Yet, where his real interests were involved, as in political matters, he did probe the relations between form and practice. He says, with regard to the title of sachem, "how far these titles were hereditary in that part of the family of the sachem who were of the same tribe [clan] with himself, becomes the true question to consider" (Morgan 1954,I:83). That he answered the question inadequately, so that it waited until Goldenweiser for a partial solution, is another matter.

Hence, despite his innovations in collecting terminological data by schedules, and in the native language, Morgan was severely handicapped at the very start of his comparative studies. He was not conditioned by his Iroquois experience to inquire into social behavior and marriage practices among the Indian tribes that he studied, and thus to find a major part of the modern answer to the question: why the "classificatory" system? Nor were conditions on the newly established reservations ideal for field work. White agents, and even missionaries of long experience, often had great difficulty in interpreting, so that Morgan came to prefer Indian informants who knew a little English, where such could be found. He also discovered that women were the best informants on kinship: "It was not always possible to complete a schedule without consulting the matrons of the tribe" (1871:136).

Morgan was aware that kinship terminology is systematic, even though not simple. The American Indian system, he said, "is so diversified with specializations and so complicated in its classifications as to require careful study in order to understand its structure and principles" (1871:132). It is on this point that Morgan's comparative method was deficient: while he was concerned with the *similarities* that made the kinship systems "classificatory," he was not concerned to the same degree with the differences that he noted—differences that in modern perspective give us kinship systems, such as the "Crow" and "Omaha," which are based on different principles of classification, in part, at least. And as the Seneca model gradually hardened into the American Indian System, he increasingly ignored minor variations as possible indicators of change.

Morgan recognized the great importance of linguistics, and especially the significance of cognates and other linguistic features, for determining genetic relationships between tribes, and the linguistic classifications he used for the eastern United States were not very different from those later established by Powell. But Morgan, with his growing conviction that the American Indians were one in race and origin, thought there was evidence in the kinship terminologies for an ultimate linguistic unity as well. He believed that kinship terminology was more stable than other aspects of vocabulary, and thus would reflect earlier relationships more clearly.

Morgan began his examination of the American Indian systems by using the Iroquois, specifically the Seneca, as a standard for comparison. In his early account of Seneca kinship in *The League of the Iroquois*, he analyzed Seneca terminology in detail, relating the kinship groupings to clan membership (1954,I:81), and noting the merging of collateral with lineal kin. He was also impressed with the Iroquois rules of exogamy in which marriage was forbidden with consanguineal kin. In the more detailed account of Seneca kinship given in *Systems*, Morgan utilizes a series of diagrams to present the system as a whole from the standpoint of both male and female egos. But these diagrams, while they fit the logical and analytical purposes he had in mind, are borrowed from Roman models and fail to present the Iroquois system in adequate fashion. Morgan was puzzled by the Seneca use of "cousin" terms between the children of a brother and a sister, in contrast to the sibling terms used between the children of two brothers or two sisters. He thought the use of cross-cousin terminology to be a later development designed "to remove an irregularity which amounted to a blemish" (1871:158), the irregularity apparently being a logical one. The relationship of a mother's brother to his sister's son, on the other hand, Morgan believed to be a function of the mother's brother's position of authority in the matrilineal clan. This position Morgan thought to be widespread among American Indian tribes, whether matrilineal or patrilineal, although originally derived from the matrilineal system.

In exemplary fashion Morgan next compares the terminological system of the Seneca with those of their close linguistic relatives, the Cayuga, Onondaga, Oneida, and Mohawk. He finds they agree with the Seneca in both pattern and classification and vocabulary, with one important exception: they classify the father's sister with the mother instead of as an "aunt," and she in turns calls her brother's children "son" and "daughter." This deviation he finds difficult to explain in terms of long association and intermarriage of the Iroquois tribes, particularly as the Tuscarora and Wyandot follow the Seneca practice and use a cognate term for "aunt." "It is one thing to borrow a term of relationship and substitute it in the place of a domestic term of equivalent import, but quite a different undertaking to change an established relationship and invent a new term for its designation" (1871:165).

With regard to the classification of the father's sister, the Iroquois were divided rather evenly. We can see now in the light of Lafitau's earlier researches that Morgan made the correct choice in selecting the Seneca pattern as the standard. But in the light of his interpretation of the Malayan (or Hawaiian) system as an earlier stage in the development of systems of kinship terminology, the classification of the father's sister as "mother" by the Iroquois would have to be interpreted as a survival, and thus place the Iroquois on a lower level of American Indian development rather than with the "highest rank." If Morgan had seriously investigated this important variation, he might have discovered that it was an initial step in the modification of the kinship system under white acculturation or changed conditions, and that comparable shifts were underway in the Southeastern tribes at the same period. For when Morgan studied the Iroquois in the nineteenth century they had been under white pressures for over 250 years.

But for Morgan, the most remarkable fact with reference to this system was that "it is identical with the system now prevailing amongst the Tamil, Telegu, and Canarese peoples of South India. . . . The discrepancies between them are actually less, aside from the vocables, than between the Seneca and the Cayuga" (1871:166). This last statement might well have caused Morgan to pause and reconsider his basic assumptions, both as to change and origins. In particular, it should have led him to reexamine his negative answer to the question of "whether in any portion of uncivilized society, as now organized, there are at present operating causes adequate to the production and therefore to the constant reproduction of this remarkable system of relationship" (1871:474). For while Morgan did an excellent technical job of comparison, controlling it with linguistic and other checks, he had ruled out the alternate working hypotheses of independent invention or borrowing which were actually the keys to the interpretation of many of the parallels which he found.

IV

The next major grouping that Morgan discusses is composed of the Siouan-speaking tribes of the Prairie and Plains regions. This group, including the Dakota, the Central Siouans, and the Village Tribes of the Upper Missouri, shows a number of important variations in social organization and kinship which Morgan noted without appreciating their implications. The Dakota groups—Santee, Teton, and Yankton—plus the closely related Assiniboin had expanded westward from the Minnesota region in historic times. Morgan recorded the terminologies of eleven out of thirteen named bands and found them identical in pattern and cognate in vocabulary. Comparing the Yankton with the Seneca kinship system he found them identical in "ten indicative features," and in minute agreement throughout, including the affinal patterns. Morgan further noted that "the terms of relationship are the same words, in nearly every instance, under dialectic change. This shows that the terms have come down to each nation as a part of the common language; and that the system, also, was derived by each from the common source of the language" (1871:175).

Though Morgan is here anticipating part of Sapir's (1929) famous classification, his determination of cognates by inspection is premature;

it is clear from later research that the Seneca and Yankton systems have not descended unchanged from a common prototype though certain terms may ultimately prove to be cognate. The reduction of the comparison to ten "indicative relationships," restricted for the most part to close consanguineal kin, made it easier to ignore variations and resulted in the overlooking of important clues. Thus, if Morgan had examined his Dakota schedules more carefully he would have discovered that the "cousin" terms were derived from the terms for "siblings-in-law," and he might have been led to a more careful investigation of the affinal system and rules of marriage. Nor does Morgan concern himself with the possible significance of the lack of clans among the Dakota. He was already impressed with the enduring nature of the kinship system: "We shall be led step-by-step to the final inference that this system of relationship originated in the primitive ages of mankind, and that it had been propagated like language with the streams of the blood" (1871:176).

The Central Siouans of the Missouri region formed a reasonably compact grouping and Morgan was aware that they were derived from the same source as the Dakota dialects. He also found their systems of consanguinity and affinity to be one and the same. They agree with the Dakota in the ten indicative features of the "classificatory" system, but with regard to cross-cousins Morgan discovered a striking difference. The mother's brothers' children, instead of being called "cousin," are classed as "mother's brother" and "mother," and this pattern descends in the male line indefinitely; correlatively the children of the father's sister are "nephew" and "niece," or "son" and "daughter."

Morgan carefully checked this strange terminological usage on a number of reservations and found it uniform. If he had not been so strongly attached to the Iroquois system as the model for a clan-organized society, the correlation of the "line of uncles" with the mother's patrilineal clan might well have been noted and the "Omaha" pattern of kinship defined. For these Central Siouan systems, together with the cognate Winnebago, provided much better evidence of clan orientation in their kinship systems than did the Iroquois and Dakota, as Lowie (1917:152–54) long ago pointed out. Morgan's own explanation was that "a mother's brother and his lineal male descendants are thus placed in a superior relationship over her children with the authority the avunculine relationship implies in Indian society" (1871:179), but if he had inquired of his Central Siouan informants as to the actual role played by the mother's brother in these patrilineal societies he would have found it quite different.

Morgan's schedules for the Village Tribes of the Upper Missouri region,

the Mandan and Hidatsa, with the related Crow of the Plains, were incomplete, but he found sufficient evidence to establish their general relationship to the "classificatory" system. Morgan was unable to establish
the terms for cross-cousins among the Mandan, but recorded the father's
sister as "aunt," male speaking, but "mother" with a female ego. The
Hidatsa classed the father's sister as a "grandmother," and the mother's
brother as an "older brother," whereas the closely related Crow called
the father's sister "mother." Both the Crow and Hidatsa were recorded
as classifying the father's sister's children with the father and mother but
the further extensions of this pattern were not noted. Morgan states that
this form of classification will appear among the Gulf and Prairie tribes,
but as we shall see below, it appeared in a form which prevented Morgan
from realizing the nature of the parallelism, and discovering the "Crow"
type of matrilineal kinship. The partial parallels with the Iroquois in the
classification of the father's sister with the mother apparently escaped
Morgan's attention.

The Gulf Nations, the Choctaw, Chickasaw, Creek and Cherokee, were
well-known and important tribes already removed to reservations in
Oklahoma. Early in 1859 Morgan had received detailed schedules on the
Choctaw from Edwards, Copeland, and Byington, veteran missionaries
who spoke the language and knew the Choctaw well, and he later received additional schedules for the remaining tribes from other missionaries. Here the descendants of the father's sister were "father" and
"father's sister," for a male speaker, and "father" and "grandmother" for
a female speaker. But the father's sister's *son's* son is also recorded as
"father," this relationship term continuing in the *male* line. "The analogue
of this is found in the infinite series of uncles among the Missouri nations,
applied to the lineal descendants of my mother's brother" (1871:191).

I have elsewhere (1937) discussed the Choctaw and other southeastern
kinship systems and have attempted to put them in historical and accul-
turational perspective. It seems clear from the researches of Spoehr
(1947) and others that the Choctaw and other Southeastern tribes formerly had kinship systems of a "Crow" type, with the line of fathers and
father's sisters descending through the *female* line, but that they were
in the process of changing the pattern of descent when recorded for Morgan. He was thus prevented from discovering the "Crow" type of matrilineal kinship among these tribes and in perceiving its similarity to those
of the Mandan and Hidatsa, as well as possibly discovering the correct
analogy between these systems and those of the Central Siouans—that
they are both related to the pattern of unilineal descent. But Morgan

might well have engaged in a more adequate comparison of the Iroquois and the southeastern tribes, since the parallels in social organization and political structure were detailed and extensive. But by this time the other goal loomed larger: "If identity of system proves unity of origin, all of the Indian nations thus far named are of one blood" (1871:193).

Morgan was concerned to some extent with the "deviations from uniformity" which he found in comparing the various American Indian systems, principally those with regard to uncle and aunt, nephew and niece, and cross-cousins. He compared the various Siouan-speaking tribes in an attempt to determine which pattern of cross-cousin nomenclature was the oldest. Since there is no doubt that the pattern found among the Iroquois and Dakota "is the most perfect form," Morgan (1871:193) concludes that the Omaha and Crow-Choctow types are the older, and of these the latter is the most ancient. "A critical examination of all the forms of the system of relationship will show that its development is under the control of principles within itself; and that the direction of the change when attempted, was predetermined by the elements of the system."

The Prairie Nations, the term Morgan employs for the Pawnee and Arikara, were little known and Morgan was not able to collect a full schedule of terms. He was impressed by the extension of kinship terms up and down four generations from ego, and he recorded the classing of the father's sister with the mother, and her children as father and mother. This pattern is recognized as descending in the *female* line, which Morgan considered a variant from the Choctaw form. Hence, the "Crow" pattern of terminology was never clearly recognized, even though here clearly defined.

Morgan concludes his discussion up to this point with the statement: "The constancy and uniformity with which the fundamental characteristics of the system have maintained themselves appear to furnish abundant evidence of the unity of origin of these nations, and to afford a sufficient basis for their classification together as a family of nations" (1871:199).

V

Morgan next turned his attention to the great Algonkian family which occupied the territory around the Great Lakes, with outliers in the Plains and down the Atlantic coast. The Ojibwa system, it will be remembered, started Morgan on his comparative study, and it became the standard for the Great Lakes tribes, such as the Ottawa, Potawatami, and Cree. The similarity between the Ojibwa and Iroquois-Dakota systems he finds so great as "to excite astonishment." Except for the use of step-relationship terms for father's brother and mother's sister, and for their children, among the Ojibwa and other Great Lakes tribes, Morgan considered the consanguineal and affinal terminologies to be essentially the same as those of the Iroquois and Dakota. But these differences are crucial in terms of Morgan's conception of "classificatory" systems; he prejudges the issue in part by the use of "step-father" and "step-mother" as translations of terms not at all obviously related linguistically to the terms for father and mother. And in a footnote he suggests: "I think, if re-examined, it will be found that my mother's sister is my mother, and my father's brother my father, *Ego* a female, and that my sister's son, *Ego* a female, is my daughter" (1871:204, footnote 1; ["daughter" is an error, should be "son"]).

Here, also, as in the Dakota case, the terms for cross-cousin are clearly derived from those for siblings-in-law; and, further, the terms for father's sister and mother's brother are similar to, or identical with, the terms for parents-in-law. If Morgan had inquired into the marriage practices of the Ojibwa and their neighbors he would almost certainly have discovered the custom of cross-cousin marriage, which was still extensively practiced among the Canadian Ojibwa and Cree when Hallowell studied them (1937), though perhaps already given up south of the border. The discovery of a close relationship between cross-cousin marriage and kinship terminology, which had to wait for Rivers (1914), might have diverted Morgan from his dependence on the past to explain the details of the "classificatory" system; at the least it would have suggested some possible differences in origin of the Ojibwa as compared with the Iroquois.

The Ojibwa, Ottawa, and Potawatami all possessed patrilineal, exogamous clans, but the Cree, with cognate terminology for the most part, were clanless. The Central Algonkian tribes, inhabiting the prairies and parklands of what are now Wisconsin, Illinois, Indiana, and Michigan all had kinship systems of the same basic pattern as those of the Central Siouans, and specifically a classification of cross-cousins in which the mother's brother's children were "mother's brother" and "mother," and correlatively the father's sister's children were "nephew" and "niece," or "son" and "daughter," depending on the sex of ego. The Central Algonkian tribes likewise classified the father's brother with the father and the mother's sister with the mother, thus confirming Morgan in his view that the step-relationships of the Ojibwa were "simply a refinement upon an original system" (1871:205). He also noted the parallel differences between the various systems for classifying cousins among both the Siouans and Algonkians: he interpreted this not in terms of diffusion or as the result of similar causes, but as evidence for a similar pattern of change in a predetermined direction (1871:211–12).

To this group Morgan adds the Cheyenne, whose system of terminology is "classificatory" though the terms for cousins were not obtained. Morgan suggested that they probably followed the Omaha pattern, but later research (Eggan 1955a) indicates that the Cheyenne classified cross-cousins with siblings, along with a majority of other Plains tribes. Morgan believed that sibling terms were originally used for cross-cousins, in accordance with life in the "communal family," but that with the advent of clan organization separate cross-cousin terms were developed. Presumably Morgan would have placed the clanless Cheyenne as intermediate between the Malayan and Ganowanian systems, but this is not certain. When Morgan later notes the use of sibling terms for cross-cousins among the Gros Ventre, he merely says: "This last classification is not in accordance with the principles of the system" (1871:227).

Examining the terms of relationship among the Algonkian nations thus far considered, Morgan observed that they "are, for the most part, the same original words under dialectical changes. From this fact the inference arises that the terms, as well as the system, have come down to each from a common source; thus ascending to the time when all of these nations were represented by a single nation, and their dialects by a single language" (1871:217). That the Central Algonkian languages are genetically related is well known from Bloomfield's work. Recently Charles Hockett (n.d.) has reconstructed proto-Central Algonkian kinship terms and finds clear evidence of a system based upon cross-cousin marriage. Driver and Massey (1957:437) report a recent unpublished reconstruction of proto-Siouan kinship terminology by Hubert Mathews which suggests that an Omaha type of structure was basic to Siouan kinship. If these reconstructions are valid, the Central Algonkians and the Central Siouans, instead of representing parallel developments, would be convergent, with diffusion and interaction possibly playing an important role.

Morgan goes on to examine the Eastern Algonkians, where he finds a considerable number of variants on the basic "classificatory" system which are ascribed in part to disintegration and in part to error; and the Blackfoot, Blood, and Piegan, whose partially recorded systems resemble those of the Great Lakes. The twenty-four Algonkian tribes Morgan surveys are considered to be identical in major features to the "classificatory" system. He also notes that: "There is a not less striking identity in the classification of marriage relatives, amongst the widely separated Algonkian nations, which it would have been interesting to trace had it been necessary to strengthen, from this source, the principal argument for unity of origin. The marriage relationships, standing alone, would have been sufficient to demonstrate this question" (1871:228). As we have seen above, attention to the marriage system in terms of behavior, and the relations of affinal to consanguineal terminology, would have been even more useful.

In succeeding sections Morgan analyzed the more fragmentary data secured on the Athabaskan-speaking peoples, the tribes of the Columbia River region, the Shoshoni and Ute, scattered Pueblos, and the Eskimo, and found greater divergences than among the kinship systems so far considered. The tribes of the Columbia River region, in particular, which Morgan believed to be the source of dissemination of the American Indian stocks, showed considerable diversity, both in language and in kinship. The Spokane, for example, one of the Salish-speaking tribes, was found to have a different terminological system for males and females, and in addition made some discriminations not provided for even by Morgan's elaborate schedules. But all of these groups in one way or another were judged worthy of admission to the "classificatory" system, with the sole exception of the Eskimo which in "the greater and most important fundamental characteristics of this system . . . is wanting" (1871:277). Morgan wasn't quite willing to place the Eskimo among the "descriptive" systems, even though it tended strongly in that direction, so he classed it somewhat reluctantly with the Ganowanian, Turanian, and Malayan systems.

VI

From Morgan's standpoint his great discovery with regard to kinship was the classificatory system of relationship. Rivers gives him full credit:

I do not know of any discovery in the whole range of science which can be more certainly put to the credit of one man than that of the classificatory system of relationship by Lewis Morgan. By this I mean, not merely was he the first to point out clearly the existence of this mode of denoting relationship, but it was he who collected the vast mass of material by which the essential characters of the system were demonstrated, and it was he who was the first to recognize the great theoretical importance of his new discovery (1914:4–5).

Rivers goes on to point out that Morgan was largely to blame for the rejection of the importance of this discovery by his critics, since

He was not content to demonstrate, as he might to some extent have done from his own material, the close connection between the terminology of the classificatory system and forms of social organization. There can be little doubt that he recognized this connection, but he was not content to demonstrate the dependence of the terminology of relationship upon social forms, the existence of which was already known, or which were capable of demonstration with the material at his disposal. He passed over all these early stages of the argument and proceeded directly to refer the origin of the terminology to forms of social organization which were not known to exist anywhere on the earth and of which there was no direct evidence in the past (1914:5–6).

Rivers' own contributions to the rehabilitation of Morgan's views, including the demonstration of the close connection between kinship terminology and certain forms of marriage, and the conception of systems of relationship as a key to the history of social institutions, is well known. I have elsewhere (1955b:519–51) discussed the significance of Rivers' contributions when applied to the social organization of the Algonkian-speaking peoples of Northeastern North America where cross-cousin marriage is an important social institution. But of still greater importance has been the recognition that the kinship usages of a people constitute a social system composed of *both* terminology and social behavior, of which marriage is only one aspect.

The basic reason why Morgan failed to make the most from the materials on kinship that he collected would seem to be that he was not primarily interested in understanding kinship systems as such, but rather in using them as means to other ends. His frames for comparison were adequate, and he utilized linguistic and other controls, but as the "evidence" for the ultimate unity of the American Indians and their derivation from Asia seemed more and more definite, the rigor of the comparison became more relaxed. We have noted that alternate explanations to derivation from a common source, such as independent invention or borrowing, were ruled out in advance, and when Morgan returned to them it was not to test them against the data but to emphasize the correctness of the original assumptions. In the light of our present knowledge of kinship systems, we tend to emphasize the influence of common factors in bringing about similar social systems. Similarly, the assumption of the stability of the terminological system over long periods, and in the face of linguistic change, was never seriously examined, although the Iroquois tribes offered an important example of possible change in the classifications of the father's sister, and the classifications of cross-cousins in other linguistic stocks offered clear evidence of variation over relatively short periods. In recent years cross-cousin terminology has formed the basis for both Spier's (1925) and Murdock's (1949) classifications of kinship systems, and offers an index to the social structure as well. Today we might well reverse Morgan's assumption and consider the terminological patterns as relatively sensitive indicators of social change. Spoehr's (1947) study of changes in Southeastern tribes under acculturation makes this conclusion clear, and it is supported by my own (1937; 1950; 1955a) researches in the Southeast, Plains, and Pueblo regions.

If Morgan had been more concerned about the possible alternate explanations of kinship patterns and their stability, and if he had investigated the variations which he found with the same enthusiasm that he did the similarities, he would have been in a position to contribute a great deal more to the theoretical study of kinship than he in fact did. And the comparative method might have been salvaged and restored to usefulness rather than being abandoned by American ethnologists after Boas' (1896) attack.

From a larger perspective, Lowie has wondered what Morgan's scheme

might have been like if chance had first thrown him among the clanless Paiute, the wealth-craving Yurok, the pedigree-mad Polynesians, or the monarchial Baganda. Proceeding from the Seneca and encountering for hundreds of miles nothing but broadly comparable social structures, Morgan prematurely generalized what primitive society was like, even though on an apparently wide inductive basis. And when he had once formulated the generalization, he could dismiss contradictory evidence from the Columbia River tribes with the cheap auxiliary hypothesis that their clan organization had fallen into decay (1936:174).

It is true that Morgan believed that of the nations north of Mexico "the Iroquois deservedly hold the highest rank," and his view of kinship was forever complicated by the fact that the Iroquois system of terminology, with its balanced bilateral character, did not rest conformably on a matrilineal clan system, as he supposed. Hence he was not able to isolate types within or outside the classificatory system, nor to see the correlation of unilineal clans with "Omaha" and "Crow" systems. The task of understanding the Iroquois social system and its development still faces anthropologists, and Morgan's critics have added little to our basic knowledge. However, Merlin Myers' forthcoming structural-functional analysis, based on recent field work in Canada, should dispel some of the mystery, and Harry Basehart's historical study, when published, will contribute further to our understanding.

But Morgan cannot be held responsible for the fact that so many of the tribes he studied at first-hand happened to have broadly similar social systems. He expended considerable effort to reach as many tribes as were accessible to study in the 1860's; he could not know that Northern and Eastern North America would turn out to be a single major culture area (in, for example, Kroeber's [1939] classification), in contrast to the much greater differentiation in Western North America. Lowie's strictures with regard to premature generalization are more relevant. Morgan's major generalization with regard to the "classificatory" system was made early and defended at every turn, despite mounting evidence that it was not universal. Even the Ojibwa terminology which began the comparison did not fit the main "indicative features" of the "classificatory" system.

Leslie A. White has evaluated Morgan's contribution to kinship as follows:

Although Morgan failed to see that kinship in human society is primarily and essentially a social phenomenon and only secondarily and incidentally a biological matter, he did discover and appreciate the fact that relationship terms are sociological devices employed in the regulation of social life. A relationship term is the designation of an individual or class of individuals that is socially significant. Every society of human beings is divided into social classes or groups, which, with reference to any individual in the society, are designated with kinship terms such as "uncle," "sister," "mother-in-law," etc. One's behavior toward one's fellows varies, depending upon the category of relationship in which the person stands. Since the categories are labelled with kinship terms, a close functional relationship obtains between kinship nomenclature and social organization and behavior. These are the views and postulates upon which a modern school of social anthropology bases much of its work. They were discovered, elucidated and established by Morgan many decades ago. (1948:144).

With much of White's evaluation we can readily agree. Morgan clearly recognized the social importance of kinship and was aware that the terminology formed a definite system. With regard to the functional relationships obtaining between kinship nomenclature and social organization behavior, Morgan recognized such relationships macroscopically, but was little concerned with them at the level of the individual tribe. The Malayan (Hawaiian) system he related to particular forms of marriage, and the Ganowanian, or American Indian system he correlated with clans. Only rarely, as in the case of the mother's brother, does he attempt to relate particular terminology to special status or behavior. Modern social anthropology is built in part on Morgan's discoveries, but much of its progress has been in the directions which Morgan neglected—the detailed structural and functional analysis of individual tribes and communities.

In modern perspective certain of Morgan's assumptions and discoveries with regard to kinship require modification. Kinship terminology is no longer considered to be the stable institution Morgan envisaged, enduring over centuries and furnishing evidence of genetic relations no longer apparent otherwise. The unity or diversity of the American Indians as a race, and their ultimate derivation from Asia, rest today on other evidence than kinship terminologies. The evolutionary stages of family development are no longer tenable. Even the "classificatory" system, now that the dust of controversy has settled, has less significance than Morgan envisaged, although it is still an important theoretical concept (cf. Radcliffe-Brown 1941).

But even so it is remarkable how close to the truth he actually came. He grasped the essential principles and considered the possible explanations. That he rejected the explanations that modern social anthropology accepts was in some measure due to the intellectual fashions of the time. And there is much else that remains. The insights that Morgan achieved through saturation in kinship for a decade are scattered throughout *Systems,* waiting to be utilized. And above all there are the raw data that he collected on kinship terminologies which become increasingly valuable as we learn more about kinship systems. It may well be that Morgan himself is the best evaluator of his contributions to the study of kinship. After summarizing what he has done, in the Introduction to *Systems,* he says: "The tables, however, are the main results of this investigation. In their importance and value they reach far beyond any present use of their contents which the writer may be able to indicate. If they can be perfected, and the systems of the unrepresented nations be supplied, their value would be greatly increased" (1871:8). Of his methods of comparison he was properly modest:

If these tables prove sufficient to demonstrate the utility of systems of relationship in the prosecution of ethnological investigations, one of the main objects of this work will be accomplished. The number of nations represented is too small to exhibit all the special capacities of this instrumentality. The more thoroughly the system is explored in the different nations of the same family of speech, especially where the form is classificatory, the more ample and decisive the evidence will become which bears upon the question of their genetic classification (1871:809).

In his emphasis upon *systems* of relationship and their controlled comparison Morgan is much closer to modern scholarship than were many of his critics. After a long interval of neglect Morgan's *Systems of Consanguinity and Affinity of the Human Family* is coming into its own and the data in the tables are being expanded by the addition of new tribes and deepened by the collecting of contemporary materials from the same tribes. There is even talk of reprinting *Systems*. And on the basis of his pioneer insights into kinship new methods of investigation have developed which do in fact carry us far beyond the stage which Morgan had achieved. He predicted this eventuality and would be puzzled by the length of time it has taken us to get this far beyond him.

BIBLIOGRAPHY

BOAS, FRANZ
  1888 "The Central Eskimo." *Annual Report of the Bureau of [American] Ethnology*, 6(1884–85):399–669.
  1896 "The Limitations of the Comparative Method of Anthropology." *Science*, 4:901–908.
DRIVER, HAROLD E. and WILLIAM C. MASSEY
  1957 "Comparative Studies of North American Indians." *Transactions of the American Philosophical Society*, 47:165–456.
EGGAN, FRED
  1937 "Historical Changes in the Choctaw Kinship System." *American Anthropologist*, 39:34–52.
  1950 *Social Organization of the Western Pueblos*. Chicago, The University of Chicago Press.
  1955a "The Cheyenne and Arapaho Kinship System." In *Social Anthropology of North American Tribes*, revised edition, ed. by Fred Eggan, pp. 35–95. Chicago, The University of Chicago Press.
  1955b "Social Anthropology: Methods and Results." In *Social Anthropology of North American Tribes*, revised edition, ed. by Fred Eggan, pp. 485–551. Chicago, The University of Chicago Press.
EVANS-PRITCHARD, E. E.
  1951 *Social Anthropology*. London, Cohen & West.
HALLOWELL, A. IRVING
  1937 "Cross-Cousin Marriage in the Lake Winnipeg Area." *Twenty-fifth Anniversary Studies*, ed. by D. S. Davidson. *Publications of the Philadelphia Anthropological Society*, 1:95–110.
HOCKETT, CHARLES
  n.d. "A Reconstruction of the Proto-Central Algonquian Kinship System." Unpublished manuscript.

KROEBER, A. L.

1939 "Cultural and Natural Areas of Native North America." *University of California Publications in American Archaeology and Ethnology*, 38.

LOWIE, ROBERT H.

1917 *Culture and Ethnology.* New York, Boni & Liveright.

1936 "Lewis H. Morgan in Historical Perspective." In *Essays in Anthropology Presented to A. L. Kroeber in Celebration of his 60th Birthday*, pp. 169–181. Berkeley, University of California Press.

1937 *The History of Ethnological Theory.* New York, Farrar & Rinehart.

MCLENNAN, J. F.

1886 *Studies in Ancient History.* 2nd edition. London, Macmillan and Co.

MORGAN, LEWIS H.

1954 *League of the Ho-dé-no-sau-nee or Iroquois.* Reprinted by Human Relations Area Files, New Haven, 2 vols. (From edition of H. M. Lloyd, 1901, based on 1851 edition.)

1871 "Systems of Consanguinity and Affinity of the Human Family." *Smithsonian Contributions to Knowledge*, 17.

1877 *Ancient Society.* New York, Henry Holt & Co.

MURDOCK, GEORGE P.

1949 *Social Structure.* New York, The Macmillan Company.

RADCLIFFE-BROWN, A. R.

1941 "The Study of Kinship Systems." *Journal of the Royal Anthropological Institute*, 71:1–18.

1950 "Introduction." In *African Systems of Kinship and Marriage*, ed. by A. R. Radcliffe-Brown and Daryll Forde, pp. 1–85. London, Oxford University Press.

RIVERS, W. H. R.

1900 "A Genealogical Method of Collecting Social and Vital Statistics." *Journal of the Royal Anthropological Institute*, 30:71–82.

1914 *Kinship and Social Organization.* London, Constable & Co., Ltd.

SAPIR, EDWARD

1929 "Central and North American Languages." *Encyclopaedia Britannica*, 14th edition, 5:138–141.

SPIER, LESLIE

1925 "The Distribution of Kinship Systems in North America." *University of Washington Publications in Anthropology*, 1:71–88.

SPOEHR, ALEXANDER
   1947 "Changing Kinship Systems." *Field Museum of Natural History, Publications, Anthropological Series,* 33:151–235.
STERN, BERNHARD J.
   1931 *Lewis H. Morgan, Social Evolutionist.* Chicago, The University of Chicago Press.
TAX, SOL
   1955 "From Lafitau to Radcliffe-Brown." In *Social Anthropology of North American Tribes,* revised edition, ed. by Fred Eggan, pp. 445–481. Chicago, The University of Chicago Press.
WHITE, LESLIE A.
   1948 "Lewis H. Morgan: Pioneer in the Theory of Social Evolution." In *An Introduction to the History of Sociology,* ed. by H. E. Barnes, pp. 138–154. Chicago, The University of Chicago Press.
   1957 "How Morgan Came to Write Systems of Consanguinity and Affinity." *Papers of the Michigan Academy of Science, Arts, and Letters,* 42:257–268.

* * * *

Alfred K. Guthe

ROCHESTER MUSEUM OF ARTS AND SCIENCES

THE CULTURAL BACKGROUND

OF THE IROQUOIS

One of the archaeological problems in northeastern North America is that of the cultural origins of the northern Iroquois. For many years, Parker's theory of a recent Iroquoian migration into their historic homeland had been accepted. He postulated that the Iroquois tribes once lived near the mouth of the Ohio River and were pushed up the Ohio into the northeast and the Carolinas (1922:155–161). He estimated that the Iroquois were in the New York area around 1300 A.D. (*Ibid.*: 100). Recently MacNeish (1952) undertook the analysis of Iroquoian pottery. He defined many pottery types and associated them with the Mohawk, Oneida, Onondaga, Cayuga, Seneca, Erie, Neutral-Wenro, and Huron tribes of the Iroquois. Types were not defined for Susquehannock pottery because MacNeish was not able to examine large collections of it. However, similarities between the pottery of this tribe and that of the Cayuga were noted, suggesting these two tribes share an ancestral culture.

During recent years this problem has received renewed attention. The definition of Iroquois pottery types has revived interest in the cultural background of the northern Iroquois. It has provided students of northeastern archaeology with a single frame of reference. The designation of a site as that of an Iroquoian occupation is now based upon something more than subjective judgment. By using what is called the "Direct Historic Approach," MacNeish first analyzed pottery from historically documented sites. He then identified pottery from prehistoric sites as generically connected with pottery from historic sites by means of seriation or overlapping pottery types and ceramic trends. This resulted in the identification of prehistoric pottery types with specific tribes. Thus, it is now possible to associate certain sites of Indian occupation with specific Iroquoian tribes. Having determined the pottery types, it became possible to trace the development of various of these types. This analysis led MacNeish to conclude that certain Iroquois pottery had developed from certain pottery types in the Owasco culture (MacNeish 1952). Owasco is the archaeological culture which precedes the Iroquois in the same region. It is recognized as evidence of a late prehistoric occupation in much of New York State (Ritchie 1944:29). Related cultural material in Ontario and Michigan has been identified. It may not be classic Owasco, but it is generically close (Kidd 1954). Knowing this, MacNeish generalized that there was a tendency for the Owasco culture to develop into an Iroquoian type of material culture. In this development, cultural assemblages which can be identified as those of specific tribes can be recognized (MacNeish 1952:89).

The replacement of Parker's migration theory by MacNeish's Owasco-Iroquois development hypothesis met with general approval when it was presented. Parker's theory had begun to lose favor since corroborative evidence was not unearthed in the Ohio Valley and other territories through which the migration would have had to pass. In 1944, Griffin even postulated that the Iroquois culture might have developed from a Middle Woodland culture in the area (Griffin 1944:372). While based primarily on the study of pottery, the generalization that the Owasco culture, with its local variation, contains the antecedents of all Iroquois culture traits has tended to be accepted by many workers in the northeast without question. This paper will consider the validity of the generalization. Such a view appears to be inconsistent with our understanding of the culture processes affecting persistence and change in cultures. It doesn't explain the presence of certain nonceramic culture traits in some Iroquois cultures. It will be demonstrated that all Iroquois traits cannot be derived from the Owasco culture.

Two variables are involved in the following discussion. They are time and culture. Uncertainties and unknowns exist in each of these. Archaeologists lack information on the exact time of a site's occupation. A relative sequence for the larger cultural groups has been presented for New York State (Ritchie 1951). But the precise temporal relationship between the several sites exhibiting evidence of occupation during these larger groups is not available. Radiocarbon dates are very helpful and have generally corroborated the relative sequence of cultures. However, the margins of error presented with each radiocarbon date make it impossible to determine an accurate time scale for sites within each of the cultural periods. A possible error of 300 years (±150 years) covers a span of several human generations, a rather long period during which changes could take place. Sites occupied during different seasons of a year or sites occupied for only a decade cannot be separated temporally through the use of radiocarbon dates.

The cultures with which the archaeologist deals are not complete cultures in an ethnographic sense. They are only "fossils" of cultures. The artifacts which the archaeologist recovers are only those whose physical characteristics and associations are such that they are preserved in the earth. Because of varying soil conditions certain types of artifacts such as bone and antler may be found on one site but not another. However, if the major portion of a cultural assemblage is found in two or more sites, it is customary to assume they represent the same culture. The archaeologist can do no more than speculate as to the probable language, social structure, and religious concepts of the culture with which he deals. Still, armed with ethnographic reports of nonwestern cultures, he can present shrewd guesses as to the nature of these parts of the culture.

The combination of temporal inaccuracy and the finding of only cultural fossils with which to deal means that information on the geographic distribution of specific traits must be somewhat unreliable. Even if all the sites of Indian occupation had been excavated in an area, there is no certainty that similar traits were used in each during more than a general time period. It is quite possible that traits developed at one point in time have persisted in areas peripheral to the region of initial development. It is also possible that the people in the region of original development have abandoned the use of that trait (Wissler 1922:296).

The archaeologist must proceed as if these variables were more or less constant in order to organize his findings into a meaningful story of culture history.

Returning to the Owasco-Iroquis cultural relationship, it is obvious that comparisons must be made of the traits found in each of the cultures. Some of this has been done. Ritchie has summarized the similarities between them and lists 34 lithic, bone and antler, burial, and settlement traits which are found in both cultures (1944:41–46). MacNeish reports he has found that 31 of 36 nonceramic traits common to all northern Iroquois groups occur in the late Owasco culture (1952:82). While this lends considerable support to the new theory, the Iroquois traits which are not late Owasco traits must be explained. Can they be logically derived from Owasco traits? Were trends in these directions evident in that culture? Although answers to these and other questions may never be more than speculations, it is clear that some insights and possible approaches toward the answers can be obtained through the application of principles developed by students of culture history. The processes of culture change and persistence which anthropologists have defined are certainly pertinent.

New traits appearing for the first time may be the result of developments or new applications of old principles existing within a culture. On the other hand, they may have been introduced to the culture through contacts. In the first instance, a relationship between traits of the earlier and later forms of a culture can be demonstrated. In the latter instance, traits similar to new ones should be found to exist in cultures which existed in the neighboring areas during the same general time period, or with cultures which can be proven to be related in a more distant area (Kroeber 1948:345-370).

It is my contention that certain traits appearing in late Owasco culture can best be explained as imports, not local developments. They are therefore evidence of diffusion rather than invention. If this can be supported, there is justification in stating that the Iroquois culture is a mixture of traits, some of which are derived from the Owasco culture, and others of which were received through contact with another culture, or cultures. This does not necessarily mean an invasion of the area by another group of people. The new traits could have been received as a result of contacts between the Owasco people and their neighbors.

Since many nonceramic traits are common to both the Owasco and Iroquois cultures, indication of the introduction of new traits from a non-Owasco culture will be found only by considering the difference between the cultures. At the present time, the more significant ones are: village size and location, earthworks, ossuaries, and floor plans of structures.

Information available on the size of villages during the Late Woodland and Early Historic periods of occupation is limited. The village areas of only a few sites of these periods have been examined. Most of our information comes from pits filled with refuse, refuse dumps, and, in the case of historic sites, from graves.

Owasco villages during the Late Woodland are described as large (Ritchie 1956:77). A search through the literature reveals that the reported sites covered areas of varying acreage. The Castle Creek Site, an Owasco station, covered approximately 33,000 square feet or less than an acre. The Partridge, or Bainbridge, Site, another Owasco station, covered 11,200 square feet (Ritchie 1944:68–71). The Sackett Site, another Owasco station, covered about three acres although the principal ditch considered as enclosing the village area was ellipsoidal, measuring 243 by 202 feet. Thus the village proper is only slightly more than an acre in area (Ritchie 1936:7, 11). Although 22 Owasco sites are discussed in Ritchie's *The Pre-Iroquoian Occupations of New York State* (1944:57–101), the area covered by each occupation could not be given. Another Owasco site, the Morrow Site near Honeoye, New York, also contained a ditch believed to enclose the village area. This ditch enclosed a roughly oval area approximately 180 feet in diameter, or less than an acre. Early historic Iroquois villages were comparable in size.

During the intervening time, perhaps some 400 years, it is to be expected that the village size would remain somewhat the same size. The subsistence pattern was based upon horticulture in both cultures. Certainly an increase in knowledge regarding horticultural techniques is to be expected. Thus the village population would tend to increase. However, this does not always appear to be the case. We find most early prehistoric Iroquois sites to be small settlements. (Early prehistoric Iroquois sites are identified chiefly by the presence of pottery defined as Iroquois in type.) Ritchie describes the Chance Horizon sites as small and consisting of scattered shallow refuse deposits. These, he believes, indicate a very limited population (Ritchie 1952:13). They are early Mohawk sites located in the Mohawk River drainage. Perhaps the Getman Site, a recently-excavated Chance Horizon site, will lead to a modification of this statement. During the summer of 1957, Ritchie supervised the excavation of a portion of this site uncovering evidence of a palisade enclosing the village. The palisade was almost circular with a diameter of approximately 320 feet, thus enclosing an area of more than one and a half acres (Ritchie 1958:10). The study and analysis of material from this site has yet to be completed. If it proves to be early in the Chance Horizon, at least one early prehistoric Iroquois village was large in size.

Other early prehistoric Iroquois sites are known in western New York. The Hummel Site in Ontario County has been cited as a link between the Owasco and Cayuga Iroquois because of the pottery found there (MacNeish 1952:83). Following MacNeish's study of the excavated material, additional work was done on the Hummel Site by members of the Lewis H. Morgan Chapter, New York State Archeological Association, and the Rochester Museum of Arts and Sciences. Evidence of occupation extended over an area of 400 by 200 feet, or almost two acres. This evidence was scattered, but there were several areas of refuse concentration. These are believed to have been the location of dwellings (Guthe 1955).

In Chautauqua and Cattaraugus Counties, early prehistoric Iroquois sites have been reported in considerable numbers (Parker 1922:494–499; 509–523). Few of these are described in sufficient detail for present purposes. The information on the area of some of these indicates varying sizes of villages. The Westfield Site covers more than three acres. Other sites were of comparable size or smaller (Guthe 1958a:25–48).

From this brief summary, it is evident that the early prehistoric Iroquois sites vary in size. Some were quite large, others smaller. But size of area occupied is not an accurate measure of population size. A small population could occupy a large area over a short period of time, moving their living area only a few feet each year or less. Or a large population could occupy a small area. The depth of refuse on a site is therefore of importance.

It is doubtful that settlements were standardized as to size and population. It may be that the smaller sites were occupied only during certain seasons of the year. This practice existed among the Iroquois (Fenton 1951:42). If this same practice was followed by their ancestors, larger early prehistoric Iroquois villages should occur. Perhaps the Getman Site is one, but others are still to be located. In any event, the problem of determining the relationship of the large and small villages still exists.

Site locations are of interest in evaluating the possibility that the small sites may be seasonal camps. Several Owasco sites are found on hilltops that provide protection by their natural situation. In addition to this natural protection, some were at least partially surrounded by palisades, or ditches, or both (Ritchie 1944:67, 76; Guthe 1958b). Other Owasco sites are located on the banks of lakes and streams (Ritchie, Lenig, and Miller 1953; Parker 1922:340–343). Some of the early prehistoric Mohawk sites are found on high, well-drained land (Ritchie 1952:13). Several early prehistoric Iroquois sites in the Seneca area are located on hilltops and at some distance from a major stream or lake. Hilltops or valleys were chosen for early prehistoric settlements in southwestern New York. Early historic Iroquois villages in Seneca, Mohawk, and Cayuga areas were also placed on hilltops. Some of these were surrounded by palisades (Grassmann 1952:102).

It has long been held that villages were placed on hilltops as a defensive measure. Perhaps this is so, but the need for this protection has never been clearly indicated. Was it to aid in fending off attacks? Was it that hilltops were selected for settlement by horticultural groups in order to leave the valleys and flood plains open for cultivation? The choice of terrain may have been governed in part by the reason for settling; that is, hunting, fishing, or cultivating. At any rate, hilltops were not invariably selected by the Owasco and Iroquois.

The location of settlements on hilltops has led some to designate them as fortified villages. But to say that a village was fortified is somewhat misleading unless the nature of the fortification is clearly stated. In the literature one may find a village described as fortified merely because it is located on the top of a steep-sided hill. A village may be recorded as fortified because it is on the top of a ridge extending into a valley. Occasionally, the natural fortification on three sides will be augmented by the erection of an earthen embankment across the fourth side. The other extreme of fortification is represented by a village completely enclosed by an artificial embankment or a ditch, or both. It is believed that the earth for the embankment was usually obtained by excavating a ditch. Generally, it is assumed that the embankment served as a foundation for a palisade of upright poles. Investigation of some of these embankments has produced no evidence of post molds, an indication of the former presence of a palisade. This suggests that some embankments served a purpose other than that of defense.

It is suspected that all earthworks in the Iroquois area were not intended as fortifications. Some were erected in valleys, others on hilltops. Some may have been associated with the religion of the early prehistoric Iroquois. The size and shape of the area enclosed by an embankment may be pertinent to this explanation. The area enclosed varies from about one-eighth of an acre to 16 acres. The occupational refuse within these may form a thin deposit a few inches in depth, or it may be 10 to 12 inches in depth. Occasionally it will be more concentrated in specific spots. Many of the circular enclosures contain a thin refuse mantle. This could indicate a short period of use or recurring visits at regulated intervals of time. The effort involved in constructing an earthwork would seem to argue in support of recurring visits.

A consideration of the distribution of earthworks reveals that they are numerous in western New York and occur on sites of the Whittlesey Focus in northeastern Ohio. They have also been reported in the area east of Lake Ontario (Parker 1922:132) and in southern Ontario (Thomas 1894: 540; Lee 1952:66–68). Many are associated with early prehistoric Iroquoian material. The absence of earthworks in other parts of Iroquois territory can be interpreted in two ways. Either earthworks represent a localized development or they were a culture trait which was introduced only to the western area of Iroquois occupation during early prehistoric Iroquois times.

Ditches are found on three Owasco sites. Possibly earthworks were associated with these, but positive proof of their presence is lacking. One of these sites is the Sackett Site, near Canandaigua, New York, in which pottery was found which is a probable ancestor for Seneca and Cayuga pottery (MacNeish 1952:83). Another is the Morrow Site, near Honeoye, New York, which yielded pottery resembling some of that found on the Sackett Site. The Castle Creek Site was also enclosed by a ditch, but here the posts of the palisade had been set in the ditch (Ritchie 1944:67). While this presence of ditches in Owasco sites would seem to be a probable source of ditches and earthworks in Iroquois sites, the distribution of early prehistoric Iroquois sites with earthworks does not coincide with that of the sites which the pottery analysis suggests are the probable successors to the above mentioned Owasco sites. The presence of earthworks on western Iroquois sites seems to be due to non-Owasco sources. As a matter of fact, the area in which earthworks are most numerous is not recognized as one in which the Owasco culture is found. The latter culture does not extend west of the Genesee Valley in New York (Ritchie, Lenig, and Miller 1953:6). However, pottery and other traits representing a Late Woodland occupation in western New York, eastern Michigan and southern Ontario are certainly related to the New York Owasco and can be labeled Owascoid (Kidd 1954; Greenman 1937: 95). MacNeish postulates that the Erie, Neutral, and Huron are derived from the "Ontario Owasco" (1952:87).

A trait showing the same distribution as earthworks is the practice of burial in ossuaries, or multiple burials of human skeletal material. In many of these, incomplete individuals are represented indicating they were secondary burials. Ossuaries are found in many sites on which there are earthworks, but there is no absolute correlation. Some ossuaries are not associated with earthworks, and vice-versa. Not only this, but the cultural identification of ossuaries is not always possible since they rarely contain artifacts (Parker 1922:423). However, a number of those which can be identified through cultural associations are Iroquois. The early prehistoric Iroquois ossuaries are smaller in size and contain the skeletal material of fewer individuals than the later ones. The Westfield Site, in Chautauqua County, New York, is, at least in part, an early prehistoric Iroquois occupation. Six ossuaries, one containing 125 individuals, another only four individuals were located here. The Ossossane ossuary in Simcoe County, Ontario was made in 1636 A.D. and is historic Huron. It contained the remains of an estimated 1,000 individuals (Kidd 1953:364, 378). Do the small ossuaries of the early prehistoric Iroquois indicate that a smaller population existed at that time? Were burials in ossuaries made more frequently in earlier times than they were during the historic period? Did the villages of historic Iroquois represent a greater consolidation of the population than existed during prehistoric times?

The investigation of villages which can be identified with ossuaries could provide some insight into these questions. The number of dwellings indicated by the post mold patterns could enable one to estimate the population of the village. However, the excavation of village areas in the northeast is just beginning and none are clearly associated with an ossuary. Nevertheless, some information on house patterns is available. The floor plans of structures have been located through the excavation of sites in Ontario, New York, and Pennsylvania.

In Ontario, Emerson uncovered the floor plan of a long house on the Warminster Site. It measured about 24 feet in width and 72 feet in length. One end was square, the other rounded. Three entrances were noted. One was on the east, another on the west and the third on the south side of the structure. This site may be that of the village of Cahiague occupied in 1615 A.D. It is an historic Huron village (*Proceedings: The Fourth Conference on Iroquois Research* 1949:17).

An historic Seneca village area contained at least one long house. Although the rows of post molds remaining from the wall supports were not clear, due possibly to repairs and perhaps the superposition of a second structure, the length of the structure was 56 feet. The square ends were approximately 23 feet in width. This floor pattern was located on the Factory Hollow Site near West Bloomfield, in Ontario County, New York. It has been established as an occupation of about 1600 A.D. (Guthe 1958c:37).

The Mohawk-Caughnawaga Site, near Fonda, New York, was occupied between 1667–1693 (Grassmann 1951). Excavations, directed by Father Grassmann, uncovered the floor plans of at least five structures. Three of these were dwellings. One measured 20 feet in width and 98 feet in length. Another was 21 feet wide and 68 feet long. The third was 23 feet wide and 85 feet long (Grassmann, correspondence).

To the south in Susquehannock territory, along the Susquehanna River in Pennsylvania, the post molds indicating the former presence of a long house were located by W. Fred Kinsey. This is on the Leibhart Site near Wrightsville. It is thought to have been occupied about 1650–1675 A.D. The post mold pattern indicated a structure approximately 92 feet long and 24 feet wide (Kinsey 1957:180).

It is certainly clear that the Iroquois were living in long houses during the early historic period. The construction of long houses during the prehistoric Iroquois period in Mohawk and Huron territory has also been demonstrated.

The Getman Site, an early prehistoric Iroquois occupation of the Chance Horizon, is located in Montgomery County, New York. The floor pattern uncovered here was rectangular. It measured about 90 feet in length and 22 feet in width (Ritchie 1958:10). Evidence of another long house on a Chance Horizon site is suggested by a line of post molds on the Deowongo Island Site in Otsego County, New York (Ritchie 1952:9).

In Huron territory, Emerson has located the floor plans of 17 long houses on two prehistoric sites. One of 16, on the Woodbridge Site, York County, Ontario, was 28 feet wide and 170 feet long. Entrances were on the south and east of the structure (Ritchie 1950:356). This is an early prehistoric Huron site (MacNeish 1952:85). Another house floor was located on the Balsam Lake Site, near Coboconk in Victoria County, Ontario, which measured 30 feet by 150 feet. This site is similar to the Black Creek Site, so is also early prehistoric Huron (Anonymous 1951: 285–286; MacNeish 1952:85).

The Crawford Site, in Lambton County, Ontario, revealed post mold patterns of seven long houses. They were rectangular measuring about 20 feet in width and 58 to 85 feet in length. It is an early prehistoric Iroquois site, probably proto-Huron-Neutral in culture (Jury 1948).

The time at which dwellings with rectangular floor plans first appear seems to agree closely with the appearance of Iroquois pottery types in the area. The Castle Creek Site, in Broome County, New York, is a late Owasco occupation with indications of circular house floors (Ritchie 1944:67). This site contained Owasco pottery, but some of it shows Iroquois traits (Ritchie 1934:50–51). The Sackett Site, an Owasco village near Canandaigua, New York, also contained evidence of circular house floors. These were about 10 feet in diameter (Ritchie 1936:39–43). A third Owasco site yielding evidence of circular house floors is the Bates Site in Chenango County, New York. The evidence for these is somewhat inconclusive since Ritchie reports no one house floor could be entirely defined (1958:10).

From the scattered and limited evidence, prototypes for the rectangular long house structure are not to be found in the Owasco area. The shift from a circular floor plan to a rectangular one appears to be a rather complicated architectural feat. Stimulus to build a larger dwelling might be provided by an increase in population or the desire to concentrate greater numbers of people under a single roof. Ritchie speculates that the clan structure had not been developed during the Owasco culture (1958: 10). While this is entirely possible, structures with rectangular floor plans have been reported for a site with Owascoid cultural material. Evidence of two such structures was found on the Younge Site in Lapeer County, Michigan. In reporting these, Greenman calls them enclosures. One measured 585 feet in length and 25 to 30 feet in width. The other was 252 feet long and 25 to 30 feet wide (1937:5). The length of these exceeds that reported for any Iroquois long house. It is possible that the Younge enclosures are not prototypic of the long house. However, it does indicate that rectangular structures were being built. Greenman carefully considered several possible interpretations of their use. He concludes that they were probably erected as part of a ceremony like the Huron burial rite (*ibid.:* 96). While it is often fallacious to use a single example of a cultural feature as proof of an argument, the evidence on the Younge Site does suggest that the source of structures with rectangular floor plans may well lie outside of the Owasco homeland in the central part of New York State.

This review of selected culture traits found in Iroquois sites does not completely support an Owasco origin for Iroquois culture. It suggests that there were multiple sources for the Iroquois, one of which was the Owasco culture. Such a conclusion is not at variance with the understanding of culture processes. A culture is receptive to its own past and also to culture traits developed in other cultures. This is why the process of diffusion is so often recorded as a factor in culture change. In other words, it would be impossible to find a culture comprised of traits which could be explained only as due to developments taking place within that culture.

Present evidence indicates that at least some ceramic, lithic, and bone artifacts representing the Iroquois culture are derived from the Late Woodland Owasco culture which preceded the northern Iroquois in their geographical situation. It is also evident that the practice of horticulture and residence in villages on hilltops was a common characteristic of both the Owasco and Iroquois cultures. The fortification of these villages by means of a surrounding palisade is also common to both cultures. Still the presence of similar traits in the Late Woodland cultures to the west and south of the Iroquois region should not be overlooked.

Traits comprising part of the prehistoric Iroquois culture in western New York and Ontario and not now known to be present in the Iroquois culture of eastern New York include the practice of constructing earthworks, particularly circular ones, and the practice of burial in ossuaries. Ossuaries and rectangular house floors are not part of the Owasco complex. Sources for these traits are unknown at this time, but they may have been introduced to the Iroquois from somewhere to the west or south of their area.

The principal conclusion which has been reached is that culture theory and the present distribution of certain Iroquois traits do not enable one to derive all of Iroquois culture from its archaeologically known predecessor in New York State, that is, the Owasco culture. Obviously, the determination of the cultural background of the northern Iroquois must await further research. At this time programs for the investigation of settlement patterns and skeletal characteristics of the northeastern Indians have been initiated. They should produce additional data of value to the student of northeastern culture history.

BIBLIOGRAPHY

ANONYMOUS
1951 "Notes and News: Northeast." *American Antiquity,* 16:285–287.

FENTON, WILLIAM N.
1951 "Locality as a Basic Factor in the Development of Iroquois Social Structure." In *Symposium on Local Diversity in Iroquois Culture,* ed. by William N. Fenton. *Bureau of American Ethnology Bulletin,* 149:35–54.

GRASSMANN, THOMAS
1951 "The Mohawk-Caughnawaga Excavation." *Bulletin of the Eastern States Archeological Federation,* 10:9.
1952 "The Question of the Locations of Mohawk Indian Village Sites Existing During the Historic Period." *Pennsylvania Archaeologist,* 22:98–111.

GREENMAN, EMERSON F.
1937 "The Younge Site." *Occasional Contributions from the Museum of Anthropology of the University of Michigan,* 6.

GRIFFEN, JAMES B.
1944 "The Iroquois in American Prehistory." *Papers of the Michigan Academy of Science, Arts, and Letters,* 29(1943):357–374.

GUTHE, ALFRED K.
1955 "The Hummel Site (Can. 23–3)." *Museum Service, Bulletin of the Rochester Museum of Arts and Sciences,* 28:10–11.
1958a "The Late Prehistoric Occupation in Southwestern New York: An Interpretive Analysis." *Research Records of the Rochester Museum of Arts and Sciences,* 11.

Alfred K. Guthe

1958b "The Morrow Site." *Bulletin of the Eastern States Archeological Federation*, 17:11.

1958c "A Possible Seneca House Site, A.D. 1600." *Pennsylvania Archaeologist*, 28:33–38.

JURY, WILFRID

1948 "Crawford Prehistoric Village Site." *Museum of Indian Archaeology, The University of Western Ontario, Bulletin of the Museums*, 7.

KIDD, KENNETH E.

1953 "The Excavation and Historical Identification of a Huron Ossuary." *American Antiquity*, 18:359–379.

1954 "A Woodland Site near Chatham, Ontario." *Transactions of the Royal Canadian Institute*, 30:141–178.

KINSEY, W. FRED

1957 "A Susquehannock Longhouse." *American Antiquity*, 23:180–181.

KROEBER, A. L.

1948 *Anthropology*. New York, Harcourt, Brace and Company.

LEE, THOMAS E.

1952 "A Preliminary Report on an Archaeological Survey of Southwestern Ontario for 1950." *National Museum of Canada, Bulletin*, 126:64–75.

MacNEISH, RICHARD S.

1952 "Iroquois Pottery Types. A Technique for the Study of Iroquois Prehistory." *National Museum of Canada, Bulletin*, 124.

PARKER, ARTHUR C.

1922 The Archeological History of New York. *New York State Museum Bulletin*, Nos. 235–238.

Proceedings: The Fourth Conference on Iroquois Research.

1949 Mimeographed. Washington, D.C.

RITCHIE, WILLIAM A.

1934 "An Algonkin-Iroquois Site on Castle Creek, Broome County, N.Y." *Research Records of the Rochester Museum of Arts and Sciences*, 2.

1936 "A Prehistoric Fortified Village Site at Canandaigua, Ontario County, New York." *Research Records of the Rochester Museum of Arts and Sciences*, 3.

1944 "The Pre-Iroquoian Occupations of New York State." *Rochester Museum of Arts and Sciences, Memoir*, 1.

1950 "News and Notes: Northeast." *American Antiquity*, 15:354–356.

1951 "A Current Synthesis of New York Prehistory." *American Antiquity,* 17:130–136.

1952 "The Chance Horizon." *New York State Museum, Circular,* 29.

1956 "Prehistoric Settlement Patterns in Northeastern North America." In *Prehistoric Settlement Patterns in the New World,* ed. by Gordon R. Willey, pp. 72–80. *Viking Fund Publications in Anthropology,* 23.

1958 "The Development of Aboriginal Settlement Patterns in the Northeast: A Progress Report." *Bulletin of the Eastern States Archeological Federation,* 17:9–10.

RITCHIE, WILLIAM A., DONALD LENIG and P. SCHUYLER MILLER

1953 "An Early Owasco Sequence in Eastern New York." *New York State Museum, Circular,* 32.

THOMAS, CYRUS

1894 "Report on the Mound Explorations of the Bureau of Ethnology." *Annual Report of the Bureau of [American] Ethnology,* 12:17–722.

WISSLER, CLARK

1922 *The American Indian.* 2nd edition. New York, Oxford University Press.

* * * *

William G. Haag

LOUISIANA STATE UNIVERSITY

THE ARTIST AS A

REFLECTION OF HIS CULTURE

Art is an activity found in some form in every existing society. It has a complex history extending into the distant past. Art is a distinctly human phenomenon and, as such, it is properly within the realm of anthropological examination. Art has been defined in several ways, but as used here, it means that activity in which one renders intelligible his personal experiencing of the cosmos through the media of written or oral literature, of plastic or graphic representation, of architecture, of music, of drama, and of the dance.

Ecologically successful organisms in the world today became so primarily because of adaptation. The student of biological evolution sees adaptation as both an effect and as a process. Nonetheless, he seeks organic structures that appear to be least adaptive or are free of direct association or relationship with the physical environment in order more readily to discover the nature of change. Human culture is also adaptive. That culture form best adjusted to its total environment is most successful. The student of human behavior sometimes operates similarly to the biologist. He looks to traits that are largely independent of the economic institutions of given societies for insight into the particular ethos of those societies. Religion, certain social organizations, art, and several other activities obviously may operate independently of the major subsistence institution. Of course, this latter must be successfully operating before the former endeavors can be effected.

The fine arts are thus an adaptation to a given environment but they are essentially nonutilitarian in the above sense; for example, their form and content are largely free of economic conditioning. This fact renders art an ideal area of human behavior for analyzing the nature of the relationship between the artist and his cultural environment.

Today art is an endeavor so generally removed from everyday life that many serious art philosophers look upon it as the last great refuge of human freedom. To these philosophers and other students of human behavior, it seems obvious that the increasingly totalitarian orientation of our Western states moves on apace in the direction of greater control of all of man's economic activities. Still, many feel the realm of art will be available for complete freedom of expression. Pure art is wholly without obligation to the public and is not for sale on Madison Avenue. Because of this exultant sense of freedom, artists rarely think of themselves in any other terms. They think they are entirely unrestrained in their choice not only of the medium of expression, but the form and content of their art as well.

This narcosis is emotionally induced: Art is not free. Artists are relentlessly grasped by the strongest but subtlest force that moves the world, that is, cultural determinism. Every change in the artistic taste of the times is engendered and nourished in a realm beyond the "minds" of artists. Yet one of our society's cherished beliefs is that culture is something immanent in the minds of men or emanating therefrom. Despite this general belief, there are some artists, philosophers, and critics who are quite aware of the true locus of creativeness in the artistic realm. That place, of course, is the culture—the normative, stylistic, consistent behavior of which the artist is a participant and a partaker. The desire to believe in free will is so strong in most men that to demonstrate that all art is a reflection of the cultural milieu is no easy task. "The artist's greatest and most necessary illusion is the illusion that he is creating. Rob him of that belief and you have shorn him of his power" (Carpenter 1942:30). Nevertheless, all phases of art attest to this illusion as even a cursory examination of the arts will reveal.

To the teleologically-oriented student, the fine arts appear to have a function in the world of man, a function quite as important as the sciences. Certainly, some observers of the artistic behavior of man would conclude that all such acts of man are controlled by him. Thus Roy Harris argues,

On and on, man has led himself in his search for the satisfying interests of an ever-expanding, ever-more-complex world of perception—always leading to new conceptions from within himself. Half-mad with discontent, half-ecstatic with joyous discovery, he has gropingly created always in his own image. He has created polytheistic gods and monotheistic gods, all superlatively endowed with his own most desirable attributes. From his minute examination of himself and his environment, he has created systems of thought, of trade and commerce, of government. He has created the arts and the sciences and crystallized all of them into tradition; to which he in turn has passionately avowed undying allegiance, until he himself created new pathways toward those horizons to which time forever lures him (Harris 1942:20).

Harris epitomizes the widely-held belief that man has been in control of most of his history. Man has cherished an attitude of psychological superiority to anything that has broadened his horizons and he has behaved as though he were the motivating force, if not the control of all cultural development. Collingwood (1925:7) has said of art, "it means that frame of mind which we call artistic, the frame of mind in which we are aware of beauty. . . . The awareness of beauty is at once the starting-point and the culmination, the presupposition and the end, of all art." Collingwood has also asserted that children show a high degree of artistic power, that an artist paints only for himself, and that period styles are only constructs. Whereas we argue it is difficult to realize generalizations in the area of the arts if such psychological interpretations are used, Collingwood, of course, would say it is needless as well as impossible. In contradistinction to the above position, we suggest that any definitions of art that are based primarily upon psychological factors must be largely rejected.

Music, of all the arts, offers the richest field of study and analysis of wherein lies the creative force of the artist. Music at any given period of time will probably manifest several styles. Usually one style among them is most acceptable, but, as in painting and sculpture, even the departures from the normative style will have recognizable styles of their own. Harris believes that the "basis of artistic creation in music can only be found in humanity itself." More explicitly, Harris means, "All music has been created by individuals. Each part of every rhythmic design, every melodic contour, every harmonic cadence, every contrapuntal device, every form sequence, every instrument, all notation, was conceived once by an individual" (Harris 1942:25). Such a conclusion is inescapable. It is obvious; were it not so, evolution in music would cease. It is by this mechanism—these infinitesimal increments contributed by individuals—that all cultural change and growth takes place.

A critical look at jazz, a unique contribution to the arts by American culture, reveals its origin in the classics. Harmonically, jazz owes much to the classics; even the instruments used are relatively old. The distinguishing quality of jazz is its approach to 4/4 music, but ringing through all creative effort in music from earliest classics to jazz is the feeling of improvisation. Jazz is just now catching up with the improvisations in the classic realm. Schönberg and Webern, "serious" composers of recent decades, departed completely from traditional classical melody and tonality in their inspired "improvization." The modern "progressive" jazz musicians have gone nearly as far afield; when they went so far astray as to be intelligible only to an esoteric few, it was no longer music. The ultimate experiment was applying mathematical formulae to composition —even a composing machine has been invented recently. Of course, this is a perfectly logical and scientific approach to musical composition, but it is not art.

The important point is the continuum in music; each musical style is drawn from the idiom of the preceding period. The artist's greatness lies in the manner in which he renders his interpretation of the style. In every creation the fathering musician is also the son of the grandfather and his work will show some inheritance from that generation. The modern composers, Klebe and Berg, are as much the offspring of Schönberg as jazz-pianists Bruebeck and Wilson are the descendants of Morton, but all these creatives artists carry the "genes" of Mozart and Beethoven. All composers must feel they are adding something to the musical world. Sean O'Faolain (1949:74) once observed "What the artist does is not to create but to recreate." *Recreate* means, "to give fresh life to," rather than *re-create*, "to create again." The creative process in music is invariably recreative, but to believe otherwise is far more gratifying to one's digestive tract.

Nowhere, perhaps, so much as in music is genius thought to play such an important function in producing original form and content. But nothing is more obvious to the dispassionate observer than the fact that no artist is any good until he begins to have a sweat-beaded brow. As in scholarly endeavor, the difference between good and bad musicians is almost entirely a matter of hard physical labor. Oscar Thompson concluded that music was like love—those who make it a life work can speak best about it. Musical ability may assert itself at a tender age, but in the course of time maturation catches up with that phase and unless the ability is exploited by unusual energy, the prodigy becomes another modal citizen.

Ascertaining the manner in which professional standards are fixed in such a field as music may seem beyond our grasp. On the contrary, a little reflection will disclose wherein lies the king-making power among musicians. No artist is judged to be of high enough quality for concert work until his teacher or teachers consider he has mastered the requirements of excellence. Music teachers, like college professors, draw their standards of excellence from the preceding generation. The public cannot possibly be the judge of musical superiority, for only a trained ear can be a trained judge. We have at our command only a vague language to describe these high standards of excellence, but even a music lover, unversed in specific rules of musical rendition, can recognize good quality in music. Thus, it may be argued, there is something beyond the individual musician, beyond the creativeness of the teachers, and beyond the demands of the public that sets the standards or normative expectations in music. That something, of course, is the cultural idiom. It is quite evident that musical form and content vary from place to place, from time to time, and from society to society. As an example, African Negro music depends almost wholly upon rhythmic quality; Western music is steeped in melody. Surely, the recognized music of quality of our time is a product of the past (Haag 1957:74).

In painting as in music there is a large measure of feeling of control on the part of the artist.

Yet the artist's confidence in his own unlimited power to create is fallacious. Though false, it is necessary; for if he loses this illusion he can no longer act. Yet even in his action the critical onlooker can see that the sense of freedom is deceptive. For otherwise, how is it that to the trained beholder every painting proclaims not merely its maker, but also its date and its environment? If the artist were wholly free to create, why should not each of his creations be completely unique, instead of showing a manner appropriate to a school or group, which in turn takes its ordered place within a phase or style pointing back to its predecessors and forward to its successors? Even El Greco and Van Gogh, however erratically different from their contemporaries, fit intimately their particular time and place within the evolution of painting. It is of course the old dilemma of the freedom of the human will: we may act freely according to our judgment, choice, and desires; but our judgment, choice, and desires are motivated and conditioned by our own past and by the present world surrounding us (Carpenter 1942:30–31).

Carpenter is an unusual example among art critics in indicating so clearly this awareness of the nature of creativeness. He is proclaiming that if a painting cannot be classified it cannot be art. It is neither a refutation of this statement nor an anomaly that anachronisms do occur. Van Gogh and El Greco were ahead of their time in the evolution of art, just as Mendel was in genetic theory. Their appearance was inevitable and eventually they fell into their niche. The very fact that one may see

—even though this be in historical perspective—a definite evolutionary pattern to art is evidence that artists either adhere to norms or simply do not get recognition.

From the viewpoint of historians who have tried to reconstruct the precise order of development, without presuppositions about cycles, there is a continuity in the Near East and Europe from the Neolithic period to the present—perhaps best described as a tree with many branches—in which the most advanced forms of each culture are retained to some extent, in the early forms of succeeding cultures (Shapiro 1953:302).

"In historical perspective the situation of the modern painter is clear. His art is not his own creation, but stretches for centuries behind" (Carpenter 1942:56). These are succinct statements from the determinist's thesaurus, but not all observers draw the same conclusions from identical data.

At least one recognized art philosopher has concluded that nothing except the history of art may be learned from a review of the form and content of past art (Fiedler 1949:15–16). This argument implies that a critical study of the art forms of the past would not reveal generalities and "laws" of approach to problem and other developmental phenomena that might enable us to understand the present situation. Hence, a history of art, argues Fiedler, may not be used as a measure of culture history, and by the same token, a philosophical consideration of art contributes something to philosophy but nothing much to art. Of course, one must agree with Fiedler (1949:27) that "The understanding of art can be grasped in no other way than in terms of art." Nevertheless, there are generalities and uniformities which may be detected in the analysis of the painting of the past; it is this fact that enables us to classify paintings by their shared characteristics, and label them with "school" designations such as "Impressionism," "Cubism," and "Expressionism." Through this knowledge one may be reasonably successful in predicting the trend that painting may take in the future. Carpenter (1942:58) indicates this determinism when he states, "The style of tomorrow, must therefore, evolve out of the practices and conventions of today."

Art historians and art philosophers agree that a new period of artistic endeavor was launched by Giotto, Cimabue, and Duccio, or at least it is exemplified by their works and their time. This innovation was more than a heightened sensitivity to realism; it was a psychologically different mode of expressing emotion (Malraux 1953:261). Carpenter aptly terms all the ensuing period "The Great Tradition," and finds in its seven centuries a history of mastering the technical difficulties of devising two-dimensional representations of a three-dimensional world. This, now, largely has been accomplished, and artists are casting about for new means of vitalizing the exhausted tradition. Painting today is characterized by extremes in experimentation. The very fact that it is replete with the grotesque, the pseudoprimitive, the African-inspired, and the color "sampler" attests to this search. "Our [American] painters are no longer strumming outworn melodies; they are searching the higher rhythms, the new dynamics" (Boswell 1940:90). The search will surely parallel the same development as in music, and one may expect at any moment a "painting machine" that faithfully reproduces the correct balance of color and form.

Despite Fiedler, even a cursory examination of the history of art reveals more than history—it clearly shows there has been one continuing thread for at least fifteen thousand years. This constantly varying but always discernible golden thread is realism. Man has at all times and all places continuously sought to depict realistically his experiencing of his world and always he has done so in terms of the cultural milieu in which he operates. Despite the extremes of our society, most of modern art is more definitely tinged with realism than a quarter century ago, but the experimenters continue to hurl, slosh, cannonade, flick, dribble, and piddle paint on canvas. As one stands amidst the spattering of action painting there is an encouraging note—even Jackson Pollock is labelled "the New Realism," like a signpost pointing out the road sought in all painting.

Carpenter (1942:49–50) has examined this experimental phase in the modern artist and concludes:

Only surrealism has offered a really new avenue of escape by applying the rehabilitated creed of objective accuracy not directly to the everyday world of sight but to that shattered and disintegrated world which impressionism and futurism and all their followers had produced. . . . At best, even if some suggestive evocation of such a world is possible, surrealism has handicapped itself by choosing a level of experience shared by distorted mirrors on amusement piers, dreams and nightmares, fantasy and fooling. We well may wish for painting a better future and a worthier fate.

It is not in the graphic arts alone that a creative force external to the artist may be discerned. The trends in most cultural traits or institutions are always progressive—that is, toward greater complexity—until fundamentals are enunciated. Then the object or the idea may be stripped of "mistakes" or nonessential parts, which is to say, it is *stylized*, reduced to the form and the function that the styles of the times demand. The process by which items or clusters of culture traits become successfully established in a given culture is the subject of many articles and books but where it pertains to art, Jenkins (1958) has clearly delineated the subject. This philosopher documents (p. 14) the theory that, "Art, science, and other of man's higher activities and artifacts have their ultimate source in the human effort to adapt to the environment." Thus adaptation may be considered the reason and the cause of progress in culture, even art. That is, those activities that better serve the needs of man have greater survival value. This idea of "adaptation" is the key word in our argument of the relationship between the artist and his culture.

Roger Fry, an artistic Lazarus of the early part of this century, once wrote a naive but neat essay, "A Possible Domestic Architecture." By citing his own house-building experience, he carefully made the point that such domestic architecture was possible. He ignored architectural or non-functional considerations until personal needs in number and arrangement of rooms were first satisfied. "The artistic or architectural part of the house was confined, then, merely to the careful choice of proportions within certain fixed limits defined by needs, and neither time, money, nor thought was expended on giving the house the appearance of any particular style" (Fry 1947:277). This relegates architecture as an aesthetic activity to the same category as does the New Englander when he asserts that he would build his house himself and then send to Boston for a man to "put on the architecture."

Fry believed that through many repetitions of this "indifference to public opinion," a genuine architectural style might arise. He admitted a considerable amount of criticism from his neighbors regarding the appearance of his house, and this force of public opinion alone should have convinced him of the error of his judgment. One may exercise this kind of artistic freedom, if he can withstand the resulting social disapproval. It must be concluded that nothing "genuine," nothing that is adaptive—meaning accepted by the culture as normative—can possibly flourish that flaunts public opinion. Any such items would appear almost by definition to have no affect upon the culture, that is, they are not an integral part of the typical culture behavior. To enter the stream of culture, to be integrated into the milieu, to be accepted and shared by others, an innovation must meet and pass a certain test. That test is neither the efficiency nor beauty of the item, but conformity to the "tyranny of styles and fashions" which the artist must follow and placate.

Especially in architecture is it axiomatic that the useful will survive (Carpenter 1942:59). Perhaps this may be understood more easily in a building than in a painting, for much of construction must be functional and utilitarian. Painters were inhibited in development by the slowness of technical advances in the unfolding of the Great Tradition. Architects, too, could not operate except within the confines of technological development.

The dead end in which architecture found itself in the nineteenth century, with its Greek and Gothic revivals, shows how incapable the architects were of renewing their art within the limits of traditional techniques. It was the discovery of new materials—steel, glass, and later reinforced concrete—which, thanks to the aid of industry, saved architecture by giving it new structural possibilities and opening up new horizons (Damaz 1956:21).

Neither architecture nor painting could turn back to original forms and try again. Only by working within the dictates of contemporary attitudes can architecture continue to function as a distinct art form. If architects bow their heads to constructional demands, they will become craftsmen, not artists. The form that prevails will be that of the stronger cultural force; if functional criteria gain greater cultural acceptance than aesthetic criteria, the former will dominate building design.

A vivid example of the grip of cultural determinism upon the architect may be seen in a recent local development in Southwestern Louisiana. In 1957 a hurricane destroyed over 90 per cent of the dwellings in the coastal community of Cameron. The great destruction was caused by high tide waters rather than winds, and houses were swept from their foundations. In a study of rebuilding trends in the area, Kniffen and Wright (1958) found that of nearly five hundred new houses constructed since the hurricane, *only four* were built on piers or stilts in an old-fashioned, flood resistant way. All others are modern ranch-style, built directly on the ground on concrete slabs. This style is that of inland cities whereas houses built on stilts are obviously coastal storm adaptations. Before any rebuilding began, a team of architects tried to publicize the need for elevated houses to prevent a recurrence of similar destruction when the inevitable hurricane strikes again. But their efforts were in vain; Kniffen concludes that these residents would rather be dead than out of style.

A much-discussed book of recent years is another revenant, *The Architecture of Humanism* by Geoffrey Scott. First published in 1914, the book has been revived because its message may be added to others that justify current American architectural forms essentially because they are sound in function. Perhaps the quintessence of Scott is to be found in the following: "A metaphor is, by definition, the transcription of one thing into terms of another, and this fact is what the theory under discussion claims. It claims that the architectural art is the transcription of the body's states into form of buildings" (Scott 1956:161). Obviously, the book says much more than this, but it is another plea for a sound architectural style characterized by the "proved" of yesteryears. The current trend in America toward pierced walls, grillwork, filigree, *adornos,* and textured effects suggests there will be a long period of experimentation before any "honest" architectural style may evolve. However, in Europe the wedding of architecture and the graphic arts already has progressed to the stage of public announcements of the ensuing nuptials. It is interesting to note that the title of the French text for Paul Damaz' book (which is set in parallel pages of French and English) is *Synthèse des Arts* (Damaz 1956).

Art styles characteristic of Western civilization have been used as criteria of evolutionary trends and directions of change within the culture as a whole. Some of these studies have utilized one aspect of the culture as an indicator of the changes within the major institutions of the entire culture. Such a study of this nature is Toynbee's monumental *A Study of History* (1947), in which religion is used as the key to the general ethos of periods in Western and several other civilizations that have contributed to the history of our culture. Another type study is that illustrated by Spengler's *Decline of the West* (1946), in which is utilized a variety of traits of civilizations in order to discern the course of this development. Among the things treated by Spengler were the fine arts. Flinders Petrie, the renowned Egyptologist, used the latter only in his *The Revolutions of Civilization* (1941). He constructed a developmental cultural sequence for the Western world, and also dealt with the rise and decline of art forms themselves. Of course, it is commonplace for us to characterize the whole life way of certain periods by the names with which their corresponding art expressions are recognized, such as "Romantic," "Baroque," and "Modern."

If we may recognize the validity of characterizing our own society at various periods of its history by its prevailing art form, primitive society should have a similar application. This area has been extensively studied, though actually but rarely by competent students. One such student of a well-known region, West Africa, has said:

Art styles, such as those which distinguish the schools or periods of European painting and sculpture, are found in African art. The African carver is influenced by the work of his contemporaries and predecessors in much the same way as the European or American artists, and this influence can be recognized no matter how much emphasis may be placed upon novelty or originality (Bascom 1953:35).

Much too frequently, modern painters, such as Picasso, have tried to adapt the art forms of West Africa to recent applications. This has not proved entirely successful; the African idiom is anomalous outside its cultural hearth, and, when employed elsewhere, the inspirational origin is blatantly obvious. Of the innumerable discussions of the art of West Africa, rarely, if ever, has one been written from the standpoint of the native artist. Nearly all such critical works are judged from the modern European or American background.

Experience, however, has often shown the danger of trying to guess the objectives or intentions of an artist simply by looking at his work. Where the cultural backgrounds of artist and critic are not the same, this danger is far greater, and the interpretations of the critic may be completely at variance with what the artist himself was trying to accomplish (Bascom 1953:40).

The clues that reveal the locus of stimulus of the native artist are to be found in his cultural heritage and its present configuration. Often this artist is wholly unconscious of this stimulation, but he tends to conform to art styles that have meaning only in their own cultural setting. The archeologist who uses pottery types as the key to his cultural history is using art styles that are largely unconsciously subscribed to by a large segment of native artists.

Can we not extend analyses of the role of cultural determinism to all phases of the fine arts? Embler's excellent articles (1951, 1952, 1954) on metaphor cogently explore this single aspect of literary effort. One could profitably examine other aspects of literature. Kroeber and Shapiro have painstakingly developed this theme for style in several other fields (Kroeber 1957; Shapiro 1953). Jenkins (1958) has shown that such analyses may be applied fruitfully to all aspects of human behavior. The importance of considering other than the fine arts must be subordinated to the matter of the moment, namely, that the artist reflects the idiom of the whole culture.

In ancient Sumer, astrologists confidently were predicting what was to come, but long before that time men sought clues or omens to lighten the gloom of the future. This striving to increase predictibility remains the goal, the reason, the justification for science today. Through many centuries scholars have sought to synthesize the history of the world and from it extract an indicator that could be used not only as a measure of progress in the past, but of direction and rate in the future. Because of relatively great freedom from economic determinism, the arts may approach this ideal device more closely than any other area of human behavior.

Culture evolves as energy utilization increases and those aspects of the culture that do not use energy sources external to man are thus independent of that external source (White 1949:365). Art, in all its forms, falls almost wholly within the area of man's activities that do not draw upon external energy sources. However, the evolution of art has been dependent upon technological evolution in that many art forms depend upon the media which they use. Art has changed more slowly than technology, but has always, perforce, reflected the technological progress. As better pigments were produced, as steel chisels replaced bronze, and as the piano replaced the harpsichord, so did resulting art forms show greater degrees of accuracy in desired rendition, thus greater communication of the "message" of the artist.

Evoking cultural determinism as an almost metaphysical force that drives man in certain channels has been challenged repeatedly. Not even the "as if" philosophy can be countenanced by most critics of cultural determinism. The belief that man behaves *"as if"* his culture determined the course of his actions has been called mysticism by some. It is hardly necessary to point out that there have been several able defenders of cultural determinism and numerous examples could be cited that show how clearly man does behave as though there were some real and tangible relationship between his culture and his actions. Man *does* act as though his actions were determined by some foregoing state in his culture; whether he does this consciously or not may be disregarded for the moment. Such behavior is natural since it is adaptive behavior. It is cultural, and since all cultural behavior is natural, it is an extension of organic evolution, but an extension so great as to constitute a uniquely different mode of behavior. As do all plants and animals, man reacts to his environment, and those reactions that more nearly coincide with the demands of the environment—cultural and physical—will have survival value. In this respect cultural mutations have results identical with genetic changes.

The complex societies offer so many more possible solutions to problems, so many more tools for accomplishing tasks, that their rate of cultural change is vastly greater than among simpler cultures. Western civilization provides the additive factor of placing a high premium upon success. This drive to succeed pervades all the arts as well as the sciences. Yet ambition and hard work (the latter having been singled out as essential to greatness) are not sufficient to guarantee success. At most, the artist can originate but little. "No single artist has ever been responsible for more than a contributory impulse to his art" (Carpenter 1942:33). Though it may sound paradoxical, whatever is contributed must be recognized and accepted to have been a contribution. Flowers of artistic creation that bloom unseen do not perfume the cultural air; a genius is a genius only by definition and recognition (White 1949:201). Hence, the artist must communicate in order to be recognized and communication can come only through the cultural idiom.

Herein lies the reason for constancy of realism in art. It is ever a goal of men in all cultural activities. Continual sharpening of our concepts to fit better our precepts is the spirit of all intellectual activity in virtually all periods of our history. The requirements of realism in the arts may vary from time to time in any culture but these desiderata are always couched in the contemporary language of the culture. "The sense of beauty" is always dictated by the cultural history. Artists are those members of the society who deal with this aspect of the culture. Only when they are communicating their objectives are they recognized as successfully filling their roles. Successful communication will depend upon the degree of the artists' reflection of the stylized, conventionalized idiom of their culture.

BIBLIOGRAPHY

BASCOM, WILLIAM R.
  1953 "West African Art." In *Handbook of West African Art,* ed. by Robert E. Ritzenthaler, pp. 7–44. Milwaukee, Bruce Publishing Company.
BOSWELL, PEYTON
  1940 *Modern American Painting.* New York, Dodd, Mead and Company.
CARPENTER, RHYS
  1942 "The Basis of Artistic Creation in the Fine Arts." In *The Bases of Artistic Creation,* by Maxwell Anderson, Rhys Carpenter, and Roy Harris, pp. 30–59. New Brunswick, Rutgers University Press.
COLLINGWOOD, R. G.
  1925 *Outlines of a Philosophy of Art.* London, Oxford University Press.
DAMAZ, PAUL
  1956 *Art in European Architecture.* New York, Reinhold Publishing Corporation.
EMBLER, WELLER
  1951 "Metaphor and Social Belief." *ETC.,* 8:83–93.

1952 "The Novel as Metaphor." *ETC.*, 10:3–11.

1954 "Design as Metaphor." *ETC.*, 13:93–105.

FIEDLER, CONRAD

1949 *On Judging Works of Visual Art.* Berkeley, University of California Press.

FRY, ROGER

1947 "A Possible Domestic Architecture." In *Vision and Design*, pp. 272–278. New York, Peter Smith.

HAAG, WILLIAM

1957 "The Arts That Survive." *Delta*, 11:71–76.

HARRIS, ROY

1942 "The Basis of Artistic Creation in Music." In *The Bases of Artistic Creation*, by Maxwell Anderson, Rhys Carpenter, and Roy Harris, pp. 19–29. New Brunswick, Rutgers University Press.

JENKINS, IREDELL

1958 *Art and the Human Enterprise.* Cambridge, Harvard University Press.

KNIFFEN, FRED AND MARTIN WRIGHT

1958 "Disaster and Reconstruction in Cameron Parish, Louisiana." (Abstract) *Annals of the Association of American Geographers*, 48:275.

KROEBER, A. L.

1957 *Style and Civilization.* Ithaca, Cornell University Press.

MALRAUX, ANDRÉ

1953 *The Voices of Silence.* Garden City, Doubleday and Company.

O'FAOLAIN, SEAN

1949 "Romance and the Devil." *The Atlantic Monthly*, 183:73–75.

PETRIE, W. M. FLINDERS

1941 *The Revolutions of Civilization.* New York, Peter Smith.

SCOTT, GEOFFREY

1956 *The Architecture of Humanism.* Garden City, Doubleday and Company.

SHAPIRO, MEYER

1953 "Style." In *Anthropology Today*, prepared under the chairmanship of A. L. Kroeber, pp. 287–312. Chicago, The University of Chicago Press.

SPENGLER, OSWALD

1946 *The Decline of the West.* Translated by C. F. Alkinson, 2 vols. New York, Alfred A. Knopf, Inc.

William G. Haag

TOYNBEE, ARNOLD
   1947 *A Study of History.* Abridgement of Vols. I–VI by D. C. Somer-
      vell. New York, Oxford University Press.
VAIHINGER, H.
   1925 *The Philosophy of "As If."* New York, Harcourt, Brace and Com-
      pany.
WHITE, LESLIE A.
   1949 *The Science of Culture.* New York, Farrar, Straus and Company.

* * * *

Frank E. Hartung

WAYNE STATE UNIVERSITY

BEHAVIOR, CULTURE,

AND SYMBOLISM

Social psychology is the study of that aspect of the totality of the individual's actions that is the result of social and cultural experience. As a discipline it owes much to anthropology, with an important part of the debt being the cultural analysis developed by Edward B. Tylor, who was interested in the explanation of human thought, will, and action (Tylor 1873:viii). There are, in fact, historical and empirical grounds for the view that it is just as logical to refer to *cultural* as to *social* psychology. Tylor's significance for social psychology can be briefly stated. He showed that social and cultural phenomena must be described, analyzed, and interpreted in social and cultural terms.

This paper is devoted to a social psychological exposition of four of Tylor's propositions. First, cultural and social phenomena require a cultural and social description and explanation. Second, human behavior is cultural and social behavior, which characteristically involves the use of symbols and tools. Third, culture and society are behaviorally creative in their effect on the individual human being. Fourth, the process of cultural and social change is a rational process in the sense that it is an orderly process possessing its own principles. These propositions are, of course, no longer exclusively Tylor's, if, indeed, they ever were. They do indicate, nevertheless, the dependence of social psychology on cultural anthropology.

It is possible that much confusion concerning the relations of the individual to culture and society results from the failure to recognize that these relations can be correctly stated in several ways. This is important in the analysis of the individual's behavior because much of what he does is not "his" in the sense of his having originated or invented it. One way of stating the relationship is to regard culture and society as being external to, temporally prior to, and physically independent of, any given person, and as exercizing a constraining influence on his behavior. This is the viewpoint assumed in any evolutionary study and in any culturological study. Whatever happens to the individual, he is always in a sociocultural environment. His sociocultural behavior is controlled by custom, institutions, language, and technology.

The organism-environment relationship can also be stated from the viewpoint of the species. From this viewpoint the organism determines its environment through the potentiality of its responses. The greater the potentiality of response, the more complex may become the environment that can be exploited. This in no way asserts that the species, or any member of it, creates the physical environment by its response. It merely asserts that from the totality of the external environment a species carves a segment to which it is capable of responding in terms of its capacities. All organisms exploit the environment in order to exist. Culture and society are the means of exploitation that are employed by man.

Different species thus exploit natural resources differently, determining their own environment in terms of their own behavior. A waterfall obviously does not exist for fish as a source of electrical power, but it can for man. Man swims, digs, climbs, and flies, but the relation of stimulus and response in these behaviors is qualitatively different from the relation of stimulus and response for fish, worms, apes, and birds. The immediate environment in which human beings live is cultural and social; they, and only they, have developed such an environment. Man has only indirect contact with the environment that exists over and beyond the sociocultural, and which may for the purpose of convenience be termed the physical. We can, it seems, never know the latter as it exists in its own right, because it is mediated to us through sociocultural experience. Even a tornado is not just a physical event to us. It may be the occasion for further scientific research, or it may result in personal or financial tragedy; its significance for us is not physical but rather cultural and social. Symbolism, predominantly in the form of verbal language, is the primary means through which our contact with the physical environment is mediated. Symbolism both gives us knowledge with which to interpret our experience and enables us to modify and further increase the initial knowledge.

The human central nervous system, including the cerebral cortex, makes possible the covert beginnings of alternative responses in relation to any given object, for the completion of an act already started, in advance of the completion of that act. It therefore makes possible the use of reflective choice in selecting the alternative that will finally be the response. The utilization of reflective choice means that the completion of an act (response) is delayed until the alternatives are more or less thoroughly tested symbolically. The process is symbolic because the individual employs language to indicate what the alternatives may be and what their respective results may be. The response is thus symbolically delayed and the estoppel of all those responses save the one that is selected is also symbolic. Selective choice therefore bears no behavioral, cultural, or psychical resemblance to the noncultural and nonsymbolic delayed reaction of animals that was so ingeniously and imaginatively studied some time ago by Walter S. Hunter (1923:36–38; 1928), and which has more recently been investigated in reference to chimpanzees by Cowles (1937), Wolfe (1936), and Yerkes (1943).

Symbolically delayed response is necessary to reflective behavior; without it no deliberate control over behavior could be exercized. The implicit testing and the selection of his overt response by the individual in situations requiring adjustment would not be possible if his overt actions could not be delayed until this implicit testing and selection were carried through. There would be no reflection; instead, instinct, reflex, or habit would control response.[1] Selective choice is what pragmatism refers to as "intelligent behavior" (Dewey 1930:Part III). From this viewpoint intelligence is the ability to solve problems of the present in terms of probable future consequences, as those consequences are indicated on the basis of experience, that is, the past. It is an ability dependent upon and resulting from the learning of language. Both past experience and a conception of the future are thus necessary to intelligent behavior, as here defined. This is true whether one is confronted with a third raise in a game of poker, an unannounced examination in the classroom, or the testing of an hypothesis.

Some subhuman species seem to exhibit some awareness of the future in their present behavior, in the sense that an anticipation of their future behavior appears to be causally determinative of their present behavior. Squirrels are often cited as examples. These animals, it can be shown, do not have the concept *time*—the past, the present, and the future—as an

---

[1] This statement stresses the repetitive and routine aspect of habit. While reflection is a component of some of our routine conduct, the concern at present is with the automatic aspect of habit.

object in their experience, to which they respond. A contrast of this future-in-the-present behavior will perhaps clarify the difference in this respect between man and animals. A relevant instance is the problem of social security. Squirrels behave in such fashion today as to assure a supply of food tomorrow. A squirrel secretes nuts in various places during the late summer and fall, uncovering and eating some of them during the winter. We cannot conclude from this that the squirrel is thrifty because it remembers the previous winter during which it endured semi-starvation. Squirrels are born in the late spring and early summer. When reared apart from all other squirrels, so that they cannot learn from any others, they will still secrete acorns as their parents did. This indicates that experience could not possibly determine this activity. The squirrel acts on the basis of impulses that are hereditary.

The thrifty man, however, has in the present some conception of the future, a conception to which he responds as if it were an object.[2] Of the possible alternative responses a selection is made that determines the behavior of the present. The thrifty man may have lived on welfare or held a Works Progress Administration job during the depression of the 1930's. Having become accustomed to a certain standard of living he may want to retain it as much as possible after he is retired. He may know that life-expectancy is increasing in this country, that industry tries to discharge its employees after they are about fifty years of age, and that he cannot save enough to carry himself after he is retired. He may reject the alternative of living with his children; he may want to be independent and his children probably could not afford to support him if they wanted to. The alternatives are all rejected save one: an old age pension. He may continue to live to the limit of his income, and perhaps not beyond it. He may even save a little in addition, and buy some life insurance. His selection of the pension as the solution to the problem of the future will help to determine various aspects of his behavior. The consequences will be seen in loyalty to his union, in his standard of living, and perhaps even in his mental and physical health, because his belief that a fairly comfortable old age is possible may relieve him of a chronic worry and make it easier to live with himself and with others. So the thrifty man saves through bank deposits, life insurance, and old-age contributions. An animal psychologist might say that he was hiding nuts. A social psychologist, however, would say that he was engaging in symbolically

---

[2] *Object* is used throughout this paper in the technical sense of referring to any entity of which one takes cognizance. It thus includes concepts, events, ideas, and relations, as well as physical entities.

delayed behavior, a kind of behavior that the anthropologist would characterize as being culturally determined.

Symbolism, which is exclusively man's possession, is necessary to reflection. Not all symbolic responses, however, indicate that deliberate reasoning directed toward some specific end has occurred. The sequences of thought that we may have perhaps do not even usually lead to some goal. A good deal of our thinking consists of a succession of ideas that are suggested, one by another. It is a kind of spontaneous reverie, often termed "day dreaming," which the psychoanalysts label "free association" and which William James called "irresponsible thinking" (James 1890, II:325). The items in this type of thought, in which everyone engages, are not theoretical abstractions but rather concrete items. While looking at the clouds, for example, I recall the recent lunar eclipse. This reminds me of the telescope that has been put into service on Mount Palomar, which recalls the friends in California to whom I owe a letter. The thoughts, as a rule, consist of such a succession. Having thought of one, we realize now that we are thinking of another, to which we hardly know how we have passed. If an abstract quality enters, it arrests our attention only momentarily, fades into something else, and indeed is never very abstract. In general, we think less often of qualities than of whole things, just as we may experience them.

Free association, then, is not reasoning and is not intelligent behavior as defined above, even though it is certainly symbolic. There is another type of coupling of items by association, which is regarded by many as being an act of reasoning. This is the coupling of a response to a stimulus that is referred to as *conditioning*. When the stimulus and the object that it indicates are both items that have previously been coupled in experience, the type of response is common to man and many subhuman species. The response is said to be conditioned, and the coupling apparently results from a more or less prolonged repetitious association by contiguity. The conditioning may be formed either accidentally by the organism, or deliberately for it, if it is placed in an appropriate situation by some agent such as an experimenter. In either case the association of stimulus and response involves none of the intentional combining and comparing that occurs during reasoning. In conditioning the combining is done *to* and *for* the subject; in reasoning the combining and comparing are performed *by* the actor.

In conditioning the stimulus A is obeyed and the result is the response B. By contrast, in reasoning A may suggest responses B, C, and D, with the motor or overt phase of the act held in abeyance until their probable consequences have been implicitly tested and compared and one has been chosen. In conditioning the same response follows upon a given stimulus, while in free association the objects of experience merely suggest other objects. By contrast, in reasoning a response is deliberately sought, as a means to some proposed end. The alternative responses that are held in abeyance until one is selected are not suggested immediately by a previous thought as in free association, nor are they expressed immediately in glandular or motor activity as in conditioning. The final response in reasoning may be foreign to our previous experience; it may be some new behavior, a response that mere conditioning could never have elicited. The behavioral difference between conditioning and free association, on the one hand, and reasoning on the other, is that the former are only repetitious, whereas reasoning may be creative.

The distinction between conditioning, free association, and reasoning can be summarized as follows:

Conditioning: Occurs in the behavior of animals and man. Results in the repetition of old behavior; cannot result in new behavior.

Symbolism: Occurs in the behavior of man only.
Free association is similar to conditioning in that it results in repetition and cannot produce new behavior. *Reasoning* can result both in the repetition of old behavior and in new behavior. It is behaviorally creative.

Conditioning is a term often loosely used to refer to all types of learning. In the classic sense of the term, however, as it was developed and applied in Pavlov's physiological researches, it was not intended to account for the appearance of new behavior, and it was not so utilized (Pavlov 1910, 1927). The experimental work dealt with reflex (or constitutional or instinctive) responses. It was therefore wholly unconcerned with the cultural behavior that characterizes human beings. Cultural behavior is not displayed by the newly born infant. If behavior could be learned during the fetal period it would not be cultural. When people read the term "conditioned response," they are likely to assume that the response (reflex) has been changed, whereas it is the stimulus that has been changed. Even psychologists on occasion commit this very common mistake.

The concept of time can be used to exemplify briefly the previously stated proposition that symbolism occurs in the behavior of man only. He seems to be the only species that has developed *time* as a concept.

All organisms, of course, have temporal and spatial experience in that they occupy some space and live for some time. Temporal experience, however, is quite different from the concept *time*. Chimpanzees, in many respects the closest in behavior to man of all the anthropoids, seem to have an extremely limited capacity for dealing with temporal-spatial situations. This seems to be fairly certain, to judge from the studies of Yerkes, Köhler, and others. According to Köhler, the chimpanzee's ability to deal with such situations seems to be limited to its "optical apprehension of the situation" (Köhler 1926:277). This is confirmed by the later findings of Yerkes and Nissen, who consider as "most significant the evidence that delayed response, in the absence of spatial clues, is either extremely difficult or impossible for most chimpanzees" (Yerkes and Nissen 1939:585). Riesen investigated the possibility of teaching chimpanzees to use symbols. His subjects failed to learn visual discrimination when the delay in rewards given to them was greater than four seconds. Riesen said that he could not find in the literature of comparative psychology any "instance of animal learning with delayed reward, which depended unequivocally upon non-spatial stimuli" (Riesen 1940:50).

A probable source of confusion concerning symbolic behavior arises from the fact that man uses both symbols and signs, whereas animals use only signs. Frequently no distinction is made between symbol and sign, both being regarded as signs (White 1949:27). A symbol is an object to which any meaning can be assigned. It can thus have any kind of form. Its meaning is derived from its context, and cannot be derived from either its physical qualities or the sensory experience that it may cause. Thus the color yellow is in one context an order not to cross into the traffic lane on one's left, and in another context is an accusation of cowardice.

A sign is an object whose function is to indicate another object. The meaning of a sign may be inherent in its physical form, and may also be ascertained through sensory means. Thus the return of the swallows to Wisconsin Dells in early May indicates the imminent opening of the tourist season there, and the ringing of the bell in Pavlov's experiments indicated the coming of food-powder.

Animals manifestly employ signs; if signs and symbols are equated, the erroneous conclusion very likely will be drawn that animals can think and reason. One of the primary values of White's analysis of symbolism is that it shows the necessity, in the analysis of behavior, of making a sharp distinction between the symbolic behavior of man and the signal behavior of animals (White 1949:22–39). Man, with symbolism, can give as well as receive; animals, with signs, can only receive. An animal can be likened to a radio receiving set, but a man, with symbolism, is similar to the radio station that can send messages as well as receive them (White 1949:29).

Mead's analysis of symbolic communication (Mead 1934) is in conformity with White's position and can be briefly stated as follows. In symbolic communication the person, in addressing a symbol to another, simultaneously stimulates both himself and the other to respond to that symbol or series of symbols, indicating to himself through his tendency to respond, the probable meaning of the symbols. An animal, however, in gesturing or moving toward another animal, stimulates only the other animal. It does not at the same time stimulate itself to respond to its own movement as the other animal is stimulated to respond to it.

It is the cultural process of symbolic communication that brings objects, *as objects,* into existence for those who are involved in it. Language is therefore not the expression of something that is antecedent to language, and it is not an expression of thought that is in the individual's mind prior to his acquiring language. An essential aspect of language is a cooperation in which and through which the behavior of each person is regulated and modified. The cooperation is unique in that both the linguistic gesture (vocal or written) and the response to it involve two parties in a similar and contemporaneous response; each enters into his own and the other's behavior. Each party, in himself tending to respond as the other tends to respond, indicates to himself the probable meaning of the situation. *Meaning* is in this view objective, as being the resultant of the cultural act of symbolic communication. Meaning is thus primarily a quality of behavior, and only in the most secondary sense a quality of objects.

The above view of meaning finds meaning to arise in collective, symbolic activity; a *sound* is not a *word* and does not become so unless and until it acquires meaning. A sound becomes a word or symbol when its use establishes a community of action. The response to the word as a symbol is a selective response to that aspect of the object that is involved in action. One facet of the total object is responded to, and the rest of its properties or qualities ignored. Because of this type of selective response, objects are said to be abstracted from the environment as a resultant of the behavior of those involved in the communicative process. The one aspect of the object to which we pay attention is all that we need to know of it for our purposes; indeed, it seems that we cannot know it completely in all of its aspects.

Thus the meaning of an object is relative to the behavior of those who use it. Two implications of this view may be indicated here. First, any object may be conceived in an indefinite number of ways. Second, there is no one, and only one, true way of conceiving objects. A quality that is essential in one situation may be irrelevant in another. When William James, for example, wrote his chapter on "Reasoning" (James 1890), he commented that emphasis and selection seemed to him the essence of the human mind, but that in other chapters other things seemed more important. Helen Keller saw the world through her fingertips, and said, "If I had made a man, I should certainly have put the brain and soul in his fingertips" (Keller 1939:116).

The aspect that we select and emphasize, furthermore, also characterizes us to an extent because it reveals our purpose and tends to predict our behavior toward the object in that situation. The meaning of objects is variable; from culture to culture, class to class, and to some degree, from person to person. There is a widely held belief that the object exists first and that we then name it. In avoiding a metaphysical discussion at this point it will be sufficient to state that an object exists *as an object for us* only after we have first given it meaning in the process of symbolic communication. When new objects appear during this process, they also have been abstracted from the environment. The objects of everyday human life have appeared as the resultants of this process, and so has the entire realm of scientific objects and identities (Mead 1934:80).

This abstraction is now most complete in physical and mathematical science; as Dewey says, scientific symbols express the behavior of objects in relation to each other (Dewey 1929:255). In scientifically considering objects in the most general and abstract fashion it becomes possible to solve such diverse problems as perfecting the aim of firearms, and the designing of ships and airplanes. The trajectory of a bullet is ascertained by considering it abstractly as a body in motion that is subject to the operation of certain forces, and not by considering it as a means to kill a deer or a man.

Scientific objects, then, appear in human experience as a consequence of the same process of symbolic communication that has resulted in the common sense objects of daily use. Many people make an unjustifiably sharp distinction between scientific thought and action and ordinary thought and action. Scientific behavior does involve systematic, logical reasoning; it is behavior conducted according to stricter rules than usually obtain in ordinary behavior. But the appearance of new meanings and new objects under these stricter rules is much more similar to what occurs in ordinary behavior than is usually supposed. This is because the rules of logical reasoning relate to the economy and the efficiency of thought and behavior, and do not relate to meaning as such. These rules govern to a great extent what we term experimentation, in which new combinations of meanings are found that have satisfactory consequences for certain ends (Dewey 1955:29). One finds in theoretical physics an agreement with the propositions that meaning arises out of behavior and that the rules of right reasoning apply to the efficiency of thought and not to meaning as such. This is, at least, the view of Eddington in his discussion of the downfall of classical mechanics. He shows that our instrumentally-unaided judgments of distance, size, location, space, and time are "crude versions" of measurements taken with scientific instruments (Eddington 1928:17).

New objects can be distinguished and the conceptions of old ones modified because we are able symbolically to analyze both the situations in which we are involved and the problems that confront us. It is on the basis of this continuous activity that man has achieved a positive and significant, even though admittedly only partial, control over his environment. Many thousands of years ago, as revealed by archeology, the cultural environment was quantitatively not much different from that of subhuman animals.[3] The evolution of culture, however, has led to the present control over our physical environment. The building of cities and aqueducts, the developing of systems of transportation and communication, and the harnessing of different forms of energy through the domestication of animals and plants, the use of fuels, and nuclear fission, have made man the dominant species. Culture has enabled man to distribute himself more completely over the earth than has any other species.

Man's environment consists partially of objects that are his own products. These objects are tools and concepts. They are introduced into the cultural act between its beginning and its end, and thus can be made to serve the purposes that man has developed. The use of tools emphasizes the significance of the symbolically delayed response. The beaver, for instance, although capable of much learning, is strictly limited to its own physical organs in building its dams and houses. Its teeth and tail are most important in this regard. The construction activity of the beaver appears not to change from one generation to another. Its dams today

---

[3] There is, of course, much difference between 500,000 years ago, and 20,000 years ago, and the difference between *no* culture and *some* culture is theoretically crucial. Limitations of space prevent a consideration of these two points.

seem to be no different from what they were when Lewis Henry Morgan studied them about a century ago. It is not proper to speak of architecture in connection with the beaver's work, but only in connection with man's greater or lesser skill in planning and building structures. It is not merely that man's buildings have changed, in the form of different styles and materials, although this is important enough in its own right. What is of importance is that this change has been made possible because of man's ability to analyze and to reconstruct a situation before bringing overt activity into play to complete the action. In this reconstruction symbols and tools have been of great moment because they make possible the physical manipulation of the environment in achieving a desired end. The physical and mental products of human action bring the physical environment under man's control.

The use of concepts and tools for the solution of problems involves an estimation of the probable consequences of alternatives, as these alternatives are indicated on the basis of the past. As George Herbert Mead puts it several times, the scientist or the engineer estimates the response of nature in terms of such phenomena as stresses and strains. On the basis of this estimate, he plans a course of action designed to meet the stresses that will develop. It is during this phase of the cultural act that new concepts are developed, which are instrumental in helping to manipulate the environment so as to reach given ends. The concepts appear in situations that call for adjustment on the part of those involved, in that the situation cannot be handled on the basis of habit or routine. The new concepts, and new tools also, thus tend to be developed in problematic situations, and they give man control over his environment to the extent that they are successful in the solution of problems.

The process of solving problems is never completed, however, because new adjustive situations are continually encountered that entail the modification of old tools and concepts, and that sometimes even require their being discarded. This means, in turn, that man's conception of the universe and of himself is constantly being revised on the basis of new or modified conceptions. Thus there is an inherently dynamic aspect to culture and human society, which results from a combination of two components. First, new situations requiring adjustive behavior continually arise. Second, the cultural consequences of new conceptions and tools are largely unpredictable, especially those consequences that extend beyond the immediate problems and those that are somewhat distant in time. Even though predictability is limited, subsequent study, as Tylor showed, reveals that the process of cultural change is rational

(Tylor 1873,I:22f.;II:477ff.).[4] An example from an early history of modern science will perhaps help to clarify this highly complex process.

Galileo (1564–1642) arrived at his conception of force and motion through his analysis of a problem of motion created by technological advance, and which could not be solved by the then dominant Aristotelean physics. The problem was created by the motion of a projectile discharged from a catapult, sling, or bow; and, particularly, by a projectile discharged from a firearm. It had become evident long before Galileo's time that a projectile does not always move as it should according to Aristotelean physics. Galileo's analysis led him to the conclusion that the answer to the problem was to be found in the conception of force, and not in the nature of the projectile. According to Aristotle's physics lighter bodies fall at a slower rate than heavier bodies, and force is that which produces motion or velocity in a body. A corollary of this is that the body should cease to move when the force ceases to act upon it. This conception of force is, of course, confirmed empirically countless times daily (Margenau, *et al.* 1949:10f.). When, for instance, I cease exerting force upon a pen it will cease to move; or, if I release a stone it will fall to the ground. In many other instances, however, the results are different: when the arrow is shot or the powder exploded the force ceases to act upon the body which nevertheless continues in flight for some time over a given distance. Catapults, slings, and bows were, of course, used for centuries prior to Galileo's time. The discrepancy between theory and observation was apparently not raised, however, as a general theoretical problem until the sixteenth and seventeenth centuries brought technical problems in the design and contruction of firearms that medieval theory and practice could not solve. The problem of aim was directly related to the path of the projectile: what was its motion through the air, how was its trajectory to be computed, and so on.

Galileo published his analysis of force and motion in his *Dialogues Concerning Two New Sciences* (1638). The work is developed in rigorous Euclidean fashion and is delightful reading even today. His fundamental achievement was the successful analysis of the motion of falling bodies, his work, he said, being merely the beginning of this "vast and most useful science."

Galileo began by referring to an example of work performed by craftsmen, and to observations made by himself, in which observations he at-

---

[4] For example, Tylor said of the evolution of primitive religions that "the principles of their formation and development . . . prove to be essentially rational, though working in a condition of intense and inveterate ignorance" (Tylor 1873,I:22).

tempted to indicate to himself the reaction of one element in a physical situation to the action of another element. He had been watching pile-drivers, and in meditating upon the problem of motion, conceived the weight as being a freely falling body. He noticed differences in effect as the weight traversed varying distances. The different effects, he reasoned, must be due to differences of impact, and the latter differences must be related to the distance of the fall. Galileo wanted to formulate a theory relating increase of speed to the fall. "And this, at last," he said, "after repeated efforts we trust we have succeeded in doing." He was, in social psychological terms, attempting to conceive the role of a physical object in a situation involving fall. He was confirmed in his belief that he had conceived this fall as it actually occurs, he said, mainly by the consideration of experimental results that seemed to agree with and "exactly correspond with" those properties that had been, one after another, demonstrated by him (Galileo 1946:154).

Galileo had considered certain possible actions of an object in a given situation, and rejected all but one. His own activity so far had consisted only of observation and reflection. He still had the problem of demonstrating that this was in fact the behavior of a freely falling body. He could not rest content with the results of what can be called clinical observations because the interpretation of those observations ran counter both to a conception of force and motion more than two thousand years old, and to the daily empirical confirmation of these ancient conceptions. He had no equipment at hand with which to undertake a test of his hypothesis, and thus was led to design his famous experiment of the inclined plane, a triumph of the scientific imagination (Galileo 1946:171–72). The significance of this experiment for the present discussion is that its preparatory phases had to be conducted before there was overt activity on Galileo's part. He had to conceive the various parts of the apparatus, their relations to each other, and their part in the solving of his problem, before he could construct them. He even had to invent a kind of clock with which to measure time. He interposed his conceptual tools between the beginning of the act, and the completion of the act, in that experiment that is justly so often referred to as the most famous in the history of science.

In *Two New Sciences* Galileo gave the first complete statement of the method of inquiry that science was to use in the succeeding centuries. He developed this method from two general sources: first, from the formal training contained in the traditional "liberal arts" education of his time; second, from the empirical data provided by the work of such artisans as shipwrights and gunners, to whom he freely acknowledged his debt. Technological advance, as previously stated, confronted him with the problem of force and motion that could not be solved by medieval science. His analysis led him to formulate a definition of force in terms of the motion of any object whatever, not only of tables, knives, and carts, but of projectiles as well. Since the old definition of force could not account for the motion of any object whatever, it would have to be modified in some way, or else discarded. It was discarded. It follows from the Galilean conception that when force ceases to operate on a body, the body will not cease moving, but rather it will cease to change its velocity or its direction. Thus the theoretical problem created for Aristotelian physics by the motion of a projectile simply disappears when the Galilean conception of force is accepted.

It was the discarding of Aristotle's conception of force and motion which indicated that the meaning of Galileo's conceptions extended far beyond physics and mathematics. It also led, unpredictably, to the personal difficulties of Galileo with the Roman Catholic church and to the violent opposition of that church to science, an opposition unequalled until the publication of Darwin's *Origin of Species* in 1859. The religious implications of Galileo's mathematical and physical work arose because the Roman church had imbedded Aristotle's metaphysics in the matrix of its theology. Since there was no major concept in Aristotle's metaphysics that was not already in his physics, the discarding of the latter involved also the discarding of its attendant medieval Thomistic theology (Northrop 1947:27–28). This logically meant, of course, the discarding of the medieval conception of man, God, the world, and the universe. The consequences of the first ball that Galileo rolled down his inclined plane seemingly are even yet not fully realized.

The significance of Galileo's work for physics was the appearance of new physical and conceptual objects. Although "force" and "motion" were known prior to 1638, they were not the same concepts after 1638. It was through Galileo's analysis and reconstruction that the new conceptions were developed. From them an unforeseen consequence at least partially resulted: a new ideology of man and the universe. This new ideology, which can conveniently be termed scientific, contains a host of new concepts. Margenau has aptly remarked that science defines a dynamic kind of reality, one that changes and grows as our understanding changes and grows (Margenau 1950). It is through this analytical behavior, of which Galileo's could be cited as an extreme example, that symbolic communication is responsible for both common sense and scientific objects, objects that have been abstracted from the total structure of behavior and events, and that are instrumental in the continual appearance of new objects and new meanings.

Many of the consequences of the scientific attack upon the problem of force and motion were unpredictable at the time that research on the trajectory of a projectile started, and were still unpredictable at the time that Galileo studied the problem. It was not even realized that the "merely technical" problem of the path of a projectile would be transformed into a problem of "pure science" before it could be solved. And, once transformed by Galileo, the major consequences of the development of physical science and a scientific ideology, and of the conflict between science and religion, could not have been predicted. It seemed, furthermore, as if matters proceeded independently of the actors involved, and at least part of this evolution occurred against the wishes and strenuous efforts of the Roman Catholic clergy and church. Science developed according to its own internal logic, its progress logically advancing the scientific ideology, with conflict resulting when the church undertook to challenge the movement.

The above discussion has been in personal terms, "Aristotle's physics" and "Galileo's physics," as if the views of these men were their own personal property, for which they were individually responsible. The previous paragraph, however, suggests that references to names and persons could have been omitted. The conception to be derived from a social psychological study of the evolution of science is that of different cultural subsystems in competition and cooperation with each other. Certainly Galileo—without intending to detract in any way from his genius or his firmly established fame—is not to be held personally responsible for either the conceptions he held before turning to the study of motion, or for the conceptions that he developed as a result of that study. He took his place, as everyone does, in an ongoing cultural process that supplied him with certain skills, drawn in general from his formal education and from the work of artisans. The very problems on which he worked were not of his own making, since the general orientation toward them had been developing from the time that artillery began to be used in the fourteenth century. Generations of men had been confronted with the discrepancy between what they should have observed according to Aristotelean physics, and what they did in fact observe. Force and motion, however, did not become problems until a cultural development, namely, the invention of firearms, rendered the old conceptions inadequate. Galileo is therefore not to be held responsible for the problems on which he worked, nor for the socially accumulated knowledge that made their solution possible, nor even for the solutions themselves, except for the specific form in which he stated them. This discussion, then, has not been concerned so much with what Galileo did. It has rather been concerned with what was done for him and to him (as against what went on within him) as a consequence of his entering the stream of culture and the social process at a given time and place. Cultural and social experience was behaviorally creative for Galileo, as it is for everyone.

One implication of the social psychological analysis of symbolic behavior and the use of tools can be briefly stated. The use of symbols and tools provides man with the means for the rational solution of problems. It is not only that the individual uses them, but the community also. It is unnecessary to embrace the anthropocentric illusion that man controls civilization (White 1949:Ch. 12) just because he can rationally solve problems, and on occasion does so. Any act of reasoning is an act of an individual who is able to reason because, having become a participating member of the human community he has learned to symbolize, which is the means of reasoning. Somewhere John Dewey says that language is "the mother of tools" because it enables us to use ourselves instrumentally in the achieving of given ends. Rationality, as a part of culture, is external to and independent of any given person, and exercizes a constraining influence on his behavior. Culture inevitably imposes rationality upon every person, in greater or lesser degree.

BIBLIOGRAPHY

BURTT, E. A.
  1949 *The Metaphysical Foundations of Modern Physical Science*. New York, Harcourt, Brace and Company.

COWLES, JOHN T.
  1937 "Food Tokens as Incentives for Learning by Chimpanzees." *Comparative Psychology Monographs*, 14(5).

DAMPIER, SIR WILLIAM
  1949 *A History of Science*. 4th edition. New York, The Macmillan Company.

DEWEY, JOHN
  1929 *Experience and Nature*. Chicago, Open Court Publishing Company.

1930 *Human Nature and Conduct.* New York, The Modern Library.

1955 "Unity of Science as a Social Problem." *International Encyclopedia of Unified Science,* 1:29–38.

EDDINGTON, ARTHUR

1928 *The Nature of the Physical World.* Cambridge, Cambridge University Press.

GALILEI, GALILEO

1946 *Dialogues Concerning Two New Sciences.* Translated by Henry Crew and Alfonso de Salvio. Evanston, Northwestern University Press.

HUNTER, WALTER S.

1923 *General Psychology.* Chicago, The University of Chicago Press.

1928 *Human Behavior.* Chicago, The University of Chicago Press.

JAMES, WILLIAM

1890 *The Principles of Psychology.* 2 vols. New York, Henry Holt and Company.

KELLER, HELEN

1939 *The World I Live In.* New York, D. Appleton–Century Company.

KÖHLER, WOLFGANG

1926 *The Mentality of Apes.* New York, Harcourt, Brace and Company.

MARGENAU, HENRY

1950 *The Nature of Physical Reality: A Philosophy of Modern Physics.* New York, McGraw-Hill Book Co.

MARGENAU, HENRY, WILLIAM W. WATSON and CAROL G. MONTGOMERY

1949 *Physics: Principles and Applications.* New York, McGraw-Hill Book Co.

MEAD, GEORGE HERBERT

1934 *Mind, Self, and Society.* Chicago, The University of Chicago Press.

NORTHROP, F. S. C.

1947 *The Logic of the Sciences and the Humanities.* New York, The Macmillan Company.

PAVLOV, I. P.

1910 *The Work of the Digestive Glands.* Philadelphia, J. B. Lippincott Co.

1927 *Conditioned Reflexes.* London, Oxford University Press.

RIESEN, A. H.

1940 "Delayed Reward in Discrimination Learning by Chimpanzees." *Comparative Psychology Monographs,* 15(5).

TYLOR, EDWARD B.

1873 *Primitive Culture.* 2 vols. 2nd edition. New York, Henry Holt and Company.

WHITE, LESLIE A.

1949 *The Science of Culture.* New York, Farrar, Straus and Company.

WOLFE, JOHN B.

1936 "Effectiveness of Token-Rewards for Chimpanzees." *Comparative Psychology Monographs,* 12(5).

YERKES, ROBERT M.

1943 *Chimpanzees.* New Haven, Yale University Press.

YERKES, ROBERT M. and H. W. NISSEN

1939 "Pre-Linguistic Sign Behavior in Chimpanzees." *Science,* 89:585–587.

* * * *

James H. Howard

UNIVERSITY OF NORTH DAKOTA

THE CULTURAL POSITION OF

THE DAKOTA: A REASSESSMENT

The problem of the relationship of culture to environment is one which continues to intrigue anthropologists. Although the old idea of environmental determinism in the strict sense has now been discarded by almost all students in the field, the way in which cultures shape themselves to different environments is a subject which deserves further attention. In this paper I propose to analyze the various subcultures of a single American Indian tribe,[1] the Dakota or Sioux,[2] with this problem in mind.

---

[1] In calling the Dakota a *tribe* I am following the usage of the Dakota themselves and several generations of historians and anthropologists. Perhaps a more accurate term would be *people;* that is, an aggregate of people or an ethnic group without formal political organization as a single unit but united by a common language, traditions, and feeling of nationality. The political subdivisions of the Dakota tribe or Dakota people I have termed *bands;* that is, a politically autonomous group with a permanent chief. There is one important qualification—because of their size the *sub-bands* of the Teton band should be regarded as more or less equivalent to the *bands* in the remainder of the tribe.

[2] There are several reasons for preferring the term *Dakota* for use in reference to this tribe rather than the more popular *Sioux*. Dakota is the tribe's own name for itself (with the variants *Nakota, Lakota,* used by the Middle and Teton divisions, respectively). Since two of our states bear this name the term can hardly be said to be unfamiliar. Dakota say that it means "friends" or "allies." The term *Sioux* is resented by many Dakota, as it is derived from the Ojibwa *Nátɔwèsiwɔk,* meaning "snakes" or "enemies." Aside from its pejorative connotations, there is a further objection to the word. It is continually subject to confusion with the term *Siouan,* applied to the linguistic stock to which the language of the Dakota belongs. Although most anthropologists understand this, the layman, on seeing "Siouan" for the first time, quite naturally assumes it is the adjectival form of "Sioux." Hybrid terms such as *Dakota-Sioux,* employed by those who would skirt the issue, only add to the confusion.

Perhaps no other tribe of American Indians is as familiar to the general public as the Dakota. Famous for their stubborn resistance to the encroachments of the Whites, the Dakota remain the favorite prototype for Indians in western films, romantic novels, and wherever else "real Indians" are needed. The picture of Dakota culture presented in these popular media, while not always a false one, is at best very one-sided, for it is inevitably only the Teton, the westernmost division of the tribe, who are depicted.

Traditionally the Dakota tribe is divided into seven bands, the *Očéti-šákowį* or "Seven Council Fires" of tribal lore. However, for purposes of cultural analysis, a threefold division of the tribe seems more suitable. These three divisions are, in fact, recognized and named by the Dakota themselves. The first of the three, the *Eastern* or *Santee* division, comprises the Mdewakanton, Wahpekute, Wahpeton, and Sisseton bands. The second, the *Middle* or *Wičiyela* division, is made up of the Yankton and Yanktonai bands. The third, the *Western* division, consists of a single band, the Teton. This last group, however, probably outnumbered all of the other six bands combined, at least in the nineteenth century. At the present time the tribe numbers about 42,000, of which approximately 23,000 are Teton, 10,000 *Wičiyela*, and 9,000 Santee.

Each of the three divisions of the Dakota tribe represents a unique adaptation of American Indian culture to a particular environment. Furthermore, since the Middle and Western Dakota groups at one time possessed a culture identical with that of the Eastern Dakota, and shared the same territory with them, we have here the sort of "control" situation necessary for an experiment of the "natural" type. Changes from the older Dakota culture, as represented by the Santee bands, can be interpreted as responses, on the part of the *Wičiyela* and Teton, to new locales and cultural influences as they moved west (allowing of course for some changes, presumably minor, in the culture of the Santee groups subsequent to the separation). To illustrate this I shall present a brief synopsis of the culture patterns of each of the three divisions named above, pointing out similarities and differences on both the division and band levels.

THE SANTEE OR EASTERN DAKOTA

In their culture, the Santee or Eastern Dakota most closely resembled the Central Algonquian tribes, particularly the Minnesota and Wisconsin Ojibwa, the Prairie Potawatomi, and the Meskwaki or Fox. The territory of the Eastern Dakota was the southern two-thirds of Minnesota with adjacent portions of North and South Dakota and Iowa. This was a land of lakes and forests, interspersed with areas of parkland and prairie.

The economy of the Santee was nicely adjusted to this environment, and rested upon a base of hunting, fishing, gathering, and horticulture. The first two of these activities were carried on by males, the last two by females. The Santee are known to have hunted the bison, at least in the nineteenth century, but this animal was certainly not so important to them as it was to the Middle and Western Dakota. Moose and deer were the most common quarry. The lakes and streams of the area provided a variety of fish. Spear fishing took place at river rapids and on the lakes. At night, birchbark and pitch torches aided the spearmen. Large nets were also employed in lake fishing.[3] Important wild foods were wild rice, maple sugar, and *típsina* (*Psoralea esculenta*), the wild prairie turnip. The latter was removed from the ground with a digging stick. It could be eaten raw, boiled in soup, or fried. Women tended large gardens, growing corn, beans, squashes, pumpkins, and tobacco (Skinner 1919:167). The late George Will, in his studies of Indian corn, found a distinct variety in the possession of the Santee who fled to Canada following the Minnesota Uprising (personal communication, 1951). This would seem to indicate that corn horticulture was a complex of respectable antiquity with the Eastern Dakota.

The common summer dwelling of the Santee was a large gable-roofed house of bark called the *Típi-tànka*, literally "House-big" (Mayer 1932:104–108). In winter small hemispherical cattail-mat or bark wigwams were used, as well as conical dwellings covered with hides or bark (Skinner 1919:165). Skinner mentions that sometimes the hemispherical lodges were earth covered, but it seems clear that these were not earthlodges in the usual sense of the word. Lloyd Wilford reports that no archeological remains of Dakota earthlodges have appeared in Minnesota (personal communication, 1953).

The *Típi-tànka*, or gable-roofed dwelling, had a sleeping and lounging platform about five feet wide and two and a half feet above the floor which extended around the inside of the house (Mayer 1932:106). Braided cornhusk floor mats and woven cattail mats were used on the floors and lounging platforms and to line the walls (Skinner 1919:165).

---

[3] William Chatfield, an Ojibwa informant of Cass Lake, Minnesota, stated that older people of his tribe had often mentioned that it was a dispute over stolen fish nets which triggered the sanguine wars between the Ojibwa and the Dakota which led, ultimately, to the expulsion of the Dakota from the greater part of their territory in Minnesota.

Over the door, which was at one end of the *Típi-tànka,* was a flat roof or shed extending some eight or ten feet from the building and supported by posts. This served as an outside lounging platform and was also used for drying corn and other vegetables. On hot summer nights it served as a sleeping platform (Mayer 1932:108). A medicine pole usually stood near each *Típi-tànka* (Mayer 1932:109).

Both dugout and birchbark canoes were used by the Santee. When not in use, the birchbark canoes were often stored on the shed of the *Típi-tànka* (Mayer 1932:109). Skinner found dugouts still in use among the Wahpeton and Sisseton Dakota in 1919 (1919:167).

All of the Santee bands were divided into exogamous patrilineal clans. These clans were usually named after localities rather than animals, birds, or other natural phenomena. Occasionally, however, we encounter a name referring to an animal taboo, such as the *Maġá-yùtešnì* or "Eat-no-geese" clan of the Mdewakanton (Riggs 1893:157). Such clan taboo names are common among the Omaha, Ponca, and other Southern Siouan tribes. As was the case with the Southern Siouans, each Santee clan had a specified place in the ceremonial camping circle, which was formed on the tribal bison hunt and for certain ceremonies.

Though definite information is lacking, it seems likely that the large *Típi-tànka* of the Santee was a clan dwelling. In winter the Santee village groups and clans split up into smaller groups consisting of from one to three families, which moved to favorable hunting and trapping territories. This pattern of fractionation during the winter months to ensure a better food supply was also customary among the Ojibwa and other neighboring tribes. In the spring the clans and bands re-grouped in the summer villages to plant gardens, conduct tribal ceremonies, and organize large hunting and war expeditions.

The Santee Dakota, like the Southern Siouans, might be said to have possessed a "government by kinship." Kinship and clan affiliation seem to have loomed greater than personal ability in the selection of leaders. The principal governing body was the band council. Each clan within the band furnished 20 *wakičonze* or councilors (Skinner 1919:173). The councilors' lodges were set up in front of their respective clans when the band was camped in the ceremonial circle arrangement. In times of decision these *wakičonze* sat in council with the chief of the band. All councilors had equal authority, but each clan customarily voted as a unit (Skinner 1919:173).

The office of band chief was hereditary among the Santee, passing from a father to his eldest son. As leader of the band, each chief appointed a head *akíčita* or "soldier," perhaps better expressed in English as "policeman" (Skinner 1919:173). This man's duty was to keep order in the village and to enforce the orders of the band chief and the council. He was assisted by other *akíčita*, appointed directly by the council, and the entire group made up the *tiyótipi* or "soldier lodge." Among the Santee, *akíčita* were selected from various warrior societies on the basis of personal merit. An entire warrior society was never selected for *akíčita* duty.

On the tribal bison hunt, four "hunt chiefs" were selected by the council. For the duration of the hunt these men were in complete charge of the group, possessing almost dictatorial powers, and outranking the band chief. They were assisted by the *tiyótipi*. Persons who went ahead of the main group and scared the game were whipped by the "soldiers," who also cut to pieces the offenders' lodge covers and other equipment. The authority of the hunt chiefs, however, lasted only during the hunt, after which they returned to their former status.

In dress, the Santee more closely resembled the Central Algonquian tribes than the other Dakota bands to the west. Men generally banged their hair in front and cut it short in back, and braided the remaining hair into four braids, two of which fell on either side of the forehead in front and two behind the ears in back (Skinner 1919:164). The Wahpeton are said to have roached their hair at one time (Skinner 1919:164). Old photographs in the collections of the Minnesota State Historical Society show a variety of headdresses in use by Eastern Dakota men. These include the porcupine and deer-tail roach headdress and the finger-woven sash turban, which were often worn together. A peculiar style, also affected by the Ojibwa and Prairie-Potawatomi, consisted of an otterskin fillet in which four bone cylinders, holding eagle feathers, are arranged at equidistant points. Some of the time, especially in winter, an ornate capouche or hood was worn (Winchell 1911:opposite 504, Fig. 14). Sometimes this was sewn directly to the hunting coat, in which case it is termed a capote. In winter this hood warmed the ears and in summer it kept off mosquitoes (Mayer 1932:126–127, 130). According to Skinner the Plains warbonnet was used to some extent by the Santee (1919:164). One wonders, however, if this was the true Plains warbonnet of the loose, flaring, type or the upright bonnet common in the Woodland area, and used by such distant groups as the Cherokee and Iroquois.

Santee shirts were of buckskin, but unfringed (Skinner 1919:164). The breechcloth was of the type which passes between the legs and hangs over the belt about a foot in front and in back. Leggings were tight and had large ankle flaps (Skinner 1919:164). There was a seam down the front to which a short fringe, half an inch long, was fastened. Carver illustrates a "Naudowessie" man wearing a peculiar triangular shaped knife sheath on his chest (1956:pl. 3). This article of apparel seems to have been characteristic of the Eastern Dakota. It appears almost a century later in portraits of Chief Little Crow. Another favorite item of neckwear was the bear-claw necklace.

Santee moccasins were soft-soled, puckered to a single seam over the instep, with very large ankle flaps (Skinner 1919:169). Later the Ojibwa style moccasin with smaller ankle flaps and a beaded vamp came into general use. Both types are excellently suited to stalking game on a Woodland underfooting of pine needles and moss. Both would be poor protection against the prickly pear and bunch grass stubble of the High Plains.

Santee women wore the two-piece Central Algonquian style dress, consisting of a wrap-around skirt, ornamented with ribbonwork appliqué at the hem and up the front, and a loose blouse (Skinner 1919:164). These blouses were often ornamented with a profusion of silver brooches. Santee women generally wore their hair in a single braid down the back and ornamented this with a beaded wrapping from which hung many ribbons or oblique-beaded bands. Several strands of beads were usually worn about the neck.

Curvilinear floral designs became popular with the Santee during the nineteenth century, almost completely replacing the older geometric and zoomorphic designs. At the present time such "flower beadwork" is still seen on both men's and women's dancing costumes.

The Sisseton were more Plains-like in their dress than the other Santee. Sisseton men wore their hair in two braids, one at either side of the head just behind the ears. These were often wrapped with otterskin. Their shirts and leggings were Plains-like in their long fringes, and their moccasins were often, though not invariably, of the hard-soled Plains type (Skinner 1919:165).

According to Skinner all of the Santee bands made pottery of pounded clay tempered with crushed rock. Decoration was applied by stamping the unfired vessel with a carved paddle. Before firing, the vessel was smeared with glue (Skinner 1919:165).

Skinner's informants recalled that their division of the tribe had once used flint knives, scrapers, and arrowpoints, as well as similar objects of bone. He collected a double-pitted hammerstone which was still in use. These Santee informants also mentioned the use of grooved mauls and grooved stone axes to break up firewood—traits which apparently survived until a very late date with these people. Smaller mauls were used to crush berries, chipped flint axes to chop wood (Skinner 1919:166).

Horizontal wooden mortars of Central Algonquian type were used to pound corn. Distinctively, Santee pestles were merely crude, heavy sticks (Skinner 1919:166). Wooden bowls were tastefully carved. Bowls with carved animal head decorations were reserved for use in the Medicine dance. Wood and bison horn spoons were also manufactured (Skinner 1919:165).

Like their neighbors to the east, the Santee wove square cedar and basswood fiber bags of the Central Algonquian type. Square woven tobacco pouches, which Skinner notes as a Central Algonquian style, were worn about the neck (Skinner 1919:166).

The Mdewakanton and Wahpekute used barrel-shaped hide parfleches, the Wahpeton and Sisseton a box type and a flat rectangular type more reminiscent of the Plains (Skinner 1919:166). All of the Santee bands made and used birchbark vessels. Tumplines of moosehide were used in back packing and by women in carrying the cradle board. Santee cradle boards were of the solid-piece style typical of the Eastern Woodlands (Mayer 1932:126; Skinner 1919:166).

The principal weapon of the Santee was the long bow. For close fighting, the ball-head and rifle-stock warclubs were employed (Skinner 1919:166). The ball-head warclub and a characteristic triangular dagger (contained in the peculiar chest sheath mentioned above) are pictured by Carver (1956:pl. 4).

Among the musical instruments of the Santee were the double-headed tambour drum and the tall wooden water drum. The water drum was apparently used for all major ceremonies, including the Sun dance (Eastman 1849:xxii). Musical rasps of bone, with tin plate resonators, are described by Mrs. Eastman (1849:xx). The tin plate resonators had very likely replaced earlier ones of gourd. Deer hoof and gourd rattles were also used, the latter, especially, by shamans and in the Medicine dance. Mnemonic song records were either incised on flat boards or birchbark. These were used mainly to record Medicine dance songs (Skinner 1919:167).

Deer hides were dressed over an inclined log in Northern and Central Algonquin style, but bison hides were staked out on the ground for tanning, a practice more characteristic of the Plains (Skinner 1919:167–168). Both elk antler and wooden scrapers were used to tan buffalo robes (Skinner 1919:167).

Popular Santee field games were snow snake, lacrosse, and shinny.

Most gambling was done via the mocassin game. The folklore of the Santee is very similar to that of the Central Algonquian tribes, with one important exception: the culture hero does not seem to be connected with the Medicine dance ceremony in any way. Prominent folk-characters are the culture hero, Spider; *Wíyą-nùpapi* or "Double woman"; and *Čą́-otìdą* the "Little-tree-dweller," a malicious elf. A prominent cult surrounded this last figure (Howard 1955). Tales of "Windigo" type cannibals are also present.

The chief ceremonies of the Santee were the Medicine dance, which resembles the Algonquian Midewiwin; the Sun dance; the Thunder dance; and the Little-tree-dweller ritual. A distinctively Santee dancing society was called the "Raw Fish Eaters." Members dressed and danced in imitation of the cormorant (Lowie 1913:123–124). This dance serves to demonstrate the importance of fish in Eastern Dakota economy.

Carver mentions an interesting ceremony, already obsolescent in his time, involving sexual intercourse of a ritual nature. This rite was known as the Wild Rice feast, and may have been performed to ensure the fertility of this important staple. A young woman of high rank invited forty of the principal warriors of the village to her lodge where, "having feasted them with rice and venison, she by turns regaled each of them with a private desert, behind a screen fixed for this purpose in the inner part of the tent" (Carver 1956:245–246). The woman was thereafter held in great respect by the tribe, and married one of the principal chiefs.

The Santee were the only division of the Dakota which possessed the institution of bride-service. A youth, when he had selected a girl as his bride-to-be and reached an agreement with her parents, went to live for a year in their house, hunting and performing menial tasks for the family. If he had demonstrated during this time that he was able to support a wife, he married the girl at a public feast, which was concluded by the groom's carrying off the bride on his back (Carver 1956:372–374).

The Santee were and are still considered by other Dakota to be great magicians and shamans. Members of the Medicine dance particularly were thought to be great wonder workers.[4] The characteristic plant of the Santee shaman was the fern, rather than the sage of the *Wičíyela*

---

[4] The Santee reputation for magic still persists to some extent. In 1946 a white man, a resident of Sisseton, South Dakota, told how an old Santee had recovered the body of a drowned person from a nearby lake. "We don't know how he did it—those old Indians know things that give you the creeps. He went out in his rowboat alone. All he had with him were a gunny sack and a rake. Pretty soon he came back with the body. We were watching him with field glasses but we can't figure out how he did it. We think he had trained otters."

and Teton practitioners. The floor of the lodge in which a shaman conducted a curing ritual was covered with fern leaves.

Two forms of burial were practiced by the Santee. The first form, burial in the ground with a small house built over the grave, was practiced also by the Ojibwa, Potawatomi, and Winnebago. The second, tree or scaffold burial, is more characteristic of the Plains area.

Though broken and scattered since the Minnesota Uprising, members of the various Santee bands are proud of their status as members of the "oldest" or "original" division of the tribe.

THE WIČÍYELA⁵ OR MIDDLE DAKOTA

While first encountered in the Leech Lake region of north central Minnesota in the latter part of the seventeenth century, this division of the Dakota tribe began a westward movement shortly afterward. In the process of migrating the group divided, the Yankton moving southwest to southeastern South Dakota and nearby parts of Iowa and Minnesota, the Yanktonai further north to southern North Dakota on the eastern side of the Missouri as far north as the present town of Washburn, North Dakota, and along the James and Big Sioux drainages in eastern South Dakota. This territory includes the Missouri Coteau, and is characteristically parkland and prairie, as distinguished from the "short grass" country west of the Missouri. Today it is used chiefly for cultivation, while the country west of the river is typically cattle country.

In moving into this area, the Yankton band encountered the Ponca, a small group of the Thegiha division of the Siouan stock. The Ponca and Yankton seem to have gotten on well together from the first, and the Ponca set aside a part of their traditional territory for the use of the Yankton, in return for their military support. Farther north, the Yanktonai encountered and displaced upstream the Caddoan-speaking Arikara and the Siouan-speaking Mandan and Hidatsa. Much of the subsequent cultural change on the part of the Yankton and Yanktonai can be explained in terms of their contacts with these semi-sedentary riverine groups, whose culture was well adapted to the Missouri Coteau environment. One might say that the *Wičíyela* literally "fell into" the environmental

---

[5] The term *Wičíyela* is said to refer to the "childish" or simple, direct, manner of speech employed by the Middle Dakota. Certainly, when compared with the Teton dialect, the speech of the Middle Dakota appears simple, lacking the flowery elaborations of the former.

niche vacated by these earlier inhabitants. At any rate, by the beginning of the reservation era they had approximated the cultural patterns of the riverine tribes to a remarkable degree.

The economy of the Middle Dakota, like that of other Missouri River groups, rested upon a base of hunting, fishing, gathering, and river-bottom horticulture. Great tribal bison hunts took place twice a year, in midsummer and late fall, a practice also followed by the Ponca, Arikara, Mandan, and Hidatsa. Bison, elk, deer, and antelope were also hunted throughout the year by individuals and small groups. Small game was taken with rabbit sticks, similar to those of the Hopi and other Southwestern tribes (Hurt 1950:1–2).

Fishing, though not as important as to the Santee, was practiced to some extent. It was, however, fishing of a quite different sort. Large weirs were built near villages (Kingsbury, quoted by Hurt 1953:2). Willow branch seines weighted with grooved stones were used to take fish in the James, Turtle, and certain other rivers of the region which are shallow and suited to wading. Several men formed a line, wading with the seine. At intervals the ends of the seine were brought together and the imprisoned fish killed with spears. Bow-and-arrow fishing was also practiced on the numerous glacial lakes of the area. One Lower Yanktonai, John Saul, continued to fish with a bow and arrow till the 1940's (Howard 1951a).

The gathering of tipsina and other wild foods was also important to the Middle Dakota. Horticulture was practiced by the women of the two bands, who raised at least three varieties of corn, two types of squash, and at least three varieties of beans (George Will, personal communication, 1950). The Yanktonai possess a myth which explains how they secured the first corn from milk which dripped from the udder of a supernatural buffalo cow. This indicates some antiquity for the use of corn by the *Wičiyela*. The late No-two-horns, an Upper Yanktonai chief, reported that back scratchers made of corncobs with wooden stick handles were important objects in the bundle of an ancient member of his band. These had been used by at least six generations of Yanktonai. Further evidence is found in Peter Pond's report of being served a bowl of corn meal soup by his Yanktonai hosts (Pond 1908:349). Skinner notes that the Yankton raised corn aboriginally (1919:174).

Three different types of dwelling were used by the Middle Dakota: the skin tipi, the skin-covered wickiup, and the Plains earthlodge. Although definite information is lacking, it appears that the Yankton band used only the first two of these. The Middle Dakota tipi was of the standard three-pole foundation type. Wickiups resembled the dome-shaped and elongated cattail mat and bark houses of the Santee and the Central Algonquians, but were covered with hides rather than bark or mats.

The Yanktonai earthlodge was very likely derived from the Mandan, Hidatsa, or Arikara in the early part of the nineteenth century. It resembled the lodges of these three tribes in nearly all respects (Hurt and Howard 1950). The locations of three Yanktonai earthlodge villages are now known: one a mile and a half north of Ft. Yates, North Dakota; one near Armadale Island, near Melette, South Dakota; and one near Ft. Thompson, South Dakota. Two lodges of the first village mentioned were excavated by a party from the North Dakota State Historical Society in 1957. Although small, measuring approximately thirty feet in diameter, they were otherwise of classic Missouri River style.

Perhaps the most famous Yanktonai earthlodge village was the one at Armadale Island. This village was visited in 1863 by Captain Tripp, of the 41st Iowa Cavalry. He records that it then contained fifteen earthlodges, arranged in a circle 165 feet in diameter. In the center of the plaza was a medicine pole and lookout station. The lodges were of varying dimensions. Tripp estimated that some would accommodate seventy-five Indians, others about twenty-five. Forty acres of land had been broken up nearby. About half of this was in corn, the remainder in beans, peas, turnips, potatoes, and other vegetables. A large fish trap had been built in the James River, just west of the village (Kingsbury, quoted by Hurt 1953:2).

To travel on the Missouri, James, and other rivers of the region, the Middle Dakota employed the bullboat, another trait undoubtedly adopted from the Mandan, Hidatsa, or Arikara. An example of such a bullboat, manufactured by John Saul, is in the University of South Dakota Museum in Vermillion. This bullboat is round, but models seen among the Upper Yanktonai of Cannonball, North Dakota, are shaped much like an ordinary rowboat.

At one time the Yankton and Yanktonai seem to have been divided into clans like the Eastern Dakota. This is indicated by the survival of taboo names of the type used in reference to clans by the Southern Siouans for certain sub-band and village groups. One sub-band of the Yanktonai is called *Pteyútešni*, literally "Eat-no-buffalo-cows," clearly a buffalo clan taboo name. Another sub-band is called *Kiyúksa*, literally "Breakers-of-the-rule" (of clan exogamy). By the time scientific investigation of these bands was undertaken, however, clans were not present.

As with the Santee, government was by a council, assisted by the *tiyótipi* or "soldier lodge." Chieftainship tended to be hereditary, but if a chief's eldest son was deemed unfit, he could be passed over for the next in line. *Wičíyela* organization for the bison hunt was identical with that of the Santee.

The dress of the Yankton and Yanktonai resembled that of the Upper Missouri village tribes to a great degree. Men wore their hair in three braids, two at the sides of the head and a third, wrapped in otter fur, hanging down the back. In front the hair was worn in bangs, leaving a lock hanging over the brow and nose. At either side of the forehead hourglass-shaped ornaments of dentalium shells were tied to the hair, with pendants of the same material hanging down as far as the shoulders. Fur fillets were worn by some men, and the warbonnet was used to some extent. Yankton chiefs, judging from old photographs, favored the finger-woven sash turban. The roach headdress was introduced with the Grass dance ceremony, and remains the most popular dance headgear today.

Fringed buckskin shirts were worn which are indistinguishable from those of the Teton Dakota, Cheyenne, and other High Plains groups. Both breechcloth and leggings, however, are distinctive. The Yankton and Yanktonai breechcloth is of the "riverine" style, tucked in over the belt for a few inches in back and hanging out over the belt for about a foot in front. This type of breechcloth is almost invariably ornamented with ribbonwork in a "V" design in back. Leggings were unfringed, but looser than those of the Santee. Instead of the characteristic Plains beadwork up the side, Yanktonai leggings had a large quilled or beaded rosette or a box-like design at the bottom.

In late years moccasins were of the hard-soled Plains type, but earlier illustrations show soft-soled footwear, puckered to a single seam up the top. A favorite item of neckwear for men was the "Crow" necklace, which consisted of several strands of cut bone beads, each strand longer than the one above.

Women wore a one-piece dress, often ornamented at the top with a cape-like piece completely covered with dentalia. Moccasins were likewise distinctive, having the high buckskin top or leg-wrap common among Mandan, Hidatsa, and Arikara women. The distinctive oval-shaped woman's belt pouch also appears to be derived from the upriver tribes. Heavy necklaces of vertical bone "hair pipes" are more reminiscent of the Plains.

Both the Yankton and the Yanktonai made fine pottery, but only small vessels. Larger pottery vessels were obtained through trade with the Arikara and Mandan (Hurt 1950:1).

Both flat and barrel-shaped parfleches were used. Baskets, of the type made by the Arikara and Mandan, were manufactured, at least by the Yanktonai. Vertical mortars, set into the floor of the earthlodge, were used to pound corn, while smaller ones were used to grind medicines and perfumes. Pestles were shaped like elongated dumbbells. Another sort of mortar, used to pound dried meat and berries, was made from the skin of a bison's head. Hides were tanned by staking them out on the ground in the Plains fashion.

Baby hoods of the soft Plains type, often completely quilled or beaded, were used by the Yankton and Yanktonai. A baby, bundled in such a hood, might be carried in a woman's arms. If she wished to carry the baby on her back the hood was fastened to a wooden frame shaped something like football goalposts.

In both hunting and warfare the Middle Dakota employed the short bow, as it was best adapted for use on horseback. Soft hide armor and shields are mentioned for the Yanktonai by Pond (1908:354). Although the Woodland style ball-head and rifle-stock warclubs were highly valued by the Middle Dakota, they served principally as items of dance regalia. For actual fighting, the stone-head Plains type club was preferred.

Wičíyela musical instruments included the single-head tambour drum, the large dance drum (in size and shape like a modern bass drum), and the tall water drum. This last was used only in the Medicine lodge ceremony. Deerhoof, gourd, and hide rattles were used. Gourd rattles were rare, and their use was restricted to shamans and members of the Medicine lodge. Mnemonic song boards of the Santee type were used to record Medicine lodge songs.

The Sun dance was perhaps the most important religious ceremony of the Middle Dakota. Important also was the Woodland Tree-dweller cult. The Medicine lodge ceremony, though highly regarded, was rarely performed, and disappeared early in the reservation era (Gilette 1906). It seems to have more closely resembled the Arikara Medicine lodge than the Ojibwa Midewiwin, and consisted of a sort of superorganization of shamanistic groups, such as the Bear, Buffalo, Wolf, and Tree-dweller cults (Eva Littlechief, personal communication, 1951).

The Blue bead ceremony was apparently practiced only by the Middle division of the Dakota, who shared a reverence for blue glass beads of native fabrication with the Mandan, Hidatsa, Arikara, and Cheyenne. The *Wičíyela* Blue bead ceremony, which survived until 1913, involved the parents of a beloved child giving away vast amounts of goods in return for the privilege of ornamenting their child's forelock with a blue bead or pendant.

Another ceremonial complex shared by the Middle Dakota and the Upper Missouri village tribes was ritualized eagle trapping of the type so well known among the Hidatsa and Mandan (Howard 1954). The pronounced age-grading of *Wičíyela* warrior societies can also be attributed to influence from the village tribes upriver.

Wičíyela shamans, as noted above, were divided into different classes according to specialties. Those who had been blessed by the bison were the tribal surgeons. The bear shamans were skilled in the use of herbal medicines, while the Little-tree-dweller shamans specialized in the treatment of headaches.

Popular field games of the Middle Dakota were shinny, lacrosse, and hoop-and-pole. At least four variants of the last game were known, in one of which rabbit sticks were thrown at the rolling hoop. The most popular gambling games were the hand game and the plum shooting game, the latter played mainly by women. The moccasin game was sometimes played when the *Wičíyela* met Santee or Ojibwa, who were unfamiliar with the hand game. The folklore of the Middle Dakota is quite similar to that of the Santee bands. Tales of "Windigo" type cannibalism, however, are absent.

Among the Yanktonai, marriage was by purchase. Pond noted this practice in the first half of the eighteenth century (1908:354), and it persisted until the early 1900's. Eva Littlechief, an Upper Yanktonai informant, said that her father, Chief Red-fish, had sold her to an old man when she was still a girl.

Scaffold burial was the only type reported by Yankton and Yanktonai informants for the prereservation period. The Yanktonai believed that if a person were buried in the ground his ghost would come back to haunt the living.

The *Wičíyela* or Middle Dakota regard themselves as the elite of the Dakota tribe. Their clothing, they state, was plain but elegant. It was not ragged like Santee garb, nor overly flashy like that of the Teton. In their own opinion, the *Wičíyela* are also handsomest physically. The Santee they describe as small, and the men, they say, usually have scraggly goatees and mustaches. The Teton are described as tall and gangling with big noses.

The *Wičíyela* despise the Santee but fear their magic. Santee shamans are known to be able to fly through the air and cover vast distances in a short time, and will avenge any fancied slight with black magic. There were no harlots among the *Wičíyela*, they say, until the Santee introduced powerful love medicines secured from the Ojibwa.

While the *Wičíyela* respected the warlike prowess of the Teton, they considered them rather crude "country cousins" whose clothing was generally too flashy and whose manners were a bit rough. The attitudes of the Middle Dakota in regard to the Teton are very reminiscent of those of the Missouri River village tribes in regard to nomadic groups in general.

Although the *Wičíyela*, being Dakota, were traditional enemies of the Mandan, Hidatsa, and Arikara, there were many peaceful interludes which permitted cultural exchange. In the winter of 1851–52, according to several Dakota "winter counts" or calendrical records, an Arikara chief named "Red Elk" and his people wintered with a group of Upper Yanktonai near the present town of Washburn, North Dakota. Likewise, Medicine-bear's band of Yanktonai contained many people descended from captured Nuptadi Mandan women, including Chief Medicine-bear himself (Alfred Bowers, personal communication, 1957). As a result, this band felt an affinity to the Mandan and often went on the bison hunt with them.

In the case of the Yankton, Ponca informants reported that relations between their tribe and this band of the Dakota had always been friendly, even when the Ponca were being subjected to intensive raiding by the Teton. These varied contacts with semi-sedentary Missouri valley horticulturalists seem to have given Middle Dakota culture its characteristic stamp.

THE TETON OR WESTERN DAKOTA

Traditionally the western division of the Dakota tribe consisted of but a single band. This "band," however, was larger than all of the other six bands of the tribe combined, and it is therefore important to note the various sub-bands. There were seven of these:

1. Hunkpapa
2. Miniconjou
3. Sihasapa or Blackfoot
4. Oohenonpa or Two-kettle
5. *Sičángu* or Brulé
6. *Itázipčo* or Sansarc
7. Oglala

The name Teton is derived from *Títonwàna*, "Dwellers on the Plains." This division was first encountered in 1680 on the Mississippi River in central Minnesota. By 1700 they had moved westward to the Lake Traverse region in northeastern South Dakota, and by 1800 the various sub-bands were scattered along the Missouri in South Dakota. Subsequently, the Teton ranged southward into Nebraska, westward into Colorado, Wyoming, and Montana, and north into western North Dakota, Manitoba, and Saskatchewan. Bitterly resisting the incursions of the whites, they acquired notoriety and, when warfare had ended, fame. Today they have come to be considered the Plains Indian *par excellence,* and from them have come most of the popular ideas about the Dakota, and indeed, about Indians in general.

The bison was the mainstay of the Teton, and the various sub-bands traveled widely following the herds. This steady meat diet was varied with tipsina and other wild foods gathered by the women. Occasionally, women planted corn and other vegetables in small gardens, but more commonly such foods were secured by raiding the Arikara, Pawnee, Ponca, and other horticulturalists. Fish were despised as "unclean" food.

The tipi was the principal dwelling of the Teton, and some tipis were large enough to permit dancing inside. Occasionally, a hide-covered wickiup was built as a temporary shelter, and several winter accounts mention that the Sansarc sub-band built and lived in earthlodges in the winters of 1815–16 and 1816–17 (Howard 1951b:4–8). The tipi, however, was the principal type of dwelling of the Teton, both in summer and winter.

The characteristic local group of the Teton was a loose sub-band. The membership of such a sub-band was rather fluid, and families could join or withdraw from the group as they chose. While camping with a particular group, however, a family was subject to all of its rules and sanctions. Clans, presumably present at an earlier period, had completely disappeared among the Teton by the time they were subjected to scientific investigation. Linguistic survivals, in the form of sub-band taboo names of the type used in reference to clans by the Southern Siouan tribes, indicate their former presence.

The chief of each sub-band was chosen by a council of all adult males over forty years of age. Once chosen, however, the personal qualities of the chief and his success in leading the group in war and in the chase determined the size of his following, as people were free to leave the camp of an unpopular man. No one was barred from chieftainship by birth, and members of other bands of the Dakota and even of enemy tribes sometimes became chiefs among the Teton. Thus we find "Osage" and "Shawnee" sub-groups among the Brulé, led by members of these tribes who had been taken captive as children and had grown up as

Teton. Such a thing was unheard of among the Eastern Dakota, where clan and family affiliation were all-important in selecting leaders.

Although details of organization differed from sub-band to sub-band, the council and chief emerge as the principal governing body. Some sub-bands, such as the Oglala, elected four "shirt wearers" or supreme councilors to sit with the chiefs and council (Wissler 1912:7). The orders of this group were carried out by four *wakičun* or head councilors, who were assisted by two head "soldiers" and a larger soldier group of lower rank (Wissler 1912:8). Often an entire warrior society was selected for *akičita* or "soldier" duty (Wissler 1912:13).

Theoretically, the council acted as a balance to the power of the chiefs, but in actuality many chiefs possessed almost dictatorial power. This was particularly true in the case of such men as Sitting Bull and Red Cloud, who often paid little heed to the words of the council. On at least one occasion Sitting Bull ordered a horse thief put to death, an assumption of authority that would have been impossible for a Santee or *Wičiyela* chief.

In their dress, the Teton were typically High Plains Indians. Both men and women wore their hair in two braids, one at either side of the head. Men often wrapped their braids in otterskin or red strouding. Shirts were elaborately decorated with long fringes and ermine skins, and quillwork or beadwork bands were sewed on the arms and over the shoulders. At the front and back of the neck, a rectangular or triangular ornament was sewed. The triangularly shaped ornament may have been derived from the Santee knife sheath. Teton breechcloths were usually long and narrow, often reaching to the ground. Leggings were loose, for comfort on horseback, and were usually ornamented with a beaded strip up either side.

Moccasins were of the hard-sole Plains type, and often had fancy quillwork cuffs and instep ornaments. A favorite item of neckwear was a breastplate of bone "hair pipes." Long trailing warbonnets suited for display on horseback, were favored by the Teton. Another characteristic headdress consisted of a strip of quillwork about the size of a foot ruler, with a bison tail pendant at the bottom. This was worn, with one or two upright eagle feathers, at the back of the head. Members of the three northernmost sub-bands, the Sihasapa, Sansarc, and Hunkpapa, occasionally affected riverine styles of dress, such as the "box design" leggings, the riverine breechcloth, and the "Crow" necklace.

Teton women's dress was also elaborate. The yokes of dresses were often heavily quilled or beaded, or a dress might be covered with rows of elk teeth. "Hair pipe" breastplates or necklaces, similar to those of the men but with the pipes fixed vertically rather than horizontally, were worn at dances. Heavy concha belts of German silver had pendants which dragged on the ground when the woman was not on horseback. The knee-length women's leggings were often solidly beaded. A complete woman's costume might weigh forty pounds.

Among the Teton, warfare was an all-important activity. An elaborate system of warrior societies developed, and often there was an intense rivalry between certain pairs of societies.

The Sun dance, Alowanpi, and Horse dance ceremonies were the foci of great summer encampments which might contain thousands of individuals. The Medicine lodge as an organized group was absent, but shamans occasionally gathered to demonstrate their powers (Wissler 1912:95). Shinny and various forms of hoop-and-pole were the principal field games, while the hand game was a favorite winter pastime.

Marriage was by purchase and some brides commanded a price of a hundred ponies. Burial was invariably of the scaffold type.

Teton folklore reflects the great emphasis upon warfare which dominated the thought of this division of the tribe. Stories of witchcraft are relatively unimportant. In Teton folktales the Little-tree-dweller appears as a grassland spirit (Walker 1917:89).

During the late historic period, the Teton were rich in horses, buffalo robes, and trade goods. They had a tremendous *esprit de corps* and a flair for doing things in the grand manner. Poorer groups, such as the Middle Dakota, and especially the Santee, were scorned and termed "women." Clearly, Teton culture of the eighteenth and early nineteenth centuries was a burgeoning thing. Even today, after several generations of reservation life, the Teton possess an *hauteur* and at the same time an openness of character which clearly distinguishes them from both the Middle and Eastern divisions of the tribe. This is often expressed in extravagant gifts to visitors at Grass dances.

SUMMARY AND CONCLUSIONS

The above data serve to indicate some of the many differences between the various divisions and bands of the Dakota tribe. Three principal points have been demonstrated:

1. In any future studies the three great divisions of the Dakota must be distinguished from one another. The days of the facile characterization of the entire tribe as "wandering nomads" are past.

2. Since these various differences grew up in the relatively brief period

subsequent to the entry of the *Wičíyela* and Teton into the Plains, they demonstrate the speed with which cultures may adapt to new situations. The close cultural resemblances between the Santee and the Central Algonquians, the *Wičíyela* and the Upper Missouri village tribes, and the Teton and the tribes of the High Plains indicate that many traits and complexes which have come to be considered "tribal" by American anthropologists are more truly of a regional nature. Many of these traits and complexes appear to be environmentally conditioned.

3. The data support the thesis that "government by kinship" is intimately associated with a settled, usually agricultural, way of life (as represented by the Santee Dakota), whereas among more nomadic groups (as represented by the Teton), social groupings tend to be more fluid, and personal qualities loom more important than kinship in the selection of group leaders.

BIBLIOGRAPHY

CARVER, JONATHAN
  1956 *Travels Through the Interior Parts of North America in the Years 1766, 1767, and 1768.* 3rd edition. Minneapolis, Ross & Haines, Inc.
EASTMAN, MRS. MARY
  1849 *Dahcotah; or Life and Legends of the Sioux Around Fort Snelling.* New York, John Wiley.
GILETTE, J. M.
  1906 "The Medicine Society of the Dakota Indians." *Collections of the State Historical Society of North Dakota,* 1:459–474.
HOWARD, JAMES H.
  1951a "Dakota Fishing Practices." *University of South Dakota Museum News,* 12(5):1–3.
  1951b "New Notes on the Dakota Earth Lodge." *Plains Archeological Conference News Letter,* 4(1):4–10.
  1954 "Yanktonai Dakota Eagle Trapping." *Southwestern Journal of Anthropology,* 10:69–74.
  1955 "The Tree Dweller Cults of the Dakota." *Journal of American Folklore,* 68:169–174.
HURT, WESLEY R.
  1950 "Notes on the Dakota Indians." *University of South Dakota Museum News,* 11(12):1–3.

James H. Howard

1953 "House Types of the Santee Indians." *University of South Dakota Museum News*, 14(11):1–3. (Quoting from George W. Kingsbury's *History of Dakota Territory*, vol. 1, pp. 306–307.)

HURT, WESLEY R., and JAMES H. HOWARD
1950 "Two Newly Recorded Dakota House Types." *Southwestern Journal of Anthropology*, 6:423–427.

LOWIE, ROBERT H.
1913 "Dance Associations of the Eastern Dakota." *Anthropological Papers of the American Museum of Natural History*, 11(2):101–142.

MAYER, FRANK B.
1932 *With Pen and Pencil on the Frontier in 1851; the Diary and Sketches of Frank Blackwell Mayer*, ed. by Bertha L. Heilbron. St. Paul, Minnesota State Historical Society.

POND, PETER
1908 "The Journal of Peter Pond." *Collections of the State Historical Society of Wisconsin*, 18:314–354.

SKINNER, ALANSON B.
1919 "A Sketch of Eastern Dakota Ethnology." *American Anthropologist*, 21:164–174.

RIGGS, STEPHEN R.
1893 "Dakota Grammar, Texts, and Ethnography," ed. by James O. Dorsey. *U.S. Geographical and Geological Survey of the Rocky Mountain Region. Contributions to North American Ethnology*, 9.

WALKER, J. R.
1917 "The Sun Dance and Other Ceremonies of the Oglala Division of the Teton Dakota." *Anthropological Papers of the American Museum of Natural History*, 16(2):51–221.

WINCHELL, N. H.
1911 *The Aborigines of Minnesota*. St. Paul, The Pioneer Company.

WISSLER, CLARK
1912 "Societies and Ceremonial Associations in the Oglala Division of the Teton-Dakota." *Anthropological Papers of the American Museum of Natural History*, 11(1):1–99.

✳ ✳ ✳ ✳

Wesley R. Hurt

STATE UNIVERSITY OF SOUTH DAKOTA

THE YANKTON DAKOTA CHURCH:

A NATIONALISTIC MOVEMENT

OF NORTHERN PLAINS INDIANS

Two patterns usually have been followed by Indians in their adaptation to the general Anglo-American culture. Some individuals have identified themselves with this new cultural group and have adopted the new way of life while others have classified themselves as Indians and have attempted to retain aspects of their traditional culture which they consider important. Individuals of the latter type have joined intertribal movements in their attempt to preserve native cultural values and customs. In this category are Indians who joined the Ghost Dance, the Peyote Cult, or those who participate in the Pan-Indian movements as described by James Howard (1955) and Ernest Schusky (1957).

Recently there has emerged a third pattern of adaptation among Indians in the Northern Plains. In several urban centers such as Yankton, South Dakota, and Sioux City, Iowa, Indians have organized churches which have as a major objective the preservation of the racial identity of American Indians. These churches de-emphasize tribal and cultural identity. In addition, the leaders of these churches consider their organizations to be American Indian nationalistic movements.

Undoubtedly many factors led to the development of these Indian churches. The institutions provide a social and religious group for Indians moving into urban centers: they aid these immigrants in social-economic adaptation through cooperative effort. Indian leaders find in these organizations a means of acquiring a following normally denied to them in communities largely populated by non-Indians. None of these functions, however, appears to explain entirely the nationalistic character of the Dakota churches. On the other hand, these churches seem to be a reaction by the Indians against the low status assigned to them by their non-Indian neighbors because of their Indian descent.

Many Northern Plains Indians have been able to improve their status in urban communities by accepting the new American cultural traditions. It is difficult, however, for an individual with a high degree of Indian blood to overcome the stigma of his racial descent in an urban community of the Northern Plains. There are several possible reactions to this low status: to conceal their racial descent, to make an attempt to prove that all races have equal capabilities, or to remain indifferent. This reaction to low status on the basis of racial descent may be a major factor in the present day African and Asian nationalistic movements.

THE CHANGING STATUS OF
THE NORTHERN PLAINS INDIANS

During a period of two hundred and fifty years of contact with people of European descent the Northern Plains Indians have had various statuses assigned to them. These have been:

1. THE STATUS OF A BUSINESS PARTNER. Initially the Plains Indian was treated as an equal in a business relationship with the French and British fur traders. This status did not radically change during the period of American fur trade, *c.* 1803 to 1842.

2. THE STATUS OF HOSTILE TRIBES WITH AN INFERIOR CULTURE. The years between 1842 and 1890 were characterized by intense warfare between the Plains Indians and the United States. Those who did not remain on reservations were treated as hostile enemy tribes. The warfare was justified on the grounds that the Indians had an inferior culture.

3. THE STATUS OF SUBJUGATED PEOPLES WITH AN INFERIOR CULTURE. The Indians who surrendered and moved onto the reservations after about 1870 were treated as prisoners of war. The government began many programs after this date to force the Indians into adopting the American cultural pattern. Implicit in these programs was the theory that the In-

dian's way of life was inferior but that he was capable of learning the new culture. The Indians' status as "wards" or subjects was legally removed by granting them citizenship in 1924.

4. THE STATUS AS CITIZENS WITH AN INFERIOR CULTURE AND INFERIOR RACIAL CHARACTERISTICS. Although the Indians were often considered to be people with inferior racial characteristics, this status became more generally accepted through time as a result of the non-Indians' becoming increasingly impatient and disillusioned over the slow rate at which the Indians adopted the new American culture.

Below is a more detailed presentation of the changing status of the Northern Plains Indians.

The British and French fur traders coming into contact with the Plains Indians during the eighteenth century established a business partnership with them. Intermarriage with the Indians was sought and looked upon as a desirable way of cementing trade relations.

There was no immediate change in Indian-White relations as a result of the Louisiana Purchase of 1803, which now made the Plains Indians subjects of the United States. Treaties made in the period between 1803 and 1825 were of the "peace" type commonly signed between sovereign European Nations. These treaties attempted to insure friendly relations and to obtain from the Indians an acknowledgement of the sovereignty of the United States. While the Indians were recognized as subjects there was no open statement that they belonged to an inferior race or had a culture of low status.

A change occurred with the entry of the colonists into the eastern part of the Northern Plains in 1825. After that date the treaties were concerned with territorial cession of Indian land. A period of active hostilities was generated between the two racial groups in 1842 with the onset of American emigration through the Plains. In 1858 the first reservation for the Dakota Indians was established in South Dakota. This reservation and others established at later dates had two functions: to confine the Indians in an area removed from transcontinental lines of travel and to protect the Indians from the encroachment of American settlers. The treatment of the Indians as prisoners on the reservations resulted in a further lowering of their status.

Once on the reservations, the Indians became subject to many attempts to change their culture. Intensive efforts to Christianize them were started with the Santee Dakota bands at Fort Snelling, Minnesota, by Protestant missionaries in 1835 (Barton 1919:13). The ability of these missionaries, such as Thomas S. Williamson, to cure illness in cases where the medicine men failed shattered the faith of some of the Santee in their own leaders (Barton 1919:23).

After the "Sioux Outbreak" of 1862 a large number of the Santee became ready converts to Christianity. Many were placed in prison, all power was stripped from the chiefs, and they were in a state of starvation. The missionaries who attempted to protect them were embraced as a last recourse. In 1866 the Santee were moved to a reservation in northern Nebraska and John P. Williamson, the son of the Williamson of Fort Snelling, joined them. In time several of the Santee became missionaries and worked with neighboring tribes.

In 1871 John P. Williamson moved to the nearby Yankton reservation in South Dakota. At this time the Yankton were not thoroughly subjugated and Williamson and his associates had much less success in persuading these Indians to give up their old customs. In 1868, Williamson and some of his converts petitioned the Commissioner of Indian Affairs for the legal right to stop by force such Dakota ceremonies as the Grass Dance (Barton 1919:181). These requests, with those of other missionaries, in a few years led to the Federal policy of prohibiting the Plains Indians by force from practicing their religious ceremonies and dances (Brown 1953:10). Some of the Indians gave up their traditions under the pressure of the missionaries and the Federal government but others practiced them in a clandestine fashion.

During the initial phase of the reservation period the American government issued rations to the Indians as an inducement to live on the reservations. The destruction of the game animals also made rations necessary. At this time neither the Americans nor the Indians regarded the rations as an act of charity nor were the Indians who accepted them regarded as an inferior type of human being.

With the discovery of gold in the Black Hills in 1874, thousands of miners entered the territory reserved for the Teton Dakota; thus a period of intense warfare began. Open hostilities were brought to an end with the arrest and death of Sitting Bull and the massacre at Wounded Knee, December, 1890.

While the Americans followed a policy of exterminating the hostile Indians, a different policy prevailed for those Indians who remained on the reservations. George Hyde has documented in detail the influence of the philosophy of a group of "friends of the Indians" who lived in the eastern United States (Hyde 1956:145–163). This group believed that the Indians could and should be changed into typical American self-sufficient farmers in a short period of time. Through their efforts Congress and the Bureau of Indian Affairs accepted this philosophy as a basis for the policy that prevailed until the passage of the Indian Reorganization Act in 1934. One program to accomplish the rapid assimilation of the Indians was aimed at breaking the control of the chiefs. Uncooperative chiefs and their followers were imprisoned or were not issued rations. As a result many Indians deserted the chiefs who resisted this pressure. Another program was initiated in the Treaty of 1868 which provided for compulsory education of children (Mattison 1955:164). The school teachers derided Indian customs and punished children who spoke their native language. The "Eastern Indian friends" group laid the foundation for the off-reservation boarding school system by founding the school at Carlisle, Pennsylvania. A further effect of the philosophy of the Eastern group was the passage of the Dawes Act in 1888 which allotted land to individual Indians in an effort to free them from tribal control. The continued faith of the American people in the Indians' ability to adopt the new cultural pattern is reflected in the granting of citizenship to them in 1924.

By 1934 public feeling had been aroused by many non-Indians against the continual devaluation of American Indian culture. A result of this change in attitude is revealed in the passage of the Indian Reorganization Act. Provision was made for the Indian tribes to organize with a charter, a constitution, an elected tribal council, and a tribal court. Indians were permitted to revive their clandestine religious ceremonies such as the Peyote Cult and were aided in the development of handicraft industries.

This new attitude of raising the status of American Indians both as a racial and culture group was not shared by all non-Indians. In fact those non-Indians who lived near reservations in the Northern Plains were gradually accepting the concept that the Indian was inferior not only in culture but by descent. During the 1930's many of these non-Indians in the Northern Plains ceased to regard public welfare programs and other services furnished to Indians as just compensation for land loss. The belief became prevalent that a recipient of welfare, either an Indian or non-Indian, was an inferior type of human being. Also many non-Indians became impatient with the long time the Indians were taking in adapting to the White Man's culture. Dissatisfaction arose over the Indian's absenteeism from employment, his disregard for time as measured by the clock, and the unwillingness of many Indians to save money. In addition, the relatively higher rate of Indian crime and alcoholism convinced many non-Indians that the Indians were incapable of adapting to the American culture because of their racial descent.

Local newspapers at this time were quick to identify a criminal's race if he were Indian. Since World War II, as a result of pressure by the Bureau of Indian Affairs and more enlightened public opinion, "No Indians Wanted" signs have been taken down in commercial establishments in Nebraska and South Dakota. Employment discrimination, however, appears to be worsening in the area.

NATIVISTIC MOVEMENTS OF
THE NORTHERN PLAINS INDIANS

The first major intertribal reaction of the Northern Plains Indians to the attack on their cultural traditions and persons by the Americans was the Ghost Dance. This nativistic movement was started by a Nevada Indian named Wovoka (Mooney 1896). Wovoka claimed that in a dream he was made a prophet and instructed by the gods to tell the Indians that if they would be good, obedient, and perform certain dances and rituals the game animals would be restored, the Whites vanquished, and the Indians would be united with their friends in the other world. In this reaction there was no attempt to accommodate the Indian to the new American cultural patterns. The Dakota tribes sent a delegation to Nevada to find out about this new religion and, after its return, the Ghost Dance was instituted on many reservations in the Northern Plains. The Federal government, fearing trouble, attempted to stop the dancing. A military force was sent to arrest Sitting Bull, one of the main leaders. Sitting Bull resisted arrest and was killed on December 15, 1890. The threat of force by the Americans and the disillusionment of the members because the prophecies of Wovoka did not come true caused the Ghost Dance to die out in a few months.

Within a few years the Peyote Cult, another nativistic movement, spread into the Northern Plains. According to Aberle and Stewart, the Peyote Cult was introduced to Pine Ridge, South Dakota, about 1904 (Aberle and Stewart 1957:9). From that date until the present Peyotism has spread to nearly all the other reservations of the Northern Plains. Peyote membership in this area consists mainly of Indians living on reservations who desire to continue certain aspects of their traditional values and customs. Peyotism, while basically an attempt to preserve Indian culture, is blended with elements of the Christian doctrine. Its members have attempted to improve the low status of this church by obtaining legal charters as a sect of the Christian Church and by making claims that they are Christians. Although the movement is Pan-Indian in character local units preserve certain features of their old culture pattern.

THE YANKTON DAKOTA CHURCH

The Indians in the Northern Plains did not organize any intertribal movements to counteract their increasingly low status, attributed to racial descent, until the last few years. One of the first institutions of this type to be developed was the Dakota branch of Christ Church, Episcopal, Yankton, South Dakota. Since this group has not yet been given an official name, in this paper it will be called for convenience, "The Yankton Dakota Church."

One of the leaders of the Yankton Dakota Church published an article describing the founding and objectives of this group, excerpts from which appear below: (Hayes 1957:1–3).

It is the belief of these people that most Indians have a strong sense of nationalism. Even though all of these people want their children to go farther than they in everything good America has to offer; they also want to remain Indians most of all the proper kind of an Indian. . . .

How do you do all this: well like all buildings you must have a good foundation and that was close by . . . the rock of the great Christian faith. . . . The church being the great Christian body that it is, granted permission to try. So on the 16th of October, 1955, under the leadership of Steven Moose, a catechist of 30 years experience, assisted by George Selwyn of Bloomfield, Nebraska, and in the home of Stanley Jones who became its first warden and with only 8 people present this group was born.

Being allowed to maintain their identity within the church this group has grown from 8 people to 28 families. . . . Each Sunday evening they hold services both in Dakota and English; in the winter in the homes of the members, in summer out of doors.

They handle everything by themselves that they have qualified for. . . . In all other phases of life they integrate as far as their individual ability will allow. Each member could be called a Christian Patriot. . . . Yes, they are Christian Indian Patriots who love God deeply, and have a deep sense of duty toward their race.

Why was it called the Dakota group? Well no doubt because it is Dakota country; they could have been called the Indian group for they come from the four winds, and have learned to think not as a family, an individual group or a tribe, but as Indians; Christian Indians. . . .

I am very proud to be a member of this group and find a spirit in the air that is hard to explain. Let me give you an example of what I mean. Not long ago a man asked me why we didn't ask the church [Episcopal] to build us a meeting place; he doesn't know these people for they have learned to try like a man called Moses, and a group of people who lived long ago. What they get will come from God, and their own doing.

The statements quoted above make it clear that the Yankton Dakota Church in the eyes of one of its leaders is part of a nationalistic movement intent on proving the equality of Indians by emphasizing self-reliance and their ability to manage their own affairs. The desirability of accepting the modern American culture is acknowledged and the tribal and cultural affiliation of an Indian is considered unimportant. Actions taken in the meetings of the Yankton Dakota Church bear out the philosophy expressed by Hayes. It should be emphasized, however, that many of the members have affiliated with the church, not because of nationalistic aspirations but for religious and social reasons. One member stated that he could not afford to buy good enough clothes to attend the regular services of Christ Episcopal Church in Yankton.

The Yankton Dakota Church contains several committees and affiliated organizations. The church as a whole is governed by an annually elected body of four officers and is affiliated with the Christ Branch of the Episcopal Church of Yankton. Within the church structure is a Young People's Fellowship group, a women's auxiliary called the Martha and Mary Guild, and a Social and Recreation Committee, each governed by four officers who are elected annually. The men's group within the Church forms a local branch of the Brotherhood of Christian Unity, a national organization of Episcopal Indian men. Within the church framework is the Yankton Tribal Council which sponsors a surplus commodity program. The church also sponsors a Boy Scout troop, a Girl Scout troop, a boy's baseball team, and a girl's baseball team. With the exception of the committee called the Yankton Tribal Council, the structure of the church does not differ greatly from that of any other Episcopal church in the area.

It is difficult to determine the actual membership of the Yankton Dakota Church. The church leaders claim that about thirty families are members. However, the writer interviewed about forty household heads who claimed affiliation. The discrepancy was probably caused by the fact that some of those who claimed affiliation were baptized as Episcopalians, but never attended the services of the Yankton Dakota Church. At an ordinary service of this church the attendance averages about thirty individuals but at a church party the attendance swells to more than a hundred people. During a survey made in Yankton from September 1957 to June 1958, approximately seventy married couples and unmarried adults were encountered. It is probable that most households were located in this survey. Therefore about 40 per cent of the Indians resident in Yankton are affiliated with Yankton Dakota Church.

Since the majority of the adult Indians who live in Yankton are from the nearby Yankton and Santee Reservations, this same proportion is reflected in the church membership. Other adult members were born on reservations throughout the Northern Plains. No difference was observed between the percentage of Indian blood of the members and nonmembers of the church.

The main reason given by local Indians for not joining the Yankton Dakota Church was that they belonged to other Christian sects. Open disapproval of the Yankton Dakota Church was expressed by only one Indian, a Catholic, who stated that this church would retard the assimilation of the Indians. One woman of mixed blood attends the regular morning services of Christ Episcopal Church. She stated that she did not affiliate with the Dakota group because she did not want her friends to know that she was an Indian. Within the Yankton Dakota Church there are several individuals who are members of other Churches and there is also one non-Indian married to an Indian woman member. This non-Indian holds a position as a church officer.

The educational level of the members of the Yankton Dakota Church varies from older Indians with a few years of school to those with college degrees. Some of the members are students at Yankton College. The church leaders as a whole are Indians with a high reputation in the non-Indian community. On the other hand there are members with reputations for alcoholism, prostitution, and job absenteeism.

The Yankton Dakota Church has a varied activity program. The major event is the Sunday evening service held in members' homes during the winter and under an arbor of branches in the backyard of a member during the summer. The church officers have made plans for building a structure outside the city. The religious services are led by a catechist who gives sermons in the English and Dakota languages. Hymns are sung in Dakota. The older members prefer the sermons to be given in Dakota and the middle-aged and younger members prefer English. Few people of the latter groups can speak the Sioux language. After a service, refreshments are served and business matters are discussed. The minister of the Christ Episcopal Church is invited occasionally to give sermons.

The Martha and Mary Guild meets in members' homes once a week.

One of the main activities of the guild is making quilts to sell in fund-raising campaigns. Annually they hold a bazaar to raise funds for the Niobrara Conference, an annual convocation of Episcopal Indians.

The Young People's Fellowship is a social religious group meeting once a week in the members homes. This group also has fund raising campaigns.

Parties are sponsored in the basement of Christ Episcopal Church by the Social and Recreation Committee. Events such as Christmas and New Year's and other American Holidays are celebrated with pot luck suppers, typical modern games, and square dances.

An organization affiliated with the Yankton Dakota Church is the Yankton Tribal Council. The catechist of the church and the county welfare director began efforts in 1955 to obtain food under the Federal Surplus Commodity Program for needy Indians in Yankton. They worked out an arrangement whereby Christ Episcopal Church furnishes the space for storage and distribution of these commodities and the Yankton Dakota Church pays for the cost of transportation from the government warehouse in Sioux Falls. The first year the Christ Church agreed to underwrite the cost. A Yankton Tribal Council was organized with the duty of raising funds and administering the local commodity program. The first year the council was not able to raise funds for all of the transportation costs by bazaars and bake sales. In the winter of 1957 the council started the system of charging $2.50 a month to each household head who drew commodities. Some families paid without drawing the rations, while a few who did not pay asked for their share.

As noted above, one of the main problems of the Yankton Dakota Church is in financing its various activities. Outside help is frowned on and sometimes refused. Several events have happened in the church which reveal the value placed on self-reliance. In order to hold services in the member's homes the church needed a portable organ. Money was borrowed from a local bank, and by taking up collections in the church they were able to pay back the note before it came due.

A business meeting was held to plan for the Christmas party in 1957. One of the older church officers proposed that they ask the local non-Indian community for money, clothing, and toys to distribute at the party. This suggestion caused great chagrin among many of the members and a majority defeated the motion.

A field representative of a project sponsored by an Indian aid organization of New York approached the church members at a business meeting and offered financial and technical assistance for a community development project. The church officers refused to cooperate with this project stating that they were able to take care of their own problems. When the church organized a Boy Scout troop they solicited equipment from Indians and refused to accept any contributions from non-Indians. This same self-reliance is reflected in the event described by Hayes in the members' refusal to ask for aid from the Episcopal Church for a building.

Strong pressure is placed by the church officers on members who are alcoholics and who absent themselves from work. These leaders admit that this pressure has not been very successful and that some of the members have become worse through time. The officers also function as go-betweens in relations between the public welfare office and the employers of Indians on the one hand, and the members of the church on the other.

The attitudes of the non-Indians of Yankton and the officials of the Episcopal Church toward the Yankton Dakota Church vary. The writer has made only a brief survey regarding these attitudes and the following statements are based on only a few cases. The minister of Christ Episcopal Church of Yankton is a sponsor of the group and extends all the aid and cooperation possible. He occasionally gives sermons and lectures to the group and writes articles for the *B.C.U. Digest,* a publication of an affiliated organization. According to informants there is a split in attitude among the clergy of the South Dakota Missionary district regarding the sponsorship of separate Indian churches. Younger members of the clergy are opposed to segregation in the churches. The Yankton county officials as a whole vary in attitude from indifference to mild approval. Several employees of the Bureau of Indian Affairs with whom the writer discussed the church expressed the opinion that such organizations retard the assimilation of the Indian.

THE BROTHERHOOD OF CHRISTIAN UNITY

A group of about sixteen men in the Yankton Dakota Church form a local group of the Brotherhood of Christian Unity. The Brotherhood is an Indian men's organization of the Episcopal Church founded eighty-six years ago by three Indian Episcopal ministers, Messrs. J. P. Deloria, David Tatiyopa, and Felix Bronut. Branches were organized in the Episcopal missions on reservations in the Northern Plains. At its climax the organization had about 1200 members, but in time it dwindled to no more than 200 members. A recent revival has taken place under the stimulation of the Yankton Dakota Church.

The Brotherhood of Christian Unity was modeled after St. Andrew's Guild, a men's organization of the Episcopal Church. According to its constitution and bylaws the objective of the Brotherhood is "to oppose what is evil and help what is good, . . . till we all come in the unity of the faith, Eph. 4:13." Originally the institution functioned as a devotional society and as a group to raise funds for Indian education at Hare School, Mission, S.D. and St. Katherine School, Wakpala, S.D. Many of the leaders of the revived brotherhood, however, have the same nationalistic aspirations of the Yankton Dakota Church. The following are quotations taken from the organization's publication, the *B.C.U. Digest* of 1957, page 3,

Notice to all BCU Men— You will find here four things that represent the BCU. . . . let's give them all we have. W.F.T. (1) That we show by our accomplishments that we are good, intelligent, and worthy. (2) That we prove to the world that we can compete on an equal basis. (3) That we see to it that our children get a better education than we have. (4) Be prepared; be ready to do whatever it is God requires us as Christians to do, for this will deliver us from the Egypt of today.

Within the revived Brotherhood of Christian Unity are seven branches scattered through the Northern Plains. The leaders plan to conduct a nationwide campaign for membership among all eligible Indians. The leaders of the seven branches convene once every three months for a business meeting. Once a year an annual meeting of all members is held.

About fifty Indians attended in 1958 one of the tri-monthly business meetings, which was held in Yankton. The meeting began with a noon day dinner in the basement of Christ Church. This was followed by a program which included a business discussion, reports by branch officers, elections of officers, all interspersed with prayers and hymns in the Dakota language. Collections were taken for the sick and for the general fund. At the election of officers the women and children were not allowed to vote. After the program the group had an evening meal.

Major items discussed in the business meeting were the plans for the next annual meeting to be held in 1958 at Lake Andes, South Dakota, and the method of financing the monthly publications of the group. A member asked the advisor of the organization, an Indian Episcopal minister, if he thought it was a good idea to cease publishing the *B.C.U. Digest* and to send the news to the *South Dakota Churchman,* the official organ of the South Dakota Episcopal Church. The advisor answered by stating that other organizations such as the American Legion had their own publications and so should the B.C.U. He emphasized that the

B.C.U. Digest was a help in bringing Indians together and preserving their identity and integrity.

Financing the publications of the Brotherhood of Christian Unity is a serious problem. Each local branch is supposed to make a contribution, but the amount raised has never been sufficient. As a result publications are issued at infrequent intervals and the officers themselves make partial payment for the printing. One of the main features of these publications is the printing of biographies of outstanding Indian leaders in the United States.

OTHER NATIONALISTIC
NORTHERN PLAINS CHURCHES

In Sioux City, Iowa, and Mobridge, South Dakota, Indian churches have recently been organized under the inspiration of the Yankton Dakota Church. According to an informant, the Dakota Indian Center in Sioux City became an official project on January 12, 1958, in an Indian's home. A planning committee was organized at that time, with a chairman, a public relations and promotion officer, and a secretary. Although started as a branch of the Episcopal Church, the planning committee decided to emphasize nondenominationalism to attract more members. A women's guild was organized but as yet no Brotherhood of Christian Unity. There are, however, individuals who belong to the B.C.U.

As yet this newly formed church has not been studied in detail but certain differences from the Yankton Dakota Church already are apparent. The Sioux City group plans to establish a community center building and did not hesitate to ask for aid from an Eastern "friends of the Indian" organization, the same institution which had been rebuffed by the Yankton. The leaders of this group do not appear as hostile toward the non-Indians as do the Yankton. Perhaps this difference in attitude can be attributed to the fact that the minister of the Sioux City Indian Church is an ordained Episcopal minister and that some of the other leaders are employed by civic and state organizations of Iowa. At the moment it is impossible to predict what trend this Sioux City Church will take as it expands in membership.

An Indian church has been organized in Mobridge, South Dakota. The writer is unfamiliar with the group.

The Indians in Sioux Falls, South Dakota, have been unable to organize a unified group. An organization called the Council of Seven Fires has been formed by extremely hostile Indians who present almost paranoid characteristics. In the Council are also a group of Anglo-Americans who have taken up the Indian "cause." One of the major activities of the organization is the writing of letters to the readers' columns of South Dakota newspapers complaining of the bad treatment the Indians have received in the past and are now receiving. The explanation of Yankton informants for the lack of attraction of the Council of Seven Fires for Sioux Falls Indians is that some of the sponsors are Anglo-Americans. Several of the members of the Council of Seven Fires resemble the Pan-Indians of Oklahoma in that they are attempting to revive certain aspects of Indian culture. One of these individuals lectures on Indian folklore, art, and handicrafts to various Anglo-American organizations.

RECENT PAN-INDIAN MOVEMENTS

James H. Howard has described the "Pan-Indian Culture of Oklahoma" which shares certain traits with the Yankton Dakota Church and the Brotherhood of Christian Unity (Howard 1955). Howard states:

During the nineteenth century many Indian tribes from the Southeastern, Northeastern, and Plains areas were settled in various parts of the territory now included in the present state of Oklahoma. With the collapse of the old tribal life prior to and immediately subsequent to their placement on reservations in Indian Territory, a stage of acculturation was reached which seemed to presage complete assimilation. Technologically, economically, in social organization, and religion the various Indian tribes seemed to be rapidly approximating white culture.

This was, however, more apparent than real, for rather than becoming nondistinctive members of the dominant culture, many Indians have instead become members of a supertribal culture, which we here term *pan-Indian*. By *pan-Indianism* is meant the process by which sociocultural entities such as the Seneca, Delaware, Creek, Yuchi, Ponca, and Comanche are losing their tribal distinctiveness and in its place are developing a nontribal "Indian" culture. Some of the elements in this culture are modifications of old tribal customs. Others seem to be innovations peculiar to pan-Indianism.

Particular factors fostering pan-Indianism that may be separated from the general matrix of acculturation are (i) the mild racial discrimination found in Oklahoma, (ii) the common economic base of most Oklahoma Indians, (iii) intermarriage between members of different tribes, (iv) increased geographic mobility, and (v) Indian school contacts. . . . [It] is . . . one of the final stages of progressive acculturation, just prior to complete assimilation (Howard 1955:215, 220).

Some of the cultural traits listed by Howard in the Oklahoma Pan-Indian culture are the Peyote Cult, the "pow-wows" with such dances as the War Dance, the generalized dance costumes, and the election of pow-wow "Princesses" (Howard 1955:217–219).

William W. Newcomb has described the Pan-Indian aspect of the present day culture of the Delaware Indians of Oklahoma. He notes the possibility that racial discrimination may be a factor which encourages the Pan-Indianism but discounts its effect on the Delaware because he can find so little evidence of prejudice in the local area (Newcomb 1956:121). He states:

Pan-Indianism has been made possible by the fact that through acculturation Indians of very diverse backgrounds have come to share a common language and participate in the same economy. . . . Pan-Indianism may also be explained as an attempt, perhaps largely unconscious, by a minority group composed of many different tribal remnants to find unity and strength in common customs. In a sense, it is a final attempt to preserve a distinctness of being which a dominant civilization has tried to destroy. But in another sense it may be regarded as an effort to glorify or enhance a minority group status which the dominant majority has insisted be preserved (Newcomb 1956:128).

The Pan-Indian movement in the eastern United States has been analyzed by Ernest Schusky (Schusky 1957). In its basic features the Eastern movement is similar to that of Oklahoma although it is much poorer in cultural traits. The main feature is a series of "pow-wows" with Indian dances and stands selling souvenirs. The dancing and costumes are composite and closely resemble those of the Plains Indians. A secondary aspect is a group of small commercial museums established by Indians in New England.

Schusky noted that the generalized culture is spread by Eastern Indians visiting other Indians in the West and by Indians from throughout the United States who have moved to Brooklyn (Schusky 1957:121–122). He discounts the effects of race prejudice as a causal factor in the Eastern Pan-Indian movement, although he acknowledges that this factor may be present in the groups which have a high percent of Negro blood. Schusky observes that in the movement are many individuals who can easily pass into the local Anglo-American society on the basis of their behavior and physical appearance.

As factors generating the Eastern Pan-Indian movement, Schusky suggests (1) the commercial aspect—it pays certain individuals to be an Indian; (2) the sharing of in-group feelings; and (3) the fact that Indians hold deep historical and traditional roots in their home localities. He concludes that Pan-Indianism need not necessarily be thought of as only an acquirement of new "Indian" elements but also as an incorporation and revival of cultures and societies (Schusky 1957:123).

Evon Vogt in a recent discussion of the factors in the persistence of American Indian culture traits as revealed by Pan-Indianism states, "It is my impression that we have tended to de-emphasize recently, in our analysis of United States Indian data, what is perhaps the most important factor of all; our persisting Anglo-American 'racial' attitude, derived historically from Puritan Colonialism, which devaluates other physical types bearing different cultural traditions" (Vogt 1957:144).

As yet there has not been developed in the Northern Plains a Pan-Indian culture of the types found in Oklahoma or the eastern United States. Many of the specific culture traits are now present on the reservations such as the Peyote Cult, and the "pow-wow" variety of dancing and celebrations. However, in the Northern Plains, the majority of Indians still live on reservations and make an attempt to preserve at least partially their tribal identity. In Oklahoma and the eastern United States the Indians no longer live on reservations, with a few exceptions. It is reasonable to assume that as the reservations of the Northern Plains are terminated a more generalized culture of the Oklahoma type will develop among those Indians who desire to preserve Indian values and cultural traditions.

The movement of the nationalistic organizations among the urban Indians of the Northern Plains is similar to Pan-Indianism in its de-emphasis on tribal identity. The Northern Plains nativistic movements, however, differ radically in that such groups as the Yankton Dakota Church make little or no attempt to preserve traditional Indian culture nor are they a blend of various Indian cultural traits. In fact they place high value on the Anglo-American way of life. In these organizations the emphasis is on demonstrating that American Indians have capabilities equal to those of other races. These two factors seem to explain the differences in the Yankton Dakota movement and Pan-Indianism. Prejudice and discrimination apparently is much stronger in the Northern Plains and the Indians feel under pressure to prove themselves. In addition, the urban Indians of the type who join the Yankton Dakota Church or the Brotherhood of Christian Unity are much more acculturated than those who participate in the Pan-Indianism of Oklahoma or the eastern United States.

SUMMARY AND CONCLUSIONS

Since the time of contact the American Indian has been forced to adjust to the changing status assigned to him by peoples of European descent. Frequently he has reacted in intertribal movements. The Ghost Dance, which spread to the Northern Plains, was a major reaction to his subjugation by the Anglo-Americans. This religious cult had the function of restoring the tribal cultures and eliminating the hated Anglo-Americans by magic.

After the Indians were settled on reservations they became subject to a series of programs aimed at forcing them rapidly to adopt the Anglo-American culture. The designers of these programs assumed that Indian cultures were inferior. After the failure of the Ghost Dance prophecies the Indians were convinced of the futility of trying to dispossess the Anglo-Americans. A new movement, the Peyote Cult, soon diffused into the Northern Plains. A basic aim of this cult was the preservation of generalized Indian values and customs. To protect the members against arrest and to improve their low status, charters were obtained in several states legalizing the Peyote Cult as a Christian sect. The rituals and doctrines of the Peyote Cult were blended with Christian traits as a result of the long contact with missionaries. The members of the Peyote Cult generally live on reservations in the Northern Plains.

In the Southern Plains the Peyote became a major element in the gradually evolving generalized, nontribal Indian culture, which has been recently referred to as "Pan-Indianism." This movement in less rich detail has spread into other areas of the United States such as New England. Basic traits included annual "pow-wows" with generalized Indian dances and costumes plus souvenir stands. Tribal affiliation is de-emphasized. Causal factors include (1) mild discrimination (2) the termination of reservations (3) intermarriage (4) common schools and similar economic status and (5) commercialism. Racial prejudice does not appear to be an important causal factor for in the areas where Pan-Indianism flourishes it is becoming increasingly difficult for the Anglo-Americans to recognize an Indian by his appearance and behavior.

In the Northern Plains the off-reservation, acculturated Indian is still subjected to racial discrimination. In addition, he still is physically visible to the Anglo-Americans, so that it is difficult for him to conceal his descent. Since the 1930's many more Anglo-Americans have reached the conclusion that the Indian is a member of an inferior race and have assigned this status to him. This conclusion was a result of the Anglo-Americans' disillusionment over the failure of the majority of Indians in adopting the new culture pattern.

The urban Northern Plains Indian has reacted to racial discrimination by becoming apathetic, attempting to conceal his descent, or by joining nationalistic movements such as the Yankton Dakota Church or the Brotherhood of Christian Unity, which have as a major objective the demonstration that the Indian has capabilities equal to those of any race. In these movements there is no attempt at cultural revival for the members are too highly acculturated.

BIBLIOGRAPHY

ABERLE, DAVID F. and OMER C. STEWART
  1957 "Navajo and Ute Peyotism: A Chronological and Distributional Study." *University of Colorado Studies, Series in Anthropology,* 6.
BARTON, WINFRED
  1919 *John P. Williamson: A Brother to the Sioux.* New York, Fleming H. Revell Co.
BROWN, JOSEPH EPES
  1953 *The Sacred Pipe, Black Elk's Account of the Seven Rites of the Oglala Sioux.* Norman, University of Oklahoma Press.
HAYES, JAMES
  1957 "Christ Church? Dakota People of Yankton." *The B.C.U. Digest,* Yankton, S.D., 1(3):1–3.
HOWARD, JAMES H.
  1955 "Pan-Indian Culture of Oklahoma." *The Scientific Monthly,* 81:215–220.
HYDE, GEORGE E.
  1956 *A Sioux Chronicle.* Norman, University of Oklahoma Press.
MATTISON, RAY
  1955 "The Indian Reservation System on the Upper Missouri, 1865–1890." *Nebraska History,* 36:141–172.
MOONEY, JAMES
  1896 "The Ghost Dance Religion and the Sioux Outbreak of 1890." *Fourteenth Annual Report of the Bureau of [American] Ethnology for 1892–1893,* Part 2.

NEWCOMB, WILLIAM W., Jr.
  1956 "The Culture and Acculturation of the Delaware Indians." *Anthropological Papers, Museum of Anthropology, University of Michigan,* 10.
SCHUSKY, ERNEST
  1957 "Pan-Indianism in the Eastern United States." *Anthropology Tomorrow,* 6(1):116–123. Anthropology Club of The University of Chicago.
VOGT, EVON Z.
  1957 "The Acculturation of American Indians." *The Annals of the American Academy of Political and Social Science,* 311 ("American Indians and American Life"):137–146.

* * * *

Barbara Savadkin Lane

BERNICE P. BISHOP MUSEUM

VARIETIES OF CROSS-COUSIN

MARRIAGE AND INCEST TABOOS:

STRUCTURE AND CAUSALITY

Students of social structure for some time have been concerned to
explain the varieties of prescribed cross-cousin marriage regulations found widely distributed in various ethnographic areas. They have
not reached any general agreement regarding either the causes for the
several types of prescription or for their disproportionate incidence. The
failure to arrive at general agreement suggests that a new approach to
the problems is indicated. This essay probes some of the limitations in
present methods of analysis in order to indicate more fruitful lines of investigation.

Three major types of prescriptive cross-cousin marriage regulation have
been identified: (1) symmetrical cross-cousin marriage (ego marries
MoBrDa who is structurally also FaSiDa); (2) asymmetrical patrilateral
cross-cousin marriage (ego marries FaSiDa, but is forbidden to marry
MoBrDa);[1] and (3) asymmetrical matrilateral cross-cousin marriage
(ego marries MoBrDa, but may not marry FaSiDa). Additional variations
are reported involving usually the substitution of some other relative such

---

[1] Needham (1958) has recently questioned the existence of kinship systems based on
prescribed patrilateral cross-cousin marriage. I think that the problems which he
raises can be satisfactorily disposed of and the practical feasibility of such systems
demonstrated, but the problem need not concern us here as the present paper deals
only with symmetrical and matrilateral types.

as certain "second" cross-cousins (that is, MoMoBrDaDa) or the parent or child of a cross-cousin (that is, MoMoBrDa, MoBrDaDa). These additional types also can be categorized as symmetrical, patrilateral, or matrilateral.

Recent studies have examined the structural implications of various sorts of prescribed cross-cousin marriage regulations. Such studies, while extremely useful in highlighting contrasts between the various kinship systems incorporating these rules, have two serious limitations. First, the "type" kinship systems which they examine are necessarily assumed to have a stability, a static quality which does not exist as a social reality. Kinship systems, like all other cultural systems, are constantly undergoing change through time by exposure to changing cultural conditions and by independent development. In consequence of this, a kinship system— of whatever type—includes in its present form and structure components of its previous make-up. The directions of its future development are likewise limited and in part predicated by its present character.

This fact has two important corollaries. First, it implies that the antecedents of any given kinship system as well as its future possibilities often should be ascertainable on the basis of internal evidence. As a matter of record, the histories of a number of kinship systems have been reconstructed through techniques of analysis based upon this premise.[2] Second, it means that an awareness of probable antecedents and an understanding of future possibilities may illuminate the structural properties of a kinship system at any given moment in its history. This point is important because failure to see present properties in temporal perspective can lead to invalid inferences.

The second major limitation of structural-formal analysis is that it necessitates the study of each type of prescribed marriage rule as an institutional isolate and thereby precludes an analysis of functional-temporal interrelationships of the various types.

The thesis of this essay is that differing rules of prescribed cross-cousin marriage may characterize a given kinship system in different stages of its development. By differing rules here I mean not only that a system may progress from symmetrical first cross-cousin marriage to symmetrical second cross-cousin marriage, for example, but that a system may at one time be characterized by a rule of symmetrical cross-cousin marriage and at a later time embody a rule of asymmetrical cross-cousin marriage (either patrilateral or matrilateral), and vice versa. Further I submit that in any particular instance the sequence or alternation of prescriptive rules

---

[2] Cf. Lévi-Strauss (1949), de Josselin de Jong (1952), Lane and Lane (1958).

will always be associated with a systematic extension of incest taboos and attended by an increasing complexity in the social structure.[3] Third, I suggest that the particular sequences which occur will differ according to the rules of marital residence and methods of tracing descent operative in any given society. No one of these views is new or original. Each has been proposed and to some extent investigated by previous writers. However, to my knowledge, no one has as yet applied all these criteria simultaneously and systematically to the known varieties of prescriptive cross-cousin marriage in order to derive evolutionary stages with reference to which any particular kinship system or any type of marriage prescription may be viewed.

I will not attempt to present here an over-all scheme of such evolutionary stages. Instead this essay is confined to an exposition of how such stages may be derived. For present purposes discussion is limited to the Kariera, Karadjeri, Ambrym, Aranda, and Murngin systems. All of these have in common patrilocal residence, "double descent," and sections. In each case patrilineal descent is associated with local groups and matrilineal descent is derived from nonlocalized matrilineal moieties which divide the members of any one patrilocal-patrilineal group into alternating generations.

The Kariera four-section system is characterized by two explicit matrilineal moieties intersected by two implicit patrilineal moieties. With respect to marriage regulation, two kinds of patrilocal-patrilineal groups are recognized. One kind contains "sisters" whom ego may not marry; the other kind contains his cross-cousins whom he must marry. Cross-cousin marriage is symmetrical and sister-exchange is practiced. A man marries his MoBrDa who is also structurally his FaSiDa. Women are exchanged directly and reciprocally between men of two local descent groups (see Figure 1). According to de Josselin de Jong (1952:15), "the Kariera strongly recommend matrilineal c[ross] c[ousin] marriage (mo. bro. da. marriage), although according to the section system matrilateral and patrilateral cross-cousins are equivalent, being, for that matter, identical as a rule." It is worth noting that if this preference for matrilateral over patrilateral cross-cousin marriage developed to a degree that the former were prescribed and the latter proscribed, a system of the Karadjeri type would result.

The Karadjeri have a rule of asymmetrical matrilateral cross-cousin

---

[3] Even if claims of occasional shifts in the direction of decreasing complexity should be substantiated, this in no way negates the general trend from lower to higher levels of integration.

marriage. A man must marry his MoBrDa; he may not marry his FaSiDa. Systems of this type must differentiate a minimum of three kinds of local groups; one containing "sisters" whom ego may not marry, one containing patrilateral cross-cousins whom he also must not marry, and a third containing matrilateral cross-cousins with whom marriage is prescribed (see Figure 2).

Under such a system sister-exchange is not permitted. Yet the kinship terminology recorded for the Karadjeri (Elkin 1932:300–301) strongly suggests that the Karadjeri must at one time have practiced sister-exchange. How else are we to explain the fact that FaSi and MoBrWi are called by the same term (*tabalu*), MoBr and FaSiHu are called by a single term (*kaga*), Si (m.s.) and WiBrWi are equated (*kabadzu*), while all four cross-cousins may be called by one term (*dzambad*)?

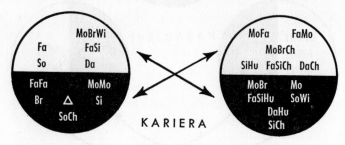

Figure 1. THE KARIERA TYPE. FOUR-SECTION SYSTEM WITH SISTER-EXCHANGE. MALE EGO MARRIES MoBrDa/FaSiDa. CIRCLES REPRESENT LOCAL PATRILINEAL DESCENT GROUPS. SHADED AREAS DESIGNATE ONE MATRILINEAL MOIETY; UNSHADED AREAS THE OTHER. ARROWS INDICATE THE DIRECTION IN WHICH WOMEN MOVE AT MARRIAGE.

Furthermore, although the Karadjeri are reported to have four sections, I fail to see how this arrangement could work if a distinction is made between MoBrDa and FaSiDa. Josselin de Jong (1952:44) puts the situation thus: "The Karadjeri have 4 sections, but recognize 3 patrilineal lines of descent: mo.mo.bro. is not identified with fa.fa., as in a real 4 section system of the Kariera type, and, on the other hand, fa.mo.bro. is not distinguished from mo.fa., as in a system of the Aranda type. Standard marriage is exclusively matrilateral (mo.bro.da.). This situation implies of course that 2 of the 4 sections are subdivided into 2 unnamed subsections. . . ." This interpretation agrees in substance with the six-section system diagrammed in Figure 2.

We have seen thus far that the Kariera type could lead to a Karadjeri type and that for the Karadjeri proper there is reason to suspect a previous Kariera type stage.

Turning now to the New Hebrides, we find a six-section system of a type apparently unreported in Australia. Since the Ambrym system is not so well known as the Australian types, I will describe it in somewhat more detail.

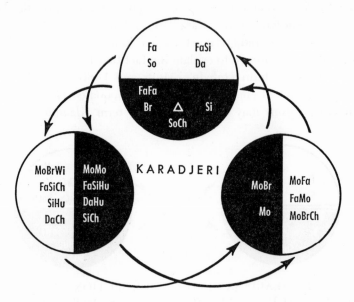

Figure 2. THE KARADJERI TYPE. SIX-SECTION SYSTEM WITHOUT SISTER-EXCHANGE. MALE EGO MARRIES MoBrDa ONLY. CIRCLES REPRESENT LOCAL PATRILINEAL DESCENT GROUPS. SHADED AREAS DESIGNATE ONE MATRILINEAL MOIETY; UNSHADED AREAS THE OTHER. ARROWS INDICATE THE DIRECTION IN WHICH WOMEN MOVE AT MARRIAGE.

The Ambrym system is characterized by double descent in which exogamous matrilineal moieties bisect three categories of patrilineal sibs so that six sections result. Residence is patrilocal and the sibs are localized while the moieties are not. Adjacent generations in any one local patrisib belong to opposite moieties. A particular sib may be found in more than one part of the island, but in all instances the sibs are claimed to have a local origin. If single sib villages occur, these are exogamous, but composite villages (that is, in which native born males are not all members of the same sib) appear to be the norm. In composite villages, male sibmates' houses are clustered together and form subdivisions of the village which are exogamous. Where intra-village marriage occurs, it is always exogamous with respect to these subdivisions of the village. The pre-scribed marriage is with mother's brother's daughter's daughter who is structurally also father's sister's daughter's daughter. Sister-exchange is required. The prescribed marriage mate may also be mother's mother's brother's daughter who is structurally also mother's father's sister's daughter [4] (see Figure 3).

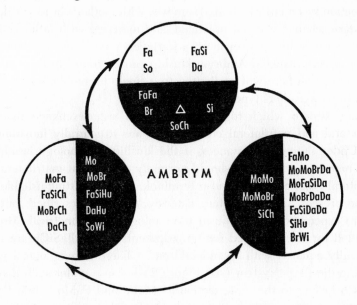

Figure 3. THE AMBRYM TYPE. SIX-SECTION SYSTEM WITH SISTER-EXCHANGE. MALE EGO MARRIES MoBrDaDa/FaSiDaDa. CIRCLES REPRESENT LOCAL PATRILINEAL DESCENT GROUPS. SHADED AREAS DESIGNATE ONE MATRILINEAL MOIETY; UNSHADED AREAS THE OTHER. ARROWS INDICATE THE DIRECTION IN WHICH WOMEN MOVE AT MARRIAGE.

It is instructive at this point to contrast the Ambrym system with the Kariera and Karadjeri types. The Ambrym system agrees with the Kariera in that both practice sister-exchange. Leach (1951:26) in a discussion concerned primarily with the ways in which women are exchanged in marriage among local descent groups classes the Ambrym system with the Kariera type. This is precisely the point at which it is necessary to distinguish the Kariera and Ambrym situations. Reference to Figure 3 will show that the Ambrym system, like the Karadjeri, requires three kinds of local descent groups and, as in the Karadjeri system, men of

---

[4] Cf. Lane and Lane (1956) for a detailed exposition of this point.

any one local descent group exchange women with men of at least *two* other descent groups. In both of these features the Ambrym system resembles the Karadjeri type rather than the Kariera despite the practice of sister-exchange.

This situation accords with evidence presented elsewhere (Lane and Lane 1958) that the present Ambrym kinship system developed out of a six-section system in which marriage was with mother's brother's daughter, sister-exchange was not practiced, and marriage with father's sister's daughter was forbidden—in short, a Karadjeri type. Since a detailed discussion of reconstructed Ambrym kinship can be found in the reference cited, exposition here will be limited to a single terminological indicator of the prior Karadjeri type stage.

In any system which regularly prescribes sister-exchange marriage, matrilateral and patrilateral cross-cousins are structurally indistinguishable. Under these circumstances, if the kinship terminology is adjusted to the marriage system, we should normally expect that matrilateral and patrilateral cross-cousins are also terminologically indistinguishable. Under the present Ambrym system sister-exchange is prescribed, but contrary to expectation, cross-cousin terminology is asymmetrical. MoBrCh are called by the term used for "grandparents" while FaSiCh are terminologically equated with "grandchildren." [5] These terminological usages fit a Karadjeri type system (see Figure 2) because under such a system MoBrCh belong to the same section as MoFa and FaMo, while FaSiCh belong to another section along with DaCh. The present seemingly inexplicable cross-cousin terminology at Ambrym is thus explained by a prior Karadjeri type phase.

Returning to Australia, the eight-section Aranda system is characterized by symmetrical second cross-cousin marriage. The prescribed mate is MoMoBrDaDa who is also structurally MoFaSiDaDa, FaMoBrSoDa, and FaFaSiSoDa due to prescribed sister-exchange. In this system four lines of patrilineal descent are distinguished, while the intersection of these by matrilineal moieties creates the eight sections (see Figure 4). The Aranda type thus involves a greater complexity than any of the types we have considered heretofore. Despite this, it closely agrees with the Ambrym system in that sister-exchange is practiced and men of any one local descent group exchange women with men of two other kinds of local descent groups. The eight-section Aranda system differs from the

---

[5] This results in the possibility of Ego addressing a single individual as both grandparent and grandchild—a situation which even the natives find confusing.

six-section Ambrym system only in differentiating a fourth line of descent with a concomitant change in the prescribed marriage mate. The form and structure of the two types are otherwise identical.

At this juncture it is necessary to return to a consideration of the Karadjeri type. We noted earlier that this type requires a minimum of three different kinds of local descent groups. Reference to Figure 5 will

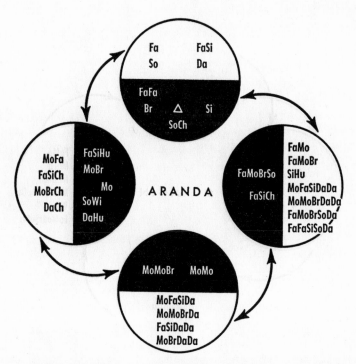

Figure 4. THE ARANDA TYPE. EIGHT-SECTION SYSTEM WITH SISTER-EXCHANGE. MALE EGO MARRIES MoMoBrDaDa/MoFa-SiDaDa. CIRCLES REPRESENT LOCAL PATRILINEAL DESCENT GROUPS. SHADED AREAS DESIGNATE ONE MATRILINEAL MOI-ETY; UNSHADED AREAS THE OTHER. ARROWS INDICATE THE DIRECTION IN WHICH WOMEN MOVE AT MARRIAGE.

show that the same marriage prescription can be diagrammed for a system differentiating four kinds of local groups. Theoretically, the ring could be extended indefinitely but for present purposes we will consider a type characterized by asymmetrical matrilateral cross-cousin marriage which distinguishes four kinds of local groups. According to some interpretations (de Josselin de Jong 1952:42) the Murngin system fits this type. For those who agree with de Josselin de Jong, we may call this the Murngin type. For those who interpret the Murngin system otherwise, this type can remain for the present a hypothetical construct.

For our purposes the important point is that a system embodying a rule of asymmetric matrilateral cross-cousin marriage which recognizes four kinds of local patrilineal groups can shift to an Aranda type simply

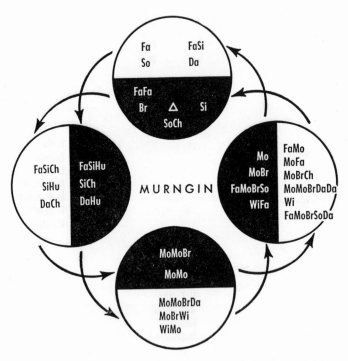

Figure 5. THE MURNGIN TYPE. EIGHT-SECTION SYSTEM WITH-OUT SISTER-EXCHANGE. MALE EGO MARRIES MoBrDa ONLY. CIRCLES REPRESENT LOCAL PATRILINEAL DESCENT GROUPS. SHADED AREAS DESIGNATE ONE MATRILINEAL MOIETY; UN-SHADED AREAS THE OTHER. ARROWS INDICATE THE DIREC-TION IN WHICH WOMEN MOVE AT MARRIAGE.

by adopting a rule of sister-exchange. This would come about automatically if incest taboos were extended to MoBrDa. In other words, a system of this type would automatically convert to an Aranda type in precisely the same way that a Karadjeri type converts to an Ambrym type and for precisely the same reasons. These shifts are diagrammed in Figure 6.

Figure 6 represents in diagrammatic form several integrative levels of differing complexity represented by known kinship systems. The arrows connecting one system with another indicate directions in which shifts can occur. In each case it will be noted that an extension of incest taboos is correlated either with an increase in complexity of social structure (that is, Kariera to Karadjeri) or a higher degree of integration (that is, Karadjeri to Ambrym). To put it another way, the shift from a Kariera to a Karadjeri type increases the kinds of local groups which interact. The shift from a Karadjeri to an Ambrym type consolidates this gain by instituting direct and reciprocal exchange of women among men of all three kinds of groups.

It is important to note what Figure 6 does *not* represent. The fact that the Kariera type occupies the lowest level of complexity and that Karadjeri systems may arise from a Kariera type does not imply that all section systems necessarily begin with a Kariera stage. Likewise, the fact that the Murngin type can shift to an Aranda type does not imply that this is the only direction in which this type may develop. As a matter of fact, I strongly suspect that the Murngin system was in the process of evolving along quite different lines, but this analysis lies outside the scope of the present essay as do a number of other possibilities and permutations that involve other residence rules and methods of tracing descent.

Even the types represented in Figure 6 have not been exhaustively analyzed. For example, no consideration has been given to the problem of whether shifts take place from Karadjeri to Murngin or from Ambrym to Aranda types, and if so, by what means. It has often been asserted that Kariera type systems convert directly to Aranda type systems by simultaneous extension of incest taboos to both first cross-cousins. This assertion has not been investigated here, but the problem should be susceptible to the same sort of analysis as that applied to the Karadjeri and the Ambrym systems. If the claim cannot be substantiated, then one of the most vexing problems in this area of social structure is eliminated—namely, why should some systems of Kariera type extend incest taboos simultaneously while others have obviously done so asymmetrically.

Turning to another area, the exposition that symmetric and asymmetric marriage systems may have temporal-functional interrelations demonstrates the invalidity of certain inferences drawn from purely structural-formal analysis: for example, Leach's conclusions that Karadjeri and Murngin type systems are inherently unstable, that they imply status differentiation between the wife-giving and wife-receiving groups, and that these differences are reflected in political structure (Leach 1951: 52–53.)

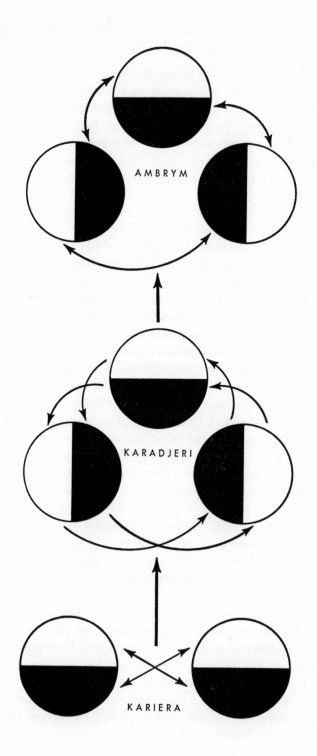

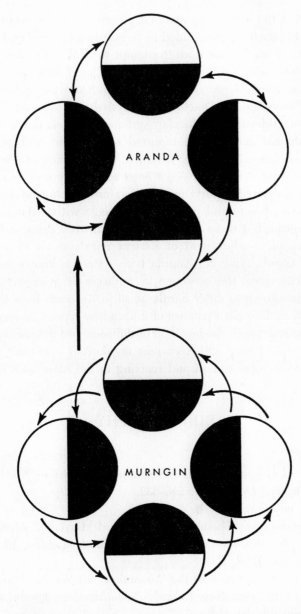

Figure 6. (Facing page and above) EVOLUTIONARY STAGES SHOWING
PROGRESSIVELY HIGHER LEVELS OF INTEGRATION CORRELATED
WITH SYSTEMATIC EXTENSION OF INCEST TABOOS. CIRCLES
REPRESENT LOCAL PATRILINEAL DESCENT GROUPS. SHADED
AREAS DESIGNATE ONE MATRILINEAL MOIETY; UNSHADED
AREAS THE OTHER. ARROWS INDICATE THE DIRECTION IN
WHICH WOMEN MOVE AT MARRIAGE.

Barbara Savadkin Lane

As stated at the outset, the material presented in this essay and summarized in Figure 6 is not intended to constitute an all-embracing scheme
of evolutionary stages, nor does it attempt to deal with all known sorts
of prescriptive marriage regulations or associated kinship systems. Instead, I have tried to present material to indicate the potentialities of
this line of investigation. Diachronic analysis has illustrated forcibly the
possibility of understanding kinship systems in which the terminologies
employed do not accord with reported social forms and practices. It
seems entirely conceivable, for instance, that systems of the Ambrym
type exist in Australia and have not been adequately reported or clearly
understood. Scattered reports in the literature mention systems with a
rule of sister-exchange and prescribed marriage with a daughter of the
first cross-cousin, but these situations are summarily dismissed as representing incomplete adjustment of Kariera type systems to neighboring
systems of Aranda type. No Aranda type system is known in the New
Hebrides. Therefore, the existence in Ambrym of a six-section system
which can be shown to differ hardly at all in structure from the Aranda
type, as well as the prior existence of a Karadjeri type at Ambrym should
destroy once and for all the bugaboo of diffusion and demonstrate clearly
that we are faced here with recurrent regularities operating under the
same sorts of cultural stimuli and reacting to the same sorts of cultural
laws.

BIBLIOGRAPHY

ELKIN, A. P.
1932 "Social Organization in the Kimberley Division, North-Western
Australia." *Oceania*, 2: 296–333.
DE JOSSELIN DE JONG, J. P. B.
1952 "Lévi-Strauss's Theory on Kinship and Marriage." *Mededelingen
Van Het Rijksmuseum Voor Volkenkunde*, Leiden, 10:1–59.
LANE, R. B. and B. S. LANE
1956 "A Reinterpretation of the 'Anomalous' Six-Section Marriage System of Ambrym, New Hebrides." *Southwestern Journal of Anthropology*, 12:406–414.
1958 "The Evolution of Ambrym Kinship." *Southwestern Journal of
Anthropology*, 14:107–135.
LEACH, E. R.
1951 "The Structural Implications of Matrilateral Cross-Cousin Marriage." *Journal of the Royal Anthropological Institute*, 81:23–55.

Lévi-Strauss, C.
    1949 *Les Structures Elémentaires de la Parenté.* Paris, Presses Universitaires de France.
Needham, R.
    1958 "The Formal Analysis of Prescriptive Patrilateral Cross-Cousin Marriage." *Southwestern Journal of Anthropology,* 14:199–219.

* * * *

Betty J. Meggers

SMITHSONIAN INSTITUTION

THE LAW OF CULTURAL

EVOLUTION AS A

PRACTICAL RESEARCH TOOL

In the long-term feud between evolutionism and anti-evolutionism in American anthropology, there has been one point of mutual
agreement: evolutionary formulae do not apply to particular cultures or
to regional cultural sequences. Boas once commented that "it would be
quite impossible to understand, on the basis of a single evolutionary
scheme, what happened to any particular people" (Boas 1948:286).
Even a sympathetic student of cultural evolution like Steward has
objected that "White's law of energy levels . . . can tell us nothing about
the development of the characteristics of individual cultures" (Steward
1953:318). White has agreed with this assertion: "the evolutionist's formulas . . . are not applicable to the culture history of tribes and were
not intended for this purpose" (White 1945:346). The effect of such
unanimity has been to remove evolutionary theory from the practical tool
kit of the field anthropologist to the high plane of philosophical discussion. It will be the purpose of this paper to dissent from the view that
evolutionary theory has only limited and generalized applicability and to
suggest how it can be used as a guide in understanding the dynamics of
individual cultures.

The law of energy and cultural evolution was first set forth by White
in 1943 and restated by him in 1949. This law is based on the recognition that all cultures are composed of three general classes of phenomena:

technology, social organization, and philosophy. Of these, technology is primary and determines the content and form of the other two components. This, in White's view, reduces the explanation of cultural development to the same terms that physicists use to describe the rest of nature: matter and energy. Culture becomes "an elaborate thermodynamic, mechanical system" (White 1949:367), with its functioning "determined by the amount of energy harnessed and by the way in which it is put to work" (*op. cit.*, 368–9). The content of any particular culture depends on the amount of energy that can be controlled and the efficiency of the technological means of putting this energy to use. Expressed in a simple formula, $E(nergy) \times T(echnology) \longrightarrow C(ulture)$. The implications of this formula are three-fold: (1) if there is no increase in energy (E) or improvement in technology (T), the culture (C) will remain stable; (2) if either energy or technology or both are increased or improved, the culture will increase in complexity; (3) if either the energy or the technology or both are diminished, the culture will decline in complexity.

The energy available to a culture may be derived from several sources. In the beginning man had only his own body to draw upon. White (1949:369) has calculated that this amounts to about $\frac{1}{20}$ horsepower per capita. This level of energy output can achieve more with efficient tools than with inefficient ones, but the latitude is slight. Certain other resources available in nature, such as fire, water, and wind, can be used for specialized purposes, but their energy contribution in primitive cultures is small. It was only with the domestication of plants and animals that a major new source of energy was tapped for culture building. More food could be acquired per man hour of labor than before, and each improvement in agricultural technique had the effect of enhancing the productivity of human labor. The cultural consequences were impressive; all the great civilizations of antiquity came into being with a rapidity that is in sharp contrast to the slowness of culture change during the preceding millennia of human existence. More recently, another major energy source has been put to work: fossil fuel (coal, oil, gas). The effects of the use of fuels have been pyramiding since the initial impact we know as the Industrial Revolution. Today, we are on the threshold of harnessing a fourth major culture-building force, atomic energy. If successful on a large scale, this achievement should be no less striking in its consequences than the previous additions.

Traditional anthropology is concerned only with pre-Fuel Age cultures, whose energy resources are limited to human muscle and to domesticated animals and plants. Within this restricted frame, the law of cultural evolution has generally been either dismissed as obvious or ignored. This reaction appears to be based to some extent on a misunderstanding of what such a law can be expected to reveal and how it might be applied. James Jeans, a leading physicist, has said of the laws of physical science: "The obvious path of scientific progress would seem to lie in the direction of inquiring what consequences are involved in supposing these laws to be of universal scope, and then testing these consequences against the ascertained facts. . . ." (Jeans 1930:180). In order to consider the law of cultural evolution from this point of view, we must determine first what consequences are implied if the law is assumed to be valid and, second, whether individual cultures exhibit these inferred consequences.

In all real situations, the consequences of a scientific law are masked by the action of variables that the formulation of the law holds constant. When the law is applied to specific problems, these variables must be considered and weighed. In the case of the law of cultural evolution, one of the principal variables is environment, which under differential circumstances may alter, slow, or speed up the "ideal" reaction. The amount of energy controlled or controllable by a culture may be limited by features of its habitat, such as lack of agricultural potential or the absence of coal or oil deposits. If the energy sources are all potentially available, certain technological improvements may be ruled out by lack of suitable raw materials.

If we follow the procedure indicated by Jeans and look for consequences that could be expected if the law of energy and cultural evolution is of universal scope, there are several tests that can be made. One is to see whether cultures can be classified into general types, and, if so, whether the types are associated with differences in the level of energy resources controlled and the efficiency of their use. If such a classification is possible, it will indicate not only that the variability in E and T is significant culturally, but that it reaches a series of "critical" intensities, each of which produces a particular kind of general cultural change. If the variability of E and T is continuous, it should be possible to arrange cultures in a series of increasing complexity, but not to group them into a small number of types.

Another way of testing the law is to examine one of the sources of energy: agriculture. One of the important variables influencing the effectiveness with which this energy resource has been exploited by different cultures is the environment. If agricultural energy is an important factor in cultural evolution, differences in agricultural potential of environments should be reflected in differences in the level of development of the associated cultures. A third test is to trace the development of a culture over a period of time, to note any changes that occur in social and economic organization, settlement pattern, and so on, and to see whether these changes can be related to changes in E(nergy) or T(echnology).

TEST 1: CLASSIFICATION
OF CULTURES INTO TYPES

The most recent effort to arrive at a series of universally valid culture types was made in 1955 by the Washington Summer Seminar of the Society for American Archaeology (Beardsley *et al.* 1956). Taking community patterning as its point of departure, this analysis distinguishes seven basic types. Arranged in the order of increasing sedentariness these are: Free Wandering, Restricted Wandering, Central-Based Wandering, Semi-Permanent Sedentary, Simple Nuclear Centered, Advanced Nuclear Centered and Supra-Nuclear Integrated. Each type has economic, sociopolitical, and religious features that set it apart from the others, as well as a distinctive community pattern. As a consequence of the functional integration of these various aspects, a culture identified as having a Semi-Permanent Sedentary community pattern can be deduced to possess the associated general cultural complex: a simple, kinship-based social organization; pottery-making, weaving, and other crafts practiced on an individual basis; supernaturalism focused around shamanistic dealings with a spirit world, and so on (Beardsley *et al.* 1956:140–141). Similarly, an Advanced Nuclear Centered community will be characterized by social stratification into well-developed classes; strong, centralized political control; advanced division of labor and craft specialization, with consequent standardization of products; and supernaturalism expressed by a hierarchy of priests serving a pantheon of gods in special temples and courting their favor by offerings, prayers, and sacrifices (*op. cit.*, 143–144).

The differences between these seven cultural types are the direct result of differential productivity in subsistence resources per man hour of labor expended, and this can be directly observed in the differing amounts of human energy that are diverted into nonsubsistence activities. The subsistence resources are not always identical in all cultures belonging to a single culture type, but they must yield an equivalent energy return.

For example, it was possible to recognize at least three forms of subsistence that support a Central-Based Wandering type of community pattern, in which the community wanders part of the year and spends the remainder at a camp or "central base." These are "1) a storable or preservable wild food harvest, such as acorns or mesquite beans; 2) a locally abundant food, such as shellfish; and 3) incipient agriculture producing a small harvest" (Beardsley *et al.* 1956:138). Among the types of community patterning dependent on agriculture, it is possible to correlate increasing cultural complexity with increasing realization of the potentialities latent in agriculture as a subsistence base. Different degrees of efficiency in agricultural technology—incipient, exploitative, conservational, or intensive—are linked with striking closeness to differences in cultural complexity (*op. cit.*, fig. 1). The occurrence of transitional cultures is rare, suggesting that the efficiency of agricultural exploitation has to reach a certain "critical" point before the energy available for culture building is sufficient to produce a major cultural effect. When that point is reached, there is a rapid development into the next cultural type, followed by another period of relative stability. If E and T were freely and continuously variable, one would expect that cultures could be arranged in a series, but that there would be little tendency to clustering. Thus the fact that cultures can be classified into a small number of types not only supports the validity of the law of cultural evolution, but throws additional light on details of its operation.

TEST 2: ENVIRONMENT, AGRICULTURE, AND CULTURAL DEVELOPMENT

If agriculture is a significant culture-building force and environment is an important determinant of agricultural productivity, then it should be possible to find some correlation between the level of development that a particular culture has reached and the agricultural potential of the environment that it occupies. Although environment has generally been recognized as affecting culture to a greater or lesser extent, efforts to specify this relationship have been hampered by the fact that environments are usually classified in terms of geographical characteristics rather than in terms of their most significant aspect from the point of view of cultural evolution, namely, subsistence potential. An attempt to differentiate environments on this basis has produced a four-fold classification into Type 1, areas with no agricultural potential; Type 2, areas with limited agricultural potential; Type 3, areas with increasable agricultural potential and, Type 4, areas with unlimited agricultural potential (Meggers 1954:803–804).

Each of the four types of environment offers different possibilities or sets different kinds of limits on local cultural development. Where agriculture is ruled out by unfavorable climate or topography (Type 1) and the energy available for culture building cannot exceed that of man's own body (except in a few places where domestic animals can be substituted), cultures have remained on a hunting and gathering level. Where environmental conditions mitigate or destroy the value of fertilization, crop rotation and other techniques of maintaining soil fertility (Type 2) and agriculture realizes only a relatively small fraction of its energy potential for culture building, the relatively primitive Semi-Permanent Sedentary type of community pattern is characteristic. In environments of increasable (Type 3) or unlimited (Type 4) agricultural potential, the amount of return that can be extracted from agriculture is practically unlimited and realization of the full potential depends upon technological advances. Consequently, these environments can support a wide variety of cultural types.

The general relationship between agricultural potential of the environment and cultural development has been phrased as a law of environmental limitation on culture: "the level to which a culture can develop is dependent upon the agricultural potentiality of the environment it occupies" (Meggers 1954:815). This is a corollary to White's general law of cultural evolution. It describes the same process—an increase in cultural output derived from an increase in energy input—but focuses on energy derived from agriculture. In addition, it brings in one of the important determinants of differential agricultural productivity when the third dimension of space is added to the temporal-formal evolutionary process. If in White's equation, $E \times T \longrightarrow C$, we hold energy constant at agriculture and make environment the variable expressed by E, then as E is altered from Type 1, to Type 2, 3, or 4, different possibilities arise for agricultural and consequently cultural development. The position of technology in the equation is the same as when E stands for "energy": it is improvable only within the limits set by E. In environments of Types 1 and 2, the technological innovations that can increase the efficiency with which the energy resources are utilized are few. In Type 4, the environment is highly productive even with a relatively primitive technology. In Type 3, however, technological differences are of major significance in the realization of the potential latent in the environment. Because of the large number of local historical factors that may affect improvements in technology, there is a wide variation in the extent to which this potential has been realized. The analysis of these variables should explain why a particular culture did or did not make the fullest use of the agricultural potential of its environment.

TEST 3: CULTURAL STABILITY
AND CULTURAL CHANGE

If the law of cultural evolution is valid, it should be possible to correlate significant changes in the content of a culture with a change in the amount of energy under control or an improvement in the technology by which existing energy is utilized. In order to limit the scope of the examination, examples will be chosen to illustrate three types of culture process: progression, stability, and regression.

It should be noted, by way of introduction, that good case studies are difficult to find because little attention has been paid to the kind of analysis advocated here. Crucial data are sometimes missing, and consequently some of the examples do not illustrate the point as clearly as might be desired. Attention should be focused on the kind of analysis being made rather than on the validity of the interpretation in regard to the particular culture used as the example.

Case 1: Progression

TANALA. The law of cultural evolution specifies that an increase in energy resources will produce an alteration in the general cultural product. Well-described examples of this transformation are rare, but Linton (1936:348–354) provides an excellent one in his description of the Tanala, a hill tribe of western Madagascar. Some 200 years prior to Linton's visit, the Tanala had been a typical Semi-Permanent Sedentary group, subsisting by slash-and-burn cultivation of dry rice. The village was moved periodically as nearby lands lost their fertility. Family members worked together to clear the land and shared the produce, which was not sufficient for the accumulation of a surplus. There was no social stratification, no private ownership of land, no unequal distribution of wealth.

The introduction of wet rice cultivation initiated a series of changes in the culture that converted the community pattern into Simple Nuclear Centered. Wet rice cultivation has a conservational effect on soil fertility, with the result the village no longer had to be moved periodically because of exhaustion of nearby fields. With the investment of labor in hillside terracing and the construction of irrigation canals, larger areas could be brought under cultivation. These fields became privately owned. Although the cultivable portion of the terrain had always been limited by soil suitability and elevation, with shifting cultivation all land was accessible to everyone and inequalities were balanced out. Now certain families had the advantage over others. Differences in wealth developed, and sharing ceased to be practiced within joint families. Increasing social and economic differentiation brought concentration of power in the hands of a few and finally culminated in domination by one clan, whose head became the king. As Linton comments,

It was a far cry from the mobile, self-contained Tanala villages with their classless society and strong joint families to the Tanala kingdom with its central authority, settled subjects, rudimentary social classes based on economic differences, and lineages of little more than ceremonial importance. However, the transformation can be traced step by step and at every step we find irrigated rice at the bottom of the change (1936:353).

CHEYENNE. Control over an increased amount of energy does not always result in increased sedentariness. Under certain circumstances, increased energy for culture building is provided by a subsistence that requires greater community mobility. From the point of view of the law of cultural evolution, the transition from Semi-Permanent Sedentary to Equestrian Hunting made by certain tribes of the North American Plains in early post-European times represents such a cultural advance. Prior to the introduction of the horse, buffalo hunting was a difficult task. On the eastern edges of the plains, tribes like the Cheyenne found primitive agriculture a more secure subsistence resource. They lived in small earthlodge villages, which were moved periodically, and the archeological remains suggest their culture was typical of that associated with a Semi-Permanent Sedentary community pattern in other parts of the world.

The coming of the horse put into the hands of such Indians a tool for the large-scale exploitation of the buffalo. For the first time hunting could be depended upon to feed large groups of people on a permanent basis. However, the effective exploitation of this food supply required a wandering type of community pattern, and the Cheyenne along with other Semi-Permanent Sedentary tribes made the transition. Horses became valuable because of their subsistence role, and owning them provided a basis for differences in wealth and influence and for social stratification. The greater efficiency of hunting released labor for non-subsistence activities, but community mobility prevented the utilization of this labor for the kinds of development typically associated with sedentary groups. Instead, it was diverted into competition within and between groups for prestige and property. The change from agriculture to buffalo hunting did not effect as marked a change in Cheyenne culture as the change from slash-and-burn to permanently productive agriculture did in that of the Tanala, but it can be shown that large population concentrations were supported and social stratification became more marked. Similar changes have been documented for the Blackfoot (Ewers 1955:299–320), who were pedestrian hunters before the introduction of the horse.

Case 2: Regression

THE AZTEC EXPLOITATION OF THE TEOTLALPAN. If an increase in energy resources or their control results in increased cultural complexity, a decline in energy resources should result in a decline in cultural complexity. Examples of this kind of transformation are largely inferential, being derived from archeological remains rather than direct observation. In Mesopotamia, the southwestern United States, at the mouth of the Amazon, and in other parts of the world, it has been observed that regions at one time occupied by rather highly developed cultures are now sparsely inhabited by scattered, more primitive groups.

An analysis of this kind of situation has been made by Cook (1949) for the Teotlalpan, a semi-arid region twice dominated by high cultures, first the Toltec and then the Aztec. Prior to these conquests, this part of Central Mexico was populated by the Otomi, who lived by hunting, gathering, and limited agriculture. Under Toltec domination, agricultural exploitation was expanded and intensified, resulting in a considerable increase in population density. After the Toltec withdrawal, the subsistence exploitation of the Teotlalpan apparently largely reverted to its earlier pattern. A second and longer period of agricultural development was initiated between the thirteenth and sixteenth centuries by the Aztec, who succeeded so well in exploiting the potential of the area that population density reached 530 persons per square mile (Cook 1949:58). However, various factors, some natural and some the result of insufficient application of conservational techniques, initiated a transformation in the agricultural potential of this seemingly Type 3 region. Extensive deforestation brought erosion and lowering of the water table, and these in turn led to crop failures or gradually lowering yields. Cook feels that a crisis was imminent when the Spanish arrived:

> So far as the Teotlalpan is concerned, it is quite clear that had Aztec (or Nahua) domination continued unchecked for another century or two, soil erosion, deforestation, and land deterioration would have reached the point where agriculture could not have supported the existing population, not to mention any further increase. At that crucial point the only solutions would have been famine and death, or wholesale emigration, which would have spelled the end of Aztec power and domination (Cook 1949:54).

It would be unrealistic to suggest that every example of cultural regression is to be directly traced to subsistence failure. However, where some other cause is not obvious, it would seem worthwhile to investigate the possibility of decline in the subsistence resources. This is particularly pertinent in cases of invasion or colonization, where the newly settled territory may require different techniques than the homeland for permanent intensive agricultural exploitation (for example, the Inca efforts to expand to the eastern lowlands), or may be of lower agricultural potential (cf. Meggers and Evans 1957:26–32). However, climatic shifts or insufficient technical knowledge to cope with problems of conservation can alter the agricultural potential of the local area in the direction of declining yield, with consequent cultural effects.

Case 3: Stability

BASIN-PLATEAU TRIBES. When contemporary hunting and gathering cultures are used to exemplify cultural stability, this procedure is often denounced on the grounds that since such groups have as long a history as our own, an equal opportunity for change must be inferred. The question is not, however, whether there has been time for change, but rather what kind of change could have taken place. All of the hunting and gathering groups that survive today inhabit Type 1 areas, where agriculture is impossible. Energy available for culture building is thus restricted to the $\frac{1}{20}$ horsepower per capita available from the human body. This low level sets very narrow limits to cultural variability. Limits of another kind come from the natural resources of the particular environment, which not only favor but frequently require a certain kind of adaptation. Steward, noting that primitive hunters and gatherers around the world share certain simple sociopolitical patterns, undertook a detailed analysis of tribes of the Basin-Plateau area to discover the cause. He found that:

"Most of the Basin-Plateau people lived at a bare subsistence level. Their culture was meager in content and simple in structure. Pursuits concerned with the problems of daily existence dominated their activities to an extraordinary degree and limited and conditioned their institutions" (1938:1–2).

By detailed investigation of the environment, the nature of the food resources, techniques required for their exploitation, and problems of food storage and distribution, Steward was able to show that even such specific traits as patrilineal descent, kinship obligations, property ownership, and relationship between spouses are directly related to the subsistence pattern.

The existence of so tight an integration on a primitive food-gathering level implies that very little alteration will take place in the culture as long as the environment remains stable. Changes that occur will be in features not intrinsic to survival, such as games, folklore, minor variations in dress and ornament, and perhaps methods of disposal of the dead (for example, interment versus cremation). If this conclusion is valid, it would be unrealistic to deny that living food gatherers may represent a way of life of great antiquity and stability. The fact that cultures with limited food resources remain primitive substantiates the laws of cultural evolution as forcefully as do examples of cultures that increase in complexity as energy resources or technology are improved.

Case 4: Subsistence and Social Organization

SOUTHERN ATHAPASKANS. Few attempts have been made to trace the relationship between specific varieties of unstratified social organization and specific environments or subsistence patterns, but there is one interesting study of this sort (Kaut 1957) dealing with the Southern Athapaskans. Close linguistic and cultural similarities permit the inference that the seven component tribes have diverged from a common ancestry. Analysis suggests that certain of their present differences can be explained functionally as recent adjustments to habitats with different subsistence resources. As Kaut explains:

The Chiricahua and Mescalero were two distinct non-farming, hunting and gathering peoples who inhabited the severe ecological region of the middle Rio Grande and northern Chihuahua. The Jicarilla, who occupied the region between the head of the Rio Grande and the Canadian River, were agriculturists as well as hunters and gatherers. Plains influence was apparent in their material culture, and they practiced limited buffalo hunting. From what little we know of the Lipan, they were offshoots of the Jicarilla who also engaged in agriculture, and hunted and gathered along the upper reaches of the Pecos until they were pushed south toward the Gulf of Mexico by the Comanche and others. The Kiowa Apache were typically Plains-oriented, forming one band of the Kiowa camp circle and operating as such in the annual Sun Dance. Of all the Athapaskan groups, the Navaho seemed to have been the most agricultural. They occupied the area directly west of the upper reaches of the Rio Grande in New Mexico and Arizona. The Western Apache were also agriculturists on a limited scale, settled in the region which includes the upper drainage of the Salt and Gila rivers in Arizona (Kaut 1957:3).

Since these tribes closely resemble each other in material culture, general social organization and religion, as well as in language, it can be assumed that their differentiation is relatively recent. Differences in details of kinship terminology and behavior must therefore be the result of evolution from a single form. In tracing this evolution, Kaut suggests that "each difference in patterning of the relationships between particular segments of the kin group (or extended imputed kin grouping) appears to be related to differences in subsistence basis and total ecological adaptation" (Kaut 1957:33). In more specific terms,

The Mescalero and Chiricahua organization, primarily set in a severe hunting and gathering ecologic adaptation, represents an extension of nuclear family relationships with great stress upon sibling solidarity so that groups of close relatives formed cooperating units. Kiowa Apache, Jicarilla, and Lipan— the groups to the east—relied more on the buffalo hunt and/or agriculture and developed a clearly defined organization in which generational opposition formed the basis for cooperation and training. This type of organization, with its greater emphasis on the band, seems to have been geared to permit interaction between larger groups of relatives rather than restricting cooperation to close relatives as did the organization of Mescalero-Chiricahua local groups. Finally, among the Navaho and Western Apache, more thoroughgoing agriculture and a much less nomadic life were related to a matrilineal clan system which extended both generational and familial principles in such a way that whole communities made up of local groups were interrelated and could operate together in corporate enterprises (*op. cit.*, 81).

Translated into the terms of the law of energy and the evolution of culture, this correlation throws into relief a small segment of the process by which a minor alteration in the energy resource produces a minor change in social organization, although the latter continues to be kinship based. As an analysis of the evolution of Southern Athapaskan social differentiation, Kaut's study is of great interest, but viewed in the larger framework of cultural evolutionary theory, it takes on broader significance and deserves the attention of others than specialists in kinship analysis.

CONCLUSION

This brief consideration of the application of the law of energy and cultural evolution to the data of anthropology has been undertaken for two reasons. One has already been stated: refutation of the commonly held conception that the law applies only to general and theoretical problems. On the contrary, it is a vital factor in every real situation and can provide an explanation even for small-scale changes in social organization. Recognition of the common principle operating in all of the examples just cited increases the value of each study. Instead of being restricted to a local situation, the findings become significant in the formulation of the universal principles explaining cultural development.

The second purpose of this paper is to stress the need for more studies of the kind used as examples. Perhaps because of the impression that the law of cultural evolution cannot be applied to particular cultures, very little attention has been paid to field testing of its implications. However, field work offers a fine substitute for laboratory investigation, often mentioned as a lack in anthropology's scientific method. One can take Eggan's question: "Why did tribal groups coming into the Plains from surrounding regions, with radically different social structures, tend to develop a similar type?" (1954:757), and, following the law of energy and cultural evolution, predict that it was because the new subsistence pattern favored one form of integration over all others. Field work after the manner of Kaut's investigation of Southern Athapaskan social organization should provide "experimental results" to test such a prediction. To take another example, one might analyze the energy potential of a particular type of environment and the energy requirements of a particular type of culture and conclude whether or not the culture could have developed in the environment it occupies or whether it was intrusive. An attempt to apply this reasoning to Maya culture (Meggers 1954) resulted in the hypothesis that classic features were intrusive. Although proof or disproof of this interpretation is not yet available, a recent analysis of calendrical monuments (Coe 1957) has led to the conclusion that the Maya ceremonial complex was an introduction into the Guatemalan lowlands rather than a local development.

One of the hindrances to the development of anthropology as a science has been the confusing complexity of its data, which has led to a feeling of hopelessness that any useful generalizations can be achieved. The hostile reception toward attempts at the recognition of cultural laws has been tempered in recent years, but there is still a tendency to reject them summarily at the first opportunity. In physics, when an experiment seems to invalidate a law, the experiment is repeated and carefully analyzed for flaws before its results are accepted. In anthropology, however, any situation that seems superficially to be irreconcilable is seized upon to demolish the law without further ado. There has been little serious attempt to analyze the data in the manner of a scientific experiment, to discover factors that might explain seeming contradictions, or to determine whether the cause of the apparent lack of conformation to the expected results might not stem from a faulty analysis of the situation under examination. Until we learn to subject cultural theories to the kind of "experimental" investigation illustrated in the cases briefly summarized here, we will have no true way to measure their validity.

Anthropology, in its development as a science, has spread in many directions, taken up various methodologies, and espoused a number of theoretical points of view, some of them contradictory. As more facts were collected, those alternatives not supported by the evidence died out. Unfortunately, however, disproof of some theories resulted in loss of confidence in the remainder and cultural theory went into almost total eclipse. It is becoming increasingly obvious that anthropology cannot continue indefinitely as a repository of miscellaneous data susceptible to only the loosest kind of theoretical integration. There seems to be growing recognition among anthropologists that a theory of cultural development of the kind drawn upon in this paper can be used to integrate and illuminate many types of data on culture. Extensive testing in the field is the next essential step.

BIBLIOGRAPHY

BEARDSLEY, RICHARD K., PRESTON HOLDER, ALEX D. KRIEGER, BETTY J. MEGGERS, and JOHN B. RINALDO
> 1956 "Functional and Evolutionary Implications of Community Patterning." In *Seminars in Archaeology: 1955*, pp. 131–157. *Memoirs of the Society for American Archaeology*, 11.

BOAS, FRANZ
> 1948 "The Methods of Ethnology." In *Race, Language and Culture*, pp. 281–289. New York, The Macmillan Company.

Betty J. Meggers

COE, MICHAEL D.
1957 "Cycle 7 Monuments in Middle America: A Reconsideration."
American Anthropologist, 59:597–611.

COOK, SHERBURNE F.
1949 "The Historical Demography and Ecology of the Teotlalpan."
Ibero-Americana, 33.

EGGAN, FRED
1954 "Social Anthropology and the Method of Controlled Comparison."
American Anthropologist, 56:743–763.

EWERS, JOHN C.
1955 "The Horse in Blackfoot Indian Culture." *Bureau of American
Ethnology Bulletin*, 159.

JEANS, JAMES
1930 "The Physics of the Universe." *Smithsonian Institution Annual
Report for 1929*:161–181.

KAUT, CHARLES R.
1957 "The Western Apache Clan System: Its Origins and Development." *University of New Mexico Publications in Anthropology*, 9.

LINTON, RALPH
1936 *The Study of Man*. New York, D. Appleton–Century Company,
Inc.

MEGGERS, BETTY J.
1954 "Environmental Limitation on the Development of Culture."
American Anthropologist, 56:801–824.

MEGGERS, BETTY J., and CLIFFORD EVANS
1957 "Archeological Investigations at the Mouth of the Amazon."
Bureau of American Ethnology Bulletin, 167.

STEWARD, JULIAN H.
1938 "Basin-Plateau Aboriginal Sociopolitical Groups." *Bureau of
American Ethnology Bulletin*, 120.
1953 "Evolution and Process." In *Anthropology Today*, prepared under the chairmanship of A. L. Kroeber, pp. 313–326. Chicago, The
University of Chicago Press.

WHITE, LESLIE A.
1943 "Energy and the Evolution of Culture." *American Anthropologist*,
45:335–356.
1945 "Diffusion vs. Evolution: An Anti-Evolutionist Fallacy." *American Anthropologist*, 47:339–356.
1949 *The Science of Culture*. New York, Farrar, Straus and Company.

* * * *

W. W. *Newcomb, Jr.*

TEXAS MEMORIAL MUSEUM

TOWARD AN

UNDERSTANDING OF WAR

INTRODUCTION

The clank of a tank's treads on a darkened Budapest street, the blood of a United States Marine reddening the snow near the Yalu River boundary of North Korea, an Egyptian conscript surrendering to an Israeli soldier during a brief struggle in the Gaza Strip are isolated incidents which illustrate a chronic condition of the modern world—war. It has probably been impossible to pick up an American metropolitan newspaper any time during the present century and fail to find many columns devoted to wars just past, in progress, or impending. And the most disastrous calamity of all—the holocaust of an atomic world war—hangs daily over our heads, we are told, threatening utter destruction of civilization, perhaps of all mankind.

Despite the fact that anthropology more than other sciences is concerned with social and cultural wholes and their interrelationships, few anthropologists in recent years have shown more than a passing interest in the causes underlying war.[1] Nearly two decades ago Malinowski wrote that anthropologists

---

[1] Since 1950 the *American Anthropologist* has published only one paper which dealt specifically with war. This article, of which I was the author, was concerned only with the causes of war in the Plains culture area of native North America. The first twelve volumes of the *Southwestern Journal of Anthropology* have a slightly better record, having published four articles which deal descriptively or analytically with American Indian warfare. So far as I am aware only one anthropologist in recent years has published an ethnological study of warfare (*Primitive War* by H. H. Turney-High).

should be able to tell us what war really is. Whether war is a cultural phenomenon to be found at the beginning of evolution; what are its determining causes and effects; what does it create and what does it destroy—these are questions which belong to the science of man. The forms, the factors, and the forces which define and determine human warfare should, therefore, be analyzed in a correct anthropological theory of war (Malinowski 1941a:522).

But no general anthropological theory of war has subsequently appeared, and precious little additional light has been shed on warfare since these words were written. Why is this so? Are the chronic conflicts we call wars somehow so special and different from other cultural events that anthropologists can have little or nothing of value to say about them? Have anthropologists been unable to devise conceptual tools which can lead to a better understanding of warfare? Why is it that a human activity of such profound importance can be so thoroughly neglected by the very discipline that should be most interested in it?

We do not have far to seek for the answer to these questions. It is as apparent as it is damning: anthropologists have avoided investigations of the causes of war, and have proposed no "anthropological theory of war" because they have not generally equipped themselves with conceptual points of view which could possibly lead to an adequate understanding of war. Many, in fact, seem to embrace such sterile, even vestigial, cultural concepts that they can scarcely perceive the problems of warfare, let alone their solution. One of the purposes of this paper is to suggest why a number of the currently fashionable cultural concepts are inadequate for explaining the forces that involve tribes and nations in wars. But it is doubtless of more value to suggest a more effective method by which the origins, the reasons, the causes of wars may be sought. Hence, the main object of this paper is to describe the system, the conceptual point of view, by which the causes of warfare may be more fully comprehended. This is not to say that there have been no adequate analyses of specific wars, for there have. Nor are any new or revolutionary concepts propounded here. On the contrary, the conceptual approach advanced is that of culturology as proposed by Leslie A. White (1949). This paper is intended as an extension and elaboration upon concepts first formulated in their modern form by him. Whatever defects attach to my proposals are of course my responsibility and not his.

What Is War?

Many different kinds of activity, human and nonhuman, individual and collective, have at one time or another been called war. The word has been used in so many different ways that at the outset a minimal definition is necessary. For the purposes of this paper *war is considered to be an armed conflict between autonomous cultural bodies.* The use of 'cultural' means that war is considered to be wholly and uniquely a human activity. It implies that its causes are unique and that little if anything can be learned about human warfare from various sorts of subhuman conflict.

The closest parallels to human warfare to be found in the animal kingdom are, oddly enough, expressed by the activities of a few species of ants, which are far removed taxonomically from *Homo sapiens.* The resemblances between warfare and the activities of some ants stem from the fact that ants are also highly social creatures. Their predatory raids are similar to rather simple military campaigns in their division of labor and tactics. They are also superficially similar to some wars in that their purpose or reason for being is broadly economic (that is, ant campaigns are carried on to obtain food or captives). But, the nature and form of ant campaigns are governed by inherited behavior patterns. The raids of one species of ant are waged in an identical manner by every colony of that species. Similarly, their campaigns vary from generation to generation only in so far as their genetic equipment changes. And normally ant campaigns are interspecific raids rather than intraspecific contests. These characteristics indicate that ant campaigns are of an entirely different nature than human warfare. An understanding of ant conflict does no more to enlighten us about the nature and causation of human warfare than intimate knowledge of the forces which control a wild stallion and his herd of mares reveals about why some human groups practice polygyny.

Many animals, including many mammals, fight among themselves. These conflicts are usually individual contests—over females, over territories of individuals, and the like. And even though, as with some subhuman primates, group fights occur, these should not be confused with wars. The impulses which drive sub-human organisms into conflicts with their fellows are not similar to the factors which push sociocultural groups into conflicts with one another. The former are rooted in the genetic makeup of the organism, the latter in the cultures of the contending groups.

The words "war" and "warfare" are also commonly used for man's systematic efforts to exterminate various nonhuman creatures. But "warfare" against the boll weevil, typhus, ticks, or coyotes is something far different from the American War for Independence, the Napoleonic wars, or World War II. From the viewpoint of mankind in general, these assaults on other forms of life are constructive and beneficial, or at least are thought to be, whereas wars are directly destructive of human life and property. And since these campaigns are directed against other forms of life, they fall outside of the present usage of the term war.

I

The Analyses and Explanations of War

The various investigators of war have proposed almost as many reasons and causes for wars as their imaginations have been able to conceive—a considerable number. Generally, however, their analyses and hypotheses fall into one or another of four categories: (1) that men are inherently, genetically predisposed to be pugnacious and warlike; (2) that wars are caused by war-making forces; (3) that psychological conditions of individual men cause wars; and (4) that wars are cultural and social struggles explainable in terms of antecedent and concomitant cultural events and forces.

1. THE GENETIC THEORY. The theory that men are genetically predisposed to be combative and warlike has been refuted a number of times, and the evidence or lack of evidence cited in support of this point of view scarcely needs to be reviewed here (see White 1949:129–135; Cantril 1950:17; Malinowski 1941b:23; Wright 1942, Vol. II:1198). Many who have investigated this problem have done so with the prior hope that an inborn love of martial glory, the instinct of pugnacity, were myths. There would be no hope for world peace if the warlike urge were inherent. As technological ingenuity spawned increasingly lethal machines, men would presumably carry out the dictates of their germ plasm and succeed eventually in exterminating one another. There is no evidence, however, that suggests men are organically destined to be warlike. From a biological standpoint, the human organism is hardly equipped for a violent, warlike career. It is only with cultural appliances and as cultured beings that men become dangerous foes, both to other animals and to fellow men. Fighting wars, in fact, runs counter to the powerful urge toward self-preservation present in every organism, including man. Some other animals occasionally sacrifice their own lives in defense of their young, or perhaps for their mates, but the awareness of their own imminent self-destruction in such cases must be dim or lacking. Men too, may sacrifice their lives as do subhuman creatures, but it is only man in the grip of powerful cultural forces who can habitually, consciously, joyously, and en masse be led to offer up their lives in war.

As ethnographic information has increased, it has become clear that warfare (as defined here) is virtually absent among some primitive tribes. This fact alone is strong evidence discounting any warlike predisposition of the human organism. But even in Western civilization, it has been shown that an "inborn" love of fighting is not particularly evident. White has noted, for example, that:

in modern nations pugnacity has been "bred so weakly in our bones and marrow" that every nation has to resort to conscription. And despite such stinging epithets as "draft dodger," the number of men who prefer the degradation of prison to the glory of war is considerable. Thus it would appear that the lust for fighting and killing is not overriding in primates in general or in man in particular (White 1949:131).

2. TAUTOLOGICAL THEORIES. Tautologies or very similar devices have been utilized in some attempts to explain warfare. They would hardly be worth mentioning were it not for the fact that such verbalistic pseudo-explanations continue to appear occasionally. Ruth Benedict, for example, remarked that ". . . it is commonplace that men like war. . . . Over and over men have proved that they prefer the hazards of war with all its suffering" (1942:763). This is no doubt an accurate description of some men in some cultures, but offered as the agency responsible for war it is useless or worse. The question remains unanswered: Why do men like war? Another anthropologist suggested that the Plains Indians would not have been interested in war if they "had not been warlike" (Linton 1936:463). This is akin to saying that if tomatoes were not tomatoes they might be grapes, and utterly fails to lead toward understanding.

3. PSYCHOLOGICAL THEORIES. At the present time, psychologically oriented "explanations" of warfare tend to dominate the thinking of both anthropology and the social sciences. Psychological explanations, of course, explain how and why individuals are brought to fight wars. They attempt to explain the motivations, the forces which lead men to sacrifice their lives and take those of others. But explaining the forces which lead a particular individual to become a warrior or soldier or to be pugnacious and aggressive no more explains why that individual's tribe or nation is fighting another nation than a knowledge of the chemical composition of a boulder reveals the reasons why it rolls downhill when pushed.[2] The knowledge of what makes men fight is no doubt of tremendous value, and my remarks are not meant to disparage the usefulness of such in-

---

[2] It might be remarked parenthetically that the chemical reactions and alterations in a soldier's body during or before battle would be interesting and perhaps valuable to know, but like the psychologies of the individuals involved, such information would not and could not tell anything about why nation A went to war with nation B on X date instead of with Nation C on Y date, or not at all.

vestigations. But a great deal of misunderstanding and confusion has been created by trying to explain the cultural phenomenon of war by falling back to the level of individual psychology. *The reasons which lead individuals to fight are of a different nature than the causes which lead a nation to fight another nation at some particular time and place.* Warfare is a cultural phenomenon, and hence its explanation must be cultural, not psychological or chemical. Or as White has put it, "Warfare is a struggle between social organisms, not individuals. Its explanation is therefore social or cultural, not psychological" (White 1949:132).

A number of writers have discussed the motivations which induce individuals to go to war. These include the sexual success of soldiers, the prestige attendant upon wearing a uniform, boredom with a colorless existence, the desire to escape a nagging wife, or an intolerable family situation, and many others (Turney-High 1949:142–152; White 1949:132–133). Doubtless these are accurate descriptions of the motivations of soldiers and warriors in various societies. But to invoke them as causes of war is misleading. It is difficult to understand how a serious student would dare to state—at least in effect—that World War II was caused by the fact that many American husbands wanted to get away from intolerable wives, or even that Germany went to war because considerable prestige accrued to a youth who wore a Nazi uniform. Perhaps it is because of this obvious absurdity that in recent years the most popular psychologically oriented attempt to explain warfare is what may be called the "frustration-aggression" hypothesis. We learn from Kluckhohn, for example, that one of the causes of war

is the inhibited aggression engendered by the socialization process. Anger, openly expressed toward parents and other elders, does not ordinarily work very well. It is therefore repressed, providing a canker of hate and resentment that may release its energy in fighting the battles of a group, a social class, or a nation (1949:224).

The argument is presented at greater length on a later page:

Some frustration and deprivation is inevitable in the production of responsible adults. But the resultant tensions can be drained off more effectively than most human societies have done in the past through socially useful competition, through socially harmless releases for aggression, as in sports, and in other, as yet undiscovered ways.

Those who are insecure themselves manifest hostility toward others. It will be by diminishing both the realistic and unrealistic causes for anxiety in the world that the psychological bases for war can be controlled. Of course, war is not the only direction which violence can take. Ordinarily, aggression release within a society is inversely proportional to outlets outside. . . . Some cultures, at their flowering, have been able to channel most of their free-floating hostility into socially creative channels: literature and the arts, public works, invention, geographical exploration, and the like. In most cultures, most of the time, the greater part of this energy is diffused into various streams; into the small angry outbursts of daily living; into constructive activities; into periodic wars. . . . Finally, it should be noted that, since it takes two or more nations to make a war, a psychological climate of uncertainty, confusion, and apathy can endanger peace as much as dammed up hostility (1949:278).

Another anthropologist, H. H. Turney-High, has also joined the ranks of the frustration-aggressionists. In *Primitive War* he describes a number of reasons why men fight, but he does not distinguish, so far as I can judge, between the motivations of warriors or soldiers, and the cultural forces which bring about wars. He says:

A very profound motive for going to war is to resolve life's tensions, to escape from unhappiness caused by frustration in other realms of existence. War is one of the most effective devices ever invented for this cathartic purpose (Turney-High 1949:141).

Again on the next page:

Man's balked wishes and denied ambitions in time tie him into tight knots of frustration, crying for release. War is one such release. It allows desires disapproved within the group to find an approved outlet. The piping times of peace are often boresome except for the very fortunate. *Ennui* seems to be a price of domestication, and man, the self-domesticated primate, suffers from it more severely than any other creature. . . . The real struggle of fighting is more thrilling than the mock opposition of games; the real manhunt is incomparably more stimulating than the slaughter of animals. War is the great trigger-release of pent-up emotions, and it is apparent that more than one tribe has realized this (Turney-High 1949:142).

Anthropologists are not alone in subscribing to frustration-aggression as the cause of war. Gordon Allport, a psychologist and one of the contributors to a UNESCO book entitled *Tensions that Cause Wars* (to which significantly no anthropologists contributed), summed up his paper by saying:

Personal aggressiveness exits in large amounts, in devious forms, and plays many unhappy tricks with our own essential longing for friendship, love and peace. Mental hygiene is profoundly concerned with these ravages of hate, anxiety, envy in the personal life. In complex ways such individual states of mind intrude themselves into international relations. . . . (Allport 1950:53).

One of the more pessimistic exponents of the frustration-aggression hypothesis is Kimball Young, also a psychologist, who writes:

while we may discount the notion of innate pugnacity which operates for its own sake, we do find a basis for the larger conflict and aggression in the individual's experience: in the blocking of his drives and in his interaction with others in attempting to fulfill these drives. Second, culture and society direct this early aggression upon races, religions and nations. Hence to deal with the problem effectively, we must ask: Can you eliminate the development of aggression in individuals? And can you redirect or change the cultural objects of aggression, that is, can you eliminate or reduce group struggles by altering institutions and groups? Our wish is that we could work at both these levels, but it is questionable that much can be done. Surely we may be able to reduce the intensity of aggression in the individual at the early and formative years, but that we can eliminate it seems very doubtful (Young 1941:20).

These examples have been selected not because they represent particularly extreme views, but because they seem to be fairly representative of the recent thinking about war.[3] Even to a non-psychologist, it is apparent that the frustration-aggression hypothesis is unsatisfactory as an explanation of why individuals fight and become pugnacious, and it is completely unacceptable as an explanation of the causes of warfare. It places unwarranted stress upon the frustrations of life and their "inevitable" aggressive outlets. The love of adventure, boredom with a routine life, desire to see the world and similar factors are strong motivations which induce individuals in various cultures to become soldiers or warriors (although some investigators would even force these factors into a context of frustration-aggression). Man does not live by frustration alone, nor is pugnacity solely a result of frustration.

Another equally serious defect in this theory, and particularly as an explanation of the causes of war, concerns the ways by which aggression is suddenly uprooted and transferred to certain enemy nations. We learn, for example, that "most people under the threats of danger to their state transfer these aggressions to the objects of political opposition" (Young 1941:20). But, as Malinowski put it, "aggression, like charity, begins at home" (1941b:24). How are aggressions so easily displaced from their original loci (wives, mothers, fathers, employes, and so on)? How can they almost instantaneously be refocused by an entire populace on a single, remote, and perhaps poorly-known enemy? What happens during long periods of peace? Are these aggressions automatically released in other ways? And if so, does not the entire hypothesis collapse? Many other similar questions might be raised, but there is hardly need to do so. The frustration-aggression theory accounts for the forces, or

---

[3] This is not intended to imply that a majority of psychologists now employ frustration-aggression theories as general explanatory devices.

some of the forces, which impinge on individuals and frustrate them. These are apt to result in a pugnacious spirit and in aggression of various sorts. But this is a far cry from an explanation of why certain cultures go to war with others at certain times. As White has remarked, "It is all too frequently assumed that a sociocultural phenomenon has been explained when one has isolated and defined the psychological experiences of an individual within that sociocultural context" (1949:134–135).

The attempt to explain war by recourse to the frustration-aggression hypothesis is but one step removed from the discredited "genetically pugnacious" hypothesis. Since frustration is present in various amounts in all societies, latent aggression which allegedly leads to war, is always lurking about in the neural underbrush. Of course, if we are to believe the frustration-aggressionists, at some future date they will create frustration-less societies, or at least be able to provide "harmless" outlets for aggression. (Many of them seem to propose something very similar to global games of ring-around-the-rosie.) War becomes inevitable, then, for the time being, and for the more pessimistically and deterministically inclined frustration-aggressionists, eternally inevitable.

It is significant to note, too, that in modern nations aggressive, pugnacious individuals are less useful and probably make poorer soldiers than they once did. Pugnacity is quickly spent, and the modern soldier, if anything, needs patience and perseverance. The soldier is becoming less the man who wields the bloody bayonet or fires when he sees the 'whites of their eyes' and more the calm, detached technician who operates a computer or pushes a button, far distant from the enemy. Thanks to the gadgetry of a highly industrialized age, pugnacity and aggressive urges serve the individual ill; technical skill and a serene psychological state serve him better.

In sum, it is apparent that such theories as those of the frustration-aggressionists are not only deficient as explanations of the forces which lead individuals to be pugnacious and to fight in wars, but are beside the point as explanations of the causes of wars. No matter how such theories are twisted they do not and cannot explain *at all* why a particular nation fought another nation when and where it did, and not at some other time or place, or not at all.

It is not very surprising that psychologists and perhaps other social scientists have not attempted to use cultural concepts to solve cultural problems. But it is curious that most of those few modern anthropologists who have concerned themselves with the causes of war should have turned their backs upon their cultural birthright, and for the most part embraced inadequate psychological theories. Why have so few anthropologists grappled with this problem? Why, when they have, have they been seduced by noncultural, psychologically questionable theories? There seems to be but a single answer: Many if not most of their conceptions of culture are incapable of providing an understanding of the causations of warfare. If culture is conceived to be ultimately reducible to psychology, or if it is thought of as an "abstraction" or as a "theory" as is now popular (Kluckhohn 1949:23–24) then the viewpoint that war is something more than an extension of individual fights undertaken for psychological reasons is seriously impaired, if not made impossible. Similarly, the disinterest and general neglect of the problems of the causation of war may be attributed to such conceptions of culture. Either these conceptions have led investigators away from this type of problem, or perhaps they have been dimly aware that they were inadequate for the task.

As White has suggested, the trend of ethnological thinking

is away from the conception of culture as objective, observable things and events in the external world and toward the conception of culture as intangible abstractions. We deplore this trend because we believe that it is veering away from a point of view, a theoretical standpoint, that has become well established and has proved itself to be fruitful in the tradition that is science: the subject matter of any science is a class of objectively observable things and events, not abstractions. This shift in conceptions of culture will, therefore, only make the achievement of a science of culture more difficult (White 1954:467).

In brief, then, the widespread avoidance by anthropologists of the challenging problems of warfare, and the inadequate explanations of the causes of war by those few who have shown interest in these problems, must be blamed squarely on this trend in ethnological thinking.

II

4. A CULTUROLOGICAL VIEW OF WAR. A culturological approach to war is based on the position that since war is a cultural phenomenon, its causes are sought within the cultures of the contending groups. Whether or not a culture is warlike, and the way in which it conducts warfare, are determined by the nature of other aspects of that culture and the conditions of its relationships with other cultures. But more specifically, what in the nature of a culture determines warlike potentialities? The answer to this question is as well known as its importance is disregarded. To put it

simply, whether or not a culture can be warlike, as well as the basic form its wars will take, is dependent to a large extent upon the technological development of that culture. At certain technological levels warfare may be absent, at others it is apt to be chronic. In fact, if we take into consideration the entire known spectrum of human cultures we find that there are but four distinctive types of conflict. Each of these types is associated with, and the nature of its warfare determined by, certain technological means of exploiting the environment.

Type 1 Warfare. Cultures with the rudest and poorest means of exploiting nature are sometimes peaceful. These "wild food gatherers" have either existed in remote areas of the world where they could not benefit from the technologic advances made elsewhere (like most of the native tribes of Australia), or they were located in unproductive areas where the more advanced techniques of exploitation were impossible or unknown. The tribes of the Great Basin area of North America are a good illustration of the latter (Steward 1938:238). There are a number of excellent reasons for these most primitive of cultures to often be peaceful. Economic motivations for war are normally slight. Neighboring bands or tribes of similar cultural status have no surplus goods or foodstuffs to attract potential aggressors. And frequently, possible opponents are so scattered and far apart that to come together in conflict is a difficult feat. Nor are captives of any economic value. They cannot be used as slaves since they cannot create a surplus for their masters, and masters have no coercive economic advantage over their captives. Conquest of additional territory is seldom a reason for war since a band of hunters and gatherers can exploit only a limited extent of territory. The subsistence quest is a full-time one, and it is only rarely that the larder provides enough extra materials and foodstuffs to sustain war. Because political organization is rudimentary, well organized bodies of warriors, obeying the commands of a superior, are rare or absent. Infringement upon another band's territory is perhaps the most important cause for conflict. But conflicts are generally so infrequent, brief, unorganized, and involve so few individuals that they must be considered as a distinctive form of warfare.

Type 2 Warfare. The second category of conflict is commonly designated as primitive warfare (Wright 1942, Vol. 1:62, 546, calls this type of war "social"). It is associated with a wide range of preliterate cultures, but cultures which are below a level of technology based on animal husbandry and developed agriculture. These cultures include many hunters, a number of tribes that combine hunting with gardening, as well as some cultures whose subsistence is primarily horticultural, but who for one reason or another are not distinguished from hunters and gatherers in their total productivity. Whatever the exact nature of the technologies of these cultures, they are not so productive as to have achieved cities, social stratification, or states. The type of conflict characteristic of these societies is often noneconomic, sporadic, and frequently nonlethal or nearly so. Malinowski described this form of war as "Armed and organized head-hunting, cannibalistic, and sacrificial raids, for sportive or religious purposes, but without culturally constructive significance" (Malinowski 1941b:28).

Contests of this sort have been the source of some difficulty for investigators, and many definitions of war have sought to differentiate between this primitive type of conflict and modern war. Turney-High, for example, distinguishes "true" war from this "primitive" war by specifying that "true" war must have: (1) tactical operations, (2) definite command and control, (3) campaigns that are something more than brief raids, (4) a clear motive that is a group rather than an individual one, and (5) adequate supply (Turney-High 1949:30). He also observed that "primitive war, in spite of the dancing about, honors-counting, scalping, and head-hunting, was remarkably tame. Perhaps this is because it so rarely was thoroughly economic" (*ibid.*, 196). I have also attempted to distinguish between these two forms of conflict by defining war as "a type of armed conflict that takes place between societies, meeting in competition for anything that is valued by the groups involved, usually consisting of territory or certain products of this territory, such as good hunting grounds, oil-producing or agricultural lands" (Newcomb 1950: 320). My purpose was to distinguish these forms of conflict from one another, reserving the word war for only what Turney-High calls "true" war. Since, however, there seems to be no name other than war for the crude, sportive, brief, generally unorganized conflicts they will be designated here as "primitive war."

Primitive warfare is best comprehended as a transitional type of conflict—transitional between an ordinarily peaceful state of affairs and serious, deadly, competitive strife. Societies that practice primitive warfare cannot long sustain fighting men in the field, since they do not have the supplies. Nor are they typified by well-organized, strong, or centralized governmental institutions, so that raising and controlling large numbers of fighting men is difficult. Warfare against enemies of similar technological level is scarcely more productive of loot or wealth than it is among the most primitive cultures. On the other hand, small bands of warriors can be spared from time to time, for a few days or weeks, to engage in the sport of war. In short, the technological level of these cultures is not so restrictive in its effect as to preclude war. They are probably more frequently in conflict over favored hunting and fishing grounds, and other natural resources than are the technologically most primitive cultures.

Type 3 Warfare. The third form of conflict, sometimes referred to as "true" war as noted above, is associated with cultures which have reached an animal husbandry or agricultural technology. In a very real sense "true" warfare may be viewed as one of the more important social consequences of the agricultural revolution. Malinowski was thinking of cultures at this technological level when he remarked that

Wars organized for economic gain, loot, slavery, cattle-raising, or tribute occur only at a fairly high level, after accumulation of portable wealth has been achieved; or after slavery, as an industrial system, or tribute, as a political technique, have become efficient. War achieves its full cultural status with the phenomenon of conquest (Malinowski 1941b:27).

At this technological level, populations are relatively large and dense, and not all of the populace is engaged in purely subsistence activities. Cities, a complex division of labor, and states are characteristic. Social and economic organization based upon the ties of kinship has disappeared or is under severe strain. It is being or has been replaced by segmented societies, based upon property ties. The first great civilizations of the old world, Mesopotamian, Egyptian, Indian, and Chinese, are illustrative of such cultures, as the Aztec, Inca and Maya were in the New World.

There are in this and in more advanced cultures several factors which tend to promote war, to make it a more attractive activity than it ever was on cruder technological levels. For the first time war can become a highly profitable venture. Stores of grain and other agricultural produce, precious metals, and tools of all sorts, works of art, captives, and other forms of wealth constitute a rich prize for the victor. And second, land itself has become a valuable prize of war. Rich hunting grounds, favored fishing sites, and the like, are always apt to be objects of contention between even simpler societies, but for agricultural civilizations the basis from which their cultural blessings flow—fertile river valleys and other types of productive lands, mines and supply routes—must be controlled at all costs. And those who are defeated can look forward only to exploitation, slavery, serfdom, and perhaps cultural annihilation. Thus, war becomes more deadly and serious, its consequences greater; there is more to fight about, more to gain or lose. (White 1949:379–380, contains an interesting discussion of the social and political consequences of "true" war.)

Type 4 Warfare. Cultures that have tapped the energy resources of the fossil fuels and have passed through an industrial revolution have been as warlike, or perhaps even more warlike than any ever to exist before on the face of the earth. As "true" war was a consequence of the agricultural revolution, so world wars may be regarded as a consequence of the industrial revolution. Malinowski felt that world war (which was not possible in pre-industrial cultures) is a radically distinct type of conflict:

World War, that is total war, is, in the light of our anthropological criteria, as distinct from the historical wars up to 1914 as these were different from head-hunting and slave-raiding. The influence of present warfare on culture is so total that it poses the problem whether the integral organization for effective violence, which we call totalitarianism, is compatible with the survival of culture (Malinowski 1941b:29).

Instead of petty wars between relatively small states, usually lasting only a short time and not seriously involving more than a fraction of the populace, a number of nations joined together by various sorts of ties are opposed by rival coalitions of nations in gigantic world wars. Armies are counted in millions and are supported by mobilized civilian populations. Continuous battles rage over the earth for relatively long periods of time. But there is little reason to believe that the basic causes of conflict have changed appreciably. They are still competition for natural resources, for supply routes, and the like, although perhaps intensified. It is significant that industrial nations are not self-sufficient in the sense that more primitive civilizations were. All sorts of raw materials must be obtained from the far corners of the globe, and in turn markets must be found for manufactured products. In short, the necessity to acquire raw materials and markets, or conversely, the need to preserve them, adds a vital, if not an entirely new dimension to the causation of war.

It is apparent that a new and even higher technological level is rapidly being reached by modern nations. This level, utilizing and unleashing the tremendous energy of the atom, has not yet made its effect felt throughout culture, nor is it entirely clear what its effect on the nature and form of war will be. This is not the place to speculate about the possibilities inherent in this new technological revolution, although it should be clear from this discussion that revolutionary technological changes have not only been followed by social and political upheavals, but that the accompanying wars are likely to be of a new type.

So far in our outline of the principal forms of war, we have for convenience spoken as if wars always took place between cultures of the same technological level. This is of course far from being the case, and in fact neighboring cultures with differing technologies are apt to fight one another because of these very differences. The people of a technologically primitive culture are likely to view greedily the wealth of a rich and technologically advanced neighbor. Conversely, the members of a technologically dominant and expanding culture are apt to look on the lands and persons of weaker, poorer neighbors as fair game. There are many examples which might be chosen to illustrate this point, from Barbarians attacking and the Roman Empire eventually succumbing to their onslaughts, to the decimation of the Indian tribes which accompanied the European colonization of North America.

Although the forms war takes are dependent upon the degree of technological development, and "true" war does not accompany primitive technologies, this does not necessarily mean that all technologically well-developed cultures must be warlike. Whether cultures shall have wars with their neighbors, exist by armed truces, or dwell in harmonious peace is affected by a large number of other cultural as well as extra-cultural factors. How severe is the competition of another nation? What are the chances of victory if war should come? Of defeat? What manner of political alliances can be made? What is the traditional relationship with the current enemy? Does one nation by geographic happenstance lie astride and so control a vital supply route which another nation must use? In short, "Wars are fought between societies, between sociocultural systems, between tribes, and nations. It is the culture of any given situation that determines whether warfare shall be engaged in or not, and if so how, with whom and for what" (White 1949:131–132). The nature of a culture's social system, the form of its political system, the character of its philosophic system have much to do with the warring capabilities and potentialities of cultures. Is the military tradition strong? Is there a military caste? Are social institutions geared for war, or will they readily support wars? Is warfare condoned or fostered by the religious system? It should be clear that these are cultural factors, and assessing their importance is a cultural matter and not a psychological or biological problem. It should be noted also that this implies another fundamental aspect of a culturological view of war. It is that cultures are systems, made up of interrelated parts. While it is plain that the nature of warfare is determined by the technological system, this system operates within a socioreligious matrix which influences and conditions the warlike potentialities of culture (See White 1949:381–385).

To put this discussion in a slightly different manner, "true" war and "modern" wars grow out of the competition between cultures for land, natural resources of all sorts, markets, and the like. Yet these wars are not necessarily the simple result of competing economies. In modern nations especially, they are contests growing out of complex competitive situations, always conditioned by many other social, political, and ideological factors. This does not mean, however, that the facile explanations of warfare current at the outset of World War II were accurate. One such statement alleged that, "The war against the Axis in 1942 . . . is a war between two ideologies about the way to set up human societies" (Benedict 1942:763). Another suggested that World War II "is a war of social philosophies. It is what brought the war about. It is what will win or lose the war" (Aginsky 1942:525). These are interesting allegations and if true would bode ill for the future of mankind, since they imply that there can be enduring peace only when all men embrace the same, or very nearly the same, social philosophy and social organization. From what has been said here, however, it should be clear that the basic causes of wars are to be found in the realm of competitive conflict. To say that any war is caused solely by a clash of ideologies is either wholly wrong or grossly misleading.

Another distinguishing feature of the culturological approach, and an extremely helpful one in understanding the causes of war, lies in the conception of culture as a superorganic entity, obeying its own laws and moving in accordance with its own principles (White 1949:373ff.). When it is realized that cultures do have their own independent integrity, their own direction and force, and an existence apart from individuals, the distinction between the reasons why individuals fight in wars and the causes of their culture's wars comes clearly into focus. Men are drawn into the role of warrior or soldier for a multitude of reasons, as we have seen, and none of these reasons need coincide with the causes of cultural conflict. In fact, a nation may be able to produce more strongly motivated fighting men if they are ignorant of the real causes of conflict. How many American youths could be enlisted to fight the battles of the oil companies, or for the markets of southeast Asia? How many, on the other hand, could be enlisted to prevent the rape of their mothers, or to "see the world" (as Navy posters once said), or for other personal reasons?

How many men may have enlisted in the A.E.F. in World War I "to make the world safe for democracy," or perhaps more accurately because it was the thing to do, while their nation had actually gone to war to preserve vast markets and its economic stake in Europe, Asia, and Africa?

All cultures must present themselves to their members as moral bodies, or at least persuade their members to observe certain codes of conduct. This is of course a necessity if man's social world is to function. The mistake has been in thinking that since this is true of the members of any culture, it also must be true of a society's dealings and relationships with other societies. Nothing could be farther from the truth. The relations between nations have always been governed by the law of the jungle, by sheer power. This has inevitably forced nations into all sorts of rationalizations and illogical positions in defending their amoral or nonmoral dealings with others before their inveterately moral members. It has made the task of laying bare the causes of modern wars difficult since every investigator is bound to be a biased, ill-informed member of a contending civilization. Yet the student who views culture superorganically is relieved from being upset by the fact that "peace-loving nations" are frequently at war, or that (as the journalistic world assures us) the man in the street, whether it be Red Square or Main Street, does not want war although it is this man who will become his nation's soldier. The superorganicist realizes that the wishes and hopes of the individual are the result of the interplay of cultural forces which are affecting him, and that it is not the other way around.

So far this paper has been chiefly concerned with the ways by which anthropologists can achieve a better understanding of the causes of wars which have already occurred. Nothing has been said about future wars, or predictive possibilities, although prediction is a major goal of any scientific discipline. As far as warfare is concerned, a number of anthropologists have understood the trend of cultural evolution and have noted that one of its most important results has been the appearance of larger and fewer political units. The defeated, the weaker, the decadent, pacific, or merely unfortunate have been absorbed or neutralized by the stronger:

A half-dozen or so World Powers engaged in the First World War; only two great powers emerged from the second. The competition for power narrows as contestants are eliminated. The logical conclusion is, however, not simply the domination of the world by a single nation—this would be but a transitional stage—but a single political organization that will embrace the entire planet and the whole human race (White 1949:389).

Even Boas, the epitome of anti-culturology, was moved to remark that:

the history of mankind shows us the grand spectacle of the grouping of man in units of ever increasing size that live together in peace, and that are ready to go to war only with other groups outside of their own limits. Notwithstanding all temporary revolutions and the shattering of larger units for the time being, the progress in the direction of unification has been so regular and so marked that we must needs conclude, that the tendencies which have swayed this development in the past will govern our history in the future. . . . The practical difficulties that seem to stand in the way of the formation of still larger units count for naught before the inexorable laws of history (Boas 1945:100).

Unfortunately our present comprehension of human culture leads us no farther than the conclusion that the future holds in store for men a world-wide political unit, and hence one which is at peace. When or where the last conflict (or conflicts) shall take place remains at the moment beyond the predictive powers of anthropologists as well as of other men. This is not intended as a statement of ethnological impotence, only as an admission of ignorance. The developing science of culture will lead to a more perfect understanding of war and its causes. With maturity it will more clearly forecast the course of future events.

Nothing, naturally enough, has been said here about the control of warfare. When the understanding of the causes of cultural conflicts is slight, and the prediction of future wars restricted to a generality, it would be foolhardy to make any claims for control, even if any were thought possible. Many writers whose explanations of warfare are seriously defective, at least from our point of view, have said much about how to halt wars. There is no room here for a discussion of these remarks, although it should be noted that almost all such statements at best seem to be frenzied adjurations. (For a pertinent discussion bearing on this aspect of cultural conflicts see White 1949:330–359, particularly 355.)

SUMMARY

This paper has attempted to do two things: first, to suggest why anthropologists have contributed so little to the understanding of warfare, and second, to suggest a method by which the causes of war—the factors which result in cultural conflicts—may be more fully comprehended. Nonculturological explanations of warfare are unsatisfactory, misleading, and unconvincing. There has been, then, a desperate need for a more rewarding approach to the causes and problems of warfare. Culturology offers such an approach, and a number of the principal features of a culturological view of warfare have been examined here.

BIBLIOGRAPHY

AGINSKY, B. W.

1942 "Social Science and the World Situation." *American Anthropologist,* 44:521–525.

ALLPORT, GORDON

1950 "The Role of Expectancy." In *Tensions that Cause Wars,* ed. by Hadley Cantril, pp. 43–78. Urbana, University of Illinois Press.

BENEDICT, RUTH

1942 "Primitive Freedom." *Atlantic Monthly,* 169:756–763.

BOAS, FRANZ

1945 *Race and Democratic Society.* New York, J. J. Augustin.

CANTRIL, HADLEY, ED.

1950 "Common Statement." In *Tensions that Cause Wars,* pp. 17–21. Urbana, University of Illinois Press.

KLUCKHOHN, CLYDE

1949 *Mirror For Man.* New York, Whittlesey House, McGraw-Hill Book Co.

LINTON, RALPH

1936 *The Study of Man.* New York, D. Appleton-Century Company.

MALINOWSKI, BRONISLAW

1941a "An Anthropological Analysis of War," *American Journal of Sociology,* 46:521–550.

1941b "War—Past, Present, and Future." In *War as a Social Institution,* ed. by J. D. Clarkson and T. C. Cochran, pp. 21–31. New York, Columbia University Press.

NEWCOMB, W. W., Jr.

1950 "A Re-examination of the Causes of Plains Warfare." *American Anthropologist,* 52:317–330.

STEWARD, JULIAN

1938 "Basin-Plateau Aboriginal Socio-Political Groups." *Bureau of American Ethnology Bulletin,* 120.

TURNEY-HIGH, HARRY HOLBERT

1949 *Primitive War, Its Practice and Concepts.* Columbia, University of South Carolina Press.

W. W. Newcomb, Jr.

WHITE, LESLIE A.

1949 *The Science of Culture.* New York, Farrar, Straus and Company.

1954 "Review of Culture: A Critical Review of Concepts and Definitions," by A. L. Kroeber and Clyde Kluckhohn. *American Anthropologist,* 56:461–468.

WRIGHT, QUINCY

1942 *A Study of War.* 2 vols. Chicago, The University of Chicago Press.

YOUNG, KIMBALL

1941 "The Psychology of War." In *War as a Social Institution,* ed. by J. D. Clarkson and T. C. Cochran, pp. 4–20. New York, Columbia University Press.

* * * *

Edward Norbeck

UNIVERSITY OF CALIFORNIA

ECONOMIC CHANGE

AND JAPANESE

SOCIAL ORGANIZATION

After many centuries of intermittently close relations with China and six decades of contact with the West, Japan closed her doors to foreign contact at the beginning of the seventeenth century. The two and one-half centuries of the Tokugawa government (1603–1868) which followed were years of unprecedented peace, but they were also a period of relatively little cultural change. These were the years when Europe saw the sweeping changes which are labeled the industrial revolution. Self-isolated Japan, allowing none of its subjects to leave the country and admitting only a tiny and rigidly supervised trickle of Western culture in the persons of Dutch traders, had lost the stimulus to cultural expansion which diffusion has repeatedly provided the societies and nations of the world. Approximately equal in cultural development with the nations of the West at the time of arrival of the first Europeans in the middle of the sixteenth century, Japan three centuries later seemed hopelessly retarded, a small and technologically primitive nation doomed to a position of little consequence in international affairs.

But the seeds of cultural change seem long to have been germinating in Japan, awaiting an opportunity for more rapid growth. The Japanese response to the fertilization of Western science and technology has been astounding, the most rapid and drastic cultural change conjointly involving a large number of human beings ever to occur under conditions of internal peace in the recorded history of the world. Western culture was not merely accepted, it was fervently if selectively welcomed and the bearers of that culture, the individuals and nations of the West, were eagerly courted. That which advantageously fit or could be adapted to conform with indigenous patterns without serious conflict was seized, although it was inevitably cast in a distinctively Japanese mold. Western cultural traits that conferred no obvious advantages and were neutral toward established counterparts tagged along, growing less luxuriantly or not at all. Actively conflicting traits such as Christianity, which was intolerant of traditional religious beliefs and unsuited to nationalistic aims of the government, hardly penetrated or had very little growth. Neutral and amoral science and derived technology, their advantages prominently apparent, received the most zealous welcome.

Using the obviously powerful nations of the West as its models, Japan began in 1868 a program of catching up which finds no equal in velocity. Compulsory education for all, the absorption of scientific knowledge, and the use of applied science in the form of industrialization are among the important innovations which began almost immediately. By 1895 the erstwhile small, backward, and powerless nation was able to challenge in war a great international power and, until its defeat in 1945, intermittently continued to wage a successful military campaign of conquest.

These facts of the recent history of Japan are well known. The political reorganization of Japan is also well recorded. Far less well known, however, are contemporaneous and unplanned social changes of another kind, in their own way quite as sweeping and radical as the more amply documented events of industrialization and governmental remodeling. These are the changes that have come about on the familial, community, and other interpersonal levels. In these matters we are still ignorant of many details of regional differences, but the major outlines are clear. Using as a base point the conditions prevailing at the beginning of the Meiji reign (1868–1912) and proceeding to modern times, we shall sketch the history of both economic and social changes, giving emphases in the social field to alterations in familial and other interpersonal relationships. Data presented here are drawn from published accounts and in lesser part from personal field research.

In 1868 Japanese life was built mainly around agriculture, the cultivation of small plots of ground, chiefly rice paddy, by farmer-owners and tenant-farmers, both under the control of a hereditary nobility. A few cities of considerable population and a modest number of smaller urban centers had long existed as aggregations of people with specialized occupations clustered about the seats of national government or the castles of local rulers. Japan was economically self-sufficient, and commodities of many kinds were produced by specialized craftsmen. Money had been in use as a means of exchange for many centuries and organized industry had reached an embryonic stage independent of the West. But Japan at this time could hardly be described as industrialized or as having a money economy. For most of the nation, the necessities of life were either self-produced or were received by exchanging commodities. As the principal agricultural product and the mainstay of existence, rice served as the chief medium of exchange and was the standard form of revenue of national and local rulers.

In the course of their lives, ordinary men, principally farmers living in small and largely self-sufficient communities, saw little money. Wants and necessities that could not be self-produced were provided principally through kinship and through personalized ties with unrelated community members. Life revolved about the family and the small community, which was often composed chiefly of consanguineal, affinal, and ritual relatives.

The basic unit of social organization was the extended family occupying a single dwelling. Its average size for the nation as a whole or any major region, we do not know, but scattered information on communities and provinces indicates that it was large. Data on a village of Gifu Prefecture in central Japan for 1876, for example, indicate an average of 8.8 persons (Matsumiya 1947:108), and larger figures have been cited for other communities. Personnel of the extended family clustered about a nucleus composed of a male household head, his wife, and his children. To this group a varying number of other kin were added. Most commonly these were the aged parents of the household head and his young, unmarried siblings. Mature married brothers of the household head, their wives, and their children might be included if economic conditions permitted, although sisters of the household head married out. The household might thus embrace several nuclear families, but household unity was close, and the individual nuclear families had no recognized position as discrete entities.

A still larger residential kin group, the *dōzoku*,[1] was composed of a senior and founding household (*honke*) and subsidiary or branch households (*bunke*). As circumstances permitted, sons who would not inherit the position of head of the household were provided with separate lands and dwellings and became heads of branch households, which stood in

---

[1] Following Japanese usage, this term may be applied to a body of kin which is not organized into *honke* and *bunke*.

social positions inferior to that of the founding household. A whole community might be composed of a single *honke-bunke* system embracing as many as twenty-five or more households. The network might also include households composed of persons who were unrelated to the parental or founding household but who were ritually made into fictive or quasi-relatives, a course of action often followed by landless men and their families. Within the individual extended family and its ramification, the *dōzoku,* interpersonal relations of authority and submission were strongly vertical. Male heads of households held the position of greatest authority. The head of a *honke* strongly dominated heads of branch households, and ritually related households stood below the consanguineally related *honke-bunke.* Females held statuses much inferior to those of males.

Other variably important units of community social organization were cooperative associations (*kō, kumi*) composed of a single representative of each household, ordinarily the household head. These units served economic, political, religious, and other functions.

It is necessary to note that regional differences in social organization existed then as they do today. In general terms, the greatest regional differences lay between approximately the northern and southern halves of Japan—in more accurate geographical terms, between the northeastern area on the one hand, and the central and southwestern areas, on the other. These may be summarized briefly. In the northeastern area social organization emphasized kinship and quasi-kinship more strongly, and the *honke-bunke,* which had seen its greatest development throughout Japan several centuries earlier, remained well established. The eldest son inherited the position as head of the household, and the status of younger sons was markedly inferior to that of the heir. In central and most of southwestern Japan the extended family was again the fundamental social unit. The *honke-bunke* system and ritual kinship also existed but less commonly than in the northeast and in what appears to have been much less luxuriant form than in earlier times. Many of the functions performed by kin or quasi-kin in communities of the northeast were here fulfilled by nonhierarchically organized cooperative associations. In some areas of southwestern Japan, particularly the seaboard, these associations were chiefly age-graded societies applying to all members of a community. More commonly, egalitarian representation in various associations of male, female, and mixed membership was by a single individual from each household whose selection was not strictly determined by age. Inheritance was by primogeniture or, less commonly, by ultimogeniture, and matrilineal relatives appeared to have held a position of greater importance here than in the northeast.

Social arrangements in Japanese cities of the time are less clear. The cities themselves were usually sprawling aggregations of dwellings interspersed here and there with rice fields. The forms of kin organization described for rural areas certainly all existed, although probably in attenuated form, and ritual kinship was well developed. As in modern times, urban ritual kinship probably often took the form of a parent-child relationship (*oyabun-kobun*, "parent role-child role") between two genealogically unrelated individuals rather than between whole families. In this relationship the elder served as sponsor, guarantor, master, teacher, or employer, and the younger as recipient of benefactions in return for which he was expected to provide service or other economic advantage to his "parent" (cf. Ishino 1953).

The opening of Japan to Western science and technology stimulated a continuing process of change in these social arrangements which has moved at its most accelerated pace in the past decade. One of the remarkable changes which began almost at once was an enormous growth in population, from an estimated 30,000,000 in 1868 and the preceding two centuries to approximately 92,000,000 in 1958. Increase in numbers itself was, of course, influential in bringing about the social changes which have taken place since 1868, but other closely interrelated factors are also involved. Fundamental to the spurt in population were a reduction of death rates brought about by the adoption of scientific medicine and an increase in birth rates encouraged by technological and economic changes. Despite a recent decline in birth rates, the Japanese population has increased during the past ten years at a rate of approximately 1,000,000 annually.

Agricultural expansion to Hokkaido, increase in cultivated lands in other areas, and improved techniques of agronomy resulting in higher yields allowed an absolute but nevertheless limited increase of the rural population. The development of industry served indirectly in far larger measure to stimulate population growth by providing a source of livelihood for excess rural residents and their descendants. Migration to accept employment in industrial centers, especially by noninheriting sons and unmarried daughters who were not needed on the farms and whose presence there worked a hardship on their households, was quickly established as a demographic pattern which strongly influenced social relationships.

The rapid industrialization of Japan brought with it the traits which characterize industrial societies elsewhere and which have come to be regarded as their synonyms or inherent correlates: a money economy, intensive specialization in labor, a decline in the size and strength of kin units, growing impersonality in human interrelationships, and the emergence of impersonal agencies which assume many of the functions once performed by kin. The extent to which these trends exist in Japan is a matter of particular interest, especially since those directly relating to social organization seem on casual inspection sometimes to contradict tendencies noted in other parts of the world.

In 1868 approximately 85 per cent of the Japanese population depended directly upon agriculture for a livelihood (Taeuber 1951:150). In 1955, 44 per cent of the population lived in rural areas (Bureau of Statistics 1957:12). The number of industrial workers in 1955 was, however, greater than these statistics on residence indicate for the reason that the line between rural and urban occupations in modern Japan is obscured by individuals employed in both agriculture and industry. In 1946, for example, 45 per cent of the farms were reported to have workers who also engaged in part-time employment in factories or in home industries (Taeuber 1951:152), and similar conditions have continued to prevail. In 1958 approximately 40 per cent of the labor force was engaged primarily in agriculture and forestry (Levine 1958:4). The overall trend may thus be described as being toward a great but imprecisely stated increase in specialized employment in industry and in occupations peripheral to industry. At the same time, rural occupations have come increasingly to hold much in common with forms of urban specialization in labor. The rural resident, formerly a nearly self-sufficient peasant, today seldom does such things as build his own dwelling or make his own implements. He is instead increasingly dependent for survival and well-being on the efforts of manifold specialists. As farmer, fisherman, or forestry worker, his efforts have become so narrowly concentrated that he, like the industrial worker, may be described as a specialist in his own right.

With the exception of a brief period of chaos at the end of World War II, money has everywhere long been established as the prevailing and sole important means of exchange. Although traditional class distinctions evident in attitudes expressed toward the old nobility and toward the socially debased Eta class have not wholly vanished, it may be said that money has become the prime measure of individual worth.

Changes in the family and other social units have been extensive. In

1947 the average size of the family—reported by prefecture and thus including both urban and rural populations—varied between 4.0 and 5.9 persons (Izumi and Gamō 1952:40). In 1950 the national average in "normal households" of two or more persons sharing a common income was reported as 4.9 individuals, a figure which excluded approximately 1,500,000 individuals who lived alone or, if with others, shared living expenses with no one (Bureau of Statistics 1957:26–27). The old extended family including three generations and various collateral members had obviously been severed into smaller units. As early as 1920 a sample of 11,119 families revealed that 90 per cent lacked collateral members (Matsumiya 1947). The small nuclear family has in fact been the dominant familial form for more than a decade and appears to be steadily increasing in incidence. When relatives beyond husband, wife, and their children are included in the modern household, they are most commonly limited to one or both of the aged parents of the male spouse when these individuals have no other means of support.

The *dōzoku* has also been greatly weakened and has virtually disappeared in most of the country. Ritual kin membership in *dōzoku* has waned correspondingly, but the *oyabun-kobun* form of ritual kinship between individuals has retained considerable strength in industrial centers—a subject to which we shall return.

Along with this diminution in size and incidence of kin groups has come a weakening within them of authoritarian control by seniors over juniors and males over females. According to legislation enacted during the American occupation, laws of inheritance entitle offspring to equal shares of property regardless of sex, and the franchise has been extended to women. That these laws, imposed by outsiders, have continued to exist after the end of the occupation is surely in part symptomatic of social changes in Japan which antedate the laws. Subdivision by inheritance of the already tiny farm plots is not, in actuality, an economically feasible course, and the eldest son ordinarily continues to inherit farm property to the exclusion of his siblings. Brothers of the heir commonly take employment in industry, thus removing themselves from positions of subservience to him. Sisters also often follow the same course until marriage, and many continue to be gainfully employed after marriage.

Before the opening of Japan to the West, social superiority of males over females was greatest among the economically and socially privileged classes, female members of which made no direct contribution to household finances. Proceeding down the social scale to the laboring classes, where women performed work of direct economic significance as well as household tasks, the breach in authority between males and females diminished. Among fisher folk, whose social status is near the bottom of the national scale, women ordinarily tilled the vitally important agricultural plots customarily owned by Japanese fishing households, and the advantage of the economic importance thereby conferred made their position in relation to men of their society relatively high (Norbeck, 1954). Inter-class differences in the relative social positions of males and females remain evident today, but the breach in status between the sexes has everywhere diminished. Evidence also appears to indicate the weakening of the traditionally strong authority of mother-in-law over daughter-in-law (Raper 1950:219; Norbeck 1954:210). There seems little doubt that the authority of the father and household head has generally diminished, over females as well as over males.

In general, it may be said that all intra-familial relations have become democratized as compared with the past. No analysis of the undoubtedly multiple influences contributing to this trend of change will be attempted here, but it appears certain that economic factors have been potent. Regardless of the order of his birth, the son is generally better educated than the father and frequently has a greater income, circumstances which do not encourage strong paternal domination. Men who migrate to industrial centers may establish themselves in positions more highly favored economically than their brother who remained at home as the master of the farm. The importance of women as wage earners has undoubtedly contributed to their enhanced social status; in 1958 females comprised over 40 per cent of the total labor force (Levine 1958:3).

Additional indications of the diminished importance of kinship and the growth of impersonality are provided by trends of change in the use of terms of relationship. The traditional Japanese family was not merely a cooperating group of individuals but was a highly cohesive unit in which the wishes, problems, and goals of the individual were subsidiary to those of the group as a whole. All social relationships extending to the national political structure tended strongly to be patterned after the model of the family, a tendency that remains evident in present-day forms of address for distant relatives and unrelated persons.

Modern Japanese kinship nomenclature includes a large variety of terms of reference for consanguineal and affinal relatives, but—what is germane here—only a few terms of address. Only relatives older than the speaker are ordinarily addressed by the terms of relationship; relatives younger than the speaker are addressed by personal name. Terms of address are limited to four sets,[2] grandfather-grandmother, father-mother, uncle-aunt, and elder brother-elder sister, which are modified by affixes to indicate degrees of formality or informality. These terms are customarily employed in addressing the relatives which they denote. They are also often used in addressing more distant kin, for whom a variety of terms of reference but none of address exist. "Mother" and "father" are used only to address parents and parents-in-law, but any terms of the remaining three sets might be used in addressing other affines, cousins, and more distant collateral relatives. The selection of a term to be used in address is made according to the marital and household status and the age of the addressee. Thus, for example, a cousin somewhat older than the speaker might be addressed as "elder brother" or "elder sister," a cousin still older as "uncle" or "aunt," and a distant elderly relative as "grandfather." This practice nominally intensifies relationships between the speaker and the addressee, and it serves in a manner not altogether superficial to bring the relatives in question into a circle of greater intimacy.

The use of kin terms of address is not confined entirely to relatives, but with various exceptions connected with distinctions in social class between speaker and addressee, extends to embrace all members of society of appropriate age. Friends, acquaintances, and sometimes total strangers may be addressed by terms of these three sets.

Recent research (Norbeck and Befu 1958; Befu and Norbeck 1958) indicates a decline as compared with the past in the use of kin terms for relatives except those "properly" denoted by the terms of address. Even among these relatives a nascent trend seems evident toward substitution of personal name for kin term in addressing parents' siblings and own elder siblings. The same trend toward dwindling use of kin terms appears also to apply in addressing friends, acquaintances, and strangers. Investigations indicate the weakening of kin ties among upper class urban residents to the point where even the names of the parents' siblings are not always known, a circumstance which must surely have been very uncommon a century ago.

Thus far virtually all of our general statements concerning social change have been in neat accord with the correlates of industrialization and urbanization as noted in the West. But our brief and selective sketch of Japanese social change, which emphasizes end results and compares

---

[2] A fifth set denoting great-grandparents also exists, but occasion for its use are, expectably, rare. Moreover, the terms for grandparents tend to be used for these and any other relatives of great age. Husband and wife address each other by terms which are not strictly terms of relationship. (See Befu and Norbeck 1958.)

them with conditions existing at our base point, masks much that is note-worthy. If we now attempt to make a direct comparison between Japan and the United States in patterns of industrialization and trends of change in social organization, we see many differences, including developments which appear to oppose trends of change in the West.

Japanese industrialization began with a mushroom growth of cottage industry, great numbers of tiny plants employing only a few persons who were often relatives and dependents of the entrepreneur. As late as 1930 over 50 per cent of the industrial labor force was employed in firms with less than five employees and over 70 per cent in firms with less than fifty employees (Taeuber 1951:152). In March, 1952 about 93 per cent of the nation's nonagricultural establishments were small individual enter-prises and only 4.8 per cent of the total were corporations. In 1954, fac-tories with more than 500 workers each comprised less than 0.2 per cent of the total number of manufacturing plants and accounted for approx-imately 23 per cent of manufacturing employment. At the other extreme, factories with less than ten workers each represented 81 per cent of the total of manufacturing plants and employed another 23 per cent of the labor force in manufacturing. Although the trend has been toward larger enterprises, the number of factories and all other nonagricultural estab-lishments with more than 100 employees today comprises less than 0.5 per cent of the total (Levine 1958:7).

Japan has also differed greatly from the United States in the efficiency of its industrialization. Japan is indeed industrialized in the sense of producing commodities in mass by largely mechanical means and en-gaging extensively in the trade of commodities. The efficiency of its industrialization as measured in terms of per capita wealth or surplus produced and in man-hours of labor is, however, another matter, and in this respect Japan trails far behind.

In the social sphere, many differences between the United States and Japan may be pointed out. Kinship remains very important in Japan, and in its derived form of ritual or fictive kinship it survives with locally variable strength. An examination of the historic course of events since the inception of industrialization reveals, in fact, a temporary florescence of fictive kinship, an occurrence which is out of keeping with theories of the impersonalizing effect of industrialization. Outside the realm of "true" and ritual kinship, social relationships continue to be characterized by paternalism and personal loyalties. Communal associations—the fish-ermen, boat owners, and agricultural cooperatives, funeral societies, and other similar organizations so abundant in modern rural Japan—have had comparatively little development in the United States. Like fictive kinship, communal associations have had their greatest development in Japan after the nation became industrialized.

We may, in short, note both similarities and differences, and the problem is to account for them. Explanation of similarities in social organization by recourse to a hypothesis of direct diffusion from the United States or Europe is, of course, unsatisfactory. Japanese industrialization and the acceptance and development of modern science were, to be sure, in large measure consciously planned innovations. Social developments could hardly be so labeled. Such witting planning as was involved appears to have been spurred by economic and associated demographic changes and thus represents measures designed to meet needs created by these changes in the conditions of life.

A correlate of industrialization in the United States has been the growth of systems of social security subsidized by both private corporations and local and national governments. Impersonal programs of welfare providing unemployment insurance, old age pensions, sickness pay, and similar aid saw little growth in Japan under either governmental or private auspices until very recent times. Modified in both form and function by industrialization, kinship long continued to play a large share of its old roles. One still relied heavily upon his relatives for financial and other aid at times of necessity. If he lacked kin or if they were unable to provide help, he turned to friends and other unrelated persons.

The rural young man or young woman who went to the city and the urban resident without means gained employment by finding a patron, most frequently his future employer or occupational supervisor. The relationship between the two individuals was formalized by ritual into the *oyabun-kobun* institution, which morally pledged them to mutual economic support in a manner more binding than a legal contract. From the standpoint of employers, managers, and work foremen who became ritual fathers to the employees under them, the *oyabun-kobun* served as an effective method for meeting needs for labor. For the protégés in the role of "children," the *oyabun-kobun* was a surrogate of the familial life in which they had been reared, offering economic and also psychological support, and it was often the only means by which they could become economically established.

Fictive kinship applying among individuals blossomed in industry during the nineteenth century and has continued to survive although in diminishing strength. Its counterpart among familial units—that is, the *dōzoku* which includes ritually related families—also had some temporary growth in northeastern Japan after 1868 when additional lands were opened for agriculture. Here ritual kinship served as a means by which landowners were able to secure enough hands to work their increased holdings of land. At the same time it assured greater loyalty and support than could be expected of tenant-farmers.

Unfavorable economic circumstances of the nation as a whole has doubtless served to inhibit the development of extensive and effective programs of social welfare. Poorly endowed with natural resources, Japan has depended largely upon foreign trade and it must import most of the raw materials used in the products it manufactures and exports. Despite extensive industrialization, the nation has never experienced economic conditions which provided its population much beyond the level of subsistence. The lack of wealth has also strongly influenced the nature of Japanese industrialization, favoring small enterprises with limited capital and few employees. These conditions in turn provide fertile ground for the retention, if in modified form, of a personalized social order.

The hypothesis is inviting that the force of Japanese tradition also served to discourage the emergence and growth of impersonal institutions to provide for the care and well-being of the nation's population. Centuries of social life centered upon such traditions as communalism, kinship, and the extreme importance of the Japanese family might well continue to exert influence when the vital functions they performed could be handled in other ways. At the very least, it may be said that the influence of ingrained Japanese cultural traditions is evident in many ways. Fictive kinship and communal associations are social forms for which models had long existed in Japan, and they appear to have blossomed for lack of the more impersonal devices which fulfill the same functions in the United States. Cooperative associations were in fact strongly encouraged by the national government as a valuable economic measure costing the nation little, and membership in agricultural and other cooperatives was mandatory during World War II as a means by which production could be closely watched and controlled.

The influence of pre-existing cultural forms is also evident in many other ways. An example is provided by the trade-union movement in Japan, which has tended toward a proliferation of tiny and essentially autonomous unions limited to individual enterprises. Levine has called "enterprise unionism" the central theme of the Japanese labor movement and has given convincing support to his contention that it is an indigenous product "imbedded in the web of traditional Japanese culture" (Levine 1958:102). Among other conditioning factors, Levine notes that workmen carried with them agrarian backgrounds emphasizing familial ties and that the family-like social orders of the small establishments which gave most of them employment made enterprise unions the "natural" form (Levine 1958:105).

Change in the social and economic spheres has not been uniform throughout the nation, and a closer inspection of regional differences is useful. In northeastern Japan, an agricultural area with only one sizeable city (Sendai; 1955 population, 375,844), kinship has retained its strongest hold. Families in this area include more collateral members and continue to be the largest in the nation. The *dōzoku* organization, although diminished in both size and incidence, retained life until after World War II. Democratic cooperative associations basing their membership on considerations other than kinship likewise did not find development comparable with that of southwestern Japan until after the war. In rural areas of central and southwestern Japan, the family is small and tends more strongly toward the nuclear form. The *dōzoku* has generally disappeared as an effectively functioning unit, as have systems of age-graded associations embracing all members of a community. The development of egalitarian communal associations has, however, been luxuriant.

It is noteworthy that the earliest emergence and most flourishing growth of these democratic community associations occurred in central and southwestern Japan, where economic opportunities, which served to discourage authoritarian control by main households over branch households, first arose and thus weakened the *dōzoku* structure. In the cities, the nuclear family is strongly dominant and the average size of the family is the smallest, less than four individuals. Trade-unions stand out as the most prominent form of urban associations.

These regional distinctions in social structure may be summarized in the general statement that departure from the traditional is most marked as one proceeds from northern to central and southern Japan in rural areas and from small city to large city. These differences in turn reflect two major influences, variations existing at our base point a century ago and differentials in degree and nature of subsequent economic development. Northeastern Japan, with more extensive individual farm plots but less productive land, inferior natural resources of other kinds, and a colder climate prohibiting double-cropping, had lagged far behind central and southwestern Japan in industrialization-urbanization, density of population, and even in the development of efficient agricultural techniques.

In very recent years, northeastern Japan has for the first time seen relative economic prosperity, and its distinctive features of social organization are rapidly disappearing.

It is significant that the most rapid decline in the incidence, size, and functional importance of both conventional kinship and ritual kinship appears to have come about since the end of World War II. Post-war economic changes have also been extensive. Among them were the land reform program, which took farm lands out of the hands of absentee landlords with large holdings and placed them under the ownership of their former tenants, thus discouraging not only tenant farming but also the cultivation of plots by individuals bound to land-owners by ritual kinship, a status which did not give title to land and was not inherited.[3] Industry has had further growth, and, as we have noted, industrial plants have grown in size. Governmental programs of social welfare have developed rapidly. Laws enacted since the war have dealt with public health, housing, work relief through public projects, family assistance, and unemployment, accident, health, and old age insurance. Some are expansions of old laws and others, notably the legislation establishing unemployment and health insurance, are innovations. Over one-third of all wage-earners in nonagricultural enterprise are now eligible for benefits under the several insurance laws (Levine 1958:164ff.). Another noteworthy governmental innovation was the establishment of a network of public employment agencies; these were effective in eliminating private labor recruiters, who often established fictive kin relationships with the workmen they recruited. Trade unions grew phenomenally after the end of World War II. An embryonic labor movement had emerged at the end of the nineteenth century but its growth, hindered by governmental suppression, was intermittent and small. In 1940 the government outlawed all unions, and they were not again permitted until after Japan's surrender in 1945. Within six months of this time, the trade-union movement had again reached the height of its pre-war development (420,000 members in 1936), and by 1957 membership had risen to nearly 7,000,000 workers (Levine 1958:67).

In summary, contrasts which may be drawn between Japan and the United States in patterns of social change are sharp, but the similarities nevertheless seem more striking and significant than the differences. Japan appears to be following the same general path of culture change in both the economic and social spheres as societies of the West but, in consider-

---

[3] A much less democratic program of land reform initiated at the end of the sixteenth century served in a similar but less far-reaching manner to inhibit the *dōzoku*.

able part because of impoverishment in natural resources, it has progressed less far. Our state of knowledge is yet too limited to allow us to delineate sharply the range of social structures compatible with any given type of economic system. It has long been adequate, however, to show that some forms are incompatible. In the infancy of anthropology, it seemed clear that social organization strongly based on kinship was a characteristic of only technologically simple primitive or peasant societies. This idea, subsequently obscured for a time, has now long met with such general acceptance that it is regarded by many as a truism. When an attempt is made to apply the generalization to modern Japan, however, the results are at first glance puzzling because in the social realm the new and the old co-exist and much of the new bears the imprint of the old. Despite its apparent strength in modern Japan, kinship has in the past century yielded much ground to impersonal institutions arising as concomitants of industrialization. The direction of change in Japanese social organization has, in fact, been toward increasing similarity to conditions prevailing in the United States. This trend is all the more impressive in view of the vast differences which existed between the two cultures a century ago. The case seems to be one of similar influences yielding similar results.

These words do not mean to say that Japan will ever coincide in social organization with the United States even if, to present a wholly hypothetical situation, its economic structure were to become identical with that of this country. They are intended instead to point up meaningful similarities in the social realm that have accompanied similar changes in economic organization, and to warn against the danger of their becoming obscured by attention to striking but less fundamental differences.

BIBLIOGRAPHY

ACKERMAN, EDWARD A.
  1953 *Japan's Natural Resources and their Relation to Japan's Economic Future.* Chicago, The University of Chicago Press
ARIGA, KIZAEMON
  1940 *Nihon Shakai no Kenkyū.* Tokyo, Kawade Shōbō.
  1948 *Sonraku Seikatsu.* Tokyo, Kokuritsu Shoin.
  1955 "The Contemporary Japanese Family in Transition." *Transactions of the Third World Congress of Sociology,* 4:215–221.

ARIGA, K., T. NAKANO, and K. MORIOKA
1954 "The Japanese Family." *Transactions of the Second World Congress of Sociology,* 1:83–89.

BEFU, HARUMI and EDWARD NORBECK
1958 "Japanese Usages of Terms of Relationship." *Southwestern Journal of Anthropology,* 14:66–86.

BENNETT, JOHN W. and MICHIO NAGAI
1953 "A Summary and Analysis of 'The Familial Structure of Japanese Society' by Takeyoshi Kawashima." *Southwestern Journal of Anthropology,* 9:239–50.

BROWN, DELMER M.
1951 *Money Economy in Medieval Japan.* New Haven, Yale University Press.

BUREAU OF STATISTICS
1957 *Japan Statistical Yearbook, 1955–56.* Tokyo, Office of the Prime Minister.

CORNELL, JOHN B. and ROBERT J. SMITH
1956 *Two Japanese Villages.* Ann Arbor, University of Michigan Press.

FUKUTAKE, TADASHI
1952 *Nihon Nōson no Shakaiteki Seikaku.* Tokyo, Tokyo University Press.

ISHINO, IWAO
1953 "The Oyabun-Kobun: A Japanese Ritual Kinship Institution." *American Anthropologist,* 55:695–707.

IZUMI, SEIICHI and MASAO GAMŌ
1952 *Nihon Shakai no Chiikisei.* Tokyo, Kawade Shōbō.

LEVINE, SOLOMON B.
1958 *Industrial Relations in Postwar Japan.* Urbana, University of Illinois Press.

LOCKWOOD, WILLIAM W.
1955 *The Economic Development of Japan: Growth and Structural Change, 1868–1938.* Princeton, Princeton University Press.

MASUOKA, JITSUICHI
1947 "Urbanization and the Family in Japan." *Sociology and Research,* 32:535–539.

MATSUMIYA, KAZUYA
1947 "Family Organization in Present-day Japan." *American Journal of Sociology,* 53:105–110.

NAGAI, MICHIO
1953 "Dōzoku: A Preliminary Study of the Japanese 'Extended Family'

Group and Its Social and Economic Functions." *The Ohio State University Research Foundation, Interim Technical Report,* 7.

NORBECK, EDWARD

1953 "Age-Grading in Japan." *American Anthropologist,* 55:373–384.

1954 *Takashima, A Japanese Fishing Community.* Salt Lake City, University of Utah Press.

NORBECK, EDWARD and HARUMI BEFU

1958 "Informal Fictive Kinship in Japan." *American Anthropologist,* 60:102–117.

OKADA, YUZURU

1952 "Kinship Organization in Japan." *The Journal of Educational Psychology,* 26:27–31.

RAPER, A. L., *et al.*

1950 "The Japanese Village in Transition." *General Headquarters, Tokyo, Supreme Commander for the Allied Powers, Natural Resources Section, Report,* 136.

SANSOM, G. B.

1951 *The Western World and Japan.* New York, Alfred A. Knopf.

TAEUBER, IRENE

1951 "Family, Migration and Industrialization in Japan." *American Sociological Review,* 16:149–157.

* * * *

Marvin K. Opler

UNIVERSITY OF BUFFALO

CULTURAL EVOLUTION AND THE

PSYCHOLOGY OF PEOPLES

Evolution is a process by which specific kinds of integration, of matter, of life, or of culture, undergo transformations from one type to another. In each realm, physical, organic or cultural, we speak of this process as a generic one. We do not, for example, refer to various *evolutions* in the organic world from Paramecium to Aunt Polly. Nor do we confuse the process that produced Aunt Polly with the process that produced the physical world she inhabits, or the cultural world she may, more or less, participate in as she lives her life. Thus we do not talk of various kinds of cultural evolutions to explain social and behavioral developments along the human pathway from hunting and gathering to atomic energy. The process is one.

The focus in each type of evolution is upon regularities of this general process. In a science of culture, it is recognized that each kind of integration and change is dependent upon the general nature of culture itself. If the stories of cultures are to become a general science of culture, general principles of integration and change must be established. It is true, also, that this generic process may have particular aspects. That is to say, culture has such aspects as the material, the social, the ideational, and the behavioral. White has commented on anthropologists' attitudes, especially in America, toward generalizing *versus* particularizing (White 1949:55–117). It is no doubt true, in science as it is in logic, that an expansion of the scope of science occurs when wider generalizations are attempted and evolutionary principles established.

In American anthropology, as we shall see, a recent tendency has been to particularize about given cultures or geographical areas. However, this tendency has not constituted the major difficulty standing in the way of analysis of general cultural process. If our views of specific cultures, areas, or traditions in each case analyzed a kind of integration or a type of change accurately, we would undoubtedly find analyses of the general process in culture emerging naturally and somewhat inductively from these data. But few sciences are built in this fashion, and anthropology has been no exception. An exclusive preoccupation with specific cultures is a deterrent to generalization. Yet a more basic difficulty standing in the way of analysis of general process is seen when we ask not only *why*, but *how*, American anthropologists have tended to particularize. While most have avoided analyses of general process beyond single cultural or traditional boundaries, this has been done by confusing questions of integration and change with psychological interpretations. Of this confusion, White said: "Psychology and culturology deal therefore with biological and extra-somatic aspects respectively of one and the same set of events. Both sciences are essential to a comprehensive interpretation of human behavior. It is necessary, however, in order to avoid confusion, to know and respect the proper boundaries of each" (White 1949:145).

However, one aspect of culture is cultural behavior; and moreover, psychology deals not only with biological aspects of human adaptation (or "adjustment"), but with cultural or extra-somatic aspects of human behavior as well. The confusion lies in failure to link the psychological *with* cultural interpretations, and to recognize that psychology (that is, the psychology of peoples) is a result of such cultural influences as the material conditions under which a culture operates. Further, the way in which society is organized directly influences behavior. In this sense, cultural existence functions as *the* human psychological environment. The "psychologies of peoples," rather than being causal in the cultural equation, actually result from both the extra-somatic as well as the biological events White discusses. The real confusion lies not only in particularizing or in avoiding analyses beyond one cultural or traditional boundary, but in the confusions of integration and change which occur with *assumptively causal psychological explanations*.

In other words, cultural integration and cultural change, both key concepts in any evolutionary process, are often themselves blurred in American anthropology because of further basic confusions as to the role of psychology. The explanations of integration, ordinarily based on particular cultures, are usually psychological in character. Yet as we shall see, these explanations are usually proposed as causal statements of cultural change or dynamics. Psychological approaches to given cultures are used to account for both cultural stability or cultural change. Recently in American and British anthropology, such approaches have frequently been offered as alternatives to cultural evolution. Finally, psychological approaches to cultural integration replace principles of evolution by proposing that culture is, in essence, psychological in character.

This difficulty may be resolved by noting that while cultural behavior is by definition psychological, *the psychology of peoples is cultural.* The psychology of a culture becomes understandable only in the light of its being one aspect of the culture as a whole. It is a part or an aspect of culture. A generalized psychology of peoples therefore depends upon the evolution of the culture and is illumined by the material conditions of existence in that culture. Psychology is, then, a result of environmental influences in which culture and the conditions of cultural existence always operate. There is no doubt *an evolution of behavior,* not as Spencer saw it apart from and causal to cultural developments, but as an ingredient and as a *consequence* of those developments.

The fact is that integration and change, which are Spencerian concepts, figure in evolution which includes behavior as well as social forms. A kind of integration presupposes a type of change, whether we are speaking of social organization or behavior. Actually, all cultural integrations appear to be based on two essential types of phenomena: first, a material base of culture acting upon the conditions of existence within that traditional setting and changing traditions with changes in the material base; second, the manner in which these conditions of existence are socially organized. The first factor is obviously a basic motive power or causal element in cultural change. The second, affecting any actual process of transformation, is not merely epiphenomenal, although it is a result of the first factor. Rather it is present and contributes to the aim and direction of an evolutionary process.

This does not mean, in the triad of material conditions, social organization, and behavior, that behavior or psychological phenomena can mysteriously determine the direction of change; nor can they singlehandedly produce a type of cultural integration. There is no such thing as a psychology of peoples apart from the conditions of existence, but there is, indeed, such generalized psychologies connected both with material conditions and social milieu. Some have proposed that evolution in culture occurs regardless of a psychological process. To the contrary, the causal chain goes from a material base and the manner in which these conditions of existence are socially organized, to a *resultant* behavior, or psychology, of peoples. To be sure, there is no such thing as "psychology" predetermining the material base or social organization, since a generalized psychology of a people is the result of the vicissitudes of the evolutionary process. However, this does not relegate psychology to a negligible or wholly unimportant role in the actual lives of actual people. As a dependent or resultant variable, as a particular aspect of culture and evolution, as a potent force in specific human lives, and as a means of interpreting the meanings in culture, we prefer not to rule psychology out of court. In fact, uniformities in behavior and the psychology of peoples are the very stuff of culture, best studied as uniformities and typical relations in the cultural process; a generalized psychology is either a part of given integrations or of specific changes. This essay examines these positions in terms of a series of propositions and precepts stated by various teachers and colleagues with whom the author has been associated in the last three decades.

For example, one teacher, Ruth Benedict, wrote in *Patterns of Culture* of a final operating principle of "psychological selectivity" and "unconscious canons of choice" residing in each cultural pattern. This unique stamp she placed upon a cultural integration determined the formation or development of the pattern itself, according to her view. Her *Chrysanthemum and the Sword*, on patterns of Japanese culture, was attacked repeatedly for its nondynamic view, that is, for its failure to note class and regional variations and the various differences between pre- or post-Meiji Japan. More crucial, and less noticed, was the theory of cultural dynamics which she implied. According to both books, the development of total patterns is no more mysterious than the emergence of a style in art, or a type of emotional expression (Benedict 1934:24, 46–48, 237).

Benedict forgot, of course, in this analogy, that most of the affective expressions in a culture can express only the culture itself, or aspects of its organization. She failed to note, therefore, that her idea of cultural development was descriptive rather than analytic. In logic, such proofs or demonstrations are called circular. Her explanation begs the question: What in turn determines the principles of psychological selectivity which shape the culture pattern?

Benedict did not stand alone in this recourse to psychological "explanations" of cultural forms. Another of the author's teachers, Ralph Linton, wrote of a cultural basis of personality development, but this too referred merely to psychological descriptions of peoples, sometimes with historical overtones (Linton 1945; 1955). Linton provided his one exception to psychological reductionism in an analysis of shifts in Tanala culture subsequent to new modes of rice production. Otherwise, Linton implied, the tree of culture merely grew. In *The Study of Man,* his most influential work, there are triumphant announcements, running counter to the Tanala case, of technology and economic institutions reflecting a people's culture. For example, rank and status in one Polynesian culture are said to have modified the form of High Council chambers to a circular form accommodating many statuses! No doubt, the psychological bent in a culture affects technique and economy on occasion, but Linton adduced very flimsy evidence in one case to account for cultures in general. His cultural universals and alternatives, when examined, are really deep in the realm of attitude and motivational system. Thus the "tree of culture" grows, again as a shape or style, with periods, moods, regional and physiographic roots, and with an occasional impetus from a strong leader. Nothing could really explain culture. The "tree" simply puts down roots here and there in most of the world (Linton 1955).

Benedict alludes to Dilthey as sharing her view. But among her contemporaries who also stress psychological types in cultures, she might have referred equally to Sorokin's sensate and ideational cultures, or Kroeber's cultural climaxes as bearing a general resemblance to her own principle of psychological selection. Toynbee, too, prefers striking psychological examples. All these, and a host of others, postulate a history and prehistory in which forms are described and discussed in psychological terms. Sorokin's liking for medieval attitudes, Kroeber's interest in style and climax of historical patterns, and Benedict's predilection for describing polar psychological types are each emphases on given cultural systems of affect. They are intended to stand for theories of kinds of cultural development or dynamics. Sorokin so entitled his work (Sorokin 1937–1941), and Benedict entitled her first essay on the patterns in the American Southwest "psychological types," implying at the same time emergent, developing styles in culture (Benedict 1930; 1932).

Another teacher, Leslie A. White, has been more concerned with the theoretical distinctions between psychological and cultural phenomena. He has held that cultural evolution is best studied apart from psychological considerations—*as if* the individual and his psychology did not exist. Kroeber's doctrine of levels of organization provided a superorganic realm separate from psychology to be investigated by a separate science of culture. White studies culture as a thing of its own type, and in accordance with principles and techniques appropriate to such an entity. To understand this difference and the clash of doctrines adequately, we may allude next to the central position in the main stream in recent American anthropology, from which, as a matter of fact, Benedict's and Linton's work stemmed only as variations.

A fourth teacher, Franz Boas, represents this dominant position in twentieth-century American anthropology. Because of Boas' influence, and that of certain of his associates, American anthropologists came to be suspicious by and large of all general theories of cultural development. This applied equally to Graebnerian *Kulturkreislehre*, Spencerian evolutionism stressing laws of progress, or Lewis H. Morgan's anthropology, with its developing "germs of thought" and its theory of technological indicators and the influence of productive systems in cultural change. Boas advocated detailed descriptive studies of particular cultures and specific historical influences. Regarding dynamic questions, one spokesman of this school, Goldenweiser, repeatedly noted that his colleagues studied the place and function of various aspects of cultures in terms of psychological meanings to participants in these cultural systems. Thus, the American School of historical ethnology, as he termed it, disregarded general theories of development (Goldenweiser 1922; 1925). It was psychological rather than evolutionary, descriptive rather than generalizing or analytical, and devoted to the study of particular cultures and regional diffusions, rather than to the analysis of the cultural process in general. It was in this sense that Benedict and Linton, despite their modernizing tendencies here and there, represented movements well within the orbit of a nongeneralizing, particularistic, and psychological American anthropology.

This position or approach obviously applies better to questions of particular cultural integrations than to questions of integration in general. It is far distant, as a research design, from investigations of questions of general cultural evolution. To typify it theoretically, we may use the analogy of the common nursery game played by children in Japan. As in our children's game of matching digits of a hand, two Japanese children may symbolize any one of four objects by hand gestures. The objects symbolized are, for example, Scissors (two fingers), Paper (flat hand), Rock (fist), and Match (one finger). According to rules of the game, each object relates to another. Scissors can cut Paper and Match burns it. Rock blunts Scissors and breaks Match. But paper conceivably can be used to wrap a rock, so Paper stands highest in this single relationship. In other words, the possible connections of items in the series may be tested empirically. But consider the standard rule or convention by which no single item is always more effective in all relationships than any other. Science constantly seeks to isolate such selectively weighted and significant items which are constant in their effects in a total process. It explores dual relationships and connections of an item in larger configurations, to be sure, but it goes beyond this point to the elucidation of larger total processes and constant effects. One might call the Scissors-Match approach classificatory, descriptive, and historical, even though it weights one factor, in each instance differently, since it proceeds according to simple, nondynamic rules to classify and describe phenomena as they "seem" to occur. The similarities and differences in phenomena, or how "they hang together," will appeal to a descriptive classifier, like Linnaeus, or to one who is essentially an epitomizing poetic artist, like Benedict. One is essentially *describing* random relationships, not seeking invariant relations or causes. These approaches will set the descriptive tasks of a science far ahead. But the urge to describe and classify is not all of any science. Each science also seeks invariable relationships, regular processes, and laws or principles governing uniformities or similarities in a general process. Defining relations in given configurations is but a first short step towards locating regular processes in nature. Biology had its Linnaeus, but also, fortunately, its Darwin.

In American anthropology, from Boas to Benedict and Linton, static or functional relationships and historical inferences were most important, as if these led, somehow, to dynamic understanding of developmental process, or replaced it. The descriptive tasks of the science, the careful accumulation and classifying of data, *were* set far ahead. But the game continued, seemingly without end and without better-defined scientific purpose or goal. In a descriptive nongeneralizing or particularistic science, there are no parameters or set outer limits for determining probabilities and causal relationships, no search for invariant factors which are always significant, and consequently no discoveries of *regularities* in process. With Benedict, as we have seen, anthropologists were set a new descriptive task; the institutional relationships, she stated, were less important than the configuration itself (Benedict 1932; 1934). But in each such instance, as in her Southwestern studies, a psychological touchstone was sought to "explain" the emergent pattern (Benedict 1930). Linton's portrayal of specific cultures broadened at best to a larger historical delineation of particular traditions or geographic areas. But the tree of culture, even in the symbol selected to represent it—the banyan —in its growth and development, sent out aerial roots which only occasionally rooted in soil.

Edward Sapir, another gifted American anthropologist, summarized frankly and clearly in a work on *Time Perspective in Aboriginal American Culture* the bases for historical inference in continental areas. Sapir's chief contribution, aside from this monograph, was a volume called *Language.* Here, and elsewhere, Sapir sought to establish a theory of linguistic change which he appropriately called language "drift." Inspection of this theory indicates that it applied, somewhat coincidentally with Benedict's work on culture, the configurational approach to language structures, attempting to denote a genius, or special flair, or form-quality in whole families of languages. The word "drift" simply implied that qualitative or psychological tendencies in a language structure might become further adumbrated as the language changed slowly over time. It is obvious that Sapir's work just as that of Benedict or Linton falls within the orbit of the historical, particularistic, and psychological tradition of American anthropology though it stressed, at the same time, greater historical synthesis than Linton attempted. Sapir also paid much attention to psychological meanings in language as did Benedict's configurational approach in cultures. That the psychological theory of culture remained a matter of "unconscious patterning" was also made explicit by Sapir (1929). He attacked Kroeber's superorganic as an extraneous, unnecessary addition (Sapir 1917). Impressed by the subtlety and almost endless creativity of Man the Artificer, Sapir felt there could be no set limits for determining cultural regularities (Sapir 1929; 1934). In culture-personality theory, he spoke of "outlines, significances and demarcations" of conduct developed in specific cultural traditions, but such meanings or personalized interpretations required psychiatric, more than social, analysis (Sapir 1934; 1937). There was never the slightest hint in his work that any one item in a configuration weighed more heavily than all the rest. Again one finds description of psychological meanings within cultures, languages, and other forms of behavior, but these are largely categorized as unconscious patternings of conduct in society. Most crucial in understanding this penetrating and sensitive, but always elusive and nongeneralizing, quality in Sapir's work on language, culture, and personality is his feeling that human affairs are not underwritten by law or principle at all. They lend themselves only to historical and psychological description. Observing in one essay that the laws of crystallography, for example, applied to phenomena that are unchanging, Sapir contrasted human affairs as being unpredictable in advance or unceasingly changing in retrospect (Sapir 1929). This, again, is the position of the descriptive historian, not the social and cultural analyst. Despite the complexity of all systems of nature, scientists assume that the tools of analysis may be shaped to investigate any materials at hand. If, indeed, culture changes, then investigate its change. However, Sapir's talent was never so employed. In anthropological linguistics, in culture, and in personality study, or in ethnology, he developed only the descriptive and particularistic aspect of science which appealed to more pedestrian colleagues.

It is fitting that someone as perceptive as Sapir should have noticed the fact of cultural change, society's dynamism, as being a basic characteristic of culture even if this fundamental proposition about change were used in so curious or limiting a fashion. For crystallography, his "science with laws" is the epitome of a descriptive, nongeneralizing, and particularistic science, however much it is related to more dynamic disciplines. In science, moreover, we have learned that all systems of nature have their complications and time enters into all of them. To suppose a timeless, ideal type of understanding is to go back to Plato and away from a philosophy of science, or naturalism. Even in respect to atoms of a given type, we now know ordinary predictions and laws of probability give way to stochastic or somewhat less determinate rules and measures, in order better to investigate hidden probabilities, varying time values, and dynamic change. Most positively, the laws of crystals will differ from the analysis of stochastic principles applied to the radium atom, or from cultural laws in form and content. But to suppose that causal inquiry and some kind of probability, or science itself, will stop at a cultural boundary in the universe is arbitrary and quixotic in the extreme.

If one searches the positions which Goldenweiser termed the American School, one finds no variation in this point of view. Two British anthropologists, after distinguished careers in England, came to the United States where they were influential in the early 1930's. Each man, Bronislaw Malinowski and A. R. Radcliffe-Brown, adopted the term, functionalism. In both positions, the familiar point was made that an aspect of culture interpenetrates with or relates to another, and for both men such functional interrelations overshadowed an interest in historical questions. This stress on function and integration is seen clearly in Malinowski's view of the institutional parts of culture: religion, social organization, and economy, for examples. As in the Scissors-Match game, ultimately this method stressed an integration in which the parts of a culture functioned or "interrelated" with perfect equality. This lifelong preoccupation with a merry-go-round view of single cultures, with "integration" as Malinowski had described it painstakingly for the Trobriand Islands, was repeated in a series of volumes from 1927 to 1935. Malinowski held that no part of culture is basic to its final integration. Where a general theory, say of magic, is developed, it is based wholly on psychological attitudes within a cultural setting (for example, the point at which uncertainty and fear may enter in).

A. R. Radcliffe-Brown, while developing a theory favoring the study of cultural integration, was somewhat anomalous in his distaste for approaches emphasizing psychological factors to account for this phenomenon. He was also at odds with the general current of opinion favoring historical reconstruction. To him, "synchronic" research, as he called it, was the study of social organization and kinship system, and was basic to any understanding of integration. This must precede "diachronic" research, the analysis of change. Although he presumed he followed Durkheim, the only intrusion of the latter's extensive theorizing on a doctrine of cultural conditioning appeared in Radcliffe-Brown's descriptive listing of social sanctions, ritual, punitive, or collective in character. In such a system the basis for behavior is seen as social, and this conceptual system is descriptive rather than dynamic. It contrasts with the historical-descriptive theories of Boas and his followers, but yet it agrees with them that no general theories of development account for any culture or cultures in the plural. The Boasian group might study limited influences and diffusions, such as the diffusion of traits in the Sun Dance or the influence of the horse in Plains Indian cultures, but Radcliffe-Brown insisted on static, cross-sectional studies of social organization, ritual, or penal and legalistic matters, as a basis of comparative analysis. While Radcliffe-Brown rounded out his system with vague allusions, à la Spencer, to types of integration which were narrow or wide in extent, and close or loose in Durkheimian social solidarity, neither he nor the Boasian group can be safely credited with a dynamic or a generalizing position in anthropology, since both advocated studies of specific integrations.

The historical-descriptive theory of Boas and his associates was even more popular in American anthropology than Radcliffe-Brown's parallel emphasis on integration when Leslie White took up the cudgels for cultural evolutionism. There has been much discussion, entirely behind the scenes, as to whether cudgels preceded careful exposition of the evolutionary position. Of all those mentioned above, White agreed only with Radcliffe-Brown and Kroeber in separating psychological from cultural study; but at the same time his interest is focussed on process, and he stresses cultural change and evolution, whereas Radcliffe-Brown's interest was static or "synchronic." The author, having studied with White, Boas, Benedict, Linton, and others, and having had, in his formative years, extensive correspondence with Malinowski and Sapir, cannot be accused of simple partisanship. In searching for a fruitful and creative synthesis in anthropology, one must especially consider scientific theories in relationship to the purposes and methods of science in general.

A science systematically extends its exploration of an aspect of nature usually after a first descriptive-observational or classificatory phase. The theories we have reviewed in anthropology, with the exception of White's, mark such an initial period, since the main effort is to observe, describe, and classify cultural phenomena. It is instructive, therefore, to consider movements in the history of science which followed similar initial descriptive tendencies.

The Copernican revolution in astronomy and its strengthening by Galileo occurred in a setting of observation and description in which earlier confusions in the analysis of process required major correction by sound evolutionary principles. The warfare between evolution in astronomy and theological dogma was still being waged in the nineteenth century when geologists demonstrated that not only had a solar system evolved, but the earth too had developed according to definite processes. The battles of Darwin and Huxley came next, though Linnaean classification preceded them by a full century. An order of evolutionary discoveries, from the remote astronomic to the earth and life sciences in the sixteenth to nineteenth centuries, witnessed extensions of developmental principles much as our own century has begun to see them applied occasionally in psychological and social sciences. In biology, psychiatry, psychology, and anthropology, the descriptive phases preceded analytic ones.

Just as in geology, where its descriptive-exploratory schools came first, so in biology, descriptive-classificatory or taxonomic movements preceded Darwinism. In psychiatry, one thinks of early German descriptive schools and Kraepelinean classifications making their appearance. The analogies between a nonanalytic behaviorism in psychology and an equally nonanalytic functionalism in anthropology are not chance phenomena in the philosophy of science; nor are the configuration-Gestaltist movements, the clinical Freudian emphases on genetic history, or ideas of stimulus-diffusion in both the psychological and anthropological fields. For some, culture-personality theory in anthropology has meant the simplest kind of merger between descriptive psychology and descriptive anthropology, marked by the use of Freudian clinical models of the effects of childhood disciplines. Descriptive-historical positions run parallel, but these are followed by analytic and dynamic approaches in each discipline as it matures (Opler 1942; 1956a).

In the development of analytic and dynamic approaches in maturing disciplines, science integration and cross-fertilization may even give rise to new interdisciplinary fields as inventories and observational phases are at some point supplemented by such general analytic formulations. One thinks of astrophysics, biophysics, and biochemistry, geochronological and biochronological methods in archaeology, serological and genetic studies in physical anthropology, or ethnopsychiatry and comparative social psychology. While evolution operates in the physical, biological, and cultural systems of nature, it is obvious today that the Spencerian theory of an organic and psychological evolution governing social and cultural development is definitely not the key. A refinement in technique, such as geochronological dating derived from physics, has not added or detracted one bit from evolutionary principle though it has made history more accurate.

However, comparative social psychology and ethnopsychiatry can throw light on aspects of cultural evolution precisely because they deal with symbolization processes and the psychology of peoples. Rather than return to Spencerian formulations, based on ignorance, we suggest that emergent evolution is closer to the mark in that wholly new *systems* appear in nature, and require analysis, even though the novel appearances are based upon successive transformations affecting life forms. As White has noted, man's evolution from earlier primates has given rise to new forms in behavior or psychological functioning. It is his work on the importance of symbol-using in human behavior, or in culture, that points to a functional difference in the psychology of humans as the Pandora's Box of cultural emergence. Man as a social and political animal depends upon energy harnessed within specific cultures for the type of social structure which develops.

Alfred North Whitehead's idea of separate systems of evolution and organization in nature, operating on different levels, is similar to White's, as are his warnings against the fallacy of reductionism, of reducing the terms of one system (like the cultural) to those of another (like the psychological). This does not mean behavioral variations are not linked to cultural evolution, or that ethnopsychiatry is not, rightly, a part of anthropology. Such reductionism to sometimes vague and repetitious "First Principles" plagued Spencer's *Principles of Sociology*. It still plagues a good many anthropologists who castigate Spencer for what they call his ethnocentric Victorian racism, but who nevertheless "explain" whole cultures or even cultural "dynamics," as we have seen, by some bald and unadorned psychogenetic principles.

Whitehead also spoke of a fallacy of misplaced concreteness which is relevant at this point. It is not that a people's psychological functioning is unrelated to their cultural forms, Radcliffe-Brown notwithstanding, but that behavior in a most active and everyday sense is the very stuff of cultural forms. However, the approach through the individual is not, statistically, the study of normative culture or necessarily a study of its characteristic ranges of behavior. Even more important, in anthropology, the material conditions under which a culture operates constitute the setting and *binding conditions* affecting this *range* of behavior. To put the matter otherwise, that culture limits itself (and not people), is a prime example of misplaced concreteness. One fallacy lies in explaining material conditions under which a culture operates by psychological resultants; another fallacy consists in mistaking individualized affects, as in consequences of early childhood training, for group psychological norms which may or may not be consistent with them. Of all Benedict's papers on the psychology of peoples, the most useful one runs counter to ideas of psychological epitomizations of whole cultures, and is on continuities and discontinuities in *cultural* conditioning. In this paper, Benedict deals with cultural forces and conflicts influencing psychology, not the opposite, as in most of her work (Benedict 1938).

Sapir and Linton were more consistent in seeking a cultural basis for personality development (Linton 1945; Sapir 1948). However, in the Linton collaborations with Kardiner, this position is fairly negated by portrayals of cultural systems as stemming from systems of child-care. Sapir's concern with why cultural anthropology needed "the psychiatrist" is certainly ambivalent, if not contradictory, in reducing cultures to the status of mere epiphenomena, while proclaiming elsewhere the formative influence of culture. Neither Linton nor Sapir hints that the material conditions under which a culture operates, and which affect social structure, the value system, or religion, will inevitably affect the unconscious patterning of personality as well. For both men, the cultural emphases in discussions of normative personality development remained on descriptive, nongeneralizing planes, applicable only to specific cultures.

We have already noted that these theories of culture and personality apply better to discussions of particular cultural integrations than to questions of integration in general. No doubt, this delimitation troubled many anthropologists seeking psychological explanations of cultural forms.

Though violently opposed by Sapir and Linton, the tendency of those attempting wider generalizations was to confuse culture and clinic, and to find in Freudian explanations of clinical phenomena the universal explications for any human behavior (Opler 1956a). The difficulty with these last generalizing, analytic formulations is that they did not concern culture. When Benedict indicated that "abnormals" of one culture might be the "normals" of another, she displayed considerable ignorance of clinical psychiatry. When, on the other hand, Roheim and others claimed to have found psychopathology a chief characteristic in most nonliterate cultures they discussed, they entirely missed the adaptive and creative features of such societies, imputing statistical significance to shreds and patches of psychiatric evidence before they established the norms and the clinical proofs from which pathology could be inferred. Since it is our position that a general and analytic concept of integration and reintegration or change mediates between cultural evolution and the psychology of peoples, the remainder of this essay will be devoted to these relationships.

Although culture is, as Tolstoi said, "what men live by," its presence in all human groups is not haphazard or random. White has noted that energy-utilizations and symbolizations constitute its chief mechanisms, and these permit tool-specializations, productive systems, and growth of knowledge or control over nature, which, together with symbol-using, are peculiar to *Homo sapiens*. None of the categories in the above listing are immutable by their very nature. There may even be retrogression in one part of the world or another without basic interference with the evolution of culture as a whole. Two grimly destructive world wars in the twentieth century illustrate this. With progress and retrogression, with recurrent debasement of humans over continents and in remote island territories, this century has been thus far a period of contradiction, of steps forward and stumblings down blind paths of reaction. Over wide areas, advances in technological application of physical sciences have been achieved, while social science has been applied very little. The twentieth century has been to the present a century of engineering and of dangerous drifts, of speed in communication and of towering barriers, of remarkable discoveries and deepening fears. Nor is the contention of a Toynbee, that a dozen civilizations have come and gone, really reassuring. The anthropologist, with easier access to the solace of centuries, is also the most aware of the passing of social isolation in the remotest regions of the modern world. For him, the species is one under different cultural banners. As cultural processes converge in modern history, it becomes more important than ever to understand cultural process in general.

In this setting of modern times, anthropology was born with great promise. It boldly explored social relationships between the wars, and captured with some success and prodigious labor the many patterns of culture fast being caught in the current flow of intercultural communication. If culture is what men live by, science is today their chief weapon. The older social sciences could not deal adequately with man's course since they were, after all, not holistic in their approach and geographically delimited in perspective. Anthropology spanned the range of social relationships and ambitiously covered the world. It was concerned with revealing the nature of all social phenomena which are fundamentally human and cultural. Such revelations required an ever wider integration of facts, but more important, the tactic of ordering data. Such an organization of data, as we have seen, came under descriptive, particularistic, and psychological rubrics, and not under general analytic principles of cultural process. Consequently, the progress that was made was from essentially idle antiquarianism to cultural history, from the comparative method of tearing traits and complexes out of context to fit preconceptions to studies of given cultural integrations, and from isolation to active collaboration with other behavioral sciences. However, descriptions were not analysis, and this much was done without benefit of dynamic or analytic principles. It did not, for example, challenge Malinowski's merry-go-round view of culture in which nothing is basic or formative in any given integration.

To understand why anthropology turned its back on analytic tasks and exhibited studied preoccupation with data-gathering and description, one must realize that the new science, or series of sciences dealing with man and culture, developed in a period of conflict. As Lancelot Hogben has pointed out, scientific knowledge, even in its more puristic mathematical forms, reflects the organization and problems of the real world. Twentieth-century culture and society—in a half-century of contradiction—has been caught between the necessity of a science of man and culture and the very conflicts affecting science and ethics. The fear of formulating general principles may be noted in such classic essays as Boas' "Limitations of the Comparative Method of Anthropology" (1896), stating hesitantly that laws and principles of cultural development may someday be found, and again in his "Aims of Anthropological Research," thirty-six years later (1932), which despaired of any such possibility.

The contrast with White's sense of urgency in this respect and his pleas for a science of man and culture, founded on principles, is all the more noticeable when we review the meanings of anthropology in early, more hopeful periods.

From Aristotle on, the term anthropology is used. To Aristotle, despite his generous use of the organic analogy, culture was a thing *sui generis*, requiring separate study along with man, equally a product of a separate evolution. While encyclopedists of the Enlightenment stressed traditional aspects of human experience in the same scientific spirit, the data of anthropology from the sixteenth to eighteenth centuries lent themselves to speculative, if not wholly imaginative, outlooks. Yet to Rousseau, the men of the Enlightenment, and the naturalistic materialists must go credit for seeking rewarding values and meaningful ways of life in other cultural milieus.

Increasingly, however, scientists required data from cultures the world over. As American anthropology came on the scene, with men like Jefferson, Gallatin, and Morgan, the inflated myths about "primitive man" had already become fantastic and baseless. Concerted efforts of anthropology served to lay the ghosts of the "primitive mind," the White Man's "burdens," and the popular prejudgments. Regional studies and monographs revealed a wide range of customs across continents, both ethnographically and archaeologically. The visit of Humboldt to America in 1804, the linguistic classification of Amerinds by Albert Gallatin in 1836, the monumental fieldwork and publication of Lewis H. Morgan from 1850 to 1881, the founding of the Bureau of American Ethnology by J. W. Powell and William H. Holmes in the last quarter of the century, and of the Peabody Museum, largely through the efforts of Frederic Putnam in the quarter before, indicate the tempo of anthropological development in the United States. It appeared, at first, that there was no one drama of the human life cycle, no single model of cultural adaptation to the world, no universal touchstone of belief for achieving rapport with the universe, and no fixity in art style or philosophy.

In 1886, Daniel G. Brinton founded the first department of anthropology at the University of Pennsylvania, his title stressing linguistics and archaeology. Before the turn of the century, the general trend of anthropology in America was not far different from the European tradition built up from Linnaeus and Blumenbach to emphases on physical anthropology, archaeology, and broader conceptual trends implied in the names of Tylor, Bastian, and Waitz. To match Tylor and Waitz in European cultural anthropology, America had its Lewis H. Morgan.

These great synthesizers, European and American, augmented the search for facts and the organization of fast-accumulating data by an even greater concern for their context long before the fashion for functionalism. Social science, like all science, was the discovery and denoting of general regularities in *processes,* particularly in such social and cultural phenomena as were found to be essentially dynamic. There were then limits to such data. But sparse as the facts were, they were analyzed according to logical and realistically conceived method. This early trend toward a generalizing science of culture proved that anthropology was too advanced in data, methods, and perspective by 1900 to be called a product of the twentieth century. Since then, its sustained and current impact on the social sciences give it its particular claim to modernity. Other social sciences neither have the tools, nor, at times, the inclination to analyze whole cultures, intercultural relations, or cultural process. For this reason, philosophers like Cassirer have at times assumed the title of anthropologist. Historians like Toynbee, Turner, or Beard have attempted to blend historical description with cultural analysis; and psychologists, psychiatrists, and sociologists have turned to anthropology for cross-cultural perspective.

However, general dynamic analyses of culture gave way to relatively simple propositions such as the claim that major social segments of any culture are structured and have definable functions, or that man's characteristic psychodynamic tendencies in any group are also structured and reflect the interpenetrations of culture and personality. Such theories of integration are themselves formal. They are solipsismal in that they are limited to current deductions about single traditions, and incapable of further dynamic generalization. Cultures do not exist in traditional immutability, and the society embodying a tradition cannot remain static any more than its individual culture-carriers can. In this sense, a society is more or less structured, and its definable functions are merely a current balance of forces, social in origin and expression. Even psychodynamic tendencies in individuals and groups exist only as balances of forces which men like Freud saw as being often in opposition, or in the polite diplomacy of truce.

A cultural integration, far from being a sculptured, fixed, and inevitable arrangement of constants, psychological in nature, such as Benedict and others sought to describe, is constantly in a state of flux. It is only a more or less stable set of conditions for social existence found among specified groups of mankind and operating for limited spans of time. Thus cultural integrations contain within themselves the seeds of reintegration or change. Just as all grammatical structures or morphological systems of language are imperfect, or as Sapir bluntly put it, "all grammars leak," so social structures and kinship systems are merely outlines and general indicators of conduct and custom. Social organization is ordinarily most responsive to the steady and inevitable impact of material conditions of existence. Since a culture contains the traditional modes of coping with both physical and human nature, its economy and social organization will of necessity be related. When this relationship becomes tenuous through changes in economy, either the old society and cultural traditions change in a process of reintegration, or the cracks and fissures multiply and the culture dies. The past is strewn with both instances: reintegration and forward development in some traditions as society and culture develop, or disintegration, death, and decay in others. Benedict and others have written that necessity is *not* the mother of invention, either in economic or social affairs. Perhaps not, so far as the slow but rapidly increasing tempo of economic and scientific inventions goes. At any rate, on the social and cultural side, material inventions become the mother of necessity; and either necessary social changes are made or the society goes under.

At one time, anthropology had such perspectives. As early as 1844 in the United States, Gallatin, as founder and president of the American Ethnological Society, wrote into the constitution of that body, "The object of this society shall comprise inquiries into the origin, progress and characteristics of . . . man." Jenks, writing with Rivers and Morley by request of the Carnegie Institution of Washington, also stated in 1913 that "the anthropologist . . . makes his studies of both the past and the present with an eye to the future, in order that those things which vitiated or benefited the evolutionary process in the past, and which vitiate and benefit it today, may serve as guides for future generations" (1913:54). Sir Edward Tylor's closing passage of his great work, *Anthropology,* put this matter clearly as early as 1881: "Mankind is passing from the age of unconscious to that of conscious progress. . . . The study of man and civilization passes at once into the practical business of life." Either anthropology today accepts this challenge to formulate a dynamic science of culture, or we blindly and emotionally renounce the practical aspects of human existence.

Having already noted that questions of particular cultural integrations are different from the question of integration in general, we are faced with an old problem of whether mankind should be studied in unity or diversity. In biology, one thinks of Claude Bernard's famous aphorism:

"The life of the animal is only a fragment of the total life of the universe." In cultures, which grow and change not only through internal inventions and accretions, but through contact and diffusions, the life of a single culture is but an instance in the story of culture in general. In Raoul Allier's badly-titled *The Mind of the Savage* (*n.d.*), the anthropological tradition of the fundamental unity of the human species is presented, especially as it emerged in French social thought. The position of Fontenelle, so characteristic of the eighteenth century, was that culture alone made men diverse, while psychological equality and the even distribution of natural gifts argued for a fundamental unity of mankind. With Helvetius and Montesquieu, comparisons of humanity in general with man in Europe (termed "savages" by Voltaire) led to the idealization of nonliterate peoples. The classic statement of Baron de Lahontan, "They know nothing of thine and mine, have no class distinctions, but live in the state of equality nature intended," is an attempt at such dignifying, which Comte rephrased in opposition to Rousseau as evidence merely of higher potentialities always present in man.

In anthropology, early periods of discovery and first formulations provided more than descriptive data and methodological cautions. In general approaches to man and culture, anthropologists were busy laying the ghosts of exploration and conquest. Racial mentality was recognized as the empty echo of self-interested minds. Human nature was seen undergoing transformations in the crucibles of culture. What was added to eighteenth century romanticism, however, was mainly the first clause in the dictum: "Cultures are many, though man is one." Even before Boas, the second clause had been recognized in the anti-racistic emphases of the French Enlightenment, the naturalistic materialists, the schools of fundamental human unity, and the more penetrating evolutionists like Tylor and Morgan.

At this point, a reference to Theodor Waitz is instructive. Waitz, in his *Anthropologie der Naturvölker* (1859–1872), proceeds immediately from a position assuming fundamental unity of man to an analysis of what "human nature" basically includes. Here we are reminded much more pointedly of White than Boas. Culture, as a superorganic adaptation to man's need for food, shelter, and protection, as a mode of regulating human relations, and as expressed in religion, art, recreation, and knowledge, is despite manifold forms and exemplifications a generic *process* coexistent with mankind. By page 272 of the first volume, the bases of all human or cultural behavior are isolated in the ability to make tools and to symbolize, especially by means of that "specific human peculiarity, language." To be sure, in Waitz as in Boas, the shibboleth of the "primitive mind" is assaulted vigorously, but while Boas is led to present the data of cultures piecemeal and in separate and supposedly unique circumstances, the method of Waitz is synthesizing and generalizing. One is reminded here of Kroeber's critique of Boas in the essay, "History and Science in Anthropology" (1935):

> From physics Boas brought into anthropology a sense of definiteness of problem, of exact rigor of method, and of highly critical objectivity (p. 539). In brief, one may define the Boas position as . . . being aware of the requirements of cultural or human material: the need for all possible context, the strong element of uniqueness in all the phenomena, and extreme caution of generalizations savoring of the universal. All these are criteria of sound historical method; and because he observes them, Boas is right in insisting over and over again that he uses historical method. Only he does not *do* history. And that does make some difference (p. 544).

Obviously, one cannot *do* history, much less generalizations on processes in culture, until one notes similarities as well as differences. How far Kroeber was correct in intimating that a doctrine of cultural diversity led Boas to historical atomism may be seen in further examination of the latter's paper, "The Aims of Anthropological Research" (1932). After indicating certain obvious correlations between population size and food supply, Boas attacks materialistic explanations:

> We do not see how art styles, the form of ritual or the special form of religious belief could possibly be derived from economic forces. . . . Economics and the rest of culture interact as cause and effect, as effect and cause. Every attempt to deduce cultural forms from a single cause is doomed to failure, for the various expressions of culture are closely interrelated and one cannot be altered without having an effect on all the others. . . . It seems justifiable to question whether any general conclusions may be expected that will be applicable everywhere and that will reduce the data of anthropology to a formula which may be applied to every case, explaining its past and predicting the future (1932:608–9).

This tendency of history to describe the unique event led Boas to conclude that anthropology "must be a historical science . . . the interest of which centers in the attempt to understand the individual phenomena rather than the establishment of general laws." If this were history, wrote Boas, then psychology would consist in seeing "how many of our lines of behavior that we believe to be founded deep in human nature are actually expressions of our culture and subject to modification with

· 373

changing culture. . . . By a study of the universality and variety of cultures, anthropology may help us to shape the future course of mankind" (*ibid.*:612–613).

How this generous light could be shed without knowledge of the laws and principles governing cultural change and development was not considered. What art, social organization, ritual, and religion contributed to the psychic economy of individuals and the social economy of cultures was not explained. Of particular interest here is the amazing claim that close interrelation of the expressions of a culture blurs cause and effect relationships. On the contrary, it should make these all the more apparent. Obviously, this is again the merry-go-round view of single cultures. But more important for our thesis, we find that it is not a fruitful theory of integration for a single culture and even less a theory of cultural integration in general. Again, the Scissors-Match game is proclaimed to be the final aim of anthropology. It is suggested, to correct such aberrations, that if the amazingly complex material universe may be approached by formulae—not one, but several—then cultural phenomena, especially in terms of the relations of institutional aspects in change, may also be so expressed.

While, indeed, history may describe the unique event, science does not stop there. Anthropology is not mere descriptive history, but the science of man and culture. Therefore, a useful theory of cultural integration, one which explains and analyzes rather than merely describes cultures, must have general as well as specific reference.

Turning to Boas' second proposition, the notion that human psychology is merely an expression of a *particular* cultural content, how then can one explain, as Boas was fond of doing, any independent inventions? How account for such forms as clans, states, nomadic bands, totemism, shamanism, priestly cults, or indeed, any of a variety of phenomena found across continents and in remote island territories? A. A. Goldenweiser attempted in a paper called "The Principle of Limited Possibilities . . ." (1913) to set formal limits within which human creativity operates. Yet within such limits, the many minor variations on basic themes seem unrestricted, and human creativeness is certainly not at fault. Boas' statement that a change in *any* one aspect of culture changes all the rest appears unlikely in the light of survivals, cultural persistence, and traditions which resist change. Boas erroneously applied equal weight to all aspects of culture.

A notion of interests—economic, sexual, and artistic—might be helpful here, provided we rid ourselves of the extravagant idea that "anything" can happen in culture. In the human species, man must first seek food, shelter, and protection to survive, and all social systems emphasize some form or elaborated versions of these simple economic functions. There is no society which does not regulate, or formalize, social and sexual relationships. All develop ideas and practices for achieving some type of relationship or rapport with the universe. They contain in all instances forms of artistic expression and types of recreation. But in no instance are the psychological capabilities and biological or social needs separate from the meanings of a culture to its carriers. There is no formal, psychological limitation to human invention, imagination, or culture, except the material conditions under which a culture exists, and its systems for regulating conduct. Economic and technical aspects of a culture set the limits and constitute the bases of culture, and even these change. The formal similarities noted by Goldenweiser, both in technique and in the social superstructure of cultures, generally are due to similarities if not identities, as he found them, in the evolutionary process the world over.

Our review of tendencies in American anthropology reveals a series of common pitfalls. Perhaps the most common, illustrated by Benedict, Sapir, and Linton, is to treat psychology of peoples or the results of cultural conditioning and milieu as a causal explanation of particular cultures or cultural traditions. Of the three, Sapir was closest to doctrines of the importance of cultural meanings and unconscious patternings of behavior in psychiatry. Nevertheless, he was ultimately as far as Benedict or Linton from the more important point in social psychiatry that psychology reflects culture, and not the opposite. In Goldenweiser's attempt to explain away cultural similarities and generic patterns, we find the epitome of this recourse to a formal psychological principle "explaining away" cultural dynamisms. Boas' historical atomism, Radcliffe-Brown's notion of synchronic kinship studies preceding diachronic ones, and Malinowski's descriptive, nonanalytic integrations are all related as essentially static systems. It is proposed to restore ethnological theory and the psychological content of culture to their proper relationship. This the author has earlier attempted to do (Opler 1942; 1956a; 1956b).

Anthropology today requires a generalizing analysis of the complete process of cultural evolution—material, social, and behavioral. Only within this framework are particular analyses of given cultural integrations and reintegrations meaningful. While cultures are many and diverse, the unity of mankind and generic similarity of human psychological processes make each society part of a larger process. The psychological content of specific cultures, while having importance in individual lives, is one resultant of the particular conditions under which one culture operates. Anthropology has other tasks: it preserves a rich account of culture; it notes where the toll in individual lives, both biologically and psychologically, has been too great; and hopefully, it may apply principles discovered in the larger evolutionary settings to specific cultural integrations. Already in American anthropology there is every indication that a dynamically oriented, analytic, and generalizing science of culture is on the way.

BIBLIOGRAPHY

ALEXANDER, FRANZ

    1951 *Our Age of Unreason.* Revised edition. Philadelphia, J. B. Lippincott Co.

ALLIER, RAOUL

    n.d. *The Mind of the Savage.* New York, Harcourt, Brace and Company.

BENEDICT, RUTH F.

    1930 "Psychological Types in the Cultures of the Southwest." *Proceedings of the Twenty-Third International Congress of Americanists* (New York, 1928), pp. 572–581.

    1932 "Configurations of Culture in North America." *American Anthropologist,* 34:1–27.

    1934 *Patterns of Culture.* Boston, Houghton Mifflin Co.

    1938 "Continuities and Discontinuities in Cultural Conditioning." *Psychiatry,* 1:161–167.

    1946 *The Chrysanthemum and the Sword.* Boston, Houghton Mifflin Co.

BOAS, FRANZ

    1896 "The Limitations of the Comparative Method of Anthropology." *Science,* 40:901–908.

    1911 *The Mind of Primitive Man.* New York, The Macmillan Company.

    1932 "The Aims of Anthropological Research." *Science,* 76:605–613.

DILTHEY, WILHELM

    1921–1936 *Gesammelte Schriften.* 11 vols. Leipzig, B. G. Teubner.

GOLDENWEISER, ALEXANDER A.

    1913 "The Principle of Limited Possibilities in the Development of Culture." *Journal of American Folklore,* 26:259–290.

1917 "The Autonomy of the Social." *American Anthropologist,* 19:447–449.

1922 "Four Phases of Anthropological Thought." *Publications of the American Sociological Society,* 16 (*Papers and Proceedings of the Sixteenth Annual Meeting, American Sociological Society, 1921*):50–69.

1925 "Diffusionism and the American School of Historical Ethnology." *American Journal of Sociology,* 31:19–38.

1933 *History, Psychology and Culture.* New York, Alfred A. Knopf, Inc.

HALLOWELL, A. IRVING

1956 *Culture and Experience.* Philadelphia, University of Pennsylvania Press.

JENKS, ALBERT ERNEST

1913 "Report on the Science of Anthropology in the Western Hemisphere and the Pacific Islands." In *Reports on the Present Condition and Future Needs of the Science of Anthropology,* by W. H. R. Rivers, A. E. Jenks, and S. G. Morley, pp. 29–59. *Publication of The Carnegie Institution of Washington,* 200.

KARDINER, ABRAM

1939 *The Individual and His Society.* New York, Columbia University Press.

KARDINER, ABRAM, with RALPH LINTON, CORA DUBOIS, and JAMES WEST

1945 *The Psychological Frontiers of Society.* New York, Columbia University Press.

KROEBER, A. L.

1917 "The Superorganic." *American Anthropologist,* 19:163–213.

1935 "History and Science in Anthropology." *American Anthropologist,* 37:539–569.

1952 *The Nature of Culture.* Chicago, The University of Chicago Press.

LINTON, RALPH

1936 *The Study of Man.* New York, D. Appleton–Century Company.

1945 *The Cultural Background of Personality.* New York, D. Appleton-Century Company.

1955 *The Tree of Culture.* New York, Alfred A. Knopf, Inc.

MALINOWSKI, BRONISLAW

1927 *Sex and Repression in Savage Society.* New York, Harcourt, Brace and Company.

1931 "Culture." *Encyclopedia of the Social Sciences,* 4:621–646.

Marvin K. Opler

1935 *Coral Gardens and Their Magic*. 2 vols. London, George Allen and Unwin, Ltd.

MEAD, MARGARET

1953 "National Character." In *Anthropology Today*, prepared under the chairmanship of A. L. Kroeber, pp. 642–667. Chicago, The University of Chicago Press.

MORGAN, LEWIS H.

1877 *Ancient Society*. New York, Henry Holt and Company.

MURDOCK, GEORGE P.

1949 *Social Structure*. New York, The Macmillan Company.

NADEL, S. F.

1951 *The Foundations of Social Anthropology*. Glencoe, The Free Press.

OPLER, MARVIN K.

1942 "Psychoanalytic Techniques in Social Analysis." *Journal of Social Psychology*, 15:91–127.

1956a *Culture, Psychiatry and Human Values*. Springfield, Illinois, Charles C Thomas, Publisher.

1956b "Entities and Organization in Individual and Group Behavior: A Conceptual Framework." *Group Psychotherapy*, 9:290–300.

ORLANSKY, HAROLD

1949 "Infant Care and Personality." *Psychological Bulletin*, 46:1–48.

PARSONS, TALCOTT

1950 "Psychoanalysis and the Social Structure." *Psychoanalytic Quarterly*, 19:371–384.

RÓHEIM, GÉZA

1947 "Psychoanalysis and Anthropology." In *Psychoanalysis and the Social Sciences*, ed. by Géza Róheim, vol. 1, pp. 9–33. New York, International Universities Press.

SAPIR, EDWARD

1917 "Do We Need a Superorganic?" *American Anthropologist*, 19:441–447.

1929 "The Unconscious Patterning of Behavior in Society." In *The Unconscious, A Symposium*, ed. by E. S. Drummer, pp. 114–142. New York, Alfred A. Knopf, Inc.

1934 "The Emergence of the Concept of Personality in a Study of Culture." *Journal of Social Psychology*, 5:408–415.

1937 "The Contribution of Psychiatry to an Understanding of Behavior in Society." *American Journal of Sociology*, 42:862–870.

1948 *Selected Writings in Language, Culture and Personality,* ed. by David G. Mandelbaum. Berkeley, University of California Press.

SOROKIN, PITIRIM A.

1937–1941 *Social and Cultural Dynamics.* 4 vols. New York, The American Book Company.

1947 *Society, Culture and Personality.* New York, Harper & Brothers.

WAITZ, THEODOR

1859–1872 *Anthropologie der Naturvölker.* 6 vols. Leipzig, Friedrich Fleischer.

WHITE, LESLIE A.

1947 "Evolutionary Stages, Progress, and the Evaluation of Cultures." *Southwestern Journal of Anthropology,* 3:165–192.

1949 *The Science of Culture.* New York, Farrar, Straus and Company.

* * * *

George I. Quimby

CHICAGO NATURAL HISTORY MUSEUM

HABITAT, CULTURE,

AND ARCHAEOLOGY

In this paper it is my intention to present an hypothesis concerning the interaction of habitat and culture under certain specified conditions. My ultimate aim is to be able to predict culture from habitat within certain limits to be stated subsequently. Such prediction, although necessarily general, would be of considerable use in the reconstruction of the prehistory of the Upper Great Lakes region in pre-agricultural times, a long period extending back from about 500 B.C. or later to probably 10,000 B.C., for which the archaeological record is sparse.

By habitat I mean the physical environment of a region. Habitat includes the wild flora and fauna, climate and weather, soils, land forms, geological formations and the like. As used in this paper environment and habitat are the same.

Habitat may be relatively stable for long periods or it may change relatively rapidly. In the Upper Great Lakes region the environment has been more or less stable for the last 2,000 years, but during the preceding 10,000 years there were a number of radical environmental changes (Quimby 1957).

By culture I mean the same thing that Professor White does when he states:

Culture consists of material objects—tools, utensils, ornaments, amulets, etc.— acts, beliefs, and attitudes that function in contexts characterized by symbolling (making and using symbols). It is an elaborate mechanism, an organization of exosomatic ways and means employed by a particular animal species, man, in the struggle for existence and survival (White 1949:363).

Culture as a system may be divided into three aspects; technological, sociological, and ideological. "Social systems are functions of technologies; and philosophies express technological forces and reflect social systems" (White 1949:366). Thus all of culture is basically geared to the technological system.

The technological system, according to White, "is composed of the material, mechanical, physical, and chemical instruments, together with the techniques of their use, by means of which man, as an animal species, is articulated with his natural habitat" (White 1949:364). White also states that:

Man as an animal species, and consequently culture as a whole, is dependent upon material, mechanical means of adjustment to the natural environment. Man must have food. He must be protected from the elements. He must defend himself from his enemies. These three things he must do if he is to continue to live, and these objectives are attained only by technological means. The technological system is therefore both primary and basic in importance; all human life and culture rest and depend upon it (White 1949:365).

Culture may be relatively stable for long periods or it may change relatively rapidly. In past times there have been periods of thousands of years duration in which there was very little culture change whereas in more recent times the rate of culture change or development has accelerated tremendously. With regard to the development of culture, White says:

Assuming the factor of habitat to be a constant, the degree of cultural development, measured in terms of amount of human need-serving goods and services produced per capita, is determined by the amount of energy harnessed per capita and by the efficiency of the technological means with which it is put to work (White 1949:368).

For the purposes of this paper I would like to hold energy constant, and consider habitat a variable. I hold energy constant because in the pre-agricultural groups in which I am interested, only human energy, fire for heat and light, and possibly the flow of water to move boats are involved. There is no agriculture, animal husbandry, or harnessing of more elaborate kinds of energy. Under these conditions it is possible to state a corollary of White's formulation which is as follows: Assuming the factor of energy to be a constant, the degree of cultural development is determined by the habitat and the efficiency of the available technological means.

Since for purposes of this paper I am interested only in cultures based upon a hunting and fishing subsistence, cultures with essentially the same kind of technology, I wish also to hold technology constant. With the factors of energy and technology held constant, culture will vary with the habitat. A good example of this corollary lies in the comparison of Kwakiutl culture and Naskapi culture. Both have a subsistence based upon hunting and fishing as a primary part of their technology. Both utilized only human energy. Yet Kwakiutl culture is much more elaborate than that of Naskapi. The reason for this lies in the difference in habitats.

The habitat of the Kwakiutl is much superior to that of the Naskapi. The abundance and behavior of the animal food resources enables a sedentary mode of life with relatively large villages, a large population, the development of specialization, the segmenting of society, the acquisition of wealth, and the development of lineages and classes. Fish can be literally harvested, and the Kwakiutl thereby possess a culture at a level of development usually achieved only by farming peoples.

In contrast, the Naskapi, filled with fears of starvation, freezing, or drowning, live in an unfavorable habitat and eke a living from fishing and the pursuit of caribou. The Naskapi of necessity are nomadic, few in numbers, unspecialized, unsegmented, poor, and classless.

The habitat has placed a definite limit upon the degree of development of Naskapi culture. But a close look at Naskapi culture suggests that the habitat has not only limited the culture: it has been a factor in determining the form of the culture.

My hypothesis is as follows: Under certain conditions a hunting culture will develop to the limits of its habitat and in so doing, the culture will acquire forms determined by the habitat. This is possible because, as White says, Man, as an animal species, is articulated with his natural habitat, and culture as a whole is dependent upon material, mechanical means of adjustment to the natural environment. The technological system, which is both primary and basic to human life and culture, is articulated with environment. Furthermore, the three basic functions of the technology—food, protection from the elements, and defense from enemies—are most closely articulated with the environment among hunting peoples.

A hunting weapon, for instance, must be made of materials provided by the habitat. The energy for production and use of the weapon is limited to human energy. The efficiency of the weapon can be increased only by development of skill in its use and by perfection of its form in relation to its function. The perfection of its form depends for the most part upon the inherent qualities of the materials used. It is one of my assumptions (based on long familiarity with material culture) that in a relatively stable environment tool and weapons are developed to a point of perfection or near perfection. It is a further assumption that the whole technology is similarly perfected among hunting peoples, given sufficient time in a relatively stable environment. The habitat may determine the need as well as the form, and the technology must respond or the culture will perish. Life in northern Labrador is absolutely impossible for peoples of a hunting culture unless they have some efficient means of traveling upon rivers and walking over deep snow in pursuit of animal life for food and clothing.

When the technology of a hunting culture is perfected in relation to its habitat it can be said to be in equilibrium with its environment. With a technology in such equilibrium, it is to be expected that the social system as a function of the technology and the ideological system as a reflection of the social system will also tend to be in equilibrium with the environment.

For such equilibrium to be achieved habitat must remain stable for a sufficient length of time. In an unchanging habitat a nomadic hunting culture achieves at least near equilibrium with the habitat and in so doing acquires or is forced to produce the forms of culture best suited for survival in the habitat. All of this suggests that, under the conditions stated, there may be only one ideal form for any given aspect of a hunting culture in a given habitat. For instance, given the winter habitat of the Central Eskimo in the Hudson's Bay region, there is only one material, snow, readily available for house building, and only one most efficient form such a house could take, namely the dome shape. It seems impossible to conceive of any other kind of house that fulfills the requirements of abundant building material everywhere present in the habitat and a form of shelter that provides the greatest amount of enclosed volume for the least amount of surface.

The Naskapi (cf. Speck 1935) who live in the northern half of the Labrador Peninsula or New Quebec between the Atlantic Ocean and Hudson's Bay offer excellent illustrations of the articulation of habitat and culture in equilibrium. Here bands of hunters wander after bands of caribou upon which they depend for food, clothing, and shelter. The technology is tied to the habitat to such a degree that one could argue that all aspects of Naskapi technology are perfect or near perfect.

Take, for instance, the Naskapi house. This conical wigwam of poles covered with skin or birch-bark is made of readily available materials. Since over much of the habitat there is little or no soil, the butts of the poles rest against the ground and are braced by a ring of the boulders that abound in this glaciated area. Any house structure that involves posts or poles sunk into the ground is impossible over most of the northern Naskapi area in summer, and over all of it in winter; therefore the dome-shaped houses of the Montagnais and Cree are unsuitable. Given the condition that poles cannot be sunk into the ground and that the poles must be of dwarfed conifers, spruce, or fir, the conical wigwam provides the greatest volume for the least amount of surface cover. Other possible forms of shelter that could be readily constructed by wandering hunters in the Naskapi habitat such as the double lean-to are in one way or another not as efficient as the conical wigwam.

The same sort of situation obtains for snowshoes, toboggans, and canoes. All of these things are absolutely necessary for uncivilized human existence in the Naskapi habitat. And all seem to have reached a point of perfection beyond which they could not have been improved under aboriginal conditions.

In the case of the birch-bark canoe, it seems impossible that any other form made of birch-bark and a wooden frame could fulfill the cultural needs of the Naskapi as dictated by their habitat.

There are, of course, forms of bark canoes other than those of the Naskapi but they would not meet Naskapi requirements. The Kootenay style of canoe with its shovel shaped bow would plunge and sink in the heavy rapids of Labrador rivers and the clumsy canoe of the Iroquois, if it didn't sink, would be hard to maneuver, and if not dashed to pieces on the rocks would be hard to carry over portages. It is true that skin covered canoes of suitable shape are possible and the Naskapi sometimes use these when birch-bark is not available, but they are poor substitutes for bark canoes as they become water logged and are heavy. It seems obvious to me that the Naskapi birch-bark canoe is an ideal tool produced by Naskapi technology in relation to the inherent qualities of birch-bark, spruce gum, spruce root, and specific woods to fulfill a cultural need within a given habitat.

There are also illustrations of the articulation of habitat and culture in the Naskapi social system.

As Speck and Eiseley (1942:219–220) pointed out, the northern Naskapi who live by following the wandering bands of caribou are socially organized into wandering bands whereas the more southerly dwelling Montagnais, Cree, and Chippewa who hunted the family-like groups of moose and beaver are organized into family groups with concepts of ownership of hunting territories (cf. Hallowell 1949).

Do forms of marriage have any relation to habitat in the context of a culture based upon a hunting subsistence? White made some statements that seem useful here. He wrote:

Marriage and the family are society's first and fundamental way of making provision for the economic needs of the individual. . . . One set of circumstances will require one definition of incest and one form of marriage; another set will require different customs. The habitat and the technological adjustment to it, the mode of subsistence, circumstances of defense and offense, division of labor between the sexes, and degree of cultural development, are factors which condition the definition of incest and the formulation of rules to prohibit it (White 1949:321).

Since, in the above statement, all of the conditioning factors that are cultural are in themselves the product of articulation of habitat and culture (in the limited context of a nonagricultural, hunting society) it seems as if rules of incest and marriage would be (in the same context) the product of interaction between culture and habitat.

The Naskapi bands that come down the rivers leading to Richmond Gulf and Great Whale River, which I observed in the summer of 1939, claimed to marry their cross-cousins, if they marry a known blood relative. If the person to be married is not known to be a blood relative, he or she is called "cross-cousin" anyway. In short, the Naskapi practice cross-cousin marriage (cf. Strong 1929). The Naskapi, insofar as I could observe, may marry into their own band, into a band where they have kindred, or into a band where they don't have kindred. Naskapi bands are variable in size and about as unstable as the supply of food.

If the cultural function of marriage and incest restriction is to expand the range of cooperation and mutual aid between families and between larger social groups such as bands, then Naskapi cross-cousin marriage seems ideal because it is best suited to the variability and instability of Naskapi bands, particularly where bands are disintegrating for want of food. The Naskapi's Yuman system (Murdock 1949:231–232) seems, theoretically at least, more efficient than other systems possible in this habitat, because it allows more possibilities of marriages between actual blood relatives than do Eskimo or Hawaiian types of systems. If the Naskapi of a particular area were reduced to two related families, as they sometimes have been, providing cross-cousins were present, they could still marry without violating incest rules. In the same circumstances they could not do this with the Hawaiian or Eskimo types of systems, the only other types that seem at all possible for a hunting culture in a similar habitat.

On the other hand, when food is more abundant, and bands are increasing in size or are in closer geographical proximity, ties between bands are established by marriage, or ties already thus established may be reinforced by additional marriages. It thus seems to me that the marriage and kinship system of the Naskapi is the most efficient of those considered possible in a hunting culture in a habitat of the type the Naskapi occupy.

Of types of social organization (cf. Murdock 1949: 226–259) only the Eskimo and Yuman types and possibly the Hawaiian type seem possible in the Naskapi habitat. The Naskapi of course have the Yuman type of social organization. All of the other types of social organization listed by Murdock seem to me impossible in the Naskapi habitat. Consider, for instance, what would happen to social organizations like the Iroquois type or the Crow type (Murdock 1949:243–248) in the Naskapi habitat. They would disintegrate because in the Naskapi habitat they would be luxuries that in no way could be supported by the highest technology that the habitat would permit. Only cultures of great wealth in controlled habitats could afford useless appendages.

Since the ideological aspect of culture expresses the technology and also reflects the social system, I would expect to find much of Naskapi religion articulated with the habitat through the interaction of technology and environment. And it seems to me that this is so. Certainly the concepts of animals in special relation to man as well as divination, magical practices, medicinal practices, and charms for hunting (cf. Speck 1935:76–231) are obviously linked directly with survival in the habitat. In fact, one could argue that Naskapi religion is part of Naskapi technology, so closely is it tied to the production of food, protection against the elements, and defense against enemies; the three things required for survival. Each Naskapi hunter is his own shaman, and hunting is considered a religious activity.

An environmental explanation of the role of the bear in Naskapi religion is that in the northern habitat no other animal can walk like and look like a man. Eating the bear is close to cannibalism, and cannibalism is a reality in the Naskapi environment.

In the summer of 1939, I frequently heard a whistling which to my untrained ear produced a tune not unlike that of some Naskapi singing. This whistling was the sound of the wind blowing across the rocks and through the shrub-like trees of the high plateaus of the west coast and interior of the Labrador Peninsula. As the wind changed in intensity or direction and as the vegetation moved in the wind, the tones changed, thus producing the whistling sound. The Naskapi account for this whistling and for the unexplained loss of children by attributing both to the Kātcīmēdgīzu spirits. Greatly feared by the Naskapi, "They are said to come into the far interior in magical, high-bowed canoes, where they steal the Naskapi children. While their whistling may be heard they are invisible. . . ." (Strong 1929:285).

It seems to me that much of Naskapi culture and particularly its technological aspect articulates with habitat in a definite and relatively fixed fashion. Except for language I cannot think of any aspect of aboriginal Naskapi culture that is not to a considerable degree the product of the interaction of habitat and culture.

Even diffusion before European contact would be subject to the dynamics of the interaction of culture and habitat since it occurred in a framework of culture and habitat. Wissler's concept of "natural diffusion" seems to fit the picture perfectly. He wrote, "we see that the basis for diffusion of trait-complexes is environmental and, to a large degree, also economic, since . . . man preys upon the organic resources of his habitat. So the immediate factors in the determination of diffusion boundaries are the fauna and flora" (Wissler 1923:138–139). Since the upper level of a hunting culture is limited by the habitat, it would be impossible to add by diffusion any trait that would not be useful in the culture that has already achieved equilibrium in the interaction between culture and habitat. For the conservative nature of what can be diffused to hunting cultures in a restricted habitat see Quimby and Spoehr (1951).

Organized diffusion, such as that produced by outposts of civilization, for example, gold miners, could penetrate the barriers of habitat and culture, but such outposts could not exist without the support of a civilization that controls habitat elsewhere.

So, on a pre-agricultural level of culture, diffusion—itself a cultural product—is controlled by habitat, because the only context in which it can occur is the context of the interaction of culture and habitat.

From a consideration of White's concept of culture, some knowledge of Naskapi and Central Eskimo culture, and Wissler's concept of natural diffusion, it seems to me that under certain conditions a hunting culture will develop over a period of time to the limits of its habitat and in so doing will acquire cultural forms determined by the habitat.

In an unchanging habitat a hunting culture achieves at least near equilibrium with the habitat and in so doing acquires or is forced to produce the forms of culture most suited for survival in the habitat. A primitive hunting culture in a changing habitat tends to achieve a new equilibrium with its new habitat. This new equilibrium is achieved by invention through the interaction of technology and habitat or by diffusion from a culture in a similar habitat. These rules are of limited utility for hunting cultures in an environment where food resources are abundant and are of no use for agricultural societies or cultures with a technology based on the use of elaborate kinds of energy. Such cultures have become varyingly independent of habitat by controlling their environment.

If, at the pre-agricultural level of culture, habitats and cultures may be bound together in rather fixed relationships, then a number of inferences can be made that would be exceedingly useful in the reconstruction of cultural histories and limited cultural developments.

Since the sociological systems of culture depend upon the technological systems, and since the technological system is dependent upon the fauna, and since the fauna is dependent upon the flora, all of these factors could possibly be correlated.

For instance, in a habitat unsuited for agriculture, one might correlate reindeer moss with caribou, caribou with nomadic bands of hunters, whose population and range depended upon caribou population and range, and this factor would ideally correlate with one form of social organization (or at most with one of three possible forms).

Similarly one might be able to correlate water lilies with moose, moose with small groups of nomadic hunters, small groups with patrilineal families, and so on. Or one might link aspen trees to beaver, and beaver to small groups of hunters, and so forth.

The seal seems to correlate well with Central Eskimo size of population, habitation, technology, and social organization. I would even go so far as to suggest that subsistence based upon the seal is most favorable to the Eskimo type of social organization, whereas subsistence based on caribou favors cross-cousin marriage and the composite hunting band, —the Yuman type of social organization (cf. Murdock 1949).

I envision these hypotheses and ideas as archaeological aids possibly useful in the reconstruction of culture history in the Upper Great Lakes region where there was a period of about 10,000 years during which culture was based on a hunting economy. The archaeological record of this period is sparse. There are, however, adequate reconstructions of habitats based upon data from geology, especially glacial geology; paleontology; pollen analysis, and other fields of natural science (cf. Quimby 1957). In fact, much more is known about the changing habitats of this period than is known about the cultures. By combining the cultural and environmental data and analyzing and interpreting them in terms of the hypotheses and ideas presented in this paper, it is possible to better reconstruct the prehistoric hunting cultures of the Upper Great Lakes region and to learn more about the kinds of culture changes that take place in hunting cultures.

BIBLIOGRAPHY

HALLOWELL, A. IRVING
  1949 "The Size of Algonkian Hunting Territories, a Function of Eco-
    logical Adjustment." *American Anthropologist*, 51:35–45.
MURDOCK, GEORGE PETER
  1949 *Social Structure*. New York, The Macmillan Company.
QUIMBY, GEORGE I.
  1957 "The Archeology of Environment, Great Lakes Area." *Chicago
    Natural History Museum Bulletin*, 28(7):4–7.
QUIMBY, GEORGE I. and ALEXANDER SPOEHR
  1951 "Acculturation and Material Culture—I." *Fieldiana: Anthropol-
    ogy*, 36:107–147.
SPECK, FRANK G.
  1935 *Naskapi, the Savage Hunters of the Labrador Peninsula*. Norman,
    University of Oklahoma Press.
SPECK, FRANK G. and LOREN C. EISELEY
  1942 "Montagnais-Naskapi Bands and Family Hunting Districts of the
    Central and Southeastern Labrador Peninsula." *Proceedings of
    the American Philosophical Society*, 85:215–242.
STRONG, WILLIAM DUNCAN
  1929 "Cross-cousin Marriage and the Culture of the Northeastern
    Algonkian." *American Anthropologist*, 31:277–288.
WHITE, LESLIE A.
  1949 *The Science of Culture*. New York, Farrar, Straus and Company
WISSLER, CLARK
  1923 *Man and Culture*. New York, Thomas Y. Crowell Company.

Marshall D. Sahlins

UNIVERSITY OF MICHIGAN

POLITICAL POWER

AND THE ECONOMY IN

PRIMITIVE SOCIETY[1]

I

It seems paradoxical to suggest that anthropological treatments of primitive economics have often been hampered by ethnocentrism. But in fact, social and economic relations of the capitalist order have frequently been projected without warrant upon this totally different sphere. The result has been distortion and confusion.

One misleading premise has yielded the inaccurate picture of primitive economies current in the anthropological literature, viz., that these economies differ from the Euro-American in degree, not kind (Firth 1950:*passim*, especially chap. 10; 1954; Herskovits 1952:488, *et passim*). From this it follows that the theoretical categories of capitalism are universally applicable. Thus writes the anthropologically trained Goodfellow, for example: ". . . it is extremely difficult to see how the whole of the logical apparatus of modern economics can fail to apply [to primitive economies]" (Goodfellow 1950:45). We are warned that chaos would ensue if it did not (p. 4); that modern economic theory would be other-

[1] Professors Morton Fried, Elman Service and Leslie White, and Dr. David Kaplan read this paper in various stages of its preparation. The critical comments offered by these gentlemen have led to the formulation and elaboration of many specific ideas. I am grateful to all of them.

390 ·

wise "meaningless" (p. 5); indeed, all the social sciences would be discredited (p. 4). It is incredible that anthropology—having at hand comparative materials from the whole range of human history and the entire gamut of cultural arrangements—should adopt, in dealing with primitive economies, a theoretical outlook relevant to historically recent, evolutionarily advanced systems of production and exchange. The fact remains that primitive economic behavior is largely an aspect of kinship behavior, and is therefore organized by means completely different from capitalist production and market transactions (cf. White 1949:379). The inference is clear: the whole of modern economic theory, resting on the assumption of the market and its concomitants, fails to apply to primitive economies.

To the initial failure to recognize the distinctiveness of primitive economies can be traced a whole compendium of economic fallacies in anthropological theory. The very definition of an economy is at issue. Anthropologists are wont to identify the economic subsystem of a culture, an economy, with "economizing"—applying scarce means against alternate ends—which is the typical transactional feature in our society. Where there is economizing, it is argued, there is an economy (Firth 1954:15; Herskovits 1952:chap. 1). In a general sense it is true that primitives economize, that is, make allocative choices. To live is to economize, but this indicates the worthlessness of so defining an economy. The question is whether economic choices are specifically determined by the relative value of the *goods* involved. If so, as can be true only in a price setting market system, then the entire economy is organized by the process of maximization of economic value. If not, as in primitive societies where price-fixing markets are absent and social relations channel the movement of goods, then the economy is organized by these relations. To say that primitives economize tells us nothing about their economy; it is simply misleading. We are indebted to Karl Polanyi for pointing out the logical weakness of the identification of economy with economizing (Polanyi 1957a).

A great disadvantage of the adoption of modern economic theory by anthropology is that the individual, rather than the society, is then taken as the unit of analysis—"final" or "ultimate" analysis. "The process of economizing," writes Herskovits, here embracing the economy, "is essentially based on the broader organization of society. Yet the individual cannot be left out of the picture, for all forms of social behavior in the final analysis, must be referred to the behavior of individual members of a given society in specific situations" (1952:7). Or again, "the economic unit, we must conclude, is the individual operating as a member of his society, in terms of the culture of his group" (*ibid.*:8). The motivations of individuals, rather than the interaction of social forces, thus become the primary concern of economic anthropology. This concern again has its roots in a society in which economizing in terms of exchange value institutes the economic process. The action of the rationalizing individual, *homo economicus,* is here prototypical of all economic activities. But everywhere the economy is a system of social arrangements for the manipulation of goods, and should be analyzed as such, and in terms of its relation to other subsystems of culture. The individual is never prime mover; the motivations of individuals in handling goods express the method of organizing the economy, not vice versa. "The idea that economic life has ever been a process mainly dependent on individual action —an idea based on the impression that it is concerned mainly with methods of satisfying individual needs—is mistaken with regard to all stages of human civilization, and in some respects it is more mistaken the further back we go" (Schmoller 1910:3–4).

Regarding the relation between political power and the economy, which will be our primary interest, it has been explicitly and implicitly assumed that the social relations of capitalism exist in primitive societies. The result is a series of curious paradoxes that are well illustrated in Herskovits' recent book, *Economic Anthropology* (1952). Primitive economies are here represented as possessed of capital, but no capitalists (pp. 10–11); as generating a relation between riches and power (pp. 414–415) where wage labor is "practically non-existent," production is geared to the use of producers and controlled by them (pp. 110, 304); as developing a leisure, exploiting class (p. 414) where producers own the means of production and hence control their own economic destiny (pp. 31, 371). Equating wealth and power in primitive societies does justice neither to classical economic theory nor to the data. Pressed to the wall by this obvious incongruity, some anthropologists seek to solve the dilemma by adopting Veblenian theory of conspicuous consumption (cf. Bunzel 1938; Du Bois 1936; Herskovits 1952). They invent a "dual" economy, composed on the one hand of subsistence transactions governed by kinship sentiments, and on the other, a "prestige economy" dominated by the acquisitive spirit and devoted to the possession, consumption, and waste of wealth which produces a leisure ruling class. This is just a theoretical dodge, as transparent as it is inaccurate.

We shall now examine the difficulties created by the assumption that capitalist relations exist in primitive society. We then analyze several primitive economies that have become notorious for their supposed exploitative power relations. In the end we advance an hypothesis concerning the relation between political and economic power in primitive society.

II

The attribution of capital and capitalization to precapitalist economies is probably the most widespread fallacy in economic anthropology. Reference to capital varies between casual remarks—as when Childe speaks of "capital" in the form of food and labor which made possible the Urban Revolution (1948:131, 132)—to the persistent employment of the term by Herskovits (1952) and Goodfellow (1950). The anthropological literature perpetuates the confusion between physical and social realities that characterized the use of this term even before Adam Smith (see Fetter 1935; Ayres 1946). Thurnwald's definition, cited also with approval by Firth, is typical: "commodities which, by their own inherent nature, can not only maintain themselves but increase themselves" (Thurnwald 1932:10; cf. Firth 1950:9–10, 353). By this definition, capital is universal—provided one need not define "commodities." Capital, writes Herskovits, "much be present in the productive process of any functioning economy" (1952:9), notwithstanding that capitalists (that is, entrepreneurs) "do not exist" (p. 10) in primitive economies.

At best the use of "capital" in the metaphoric sense of a productive good is meaningless and contributes nothing to our understanding. The reason is that everything becomes capital. Every functioning element of a culture is capital—"an analysis of capital in the economy becomes an analysis of the whole society" (Fusfield 1957:354). This actually happens in "sophisticated" analyses of primitive economies. Goodfellow (1950) designates as capital ("a produced good used for further production") among the Bantu: grain and all food, as it supports household labor (p. 71); knowledge of agricultural techniques (p. 213); the labor power of producers (p. 218); the cattle given to magicians to make rain (p. 69). The herding of cattle becomes husbanding of capital (p. 219). Nothing is sacred to Goodfellow. The very milk flowing from the mother's breast, the investment of the profits of cattle (capital) husbandry, is itself capital, since: "In keeping children alive and making them strong it is acting as a productive good or capital, in the full sense . . . the milk given to the children or to their mothers is thus invested for further production. . . ." (p. 68). By this definition of capital we need not restrict it to humans. What of the spider's web, the bird's nest, the bee's hive?

Such metaphoric use of "capital" serves to obscure a basic social difference between primitive and capitalist economies. In primitive society, goods and resources used in production are controlled by the producers. The social relation of dependence of the (wage) laborer on the entrepreneur cannot exist. The means of production are simply means of livelihood, not of profit, exploitation or stratification. Under these conditions, they are not capital (cf. Fortes and Evans-Pritchard 1940:8). In the modern economy, means of production are privately owned capital investments of entrepreneurs. The dependence of the laborer on the entrepreneur is here characteristic; hence, the subordination of the former to the latter in the total society. There is exploitation in the unequal claims to income of the owner and laborer, or in the Marxian sense of appropriation of surplus value by the entrepreneur. If it were not so, there would be no profit and the owners of the means of production would be unable to activate them. Here private ownership of the means of production transforms these into capital, the owners become capitalists, the producers are wage laborers and the relation between these groups is both exploitative and stratified.

Capital is not an inherent quality of a thing. It is the way a thing is used in a particular social system; ". . . capital is not a thing, but a social relation between persons, established by the instrumentality of things" (Marx n.d.:839). Anthropologists have succeeded in discovering that "property" is not a thing. Land is land, not property. It does not become property until it enters a social system in which particular persons are given rights, relative to others, to its disposition. The same is true of capital; it is not a quality of a thing. "A negro is a negro. In certain circumstances he becomes a slave. A [spinning] mule is a machine for spinning cotton. Only under certain circumstances does it become capital. Outside these circumstances it is no more capital than gold is intrinsically money, or sugar is the price of sugar. . . . Capital is a social relation of production. It is a historical relation of production" (*ibid.*:839, note 3).

To fail to distinguish between means of production controlled by producers and capital investments of entrepreneurs is to run the danger of assuming that the social relations of production are the same in both cases. In the anthropological literature, this danger too frequently materializes. Bunzel writes that in primitive society, power often ". . . becomes associated with wealth, and economic institutions take on an exploitative character. Capitalism is the most extreme expression of this identification. There is no full capitalism among primitive peoples; but there are many societies where wealth and power are at least partially identified" (1938:336). Lowie fails to see how the absence of a profit motive mitigates the exploitative character of Polynesian economies (Lowie 1948:30). Herskovits, although introducing a subtlety by adopting a Veblenian explanation of the economic basis of political power (see below), in many statements crudely asserts that the relation between wealth and power typical of capitalism exists in primitive economies. Not only, we are assured, are the economic institutions of our society found among primitives, but, "Similarly, the institutional aspects of these economic systems are comparable to our own, as where the control of wealth, resulting in socioeconomic class differences, interacts with other noneconomic institutions to influence their form and affect their role in everyday life" (Herskovits 1952:488).

It is clear that there is a discrepancy between the theory of economic anthropology and the facts of primitive life. On the one hand it is maintained that wealth breeds power in primitive society, as in our own. On the other hand, the uncontested fact that primitives control their own means of livelihood argues that the economic coercion that produces the class system of capitalism is nonexistent. Rather than abandon theoretical prejudice, some anthropologists adopt an expedient solution of the paradox, viz., Veblen's theory of the leisure class. The adoption of Veblen, however, should not be viewed as an abandonment of the classical view of the foundation of social inequality.

Briefly stated, the theory as utilized by many anthropologists is: In primitive economies producing surplus, chiefs (and priests) gain control of the surplus, become a leisure class, and through ostentatious display, waste and consumption, create an invidious distinction between themselves and the producers, thus reinforcing their power. Individual desires for prestige lie at the heart of the theory. Herskovits, for example, writes: "The surplus wealth, it is apparent, goes to two groups, those who govern, and those who command techniques for placating and manipulating supernatural forces of the universe. The members of these groups are, therefore, to be regarded as belonging to a leisure class in that they, like their families and retainers, profit from the social leisure which the economic surplus represents" (Herskovits 1952:414). Esteem is produced through, "the economic waste of useful goods. . . . The more conspicuous the display of economic advantage by the group in power before those whose duty it is to provide them with the means of supporting their position, the greater the assurance that their power will be continued and that they will be able to maintain control of the economic surplus on which this power rests" (*ibid.:*415). Herskovits' statements of the argument are sometimes contradictory, especially regarding the character of "waste," "consumption," and "possession" of wealth, the uselessness of leisure class activity, and the exploitative element of the class system. These contradictions are examined later.

An elaboration of the Veblenian concept is that primitive economies involving large scale "conspicuous consumption" are two economies in one, a subsistence economy and a prestige economy. As first proposed by Du Bois (1936) for the Tolowa-Tututni Indians, the two economies are differently organized and concerned with different kinds of goods. The prestige economy involves luxury goods, valuables and money tokens—or at least goods consumed in nonutilitarian fashion—manipulation, display and consumption of which bestows esteem. This is an acquisitive economy, characterized by inequality in possession of goods. The subsistence economy involves material need-serving goods. The objective is to gain a livelihood. Sharing and cooperation are characteristic. Herskovits has generalized the notion of a dual economy to a number of societies, his views usually conforming to Du Bois' characterization of Tolowa-Tututni (Herskovits 1952:257f., 461f.). The dual economy admirably dissolves the dilemma posed by lack of an economic coercive element in primitive society coupled with an insistence on the identification of power and wealth. In the subsistence economy we eat the cake, in the prestige economy we have it yet.

Examination of primitive leisure classes and prestige economies is the best test of the theory. However, some criticism is suggested a priori. Veblen's leisure class was a class of capitalists. The leisure class, arising concomitantly with private property (Veblen 1919:22), is an exploitative class (p. 204). "The relation of the leisure . . . class to the economic process is a pecuniary relation—a relation of acquisition, not of production; of exploitation, not of serviceability. . . . Their interest is to divert what substance they may to their own use, and to retain whatever is under their hand" (p. 209). Further, as C. Wright Mills observes, Veblen's theory does not even apply to the capitalist class in general, but to one segment of it in one period of its American development: the *nouveau riche* of the latter nineteenth century, "the Vanderbilts, Goulds, and Harrimans, . . . the glitter and the gold" (Mills 1953:xiv). It is justifiable to doubt that primitive economies, lacking a coercive element of economic dependence—let alone Vanderbilts and Goulds—could produce a true leisure class replete with conspicuous consumption.

A second criticism is a posteriori. The same data cited in support of a Veblenian interpretation of primitive social inequality clearly show that it is misleading to describe the economic activities of chiefs in terms of possession, display, waste and consumption of wealth. It is transparent from these data that prestige is gained and power supported by generosity, by giving away, by pooling and distributing, not by consuming. The chief emerges not as consumer but as distributor of tribal wealth, a function which effects equalization of consumption and stimulates many kinds of tribal activity. Hidden behind the catchwords "leisure class," "waste," "conspicuous consumption," and "display," behind the implications of invidious social distinction and exploitation, lies an entirely different economy.

The distortion introduced is almost ludicrous. In order to make capitalists out of savages, our authorities make consumption out of distribution. Thus writes Bunzel: "We find among many peoples that although wealth gives no power in the sense of control over persons, the *possession* (*or control, as in giving away*) of wealth confers prestige. Veblen was the first economist to be impressed by the use of wealth for this purpose. . . . (1938:337, italics mine). In almost every case placed before us by Herskovits to exemplify the assertion that conspicuous consumption is the basis of social inequality, the consumption is primarily distribution (Herskovits 1952:156, 160f., 225, 277, 412, 417, 428f., 461f.). More accurately, everywhere the accumulation of wealth is but one phase of the chiefly economic role as agent of general circulation; the equal and opposite phase, the redistribution of wealth, is absolutely necessary to produce prestige and sustain power. The redistributive activities of Polynesian chiefs are instructive. They so impress Herskovits that he momentarily refers to them as "conspicuous distribution." But conspicuous distribution is only one of a number of "particular manifestations of conspicuous consumption. . . ." (*ibid.:*472).

The facts are not at issue. The issue is an attempt to foist a theory based on the stratified relations of capitalist production on these facts, and in so doing, to ignore and misrepresent them. Who would argue that display sometimes accompanies the redistributive functions of primitive chiefs? But such display simply demonstrates and reinforces the social differentials arising in the economy, it does not create them. Display often accompanies the redistributive process, both in its accumulating and dispensing phases, because it has great utility as a ritual form in maintaining the organization of production and distribution. Display and the drive for prestige are generated by social forces. They are not simply inherent traits of individual natures. They do not explain the economy; it is the economy within which the individual operates that explains them. Note the different consequences of display in different economies. Where high rank is associated with public redistribution, the desire to display takes the form of generosity. Where power is derived from the private ownership of wealth, display takes the form of consumption. The common element of display should not blind us to these differences.

Are the prestige and subsistence economies really distinct in principle? Herskovits himself describes examples of conspicuous consumption in which—due to redistribution—the drive for prestige takes on the utilitarian functions of "accelerating the circulation of goods" and stimulating production (Herskovits 1952:163). The goods involved are often vital consumption goods: "The utilization of goods for . . . ceremonial consumption [*sic*] so as to gain prestige [is] among the most important and consistent elements in the use of available food resources in primitive societies" (*ibid.*:275). Pearson, an economic historian, has commented that the function of prestige in primitive economies "seems rather the reverse of that found in our own economy," since prestige indirectly acts, "as a mobilizer of relatively large quantities of material means as well as human services to be employed in a variety of ways, utilitarian and not, but which in any case, make them available to the community at large, as they otherwise could not be" (Pearson 1957:337, 338). It appears that the prestige economy and the subsistence economy are part of the same system. The prestige economy is that aspect of the system which circulates goods on a tribal scale—a process sometimes implemented by transactions of valuable tokens (as in the Trobriand kula trade). The subsistence economy is the local, domestic aspect of the system. Together they make up one tribal economy, governed throughout by the sentiments of kinship.

III

The following sketches of primitive economies are selected from those that have become well known as illustrative of exploitation comparable to capitalism or as having "prestige economies" dominated by the drive for power through possession of wealth. The purpose of the presentation is to show that there has been gross misrepresentation of these economies. The examples will also serve to develop an alternative hypothesis relating economic and political power in primitive societies.

The Chukchee

The Reindeer Chukchee of northeastern Siberia are a time-honored example of primitive class exploitation. Bunzel summarizes a typical position: "The use of property for class exploitation which most closely resembles our own use of it is found among the nomadic Reindeer Chukchee. . . . The existence of acute anxiety stimulates individuals to accumulate property and use it to control others. . . ." (Bunzel 1938:350–351).

The assertion of an economic class system is made in the face of statements to the opposite effect in Bogoras' classical ethnography. Bogoras found "no trace" of an aristocracy based on herd size (1904–1909:623). Although frequently speaking of "rich" and "poor" in terms of reindeer owned, Bogoras noted that wide extension of kinship and hence of mutual aid prevented the formation of a true class of paupers (pp. 47, 375, 624). The essential Chukchee attitude toward property may be judged from the fact that when tobacco—immensely valued—becomes scarce, it is never hoarded; rather, "the last pipeful is divided or smoked by turns" (p. 549). As capitalists, the Chukchee are clumsy indeed: they are unable to count above a few score and usually do not know the number of their herds, paying attention only to conspicuous animals (p. 51). Bogoras flatly characterizes Chukchee life as "plain, filthy and democratic" (p. 580).

Even if elements of a "businessman's culture" crop up among the Chukchee, it would be easy to trace them to the long-standing trade with Russians (regularly since 1789) and American whalers (since 1848). As a result of this now "indispensable" trade, a class of itinerant traders has arisen among the nomads themselves. "These are peaceful times," a man told Bogoras, "Wars have ceased, everybody thinks of gain" (Bogoras 1904–1909:44; cf. 61f., 686f.). Another acculturative factor that must be reckoned with is the nineteenth-century expansion and specialization of the Reindeer Chukchee. Chukchee groups near and on the coast have given up a seasonal or total maritime orientation in favor of herding, the attraction being a recent increase of reindeer. The Chukchee have expanded south and west at the expense of other groups. The significance of this growth for Chukchee "exploitation" is noted below.

The idea of class exploitation is derived from the social relations within the typical camp of a few families, the largest enduring, autonomous unit in Chukchee society. The camp is supported by a single reindeer herd. The herd is the property of one family (sometimes extended) and is under the administrative control of the family head, whom Bogoras designates the "master." If the herd is large, there will be others in the camp, "assistants," who are dependent on the herd and, therefore, the owners. These are the "poor," the exploited.

What is the origin of the assistant, and what is his social and economic relation to the master? Before peace was imposed by the Russians, some were war captives ("slaves"). Their place has been taken by impoverished families of alien tribes overrun by the recent Chukchee expansion (Bogoras 1904–1909:349, 660). Many of the assistants are Reindeer Chukchee—sons of poor families, and whole families whose herds have been wiped out by some disaster. Still others are Maritime Chukchee attracted inland by the latter-day increase of the reindeer. The recent expansion of the Chukchee and their herds, and the inherent difficulties of reindeer breeding, have largely generated the category of dependent assistants.

Often the attachers are relatives of the owners, whom the latter ~~has~~ have taken in and helped in the spirit of aid to kinsmen. As herding is difficult in certain seasons, the "rich" owner is quite anxious to procure the help of those who come in need, and frequently attempts to keep it by marrying off his daughter to an unmarried assistant. Bogoras writes of the assistants: "Such helpers are called 'dwelling mates' . . . and the owners of every large flock, when short of hands, will strive in every way to attract at least one poor family. Often these are poor relatives of the owner of the herd. If there are any young unmarried men in these families, they will be offered a girl of the master's family in marriage, thus becoming a relative of his" (Bogoras 1904–1909:83). Most single men, even war prisoners in former times, were so incorporated into the owner's family (*ibid.*:587, 617).

The social relation between owner and assistant is thus usually one of kinship. This deeply influences the economic relation, qualitatively differentiating it from the dependence of wage laborer on capitalist. Where the assistant becomes son-in-law, the obligation to herd for the owner becomes that of bride service, a custom which prevails even if the suitor is self-sufficient (Bogoras 1904–1909:579, 586, 601). The assistant, as son-in-law, stands to become economically independent: if his wife is principal heir, he will eventually control most of the herd; at worst he is given a substantial present in reindeer by his father-in-law as a customary return for bride service (*ibid.*:586). Even without marrying into the owner's family, the assistant or assisting family will normally build up a herd while serving an owner. During the period of assistantship, the attacher is fed and clothed from the owner's herd and is given an annual present of fawns by the owner. The assistant's own herd is thus built up and after a few years, he need no longer depend on the master (*ibid.*:82, 622). The economic consequence of Chukchee "exploitation" is thus the perfect opposite of capitalist exploitation: the effect of assistantship is to provide impoverished families with their own means of livelihood and hence, economic independence. Economically the relation between master and assistant is mutual aid. The recent expansion of Chukchee herds and concomitant incorporation of outsiders into Chukchee society has brought this feature into prominence. That is why Chukchee life remains "democratic"—plain and filthy as it may be.

Much has been made of the drudgery of the poor Chukchee assistant, the insinuation being that this is comparable to the hard lot of the wage laborer in the grip of the profit-hungry entrepreneur. Chukchee drudgery, however, is totally incomparable. In part it is that of bride service, common to suitors of means and "poor" alike. Mostly the drudgery of the Chukchee assistant is due to the sheer difficulty of herding in seasons when insect pests or scarcity of pasturage require frequent movement of the reindeer. At these times, all hands, *including members of the owning family, women and children,* are pressed into service and herd until they literally drop from exhaustion (Bogoras 1904–1909:82–83, 548). There are hard masters, but these are abusive to family and assistants alike (*ibid.*:619). The task-making master is not the norm; generosity and good treatment on the owner's part is the social ideal (*ibid.*:617). A few bad-tempered people should not be taken as characteristic of the social relations of a system of production.

There is no exploitative class system in Chukchee society. A man who joins a camp and cares for the herd is not even terminologically distinguished from the owner's family, but is treated, as Bogoras explicitly remarks, "as an equal and a brother" (Bogoras 1904–1909:616). It is a familial economy.

Tolowa-Tututni

The Tolowa-Tututni, Athapascan food gatherers of northern California and the Oregon coast, are the type case of the dual economy (Du Bois 1936). As described by Du Bois—and Drucker (1937) presents substantially the same picture—Tolowa villages had two economies: the subsistence economy, involving production and circulation of need-serving goods; and the prestige-economy, dealing with shell money tokens, obsidian blades, and other valuables. The former was organized by the kinship ethics of mutual aid. The latter was dominated by the drive to acquire and manipulate valuables so as to maintain prestige. The prestige economy effected two social classes; the few rich and powerful, and the many poor and subordinate.

It is clear that differential access to the means of livelihood was not the basis of "class" differentiation. So-called private fishing grounds and other vital resources were freely used within the village. Food was rarely if ever sold and was freely dispensed, evidently in the spirit of kinship, by the "haves" to the "have-nots" (more precisely, to the "do-nots") (Du Bois 1936:50–51; Drucker 1937:235, 241). If wealth breeds power, the causal relation is distinct from that obtaining in Euro-American society. It is further distinctive of Tolowa society that the acquisition of valuables did not actually *establish* prestige or power. The possession of wealth was a social prerogative in the first place. Valuables were maintained in certain families by primogenitural inheritance; they were not acquirable in quantity by the "poor." Therefore, status breeds wealth, not vice versa (Du Bois 1936:65; Drucker 1937:241–242).

Further, wealth of itself, its possession, did not define the powerful "rich-man," but only the use of wealth in certain transactions that affected the community: ". . . mere possession of a quantity of valued shells was not sufficient in itself to establish a man as a respected personage in his community" (Drucker 1937:225). What transactions did the rich-man enter into? The authorities agree that shell money was predominately used for two purposes: bride-price payment and legal compensation (Du Bois 1936:56; Drucker 1937:*passim*). Such payments must have been characteristically outside the village, that is, between rich-men of different communities. For even in recent times, village exogamy was normal (89 per cent of marriages recorded by Drucker were exogamous), and it was principally injuries to outsiders that were compounded, while those within the village were glossed over (Drucker 1937:289–293). It appears that the so-called prestige transactions are those in which the rich-men stand as village representatives, paying co-villagers' fines, arranging and subsidizing their marriages—in brief, dealing economically with outsiders. It seems justified to assert that the rich-man is given prestige socially since he acts as central agent in intercommunity economic dealings, as steward of goods associated with the village and used for village purposes. This is consistent with a lack of "class" interests:

The rich-man's fellow villagers, rather than resenting his wealth, bask in the reflected glory of his shell money dealings (Drucker 1937:252).

Close examination reveals that within the village and with regard to food itself, the rich-man exercises the same functions. The rich-man is the dispenser of food; he is the regulator of the supra-domestic aspect of the village economy. And this is crucial: the rich-man derives prestige from distributing food just as he does from handling shell-money. The rich-man does not operate differently in the subsistence economy and the prestige economy. The two economies apparently have the same principles and organization. We learn that "A feature never omitted in a description of the house of a man of wealth is the rows of well-filled storage baskets set against the walls" (Drucker 1937:234). This food is partly dispensed, without reciprocation, to the "poor." The generosity of the rich-man increases his prestige, while the people who depend on him sink in esteem (Du Bois 1936:50, 51). In addition, the rich-men provide food for village and intervillage feasts and also subsidize dances that might last up to two weeks (Drucker 1937:253, 265). Drucker does not break stride between the subsistence and prestige economies in describing the rich-man's role: "It is said that some of the richest men never worked; their henchmen hunted and fished for them. In return the rich-man gave feasts, and in lean times would share his stores with his people. He bought wives for the young men . . . accepted and held the bride prices paid for their sisters and daughters. . . . it was the rich-man who was obliged to pay compensation for wrongs his henchmen committed, to save them, and himself from retaliation. . . . he received a lion's share of any indemnities paid for injuries to one of them" (Drucker 1937:245).

The economic position of the rich-man is clarified by his social relation to his "henchmen," viz., he is their lineage head. The Tolowa-Tututni rich-man turns out to be the leading member of a patrilineage or a segment thereof. The Tolowa-Tututni village turns out to be a single, possibly segmented, autonomous paternal lineage (Drucker 1937:235, 244, 273). As head of the town-lineage, the rich-man is custodian of its corporate property. For example, he was "nominal owner of the real property of the lineage" (*ibid.*:273). These resources were free to all comers since ". . . the town consisted essentially of a paternal lineage, who jointly held the right to exploit certain tracts. . . . Thus all townsfolk, as part owners, enjoyed a right to share in the products of their territory, a right which was given more force by the stress on affection and mutual helping among a group of kinsmen" (*ibid.*:235). The genesis of the headman's stewardship is evidently the prevailing custom of primogenitural inheritance of title along with guarantee of usufructuary privilege to the heir's younger brothers. In time this creates a lineage with a senior line, having the obligation to administer corporate property of the whole. It is as lineage head, and because of that status, that the rich-man acts as representative in interlineage (intervillage) economic affairs. Consequently, as Drucker writes: "Status was indeed reckoned in terms of wealth, but only when the tokens were used for the benefit and protection of the kin group" (*ibid.*:252).

Tolowa-Tututni economy is simply a family economy extended on a lineage scale, characterized throughout by the cooperation typical of a household. The economy has indeed two aspects, a household aspect and a lineage aspect, but these are parts of the same whole. The lineage part of the economy is administered by the lineage head, who stands *in loco parentis* to his lineage. He manages the lineage property, concentrates goods circulating within the group, and dispenses these to those in need or in support of communal activities. He acts in the same capacity in interlineage transactions involving money tokens. The economic side of the rich-man's activities bolsters the social side, and vice versa. As head of the lineage he accumulates goods, and by distributing them for the benefit of the lineage, he accumulates prestige. Generosity, rather than simple acquisition, ownership, or consumption, is the principal means of reinforcing status. And the reason for the rich-man's generosity is that, "after all, he was more than just a master; he was a blood relative as well" (Drucker 1937:252). Another capitalist redskin bites the dust.

It is probable that analysis would reveal that the Yurok, neighbors of the Tolowa-Tututni and arch-capitalists of the primitive world, were economically organized in the same way. Space permits us to quote only Kroeber's tantalizing definition of Yurok chiefs as those "whose wealth, and their ability to retain and employ it, have clustered about them an aggregation of kinsmen, followers and semi-dependents to whom they dispense assistance and protection" (Kroeber 1925:3). The careful student can easily discover the same principles of economy throughout the Northwest Coast, among all those whom Radin proclaimed "The capitalists of the north." When the acculturative features of the potlatch are stripped away, it becomes nothing but the formalized redistributive mechanism of a lineage economy, generating the prestige of the chief while materially serving the general welfare (cf. Codere 1951; Drucker 1939, 1951, 1955; Barnett 1938).

Trobriands

Much "capital" has been made of conspicuous consumption and waste in the Trobriand economy (for example, Herskovits 1952:470–471). But Malinowski's clear description of a tribal, kinship economy administered by chiefs indicates only an enlarged variant of the types we have just considered. Malinowski was fully aware that the economic activities of Trobriand chiefs were without parallel in the capitalist order (for example, 1921:10–12). He writes this of the relation between wealth and power in the Trobriands: ". . . wealth is the indispensable appanage of social rank and attribute of personal virtue. But the important point is that with them to possess is to give [!]—and here the natives differ from us notably. A man who owns a thing is naturally expected to share it, to distribute it, to be its trustee and dispenser. And the higher the rank the greater the obligation. . . . Thus the main symptom of being powerful is to be wealthy, and of wealth is to be generous" (1922:97).

The economic function of the Trobriand chief is to organize the tribal economy by concentrating goods made available by the various households and reallocating them to subsidize further production and community activities. Two operations can be distinguished in the chief's role: the collection of goods and the redistribution of goods. Prestige is socially attributed to both operations. The net economic effect of the chief's activity is to promote the general interest.

The significance of the Trobriand case is the uncommon method by which the tribal economy is instituted. The corporate social units are localized matrilineal subclans. The political unit is a confederacy of subclans and villages ruled by a chief, a member of the subclan of highest rank. The key economic institution is the *urigubu,* the presentation of a large share of the yam crop to the gardener's sister's husband and/or the spouses of other of his maternal kinswomen. The ability of confederacy chiefs to concentrate wealth is given by customary chiefly polygyny. The chief marries women, as many as forty, from all important matrilines in his domain; the maternal kinsmen of the chief's wives are practically coextensive with his subjects. The chief is therefore entitled to *urigubu* from all groups in the polity. He may accumulate up to 30 or 50 per cent of the total yam crop. The chief is also titular owner of all coconuts, betel, and pigs within his area of sovereignty, and is given a share of these—although this too is phrased *urigubu* (Malinowski 1921, 1922, 1935).

In his storehouse, the chief's accumulated food is displayed, a sign of his position. However, simple display does not produce prestige, since only the chief has the right; others who might attempt large scale display would only invoke the wrath of the chief (Malinowski 1922:169; 1935,I:60, 82–83). Furthermore, the chief's ability to accumulate is matched by his obligations to distribute his wealth. The distributive obligation is necessary to the chief's prestige, helping to maintain it since, "The giving of food is an act of superiority; and generosity is the highest of privileges, as well as an appreciated virtue." (1935,I:82). Chiefly redistribution is not conspicuous consumption, not waste, not done for idle purposes, but instead provides the economic basis for tribal activities, and makes possible a certain degree of specialization of labor. The chief supports all communal productive activities. He subsidizes warfare, feeding and feasting assembled warriors. He contributes heavily to trading expeditions. He gives gifts to all who perform services for him, in this way stimulating a number of types of specialist production. And he feeds people who assemble for recreational activities and religious ceremonies (Malinowski 1921:7, 10–11; 1922:64, 87–88, 124f. *et passim;* 1935,I:26–27, 56, 230–231, *et passim*).

The obligation of chiefly generosity extends the principles of the familial economy to the larger society, creating a tribal-wide economy. What would Trobriand life be without it? To content oneself with the idea that this is just conspicuous consumption once again, is to fail to grasp its significance. Such censure cannot be passed on the ethnographer. He clearly states:

in the long run, all the wealth accumulated by [the chief] flows back to his subjects. This pooling and reapportionment, however, is not a mere idle play of changing hands. In the course of it some wealth becomes transformed into more permanent objects, and again a great many events and institutions in tribal life are organized by this process of concentration and redistribution. It is this process which allows of such industrial specialization as exists. It is this process also which makes wealth an instrument of political organization (Malinowski 1935,I:47).

Discussions of Trobriand economics which emphasize conspicuous waste have diverted the issue from redistribution. The Trobrianders do attempt to produce an absolute surplus of yams, an amount that would rot in the storehouses. In an average year, twice as much is produced as can be eaten, Malinowski asserts. It is supposed this was wasted in aboriginal times, although nowadays it is traded to Europeans. However, it is justifiable to question whether modern production for exchange has not stimulated productivity in food production. Furthermore, in the twenty-five years before Malinowski's study, productivity had undoubtedly been raised by the acquisition of metal tools and new crops (Malinowski 1922:482; 1935,I:161). Also European contact has mitigated the possibility of famine, as rice can be purchased from traders, conserving the yam supply in lean years. The economic significance of the Trobriand desire to see yams rotting evidently is related to the danger of famine. In aboriginal days, a bad year was a dread event, even engendering hunger cannibalism, and death by starvation (*ibid.*,I:161f.). A big yam crop in the previous year could mean the difference between life and death. Rotting yams would be a sign that disaster is not in the offing. Accumulating yams to the point of waste is to be understood as a prevention against possible starvation, not as a means of creating status through conspicuous waste. What is necessary for the exercise of power is dispensation of goods, not their accumulation in unusable quantities.

Throughout Oceania, the general relation between wealth and power is the same. Accumulation and redistribution by chiefs stimulates production, disseminates goods through the community, supports tribal activity, and bolsters the power of the central agent in the tribal economy. The case is no different even where shell money is involved, as a study of Douglas Oliver's recent book on the Siuai of Bougainville easily demonstrates (Oliver 1955). We have elsewhere brought together evidence to indicate that in Polynesia the economic function of chieftainship is redistribution, and this role is the foundation of political power (Sahlins 1958). We can rest our case for Polynesia here on the words reported to have been spoken by a Tongan chief upon receiving an explanation from a European on the use and value of money:

Certainly money is much handier, and more convenient, but then, as it will not spoil by being kept, people will store it up, instead of sharing it out, as a chief ought to do, and thus become selfish; whereas if provisions were the principal property of man, and it ought to be, as being the most useful and the most necessary, he could not store it up, for it would spoil, and so he would be obliged either to exchange it away for something else useful, or share it out to his neighbors, and inferior chiefs and dependents, for nothing (Mariner 1827,I:213–214).

IV

The value of the foregoing examples is that they dispel the notion that power and wealth are everywhere associated as they are in our economy.

Further, the examples may be used to develop some general statements regarding the economy and status differentiation in primitive society. To help in suggesting such propositions, we first summarize some ~~destructive~~ *distinctive* features of primitive economic systems. The wide extent of these characteristics is not only documented by the preceding discussion, but even from the studies of those who have attempted to graft capitalistic, market-oriented theory upon them.

In primitive economies, most production is geared to use of the producers or to discharge of kinship obligations, rather than to exchange and gain. A corollary is that *de facto* control of the means of production is decentralized, local, and familial in primitive societies. The following propositions are then implied: (1) economic relations of coercion and exploitation and the corresponding social relations of dependence and mastery are not created in the system of production; (2) in the absence of the incentive given by exchange of the product against a great quantity of goods on a market, there is a tendency to limit production to goods that can be directly utilized by the producers.

It is easy to document the fact that most production is geared to use (or discharge of kin obligations) in primitive economies. This is not even contested by those who adopt elements of a market theory of interpretation. To point to the general absence of price-fixing markets would be sufficient. Even among peasants where small surpluses are brought to market places, most of a household's consumption results from its own production. Thurnwald phrases this point by describing primitive economies as "direct"; that is, little circulation intervenes between production and consumption (Thurnwald 1932:105). The much-abused suggestion of Carl Bücher that much of primitive economy is "household economy" can be supported. The implications Bücher drew from this—viz., the general absence of entrepreneurial enterprise, of capital and of the dependence of labor upon the capitalist—are correct (Bücher 1907).

Control of the means of livelihood rests with producers in primitive society. Chiefs may claim overrights to resources and may enforce their rights by tabuing resources for tribal purposes, yet they cannot separate families from the land. Herskovits repeatedly notes that the means of production are in the direct possession of producers, and obliges us by pointing out the most significant implication of this fact, viz., the primitive producer, "is the master of his own economic destiny" (1952:31). To Marx, of course, this is the key difference between capitalistic and most precapitalistic economies. And Bücher tersely grasps its importance when he notes that from a household economy, relations of social dependence "manifestly cannot come" (1907:318).

A crucial implication of production for use and direct control of the means of livelihood has received comment from Leacock (1954:7). In the absence of an intensive division of labor and the exchange of specialized products or labor power on price fixing markets, production will be limited by the skills, resources and traditional requirements of the household. (Compare Pirenne's discussion of the limitations on productivity in the absence of large markets in feudal Europe [Pirenne 1936:64–66].) The economy lacks the productive incentive given by the market. Instead there is a centripetal tendency. Productivity is contained, production limited to goods that can be made given a minimal division of labor and that can be consumed by the producers. Primitive society does not inherently produce a surplus; the system of ownership and production moves to inhibit the generation of a surplus. To anticipate slightly, this centripetal tendency stands directly in the way of a tribal-wide economy. It is only overcome by the attribution of prestige to those who administer the tribal economy, thus giving them the ability to stimulate the production upon which, in turn, their economic functions rest.

A final distinctive feature of primitive economy is what Polanyi calls its "embeddedness" in noneconomic relations, primarily kinship: "The term 'economic life' would here have no obvious meaning" (Polanyi 1957b:70). Like the economy, the political system is an aspect of the kinship structure in primitive societies. Kin relations imply the very opposite of economic expropriation. It follows that political power is not based on expropriation.

Where economic relations are embedded in a kinship structure, these relations are characterized by minimization of the attempt to gain, maximization of mutual aid and cooperation—as in the modern family. Where the kin structure pervades the entire society, these must be the principles of an entire economy. It is impossible to organize the social system on a kinship basis and at the same time countenance transactions which maximize personal advantage. Polanyi attributes the absence of such transactions involving food in primitive society to the fact that "The element of antagonism, however diluted, that accompanies this variant of exchange is ineradicable. No community intent on protecting the fount of solidarity between its members can allow latent hostility to develop around a matter as vital to animal existence and, therefore, capable of arousing as tense anxieties as food" (1957a:255). In primitive societies, economy begins in the home. Home, as Robert Frost wrote, "is where if you got to go there, they got to take you in."

Here reciprocity and the pooling of resources and labor are the principal forms of transaction. The tribal economy is an extension of familial economic relations, just as the tribe itself is an extension of familial social relations. In handling wealth, the sentiments of kinship are ever present. "It may be said that primitive wealth is not of an economic but of a social nature; the man who has, by whatever means, acquired more cattle, grain, or valuables of any kind than his neighbors has not done so in order to hoard his wealth for his own benefit, but that it may be used for the good of other members of the community" (Thurnwald 1932:182–183). It is against this background that we must view the economic activities of primitive chiefs.

We can now summarize the argument which relates economic and political power in tribal societies. Social inequality does not develop from economic inequality. Rather, the origin of social inequality is the differentiation of economic roles generated by the development of a tribal-wide economy. Status differences arise concomitantly with the division of function between those who administer the allocation of goods and those who supply them in a multihousehold economy. The tribal economic system is an extended family system, characterized throughout by kinship cooperation and mutual aid. The principal administrative operation in a tribal economy, therefore, is pooling and redistribution of goods by a central agent. Everywhere, this central agent occupies a political, chiefly status and his redistributive activities subsidize the division of labor and tribal enterprise. Prestige is attributed to the chief so long as he manages goods in the general welfare. This prestige not only permits the chief to influence persons, it sanctions his call on goods. Prestige, therefore, operates to overcome an inherent tendency to limit productivity in a system of production for use (as opposed to production for exchange). Prestige is the action of a social system operating to widen the economy at the same time, and by means of increasing the powers of the administrating chief. It follows that the growth of political power and the development of a tribal economy are in direct and reciprocal relation, and both are similarly related to economic productivity.

The examples of primitive economy described in the last section clearly show that status differences are concomitants of different functions in the economy. As the circulation of goods, tribal enterprise, and tribal cooperation increase, there is increasing political distinction between the manager of goods on a large scale and the producers. Chieftainship emerges with a suprahousehold economy. Where households are for the most self-sufficient, as among the Chukchee, social authority is limited, confined to the family head. As tribal economy develops—as among the Tolowa-Tututni, and on a larger scale, the Trobriands and Polynesia— so does a tribal authority system. It is not, however, the possession nor consumption of goods that gives chiefly power, but their dispensation; hence generosity is the *sine qua non* of chieftainship. This generosity is manifested in chiefly subsidization of specialist production, communal production, of religious ceremony and other cooperative activity. It is understating the case to claim that chiefly redistribution makes a tribal economy possible—it makes tribal life possible.

What transforms the economic function of managership into a status and authority position is the attribution of prestige to this position. The greater the pooling and dispensing, the more the prestige, and hence the greater the power to influence others. Prestige is here considered as a social phenomenon. Prestige acts as an incentive to the central agent to generate and perpetuate a tribal economy. More significantly, prestige, by strengthening the chiefly demand on goods, overcomes the centripetal tendency of an economy based on production for use. The chief, backed by prestige, stimulates production beyond the immediate utilitarian requirements of the household. The chief, backed by his prestige, thereby provides the logistic basis for a suprahousehold division of labor and many forms of community cooperation. Prestige associated with pooling and redistribution operates simultaneously as an incentive to dispensation on the chief's part and an incentive to production on his kinsmen's part—thus a tribal economy.

We conclude by stressing that the growth of political power, of a tribal economy and of productivity are in direct and mutual relation. Any force or circumstance that would tend to increase productivity, tribal economy or chiefly power would also tend to increase the others. For example, military competition normally enhances the chief's political position since he organizes the tribe's defense. But defense, as a tribal enterprise, demands economic support; hence, the stimulation of production. The chief's role as military leader has a logistic side; viz., accumulating the goods required by the military effort. On the one hand, this means a chiefly call on household goods, while on the other hand, in accumulating and redistributing these goods the chief gains prestige which reinforces his position as military leader. The development in productivity, economy and polity attained by any particular society would depend on the specific conditions affecting it: available technology, environmental potential for expansion, degree of competition with other systems over resources, presence or absence of kinship systems that would facilitate extension of familial cooperation and redistribution, and the like. Considered, however, in general perspective, in the evolution of culture as a whole, productivity, the tribal economy, and political power proceed together. The higher the productivity, the more differentiated and larger the tribal economy, and the more developed the chiefly powers.

BIBLIOGRAPHY

AYRES, C. E.
1946 *The Divine Right of Capital.* Boston, Houghton Mifflin Co.
BARNETT, H. G.
1938 "The Nature of the Potlatch." *American Anthropologist,* 40:349–358.
BOGORAS, W.
1904–1909 "The Chukchee." *Memoirs of the American Museum of Natural History,* 11 (*The Jesup North Pacific Expedition, 7*).
BÜCHER, CARL
1907 *Industrial Evolution.* New York, Henry Holt & Co., Inc.
BUNZEL, RUTH
1938 "The Economic Organization of Primitive Peoples." In *General Anthropology,* ed. by Franz Boas, pp. 327–408. Boston, D. C. Heath & Company.
CHILDE, V. GORDON
1948 *Man Makes Himself.* London, Watts & Co.
CODERE, HELEN
1951 Fighting with Property. *Monographs of the American Ethnological Society,* 18.
DRUCKER, PHILIP
1937 "The Tolowa and their Southwest Oregon Kin." *University of California Publications in American Archaeology and Ethnology,* 36:221–300.
1939 "Rank, Wealth and Kinship in Northwest Coast Society." *American Anthropologist,* 41:55–65.
1951 "The Northern and Central Nootkan Tribes." *Bureau of American Ethnology Bulletin,* 144.
1955 Indians of the Northwest Coast. *American Museum of Natural*

History, Anthropological Handbook, 10. New York, McGraw-Hill Book Co.

Du Bois, Cora
1936 "The Wealth Concept as an Integrative Factor in Tolowa-Tututni Culture." In *Essays in Anthropology Presented to A. L. Kroeber*, pp. 49–65. Berkeley, University of California Press.

Fetter, Frank A.
1935 "Capital." *Encyclopedia of the Social Sciences*, 3:187–190.

Firth, Raymond
1950 *Primitive Polynesian Economy*. New York, The Humanities Press.
1954 "Orientations in Economic Life." In *The Institutions of Primitive Society*, by E. E. Evans-Pritchard, Raymond Firth, *et al.*, pp. 12–24. Glencoe, The Free Press.

Fortes, Meyer and E. E. Evans-Pritchard
1940 "Introduction." In *African Political Systems*, ed. by M. Fortes and E. E. Evans-Pritchard, pp. 1–23. London, Oxford University Press.

Fusfield, Daniel B.
1957 "Economic Theory Misplaced: Livelihood in Primitive Society." In *Trade and Markets in the Early Empires*, ed by K. Polanyi, C. Arensberg, and H. Pearson, pp. 342–356. Glencoe, The Free Press and the Falcon's Wing Press.

Goodfellow, David M.
1950 *Principles of Economic Sociology*. New York, The Humanities Press.

Herskovits, Melville J.
1952 *Economic Anthropology*. New York, Alfred A. Knopf, Inc.

Kroeber, A. L.
1925 "Handbook of the Indians of California." *Bureau of American Ethnology Bulletin*, 78.

Leacock, Eleanor
1954 "The Montagnais 'Hunting Territory' and the Fur Trade." *Memoirs of the American Anthropological Association*, 78.

Lowie, Robert H.
1948 *Social Organization*. New York, Rinehart & Company, Inc.

Malinowski, Bronislaw
1921 "The Primitive Economics of the Trobriand Islanders." *The Economic Journal*, 31:1–16.
1922 *Argonauts of the Western Pacific*. London, Routledge and Kegan Paul Ltd.

1935 *Coral Gardens and Their Magic.* 2 vols. New York, The American Book Company.

MARINER, WILLIAM

1827 *An Account of the Natives of the Tonga Islands, in the South Pacific Ocean.* Compiled and arranged by John Martin. 2 vols. 3rd edition. Edinburgh, Constable and Co.

MARX, KARL

n.d. *Capital.* New York, The Modern Library.

MILLS, C. WRIGHT

1953 "Introduction to the Mentor Edition." In *The Theory of the Leisure Class,* by Thorstein Veblen, pp. vi–xix. New York, The New American Library.

OLIVER, DOUGLAS

1955 *A Solomon Island Society.* Cambridge, Harvard University Press.

PEARSON, HARRY W.

1957 "The Economy Has No Surplus: Critique of a Theory of Development." In *Trade and Markets in the Early Empires,* ed. by K. Polanyi, C. Arensberg and H. Pearson, pp. 320–341. Glencoe, The Free Press and The Falcon's Wing Press.

PIRENNE, HENRI

1936 *Economic and Social History of Medieval Europe.* London, Routledge and Kegan Paul Ltd.

POLANYI, KARL

1957a "The Economy as Instituted Process." In *Trade and Markets in the Early Empires,* ed. by K. Polanyi, C. Arensberg and H. Pearson, pp. 243–270. Glencoe, The Free Press and The Falcon's Wing Press.

1957b "Aristotle Discovers the Economy." In *Trade and Markets in the Early Empires,* ed. by K. Polanyi, C. Arensberg and H. Pearson, pp. 64–94. Glencoe, The Free Press and the Falcon's Wing Press.

SAHLINS, MARSHALL D.

1958 *Social Stratification in Polynesia.* The American Ethnological Society. Seattle, University of Washington Press.

SCHMOLLER, GUSTAV

1910 *The Mercantile System and Its Historical Significance.* London, The Macmillan Company.

THURNWALD, RICHARD

1932 *Economics in Primitive Communities.* London, Oxford University Press.

VEBLEN, THORSTEIN
1919 *The Theory of the Leisure Class*. New York, B. W. Huebsch.
WHITE, LESLIE A.
1949 *The Science of Culture*. New York, Farrar, Straus and Company.

$*\ *\ *\ *$

Elman R. Service

UNIVERSITY OF MICHIGAN

SOCIOCENTRIC RELATIONSHIP
TERMS AND THE AUSTRALIAN
CLASS SYSTEM[1]

In any human society individuals occupy social positions which have significance in interpersonal conduct. When the names of these positions are used in address or reference, they may be called "relationship terms." Kinship nomenclature is a worldwide and well-known example of relationship terminology, but it is by no means the only one. Relationship terms in general can be divided into two distinct types, egocentric and sociocentric, and this division can be useful in the study of social organization. The problems of the Australian class system will be discussed as a rather extended illustration of the utility of this dichotomy.

I. EGOCENTRIC AND SOCIOCENTRIC
RELATIONSHIP TERMS

Every human society has relationship terms which specify kinds of social categories of persons or groups relative to others. The category of any individual depends on who the speaker (Ego) is. That is, someone may be "mother" to one Ego and "aunt," "cousin," or "grandmother" to others.

---

[1] I am grateful to Robert Carneiro, Gertrude Dole, Morton Fried, A. Kimball Romney, Marshall Sahlins, Gerald Weiss, and Leslie A. White for helpful comments.

Such terms may be called *egocentric*. But there are other relationship terms which are not egocentric. A person occupies a named position and status, or is a member of a recognized group, no matter who is addressing or referring to him. These categories are, in a sense, objective, and the reference point is the structure of the society itself rather than another person. We may call such terms *sociocentric*. A person is an "Eaglehawk" —of Eaglehawk moiety—and not a "Crow." Clan names, locality names, personal names, named generations, occupations, and even nationality and racial terms, are other examples of sociocentric relationship nomenclature.

Sometimes sociocentric terms are derived from egocentric kinship terms, and may even be the same words, but the distinction can still be made. Thus, "*my* grandfather" designates someone in the egocentric pattern, but a person may also be said to be "*a* grandfather," and this is sociocentric, referring to a socially significant generation grade of the society. A boy may be "son" to anyone of the older generation, and an older person may be "father" or "uncle" to any member of the younger generation. But each person is also "son," "father," or "uncle" in the egocentric set of kinship terms.

Conversely, there are terms which are not derived from the kinship system which are both egocentric and sociocentric. "My Lord" (in reference or address) is egocentric. But "He is *a lord*" refers to the status held in the society, no matter who is speaking. "Boss," "comrade," "captain," "husband," "wife"—a near infinity of examples come to mind.

Two persons can relate better, that is, more precisely, to each other if they can trace an egocentric genealogical relationship between themselves, particularly in a primitive society which stresses familial bonds. But lacking this knowledge, if each can be named as *a* something—an "elder," an "in-law," a "relative," a "stranger," a "nobleman," and so on —relationships of a certain character can be initiated. Suggested in this last sentence is a further and very important difference between the two kinds of terms—the context or occasion for their use.

Egocentric terms are used in small face-to-face groups which have a high degree of stability. A family is the most obvious and undoubtedly the most typical example of such a group; hence, familial relationship terms (kinship terms) form the most common egocentric nomenclature of social relationship. In a family, any member knows a great deal about everyone else, and therefore a great number of things relevant to social position do not need to be specified. At the same time, because all of the social relations are close, consistent, and quite permanent, the system of nomenclature can have considerable complexity; the terms can refer to the relationship of any person or number of persons in the group to any particular Ego. It becomes a cumbersome system, however, if the society is large and numbers of the people do not have frequent and continuing social contacts. Familial relationship ties become attenuated, and some relationships become insignificant and infrequent. On the other hand, familial terms may have to be metaphorically extended to include relationships which are significant in daily social behavior, but which are not truly familial.

It is in such larger complex societies that sociocentric terms have their greatest utility, particularly because of the frequency of contact between strangers. In such cases, broad categories are established first: One is a Rotarian, a midwesterner, a used car dealer; the other an Elk, a Californian, and a chiropractor. As the relationship continues, finer distinctions become specified. But as everyone knows from experience, certain things may be so manifest that they do not need to be stated; that one is a male or female is (usually) readily apparent, as is relative age if the disparity is great. Strength, wealth, and wisdom, for example, may or may not be obvious, depending on the culture and the circumstances. At any rate, one endeavors to place a stranger in a class or a series of classes and subclasses which are relevant to social status. The most important statuses may be designated by brief titles in formal usage, such as "Doctor," "Sir," "Professor," "Madame," "Lord," and so on.

In primitive life the family is such a basic part of society, and suprafamilial institutions are so rare, that all or nearly all social relations are formalized in terms of statuses which are in fact either directly familial or are derivatively or metaphorically so. To the extent that sociocentric nomenclatures exist, they typically refer to kinship categories. Probably the most common are moiety and clan names, and generation terms. And because the sociocentric terms are often kinship-relevant, the basic difference between egocentric and sociocentric categories is easily lost sight of by the ethnographer—both kinds are included in descriptions of "the kinship system."

The Australian aborigines have several sociocentric terms of relationship as well as egocentric familial terms.[2] There are locality names,

---

[2] Since this paper was written, an article by Romney and Epling has been published which mentions essentially the same distinction between class terminology and kinship terms (among the Kariera tribe) that I am here trying to establish: ". . . kinship terms are in large part *relative* in the sense that the term used depends upon the relation between two persons, while the section terms are *absolute* in the sense that every individual is assigned to a section by birth and he retains this affiliation throughout life." (Romney and Epling 1958:64).

totemic "clan" names, and names for whole linguistic divisions. In addition, there are categories of kindred once called "marriage classes," more recently called by Radcliffe-Brown "moieties," "sections," and "subsections," depending on whether the society has two, four, or eight of these divisions. As a generic term for these groupings, I shall use "class," intending it to be synonymous with "category," with no implication of socioeconomic status or suggestion as to its function in marriage.

If the Australian classes are seen as examples of sociocentric nomenclature, then we may assume that, as elsewhere, they function, not in the context of the internal order of a given social group, but in the meeting of people who do not know each other's egocentric kinship positions. And also, because Australian culture is a very primitive one, it follows that because sociocentric terms express the most significant characteristics of a person's position in the structure of his own society, the class terms will be derived from the kinship order.

These interpretations can be supported by statements from ethnologists of wide experience in Australia. A. R. Radcliffe-Brown once put it this way:

The relationships between one person and another in the kinship system are individual relationships. In deciding what they are appeal is always made to actual genealogical connection. Thus in Western Australia the first questions always asked of a stranger is "who is your father's father?" Similarly in all discussions as to the suitability of a proposed marriage it is the genealogical connection between the two persons that is considered. *It is true that when the genealogical connection is too remote to be traced the natives fall back on a consideration of the section or subsection or the clan to which an individual belongs* [italics mine], but this does not alter the fact that in the minds of the natives themselves they are dealing, throughout all the ramifications of the kinship system, with real genealogical relations of parent and child or sibling and sibling (Radcliffe-Brown 1930–31:436).

A. P. Elkin has stated several times that as guides to social behavior the class terms are used among people who are *not* continuously associated with each other, rather than among members of the same kinship group:

This is especially true in inter-tribal meetings. It is much easier for one group to learn the other's subsection system than to bother about all its kinship terms, and so mutual behavior during the gatherings in largely controlled by the subsection grouping, but only, of course, because fundamentally this is a grouping of kinship relations (Elkin 1954:101).

And again:

If different tribes are to meet together, and they do, they must understand their various methods of grouping relatives so that mutual behavior can be organized and respected during the time of meeting. . . . (Elkin 1954:32). The meeting of tribes for ceremonial purposes, and nowadays, too, the mixing of members of different tribes in white employ, facilitates and encourages the spread of such systems of summarizing kinship. They are naturally of very great value at intertribal gatherings, enabling camping, social activities, and marriages to be readily arranged, whereas the labour of comparing and adjusting the actual relationship through kinship terms alone in different languages, would be a very difficult process indeed (Elkin 1932:325).

If sociocentric class names function predominantly in a society's external, rather than internal, relations, and if they express the most fundamental categories of the egocentric kinship system, we wonder what those categories may be. There has been disagreement among students of Australian customs as to what the causes and purposes of the class system are, with a resulting variation in their ideas of the basic elements in its composition.

II. THE COMPONENTS OF THE AUSTRALIAN CLASS SYSTEM

The many analyses and explanations of Australian class nomenclature can be reduced to three general types. One of the earliest was propounded by Lewis H. Morgan and his disciples, Fison and Howitt. In its essentials, it consisted of the assumption that the named categories, which they called "marriage classes," were survivals of a previous custom of group marriage. This theory has long since been discredited and has no support today; hence, it may be ignored for the purposes of this paper.

Another early explanation is apparently accepted by most modern anthropologists, possibly because it has been presented so convincingly by G. P. Murdock in his influential work *Social Structure* (1949:51) and elsewhere (Murdock 1940). The essentials of this view were first argued by Francis Galton (1889) and later by Emile Durkheim (1897). A. B. Deacon, A. R. Radcliffe-Brown, and Brenda Seligman, all in the same volume of the *Journal of the Royal Anthropological Institute* (1927), proposed it again. In 1937, W. E. Lawrence made a thorough review of the literature and revised the explanation.

Galton and Durkheim felt that the four-class system was caused by the intersection of male and female descent lines, and that the purpose of the naming of the categories was to regulate marriage or prevent incest. Seligman also said that "bilateral descent," the recognition of both father's and mother's descent lines, is the cause, and the purpose is to regulate marriage (1927:375). Radcliffe-Brown (1930–31:55–58) put it this way: "The patrilineal lines of descent (I and II) constitute a pair of patrilineal moieties. The matrilineal lines of descent (X and Y) constitute a pair of matrilineal moieties. The system of four sections is constituted by the crossing of patrilineal moieties and matrilineal moieties giving four divisions in all." He further suggests that the subsection system of eight classes is caused by the presence of four patrilineal lines or "semi-moieties" instead of two. Lawrence (1937) also considers the four-class system (Radcliffe-Brown's "sections") to be formed by an intersection of two lines of descent, the patrilineal line formed by the patrilineal local group, and a matrilineal moiety. Eight classes are formed when the mother's patrilineal line is also recognized in order to prevent marriage with these relatives.

One of the characteristics of the four- and eight-class systems is that children do not belong to the class of either of the parents, but belong instead to the class of the father's father and mother's mother in the four-class system, and to the class of the father's father in the eight-class system. This characteristic has been phrased as "indirect descent," or as "alternating generations." But it is seen by Murdock, Lawrence, and their predecessors to be a result of the intersection of descent lines, and not as one of the basic and original components of the class system. And truly enough, if one draws a genealogy and assigns each person in it to a named category depending on the combination of descent lines, the same class names do reappear only in alternating generations.

This version of the components of the class system is particularly convincing if one assumes that the purpose of naming the groups is to regulate marriage, or as Durkheim put it, to "prevent incest." There is no doubt that most primitive societies do endeavor to prevent marriages with some relatives and to foster them with a certain few others. If this is the purpose of the class system, then the alternation of generations might well be merely a by-product of the intersection of descent lines. All of those mentioned as proponents of the "descent-lines" explanation state in one way or another that the regulation of marriage is the purpose of the naming of classes, and they seem to regard the distinctions between generations as insignificant and functionless, as indeed they would be in the context of marriage rules.

But there are some ethnological facts which contradict this interpretation. Radcliffe-Brown (1913:192 and 1930–31:58–59), Elkin (1954:90, 92) and W. L. Warner (1937:122–123) observed ethnographically that marriages are arranged in terms of the kinship system, not the class system. A further comment was made by Radcliffe-Brown (1951:42): "marriage systems and 'class' systems of Australia are not co-variant but vary independently. . . . Thus tribes with four 'classes' have marriage systems of any of the four types mentioned, and all four types are equally to be found in tribes that do not have four 'classes.' "

There is still another unsatisfying aspect to the "descent-lines" functional analysis; it doesn't explain very much. Some Australian tribes have no named classes, others two, four, or eight. They all have patrilineal descent [3] and are remarkably similar in most other aspects of social organization. Why do they not all use class nomenclatures? Why do the southern Arunta have four named classes and the northern Arunta eight, when they are otherwise identical? How can the diffusion of the system be explained, if its presence is caused by some strong local social function or need? These facts, particularly the well-documented cases of modern diffusion of the class nomenclature, properly impressed A. L. Kroeber (1952), and led him to describe the classes as "secondary" and "epiphenomenal" institutions, products of "play," rather than basic ones, and to suggest that there is no functional reason at all for things of that kind. Considering the distinction between egocentric and sociocentric nomenclatures, I would agree with Kroeber that the class terms have no important functional determinants within a group's *internal* order. But I would argue that there are important uses for it in a group's *external* social relations.

Radcliffe-Brown (who here contradicts one of his earlier quoted statements), Warner, and Elkin have said many times that the class terms have the same purpose as the kinship terms: They are convenient signposts for kinds of social conduct. As Elkin (1954:100–101) put it, "This makes the system a very useful method of summarizing the twenty classes of relations that an individual possesses. . . . It also makes the system a very useful guide to social behavior." And here we ought to be reminded again of the statements of Radcliffe-Brown and Elkin that the occasion for the use of class nomenclature is in the personal relations of people who do not belong to the same intimate social group. That is, the social

---

[3] For purposes of this paper, I am granting the existence of recognized descent lines. Actually, I am in accord with the suggestions of A. L. Kroeber (1952), Paul Kirchhoff (1955), A. M. Hocart (1955:193), and Radcliffe-Brown (1930–31:100, 107) that unilineal descent lines are probably not in fact recognized, but exist only implicitly as an aspect of postmarital residence customs. An additional argument against the Murdock-Lawrence theory could be made on this basis.

context of the use of class names is that which is normal to sociocentric nomenclature.

More plausible than the theory which considers the class nomenclature to be a result of isolating descent lines specifically for the purpose of regulating marriage, then, would be an analysis which included as the basic components of the class system those aspects of the kinship system which are most significant for general social conduct or etiquette, particularly when the individuals cannot establish their specific kin relationship. Such an analysis has been suggested by three people, Radcliffe-Brown, Warner, and Elkin. Each proposed it so succinctly and without argument or embellishment that it has not made much of an impression in anthropology.

Radcliffe-Brown's latest statement on the subject reads:

Both endogamous moieties (alternating generation divisions) and exogamous patrilineal moieties which divide the local groups into two intermarrying sets, are widespread. Where they exist together, there inevitably results a four-fold kinship division. If we call the generation divisions M and N, and the patrilineal moieties I and II, the four divisions are MI, MII, NI, and NII. The generation division may be regarded as "horizontal" and the moiety division as "vertical," since these two divisions cut across each other (1951:39).

Inasmuch as Radcliffe-Brown makes the above statement specifically in opposition to Lawrence, we assume that this is a final and considered judgment, and that he had given up or forgotten his earlier statement supporting the descent-lines theory. Curiously, he does not say anything about the causal or functional significance of his later interpretation.

Warner (1937:177) very briefly states a similar notion. The class system "regroups" and "generalizes" the kinship system. The first significant determinant of the groups is the separation of adjacent generations. The second is the moiety principle, making four groups. Eight classes "are achieved by dividing each kinship personality into two."

Elkin (1954:96) has offered the same idea, but phrased a little differently. He sees the separation of generations as one important function of the four-class system and the separation of cross cousins as the other. This latter function is essentially the same as that of Radcliffe-Brown's "exogamous moiety," for the effect of a moiety is to separate cross cousins (and other actual and potential in-laws). Eight subsections are formed when first cross cousins are separated from second cross cousins (p. 99).

This last point, incidentally, has long been accepted by field workers in Australia. Spencer and Gillen first noted it (1899:70–75). The eight-class system is associated with tribes whose kinship system and marriage customs do in fact separate first from second cross cousins, prohibiting marriage with the former. It should be noted, however, that not all of the tribes that specify second cross-cousin marriage have an eight-class system.

At this point, the above descriptions of the class system seem preferable to the descent-lines theory in certain respects. The class system is described as functioning in the context of generalized social behavior, particularly in inter-societal contacts, which is exactly what is to be expected of sociocentric nomenclature. Marriage customs are relevant to the formation of classes, but are not specifically and solely the determinants; nor is the function of the classes merely to regulate marriage. Marriage rules are significant aspects of the social structure and affect social behavior, but so do other kinds of rules and conditions. The regulation of marriage and the prevention of incest are universal problems and are typically dealt with, in Australia as elsewhere, in the context of egocentric kin systems or genealogies. The class system is seen by Radcliffe-Brown, Warner, and Elkin as having a much broader and more generalized social function. They have, in fact, *witnessed* its function, in large part; this is not a "viewpoint" but a matter of ethnographic fact. And because the class terms are guides to social behavior, the distinction they create between adjacent generations is seen as one of the basic and purposeful features of the system rather than as an insignificant consequence of the recognition of intersecting lines of descent.

No one argues that exogamous moieties are not one of the basic components of the class system. In much of the primitive world, relatives are regarded as consisting of two distinct kinds, "other" and "own." [4] Social behavior is always strongly influenced by this general dichotomy and in very many primitive societies this exogamous division exists as two named moieties; that is, a sociocentric terminology is applied. In Australia, it appears that all tribes have this division, whether named or not. Many Australian tribes have a two-class system which consists of two named intermarrying divisions. Named moieties are thus very familiar to anthropologists, and it is not difficult to see them as an ingredient in four- and eight-class systems. Their relation to marriage rules is a subordinate one, however. They do not "regulate marriage," but exist, rather, *because of* a rule of marriage which creates two intermarrying groups in the

---

[4] There seems to be no appropriate word for this distinction. The usual "consanguineal" and "affinal" are inadequate because in primitive society affinal relatives are ordinarily consanguineal relatives as well.

society; that is, marriage and moiety are two aspects of the same thing. Individual marriages are arranged much more specifically with particular relatives and are not affected by the presence or the absence of named moieties. Exogamous moieties separate *all* of the people into two groups, rather than being relevant merely to the position of the small proportion of people who are about to be married. It should be apparent that marriage customs are not, therefore, to be discounted as factors in the formation of moieties and further subdivisions. But the classes receive names because of certain conditions in wide, usually intertribal, social and ceremonial relations. The names merely *reflect* marriage customs, among other things.

But it would seem that generational distinctions are also significant. All anthropologists are familiar with a common form of primitive kinship terminology which uses so-called "self-reciprocal" terms between grandparents' generation and grandchildren's. But another way of putting it is to say that the kin terms distinguish parent-child generations, but not the second ascending and second descending generations. And this form of nomenclature can occur both in egocentric and in kinship-derived sociocentric systems. This should not be too unexpected if we assume that relationship terms name categories which are important in social behavior. In all human families the two adjacent generations have distinct statuses relative to each other.

In Australia, social distinctions between members of adjacent generations are very strong, and these distinctions are reflected in the kinship terminology. However, the ways anthropologists describe such systems conceal this point. The expressions "alternating generations" and "self-reciprocal terminology" focus on the fact that the class membership and kinship terms of grandparent and grandchild are the same. But the social significance is that adjacent generations are separated. Radcliffe-Brown's term "endogamous moieties" puts the emphasis on the fact that one marries within his or her own generation, but again, the most important point is that the two generations are separated terminologically.

Some Australian tribes have a two-class sociocentric nomenclature which is no more than the use of only two terms, as "M" and "N," successively, separating adjacent generations but leaving the third or alternate generations undistinguished from each other. The fact that this kind of two-class system, and the previously mentioned two-class system of exogamous moieties each exist separately around the periphery of the four- and eight-class area is, incidentally, another strong indication that these two kinds of divisions are the components of the four-class system.

A further point concerning the matter of generations may be made. Our emphasis is on the fact that adjacent generations are separated by the class terminology. But a more usual perspective, consistent with the phrasing "alternating generations," is that the alternate generations are lumped together. This view suggests that merging these generations in terminology is peculiar and must be explained. The typical explanation is that the social behavior of grandchildren with grandparents is somehow equivalent, equal, or symmetrical. As Radcliffe-Brown (1952:48–49) put it, "There is, in fact, a generalized relation of ascendancy and subordination between the two generations (that is, parent-child). This is usually accompanied by a relation of friendly equality between a person and his relatives of the second ascending generation." This seems peculiar, when it has been noted time and again in Australia, as well as in many other societies in the world, that although grandparents may be indulgent toward grandchildren, the two social statuses are the most unequal in the society, old people holding the very highest status, and children the lowest.

Instead of wondering why alternate generations are merged in terminology, it could just as well be said that those generations are left undistinguished from each other—not distinguished because there is no need to do so. As we have defined them, sociocentric terms specify some status or significant characteristic of a person when it would otherwise be unknown, or at least not readily apparent. The difference between persons separated by two generations is so obvious that there is no need to specify the difference in status. To be sure, through time a considerable disparity may arise between a person's actual chronological age and the age normal for his generation, but such a disjunction would not be usual enough and great enough to affect the scheme. But there is another reason, perhaps more important, why alternate generations need not be distinguished. By the time a person is fully adult in a society as primitive as that of the Australians, with its early aging and low life expectancy, people of the grandparental generation have died, with perhaps a few exceptions. And, of course, relationship terms are based on usual or normally expected situations, not on exceptions.

It is quite a different matter when adults of more nearly the same age meet. If they cannot avail themselves of the more precise egocentric or genealogical knowledge, the one apparently somewhat older might be of either the other's own generation or of his parents' generation, just as in a family it is possible to have a cousin or brother of nearly the same age as one's uncle. But the difference in social behavior is supposed to be considerable, even if the disparity in chronological age is not great. Thus, in a sociocentric context it is useful to have membership in one of the two adjacent contemporaneous generations defined.

A four-class system, then, is nothing more than four names for categories, each of which includes two socially significant attributes. A person is of one side or the other of the intermarrying moieties, and his is the ascendant or subordinate one of the two generations which are present among the active adults at any given period. These categories are socially significant in many primitive societies. They are, in fact, the major distinctions drawn in the widespread "classificatory system" of kinship nomenclature. A. M. Hocart, in speaking of the point of view of Fijian natives toward establishing the relationship of one person to another, said:

In short, what we seek most is the next of kin, and so we run up and down the family tree. The Fijians (and the Australian aborigines, and the rest) do not, because there is no point in doing so. All they want is such information as will enable them to place each man on the correct side in the right generation. An inquiry proceeds thus: "How are you related?" "Of the same side and generation." "Why?" "Because our fathers were of the same side and generation." Or else: "We belong to successive generations on opposite sides, because he is of my mother's side and generation" (1955:193).

Any family, anywhere, has these distinctions implicit in its organization. The question, though, is whether they will remain only implicit in the egocentric kinship pattern of terms, or whether objective sociocentric groups will be named from the distinctions drawn in the kinship system. Two-class sociocentric systems, consisting of exogamous moieties (the naming of father's and mother's "sides"), are very common in the primitive world. Separating adjacent generations by giving them sociocentric terms is perhaps less common, but still not unusual. The four-class system, composed of both these distinctions, has been considered as primarily an Australian phenomenon, though a few instances of its occurrence elsewhere have been pointed out. The eight-class system, which includes a further subdivision of the exogamous moieties by separating first from second cross cousins, is still more unusual, having only a limited distribution even in Australia.

The fact that an argument has been presented here to established the usage, purpose, and components of the class divisions does not mean that all important questions have been discussed. We still want to know why some tribes have class terms while others have not, and how the distribution of the various two-, four-, and eight-class systems can be explained. Can their origin, development, and diffusion be inferred? A review of the distribution of the various kinds of class nomenclatures is indicated in order to discover whether the perspective taken so far in this paper has any further utility in relation to the several questions which arise from the distribution pattern of the class systems.

III. DISTRIBUTIONAL PROBLEMS

In various places located on the coastal periphery of Australia there are tribes which have been described as having no class system. To be more consistent with the point of view taken here, we should say that they are one-class tribes, for without doubt every social order has a sociocentric term, frequently the name of a locality, by which it may be distinguished as a totality from other societies. But one class or none, the important features of the distribution of these groups are that they are infrequent, discontinuous, and marginal; yet they exist in the continent's most productive and densely settled areas, the coastal regions.

More widely scattered and more frequent are tribes with two classes. As mentioned earlier, they are of two distinct kinds. One is the named moiety, a dual division of the society into two intermarrying halves. A person's membership in a moiety may be taken from the mother in some tribes and in others from the father, but the effect is the same: two exogamous groups are formed; cross relatives are separated from parallel relatives; mother's own kin are distinguished from father's; and a generalized kind of behavior characteristic of the relations of affines rather than consanguines corresponds to the delineation. The egocentric kinship terms make these distinctions too, of course, but named moieties objectify, generalize, and extend the distinctions. The other kind of two-class system is created by the separation of the two adjacent generations.

As Radcliffe-Brown describes it, the division which distinguishes the two generations is "horizontal" and the moiety division is "vertical." When both distinctions are made and the resulting groups are named, the society is separated into four compartments. This system has the widest geographical distribution in Australia, and the tribes that have it are contiguous except where the eight-class system has overlaid it.

There is another kind of four-class system, limited and peripheral to the above, which has been called a system of "semi-moieties." It is merely the ordinary named exogamous moieties, but with each divided into two parts by the separation of first from second cross cousins of any Ego. It exists only when the marriage rule prescribes second cross-cousin marriage rather than first cross-cousin marriage. Affinals, potential or actual, are thus defined in a more restricted way. This distinction is not a difficult one for the Australians to make and adhere to, because post-marital residence rules cause second cross cousins to be members of different local groups from first cross cousins.

The eight-class system is simply the above form of semi-moieties bifurcated by generation. Stated another way, it is the other more usual four-class system of generation and moiety divisions with the moieties subdivided between first and second cross cousins. As in the system of semi-moieties, second cross-cousin marriage is not caused by the system, but, rather, the rule of second cross-cousin marriage is a necessary antecedent condition.

Both N. W. Thomas (1906) and D. S. Davidson (1926, 1928) felt that the distribution of these systems was significant. With one-class tribes the most marginal and scattered, two-class tribes less so, four-class systems contiguous and widespread, and with eight classes limited, but contiguous and central, something is suggested about their origin and development. The implied development could be represented by the diagram accompanying the distribution map on page 430.

A logically permissible conclusion from these data is Davidson's judgment (1928) that once there were no classes (or one), that two classes appeared and became widely distributed, that four classes appeared next out of two, and eight later, out of the four-class systems. I add to this only the reminder that there are two kinds of two-class systems, the named adjacent generations as well as the named exogamous moieties. The usual four-class system appeared when these two kinds came together. The eight-class system of semi-moieties combined with the separation of adjacent generations appeared more recently and diffused rapidly.

Why are the compound systems later and central? It is helpful, as remarked earlier, to see each one as dependent on a previous, simpler system. From this perspective we can see more clearly what the components are. But something else can be inferred from their distribution. The map reveals, in a very general way, that one- and two-class systems occur in the coastal areas where the population density tends to be greatest, and where the camps do not travel so extensively or distantly in search of food. The arid regions of least population density, where local groups must travel most widely, are in central Australia, where the four-class system, and finally the eight, originated and spread. A. W. Howitt (1889:34) commented on this ecological fact long ago, but reached the conclusion that the no-class groups represent an evolutionary advance over the four- and eight-class groups, because he regarded the classes as survivals of earlier group-marriage customs.

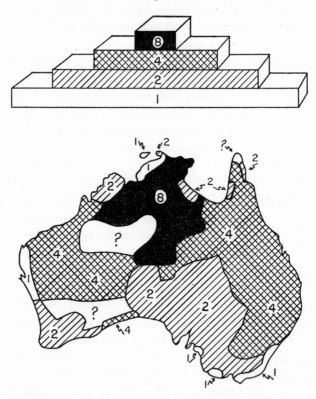

THE DISTRIBUTION MAP FOLLOWS LAWRENCE (1937:348, MAP A). I HAVE SIMPLIFIED IT BY NOTING ONLY *NAMED* CLASSES, AND I HAVE NOT DISTINGUISHED THE TWO KINDS OF TWO-CLASS AND FOUR-CLASS SYSTEMS. (Drawn by Edwin Ferdon, Jr.)

Elkin has made several observations which aid in understanding the distribution of the eight-class system. "Generally speaking it is in the drier and arid regions where this organization is more clear cut. In them, the foraging groups must be comparatively small and be separated by miles, often for weeks at a time, otherwise the sources of food would soon fail" (Elkin 1954:47). If we follow the implications of the view that class nomenclature, being sociocentric, is most useful among people who meet only sporadically and infrequently, it becomes more comprehensible why the compound systems tend to be centrally located in the arid regions.

Again, Elkin (1954:101) states, "There is little doubt that the practical usefulness of the system at meetings of an intertribal character is the cause of its spread. . . ."

The points made so far agree with Elkin's scattered statements, but it would seem that a more positive conclusion than Elkin's is justified. The practical usefulness of class nomenclature at meetings of an intertribal character is not only the "cause of its spread," but is also the stimulus which led to its origin. Discriminations among people of a social group in terms of generation differences and in-law relationships are not particularly useful among people who see each other frequently; the egocentric kinship system is sufficient and preferable. The four-part distinctions are implicit in their social order but the need for naming them sociocentrically does not exist.

Where meetings are less frequent, and the people are relative strangers to each other, the need for sociocentric terminology is greater—a stimulus is present. This would mean that in inland Australia social conditions exist which make the naming of the sections more likely there than in the more productive areas. But we must emphasize that sociocentric nomenclature in general, or any particular kind of sociocentric terminology, is not an inevitable functional consequence of these conditions. There are many ways people can codify social behavior, and it is apparent that even egocentric kinship terms can be extended—metaphorically, and by adoption—to incorporate strangers. But sociocentric terms do come about; and it is easier to understand a development of this kind when we see its utility.

The fact that sociocentric terms are used in intertribal meetings means that one system has to be used by the diverse groups that meet. If each one of the language groups had its own special system, only confusion would result. The invention of a class system, in a sense, must be something like a cooperative venture between at least two groups, with others acquiring it as its utility is manifested. As described by Elkin (1950), the eight-class system spreads at the expense of simpler ones, because, we may suppose, of its greater utility in intertribal relations. This intertribal use also has resulted in the diffusion of the system from areas where it is most useful, and where it presumably originated, to areas such as coastal Arnhem Land, where it would be less useful. This occurs because there is a belt of contiguous tribes having social relations from the former to the latter areas. The presence of a compound system in one group dictates its acquisition by the adjacent ones if social relations obtain among them.

IV. SUMMARY AND CONCLUSION

The most widely accepted explanation of the Australian class system was presented first by Francis Galton, then Durkheim and others, and finally, with some refinements, in recent years by Lawrence and Murdock. This theory holds that the recognition of both matrilineal and patrilineal descent lines creates four groups which are named in order to regulate marriage. Eight classes are formed when Ego's mother's patrilineal line is also isolated by certain marriage rules. A terminological distinction between parents' and children's generations results from the intersection of the descent lines, and is not seen as an original and fundamental part of the class system.

Another theory, briefly set forth by Radcliffe-Brown, Warner, and Elkin, describes the components of the class system as: (1) A division of the society into two intermarrying halves (moieties); (2) A distinction between adjacent generations, parents' and children's. This makes four basic compartments in the society. Eight classes are created when each of the intermarrying moieties is divided into semi-moieties, separating any Ego's first cross cousins from second cross cousins.

Both of these explanations are logical and coherent, and both propose a "purpose" to the class divisions. The purpose of naming groups formed by the intersection of descent lines is to regulate marriage; the purpose of the moiety-generational distinctions would seem to be a more generalized one, that of summarizing and simplifying the kinship nomenclature in the context of intertribal social meetings. On the face of it, there seems to be little to choose between the two views.

The distinctions drawn in the present paper between egocentric and sociocentric relationship terms, however, permit us to make a clear choice between the two arguments. Egocentric terms specify the social position of a person relative to a particular ego. Kinship nomenclature is the best known example of this type. Sociocentric terms, on the other hand, express a person's membership in a component category of the society itself; the term is therefore applied no matter who the Ego is addressing, or who is referring to him. The Australian class system is sociocentric by definition, and we find by reanalyzing the problem with this characteristic in mind that there are several reasons for rejecting the Lawrence-Murdock theory in favor of the presentation of Radcliffe-Brown, Warner, and Elkin.

Sociocentric relationship terms, in any society, differ from egocentric terms not only with respect to their point of reference—the society rather than individual persons—but also in the social context of their use. Sociocentric terms are used in the interaction of people whose meetings are sporadic and rare, people who do not know the finer and more complex status characteristics of each other, but who do need to know the most significant and gross characteristics in order to initiate an ephemeral social relationship. This expectation, based on theory, is substantiated by ethnographic descriptions of the use of the class system; it is described as functioning largely in intertribal gatherings. For this reason alone, it is reasonable to expect that the components of the class system are the generational and moiety divisions proposed by Radcliffe-Brown, Warner, and Elkin, for these are the two most important aspects of the Australian kinship order, as they are in a great many other primitive societies. The distinction drawn between egocentric and sociocentric nomenclatures reveals that the kinship system and the class system are merely two terminological facets of one social organization. The context of the use of the terms is different, but the social organization itself is a usual primitive one based on familial ties, in no way complex or unusual.[5]

So far as the purpose of the class nomenclature is concerned, then, it is the same as that of the kinship terminology. Both are systems of *relationship* terms, having to do with social behavior, and not merely the regulation of marriage. Marriage rules are not precisely irrelevant to either the formation of class nomenclature or its subsequent utility; they bear the same relationship to the classes as they do to the kinship system, for the class terms and the kinship terms are both determined by the social organization in general, of which marriage is only one aspect among many. The Murdock-Lawrence assumption that the purpose of the class system is to regulate marriage can be shown to be wrong also on other grounds, namely ethnographic fact. Marriages have been described as arranged in terms of the kinship system, not the class system. Furthermore, kinds of marriage rules do not co-vary with kinds of class systems.

---

[5] A further, but rather parenthetical, remark is relevant here. Many anthropologists have regarded Australian social organization as very complex because of the presence of the class system, and they have used this as an argument against the theory of cultural evolution; that is, they argue that evolutionists assume that a simple technology must be accompanied by a simple social organization, but technologically primitive Australians have an "advanced" (complex) kinship system: Hence evolutionist assumptions are wrong. But I hope this paper has shown that the class nomenclature is a *substitute for* the kinship nomenclature in particular contexts (and a simplification of it, in fact), and is in no way an added dimension to the social organization itself, which remains equally simple whether or not a sociocentric class terminology is used.

A further test of the utility of the egocentric-sociocentric dichotomy is made by testing its value in accounting for the distribution of the various class systems in Australia. The simplest systems exist marginally and sporadically in the coastal areas. The two-class systems may be inferred, for this reason, to be the oldest of the multiple-class systems. Four-class systems exist mostly in the interior of the continent and are contiguous to each other and widespread. Eight-class systems are a limited central block. This suggests that the eight-class system is the latest and that it includes the components of the simpler systems. Interestingly enough, we find that there are two kinds of two-class systems: one of named exogamous moieties; the other of named alternating generations. The four-class system is merely composed of both generational and moiety distinctions. Eight classes appear when each moiety is subdivided to separate first from second cousins.

The distribution of the class systems corresponds roughly to distinct ecological zones. The simplest systems occur in the coastal regions, which are the richest and most densely populated areas. The four- and finally the eight-class systems are in progressively poorer and less settled areas. The character of the social gatherings in these different zones reflects the ecological variation; in the arid interior "the foraging groups must be comparatively small and be separated by miles, often for weeks at a time, otherwise the sources of food would soon fail" (Elkin 1954:47). The use of class nomenclature, as described by ethnologists in Australia, is found among people who meet only sporadically and infrequently, just as should be expected from the general character of sociocentric relationship terms. It is therefore comprehensible why the compound systems first developed in the interior of Australia.

It should be remarked at this final point that the main purpose of this paper has not been to show that one view of the Australian class system is correct and another one wrong. The theoretical distinction between egocentric and sociocentric relationship terms, however simple and obvious it may be, is much more important. It is this idea which makes possible a choice between the two views by presenting a new kind of supporting argument for one of them, and it suggests answers to a wider variety of questions than either of the two views could supply alone.

BIBLIOGRAPHY

DAVIDSON, D. S.

1926 "The Basis of Social Organization in Australia." *American Anthropologist,* 28:529–548.

1928 "The Chronological Aspects of Certain Australian Social Institutions as Inferred from Geographical Distribution." Ph.D. Dissertation, University of Pennsylvania, Philadelphia.

DEACON, A. B.

1927 "The Regulation of Marriage in Ambrym." *Journal of the Royal Anthropological Institute,* 57:325–342.

DURKHEIM, E.

1897 "La prohibition de l'inceste et ses origines." *L'Anné Sociologique,* 1:1–70.

ELKIN, A. P.

1932 "Social Organization in the Kimberly Division, Northwestern Australia." *Oceania,* 2:296–333.

1950 "The Complexity of Social Organization in Arnhem Land." *Southwestern Journal of Anthropology,* 6:1–20.

1954 *The Australian Aborigines.* 3rd edition. Sydney and London, Angus and Robertson.

GALTON, F.

1889 "Note on Australian Marriage Systems." *Journal of the Anthropological Institute,* 18:70–72.

HOCART, A. M.

1955 "Kinship Systems." In *Readings in Anthropology,* ed. by E. A. Hoebel *et al.,* pp. 189–193. New York, McGraw-Hill Book Co.

HOWITT, A. W.

1889 "Further Notes on the Australian Class Systems." *Journal of the Anthropological Institute,* 18:31–68.

KIRCHHOFF, P.

1955 "The Principles of Clanship in Human Society." *Davidson Journal of Anthropology,* 1:1–10.

KROEBER, A. L.

1952 "Basic and Secondary Patterns of Social Structure." In *The Nature of Culture,* pp. 210–218. Chicago, The University of Chicago Press.

Elman R. Service

LAWRENCE, W. E.
1937 "Alternating Generations in Australia." In *Studies in the Science of Society,* ed. by G. P. Murdock, pp. 319–354. New Haven, Yale University Press.

MURDOCK, G. P.
1940 "Double Descent." *American Anthropologist,* 42:555–561.
1949 *Social Structure.* New York, The Macmillan Company.

RADCLIFFE-BROWN, A. R.
1913 "Three Tribes of Western Australia." *Journal of the Royal Anthropological Institute,* 43:143–194.
1927 "The Regulation of Marriage in Ambrym." *Journal of the Royal Anthropological Institute,* 57:343–348.
1930–31 "The Social Organization of Australian Tribes." *Oceania,* 1:34–63, 206–246, 426–456.
1951 "Murngin Social Organization." *American Anthropologist,* 53:37–55.
1952 "The Study of Kinship Systems." In *Structure and Function in Primitive Society.* Glencoe, The Free Press.

ROMNEY, A. K. and E. J. EPLING
1958 "A Simplified Model of Kariera Kinship." *American Anthropologist,* 60:59–74.

SELIGMAN, B. Z.
1927 "Bilateral Descent and the Formation of Marriage Classes." *Journal of the Royal Anthropological Institute,* 57:349–375.

SPENCER, B. and F. J. GILLEN
1899 *The Native Tribes of Central Australia.* New York, The Macmillan Company.

THOMAS, N. W.
1906 *Kinship Organisations and Group Marriage in Australia.* Cambridge, Cambridge University Press.

WARNER, W. L.
1937 *A Black Civilization.* New York, Harper & Brothers.

* * * *

Albert C. Spaulding

UNIVERSITY OF MICHIGAN

THE DIMENSIONS OF ARCHAEOLOGY

This paper is an attempt to describe clearly the fundamental
operations of archaeology on its empirical data. Behavioral inferences may creep in, but they will be evidence of weak-mindedness.
The goal is most definitely not a lecture on how archaeology ought to be
done; it is rather a description of what is done when exposition is incisive,
economical, and convincing. The topic is particularly suitable for a
volume honoring Leslie White, whose major work has been the systematic
exposition of interrelationships of cultural phenomena. A great gain
would result if my purpose could be realized fully: questions of fact
would be sharply separated from questions of theory, thus pointing accurately to those topics on which factual data are needed and providing
a guide for research along the most effective lines. Since all the matters
discussed here are essentially common knowledge, I have not provided
any references.

METHOD OF ANALYSIS

I assume that on an elementary level we cannot improve on the concepts
that are successful in other branches of science, especially in the physical
sciences, which enjoy a long tradition of enviable precision and clarity,
at least when viewed from the outside. These sciences can be thought
of as studying the interrelationships of the dimensions appropriate to
their specified subject matter. The subject of mechanics, for example, is
physical objects, and the dimensions in terms of which the objects are

· 437

considered are length, mass, and time. Classical mechanics can be defined economically as the study of the interrelationships of length, mass, and time exhibited by physical objects. Thermodynamics, on the other hand, can be considered a more complicated science because it deals with temperature in addition to the three dimensions of mechanics. A dimension can be thought of as an aspect or property of the subject matter which requires its own special measuring device. There are invariable rules for operating with dimensions (the examples given are not logically independent), of which we can mention:

1. The units of discrete dimensions do not possess additive properties. Any formulation of the type $L + T = x$ or $L = T$ (feet plus minutes equals x, or feet equals minutes) or "the artifact is older than it is heavy" is meaningless.
2. Ratios of discrete dimensions, usually called rates, are meaningful, familiar examples being miles per hour or pounds per cubic foot.
3. Concepts involving more than one application of the measuring instrument can be meaningful. Thus area is length squared, and volume is length cubed.
4. Dimensional equations must be homogeneous, that is, the same dimensions must appear on both sides of the equation. However, dimensionless numbers may be introduced into such equations.

SUBJECT MATTER AND DIMENSIONS OF ARCHAEOLOGY

It seems quite clear that the subject matter of archaeology is artifacts, using this term in its broadest sense as any material expression of human cultural activity and adding the qualification that I am concerned here with prehistoric artifacts. Although deciding whether or not a particular object is an artifact may be difficult, I will treat the artifact as given in this discussion for reasons of economy. The dimensions of artifacts which will be considered here are form (in the sense of any physico-chemical property of the artifact), temporal locus (meaning the dating of prehistoric events as inferred from artifacts, specifically the time of manufacture, period of use, and time of deposition of an artifact or a class of artifacts), and spatial locus (the position of the artifact in the three dimensional world). There is, I believe, general agreement that archaeologists are always concerned with these properties of artifacts, and there is an implication that archaeology can be defined minimally as the study of the interrelationship of form, temporal locus, and spatial locus exhibited by artifacts. In other words, archaeologists are always concerned with these interrelationships, whatever broader interests they may have, and these interrelationships are the special business of archaeology.

All of the rules for operation with dimensions apply to form, time, and space, and certain theoretical formulations can be dismissed at once on this basis. A statement of the type "the focus concept contains more of form than it does of time (or space)" is equivalent to the dimensional equation $F + T = x$, which is dimensionally heterogeneous and hence meaningless. Presumably what is involved here is a statement of the idea that a group of artifact assemblages having a high degree of formal resemblance to each other will usually or invariably show a compact clustering in time and in space, or in dimensional terms $\left[\dfrac{F_1}{T_1} = \dfrac{F_2}{T_2}\right]$. The dimensional equation (put in brackets to indicate that it is not algebraic) states that a systematic relationship holds between degree of formal resemblance and length of time span; since form and time appear on both sides of the equation, it is homogeneous and can be given a determinate meaning. This illustration is intended to show that reasoning in terms of dimensional analysis can be something more than a sterile formality: it can be a safeguard against unclear thinking or exposition. The dimensional equation also points directly to a very real archaeological problem: if we are to substitute real data for the symbols of the equation, then we must develop objective scales for our dimensions.

The Formal Dimension

It is plain that the formal dimension cannot be dealt with by the application of any simple kind of scale, although it is a useful concept for broad theorizing. In practice formal descriptions and comparisons are made by analyzing artifact form into a number of discrete attribute systems: color, chemical composition, weight, various lengths (and the length relationships which describe shape), and so on. These attribute systems can be treated as dimensions in their own right, and from this point of view the formal dimension is a class of dimensions. I will not attempt more than a glance at some of the obvious characteristics of formal attributes.

Formal attributes can be divided into two classes, quantitative attributes (or measurements) and qualitative attributes. Quantitative attributes, weight and length for example, vary continuously, and they can be measured by ordinary scaling devices divided into equal units. Artifacts can be compared absolutely in terms of these measurements, that is, the difference between two artifacts can be expressed in equal units of the appropriate scale (x is 25 pounds heavier than y). Relative comparisons are also possible (x is twice as long as y) if the zero point of the scale is not arbitrary. To borrow an example from another dimension, it cannot be said that Hopewell is twice as old as Middle Mississippi because the age relationship is merely a function of an arbitrarily chosen reference point in time. Quantitative attributes can be described neatly in scale units, and the numerical properties of the measurements lend themselves to straightforward statistical description and inference.

Qualitative attributes cannot be described and compared by means of any familiar scaling device. They are thought of as discrete properties of artifacts, and the scale applied is no more than a notation of presence or absence. Recognition of the qualitative attributes of an artifact seems to be largely intuitive. The observer has a personal knowledge of human musculature and sensory apparatus and of the properties of materials, and he can judge at once that the addition of a pair of side notches to a flint projectile point represents a discrete segment of the total behavior involved in making the point. Qualitative attributes which are mutually exclusive can be grouped into a dimension; thus the projectile point may be made from white flint, argillite, or some other material. This grouping provides a three-position scale within the dimension of material for describing the point and for classifying a collection of points.

In an ultimate sense, the distinction between quantitative and qualitative attributes tends to break down because any real measuring instrument must be divided into discrete steps, however small they may be. Nevertheless, the distinction remains in practice; the fineness of recorded measurements is limited only by the precision of the measuring instrument and the nature of the number system in which the records are kept, but the nature of the attribute itself limits the observation of the qualitative attribute. It is sometimes possible to transform ostensibly qualitative attributes into continuously variable properties, as when personal judgments of shades of color are replaced by measurements with physical apparatus, and the resulting gain in objectivity may prove to be valuable. However, the essentially discrete nature of many attributes is plain enough to make such a translation superfluous for many purposes, and a wholesale attempt to replace with measurements the current presence-or-absence observation of recognized attributes would have no utility. No one questions the reasonableness or objectivity of describing a vessel as having four strap handles and contrasting it with other vessels having two or no strap handles.

The distinction between quantitative and qualitative attributes is operationally relevant in a fundamental archaeological problem, the preparation of an attribute list for the formal description of a collection of artifacts. The very nature of quantitative attributes ensures that no two artifacts will yield exactly the same measurement, but it is necessary to discriminate between the unimportant and presumably random variation expected of products made by hand from materials which are not uniform and the culturally meaningful variation resulting from significantly differing models held by the makers of the artifacts. The problem can be attacked by listing in order the individual values of some measurement (say projectile point length) in a collection. If the list seems to show a pronounced clustering of values around a central point with progressively fewer values toward the extremes of the observed range, the conclusion ordinarily reached will be that the variation is of the random type. If, on the other hand, there are two or more values around which the measurements cluster, then two or more categories will be distinguished, and each can be thought of as a separate qualitative attribute such as "large" and "small." The problem is purely statistical, although in many instances it can be solved by inspection rather than by formal statistical curve fitting.

Qualitative attributes are by definition those properties of artifacts which are already recognized as representing discrete segments of behavior, and accordingly they can be placed on the attribute list without further analysis. Subsequent study may show that a supposed qualitative attribute can in fact be split into two or more meaningful classes; for example, a description of a motif as an incised triangle may disguise a significant difference between large and small or scalene and isosceles triangles. Conversely, some distinctions may be quite objective but turn out to have a sharply limited utility for the purpose of describing significant variations in patterns of attribute association. Thus triangles, rectangles, or circles might appear as decorative elements on a group of otherwise identical pots, and on this basis it would make sense to group them as a class of geometrical decorative elements. These qualifications are essentially secondary, however, and do not override the basic distinction of continuity *versus* discontinuity which is the root of the quantitative-qualitative division.

Techniques for recognizing formal attributes logically precede the next problem, that of studying artifact interrelationships in terms of formal attributes. For this problem, the recognized attributes serve as linking constants from artifact to artifact: they are the units whose presences and absences constitute similarity or difference. In some respects attributes are analogous to linguistic phonemes. They represent minimal units of meaningful behavior; they are taken to be constant for comparative and descriptive purposes; and they are articulated to form the artifact, which can be regarded as the minimal independent unit of material culture. In the simplest terms, the problem is what to do with a collection of artifacts and a list of formal attributes which the artifacts exhibit. There appear to be three possibilities in ordering a collection of artifacts with respect to their formal attributes:

1. The collection can be characterized by tallying each appearance of every attribute recognized.
2. The particular combination of attributes exhibited by each artifact can be listed, and the list can be condensed by grouping and tallying identical combinations.
3. The artifacts can be classified in terms of attribute clusters; this is accomplished by mathematical manipulation of the data provided by Types 1 and 2. This process is referred to here as cluster analysis.

Classification of Type 1 results in a number of classes having no relationship to one another except that imposed by the nature of the attribute systems. The description offered by such a classification is of the general type: red pots, 50, other colors, 50; grit tempered pots, 35; sand tempered pots, 65; bowls, 30; jars, 30; plates, 40; and so on. Tallies in sets of mutually exclusive attributes must sum to the total number of artifacts, but no other relationship is expressed. The information on relationships furnished by the physical association of attributes on the individual artifacts is wasted; we are told in the example that 35 of the 100 pots are grit tempered, but we do not know how many grit tempered pots are red.

Classification of Type 2 requires a list of all observed attribute combinations as the categories within which the individual specimens are tallied. It contains all the information presented by the attribute count plus full information on attribute association. The categories of combinations divide the entire collection according to one principle so that there is no question of which of two or more possible piles a specimen belongs to. In short, it is a complete descriptive classification which wastes no information, although its completeness is, of course, relative to the adequacy of the underlying attribute list. However, some unexploited analytic possibilities involving the relationships of attribute and attribute combination frequencies remain, and these are dealt with by the Type 3 classification.

Classification of the third type, cluster analysis, is dependent on the data of the second, and it is specifically concerned with such questions as how many of the red jars are grit tempered. Its basic feature is the comparison of the observed count for each attribute combination with the count expected on a hypothesis of attribute independence. These comparisons result in a rating on a continuous scale for each attribute combination along the lines of less than expected, about the same as expected, and more than expected. The reasoning involved is more easily exemplified than stated abstractly. Calculation of the expected tally for a particular combination under the hypothesis of independence uses only the attribute frequencies. In the example given, we can ask how many red grit tempered jars can be expected if these attributes are independent. In the total of 100 pots, 50 are red, 35 are grit tempered, and 30 are jars; if these attributes have no tendency to stick together, we can calculate that $\frac{50}{100} \times \frac{35}{100} \times \frac{30}{100} \times 100 = 5.25$ red grit tempered jars will be expected. The observed tally for the combination can range from 0 to 30 pots under the conditions specified. If the tally is actually 0, it would appear that the combination was avoided by the maker of the pots; a tally of 5 or 6 would suggest that the combination was neither avoided nor sought after; and a tally of 25 or 30 would indicate a strong tendency to group the three attributes. The last case illustrates what is meant here by an attribute cluster—a strong positive association of two or more attributes. I have ignored for the sake of clarity the sampling uncertainties which are so troublesome in real problems.

So far as I can see, classification with respect to attribute clusters exploits fully the formal information presented by a collection of artifacts since it interrelates the entire list of discriminated attributes in terms of both attribute frequency and attribute combination frequency. In my opinion, it also offers an explicit, operationally useful model of the relationships comprised under the concept of artifact type. A distinctive cluster of attributes is the consistent pattern central to the idea of type in both ordinary usage and discussions in archaeological literature. Cluster analysis is simply a full-dress exposition of the reasoning implied in the shorthand statement that type classifications are accomplished by putting together the artifacts that look alike. It is important to note that cluster analysis does not create clusters when they are not implied by the empirical data, it does not of itself explain the cultural meaning of the clusters (or lack of them) revealed by the analysis, and it will not necessarily assign every artifact to a typological pigeon hole: some artifacts may be genuinely intermediate between two clusters and others may be aberrant hangers-on of a reasonably well-defined type. It is equally important to realize that artifact types are not necessarily the most convenient and economical units for investigating possible systematic formal relationships in a set of collections; for this purpose simple attribute or attribute combination relative frequencies may serve as well.

When a formal analysis of two or more collections has been completed, comparisons in terms of the attribute list, the attribute combination list, and the type list are possible. These orders of comparison provide increasingly sensitive scales of similarily. Thus on a presence-or-absence basis two components may have identical attribute lists but not identical attribute combination lists, and they may have identical attribute combination lists but not identical artifact types.

Still more sensitive comparisons are possible when category frequencies (reduced to proportions so as to provide standard values for collections of varying sizes) are considered. Obviously it may be possible to detect valid differences between two collections on the basis of attribute frequencies even though both possess the same list of attributes. Somewhat less obvious is the fact that two collections may differ in attribute combination frequencies although they have the same attribute list, identical attribute frequencies, and identical attribute combination lists. This situation is illustrated in Table I, in which three sets of attributes are symbolized by letters and subscripts with a total of 100 specimens and the following frequencies assumed for two collections:

A_1	35	B_1	50	C_1	25
A_2	65	B_2	50	C_2	75
	100		100		100

Comparison of attribute combination frequencies is, in fact, the most sensitive possible because the combination tallies are a complete enumeration of the formal empirical data. Comparisons of type frequencies in the sense of the type concept used here would not add information to the formal likeness scale because any difference in the attribute clusters must be a reflection of differences in combination frequencies. The artifact type has no special value for formal comparison, although it does express objectively relationships inherent in or implied by the data. The attribute associations (or lack of them) revealed by cluster analysis are already contained, so to speak, in the attribute combination tallies. Cluster analysis brings into the open relationships which in many cases do not by any means leap to the eye from a simple inspection of the combination tallies; its purpose is to provide a basis for a culturally significant interpretation of differences in combination frequencies by ordering already existing data in a new way. It provides an escape from the dilemma of regarding everything as arbitrary (in which case "arbitrary" is robbed of any definite meaning) or neatly packaged (which is manifestly not true).

TABLE 1. VARIATION IN ATTRIBUTE COMBINATION FREQUENCIES IN TWO COLLECTIONS

	Collection I						*Collection II*				
	A_1		A_2				A_1		A_2		
	B_1	B_2	B_1	B_2	Total		B_1	B_2	B_1	B_2	Total
C_1	15	8	1	1	25	C_1	3	2	9	11	25
C_2	10	2	24	39	75	C_2	15	15	23	22	75
Total	25	10	25	40	100	Total	18	17	32	33	100

Over-all characterization and comparison of collections of artifacts can be conducted at a still more generalized level at which the entire body of empirical formal data is replaced by a single number. Ranking in terms of complexity is a familiar example. The basis for judging that, for example, a Hopewell assemblage is more complex than a Lamoka assemblage is usually not the result of a formal calculation, but it is plain that a simple comparison of the number of attributes, attribute combinations, or types in the two entities would support the judgment. If one were willing to assume that any attribute has about the same complexity as any other attribute, an attribute count would offer an objective measure of formal complexity. A second kind of over-all characterization can be made in terms of the degree of attribute clustering shown by a collection. This sort of characterization in nonmathematical idiom takes the form of describing a collection in some such terms as rigidly stylized as opposed to unconstrained or imaginative. Possible mathematical devices to objectify judgments of this sort need not concern us in detail. A very simple example would be the ratio of observed attribute combinations to possible attribute combinations, and more complex statements based on contingency tables could be worked out.

The Spatial Dimension

Scaling of artifact loci is a familiar operation. It means no more than the application of a yardstick in the three ordinary directions of space to produce the latitude, longitude, and depth measurements which define a point uniquely. Spatial attributes in this sense are given; the measuring instrument can be applied directly to the artifact *in situ,* and the resulting measurements can be recorded and analyzed with the aid of all the techniques appropriate to a continuous variable.

There are, however, certain circumstances under which spatial units are given special meaning. These are the cases where artifacts occur in some sort of container, and there is consequently a relationship between them which goes beyond mere propinquity. The container may be culturally produced, examples being the grave goods of a single burial, a group of artifacts in a cache or storage pit, or the contents of a room in a pueblo. Here the entire collection of associated artifacts becomes a descriptive and comparative unit, and the spatial interrelationships of the component artifacts are presented in a formal description of the unit as a sort of superartifact. The container may be provided by natural action—a single gravel lens in a stream deposit, a stratum of debris sealed by a layer of volcanic ash, and so on—or it may be the result of combined cultural and natural activity, as in the case of strata produced by the abandonment of a site, development of an erosion surface, and reoccupation. These situations do not differ theoretically from that of the culturally produced container; the component artifacts again become a special unit of association, and for many purposes the significant spatial measurement may be simply whether a given artifact is within or outside of the container. When these special association units are present, spatial observations are interpreted in the light of the physical laws of superposition and intrusion applied to the contents of the entire unit. On the other hand, when visible strata or other boundaries yielding association units within an archaeological deposit are not present, the analysis of spatial relationships becomes an example of the general case. Thus the interpretation of vertical relationships in a massive deposit is a function of the actual vertically scaled position of each artifact.

Aside from these examples of special association, space scaling yields a set of coordinates on a continuously variable scale as another sort of attribute for each artifact, and collections of artifacts are characterized by lists of coordinate sets. One of the primary results of the analysis of such data is so obvious that it is usually thought of as simple observation rather than analysis. This result is the recognition of the very strong tendency for artifacts to occur in tight spatial clusters, that is, in archaeological sites. The site is ordinarily taken to be a given, and the assemblage of artifacts from a site is the customary unit of description and comparison. In many cases the vertical component is treated as if it were negligible; indeed, there is no other course for surface collections or thin deposits. If adequate vertical segregation is present, however, the site may be divided into two or more assemblages.

Actual techniques for analysis of the spatial coordinates of artifacts need not be described in full detail for the purposes of this paper. When strata or other boundaries giving immediately observable units are not present, the deposit can be divided into arbitrarily defined blocks for cluster analysis along the general lines discussed earlier. Excavations are often arranged to give such blocks immediately on the assumption that measuring the individual artifact coordinates would produce needlessly refined data. Such techniques in effect transform the quantitative space attributes into qualitative attributes for ease of control and statistical manipulation. It is possible to work directly with the individual coordinates treated as continuous variables if the underlying information is available and if it is judged that the expected gain in precision justifies the additional work. Finally, assemblages can be described and compared in terms of over-all size and configuration.

The Temporal Dimension

Time itself is a continuum sensed as a succession of events. There are two types of time scales, relative and absolute. Relative time scaling is simply ranking an event as before or after some other event. Absolute time scaling means placing an event with respect to a sequence of events which are thought to occur at regular intervals and which are given a standard designation by reference to an arbitrarily chosen initial point. Our absolute scale is, of course, the calendar. As I noted above, all calendars are reckoned from an arbitrary starting period so that in a strict sense relative comparisons in terms of the calendar (x is twice as old as y) are not possible, although absolute comparisons (x is 500 years older than y) are.

We can also make absolute and relative comparisons of time intervals between events and in consequence can make rate-of-change comparisons in relative terms. These aspects of chronology suggest that some confusion might be avoided if we adopt the term "time ranking" for the major type of time scale called "relative" above and generally referred to as relative chronology.

Since time scaling refers to events, not things, it is apparent that the temporal attributes of a prehistoric artifact must be prehistoric events whose occurrence is implied by the formal and spatial attributes of the artifact. The prehistoric events usually thought of as archaeologically significant—the targets of chronological inference—are the manufacture and primary deposition of the artifact. In most instances no serious question is asked about the time interval separating these two events; the general uncertainties of chronological scaling are such that the interval can be treated as negligible without serious difficulty. When the unit considered is a spatial cluster (an assemblage) of artifacts, as is usually the case, the question becomes still more complicated because a large number of events is involved. Here the goal is to define the assemblage so that the events represented by the component artifacts form a sufficiently tight cluster in time to permit the inference that no marked cultural changes took place during the time interval between the first and last events implied.

An equally plain consequence of the nature of chronological attributes is the fact that they cannot be observed directly in the way that formal and spatial characteristics can. All chronological judgments are inferences made by interpreting spatial and formal attributes in the light of physical, biological, or cultural principles. We have mentioned above the physical principles of superposition and intrusion, which allow spatial attributes to be transformed into temporal ranking. Similarly, measurement of radioactivity permits an estimate of absolute chronology based on a formal property of the artifact. These and other noncultural principles are of the highest importance because they provide a method of studying culture change over time without prior assumptions about the nature of cultural change. In short, they offer raw material for the construction of cultural theories. On the other hand, chronological judgments obtained by application of culturally derived theories of change merely illustrate what is meant by the theories; the judgments will be sound if the theories are sound and are applied correctly, but they will not be independent contributions to cultural theory. Thus one can arrange a group of assemblages in order of formal complexity of some class of artifacts common to all and infer that this arrangement is also a chronological ordering, but this procedure demonstrates nothing about formal changes in time because the ordering is a product of a prior theory about such changes.

A few remarks about chronological periods are probably in order here because of some apparent confusion in the literature and in archaeological discussions. It seems plain enough that a chronological period can be defined uniquely only by specifying unique sequent events for its boundaries in time. Nevertheless, examples of time periods defined by criteria which are actually an ambiguous succession of events are by no means unknown, and they have led to misunderstandings. Such "cultural periods" seem to have their origin in the observation that a number of assemblages in some geographical area have several artifact types in common while a number of other assemblages are characterized by quite different sets of types. In symbolic terms, there are ABCD sites (letters standing for types) and EFGH sites, and, since the spatial factor is limited, the observer falls into the habit of thinking of an ABCD period and EFGH period without further analysis. Sooner or later, however, a CDEF assemblage turns up, and it becomes apparent that something is wrong with the supposed chronological division. The new assemblage belongs to both or neither of the two original periods, and a new scheme is called for. This difficulty could have been avoided at the outset by more careful definition delineating a true division of time. If it is known that type A appeared before type E, then the periods could have been defined as: (1) from the appearance of type A to the appearance of type E, and (2) after the appearance of type E. Any assemblage having either E or A (or both E and A) can be placed in this scheme without ambiguity, and the periods can be subdivided if accumulating information makes it desirable.

INTERRELATIONSHIPS OF DIMENSIONS

The study of the interrelationship of the formal, spatial, and temporal properties of artifacts presupposes an independent scaling of each dimension considered. I have discussed in a very general way the characteristic scales and some of the scaling problems associated with each dimension, and I wish to consider now how the result of simultaneous classification in two or more dimensions leads to certain familiar archaeological concepts. The possible relationships are form-space, form-time, space-time, and form-space-time.

Form-Space

In the discussion of the formal characterization of collections of artifacts, it was asserted that artifact types could be defined solely on the basis of clusters of formal attributes. A minimum cluster is a close association of two formal attributes. But if we replace the intentionally vague concept of collection with the more restricted idea of assemblage (a spatial cluster of artifacts thought to represent something approaching a point in time), it may be possible to show a close association of a formal and a spatial attribute. Suppose that the problem at hand is a typological description of a group of vessels which are substantially identical except for the presence or absence of incised decoration on the lip, and suppose further that the collection consists of a number of assemblages. If an assemblage tally shows that plain and incised lips rarely or never occur in the same assemblage, then it would appear reasonable to recognize the two classes of vessels as distinct entities, and there is no objection to calling them artifact types. A cluster of a formal and a spatial attribute exists when the assemblage is treated as a unit of association.

Even within a single assemblage, it might be possible to show formal-spatial clustering and hence types if the special association units are considered as, for example, when the vessels with incised lips appear only as grave furnishings. Moreover, examination of the actual coordinates of the spatially segregated form variants can yield information for further inferences about the prehistoric behavior underlying the empirical data. The two types of vessels could be northern and southern or upstream and downstream variants, for example. Even the absence of any systematic arrangement of coordinates has definite implications for inferential reconstructions of behavior. A systematic time difference can be treated in the same manner; a cluster of a formal and a temporal attribute also provides satisfactory evidence for an artifact type.

A second level of form-space synthesis results from treating the assemblage as a unit of association of artifact types. The reasoning is very similar, perhaps identical, to that employed in discussing the concept of artifact type, with the assemblage playing the part of the artifact and the artifact type that of the attribute. The problem is to classify a group of assemblages with respect to their formal attributes (artifact types) so as to reveal the degree of clustering of artifact types, that is, to investigate the problem of assemblage typology. The essential raw material is a list of the artifact type combinations exhibited by each of the assemblages of the group being investigated. The method of investigation involves the familiar computing of an expected number of assemblages for various artifact type combinations under a hypothesis of independence and comparing the expected tally with the observed tally. As before, a substantial excess of observed over expected indicates a strong association of at least two artifact types, and this strong association defines a type of assemblage—a culture type. The culture type defined in this manner—as a group of assemblages possessing in common two or more artifact types having a strong positive association—seems very close to the old archaeological concept of "a culture," and it has the same faults and virtues. Specifically, it is noncommittal as to the number or nature of the artifact types forming the characterizing cluster. In fact, it implies no more than the existence of some sort of distinctive cultural entity, and the component assemblages might be virtually identical through a long list of complicated artifact types or they might barely fulfill the minimum requirements. It is plain that subclasses or subculture types can exist within a culture type. There is useful work for such concepts as the phase or the ranked (according to complexity of identifying criteria) scale of the McKern system.

A higher order of space-form relationship can be derived from the spatial position and formal typology of assemblages. If the loci of the assemblages comprising a culture type form a geographical cluster, then the area occupied by the cluster is a culture type area. Repeated examples of such culture type areas would lead to recognition of a principle of spatial coherence of the component assemblages of a culture type. Finally, the spatial clustering of culture type areas themselves can be investigated to discover whether or not there is repeated association of such areas with one geographical region. A geographical region that does show such a cluster of clusters can be considered an archaeologically defined culture area, one in which some factor is at work to produce a culturally distinct region independently of the particular types of culture characteristic of any given time period. The possibility of this kind of analysis has apparently never occurred to the archaeologists who argue that the culture area concept has no value to archaeology because variation in time inevitably produces more than one culture type in any area.

The foregoing discussion of space-form relationships is a more or less mechanical approach to some possible formulations in keeping with aims of this paper. I think it safe to hazard, however, that all archaeologists would agree to the general proposition that artifact form does in fact vary systematically in space. The relationship is a direct one: artifacts or assemblages which are formally close tend strongly toward spatial closeness. The explanation for this phenomenon is obvious, but it is drawn from observations of living cultures, not from the data of archaeology: most formal similarities are the result of person-to-person transmission of ideas and objects, and space is a barrier to this transmission. The converse of the relationship, that artifacts or assemblages which are formally distant tend strongly to be spatially distant, is no better than half true. Space is not the only barrier to transmission; time is equally effective. Hence, we expect two assemblages that are very much alike formally to be close both in space and in time. Two assemblages that are very different formally are expected to be distant in space, distant in time, or distant in both space and time.

The existence of a systematic relationship between formal similarity and spatial locus does not necessarily imply that there is any simple ratio of formal likeness to spatial distance (the time effect having been removed) which can describe the relationship adequately. If such a relationship did exist, cluster analysis would not indicate any special relationship of formal similarity to any bounded area. Similarities across all possible boundaries would be as great as similarities within boundaries. Indexes of likeness between assemblages would simply decrease at a regular ratio from any arbitrarily chosen starting point, or, if one conceded the spatial coherence of the component assemblages of a culture type, indexes of likeness of culture types would decrease at a regular rate. I am quite willing to argue that such a simple relationship does not represent adequately the empirical data. Formal similarities do tend to knot up in space, and culture areas are objectively demonstrable phenomena, not arbitrary descriptive conveniences. The explanation is again obvious, and again it is drawn from outside the limits of strictly archaeological observations. From the standpoint of human behavior, space is not a simple matter of x and y coordinates, of barriers to communication completely described in terms of miles. The real world not only presents special impediments to communication in the form of mountains, oceans, and the like, it also poses special problems of technological and social adaptation in the form of distinctive ecological areas.

Form-Time

Since time is not a directly observable artifact attribute, form-time relationships have necessarily been dealt with to some extent in the remarks on time scaling. The discussion here will consist of listing some assertions about the nature of form-time relationships and examining the empirical implications of the assertions. These assertions are that artifact form exhibits serial correlation, that formal innovations tend to cluster on the time scale, and that formal change through time tends to be unidirectional.

The principle of serial correlation of form implies that, other things being equal, there is an inverse relationship between the formal resemblance between two artifacts, assemblages, or culture types and the amount of time separating them. Put in a slightly different way, the best prediction of the formal characteristics of the material culture of a society for next year is that they will not differ much from the situation this year. The archaeological technique of seriation is a direct application of this principle; when a group of assemblages is arranged in order of formal likeness, the assemblages are also ranked in time. If a simple, consistent ordering in an index of likeness matrix or a graphic representation is not achieved, it is taken to mean that some factor other than time (sampling difficulties, spatial variation, and so on) is also represented. Evidence from living societies and stratified archaeological deposits offers ample testimony of the general correctness of the principle, and, so far as I know, there is no serious question of its applicability to time ranking.

The existence of clustering of formal innovations on the time scale is not so easily demonstrated, although the idea seems to be widely accepted and is implicit in many formulations. In the context of historic and proto-historic studies, the concept of cultural revolutions is a clear example. The view of cultural dynamics underlying the concept is that a typical mode of cultural change is the achievement of a key invention—a sort of quantum advance—followed quickly by a number of functionally related auxiliary innovations. The short periods of rapid change would be separated by relatively long periods of comparative quiescence, although not of total cultural stagnation, of course. If one accepts the view that social systems are devices for operating technological systems (as I do), there is a clear implication that the character of key inventions is technical; they are directed toward the natural environment and have a generative relationship to changes in social organization. This view is important to archaeology because archaeological data yield much fuller information on technological matters than they do on social systems. The empirical implications of such a developmental theory are clear enough: assemblages formally transitional between sequent and sharply distinctive culture types should be rare, and assemblages well within the formal boundaries of culture types should be relatively abundant. I think that the actual data do show this condition, and I suspect that the principle holds good for relationships of less spectacular dimensions than those of the grand culture types. It is this clustering tendency which makes the ambiguously defined "culture period" a useful concept in spite of its logical imperfections. The several events marking the opening or closing of the period are in fact clustered in time so that most assemblages do not seem to belong to two periods.

Unidirectionality of formal changes through time is simply the idea of cultural evolution. In strictly archaeological terms, sequent culture types in one region would be expected to show greater numbers of artifact types, not only through more formalized and more varied combinations of some stock of attributes but also through the addition of new attributes to the available list. One would also expect the sites of later culture types to be more numerous (or at any rate larger) than those of the earlier ones. These expectations are a translation into formal evidence of the behavioral concept that culture change is in the main rational: technological devices are modified and reorganized so as to increase productivity, and innovation are accepted if they are demonstrably superior with respect to productivity. Hence change tends strongly to be unidirectional. It is quite true that backsliding can occur, but it would be expected only under unusual circumstances such as climatic change. A change from an agricultural to a hunting and gathering economy in a restricted area can be imagined easily and it would not be difficult to suggest plausible explanations, but it is practically impossible to imagine circumstances short of total world disruption which would cause the abandonment of agriculture everywhere. The concept of a stage of cultural development is a combination of the ideas of unidirectionality and the key invention mode of change; there are stair-steps in culture change, and the steps lead consistently upward.

Space-Time

Time to space relationships, form being constant, are not the subject of much analysis in archaeology. Probably the most familiar generalization is that underlying the age-area concept. It is expected that the area of distribution of an artifact type will increase through time, and under some conditions a more widely distributed type is judged to have been invented earlier than a less widely distributed type. Judgments of this sort are necessarily precarious because of ecological and other conditions which can limit the spread of a type. No one expects snowshoes to be as widely spread as the use of fire, whatever their respective dates of first appearance may be. A few other remarks can be made about space-time relationships. If we consider the time-space distribution of artifacts as such, it is apparent that distribution increases in space through time, at least until the entire world is inhabited, and that space is more thickly studded with artifacts as time goes on. In short, both the quantity and the area of distribution of artifacts increases through time.

Form-Space-Time

The interrelationships of form, space, and time taken together have been foreshadowed by the discussion of the relationships of pairs of these dimensions. In a very broad sense, space and time are both expressible in terms of formal distance; the formal differences between two assemblages may be associated with either spatial distance or temporal difference or with both. If we assume that the rate of formal change has been constant in both dimensions, the interrelationship would be another example of the Pythagorean theorem. Plotting time on the vertical and space on the horizontal axis, the formal distance between a pair of points (representing two assemblages) on the graph would be the square root of the sum of squares of the time and space scales. From a dimensional point of view, such an operation implies that we have reduced time and space to the same dimension measured by a common scale calibrated in units of formal distance.

CONCLUSION

I have tried to make the common operations of archaeology somewhat more explicit than is frequently the case in archaeological discussions. The method used has been a translation of customary terminology into that of technically simpler and more elegant sciences, and the result has been a gain in precision and generality at the expense of realism. Certainly, to take an obvious example, there is a substantial discrepancy between my facile assumption of objective formal scales and the actual job of comparing the collections of artifacts from two assemblages. The question is whether or not such ideal formulations serve any useful purpose.

The answer is that these ideal formulations are implicit in actual archaeological research in any case, and there is no useful purpose served by not making them explicit. Indeed, failure to analyze the dimensional implications of statements about relationships has permitted formulations that are manifestly meaningless. Similarly, one may deny the possibility of objective formal scales, but the universally accepted judgment that Middle Mississippi culture is more complex than that of Indian Knoll inescapably implies that such scales are employed, however imperfect they may be. The sterile argument as to whether or not such scales exist can be replaced by a profitable discussion of ways and means to increase the sensitivity of formal scaling. The measure of success of any archaeological formulation is the degree to which it approaches the ideal, and the ideal is indispensable as an indicator of the direction and distance of the goals of archaeological research.

* * * *

G. S. *Vescelius*

FULBRIGHT FELLOW,
UNIVERSITY OF SAN MARCOS ARCHEOLOGICAL PROJECT

ARCHEOLOGICAL SAMPLING:

A PROBLEM OF

STATISTICAL INFERENCE[1]

Of the methodological problems with which archeologists are currently confronted, one of the most important is that of statistical inference. Archeological fieldwork consists, in large measure, of the sampling of artifact "populations," and whenever an investigator attempts to gauge the character of a population by drawing a sample from it, he enters the realm of statistical inference. If they are to collect reliable samples of artifacts, archeologists must be aware of the practical consequences of sampling theory, and if they are to interpret such samples to the greatest advantage, they must be acquainted with techniques of statistical analysis.

James A. Ford (1954b:111) has voiced a widely held opinion in arguing that "the indiscriminate application of statistical formulas to archeological problems is not an activity of a cultural scientist." One could hardly fail to concur with such an opinion; unbridled enthusiasm is scarcely preferable to utter indifference. But this is not to say that statistical techniques have no place in archeology. Indeed, in many cases, archeologists have failed to avail themselves of such techniques when they would have been of unquestionable use in the solution of their problems.

[1] I am indebted to Albert C. Spaulding, of the University of Michigan, Lester Telser, of the University of Chicago, and Gabriel Lasker, of the Wayne University Medical School, for their many valuable criticisms and suggestions.

In commenting on the role of statistical techniques in pottery analysis, Anna Shepard (1956:332) has observed that "in the guise of simple, familiar calculations they are accepted by everyone as part of the established routine, but when they appear as new and complicated formulations they are likely to arouse suspicion and controversy." Concluding that "this reaction is understandable, but not altogether reasonable or fortunate," she has entered a plea in behalf of statistics.

The British statistician M. J. Moroney has clearly expressed the utility of statistical analysis in research of the sort generally undertaken by archeologists. Moroney says:

At bottom, it boils down to this: wherever anything is measured numerically, wherever there is an attempt, however rough, to assess anything in the form of numbers, even by the simplest process of counting, then there begins to arise the necessity for making judgements as to the significance of the data and the necessity for traffic rules by which the flow of information may proceed smoothly and purposefully. In a word, there is the need for statistics (1956: 462).

In recent years, some extremely important archeological problems—those of typology and seriation—have been approached from a statistical standpoint,[2] but the more fundamental problem of archeological sampling has not been adequately explored. It is a subject which merits serious attention—one which warrants the interest of professional statisticians. I hope that it may soon be studied by someone well versed in the theory of sampling, for it is a complex subject. But I also believe that it may be broached profitably—though not without trepidation—by prehistorians themselves; hence, I should like to comment on current techniques of archeological sampling, and to suggest certain means for their improvement, in the hope of provoking discussion of this important topic.

CURRENT SAMPLING TECHNIQUES

Let us suppose that statistical information is desired about some group of artifacts at a certain site. For example, the archeologist often wants to know the proportionate number of potsherds of a particular type. In such a case, each of the sherds at the site may be said to constitute an

---

[2] Brainerd (1951b) has examined the use of mathematical techniques in archeological research from a general point of view. Kroeber (1940), Spaulding (1953a), and Lehmer (1954) have dealt with typological problems. Brainerd (1951a), Robinson (1951), Lehmer (1951), Robinson and Brainerd (1952), and Spaulding (1953b) have attacked the problem of seriation from a mathematical standpoint.

element of investigation; the totality of sherds constitutes a *universe* or *population.* If each of the sherds were readily accessible, and if each were labelled with some unique catalogue number, we could draw a *simple random sample* from that population by selecting numbers at random and picking out the sherds of matching number, whereupon we could select from the sample all of the sherds of the particular type in which we were interested. Then we could calculate their proportionate number and legitimately treat that number as an unbiased estimate of the proportion of such sherds in the population as a whole. But the simple random sampling technique is obviously impractical. Fieldworkers are forced to resort to other techniques of sampling.

In general, archeologists have been content to assume that haphazardly gathered *grab samples* are representative of artifact populations. A grab sample is defined by Cochran, Mosteller and Tukey (1954:13) as "what you get by grabbing a handful." Deming (1950:14) refers to such assemblages as "chunks," and they are also known as "unsystematic," "careless," or "opportunistic" samples. Grab samples can be made to yield bits of qualitative information, that is, they can inform the investigator of the presence of a particular type of element in some population. But they cannot be made to yield demonstrably sound quantitative information, for it is wholly unjustifiable to assume that such samples are free of bias, and the unbiased sample is the *sine qua non* of statistical inference.[3]

When an archeologist collects sherds from a site's surface in a haphazard way, or when he digs a test pit at some haphazardly chosen spot, he deludes himself if he assumes that he has thereby obtained an unbiased sample, much less a truly "random" one. The investigator who relies on grab samples ignores both the possibility of selective bias (for example, the favoring of obtrusive specimens—those which are relatively large, those which are of a particularly striking color) and the possibility of canvassing bias (that is, the favoring of some particular part of the site). It is not enough to collect a hundred, a thousand, or even ten thousand sherds from some site. If we are to draw valid inferences about the nature of the sherd population at that site, the sample must not only be of adequate size, but must also be taken in such a way as to guard against bias. As Walker and Lev have pointed out:

when a statistical study deals with observations on a finite population, say the population of a city [or that of an archeological site], an element is considered to be drawn at random if, and only if, some device is used by means of which

---

[3] I refer, in a strict sense, to undetermined bias; for when bias can be ascertained precisely, it is often possible to compensate for it.

any one element of the population is as likely to be drawn as any other element. It is completely impossible for a person to pick a book "at random" from a bookcase or even to pick a blade of grass "at random" if he looks at it. Some device designed to produce a random selection is essential (Walker and Lev 1953: 10).

Archeological surveyors (such as Ford 1936:11) frequently assume that artifacts on the surfaces of ploughed sites form typologically homogeneous populations by virtue of the fact that they have been "thoroughly" mixed in the course of cultivation. Such an assumption is unjustifiable. Wallis and Roberts (1956:338) cite, as "a classic illustration of inadequate randomization," the example of the 1940 draft lottery, in which ten thousand encapsulated, numbered slips were mixed in a bowl. "The capsules were then drawn by various blindfolded dignitaries in a public ceremony. The results showed marked departures from randomness. Apparently the difficulties of adequate mixing were not understood." Surely it would be unwise to argue that the artifacts on the surface of a site have been more thoroughly mixed than the capsules in General Hershey's bowl.

Archeologists are certainly not alone in making use of grab samples. Workers in many other fields—psychology, sociology, botany, chemistry—frequently rely on such samples. But practices which are inherently faulty cannot be excused, of course, merely on the grounds that they are popular.

CLUSTER SAMPLING

Inasmuch as grab sampling is imprecise, and in view of the fact that simple random sampling is generally impractical in archeology, investigators who wish to draw legitimate conclusions about the composition of artifact populations will have to adopt new techniques of sampling. Fortunately, an appropriate technique has already been devised. It is known as *cluster sampling*, and it has been employed extensively in the study of human populations. It can be adapted easily to the archeologist's needs, but it is a more complex technique than grab sampling; hence, it is sure to encounter a certain amount of opposition, both from time-conscious fieldworkers and from those who dislike mathematical formulations.

To those who may assert that the proposed sampling safeguards are too time-consuming, I would reply that, as Deming (1950:13) has observed, "there is no alternative if demonstrable precision is required. To say that the job can be done cheaper without them is to confuse the issue, as there can be no talk of price without a simultaneous measure of quality."

To those who view statistics with suspicion, I would reiterate my belief that the archeologist who relies on samples—and who does not?—must take every feasible precaution to guard against sampling bias, and that he must do so regardless of the "simplicity" of the inferences he means to draw. Many archeologists seem to feel that, while it is perfectly proper to manipulate simple percentages, it is pretentious to employ more "complex" statistics. But a percentage is a statistic, too, and it, too, may be devoid of meaning if derived from a poorly gathered sample. Conversely, a legitimate sample may rightly be exploited by more "complex" statistical techniques if, as is often the case, such exploitation is warranted.

I do not intend to discuss the theory, or even the general practice, of cluster sampling. For a theoretical treatment of the subject, the interested reader may consult the works of Deming (1950:135–212) and Cochran (1953:203–205); and for a practical exposition, he may turn to Kish (1953:202–211). I simply mean to show how the technique may be employed in an archeological context. For purposes of illustration, I shall deal only with the collection and analysis of surface material. It should be noted, however, that cluster sampling, and other forms of multi-stage sampling, are applicable to the solution of a wide range of archeological problems.

A *cluster* is a group of elements, for example, artifacts or artifact fragments. In cluster sampling, such groups serve, in place of single elements, as sampling units.

Fieldwork must begin with the definition of sampling units. In cluster sampling, it may sometimes be convenient to employ *natural units* such as collections from individual graves or houses, but in other instances it will be necessary to devise *artificial units*. For purposes of surface survey, an artificial unit which I shall term a *tract-cluster,* and which may be defined as a group of artifacts found on a certain tract of ground, may be delineated by establishing a grid system. The width of the grid intervals —the size of the tracts—will be determined by such local conditions as the density of artifacts, the nature of the terrain, and the size of the site itself.

Cluster sampling is undeniably more time-consuming than grab sampling, but I would suggest, to those surveyors who may be horrified at the prospect of sampling by means of a grid system, that the system need not be very cumbersome. I believe that an adequate one could be established quickly with very simple instruments: a compass, a tape, and some string. Indeed, in some instances it should even be possible to dispense with these simple tools and to accomplish the job merely by pacing.

The surveyor should estimate the density of artifacts and establish grid intervals of such a size that the average tract or plot will contain at least 50 and preferably 100 or more artifacts. This is not to say that clusters of less than 50 specimens are useless; but proportions based on small numbers are liable to appreciable distortion. Certain kinds of natural units, like graves, will regularly yield small clusters; in such cases, potential distortion cannot be avoided, but there is no reason to invite such distortion if it can be easily circumvented by taking a larger cluster.

Once the units have been defined, they should be numbered systematically. Any simple system of numerical designation will do. It might be most economical to designate tracts by means of corner coördinates,[4] although Deming (1950:141) has recommended that such units be numbered sequentially in a serpentine fashion "so as to gain the benefits of geographic stratification." Under any circumstances, it would be wise to record the positions of the various units on a sketch map.

Having defined and located the units, the investigator must decide how many clusters will be required. This means, in effect, that he must decide upon the degree of reliability with which he hopes to estimate the characteristics of the artifact population, for in cluster sampling reliability is partly a function of the number of clusters in the sample on which the estimate is based. It is desirable to increase the sample size in order to reduce the standard error of the estimate, as I shall later demonstrate.

The problems of sample size are discussed in many elementary textbooks, one of which is by Parten (1950:290–330), and I will not consider them in detail. Suffice it to say that, while there is no single optimum, a sample consisting of 5 or 10 per cent of all the clusters in the population should yield results of adequate reliability for most archeological purposes.

---

[4] Such a system is feasible only when the grid interval is of the class 10^n, for example, where it is one, ten or a hundred feet, yards, or meters. I would suggest that the following practical measures be adopted by the surveyor who chooses to designate tracts by means of grid coördinates: (1) Establish the datum point somewhere outside the boundaries of the site, so that the whole site will fall within a single quadrant of the coördinate field. (2) Identify the tracts, as is customary, by means of corner coördinates, but, the interval being 10^n, drop the last n digits of both index numbers in order to expedite the selection of random numbers.

Let $m =$ the requisite number of clusters and let $M =$ the total number of sampling units. The quantity $M/m = i$, the *sampling interval,* and the quantity $m/M = f$, the sampling fraction.

Once the values of m and M have been calculated, units may be selected for sampling. The investigator should begin by picking a unit at random, and for this purpose he may use a table of random numbers. Such tables (for example, Arkin and Colton 1950:142–5) may easily be carried into the field, and they provide the simplest means of eliminating bias in the selection of clusters. Under no circumstances should a unit be selected haphazardly. If the investigator prefers to do so, he may pick all m units at random; but it would also be legitimate to choose only the first unit at random, and to sample every ith unit thereafter (Table I, Column 1).

Whatever the process of selection, care should be taken to collect every artifact falling within the randomly chosen units and, conversely, to exclude from the sample any artifact lying outside those units.

ESTIMATES OF PROPORTION

We may now turn to a consideration of the analysis of cluster samples. Let us assume that, as is so often the case, we wish to estimate the proportionate number of artifacts of a particular type in the artifact population of a certain site. Our estimate will be based upon the proportions obtaining in a sample of clusters drawn from that population. Let $P =$ our estimate of the proportionate number of artifacts of type X in the population as a whole. In cluster sampling, $P = \overset{m}{\Sigma}x/\overset{m}{\Sigma}n$, where $x =$ the total number of artifacts of type X in a particular cluster, $n =$ the total number of artifacts in that cluster, and $m =$ the number of clusters. (The symbol Σ directs us, of course, to sum a specified quantity. For example, $\overset{m}{\Sigma}n = n_1 + n_2 + \ldots n_m$, where $n_1 =$ the number of artifacts in the first cluster, $n_2 =$ the number of artifacts in the second cluster, and $n_m =$ the number of artifacts in the mth cluster.)

The formula for P is a special case of the more general formula

$$\overline{X} = \frac{1}{m}\overset{m}{\Sigma}\overline{x}\,(nm/\overset{m}{\Sigma}n),$$ where $\overline{X} =$ the estimated value of characteristic X in the population as a whole and $\overline{x} =$ the value of that characteristic in a particular cluster:

$$\bar{X} = \frac{1}{m}\overset{m}{\Sigma}\bar{x}\,(nm/\overset{m}{\Sigma}n) = \frac{1}{m}\left[\left(\frac{x_1}{n_1}\cdot\frac{n_1 m}{\overset{m}{\Sigma}n}\right) + \left(\frac{x_2}{n_2}\cdot\frac{n_2 m}{\overset{m}{\Sigma}n}\right) + \cdots\right.$$

$$\left.\left(\frac{x_m}{n_m}\cdot\frac{n_m m}{\overset{m}{\Sigma}n}\right)\right] = \left(\frac{x_1}{n_1}\cdot\frac{n_1 m}{\overset{m}{\Sigma}n}\cdot\frac{1}{m}\right) + \left(\frac{x_2}{n_2}\cdot\frac{n_2 m}{\overset{m}{\Sigma}n}\cdot\frac{1}{m}\right) + \cdots$$

$$\left(\frac{x_m}{n_m}\cdot\frac{n_m m}{\overset{m}{\Sigma}n}\cdot\frac{1}{m}\right) = \frac{x_1}{\overset{m}{\Sigma}n} + \frac{x_2}{\overset{m}{\Sigma}n} + \cdots\frac{x_m}{\overset{m}{\Sigma}n} = \frac{x_1 + x_2 + \cdots x_m}{\overset{m}{\Sigma}n} = \frac{\overset{m}{\Sigma}x}{\overset{m}{\Sigma}n}\,.$$

In simple random sampling (and in grab sampling), the estimate of a population proportion is calculated simply as $P = X/N$, where $X =$ the number of artifacts of type X in a collection and $N =$ the total number of artifacts in that collection. In practice, a collection of artifacts obtained by means of cluster sampling may be analyzed in exactly the same way; the analyst need only count the number of artifacts of type X (for example, Σx) and divide by the total number of artifacts in the collection (for example, Σn). It is important, however, to use a different scheme of notation (Σx as opposed to X, Σn as opposed to N) in the analysis of cluster samples than in that of random samples, in order to clearly express the differences in sampling technique—differences which become important if the collection is to be analyzed in a more elaborate manner (for example, if standard errors are to be calculated).

SAMPLING ERROR

The statistic P is subject to random error, and such error is a function of many things: (1) the size of the proportion itself, (2) the number of clusters, m, in the sample, relative to the number of clusters, M, in the population (for example, the size of the sampling fraction, f), and (3) the total number of specimens, Σn, in the sample.

Archeologists have often speculated about the reliability of artifact samples, and they have sometimes tried to assess the relationship between size and reliability. Spier (1917:254) broached the subject long ago, in his classic study of Zuñi surface collections and, more recently, Ford (1936:13–14, 1949:35–36) and Bennyhoff (1952:233) have attempted to determine, by empirical means, "the desirable size of a collection necessary to obtain a fair sample of the material available on the surface of a site." Few investigators, however, have displayed an awareness of the fact that statistical techniques afford a solution to this important problem.

There is a simple measure of random error as a function of sample size, namely, the standard error, σ. The standard error is one of the commonest of statistics, and one which is frequently encountered by archeologists (in anthropometric tables, for example, and in the form of the "$\pm$" figure which accompanies a radiocarbon date). Yet I know of few instances in which it has been employed by archeologists as a means of gauging the reliability of artifact type proportions. Anna Shepard (1942:226–227) has advocated the use, for such purposes, of curves based on the standard error, and Beals, Brainerd, and Smith (1945:164–166) have used similar curves based on the probable error (a modified form of the standard error), while Lehmer (1954:76–80) has employed mean standard errors in testing the homogeneity of sherd samples. But I do not believe that anyone has ever approached the problem of sample reliability by simply calculating the standard errors of individual type proportions.

The formula for the standard error of a proportion obtaining within a simple random sample is $\sigma = \sqrt{(PQ/N)}$, where $P =$ the proportion, $Q = 1\text{-}P$, and $N =$ the number of elements in the sample. The odds are 2.15 to one against the occurrence of a deviation from P as great as or greater than σ. In other words, the chances are better than two to one that the proportion for an artifact population—the proportion which we seek to estimate by calculating P—lies somewhere within the boundaries specified by $P \pm \sigma$. If the standard error is doubled, the odds are increased to 20.98 to one, and, if it is trebled, they become 369 to one. Consider, for example, a case in which $P = 17\%$ and $\sigma = 3\%$. The chances are approximately two to one that the true proportion falls within the range $17\% \pm 3\% = 14\%\text{–}20\%$, and they are better than twenty to one that it falls within the range $17\% \pm 2(3\%) = 11\%\text{–}23\%$.

Though it is possible, in dealing with clusters, to calculate estimates of proportion in as straightforward a fashion as in simple random sampling, it is improper, in cluster sampling, to use the simple formula for the standard error of a proportion. Cochran, Mosteller and Tukey (1954:17) caution that "even if the population characteristic studied is a fraction, almost never will $p = \sqrt{(pq/n)}$ be a proper expression for 'estimate $\pm$ standard error.' In every case, a proper formula will require more information from the sample than merely the overall percentage."

The variance, σ^2, of the estimate

G. S. Vescelius

$$\overline{X} = \frac{1}{m} \overset{m}{\Sigma} \overline{x} \ (nm/\overset{m}{\Sigma}n)$$

is

$$\sigma^2 = \left(1 - \frac{m}{M}\right) \frac{1}{m} \left[\frac{1}{(m-1)} \overset{m}{\Sigma}(\overline{x} - \overline{X}) \left(\frac{nm}{\overset{m}{\Sigma}n}\right)^2 \right].$$

The variance of the estimate P is, analogously,

$$\sigma^2 = \left(1 - \frac{m}{M}\right) \frac{1}{m} \left[\frac{1}{(m-1)} \overset{m}{\Sigma}\left(\frac{x}{n} - P\right) \left(\frac{nm}{\overset{m}{\Sigma}n}\right)^2 \right].$$

The standard error is the square root of the variance: $\sigma = \sqrt{\sigma^2}$.

AN EXAMPLE

Having described the method of computing proportions and standard errors, I should like to give an example, which may serve to clarify the procedure. Let us assume that a surveyor is interested in estimating the proportionate number of sherds of a particular type on the surface of a particular site, and that he has elected to sample the sherd population by means of the technique which I have described. (An investigator would normally be interested in determining the proportions of a number of types, but there is no need to consider more than one type in the example.) Suppose that the site is about 200 yards square and that, having roughly ascertained the density of surface material, in order to determine the optimal size of the tracts, the surveyor has divided it into 400 tracts, each of which is ten yards square. Finally, let us assume that he has collected all the sherds lying on the surfaces of 20 of those tracts; that he has identified all of the specimens in each tract-cluster; [5] and that the frequencies x (the number of sherds of type X) and n (the total number of sherds) for each cluster are as given in columns 1–2 of Table I.

In order to arrive at P, the best estimate of the proportion of type X sherds in the population as a whole, the investigator must calculate (1) Σn, the total number of sherds in the sample, and (2) Σx, the total number

---

[5] The problem of unidentifiable specimens is a vexing one. It is akin to the problem of nonresponse which plagues surveyors of human populations, and there is every reason to believe that unidentifiability may constitute a serious source of bias, just as failure to respond may lead to polling errors.

of type X sherds in the sample. In the example (Table I, Columns 3–4), $\Sigma n = 2797$ and $\Sigma x = 520$. The value of P may be calculated simply by dividing Σx by Σn: $P = \Sigma x/\Sigma n = .189$, or 18.9 per cent.

TABLE 1. COMPUTATION OF P AND σ FOR A HYPOTHETICAL CLUSTER SAMPLE

(1)	(2)	(3)	(4)	(5)	(6)	(7)	(8)	(9)
Tract Number	Cluster Number	x	n	x/n	$\frac{x}{n}-P$	$mn/\Sigma n$	$(mn/\Sigma n)^2$	$\left(\frac{x}{n}-P\right)\left(\frac{mn}{\Sigma n}\right)^2$
6	1	31	95	.326	+.137	.679	.461	.063
26	2	45	126	.357	+.168	.901	.812	.136
46	3	2	218	.009	−.180	1.559	2.430	.437
66	4	6	132	.045	−.144	.944	.891	.128
86	5	21	42	.500	+.311	.300	.090	.028
106	6	15	294	.051	−.138	2.102	4.418	.610
126	7	34	140	.243	+.054	1.001	1.002	.541
146	8	78	252	.310	+.121	1.802	3.247	.393
166	9	29	76	.382	+.193	.543	.295	.057
186	10	60	125	.480	+.291	.894	.799	.233
206	11	16	40	.400	+.211	.286	.082	.017
226	12	32	68	.471	+.282	.486	.236	.067
246	13	27	244	.111	−.078	1.745	3.045	.238
266	14	23	92	.250	+.061	.658	.433	.026
286	15	42	134	.313	+.124	.958	.918	.114
306	16	10	32	.313	+.124	.229	.052	.006
326	17	12	183	.066	−.123	1.309	1.713	.211
346	18	24	200	.120	−.069	1.430	2.045	.141
366	19	5	126	.040	−.149	.901	.812	.121
386	20	18	178	.100	−.089	1.273	1.621	.144
—	—	520	2797	—	—	20.000	—	3.711

$M = 400$, $m = 20$, $\Sigma n = 2797$, $\Sigma x = 520$, $P = \Sigma x/\Sigma n = .189$, $f = m/M = .05$,

$$\sigma^2 = (1-f)\frac{1}{m}\left[\frac{1}{(m-1)}\Sigma\left(\frac{x}{n}-P\right)\left(\frac{mn}{\Sigma n}\right)^2\right] = .95 \times .05 \times .0526 \times 3.711 =$$
$.00927, \sigma = \sqrt{.00927} = .030.$

The calculation of standard errors is a much lengthier procedure:

1. Calculate x/n (the proportionate number of type X sherds) for each of the clusters. In the case of the first cluster (Column 5), for example, $x/n = 31/95 = .326$.
2. Find the difference, $(x/n) − P$, between each individual cluster proportion, x/n, and the weighted mean proportion, P. In the case of the first cluster (Column 6), $(x/n) − P = .326 − .189 = + .137$.
3. Calculate the relative size, $mn/\Sigma n$, of each cluster by multiplying m by n and dividing the product by Σn. For example, in the case

of the first cluster (Column 7), $mn/\Sigma n = (20 \times 95)/2797 = 1900/2797 = .679$. The accuracy of the computations may be checked by summing the $mn/\Sigma n$'s, for they should add up to the value of m, i.e., $m = (mn/\Sigma n)$. In the example, $m = (mn/\Sigma n) = 20$.

4. Square the values of $mn/\Sigma n$. For example, for the first cluster (Column 8), $(mn/\Sigma n)^2 = (.679)^2 = .461$.

5. Multiply the values of $(x/n) - P$ by those of $(mn/\Sigma n)^2$. For instance, for the first cluster (Column 9),

$$\left(\frac{x}{n} - P\right)\left(\frac{mn}{\Sigma n}\right)^2 = .137 \times .461 = .063.$$

6. Sum the values of $[(x/n) - P]\,(mn/\Sigma n)^2$. In the example, the sum is $.063 + .136 + \ldots + .144 = 3.711$.

7. Calculate the *sampling fraction*, $f = m/M$. In this case, m (the number of clusters in the sample) is 20, and M (the total number of tracts into which the site has been divided) is 400, hence $f = 20/400 = .05$.

8. Calculate $1 - f$. In the example, $1 - f = 1.00 - .05 = .95$.

9. Determine the reciprocal of m. In the example, $1/m = 1/20 = .05$.

10. Determine the reciprocal of $m - 1$. In this case, $1/(m - 1) = 1/19 = .0526$.

11. By multiplication, calculate the value of

$$\sigma^2 = (1 - f)\frac{1}{m}\left[\frac{1}{(m-1)}\,\Sigma\left(\frac{x}{n} - P\right)\left(\frac{mn}{\Sigma n}\right)^2\right].$$

In the example, $\sigma^2 = .95 \times .05 \times .0526 \times 3.711 = .00927$.

12. Take the square root of σ^2, for example, $\sqrt{\sigma^2} = \sqrt{.00927} = .030$. The result is the standard error. In this particular case, the investigator would be able to state with assurance that the chances are better than two to one that the proportionate number of type X sherds on the surface of the site as a whole is $18.9\% \pm 3.0\%$, that is, 15.9%—21.9%, and that the chances are better than 20 to one that the proportion is of the range $18.9\% \pm 2(3.0\%)$, that is, 12.9%—24.9%.

I do not suggest that standard errors need always be calculated; but when measures of sample reliability are urgently needed, archeologists will be well advised to devote a few tedious but rewarding hours to their calculation.

BIBLIOGRAPHY

ARKIN, HERBERT and RAYMOND R. COLTON
1950 *Tables for Statisticians.* New York, Barnes & Noble, Inc.
BEALS, RALPH L., GEORGE W. BRAINERD and WATSON SMITH
1945 "Archaeological Studies in Northeast Arizona." *University of California Publications in American Archaeology and Ethnology,* 44:1-235.
BENNYHOFF, JAMES A.
1952 "The Viru Valley Sequence: A Critical Review." *American Antiquity,* 17:231-249.
BRAINERD, GEORGE W.
1951a "The Place of Chronological Ordering in Archaeological Analysis." *American Antiquity,* 16:301-313.
1951b "The Use of Mathematical Formulations in Archaeological Analysis." *Anthropological Papers, Museum of Anthropology, University of Michigan,* 8:117-125.
COCHRAN, WILLIAM G.
1953 *Sampling Techniques.* New York, John Wiley & Sons, Inc.
COCHRAN, WILLIAM G., FREDERICK MOSTELLER and JOHN W. TUKEY
1954 "Principles of Sampling." *Journal of the American Statistical Association,* 49:13-35.
DEMING, WILLIAM EDWARDS
1950 *Some Theory of Sampling.* New York, John Wiley & Sons, Inc.
FORD, JAMES A.
1936 "Analysis of Indian Village Site Collections from Louisiana and Mississippi." *Department of Conservation, Louisiana Geological Survey, Anthropological Study,* 2.
1949 "Cultural Dating of Prehistoric Sites in Virú Valley, Peru." In *Surface Survey of the Virú Valley, Peru,* by James A. Ford and Gordon R. Willey, pp. 29-89. *Anthropological Papers of the American Museum of Natural History,* 43(1):1-89.
1954a "Comment on A. C. Spaulding, 'Statistical Techniques for the Discovery of Artifact Types.'" *American Antiquity,* 19:390-391.
1954b Letter to the Editor. *American Anthropologist,* 56:109-112.
KISH, LESLIE
1953 "Selection of the Sample." In *Research Methods in the Behavioral Sciences,* ed. by Leon Festinger and Daniel Katz, pp. 175-239. New York, The Dryden Press.

KROEBER, A. L.
1940 "Statistical Classification." *American Antiquity,* 6:29–44.

LEHMER, DONALD J.
1951 "Robinson's Coefficient of Agreement—A Critique." *American Antiquity,* 17:151.

1954 "Archeological Investigations in the Oahe Dam Area, South Dakota, 1950–1951." *Bureau of American Ethnology, Bulletin,* 158.

MORONEY, M. J.
1956 *Facts from Figures.* 3rd edition, revised. Harmondsworth, Penguin Books.

PARTEN, MILDRED
1950 *Surveys, Polls and Samples: Practical Procedures.* New York, Harper & Brothers.

ROBINSON, W. S.
1951 "A Method for Chronologically Ordering Archaeological Deposits." *American Antiquity,* 16:293–301.

ROBINSON, W. S. and GEORGE W. BRAINERD
1952 "Robinson's Coefficient of Agreement—A Rejoinder." *American Antiquity,* 18:60–61.

SHEPARD, ANNA O.
1942 "Rio Grande Glaze Paint Ware." *Carnegie Institution Contributions to American Anthropology and History,* 7 (*Carnegie Institution of Washington Publication,* 528):129–262.

1956 "Ceramics for the Archaeologist." *Carnegie Institution of Washington Publication,* 609.

SPAULDING, ALBERT C.
1953a "Statistical Techniques for the Discovery of Artifact Types." *American Antiquity,* 18:305–313.

1953b Review of James A. Ford's *Measurement of Some Prehistoric Design Developments in the Southeastern States. American Anthropologist,* 55:588–591.

SPIER, LESLIE
1917 "An Outline for a Chronology of Zuñi Ruins." *Anthropological Papers of the American Museum of Natural History,* 18(3):207–331.

WALKER, HELEN M. and JOSEPH LEV
1953 *Statistical Inference.* New York, Henry Holt & Co., Inc.

WALLIS, W. ALLEN and HARRY V. ROBERTS
1956 *Statistics: A New Approach.* Glencoe, The Free Press.

R. L. Wilder

UNIVERSITY OF MICHIGAN

MATHEMATICS:

A CULTURAL PHENOMENON

In his article "The Locus of Mathematical Reality" (White 1947; see also 1949:282–302), White formulates two seemingly opposing points of view, distilled from writings on the foundations and philosophy of mathematics: (1) "Mathematical truths have an existence and a validity independent of the human mind," and (2) "Mathematical truths have no existence or validity apart from the human mind." With suitable interpretation of the term "human mind," White observes, the apparent contradiction disappears. The first view, exemplified in the statement of the late English mathematician G. H. Hardy, "I believe that mathematical reality lies outside us, and that our function is to discover or observe it," is valid if by "human mind" one means the individual organism. The second view is valid if one interprets "human mind" to mean the human species. "Mathematical truths exist in the cultural tradition into which the individual is born, and so enter his mind from the outside. . . . But culture itself has . . . no existence apart from the human species" (White 1949:285–286).

Mathematics, White concludes, is a part of culture which each individual learns and partakes of in the same way that he assimilates other elements of his culture. It is true that mathematics grows only through the minds of individual mathematicians; but this is through the interaction of mathematical elements (derived from the cultural reservoir) in individual minds, which thus serve as catalytic agents in the cultural process. It is not surprising that frequently mathematical "discoveries" are made by independent workers simultaneously. "A genius, mathematical or otherwise, is a person in whose nervous system an important cultural synthesis takes place; he is the neural locus of an epochal event in cultural history" (White 1949:295).

In order to clarify and make his point, White devotes considerable space in his article to the nature of culture and to the manner in which it evolves. In particular, he describes the way in which mathematical, and, in general, scientific, concepts are born in the minds of individuals and added to the culture stream, as well as the manner in which they may react later with other concepts to contribute to the further evolution of mathematical ideas.

In short, his viewpoint is that without individual minds to form the collective cultural pattern, there would of course be no mathematics just as there would be no language, literature or religion; but the symbolic apparatus of culture, passed from one individual to another down through the ages, is the real bearer of mathematics, and constitutes that "reality outside us" which is sensed by so many mathematicians.

In an address before an international gathering of mathematicians several years ago (Wilder 1952), I attempted to interpret and extend White's view of mathematics. I gave what I deemed a very general and noncontroversial description of the importance of the concept of culture to the study and evolution of mathematics and to an understanding of its foundations. After studying the comments and criticisms which I eventually received regarding this talk, I had the feeling that those anthropologists who later read the paper evidenced more understanding of it than did my mathematical colleagues.

Undaunted, three years later I took a deeper plunge (Wilder 1953). Specifically, I took a central mathematical concept, that of *curve,* and traced its development and influence on the evolution of mathematical thought down through the centuries. I stressed cultural factors, as opposed to individual psychological aspects which had been emphasized in such studies as those of Poincaré (1946:383–394) and Hadamard (1949). Subsequent reactions indicate that this attempt may have been much more successful than the former.

It appears that the greatest opposition to White's view of the cultural nature of mathematics comes from those who conceive of mathematics as something absolute, universal, and irrefutable. Placing the locus of mathematics in culture, no matter how the latter is defined, appears to them to deprive mathematics of these qualities and to reduce it to a relative, parochial, and arbitrary status. Let other aspects of man's existence be deemed cultural, even his religious beliefs. But do not for a minute think that the "certainty" of mathematics allows of its being assigned a cultural locale—so seems to run the protest.

For a layman to feel this way is understandable, since to him there is probably a mystical certainty about mathematics. But for a professional mathematician to share this view despite his familiarity with the manner in which mathematics is "created" and the fact that it contains contradictions which have never been resolved in a way satisfactory to all, seems to point to lack of familiarity with the cultural point of view. But there are mathematicians whose view of mathematics can only be described as dogmatic and theological. In some this is so strong that, as others have pointed out, it seems to have formed a substitute for an earlier religious belief that was abandoned with the achievement of maturity.

Perhaps an important reason for some of the opposition to White's thesis is that his discussion (White 1947) is generally on an abstract level, and even where it descends to particulars regarding mathematical items it does not, perhaps, go far enough to make his point. For example, the invention of non-Euclidean geometry is cited, quite correctly, in support of the contention that there is nothing necessary or inevitable about Euclidean geometry: "It is now clear that concepts such as space, straight line, plane, etc., are no more necessary and inevitable as a consequence of the structure of the external world than are the concepts green and yellow—or the relationship term with which you designate your mother's brother, for that matter." Without deeper analysis, this statement might be compared to the following: "To conceive of the earth as flat is not a necessary or inevitable consequence of the structure of the external world." But then one could argue with considerable evidence (see, for instance, Tylor 1919:332) that for a primitive tribe, living in the middle of a plain, the conception of the earth as flat is both necessary and inevitable.

This second line of reasoning ignores the effect of the stage of development of a culture on its mathematical concepts. It is a long way in the growth of a culture from primitive cosmogony to even the most elementary geometry; they simply do not occur at the same stage of cultural evolution. It is quite conceivable that a culture which advances far enough to embody a geometry will inevitably construct one of the Euclidean type; but with further evolution the same culture will come to realize the arbitrariness of the assumptions of the primitive geometry and construct other equally consistent (but contradictory of the primitive) geometries. It is only in the sense that *given a certain level of culture* a Euclidean type of geometry may of necessity evolve, that such a geometry is necessary or inevitable. But this only points up the determining role of cultural evolution.

On a smaller scale, the process of cultural evolution is quite obvious, and is nowhere so clearly exemplified as in mathematics. I have in mind the development of a "formalized" theory—a theory which has been given a definite set of axioms and a prescribed set of rules of proof for its development. Here the theorems "discovered" and proved have an evident inevitability in that the following out of the given rules of deduction, and so on, virtually guarantees the ultimate derivation of the theorems. Whether Pythagoras discovered the theorem which bears his name or not (and undoubtedly he was not the first "discoverer" even if he did) is not considered today a matter of any consequence; given the axioms of Euclidean geometry and the conventional modes of proof (here not even strictly formalized), the Pythagorean theorem is an inevitable consequence—someone is bound to "discover" it. On a grander scale this evolutionary process is not so obvious, but it would be a mistake to deny that it takes place.

White's critics also err in that they forget that he is writing about *mathematics,* not folklore! And by this we mean mathematics as understood today, not primitive concepts of number or space. Even to the Greeks, who had arrived at a fairly mature postulational foundation of it, geometry represented actual space; no self-respecting mathematician today would agree to such a concept of geometry. Indeed, what we today call "Euclidean geometry" is not the same thing as the geometry of Euclid. It has evolved not only into a precise, rigorous, formal system (which the Greek axiomatic development definitely was not), but at the same time has taken its place as only one among a series of equally valid (but mutually contradictory) geometries. Despite its use as a tool in such situations as surveying, it is by no means considered to be a "description of actual space."

This brings us to a second general observation concerning the reactions to White's thesis, namely, that the individual reaction will be influenced by the level and nature of one's mathematical thinking. Thus, if one is a professional mathematician engaged in abstract research having no overt connection with any sort of application, one may be able to understand and appreciate White's views more easily than if one is an "applied" mathematician, developing a theory with the purpose of applying it to some specific physical situation. In the former case, the "environment" in which one's research lies is purely mathematical, a realm which exists only in the collective minds and literature of the professional mathematical community, the current embodiment of our mathematical culture. The act of creating new concepts in this realm easily seems a "man-made" type of behavior. To the "applied" mathematician, however, the "environment" is more than the purely mathematical, and includes a portion of the "external world"; one may be investigating wave phenomena, for instance, and setting up "laws" and differential equations with a definite purpose of prediction. Here it is easy to forget that the "reality" (wave phenomena) which one believes he is describing with his mathematical model (differential equations, and so on) is itself a cultural artifact, and that one has only extended his environment to include parts of our cultural tradition not considered as belonging to "mathematics." But so long as one keeps in mind that the concepts of wave phenomena as embodied in theoretical physics consist only of concepts, not necessarily duplicated by actual physical referents, one should be ready to concede that one's model is not a "necessary truth," accurately descriptive of an actual situation in the external world.

But, to go to the other extreme, if one's mathematical thinking has never progressed beyond the level of elementary arithmetic or geometry, one may experience the greatest difficulty in understanding White's viewpoint. A similar remark holds for those non-professional mathematicians whose mathematical training may have been somewhat extensive, but who persist, either out of a desire to be widely understood even at the expense of over-simplification, or for other reasons, in exemplifying mathematics by "$2 + 2 = 4$." Their classic conclusion is that "If ever anything is certain, it is that $2 + 2 = 4$, and consequently mathematics is undeniably the embodiment of necessary truth."

An example of this type of thinking is to be found in one of the most bitter attacks on White's views, viz. an article by Martin Gardner entitled "Mathematics and the Folkways" (Gardner 1950). Typical of the statements to be found therein is the following: "It is important to realize . . . that the process of addition does not require the witness of a human being. It operates just as effectively when no one is looking. If you drop two pennies in a child's empty bank, then two more pennies you will discover, on opening the bank, that it contains four pennies. The entire operation could, in fact, be performed mechanically and recorded on film." The only trouble with this is that Gardner is not here speaking about *mathematics*. He is merely describing a type of phenomenon which, as everyone (including White, I am sure) admits, served as a stimulus to the formation of the number concept. And despite the inability of mathematicians to agree as to what mathematics *is*, there is not the same disagreement regarding many things which it *is not*; and the above described event is not mathematics, nor even a description of a mathematical event (such as the creation of a concept).

Gardner's article is strewn throughout with the same type of confusion between the mathematical and the environmental. Regarding geometry he states: ". . . if all men vanished there would still be a sense (exactly what sense is another and more difficult problem) in which spiral nebulae could be said to spiral, and hexagonal ice crystals to be hexagonal, even though no human creatures were around to give these forms a name" (Gardner 1950:180). I submit that if there were no human to *say* such things, the phenomena described would be just phenomena and nothing more. Only after generations of men had viewed such situations did it become possible for one to say "$2 + 2 = 4$," "hexagonal," or their equivalents in various tongues. (Incidentally, Gardner's discourse on the various modes of counting, and so on, seems strange, since certainly he knew that White was aware of these things, as is every cultural anthropologist. White's remark about Newton calculating "like a Hottentot" (White 1949:287) was meant purely to point to the conceptual limitations (cultural mathematical) to which Newton would have been restricted, viz., a limited set of natural numbers rather than the continuous real number system of analysis on which his work was erected.)

It is a long way in the course of cultural evolution from such external stimuli as occur in demands for quantitative measurement, necessity to differentiate shape, and so forth, to the theories of modern mathematics. On the other hand, much modern mathematics derives from external stimuli, as in the physical example cited above, or as in the case of the new theories (for example, game theory) suggested by the social environment. Are not these new theories, as theories, just as valid mathematics as elementary arithmetic or Euclidean geometry? Yet in the case of mathematics derived from social phenomena, the resulting theories are patently dependent on the character of the social events whose patterns are being analyzed, and as such, one would hardly call these theories either necessary or absolute truth. They evolve out of and reflect the cultural milieu; nothing more. Nor would one be justified in asserting that a society, which exemplified the patterns described by the mathematical theory which it suggested, would now be doing mathematics (which is what Gardner seems to be saying of the dropping of coins in the bank).

The modern mathematician views mathematical systems as embodying abstract patterns which are conceptually descriptive of models to be found in physical, social, mathematical, or other realms. The joining of two pairs to make a foursome furnishes a model of the pattern embodied in the formula "$2 + 2 = 4$," just as an economic event provides the model of its corresponding pattern in the mathematical formulation of game theory. One might, of course, attempt to divide mathematics into that part which is culturally invariant (or universal) in the sense that it is found in all cultures in various isomorphic forms (such as the rudiments of the natural numbers), and the variant. I doubt, however, if such a division would be feasible, since we do not have enough cultures that are sufficiently advanced and proved independent of the influences of diffusion to make the test for invariance. True, all cultures seem to embody rudiments of counting—a sort of embryo mathematics—but these have usually not evolved sufficiently to afford a respectable arithmetic, much less what we could call a system of natural numbers (see below). Nor do I see any necessity for such a division, even if it were feasible. If it should occur in the future that contact is established with beings on other planets having highly developed cultures, and elements are found in these cultures isomorphic to mathematical elements in our own culture, would this make these elements any less *cultural?*

I am sure that White was not trying to break anyone's philosophical crutches by asserting that sometimes two and two do not make four; nor was he making any statements impeaching the "truth" of mathematics. For example, he says (1949:285) "Mathematical truths exist in the cultural tradition into which the individual is born. . . ." Indeed, I am afraid that Professor White may, like most nonmathematicians, have a higher regard for the so-called "truth" of mathematics than most mathematicians, who are well aware of the conventional character of most of their concepts. The wise and seasoned mathematician shuns the word "truth" unless he uses it in an obviously relative sense. He knows that in order to "prove" anything he must, if he is to avoid an infinite regression, adopt certain statements or formulae without proof (that is, "axioms"), and the "truth" of what he proves is entirely relative not only to the axioms adopted but to the *methods of proof.*

I find that this statement sometimes gives the layman a profound shock. The suggestion that there should be any question of the validity of methods of proof in mathematics seems to him unthinkable. Nevertheless, not only does modern mathematics not represent its concepts as "true," but it does not insist that its methods of proof ensure "truthful" consequences from a set of axioms. Indeed, regarding some proof meth-

ods there is such profound disagreement that we are forced into recognition of their conventional character. And as mathematics grows, new
methods of proof and stricter standards of rigor are introduced. "Sufficient unto the day is the rigor thereof."

Probably no aspect of mathematics is more revealing, so far as its cultural nature is concerned, than methods of proof. Let us consider arithmetic, since for most people this is "mathematics" and has the closest ties
with "reality." How can one *prove* theorems of arithmetic, for instance
that (1) m + n = n + m no matter what numbers m and n represent?
This theorem means that it makes no difference in what order one adds
numbers; one gets the same result. Everyone—almost everyone—in our
culture "knows" this. However, merely observing that it holds for all
values of m and n up to 100, or even to one billion, would not constitute a
proof. Arithmetic furnishes many instances of "theorems" valid for an
amazingly large range of numbers, but demonstrably invalid for certain
numbers beyond this range. I doubt if the average educated layman has
the slightest idea how one would prove the above relation (1); he'd think
it obvious, anyhow, which is of course evidence of how deeply imbedded
in his culture the "fact" lies. And the reason he could not prove it is that
the average layman, like some primitive savages, may know how to
count, but yet not know the *system of natural numbers.*

One of the wondrous features of our number symbolism is its unlimited character. No matter how great a number may be, it can be expressed in our decimal notation. And real proficiency in "counting"
consists in the knowledge of and ability to use this fact. To the mathematician, however, this has opened up the concept of the *totality of all
numbers* which forms the collection of what I referred to above as the
"system of natural numbers" (a number—1, 2, 3, and so on—such as is
used in counting, is called by the technical term *natural number* to distinguish it from other types of numbers, such as fractions, decimals,
irrationals, and so forth). To prove (1) is to show that it holds for *all*
natural numbers. At this point, one might naturally object that a proof
must therefore be impossible, since one obviously cannot try all cases.
And this is correct unless we can find a *new* method of proof which will
be adaptable to *infinite* collections. Such we have, namely the method of
mathematical induction.[1] Despite the fact that numbers form the earliest

---

[1] The method of proving by mathematical induction that a theorem about natural
numbers holds for all natural numbers consists, briefly, in proving that the theorem
holds for the number 1, and that if it holds for a number n, then it holds for the
number n + 1. For other types of infinite collections, a more general method called
"transfinite induction" becomes necessary.

mathematical artifacts, the method of mathematical induction was formulated only in modern times, and I defy anyone to find it in the world of "reality." (Of course, once one passes from counting to the totality of the natural numbers, one has already transcended "reality.") With this method, one can prove formula (1) and all similar formulae expressing properties of arithmetic, basing the argument on a few simple axioms and undefined terms, and in doing so, one is now doing mathematics!

Similar observations can be made of other parts of mathematics less familiar to the layman. The elements with which they deal may be suggested by the physical environment (for example, geometric forms). But the process of developing a mathematical theory from them is a cultural activity of the highest sort, involving the creation of a suitable symbolism (which usually undergoes a prolonged evolution before it is in a mathematically abstract form), as well as the devising of special methods (such as mathematical induction) for the purposes of a complete theory. One is reminded here of E. T. Bell's statement: ". . . the useful rule, known to the ancient Babylonians, that the area of a rectangular field can be computed by 'length times breadth,' may agree with experience to the utmost refinement of physical measurement; but the rule is not a part of mathematics until it has been deduced from explicit assumptions" (Bell 1945:4). And he might have added "by logical methods which are explicitly formulated" so far as modern mathematics is concerned. C. J. Keyser makes a similar point: "Mathematics is no more the art of reckoning and computation than architecture is the art of making bricks or hewing wood, no more than painting is the art of mixing colors on a palette, no more than the science of geology is the art of breaking rocks, or the science of anatomy the art of butchering" (quoted in Dubisch 1952:24).

Of course, one may object that no matter how abstract and seemingly removed from reality mathematics may become, it *works*—it can be applied to real situations—as witness radio, air travel, and so on, none of which would have been possible without mathematics. But just how this detracts from the cultural nature of mathematics I have never been able to make out. After all, a major function of culture is to control man's environment, and as a part of culture mathematics serves this purpose. As I stated elsewhere, "The individual mathematician can play with postulational systems as he will, but unless and until they are related to the existing state of mathematics in his culture, they will only be regarded as idiosyncrasies" (Wilder 1952:269). And since mathematics has its roots in functional relation to reality, it is not surprising that much of its superstructure, no matter how abstract, proves ultimately to be functional. The classical case of the invention and development of the theory of conic sections by the Greeks, finding no application in their day but ready to serve the astronomers of the middle ages, is a good illustration of how the cultural process may devise "tools" whose applicability await the further development of other cultural elements.

However, the "it works" argument has been exaggerated. On one level of activity, Euclidean geometry may "work"; on astronomical or submicroscopic levels it may no longer work. But these are levels not encompassed by the experience of dwellers in the market place. Even the numbers 1, 2, 3, and so on, so sacred to the seeker after the absolute, may become of questionable utility. On the cosmic level, numbers are employed which are so large as to be beyond the range of realization for the layman, for which one might as well use the term "many beyond imagination." As for the atomic level, Bridgman remarks:

numbers have been an astonishingly successful device, and it is difficult to visualize situations in which they might lead to contradiction; but no proof can be given, and it may be that situations of this sort are now arising in physics, for we know that electrons cannot be thought of as having identity, and therefore as being countable in the ordinary way. Indeed we are already pretty well convinced that the concepts of space and time have proved unsuccessful when carried inside the atom; and why may not the concept of number? (Bridgman 1936:51–52)

Mathematics reacts to its environment, physical and cultural; physical events and cultural concepts affect mathematics and influence its line of development. New concepts suggested by the environment may be "brought into being by the nervous systems of individual human beings" (White 1949:299), but unless these are given "overt expression in symbolic form" and thus passed on to the culture in which the individual participates, they will never become part of that aspect of culture that we call "mathematical." Just when they become "mathematics" is a question not easily settled; nor is it easy to state just what part is, say, physics and what part is mathematics. Even the introduction of a special classification, "applied mathematics," has not helped. There seems to be no general agreement as to what constitutes applied mathematics. A comment by d'Abro is of some interest in this connection.

The accepted distinction between pure and applied mathematics is far from satisfying. In the first place, it permits no permanent classification. As an example, let us consider the doctrine of classical mechanics. When the basic postulates of classical mechanics were established by Galileo and Newton, they were thought to express physical characteristics of the world. Classical mechanics were thus regarded as a branch of applied mathematics. But today, as a result of the theory of relativity, we know that the classical postulates do not correspond to physical reality. Strictly speaking, we should therefore reverse our former stand and view classical mechanics as an abstract doctrine pertaining to pure mathematics (d'Abro 1951,I:119–120). [It is interesting to note that classical mechanics forms part of the curriculum in many mathematics departments today.]

Of course (as d'Abro realizes; cf. d'Abro 1951,I: Chapters V, VI) much depends on the "level" at which one works. In dealing with the ordinary affairs of life such as engineering, classical mechanics and Euclidean geometry are preferable for reasons of simplicity and what seems "natural" to us (that is, cultural tradition). But when dealing with astronomical or cosmic phenomena, they are no longer adequate. Howsoever we choose to classify the tools with which we work—"applied mathematics," "mathematics," "theoretical physics," or what have you—there is no denying that they are human inventions, designed to cope with "reality," and just as cultural in nature as any other conceptual tools.

How does the professional mathematician stand to benefit from the realization of the cultural nature of mathematics? White conceives of culture as "a distinct order, or class, of phenomena, namely, those things and events that are dependent upon the exercise of a mental ability, peculiar to the human species, that we have termed 'symbolling'" (1949:363). One frequently hears mathematics called, particularly by natural scientists, "a language." Poincaré once remarked (1946:375) that "mathematics is the art of giving the same name to different things. . . . When the language has been well chosen, we are astonished to see that all the proofs made for a certain object apply immediately to many new objects; there is nothing to change, not even the words, since the names have become the same." This constitutes a tacit recognition of the mathematician's interest in pattern rather than substance.

Whether they realize the cultural nature of mathematics or not, mathematicians recognize the importance of well-chosen symbols. The development of an entire branch of mathematics can be delayed by the lack of a suitable symbolism. Indeed, no human activity is so utterly dependent on the symbolic faculty; every normal person can talk, that is, can manipulate the symbols of a natural language, but apparently few can master higher mathematics. But what many mathematicians do not realize is the importance, in good teaching of mathematics, of making a distinction between a symbolic reflex type of behavior and the use of symbolic initiative. The former lies at the basis of that type of teaching which "may enable stupid John to get a required credit in mathematics but bores the creative minded William to the extent that he comes to loathe the subject!" (Wilder 1952:266). A good illustration of the difference is found in elementary algebra where it is much easier to teach the solution of a quadratic equation than to get the student to interpret the theory in so-called "word problems," where he must choose his own symbols and their meanings; or in high school geometry, where the "easy way" is to learn the proofs, letter for letter, rather than to seek out the pattern thereof and rely on the ability to make one's own assignment of symbols if called upon to reproduce the proof. It seems that there is here a good area for the use of a little applied anthropology, not only on the elementary level cited, but on the advanced level where research methods are being introduced. Elsewhere White remarks metaphorically that "One soil or climate will foster and bring forth genius; another will not" (White 1949:231–232). Development of symbolic initiative in a subject such as mathematics is virtually a *sine qua non* if we are not to lose much potential mathematical genius.

Other areas in which realization of the cultural nature of mathematics can be beneficial are (1) foundation studies, (2) amplification of the facilities for communication (diffusion), (3) use of older works, especially journals, for the purpose of discovering and revivifying concepts or problems which "died aborning" because of the lack of suitable conceptual tools for their development or solution, but which may now be susceptible to treatment, and (4) the realization that mathematics must respond to and be influenced by other cultural activities.

Regarding (1), that is, foundation studies, it is noteworthy that mathematicians cannot agree on any suitable characterization of their subject. From the cultural point of view, this would be clearly a matter of deciding what aspects of culture are to be termed mathematical. Unfortunately this is not definitive, for mathematicians are frequently critical of one another's work, and it is not at all unheard of for one mathematician to say of another's work, "Interesting, but it's not mathematics!" Kronecker would not admit the irrationals such as π to legitimate mathematical standing! An appreciation of the cultural nature of mathematics should make clear just why we have this situation. Attempts at definition of "mathematics," "topology," and so on, are doomed to failure because they aim at marking off cultural boundaries that simply do not exist. Internal disputes over the legitimacy of certain concepts and methods of proof (such as well-ordering of nondenumerable classes, use of the continuum hypothesis, and so forth) can probably never be settled, and of themselves point to the arbitrary, nonabsolute character of mathematics. To grant the admissibility of such concepts and methods on grounds of consistency, or because of their capability to contribute to the greater development of mathematics, becomes a quite arbitrary matter to be decided ultimately by agreement, much as are other codes of behavior. (Compare White 1949:301–302.) The "existence" of transfinite numbers (whose significance for the handling of infinite aggregates is like that of the natural numbers for finite aggregates), although not admitted by some mathematicians, has nevertheless found "believers" because of its usefulness, and this despite the fact that their unrestricted use can lead to contradiction. (It is significant that most of the opponents of the use of transfinite numbers work in branches of mathematics that do not need them!) In mathematics, as in physics, one introduces new concepts if they are needed; if later they prove unfruitful, they die through neglect.

The importance of (2), amplification of the facilities for communication, needs little comment. No field of science has been subjected to more profound and prolonged diffusionary processes than has mathematics during its later period of evolution. Although there are, as I have pointed out elsewhere (Wilder 1952:270), detectable national cultural differences in the practice of mathematics, most of its methods and principles have now attained a world-wide adoption. This was not always the case; history shows that without diffusion of new materials a stage of virtual stagnation may be reached, as in the examples of both Chinese and Greek mathematics. It is interesting to note, however, that there have been cases where a lone worker develops a mathematical system in virtual isolation from the rest of the mathematical world. These phenomena, which might be called "singularities" in the cultural development of mathematics, deserve special study, particularly since they have their counterpart in other sciences (as in the case of the Mendelian theory of heredity, which, as is well known, did not find contemporary recognition and had to be rediscovered later by other workers). These singularities seem to indicate the presence of cultural elements not yet ready to develop, but nevertheless finding an isolated "genius" so sensitive to their presence as to induce premature synthesis in his mind. As a rule, as White emphasizes (1949:297) "inventions and discoveries are much more likely to take place at culture centers, at places where there is a great deal of cultural interaction, than . . . in remote or isolated regions." Consequently the case of the isolated genius should be of intense interest to the cultural anthropologist, probably more so than to the psychologist, so far as the study of the development of science is concerned.

The significance of (3), delving into older works, was pointed out elsewhere (Wilder 1953:444–445), and has proved its importance in a number of recent cases, where problems that had been dropped by an older generation as not likely of solution, have been solved by the use of tools introduced during the years since the problems were first formulated.

Regarding (4), recognition of the influence of other cultural elements on mathematics: The competition between universities, industrial concerns (including consulting agencies), and government bureaus for the research abilities of mathematicians is forcing mathematicians to notice the influence of other cultural elements on the development of their field. Mathematicians have always been aware of the impact of physics, but the recent war years and the attendant migrations of mathematicians from one country to another, as well as the necessity for investigating entirely new types of phenomena, have forced upon them the realization that their field does not evolve in isolation but is closely related to and influenced by all kinds of cultural factors.

To summarize: Mathematics is a cultural phenomenon which is in a constant state of evolution. In many of its aspects, as for example certain fundamental arithmetic and geometric concepts, it studies patterns or structures suggested by the physical, social or cultural environment. But it does not cease with these, and constantly builds new concepts atop the foregoing, often being forced to invent new methods for handling them not even glimpsed in the logic derived from experience with the "real world." Although founded in experience, it transcends experience to form a cultural activity that defies definition or consignment to an absolute status. It does not aspire to "truth," only to consistency. Those who seek truth or the absolute would be well advised to confine their search to the traditional types of theology. Mathematics is not for timid souls afraid to risk intellectual adventure.

One can predict that not only does mathematics stand to benefit from a wide appreciation of its cultural nature, but that the process is not a one-way street. For it would seem that the cultural anthropologist, reacting to White's thesis, would find in mathematics a valuable area for the exemplification of his principles, as well as a fertile field for research. Also, he may find in the newly founded areas of mathematics many tools, of a nonquantitative nature and not necessitating a knowledge of classical techniques of analysis, which are applicable to the more expeditious treatment of such items as kinship systems and other facets of cultural anthropology.

BIBLIOGRAPHY

D'ABRO, A.
  1951 *The Rise of the New Physics.* 2 vols., 2nd edition. New York, Dover Publications, Inc.
BELL, E. T.
  1945 *The Development of Mathematics.* New York, McGraw-Hill Book Co.
BRIDGMAN, P. W.
  1936 *The Nature of Physical Theory.* Princeton, Princeton University Press.
DUBISCH, R.
  1952 *The Nature of Number.* New York, The Ronald Press Company.
GARDNER, MARTIN
  1950 "Mathematics and the Folkways." *Journal of Philosophy,* 47:177–186.
HADAMARD, JACQUES
  1949 *The Psychology of Invention in the Mathematical Field.* Princeton, Princeton University Press.
POINCARÉ, HENRI
  1946 *The Foundations of Science.* Translated by G. B. Halsted. Lancaster, Pa., The Science Press.
TYLOR, EDWARD B.
  1919 *Anthropology.* New York and London, D. Appleton and Company.
WHITE, LESLIE A.
  1947 "The Locus of Mathematical Reality." *Philosophy of Science,* 14:289–303.
  1949 *The Science of Culture.* New York, Farrar, Straus and Co.
WILDER, R. L.
  1952 "The Cultural Basis of Mathematics." *Proceedings of the International Congress of Mathematicians, 1950,* 1:258–271. Providence, R. I., American Mathematical Society.
  1953 "The Origin and Growth of Mathematical Concepts." *Bulletin of the American Mathematical Society,* 59:423–448.

* * * *

BIBLIOGRAPHY OF

THE PUBLISHED WRITINGS

OF LESLIE A. WHITE

The reprinting of articles has been indicated immediately following the original published version, except that reprintings of articles in *The Science of Culture* (1949) have not been listed. This book included ten previously published essays in more or less modified form in addition to four essays written expressly for the volume.

1921

"Purchasing Power of the Dollar." *Baton Rouge State Times*, Spring.

1925

"The Concept 'Social': A Critical Note." *Social Forces*, 4:72–74.

"Personality and Culture." *The Open Court*, 39:145–149.

"Knowledge Interpreted as Language Behavior." *The Open Court*, 39:396–404.

Review of Harry Elmer Barnes, *The New History and the Social Studies*. *Social Forces*, 4:432–434.

Review of Harry Elmer Barnes, ed., *The History and Prospects of the Social Sciences*. *Social Forces*, 4:643–646.

Review of L. L. Bernard, *Instinct, A Study in Social Psychology*. *The New Republic*, 42:352.

Review of Clarence Marsh Case, *Outlines of Introductory Sociology*. *American Review* (Bloomington, Ill.), 3:740–741.

1926

"An Anthropological Approach to the Emotional Factors in Religion." *Journal of Philosophy*, 23:546–554.

Review of Harry Elmer Barnes, ed., *The History and Prospects of the Social Sciences*. *American Review* (Bloomington, Ill.), 4:452–453.

Review of Jack McLaren, *My Crowded Solitude. American Journal of Sociology,* 32:507.

1927

"Ancient Indians and Modern Pueblos." *Hobbies* (Buffalo Society of Natural Sciences), 8:3–19.

Review of Mrs. William T. Sedgwick, *Acoma, the Sky City. American Journal of Sociology,* 32:671.

Review of Bronislaw Malinowski, *Crime and Custom in Savage Society. American Journal of Sociology,* 32:1005.

1928

"Medicine Societies of the Southwest." *Abstracts of Theses, The University of Chicago, Humanistic Series,* 5:341–345.

"Summary Report of Field Work at Acoma." *American Anthropologist,* 30:559–568.

Review of Frank O. Robertson, *The Fall of Buffalo Horn. Buffalo Evening News,* February 18 ("The News Magazine Section," p. 13).

Review of Roland B. Dixon, *The Building of Cultures. Buffalo Evening News,* April 28, p. 8.

Review of Chief Standing Bear, *My People the Sioux, Buffalo Evening News,* May 5 ("Saturday Magazine Section," p. 9).

Review of Geoffrey Parsons, *The Stream of History. Buffalo Evening News,* June 30, p. 9.

Review of Mrs. William T. Sedgwick, *Acoma, the Sky City. Journal of American Folklore,* 41:177–178.

1929

"Keresan Indian Songs." *Grosvenor Library Bulletin* (Buffalo, N.Y.), 3:41–43.

Review of Leo Crane, *Desert Drums. The Nation,* 128:138.

1930

"A Comparative Study of Keresan Medicine Societies." *Proceedings of the 23rd International Congress of Americanists* (New York, 1928), pp. 604–619.

"The Sioux Indian and the Lapp Groups." *Hobbies* (Buffalo Society of Natural Sciences), 10:289–293.

Review of Raoul Allier, *The Mind of the Savage. American Anthropologist,* 32:663–665.

Review of Stith Thompson, *Tales of the North American Indians. Buffalo Evening News.*

Abstract of Edwin M. Loeb, "Tribal Initiations and Secret Societies." *Social Science Abstracts*, 2:1406.

Abstract of Elsie Clews Parsons, "Ritual Parallels in Pueblo and Plains Culture with a Special Reference to the Pawnee." *Social Science Abstracts*, 2:1408.

Abstract of Edwin M. Loeb, "Mentawei Religious Cult." *Social Science Abstracts*, 2:1409–1410.

1931

Review of Margaret Mead, *Growing Up in New Guinea*. *Birth Control Review*, 15:122.

Review of V. F. Calverton, ed., *The Making of Man: an Outline of Anthropology*. *Birth Control Review*, 15:261.

Review of Bernhard J. Stern, *Lewis Henry Morgan, Social Evolutionist*. *American Journal of Sociology*, 37:483.

Abstract of Barbara Aitken, "Temperament in Native American Religion." *Social Science Abstracts*, 3:1520.

1932

"The Acoma Indians." *47th Annual Report of the Bureau of American Ethnology for 1929–1930*, pp. 17–192.

"The Pueblo of San Felipe." *Memoirs of the American Anthropological Association*, 38.

"Evoliutsiia kul'tury i americanskaia shkola istoricheskoĭ etnologii." ("Cultural Evolution and the American School of Historical Ethnology.") *Sovetskaia Etnografia*, 3:54–86.

"The Mentality of Primates." *The Scientific Monthly*, 34:69–72.

Review of Sidney S. Broomfield, *Kachalola, or Mighty Hunter*. *American Journal of Sociology*, 38:505.

Review of Erna Ferguson, *Dancing Gods*. *American Journal of Sociology*, 37:842.

Review of Earnest A. Hooton, *Up From the Ape*. *Birth Control Review*, 16:54–55.

Abstract of Frank H. H. Roberts, Jr., "The Ruins at Kiatuthlanna Eastern Arizona." *Social Science Abstracts*, 4:12.

Abstract of Henry A. Carey, "An Analysis of the Northwestern Chihuahua Culture." *Social Science Abstracts*, 4:661.

1933

Review of Martha Warren Beckwith, *Myths and Ceremonies of the Mandan and Hidatsa*. *American Journal of Sociology*, 39:435.

Review of Francis Lambrecht, *The Mayawyaw Ritual. American Journal of Sociology*, 39:435.

Review of Hutton Webster, *Primitive Secret Societies. American Journal of Sociology*, 39:290.

Review of A. B. Thomas, *Forgotten Frontiers. American Anthropologist*, 35:533–535.

1934

"Masks in the Southwest." *American Anthropologist*, 36:626–628.

Review of George P. Murdock, *Our Primitive Contemporaries. American Journal of Sociology*, 40:266.

Review of G. C. Henderson, *The Journal of Thomas Williams, Missionary in Fiji, 1840–1853. American Journal of Sociology*, 39:723.

1935

"The Pueblo of Santo Domingo, New Mexico." *Memoirs of the American Anthropological Association*, 43.

Review of W. N. and L. A. Kellogg, *The Ape and the Child. American Anthropologist*, 37:152–153.

Review of T. M. Pearce and Telfair Henden, eds., *America in the Southwest: A Regional Anthology. American Journal of Sociology*, 40:525.

1936

Review of William T. Corlett, *The Medicine Man of the American Indian and His Cultural Background. Mississippi Valley Historical Review*, 22:578–580.

1937

"Extracts from the European Travel Journal of Lewis H. Morgan." (Editor) *The Rochester Historical Society, Publications*, 16:219–389.

"Some Suggestions for a Program in Anthropology in China." *Chinese Social and Political Science Review* (Peiping), 21:120–134.

Review of Elsie Clews Parsons, *Taos Pueblo. Journal of American Folklore*, 50:198–200.

Review of T. K. Penniman, *A Hundred Years of Anthropology. American Anthropologist*, 39:157–158.

Review of I. Vinnikov, *Materials from the Archives of Lewis H. Morgan. American Anthropologist*, 39:158–159.

1938

"Science is *Sciencing.*" *Philosophy of Science*, 5:369–389.

Review of Elsie Clews Parsons, ed., *Hopi Journal of Alexander M. Stephen. American Anthropologist,* 40:306–307.

Review of C. O. Williams, *Thraldom in Ancient Iceland. American Anthropologist,* 40:321.

1939

"Mind is *Minding.*" *The Scientific Monthly,* 48:169–171. (Reprinted in *ETC., A Review of General Semantics,* 1:86–91, 1943–44.)

"A Problem in Kinship Terminology." *American Anthropologist,* 41:566–573.

1940

Pioneers in American Anthropology, The Bandelier-Morgan Letters 1873–1883. (Editor) 2 vols. Albuquerque, The University of New Mexico Press.

"Mind is Minding—But or Still?" *The Scientific Monthly,* 50:365–366.

"The Symbol: The Origin and Basis of Human Behavior." *Philosophy of Science,* 7:451–463. (Reprinted in *ETC., A Review of General Semantics,* 1:229–237, 1944; *Language, Meaning, and Maturity,* ed. by S. I. Hayakawa, pp. 252–263. New York, Harper & Brothers, 1954; *Readings in Anthropology,* ed. by E. Adamson Hoebel, Jesse D. Jennings and Elmer R. Smith, pp. 303–312. New York, McGraw-Hill Book Co., 1955; *Readings in Introductory Anthropology,* ed. by Elman R. Service, pp. 36–45. Ann Arbor, J. W. Edwards, 1956; *Sociological Theory, a Book of Readings,* ed. by Lewis A. Coser and Bernard Rosenberg, pp. 32–40. New York, The Macmillan Company, 1957; and *Readings in the Ways of Mankind,* ed. by Walter Goldschmidt, vol. 1, pp. 7–12. Boston, Beacon Press, Inc., 1957.)

Review of Herbert O. Brayer, *Pueblo Indian Land Grants of the "Rio Abajo," New Mexico. American Anthropologist,* 42:141.

Review of Frances Densmore, *Music of Santo Domingo;* and Kenneth M. Chapman, *The Pottery of Santo Domingo Pueblo. American Anthropologist,* 42:141–143.

1941

"Nicotiana Rustica Cultivated by Pueblo Indians." *Science,* 94:64–65.

"The Cultivation of Cotton by Pueblo Indians of New Mexico." *Science,* 94:162–163.

Review of Donald D. Brand and Fred E. Harvey, eds., *So Live the Works of Men. Hispanic American Historical Review,* 21:451–452.

Review of H. P. Mera, *Population Changes. American Antiquity,* 6:368.

1942

"The Pueblo of Santa Ana, New Mexico." *Memoirs of the American Anthropological Association,* 60.

"Further Data on the Cultivation of Tobacco among the Pueblo Indians." *Science,* 96:59–60.

"The Impersonation of Saints among the Pueblos." *Papers of the Michigan Academy of Science, Arts, and Letters,* 27(1941):559–564.

"Lewis H. Morgan's Journal of a Trip to Southwestern Colorado and New Mexico, June 21 to August 7, 1878." *American Antiquity,* 8:1–26.

"On the Use of Tools by Primates." *Journal of Comparative Psychology,* 34:369–374. (Reprinted in *Man in Contemporary Society,* prepared by the Contemporary Civilization staff of Columbia University, vol. 1, pp. 58–64. New York, Columbia University Press, 1955; *Readings in Introductory Anthropology,* ed. by Elman R. Service, pp. 45–49. Ann Arbor, J. W. Edwards, Publisher, 1956.)

1943

"Energy and the Evolution of Culture." *American Anthropologist,* 45:335–356. (Revised version reprinted in *Readings in Introductory Anthropology,* ed. by Elman R. Service, pp. 50–65. Ann Arbor, J. W. Edwards, Publisher, 1956.)

"Keresan Indian Color Terms." *Papers of the Michigan Academy of Science, Arts, and Letters,* 28(1942):559–563.

"New Material from Acoma." *Bureau of American Ethnology Bulletin,* 136 (*Anthropological Papers,* 32):301–359.

"Punche: Tobacco in New Mexico History." *New Mexico Historical Review,* 18:386–393.

"Sociology, Physics, and Mathematics." *American Sociological Review,* 8:373–379.

Review of *The Unpublished Letters of Adolphe F. Bandelier, Concerning the Writing and Publication of "The Delight Makers."* *American Anthropologist,* 45:127–128.

Review of H. Bailey Carroll and J. Villasanna Haggard, *Three New Mexico Chronicles. American Anthropologist,* 45:128–129.

Review of Robert Redfield, ed., *Levels of Integration in Biological and Social Systems. American Anthropologist,* 45:376–378.

Review of Morris E. Opler, *Myths and Tales of the Chiricahua Apache Indians. Hispanic American Historical Review,* 23:357.

Review of S. F. Cook, *The Conflict between the California Indian and*

White Civilization, Parts I–IV. *Hispanic American Historical Review*, 23:744–745.

Review of Matthew W. Stirling, *Origin Myth of Acoma and Other Records*. *Journal of American Folklore*, 56:306–307.

1944

"A Ceremonial Vocabulary among the Pueblo Indians." *International Journal of American Linguistics*, 10:161–167.

"Morgan's Attitude toward Religion and Science." *American Anthropologist*, 46:218–230.

"'Rohona' in Pueblo Culture." *Papers of the Michigan Academy of Science, Arts, and Letters*, 29(1943):439–443.

Review of H. P. Mera, *Pueblo Indian Embroidery*. *American Anthropologist*, 46:391–392.

1945

"Atomic Energy: An Anthropological Appraisal." *The Baltimore Sun*, December 29, 1945. (Printed also in *The Milwaukee Journal*, January 10, 1946; and *The Norfolk Virginian-Pilot*, January 13, 1946.)

"Diffusion vs. Evolution: An Anti-Evolutionist Fallacy." *American Anthropologist*, 47:339–356.

"Education, America's Magic." *School and Society*, 61:353–354.

"History, Evolutionism and Functionalism: Three Types of Interpretation of Culture." *Southwestern Journal of Anthropology*, 1:221–248.

"Notes on the Ethnobotany of the Keres." *Papers of the Michigan Academy of Science, Arts, and Letters*, 30(1944):557–568.

Review of Carlos B. García, *La Esclavitud Prehispánica entre los Aztecas*. *Hispanic American Historical Review*, 25:112–113.

Review of Laura Thompson and Alice Joseph, *The Hopi Way*. *The Scientific Monthly*, 60:473–474.

1946

"Kroeber's 'Configurations of Culture Growth.'" *American Anthropologist*, 48:78–93.

"Lewis Henry Morgan." *Union Worthies* (Union College, Schenectady, N.Y.) 1:5–9.

"The Origin and Nature of Speech." In *Twentieth Century English*, ed. by William S. Knickerbocker, pp. 93–103. New York, The Philosophical Library. (Reprinted in *Readings in Anthropology*, ed. by Morton H. Fried, vol. 1, pp. 154–162. New York, Thomas Y. Crowell Company, 1959.)

Review of Ernst Cassirer, *An Essay on Man. American Anthropologist,*
48:461–463.

1947

"Culturological *vs.* Psychological Interpretations of Human Behavior."
American Sociological Review, 12:686–698. (Reprinted in *Readings in
Introductory Anthropology,* ed. by Elman R. Service, pp. 249–261.
Ann Arbor, J. W. Edwards, Publisher, 1956.)

"Energy and the Development of Civilization." *Publication of the U. S.
Rubber Company,* pp. 1–3. New York. (Reprinted in *The Scientists
Speak,* ed. by Warren Weaver, pp. 302–305. New York, Boni & Gaer,
1947; *Technocracy Digest,* 107:10–13, 1947; and *Great Lakes Tech-
nocrat,* 4:5–7, 1947.)

"Ethnographic Notes on Sandia Pueblo, New Mexico." *Papers of the
Michigan Academy of Science, Arts, and Letters,* 31(1945):215–
222.

"Notes on the Ethnozoology of the Keresan Pueblo Indians." *Papers of
the Michigan Academy of Science, Arts, and Letters,* 31(1945):223–
243.

"Evolutionary Stages, Progress, and the Evaluation of Cultures." *Southwestern Journal of Anthropology,* 3:165–192.

"Evolutionism and Anti-Evolutionism in American Ethnological Theory."
Calcutta Review, 104:147–159; 105:29–40, 161–174. (Reprinted as "Evo-
lucionismo e Anti-Evolucionismo na Teoria Etnológica Americana,"
Sociologia [São Paulo], 10:1–39, 1948; and as "Amerika Minzokugaku-
setsu ni okeru Shinka-shugi to han Shinka-shugi," *The Japanese Journal
of Ethnology,* 15:1–22, 1950.)

"Evolutionism in Cultural Anthropology: A Rejoinder." *American Anthropologist,* 49:400–413.

"The Expansion of the Scope of Science." *Journal of the Washington
Academy of Sciences,* 37:181–210. (Reprinted in *Readings in Anthro-
pology,* ed. by Morton H. Fried, vol. 1, pp. 15–24. New York, Thomas
Y. Crowell Company, 1959.)

"Lewis Henry Morgan: Pioneer in the Theory of Social Evolution." In
An Introduction to the History of Sociology, ed. by Harry Elmer Barnes,
pp. 138–154. Chicago, The University of Chicago Press.

"The Lewis Henry Morgan Collection." *The University of Rochester
Library Bulletin,* 2:48–52.

"The Locus of Mathematical Reality: An Anthropological Footnote."
Philosophy of Science, 14:289–303. (Reprinted in *The World of Mathe-*

matics, ed. by James R. Newman, vol. 4, pp. 2348–2364. New York, Simon and Schuster, 1956.)

Review of Franz Boas, *Race and Democratic Society. American Journal of Sociology,* 52:371–373.

Review of James Feibleman, *The Theory of Human Culture. American Sociological Review,* 12:235–236.

1948

"On the Alleged Mysticism of Emile Durkheim." (Abstract) *Central States Branch Bulletin, American Anthropological Association,* 2:12–13.

"Culturology." *Bulletin of the Philadelphia Anthropological Society,* 1:2–5.

"The Definition and Prohibition of Incest." *American Anthropologist,* 50:416–435.

"Ikhnaton: The Great Man *vs.* the Culture Process." *Journal of the American Oriental Society,* 68:91–114.

Reply to William F. Edgerton. *Journal of the American Oriental Society,* 68:193.

"The Individual and the Culture Process." (Abstract) *Science,* 108:585–586.

"Man's Control over Civilization: An Anthropocentric Illusion." *The Scientific Monthly,* 66:235–247. (Reprinted in *Readings in Anthropology,* ed. by Morton H. Fried, vol. 2, pp. 548–566. New York, Thomas Y. Crowell Company, 1959.)

"Miscellaneous Notes on the Keresan Pueblos." *Papers of the Michigan Academy of Science, Arts, and Letters,* 32(1946):365–373.

Reply to Bernhard J. Stern. *American Journal of Sociology,* 53:497–498.

"The Use and Manufacture of Tools by the Lower Primates." *Antiquity,* 22:210–211.

Review of Grahame Clark, *From Savagery to Civilization;* and V. Gordon Childe, *History. Antiquity,* 22:217–218.

1949

The Science of Culture: A Study of Man and Civilization. New York, Farrar, Straus and Company. (Paperbound reprint, New York, The Grove Press, 1958.)

"Energy and the Development of Civilization." *The Michigan Technic,* 68(1):13, 34.

"Ethnological Theory." In *Philosophy for the Future: The Quest of Modern Materialism,* ed. by R. W. Sellars, V. J. McGill and M. Farber, pp. 357–384. New York, The Macmillan Company.

"The Individual and the Culture Process." *Journal of the American College of Dentists*, 16:3–10.

"Man's Moment." (Poem) *The Scientific Monthly*, 69:93.

1950

"An Anthropocentric Illusion." *Calcutta Review*, 115:21–30, 81–95.

"The Individual and the Culture Process." In *Centennial*, pp. 74–81. Washington, D.C., American Association for the Advancement of Science.

"Professor White Predicts Anthropology." *The Michigan Daily*, January, 15, p. 2.

Review of G. P. Hammond and E. F. Goad, *A Scientist on the Trail; Travel Letters of A. F. Bandelier*. *American Anthropologist*, 52:546.

Review of S. Lilley, *Men, Machines and History;* and E. Cecil Curwen, *Plough and Pasture*. *American Anthropologist*, 52:547–548.

1951

"Lewis H. Morgan's Western Field Trips." *American Anthropologist*, 53:11–18.

"Wilhelm Ostwald (1853–1932): A Note on the History of Culturology." *Antiquity*, 25:31–32.

1952

Review of Stow Persons, ed., *Evolutionary Thought in America*. *American Anthropologist*, 54:416–417.

1953

Comments on "Problems of the Historical Approach: Theory." In *An Appraisal of Anthropology Today*, ed. by Sol Tax, Loren C. Eiseley, Irving Rouse, and Carl F. Voegelin, pp. 71–72. Chicago, The University of Chicago Press.

"The Power of Speech." In *Progress of Mankind: Prehistoric to Present*. University of Michigan Telecourse Syllabus, Lesson 2, 4 pp.

"Energy and the Development of Civilization." In *Progress of Mankind: Prehistoric to Present*. University of Michigan Telecourse Syllabus, Lesson 3, 5 pp.

"Primitive Society." In *Progress of Mankind: Prehistoric to Present*. University of Michigan Telecourse Syllabus, Lesson 10, 5 pp.

1954

"The Energy Theory of Cultural Development." In *Professor Ghurye Felicitation Volume*, ed. by K. M. Kapadia, pp. 1–8. Bombay, Popular

Book Depot. (Reprinted in slightly revised and extended version as "A Teoria da Energia no Desenvolvimento Cultural," *Sociologia* (São Paulo), 20:489–500, 1958; reprinted also in *Readings in Anthropology*, ed. by Morton H. Fried, vol. 2, pp. 139–146. New York, Thomas Y. Crowell Company, 1959.)

Review of A. L. Kroeber and Clyde Kluckhohn, *Culture, a Critical Review of Concepts and Definitions. The Scientific Monthly*, 78:122.

Review of A. L. Kroeber, *The Nature of Culture;* and A. L. Kroeber and Clyde Kluckhohn, *Culture, a Critical Review of Concepts and Definitions. American Anthropologist*, 56:461–468.

1956

"Norman Daymond Humphrey, 1911–1955." (Obituary) *American Anthropologist*, 58:548–550.

1957

"The Correspondence between Lewis Henry Morgan and Joseph Henry." *The University of Rochester Library Bulletin*, 12:17–22.

"Daniel Garrison Brinton." *Encyclopaedia Britannica*, 4:151.

"Evolution and Diffusion." *Antiquity*, 31:214–218.

"How Morgan Came to Write *Systems of Consanguinity and Affinity*." *Papers of the Michigan Academy of Science, Arts, and Letters*, 42(1956):257–268.

Review of Fray Francisco Atanasia Dominguez, *The Missions of New Mexico, 1776. American Anthropologist*, 59:361–362.

Review of Julian H. Steward, *Theory of Culture Change: The Methodology of Multilinear Evolution. American Anthropologist*, 59:540–542.

1958

"Alexander Alexandrovich Goldenweiser." *Dictionary of American Biography*, 22, Supplement 2, pp. 244–245.

Comments on Edward P. Dozier, "Ethnological Clues for the Sources of Rio Grande Pueblo Population." In *Migrations in New World Culture History. University of Arizona Social Science Bulletin*, 27:29–30.

"Culturology." (Letter to the Editor.) *Science*, 128:1246.

"On 'Legalized Incestuous Marriage.'" *Man*, 58:116.

"What is a Classificatory Kinship Term?" *Southwestern Journal of Anthropology*, 14:378–385.

1959

The Evolution of Culture: The Development of Civilization to the Fall of Rome. New York, McGraw-Hill Book Company, Inc.

Lewis Henry Morgan. The Indian Journals. (Editor) Ann Arbor, University of Michigan Press.

"The Concept of Culture." *American Anthropologist,* 61:227–251.

"The Concept of Evolution in Cultural Anthropology." In *Evolution and Anthropology: A Centennial Appraisal,* ed. by Betty J. Meggers, pp. 106–125. Washington, D.C., The Anthropological Society of Washington.

"Man, Culture, and Human Beings." *Michigan Alumnus Quarterly Review,* 66(10):1–6.

" 'Culturology' in Webster's Dictionary." (Letter to the Editor.) *Man,* 59:31.

"Summary Review." In *The Evolution of Man's Capacity for Culture,* arranged by J. N. Spuhler, pp. 74–79. Detroit, Wayne State University Press.

Review of Hans Thirring, *Energy for Man: Windmills to Nuclear Power;* and Norman Lansdell, *The Atom and the Energy Revolution. American Anthropologist,* 61:513–515.

In Press

"Cultural Evolution," "Culturology," "Exogamy, Endogamy," and "Kinship Terminology." Definitions submitted to *UNESCO Social Science Dictionary.*

"The World of the Keresan Pueblo Indians." In *Culture in History; Essays in Honor of Paul Radin,* ed. by Stanley Diamond.

"Foreword." In *Evolution and Culture,* by Marshall D. Sahlins and Elman R. Service. Ann Arbor, University of Michigan Press.

"Johann Jakob Bachofen," "Daniel Garrison Brinton," "Friedrich Gustav Klemm," "Alfred Louis Kroeber," "John Ferguson McLennan," "Lewis Henry Morgan," and "Theodor Waitz." Articles submitted to *Encyclopaedia Britannica.*

INDEX OF NAMES

* * * *

INDEX OF NAMES

Index of Names

Malinowski, Bronislaw, 2, 119, 131, 317, 318, 320, 324, 328–330 *passim*, 335, 362–364 *passim*, 368, 375, 377, 405–407, 413, 487

Malraux, André, 221, 229

Man, Edward Horace, 163, 178

Mandelbaum, David G., 3, 7, 10, 16–22 *passim*, 29, 379

Margenau, Henry, 242, 244, 247

Mariner, William, 407, 414

Martin, John, 414

Marx, Karl, xxvi, xxxv, 394, 408, 414

Massey, William C., 193, 199

Masuoka, Jitsuichi, 352

Mathews, Hubert, 193

Matson, Frederick, xix

Matsumiya, Kazuya, 339, 343, 352

Matsunaga, E., 97, 99, 108

Mattison, Ray, 273, 286

Mayer, Frank B., 251–253 *passim*, 255, 268

Mead, George Herbert, 238, 239, 241, 247

Mead, Margaret, 22, 25, 27, 29, 378, 488

Medicine-bear, Chief, 263

Medvei, C. V., 91, 107

Meggers, Betty J., viii, 302, 307, 311, 314–316 *passim*, 497

Melanchthon, Philipp, 152

Mendel, Gregor, 220

Meiji, a Japanese emperor, 71, 75, 76, 338, 357

Mera, H. P., 490, 492

Merton, Robert K., 53, 62

Meyer, Eduard, 156, 160

Mills, C. Wright, 396, 414

Mironescu, T., 91, 108

Mohr, J., 95, 108

Montesquieu, Charles de Secondat, 372

Montgomery, Carol G., 247

Mooney, James, 274, 286

Moore, Omar K., 127, 131

Moose, Steven, 275

Morgan, Lewis H., xii, xvii, xxv, xxvi, xxxi, xxxii, xxxv, xxxvii, xxxviii, xli, 17, 134, 143, 165, 167, 178, 179–198, 200, 201, 241, 359, 369, 372, 378, 420, 488, 489–493 *passim*, 495–497 *passim*

Morgenroth, J., 84, 103

Morioka, K., 352

Moritsch, P., 90, 105

Morley, Sylvanus G., 371, 377

Moroney, M. J., 458, 470

Morton, Jelly Roll, 219

Morton, S. G., 80, 108

Mosteller, Frederick, 459, 465, 469

Mozart, Wolfgang Amadeus, 219

Müller-Lyer, Franz Carl, xxvii

Murdock, George P., 31, 35–39 *passim*, 42, 45, 48, 116, 121, 132, 157–160 *passim*, 162, 163, 169–172 *passim*, 177, 178, 180, 196, 200, 378, 385, 386, 388, 389, 420–422 *passim*, 432, 433, 436, 489

Murray, Henry A., 2, 29

Myers, Merlin, 196

Nadel, S. F., 378

Nagai, Michio, 352

Nagel, Ernest, 112, 130

Naito, Koichi, 91

Nakano, T., 352

Nakayama, Miki, 74

Napoleon, 148, 151

Naroll, Raoul, 13, 29

Nathanson, J., 143

Nearing, Scott, xlv

Needham, Rodney, 288, 301

Neel, J. V., 104

Nevanlinna, H. R., 82, 101

Newcomb, William W., Jr., viii, 283, 287, 317, 328, 335

Newman, James R., 494

Newman, Marshall T., 80, 108

Newton, Isaac, xv, 476, 480

Nissen, Henry W., 237, 248

Norbeck, Edward, 337, 344, 345, 352, 353

Northrop, F. S. C., 244, 247

No-two-horns, Chief, 258

Nunn, G. Raymond, 63

O'Faolain, Sean, 219, 229

Oka, Masao, 63, 69, 78

Okada, Yuzuru, 353

Oliver, Douglas, 407, 414

Opler, Marvin K., 56, 57, 62, 354, 365, 367, 375, 378

Opler, Morris E., 52, 62, 491

Oppenheim, F., 90, 108

Orlansky, Harold, 378

Osthoff, H., 93, 107

Ostwald, Wilhelm, xxvii, xxix, 495

Ottenberg, R., 85, 108, 109

Paal, H., 89, 91, 110

Paper, Herbert H., 1

Parsons, Elsie Clews, 143, 488–490 *passim*

Parsons, Geoffrey, 487

Parsons, Talcott, 1, 35–39 *passim*, 42, 45, 48, 378

Parten, Mildred, 462, 470

Pattison, Mary (*see* Mary White)

Paul, Saint, xxv

Pavlov, I. P., 236, 237, 247